DESEGREGATING THE ALTAR

DESEGREGATING THE ALTAR

The Josephites and the Struggle for Black Priests, 1871–1960

STEPHEN J. OCHS

LOUISIANA STATE UNIVERSITY PRESS

BATON ROUGE AND LONDON

99 98 97 96 95 94 93 92 91 90   5 4 3 2 1

Designer: Amanda McDonald Key
Typeface: Goudy Old Style
Typesetter: G & S Typesetters, Inc.
Printer and binder: Thomson-Shore, Inc.

Library of Congress Cataloging-in-Publication Data

Ochs, Stephen J.
    Desegregating the altar : the Josephites and the struggle for
black priests, 1871–1960 / Stephen J. Ochs.
        p.   cm.
    Includes bibliographical references.
    ISBN 0-8071-1535-5 (alk. paper)
    1. Afro-American Catholics—History.   2. Afro-American clergy—
History.   3. Josephites—History.   I. Title.
BX1407.N4O24   1990
282'.73'08996073—dc20   89-48219
                                                          CIP

To my wife, Phyllis Linda Ouellette

Now will I praise those godly men,
  our ancestors, each in his own time. . . .
But of others there is no memory,
  for when they ceased, they ceased.
And they are as though they had not lived,
  they and their children after them.
Yet these also were godly men
  whose virtues have not been forgotten;
Their wealth remains in their families,
  their heritage with their descendants;
Through God's covenant with them their family endures,
  their posterity, for their sake.

                    Sirach 44: 1, 9–13

Contents

Illustrations

Acknowledgments

Writing this book has been, in many ways, a solitary experience. Yet it has also made me keenly aware of my dependence on others, for I have received help from numerous individuals without whose assistance I could not have completed this study.

I would first like to thank the Josephite Fathers for the hospitality and openness they have shown me throughout the researching and writing of this book. The history of black priests in St. Joseph's Society and in the Catholic church is a sensitive topic, one that is a source both of great pride and of great pain for the Josephites. They have shown remarkable courage in allowing me to wander freely through the records of their family. Individual Josephites, from the current superior general, the Reverend Eugene P. McManus, on down, have shared their observations and recollections, offered criticism and encouragement, and never failed to extend their cooperation and friendship.

The archivist of the Josephite Fathers, Peter E. Hogan, S.S.J., has been a guide to anyone working in the area of black Catholic history and a friend to me for many years. I have benefited immensely from his vast store of knowledge, unfailing good humor, and generosity of spirit; in many respects, this book is really his. I am also indebted to Father Hogan's able assistant, Bernice Jones, who cheerfully and ably responded to my numerous requests for material. Agnes Rembus, secretary to the superior general, has also on many occasions taken time from her responsibilities to provide me with statistics.

A number of scholars working in the field of church history shared their insights with me. I am especially appreciative of the detailed criticism of the manuscript that Gerald P. Fogarty, S.J., provided me. Professors George C. Calcott, Richard T. Farrell, and Lawrence E. Mintz of the University of Maryland read the manuscript in an earlier form and offered valuable suggestions for its improvement. Cyprian Davis, O.S.B., Marilyn W. Nickels, Christopher J. Kauffman, and William L. Portier all read parts of the manuscript and patiently answered my many questions concerning black Catholic and church history. William Portier also generously lent me his microfilm copy of John R. Slattery's "Biographie." Albert S. Foley, S.J., of Spring Hill College, shared his research materials on black priests with me, as did Henry J. Koren, C.S.Sp., archivist of the Holy Ghost Fathers, who furnished me with documents from the Spiritan archives and also allowed me to read drafts of relevant chapters from his book on the history of the Holy Ghost Fathers in the United States.

This book has been greatly enriched by the many individuals who granted me interviews. I extend my thanks to all of those listed in the bibliographical essay. I am also deeply grateful to the many archivists, librarians, religious superiors, and diocesan officials who personally aided me or responded to my requests for information, copies of documents, or pictures: Borgia Aubespin, S.V.D., William J. Kelley, S.V.D., Dennis Newton, S.V.D., and Francis Theriault, S.V.D., southern province of the Society of the Divine Word; Dorthea L. Baillargeon, archives of the diocese of Portland; Philip C. Bantin, archives of Marquette University; Frances B. Boeckman, archives of the diocese of Jackson; John W. Bowen, S.S., Sulpician Archives of Baltimore; Priscilla B. Bravo, archives of the diocese of Savannah; the Reverend William C. Burn, archives of the diocese of Charleston; Audrey Marie Detiege, S.S.F., archives of the Sisters of the Holy Family; the Reverend Philip R. Gagan, archives of the diocese of Saint Augustine; the Reverend James F. Geraghty, archives of the diocese of Lafayette; Jerry Hiland, archives of the archdiocese of Cincinnati; Philip Hurley, O.S.B., St. Vincent Archabbey and College Archives; Doris E. Holmes, archives of the Society of African Missions; Clinton H. Johnson, Amistad Research Center; Christine L. Krosel, archives of the diocese of Cleveland; the late Reverend M. J. Madaj, archives of the archdiocese of Chicago; Caroline Mankell, archives of the University of Notre Dame; Catherine Markey, M.H.S., archives of the diocese of Little Rock; Robert Myers, S.V.D., archives of the Chicago province of the Society of the Divine Word; the Reverend Edward F. McSweeney, archives of the diocese of Pittsburgh; Mrs. Murray Nicholson, archives of the diocese of Nashville; Charles E. Nolan and Monsignor Earl C. Woods, archives of the archdiocese of New Orleans; the Reverend James W. Oberkirch, chancellor of the archdiocese of Mobile; Margaret M.

O'Rourke, S.B.S., archives of the Sisters of the Blessed Sacrament; Patricia L. O'Rourke, Bureau of Catholic Indian Missions; James M. O'Toole, archives of the archdiocese of Boston and, later, of Chicago; Monsignor Charles J. Plauché, former chancellor of the archdiocese of New Orleans; M. Felicitas Powers, R.S.M., and the Reverend Paul K. Thomas, archdiocese of Baltimore; Alfred C. Rush, C.SS.R., Redemptorist Provincial Archives; Timothy A. Slavin, archives of the archdiocese of Chicago; Vincent Tegeder, O.S.B., St. John's Abbey Archives; Mary Kay Viellion, M.S.C., archives of the diocese of Alexandria; Monsignor Francis J. Weber, archives of the archdiocese of Los Angeles; Warren A. Willis, archives of the United States Catholic Conference; and Anthony Zito and Ann Crowley, S.N.D., archives of the Catholic University of America. Archbishop Oscar Lipscomb of Mobile personally answered many letters and through his chancellor made available to me over one hundred documents drawn from the archdiocesan archives.

The administration, faculty, and staff of the Georgetown Preparatory School have been very supportive of my research and writing. I am grateful to the late Henry St. Clair Lavin, S.J., and to David A. Sauter, S.J., former president and former headmaster, respectively, for their encouragement of this project in its early stages. I will always stand in the debt of John H. Howard, S.J., also a former headmaster of the school, who made it possible for me to complete my research. Jerome B. Coll, S.J., and Thomas A. Roach, S.J., current president and headmaster, respectively, have gone out of their way to provide me with time and resources to complete the book. I would like especially to thank James A. P. Byrne, S.J., and Bonita Hanes for their interest and their critical reading of parts of this manuscript. Joy B. Choppin, the school librarian, generously allowed me the use of her office and provided me with a quiet haven for writing in the stacks of the library. Michael J. Horsey gave unstintingly of his time, advice, and computer equipment, without which I could not have finished this project. My colleagues on the faculty, particularly Robert C. Barry, Julie A. Collins, James Quinn, and Aloysius C. Galvin, S.J., have been a source of inspiration and encouragement. M. Patricia Ready graciously typed portions of the appendices, and Daniel R. Bane tracked down numerous books for me in the Catholic University library. My eleventh-grade U.S. history students distracted me from this book and enriched my life beyond measure.

I have also been the grateful recipient of professional guidance and friendship from two mentors at the University of Maryland: Professors Alfred A. Moss, Jr., and Keith W. Olson. Al Moss's mastery of Afro-American history and his keen appreciation of the spiritual dimension of life, both of which he has shared with me, have helped me more than he knows. Keith Olson, my doctoral advisor at the University of Maryland, has over the years been to me an inspiration as a scholar, teacher, parent, and human being. He enthusiastically encouraged my investigation of this topic and strengthened the manuscript by his careful reading and insightful suggestions; what scholarship this book reflects comes in large part from his influence.

I would like to acknowledge Catherine F. Barton, Barry L. Blose, Margaret F. Dalrymple, and Beverly Jarrett, members of the staff at Louisiana State University Press who have been most helpful. I also wish to thank Christine N. Cowan, whose blue pencil significantly improved the manuscript and whose advice, friendliness, and reassurance buoyed me during the hectic days of copy editing.

Finally, I must thank the two women in my life: Meghan Elizabeth Ochs, my daughter, and Phyllis Linda Ouellette, my wife. Nightly walks and daily swims with Meg brought me out of my preoccupation with the book and into the endlessly fascinating and enchanting world of a lovely little girl. My wife, Phyllis, has, for the last fifteen years, been a source of love, understanding, support, and friendship. She endured with remarkable good humor and patience the long hours I spent at the computer composing this book. My debt to her is immeasurable, my love for her abiding. For more reasons than I can name, I dedicate this book to her.

Abbreviations

AAB	Archives of the Archdiocese of Baltimore
AAC	Archives of the Archdiocese of Chicago
AACi	Archives of the Archdiocese of Cincinnati
AAM	Archives of the Archdiocese of Mobile
ACUA	Archives of the Catholic University of America, Washington, D.C.
ADA	Archives of the Diocese of Alexandria
ADC	Archives of the Diocese of Cleveland
ADJ	Archives of the Diocese of Jackson
ADL	Archives of the Diocese of Lafayette
ADLR	Archives of the Diocese of Little Rock
ADN	Archives of the Diocese of Nashville
ADS	Archives of the Diocese of Savannah
ADSA	Archives of the Diocese of St. Augustine
APF	Archives of the Congregation de Propaganda Fide in the University of Notre Dame Archives
ARC	Amistad Research Center, Tulane University, New Orleans
ASHF	Archives of the Sisters of the Holy Family, New Orleans
AUND	Archives of the University of Notre Dame
AUSCC	Archives of the United States Catholic Conference, Washington, D.C.
GUA	Georgetown University Archives, Washington, D.C.
JFA	Josephite Fathers Archives, Baltimore
MHFP	Mill Hill Fathers Papers, in Josephite Fathers Archives, Baltimore
MSRC	Moorland-Spingarn Research Center, Howard University, Washington, D.C.
PMC	Pastorelli Miscellaneous Correspondence, in Josephite Fathers Archives, Baltimore
SAB	Sulpician Archives, Baltimore

SASA St. Augustine's Seminary Archives, Bay St. Louis, Mississippi

SBSA Sisters of the Blessed Sacrament Archives, Cornwells Heights, Pennsylvania

SJAA St. John's Abbey Archives, Collegeville, Minnesota

SMAA Society of African Missions Archives, Tenafly, New Jersey

SPA Southern Province Archives of the Society of the Divine Word, Bay St. Louis, Mississippi

SPAUSA Spiritan Archives of the United States of America, Pittsburgh

SVAA St. Vincent Archabbey Archives, Latrobe, Pennsylvania

DESEGREGATING THE ALTAR

Introduction

On May 5, 1988, the Most Reverend Eugene A. Marino, S.S.J., a member of St. Joseph's Society of the Sacred Heart and, at the time, one of twelve Afro-American Roman Catholic bishops (since grown to thirteen), was installed as archbishop of Atlanta, thereby becoming the first Afro-American prelate to lead an archdiocese in the United States. Marino's elevation represented another important milestone in the ongoing campaign of the nation's approximately 1.5 million black Catholics, including over three hundred priests, to attain effective leadership and decision-making roles within the predominantly white Roman Catholic church in the United States.[1]

Approximately one year later, in July, 1989, the national media focused on another black Catholic clergyman, the Reverend George A. Stallings, Jr., and his founding of a so-called independent African-American Catholic congregation, known as Imani Temple, in defiance of Cardinal James A. Hickey of the archdiocese of Washington, D.C., who subsequently suspended him. One of the issues involved in the dispute between priest and archbishop was whether the church afforded genuine leadership opportunities to its black members.[2] Whatever the ultimate outcome of the controversy, Stallings was able to tap into the resentment and frustration still felt by many black Catholics over their historically subordinate position within the church—a church that until well into the twentieth century excluded all but a handful of Afro-Americans from its clergy.

1. The most recent profile of black Catholics in the United States, published in 1985, placed their number at 1,294,103. Ten years earlier, archdioceses and dioceses had reported a total of 916,854 Afro-American Catholics. It seems reasonable to conclude that the rate of increase for the years 1985–1989 at least matched that of the previous decade, hence the figure 1.5 million. See John Harfmann, S.S.J., *1984 Statistical Profile of Black Catholics* (Washington, D.C., 1985), iii, 8.

2. Washington *Post*, May 6, 1988, July 11, 1989.

That exclusion both reflected and reinforced the second-class status of Afro-Americans within the Catholic church.

Bishops and superiors of religious institutes refused to accept black candidates for the priesthood for a number of reasons. Acutely aware of their church's minority status in much of the South and of the suspicion and hostility harbored by many Bible-belt southerners toward Catholicism, they avoided challenges to the region's social system and instead accommodated themselves, and the institution they guided, to existing racial ideology and practices. Moreover, most Catholics, northern and southern, lay and cleric, absorbed the widespread racism of American society and regarded Afro-Americans as their intellectual and moral inferiors, incapable certainly of mastering the academic requirements of the seminary or of remaining celibate as priests. The relatively few white Catholics who dealt with Afro-Americans often viewed them as passive children to be supervised and cared for rather than as potential partners and leaders.

The dearth of black priests deprived black Catholics of effective spokesmen within the hierarchical, cleric-dominated Catholic church in the United States and also blocked their advancement into the ranks of the episcopacy, where real power lay. The few Afro-Americans who managed to become priests between 1854 and 1934 remained the exceptions and usually operated within severely circumscribed limits, often paying a staggering emotional price for their vocations. Black Catholics ordinarily had to rely on white priests. Regardless of the good intentions of such men, the situation bred paternalism, robbed black Catholics of symbols of their dignity and worth, and reinforced their feelings of inferiority. The absence of black priests from Catholic altars belied the church's claim of universality and impeded its growth among Afro-Americans, many of whom regarded Catholicism as a white religion.

The conscious exclusion of blacks from the Roman Catholic priesthood ended only after decades of struggle by black Catholics and by several religious communities that served them and only after subtle but repeated interventions by the Holy See. Central to an understanding of the development of a black Catholic clergy are the experiences of St. Joseph's Society of the Sacred Heart, or Josephites, the community to which Archbishop Marino belongs and the lone Roman Catholic clerical society of priests and brothers devoted exclusively to ministry in the Afro-American community. During the last quarter of the nineteenth, and well into the twentieth, century, the Josephites carried the main burden of the Catholic church's meager efforts among black Americans. Originally members of St. Joseph's Society of the Sacred Heart for Foreign Missions (English Josephites, or Mill Hill Fathers), founded in Mill Hill, England, in 1866 by the Reverend (later Cardinal) Herbert Vaughan, the American Josephites became an independent community in 1893. They sought to preserve the faith of the relative handful of black Catholics in the United States and to win converts among nonchurched and Protestant Afro-Americans. In that effort, the Josephites built churches and schools throughout the South, where the majority of blacks lived. More dramatically, in the years around the turn of the century, they championed the cause of a black clergy in the United States; indeed, that issue helped define the early Josephites' mission and identity.

Under their first American superior general, the dynamic John R. Slattery, who served from 1893 to 1904, and with the support of prominent members of the Americanist wing of the hierarchy, such as Archbishop John Ireland and Bishop John J. Keane, the Josephites defied prevailing racist sentiment by admitting blacks into Epiphany Apostolic College, their preparatory seminary, and St. Joseph's, their major seminary. They raised three of them, Charles Randolph Uncles, John Henry Dorsey, and John J. Plantevigne, in 1891, 1902, and 1907, respectively, to the priesthood. Since Catholics revered the priest as Christ's representative on earth, the ordination of Afro-Americans to such an exalted station posed a potentially powerful challenge to the racism that generally existed in the church in the United States. Not surprising, given these implications, Slattery's efforts on behalf of a black clergy proved controversial and met with considerable hostility from Catholic clergy and laity alike. Opposition to black seminarians and priests was particularly insidious in that it was usually voiced privately in chanceries, rectories, and seminaries and was couched in terms of "qualifications" or "unfavorable social conditions" rather than in terms of race. Paradoxically, even some of Slattery's own policies, which were tainted by his residual racism, helped subvert his goal of producing more black priests. As the influence of the racial liberals among the hierarchy declined in the wake of the Americanist controversy, and as racial conditions deteriorated throughout the country in the early years of the twentieth century, so also did Slattery's hopes for a black clergy.

Slattery's frustration over white Catholic indifference to and often hostility toward blacks, especially clerical resistance to black priests, contributed to his growing disillusionment with the church as an agent for reform in society. In 1904, having already embraced modernism, he resigned as superior general of the Josephites; in 1906, he publicly renounced his Catholicism. Slattery's apostasy almost destroyed the Josephites and helped discredit the cause of black priests that he had championed.

Slattery's immediate successors as superiors general, Thomas B. Donovan from 1904 to 1908 and Justin McCarthy from 1908 to 1918, presided over a period of institutional drift and worsening crisis. Lacking Slattery's leadership ability and his zeal for black priests, they found dealing with southern bishops, who hounded Dorsey and Plantevigne, demanded their removal from parishes, or refused to allow them even to enter dioceses to work, extremely difficult. Faced with mounting episcopal opposition and with the shattered lives of their black Josephites, Donovan and McCarthy gradually abandoned Slattery's policy of actively recruiting blacks for the Josephites.

Louis B. Pastorelli emerged from the period of chaos following Slattery's departure and rebuilt St. Joseph's Society. Exercising informal control beginning in 1912 and then serving as superior general from 1918 until 1942, he strengthened society institutions and oversaw the expansion of missions, of black converts, and of Josephite membership. Personally ambivalent about the cause of black priests and caught between bishops who would not permit them to function in their dioceses and black Catholics who desired them, Pastorelli felt constrained to conciliate the bishops at whose pleasure the Josephites served. The "living martyrdom" endured by Dorsey and Plantevigne, who suffered repeated humiliation and rejection at the hands of southern bishops, seared itself into Pastorelli's consciousness and reinforced his conviction that the good of St. Joseph's Society, and the continued existence of Catholic missions among blacks, required that the Josephites leave the development of a black clergy to others. Pastorelli effectively closed Epiphany Apostolic College and St. Joseph's Seminary to all but an occasional mulatto, whom he accepted partly as a way of deflecting charges of discrimination by black Catholics and partly as a way of maintaining faith with the society's official position of supporting black clergy and integrated seminary education.

In the years immediately following World War I, however, Afro-American Catholic activists in Baltimore and Washington, D.C., refused to allow the Josephites to retire quietly from the struggle.

4

Led by Thomas Wyatt Turner, a biology professor at Howard University and later at Hampton Institute, they organized a protest committee that, by 1925, had evolved into the Federated Colored Catholics. They denounced Patorelli's restrictive policies at the Josephites' college and seminary and appealed for redress to the American hierarchy and to the Holy See.

Pastorelli, who enjoyed the support of the archbishop of Baltimore, remained intransigent in the face of black Catholic agitation, pointing somewhat disingenuously to the presence of one or two mulatto students at either Epiphany College or St. Joseph's as proof that the Josephites had not changed their policy and still accepted "qualified blacks." The conflict between Pastorelli and black Catholic activists left a residue of distrust and suspicion—a residue that persisted for decades and resurfaced again during the late 1960s and early 1970s.

Although rebuffed by Pastorelli and patronized by the American hierarchy, Turner and his supporters found a sympathetic hearing in the Roman Curia. In 1919 and 1920, the Holy See responded to the pleas of black Catholics and of missionaries serving among them in the United States, such as the Reverend Ignatius Lissner of the Society of African Missions, by pressuring the American episcopate to take concrete steps to provide for more black priests, including suggesting that an episcopal vicar with exclusive jurisdiction over black Catholics be appointed. Subsequently, with the approval of both the Holy See and the American hierarchy, the predominantly German missionaries of the Society of the Divine Word (Divine Word Missionaries) established a seminary in Greenville, Mississippi, to prepare black priests who would then belong to their religious community. In 1923, the seminary was moved to Bay St. Louis, Mississippi, and was renamed St. Augustine's Seminary. Unlike the Josephites, who had attempted integrated seminary education, the Divine Word Missionaries, cognizant of the limits imposed by southern racial norms, conducted a basically segregated institution.

Leadership in the development of Afro-American clergy thus passed from St. Joseph's Society to the Society of the Divine Word. The existence of St. Augustine's Seminary eased the pressure on Pastorelli and on the American bishops, enabling them to refer most black applicants to the Divine Word Missionaries and still assert their support for the cause of black priests. For the next fifteen years, Pastorelli watched the progress of the "experiment" at St. Augustine's, all the while maintaining the status quo in his own in-

stitutions. He did not abandon the ideal of promoting black vocations, but he wished to proceed with extreme caution as he watched
for signs of changed attitudes among the American hierarchy. Finding the doors of their own college and seminary usually closed to
black youths from their parishes, Josephite missionaries encouraged
black vocations in the only way left to them: by sending their young
men to St. Augustine's Seminary, often paying the fees themselves
and making personal contributions to the institution.

The climate for black priests in the Catholic church in the United
States gradually began to improve in the 1930s and early 1940s.
Such Catholic interracial crusaders as the Jesuit John LaFarge began to make their voices heard, and blacks in American society
made gains as a result of the New Deal and World War II. Black
Catholics continued to demonstrate their desire for black priests
by sending their sons to St. Augustine's Seminary. In 1934, the
ordination of the first four black priests from the seminary and
their subsequent appointment to a black parish in the diocese of
Lafayette, Louisiana, accomplished only after the intervention of
Archbishop Amleto Cicognani, the apostolic delegate, marked a
watershed in the history of the struggle for black clergy. Thereafter, St. Augustine's Seminary sent forth growing numbers of black
priests; bishops and religious communities in the North, responding
to directives from the Holy See, became more involved in black
ministries and even began to admit some black candidates into
their own seminaries.

Those developments led Pastorelli to acknowledge the need for
the Josephites to add more black priests to their ranks in order to
avoid losing face in the eyes of their black parishioners. In 1941, he
could point proudly to the ordination of the first black Josephite
priest since 1907. Still, he could not shake the habits of mind or
the fears of twenty-five years, and when he left office in July, 1942,
the Josephites had only a single Afro-American in Epiphany Apostolic College.

Edward V. Casserly, who succeeded Pastorelli as superior general, finally reclaimed Slattery's legacy for the Josephites by opening
wide the doors of the college and the seminary to Afro-Americans.
A number of factors in addition to his own keen sense of justice
enabled Casserly to overcome the hesitancy of the Josephite old
guard and to implement his policy. He benefited from the changes
in American society wrought by World War II and also enjoyed the
support of a new generation of Josephites that believed in both

the desirability and the feasibility of black priests. Key southern prelates, moreover, such as Archbishop Joseph F. Rummel of New Orleans, indicated their willingness to allow black priests to function in their dioceses. At a 1946 meeting orchestrated by Cardinal Samuel Stritch of Chicago, who was the president of the American Board of Catholic Missions and who was in close contact with the apostolic delegate, several southern prelates, led by Rummel, promised to accept qualified black candidates for their own diocesan clergies. Casserly could thus feel more confident about the reception that future black Josephites would receive from bishops in the South.

Casserly's successors continued his policy of encouraging black vocations. Throughout the fifties and into the midsixties, black students and seminarians, part of a growing number throughout the nation, comprised at least one-third of the enrollments at Epiphany Apostolic College and St. Joseph's Seminary. Archbishop Rummel's dramatic defense of black priests in the Jesuit Bend incident in 1955 clearly indicated that black Josephites could safely return to the Deep South. In that same year, the first of the black students admitted under Casserly in the midforties was ordained and assigned to New Orleans. By 1960, St. Joseph's Society counted 5 black priests among its members (the total number of Afro-American priests in the United States that year reached 106) and confidently anticipated increasing numbers in the near future.

The optimism of the early sixties, however, evaporated amidst the turmoil of the late sixties and early seventies associated with the black power movement, the Second Vatican Council, and the Vietnam War. In April, 1968, 58 black Catholic priests meeting in Detroit formed the Black Catholic Clergy Caucus and issued a statement that described the Catholic church in the United States as a "white racist institution."[3] They particularly faulted it for denying blacks leadership and decision-making roles of any substance. In something of a reprise of the post–World War I years, black and white activists, including some Josephite priests and seminarians, leveled basically the same charges at St. Joseph's Society, which was often the most visible manifestation of the church in the black community. They accused the Josephites of paternalism, insensitivity to Afro-American culture, and failure to encourage and develop black lay and clerical leadership. The resulting crisis, which had its counterpart in many other religious communities and dio-

3. St. Louis *Review*, April 26, 1968.

ceses throughout the nation, cost the Josephites most of their black seminarians and several of their black priests.

Although shaken by internal upheaval and external attack, the Josephites regrouped and reaffirmed their commitment to serving the black community, including the fostering of black leadership within their own society and within the church. By the eighties, the controversies and passions of the sixties and seventies had cooled and had given way to a more cooperative spirit between the Josephites and Afro-American leaders, which could be seen in the planning that preceded the National Black Catholic Congress held in Washington, D.C., in May, 1987. The Josephites continued to ordain black priests, albeit in smaller numbers than during the early sixties, and between 1974 and 1987 saw three of them raised to the episcopacy. The ordination of Marino as the first Afro-American archbishop in the United States testified to the important role that St. Joseph's Society still plays in the Catholic church's ministry to African-Americans and illustrated the strides made in creating an Afro-American Catholic clergy.

In their wrestling with the issue of black priests throughout their relatively short history, the Josephites attempted to deal with a question that most of the rest of the Catholic Church in the United States tried to ignore. In the process, they demonstrated varying degrees of courage and vision, timidity and accommodation. Although insensitive and flawed at times by their own unconscious racism and paternalism, the Josephites, even during the 1920s and 1930s—their time in the wilderness, so to speak—never completely abandoned their ideal of integrated seminary education. The difficulties they experienced over the ordination of black men to the priesthood illustrate the depth of the institutional racism that pervaded the Catholic church in the United States and that crippled its efforts among Afro-Americans. The story of the Josephites, however, also highlights what has been positive and sustaining in this struggle: the vision of Slattery, the trail-blazing courage of the early black Josephite priests, the remarkable contribution made by the Divine Word Missionaries and St. Augustine's Seminary, the key role played by the Holy See and its apostolic delegate in the United States in finally opening American Catholic seminaries to Afro-Americans, and the prophetic stance of black Catholics themselves, who persistently called on both the Josephites and the larger church to practice the Christianity that they professed.

Chapter I

LOST HARVEST, 1634–1871

*It is a golden opportunity for reaping a harvest of souls, which if
neganted may not come again.*
—ARCHBISHOP MARTIN JOHN SPALDING, OCTOBER 9, 1865

On November 18, 1871, a British steamer weighed anchor in South-
ampton harbor, bound for the United States. The ship carried the
Reverend Herbert Vaughan and four other priests of St. Joseph's
Society of the Sacred Heart for Foreign Missions (English Josephites,
or Mill Hill Fathers). This tiny band from Mill Hill, England, represented the most organized effort of the Catholic church to evangelize Afro-Americans in the United States. Vaughan and his men
knew that the church could claim the allegiance of barely 100,000
of the approximately 4,000,000 blacks in the United States, with
serious erosion occurring daily.[1]

Before the arrival of the Mill Hill Fathers, the church had basically failed in its mission to Afro-Americans.[2] Successive waves of
Catholic European immigration throughout the nineteenth century
had taxed church resources to the limit and left few priests and sisters available for work among blacks. The minority status of the
Catholic church in the predominantly Protestant, often hostile,
United States made ecclesiastical leaders reluctant to disturb the racial status quo, especially in the South, where the church was
weakest. Little real enthusiasm existed for the black apostolate be-

1. William A. Osborne, "A Freeman's Odyssey," *Jubilee*, III (September,
1955), 13; John T. Gillard, S.S.J., *Colored Catholics in the United States* (Baltimore, 1941), 9.
2. See Randall Miller, "The Failed Mission: The Catholic Church and Black
Catholics in the Old South," in Randall M. Miller and Jon L. Wakelyn (eds.),
Catholics in the Old South: Essays on Church and Culture (Macon, 1983), 149–70.

9

cause of the indifference and sometimes hostility of most white Catholics, both clerical and lay, to Afro-Americans.

Finally, the church in the United States made few inroads in the black community, and lost many of its own black members in the nineteenth century, because it did not allow blacks to participate fully and freely in the life of the church. Many congregations humiliated their black members by establishing segregated seating arrangements and by requiring blacks to wait to receive the Eucharist until all whites had done so first. The exclusion of all but a handful of black men from the Roman Catholic priesthood, which in effect denied Afro-Americans productive leadership roles, both symbolized and reinforced their subordinate position within the church. Prior to 1886, only the three light-skinned Healy brothers—James, Alexander, and Patrick—managed to hurdle the barriers to black ordination, and even they did not publicly identify with Afro-American causes.

The resistance of church authorities in the United States to the ordination of black priests damaged both blacks and the institutional church itself. Black Catholics were deprived of almost any visible positions of authority. The lack of black leadership, in turn, seriously compromised the church's claims to universality and convinced many non-Catholic blacks that the Catholic church was the "white man's church." The arrival of the Josephites held out hope for a renewed Catholic effort to evangelize Afro-Americans. By 1879, however, hope had turned to discouragement: the Josephites faced imminent collapse, the victims of many of the same problems that had hindered previous Catholic efforts among blacks.

One of the major problems the Josephites faced was the common conception of the priest, on whom the missionary efforts of the Catholic church depended. American Catholics viewed the priest as a mediator between God and humanity; he held the keys to the kingdom of heaven. In the words of the widely used *Baltimore Cathechism*, authorized by the American bishops at the Third Plenary Council of Baltimore in 1884: "Christians should look upon the priests of the Church as the messengers of God and the dispensers of His mysteries." The priest, therefore, did more than preach; he shared in the priesthood of Christ. Upon ordination by a bishop, he received supernatural powers to change bread and wine into the body and blood of Christ during the sacrifice of the mass and to forgive sins in the sacrament of penance. Acting as Christ's representative the priest baptized, celebrated mass, forgave sins, anointed the sick, buried the dead, and preached the gospel. Without the priest, Catholics lacked the sacraments, the means of sanctification. Catholic lay people looked up to their priest as a trusted leader, one who had attained his lofty position after years of prayer and study. Celibacy further distinguished the Roman Catholic priest from other men and underscored his sacral position. The priest, in turn, answered to his bishop, the successor to the apostles; bishops reported to the Roman Curia and, ultimately, to the pope, Christ's vicar on earth.[3]

The exalted view of priesthood shared by most white Catholics precluded in their minds the possibility of black priests. Sharing the prevailing racist ideology of their fellow countrymen, most white Catholics regarded blacks as inferior to caucasians and therefore unfit to serve as priests. Moreover, the ordination of blacks to the sacred priesthood would, at least implicitly, threaten white supremacy in the church, for it would clearly trumpet the moral and intellectual equality of blacks and whites.

No doubt it would have shocked many white Catholics to learn that the Roman Catholic church had ordained black priests at least as early as the fourth century. Beginning with the apostles, Catholic missionaries encouraged the ordination of local men to the priesthood. The Acts of the Apostles and Paul's Epistle to Titus describe how the apostles established mission churches in numerous areas and ordained local Christians to carry on the work they had begun. The successors of the apostles continued that approach. In the fifth and seventh centuries, for example, St. Patrick in Ireland and St. Augustine of Canterbury in England successfully used native priests to establish the church. In fourth-century Africa, the missionary efforts of St. Frumentius led to the conversion of Ethiopia and the subsequent ordination of black Ethiopians to the priesthood. By the seventh century, however, the triumph of monophysitism in Ethiopia removed that church from union with Rome.[4]

3. A Catechism of Christian Doctrine (New York, 1886), 42, 46, 54, 61; The Baltimore Catechism with Explanations (Chicago, 1918), 83; Jay P. Dolan, The American Catholic Experience: A History from Colonial Times to the Present (Garden City, 1985), 221–25.

4. Stephen Neill, A History of Christian Missions (Rev. ed.; Harmondsworth, Eng., 1986), 26–27, 49–50, 58–59, 64–66, 46–47; J. D. Fage (ed.), The Cambridge History of Africa: From c. 500 B.C. to A.D. 1050 (8 vols.; Cambridge, Eng., 1978), II, 430–31, 443.

In the fifteenth and sixteenth centuries, European missionaries came into contact with black Africans and occasionally attempted to promote native vocations. Portuguese Jesuits arrived in Ethiopia in the early fifteenth century. In 1614, one of their number, Pedro Paez, persuaded the Ethiopian emperor to conclude a reunion with the Roman Catholic church; short-lived, it did not survive Paez's death. Capuchin missionaries also labored in Ethiopia, raising at least two Ethiopians to the priesthood. Soon after Portuguese missionaries reached the Congo in 1490, they succeeded in converting a local king and queen. Their son, the Mani-Congo, Nzinga Mbemba, took the Christian name Dom Affonso. One of King Affonso's sons, Dom Henrique, attended a Portuguese seminary, became a priest, and on May 5, 1518, was consecrated a bishop in Rome. Bishop Henrique returned to the Congo in 1521 and died there in 1535, having failed to establish the Catholic church among his people. The Portuguese increasingly came to regard the Congo more as a source of slaves than as a potential Christian ally, and King Affonso's hopes for an indigenous Catholic church died with him in 1543.[5]

Missionaries in the Americas deviated from the traditional church policy of encouraging indigenous clergy. European notions of cultural superiority led them to deny ordination to native peoples. The governments of Spain and Portugal, exercising control over the church in their empires through the royal patronage (*real patronato* and *padroado*, respectively), which they had obtained from popes during the late fifteenth and early sixteenth centuries, refused to allow the ordination of aborigines, mestizos, "Moors," or mulattos. Religious orders appear also to have restricted membership to only those of pure European stock. Although a few mulattos in the eighteenth century managed to circumvent royal policy (Bishop Francisco de Luna Victoria, for example, the son of a black man, took possession of the see of Panama on August 15, 1751, and was transferred to the see of Trujillo, Peru, in 1759), government instructions sent to Spanish civil and ecclesiastical officials in 1709, 1760, and 1772 reiterated the long-standing prohibition against the ordination of blacks and mulattos.[6]

5. Philip Caraman, *The Lost Empire: The Story of the Jesuits in Ethiopia, 1555–1634* (Notre Dame, 1985); *New Catholic Encyclopedia*, V, 585; Basil Davidson, *The African Slave Trade* (Boston, 1980), 136–63.

6. Carl Degler, *Neither Black nor White: Slavery and Race Relations in Brazil and the United States* (New York, 1971), 214; William E. Shiels, *King and Church: The*

In 1622, Pope Gregory XV attempted to establish greater uniformity in missionary effort and to curb excessive royal control over the administration of the missions by establishing a new department of the Roman Curia, the Sacred Congregation for the Propagation of the Faith (Sacra Congregatio de Propaganda Fide), or the Propaganda. The pope entrusted the direction and administration of the church's missionary activity to the Propaganda and appointed a cardinal prefect to head it. In a series of decrees issued throughout the seventeenth century, the Propaganda urged missionaries to foster native clergy. To aid in that endeavor, Pope Urban VIII established a seminary of the Propaganda in Rome in 1627 called the Collegium Urbanum, or Urban College. It trained candidates from all nations for the diocesan, or secular, clergy. (Secular clergy are committed to pastoral ministry under the direction of a bishop, to whom they are bound by a promise of obedience. They differ from regular clergy, who belong to religious institutes—orders, congregations, societies—and who observe the rule, *regula* in Latin, of their respective institutes and are under the direction of their own superiors.) Candidates took an oath to propagate or defend the faith anywhere in the world at the pope's command. The Propaganda, however, could not exercise its authority freely, especially in the face of opposition from the royal governments of Spain and Portugal.[7]

Between the seventeenth and early nineteenth centuries, in what is now the United States, the Catholic church came into significant contact with blacks only in Louisiana and Maryland. In both areas, Catholics, including religious communities such as the Capuchins and the Jesuits, owned black slaves. The baptismal, marriage, and burial records of numerous parishes in Maryland and Louisiana, as well as the Catholic descendants of slaves and free blacks from those areas, offer witness to the efforts of the overburdened Jesuits and Capuchins to bring the faith to blacks. Dedicated priests, such as Joaquin de Portillo in Louisiana, courageously defended the religious rights of slaves against the depredations of un-

Rise and Fall of the Patronato Real (Chicago, 1961); Neill, *Christian Missions,* 149; Miriam T. Murphy, "Catholic Missionary Work Among the Colored People of the United States, 1776–1866," *Records of the American Catholic Historical Society of Philadelphia,* XXXV (June, 1924), 107; Leslie R. Rout, Jr., *The African Experience in Spanish America, 1502 to the Present Day* (Cambridge, Eng., 1976), 138–40.

7. NCE, XI, 840–43; Neill, *Christian Missions,* 152–56, 176–77; John R. Slattery, "Native Clergy," *Catholic World,* LII (March, 1891), 882–85.

scrupulous planters and insisted that the royal government enforce the protections of the slave code, the *Code Noir*.[8]

Despite their reputation as lenient taskmasters, priest slaveholders demonstrated an uneven record in their care for the spiritual welfare of their slaves. In 1763, Jesuits in Louisiana owned a plantation that included 160 slaves living in forty-five small houses. The priests reportedly provided their slaves with regular religious instruction and required their attendance at church services. On the Jesuit plantations in Maryland, however, Peter Kenney, the father visitor sent by the Jesuit father general in 1820 to inspect the Maryland Jesuit plantations, found less-than-adequate living conditions for the slaves. Despite catechesis and their required attendance at mass, Kenney characterized the slaves' lives as "a moral wasteland and a scandalous reproach to the Society." The Maryland Jesuits eventually rid themselves of their slave problems by selling their 272 slaves in 1838 for $115,000. Despite elaborate instructions to the contrary from the father general, the sale broke up some slave families.[9] The degraded status and inadequate religious instruction of blacks in Maryland and Louisiana gave little enough encouragement to the growth of Catholicism among blacks. For their part, missionaries certainly did not consider the slave quarters a potential source of priestly vocations.

Ultimately, though, the religious instruction of slaves in colonial Louisiana and Maryland depended on the zeal of lay masters—a zeal that often lagged. In 1785, John Carroll, who had recently been appointed superior of the American missions, criticized Catholic planters for "a general lack of care in instructing . . . the Negro slaves in their religion." When Bishop Luis Peñalver made his first official visit to the diocese of New Orleans in 1795, he observed that "marriage among the slaves is almost unknown."[10] The reli-

8. Gillard, *Colored Catholics*, 53–54, 65–68; James Hennesey, S.J., *American Catholics: A History of the Roman Catholic Community in the United States* (New York, 1981), 43.

9. Gillard, *Colored Catholics*, 62, 68; Hennesey, *American Catholics*, 32; R. Emmett Curran, S.J., "'Splendid Poverty': Jesuit Slaveholding in Maryland, 1805–1838," in Randall M. Miller and Jon L. Wakelyn (eds.), *Catholics in the Old South: Essays on Church and Culture* (Macon, 1983), 126, 129, 132–33, 142–43. On clerical slaveholding, see also Madeleine Hooke Rice, *American Catholic Opinion in the Slavery Controversy* (New York, 1944), 45–54; Gilbert J. Garraghan, *The Jesuits of the Middle West* (3 vols.; New York, 1938), I, 610–20; Stafford Poole, C.M., and Douglas J. Slawson, C.M., *Church and Slave in Perry County Missouri, 1818–1865* (Lewiston/Queenston, N.Y., 1986), 141–95.

10. Hennesey, *American Catholics*, 43; Gillard, *Colored Catholics*, 54.

gious indifference of many planters and the small number of priests in Maryland and Louisiana often meant that many blacks did not receive the spiritual ministrations of the church.

The shortage of priests grew more acute in antebellum America as immigrants began pouring into the United States after 1815, threatening to overwhelm the limited resources of the church. Between 1815 and 1860, the Catholic population increased from 195,000 to 3,103,000, with immigration, primarily from Ireland and Germany, accounting for two-thirds of the growth. During the 1830s, 250,000 Catholics arrived here, 700,000 came in the next decade, and nearly 1,000,000 entered the country between 1850 and 1860. Although some Irish went to such southern port cities as New Orleans, the majority concentrated in the urban areas of the Northeast. Many of the Germans established themselves on farms and in cities in the Midwest. The influx of population transformed the Catholic church into an immigrant church. As late as 1866, thirty-one of the forty-seven members of the American hierarchy were foreign-born.[11]

As bishops devoted their energies and resources to meeting the needs of the immigrants in the North, missionary efforts on behalf of blacks in the South suffered. In an 1858 letter to the Lyon Society for the Propagation of the Faith, a French-based missionary aid society, Bishop William Elder of Natchez, Mississippi, lamented that he could not enable Catholic masters to do their religious duty to their slaves, "because there are not priests enough." Archbishop James Whitfield of Baltimore clearly showed that the needs of Catholic whites took top priority when he wrote that though the slaves presented a golden opportunity for apostolic labor, he could not even meet the needs of whites, who felt deprived of the succors of religion, and that he therefore could not attend to blacks.[12]

The weak condition of the Catholic church in the antebellum South prevented it from adequately meeting the needs of either whites or blacks. In 1820, the diocese of Richmond, Virginia, embraced no more than 1,000 Catholics. In 1842, at the death of

11. Hennesey, *American Catholics*, 102; Dennis Clark, "The South's Irish Catholics: A Case of Cultural Confinement," in Randall M. Miller and Jon L. Wakelyn (eds.), *Catholics in the Old South: Essays on Church and Culture* (Macon, 1983), 196–201; Thomas W. Spalding, *Martin John Spalding: American Churchman* (Washington, D.C., 1973), 195.

12. Edward J. Misch, "The American Bishops and the Negro from the Civil War to the Third Plenary Council of Baltimore, 1865–1884" (Ph.D. dissertation, Pontifical Gregorian University, 1968), 37–38.

John England, the vigorous bishop of Charleston, South Carolina's Catholics numbered only 7,000. In 1850, only eight of the more than eighteen hundred churches in Georgia were Roman Catholic. When Auguste Martin assumed direction of the newly created diocese of Natchitoches, Louisiana, in 1853, he found 25,000 Catholics spread over 22,000 square miles, for which he had one priest and seven churches. Prior to 1850, the Natchez diocese never contained more than six priests, and the Mobile diocese never had more than twenty. Bishop John Quinlan of Mobile found 10,000 Catholics, out of a total population of 964,201 in Alabama in 1860, and counted only 9 parishes and 9 mission stations, compared with 805 Baptist, 777 Methodist, 135 Presbyterian, and 34 Episcopalian congregations. Both the Natchez and Mobile dioceses lay close to the principal Catholic center of the South, the diocese of New Orleans, which held about 170,000 Catholics in 1850. By 1860, the 737,000 Catholics in the South constituted approximately 6 percent of the total southern population.[13]

Prior to the Civil War, all of the southern dioceses except New Orleans and Charleston depended heavily on grants of money from the Lyon Society for the Propagation of the Faith because southern Catholics could not contribute enough to support their churches. The dependence of the southern Catholic church on immigrant clergy, who often failed to appreciate the culture of the South and who alienated white and black Catholics alike, further sapped its vitality.[14]

In the North, where the church enjoyed greater strength and influence, long-standing antagonism between the Irish and Afro-Americans created distrust in the black community toward the church. Friction between the Irish and free blacks, based in part on job competition, exploded into race riots on a number of occasions. In 1829, for example, a three-day running battle in Cincinnati saw Irish rioters attack free blacks, black-owned property, and fugitive

13. Gillard, *Colored Catholics*, 58; Raymond H. Schmandt, "An Overview of Institutional Establishments in the Antebellum Southern Church," in Randall M. Miller and Jon L. Wakelyn (eds.), *Catholics in the Old South: Essays on Church and Culture* (Macon, 1983), 76; Clark, "The South's Irish Catholics," in Miller and Wakelyn (eds.), *Catholics in the Old South*, 202, 204; Michael J. McNally, "A Minority of a Minority: The Witness of Black Women Religious in the Antebellum South," *Review for Religious*, XL (March, 1981), 261.

14. Randall Miller, "Failed Mission," in Miller and Wakelyn (eds.), *Catholics in the Old South*, 152.

slaves. Subsequently, most of the black population of 2,000 moved to Canada. Irish mobs also assaulted blacks in Philadelphia in 1834 and, most infamously, in New York during the 1863 draft riot. Harriet Thompson, a black Catholic living in New York City, wrote to Pope Pius IX on October 29, 1853, to complain about the treatment of blacks in New York at the hands of the Irish-born archbishop of New York, John J. Hughes. Thompson pointed out that black Catholic school children could not attend Catholic schools in New York. She also claimed that Archbishop Hughes opposed Catholic schools for black children and in general disliked the black race.[15] For many blacks, *Catholic* meant Irish, and *Irish* meant enemy.

Irish and *Catholic* also meant enemy to many Protestant Americans. During the first half of the nineteenth century, the Catholic church found itself on the defensive in the face of repeated attacks from nativists. Anti-Catholic writers, such as Samuel F. B. Morse, condemned Catholicism as "idolatrous," "foreign," and "anti-American"; Maria Monk spun salacious tales about the "horrors" of convent life in her widely read *Awful Disclosures*. Between 1834 and 1855, individual Catholics and their convents, schools, and churches were the targets of nativist mob violence in cities and towns as diverse as Philadelphia, Knoxville, St. Louis, Louisville, San Antonio, and Charlestown, Massachusetts, Helena, Arkansas, and Portsmouth, Virginia. In 1855, the avowedly anti-Catholic American, or Know-Nothing, party held forty-three seats in the 34th Congress of the United States. During the last half of the decade, the emerging Republican party consistently exploited anti-Catholic feeling for political gain. One South Carolinian expressed the prevailing sentiment in the South when he declared that priestly clothes "doubtless concealed the impurities of the devil."[16]

15. Dennis Clark, "Urban Blacks and Irishmen: Brothers in Prejudice," in Miriam Ershkowitz and Joseph Zikmund II (eds.), *Black Politics in Philadelphia* (New York, 1973), 15–19; William A. Osborne, *Segregated Covenant: Race Relations and American Catholics* (New York, 1967), 21; Harriet Thompson to Pope Pius IX, October 29, 1853, copy in Congressi, America Centrale, 16, fols. 770rv, 775r, 771rv, 774r, 773r, APF.

16. Ray Allen Billington, *The Protestant Crusade, 1800–1860* (1938; rpr. New York, 1963), 68–76, 220–34, 409, 421; Charles E. Nolan, "History of Catholic Parishes in the South Central Region," in Jay P. Dolan (ed.), *The American Catholic Parish: A History from 1850 to the Present* (2 vols.; New York, 1987), I, 253–54; William E. Gienapp, "Nativism and the Creation of a Republican Majority in the

As a result of their vulnerability in American society, Catholics attempted to avoid political or social controversy by accommodating to prevailing political, social, and racial norms. Not able to compromise on doctrinal issues, they hastened instead to demonstrate flexibility on social and political questions. Catholic social thought stressed the personal obligations of providing for families, obeying the government, aiding the poor, and complying with church law. It did not include the idea of changing economic or social conditions.[17]

Although Pope Gregory XVI denounced the slave trade in an apostolic letter, *In Supremo Apostolatus fastigo,* dated December 3, 1839, traditional Catholic moral theology, heavily influenced by Roman law, did not condemn the institution of slavery itself. Archbishop Francis P. Kenrick of Baltimore, author of the three-volume *Theologia Moralis,* the standard moral theology textbook used in American seminaries, acknowledged that slaves had definite rights to physical and moral well-being because they shared in the image and likeness of God. Kenrick maintained, however, that if slave owners minimally respected the physical and moral rights of slaves by providing food, shelter, and opportunities to practice their religion, then slavery was neither repugnant to natural law nor inconsistent with the exercise of the true faith. Although Kenrick held up gradual emancipation, consistent of course with existing laws and social order, as the ideal, Catholics in general favored amelioration rather than emancipation. Affiliation with the Democratic party, which openly welcomed immigrants and acted as something of a political shield against attacks by nativist Whigs, Know-Nothings, and Republicans, accommodation to prevailing social and economic conditions, and interpretation of traditional church teaching accounted for American Catholic toleration of the "peculiar institution."[18]

North before the Civil War," *Journal of American History,* LXXII (December, 1985), 529–59; Randall M. Miller, "A Church in Cultural Captivity: Some Speculations on Catholic Identity," in Randall M. Miller and Jon L. Wakelyn (eds.), *Catholics in the Old South: Essays on Church and Culture* (Macon, 1983), 17–18.

17. Misch, "American Bishops and the Negro," 46–47; Schmandt, "An Overview of Institutional Establishments," in Miller and Wakelyn (eds.), *Catholics in the Old South,* 76.

18. Maria Caravaglios, *The American Catholic Church and the Negro Problem* (Rome, 1974), 307–308. For a translation of relevant portions of Francis P. Ken-

Catholic social teaching and popular opinion notwithstanding, enemies of the church in the South occasionally attempted to smear Catholics with the charge of abolitionism. Bishop John England's attempt in the summer of 1835 to open a school for free blacks in Charleston led to charges that he sympathized with abolitionists. Ensuing threats of mob violence forced him to abandon the project. England had already aroused the suspicion of many South Carolinians by his service as apostolic delegate to the Republic of Haiti, a position he held from 1833 to 1837. During his stint as delegate, England became the first American bishop to ordain a black man, raising George Paddington, a mulatto, to the priesthood in Port au Prince in May, 1836. Irate South Carolinians believed that merely treating with a black republic signaled the Church's sympathy with abolitionism. England went to great lengths, including an address before the South Carolina legislature in December, 1836, to dissociate himself and his church from abolitionism.[19]

Four years later, in *Letters to the Honorable John Forsyth on the Subject of Domestic Slavery*, which first appeared in England's diocesan newspaper, *United States Catholic Miscellany*, England reiterated his personal opposition to abolitionism and his approval of the indefinite continuation of slavery so long as masters treated slaves according to Christian principles. He addressed the letters to then secretary of state John Forsyth because the secretary, upset by Gregory XVI's condemnation of the slave trade, had used a campaign speech to accuse the pope and Catholics in general of aiding abolitionism. In fact, most American Catholics regarded abolitionists—many of whom, such as Lyman Beecher, were also vocally anti-Catholic—as dangerous social radicals, as enemies of religion, public law, and the Union. Bishop Richard Vincent Whelan of Wheeling expressed prevailing Catholic opinion when he described

---

rick's *Theologia Moralis*, see Poole and Slawson, *Church and Slave*, 53–58. See also Joseph Brokhage, *Francis Patrick Kenrick's Opinion on Slavery* (Washington, D.C., 1955), 102, 110–19, 122–23; Charles P. Connor, "The Northern Catholic Position on Slavery and the Civil War: Archbishop Hughes as a Test Case," *Records of the American Catholic Historical Society of Philadelphia*, XCVI (March–December, 1985), 35–37; and Rice, *American Catholic Opinion*, 70–71, 86–109.

19. Peter Guilday, *The Life and Times of John England* (2 vols.; 1927; rpr. New York, 1969), II, 270–313, 327–28, 151–56. For more information on George Paddington, see Leo R. Ryan, "Pierre Toussaint, 'God's Image Carved in Ebony,'" *Historical Records and Studies*, XXV (1935), 40–44, 50–51, and Richard C. Madden, *Catholics in South Carolina: A Record* (Lanham, Md., 1985), 389–90.

abolitionists, along with "infidels and Red Republicans," as the most deadly enemies of the church.[20]

Some Catholic masters conscientiously attempted to provide for the physical and moral needs of their slaves, just as Archbishop Kenrick advised. Silas Dorsey, for example, furnished the seventy-five slaves on his Maryland farm with good food, clothing, and shelter. He also conducted regular religious services in the chapel on the farm and brought Jesuits to the plantation to say mass, baptize, and conduct funerals.[21]

Most Catholic slave owners, however, did not imitate Dorsey. In 1844, Bishop John Chanche of Natchez, Mississippi, wrote to the Lyon Society for the Propagation of the Faith requesting that it help him recruit priests in Europe to instruct blacks who "live in an entire ignorance of religion and die without baptism." Many Catholic masters refused to allow their slaves to attend Catholic services off the plantation for fear that their slaves would run away. As teachers of catechism, most masters performed poorly, and some even hired Protestant preachers or allowed slaves to preach to one another. With widely scattered churches, few priests, and little money, bishops could not help those masters who genuinely wanted to encourage Catholicism among their salves.[22]

Countervailing forces during the antebellum period eventually undermined even the efforts of conscientious Catholic slave owners. The segregated pews or galleries of rural Catholic churches embarrassed blacks and helped to alienate them from the "white man's church." Catholic slaves felt drawn to the slave preachers with whom they increasingly came into contact as Protestant slaveholders and slaves flooded into the Gulf region. Slave preachers presided over the "invisible institution" of prayer meetings and worship services that the slaves constructed outside the white institutional churches. Slaves identified with their black preachers and took great pride in the preachers' homiletic skills, which they viewed as evidence of black intelligence. Many Catholic slaves preferred the emotional, evangelical religion of Afro-Protestantism, with its emphasis on preaching, the Bible, conversion experience, and libera-

20. Rice, *American Catholic Opinion*, 64–70, 109.

21. Hennesey, *American Catholics*, 146.

22. Report of Bishop John T. Chanche to the Society for the Propagation of the Faith, 1844, in John T. Chanche Papers, ADJ; Miller, "Failed Mission," in Miller and Wakelyn (eds.), *Catholics in the Old South*, 157–58.

tion, to the stiff, formal Catholicism espoused by the often-foreign Catholic priests who occasionally visited the plantation and who aligned themselves with the masters. Explaining why she left the Catholic church, Elizabeth Ross Hite, a former slave of French Catholic masters in Louisiana, explained that "lots didn't like that 'ligion" because it did not allow the slaves to "shout an pray like ya wanted to." Catholic slaves lacked black Catholic priests sensitive to their needs, and white Catholic clergy, such as Bishop England, discouraged black Catholic lay preachers for fear that such un-learned men would debase Catholic teaching.[23]

By 1860, Catholic masters probably owned not more than 5 per-cent of the 4,000,000 slaves in the United States. In the absence of accurate statistics, the best estimates put the number of black Catholics at approximately 100,000, the vast majority concen-trated in the South. Compared with European immigrants, they constituted only a tiny percentage of Catholics in the United States. The largest number of black Catholics, approximately 62,500, lived in Louisiana and along the Gulf coast of Mississippi and Ala-bama; of the remainder, 15,000 lived in Maryland, and 22,500 re-sided throughout the rest of the country, including small enclaves in western Kentucky and Florida and in Charleston, South Caro-lina. The sheer numbers of Protestant slaves inevitably led to mix-ing between them and the Catholic slaves. As a result of that and the indifference of many Catholic masters, Afro-Protestantism simply overwhelmed Afro-Catholicism in the rural South. Of the rural black Catholic communities, only the colony of *creoles de cou-leur libre*, or Creole free people of color, at Isle Breville in Louisiana survived, a Catholic island in an otherwise largely Protestant sea.[24]

Black Catholics did not constitute a distinct ethnic group but di-vided along cultural, geographic, and social lines. Caste barriers separated slaves, free blacks, and Creole free people of color. The French-speaking, light-skinned, Roman Catholic Creoles of color

23. Albert J. Raboteau, *Slave Religion: "The Invisible Institution" in the Ante-bellum South* (New York, 1978), 133–43, 231–39, 272; Miller, "Failed Mission," and Miller, "A Church in Cultural Captivity," both in Miller and Wakelyn (eds.), *Catholics in the Old South*, 158–62, 39–40. See also, Machel Sobel, *Trabelin' On: The Slave Journey to an Afro-Baptist Faith* (Westport, Conn., 1979).

24. Gillard, *Colored Catholics*, 99; Miller, "Failed Mission," and Gary B. Mills, "Piety and Prejudice: A Colored Catholic Community in the Antebellum South," both in Randall M. Miller and Jon L. Wakelyn (eds.), *Catholics in the Old South: Essays on Church and Culture* (Macon, 1983), 151, 161–67, 171–94.

lived in Louisiana and along the Gulf coast of Alabama and Mississippi. They established barriers between themselves and those they
called "American blacks"—both slave and free. Often educated,
sometimes slaveholders themselves, the Creole free people of color
identified with French culture and Catholicism. At St. Augustine's
Church in New Orleans, they rented half the pews and worshiped
with the white Creoles, whom they sought to emulate. They bitterly resisted any attempts by whites to lump them with American
blacks. Isolated from other Afro-Americans, the colored Creoles,
with some notable exceptions, showed little enthusiasm for enlarg-
ing the black presence in the church by evangelizing slaves or poor
free blacks.[25]

The church's black apostolate relied primarily on the individual
efforts of interested white clergy. In New Orleans, the Ursuline
nuns instructed black girls from the 1720s to 1824, and the Car-
melite sisters began a school in the early years of the nineteenth
century. In Baltimore, Sulpician priests associated with St. Mary's,
the nation's first Catholic seminary, ministered to Baltimore's black
Catholics, most of whom were French-speaking refugees from the
revolutionary violence in Saint Domingue, later called Haiti. As
early as 1794, Louis William DuBourg started a catechism class on
Sundays for black children. In succeeding years, Jean-Marie Tessier
and James Hector Joubert de la Muraille served as catechists for
Baltimore blacks, who worshiped until 1836 in the basement of the
seminary chapel, called by the Sulpicians the "Chapelle Basse."
After they gave up work among the blacks, Peter Miller, a Jesuit,
opened the Chapel of Blessed Peter Claver in the basement of
St. Ignatius Church in 1857. The fund-raising efforts of Michael
O'Connor, a former bishop of Pittsburgh who resigned his see in
order to become a Jesuit, enabled the basement congregation to
purchase the large building, four blocks from Peter Claver chapel,
that, in 1863, became St. Francis Xavier Church, the first exclusively black Catholic parish in the United States. Bishop England
taught catechism on Sunday afternoons to blacks and opened his
short-lived convent school for free blacks in Charleston in 1835.
Ten years later, the St. Joseph Sisters of Carondolet established a
school for blacks in St. Louis. In both cases, however, white op-

25. Miller, "Failed Mission," and Miller, "A Church in Cultural Captivity,"
both in Miller and Wakelyn (eds.), *Catholics in the Old South*, 151, 40–42.

position forced the schools to close.[26] Clearly, a few isolated bishops, priests, and sisters, no matter how dedicated, could make little significant impression on several million Afro-Americans in the United States.

Evidence, however, indicates that a vibrant faith life existed among many of those blacks who were Catholic. The African-American Catholic community produced people such as the saintly Pierre Toussaint (1766–1853), a hairdresser by trade to New York City's white elite, who devoted himself to daily acts of charity to both black and white. In December of 1843, approximately 200 black men and women, meeting together in the parish hall of the Baltimore cathedral parish, established, with the approbation of the archbishop and the rector of the cathedral, a prayer group known as the "Society of the Holy Family." The society, which functioned for almost two years, met on Sunday evenings. A white priest served as director, but the members of the group elected officers and established rules. Meetings lasted for approximately two hours and featured prayer in common, instruction based usually on a scripture reading, the singing of hymns, and the raising of money for the needs of the cathedral and for the poor. Members also bought books, including catechisms and the lives of the saints, for a society library.[27]

The founding of two religious communities between 1829 and 1842 among French-speaking women of color in Baltimore and New Orleans, after an earlier abortive attempt by the Reverend Charles Nerinckx in Kentucky in 1824, testified to the ability of the black Catholic community to produce religious vocations from among its own ranks. It also held out the promise of more laborers for the black apostolate and furnished concrete proof to black Catholics that they, like whites, were called to holiness and leadership roles, albeit circumscribed, in the church. Shortly after assuming duties as the catechist for Baltimore's black Catholics in 1827, Sulpician James Joubert realized the need for a school for Baltimore's

26. Gillard, Colored Catholics, 120–21; McNally, "A Minority of a Minority," 262–63; Christopher J. Kauffman, Tradition and Transformation in Catholic Culture: The Priests of Saint Sulpice in the United States from 1791 to the Present (New York, 1988), 113–16; Miller, "A Church in Cultural Captivity," in Miller and Wakelyn (eds.), Catholics in the Old South, 37–38.

27. Cyprian Davis, O.S.B., "Black Spirituality," U.S. Catholic Historian, VII, Nos. 2 and 3 (1988), 39–40.

blacks (the city did not provide public schools for blacks until after 1865). Joubert's efforts on behalf of a school brought him into contact with Elizabeth Lange and Magdaleine Balas, two young Haitian women of color (Lange had been born in Cuba of Haitian parents). Their association led to the establishment in 1829 of the first permanent black religious community, the Oblate Sisters of Providence, who dedicated themselves to the education of black children. Joubert served as the priest-director of the community. In 1836, the Oblates opened St. Frances Academy, whose chapel served as the unofficial parish church of Baltimore's black Catholics until the opening of the Peter Claver chapel twenty years later.[28]

The Oblate community grew during the 1830s but barely survived the following decade. They lost Joubert through death in 1843, and no one replaced him as priest-director because the Sulpician superior in France ordered all of his priests to forgo "extraneous" work in order to concentrate on seminary education. The Oblates found themselves cut adrift from the white religious community; their financial condition deteriorated alarmingly, and enrollment at St. Frances Academy plummeted. They suffered such poverty that they had to turn away postulants because of a lack of clothes and money. They supported themselves and the orphans for whom they cared on the small sums that they earned from washing, ironing, and mending. By 1847 only twelve sisters remained in the community, and Archbishop Samuel Eccleston of Baltimore decided to disband them. Only the intervention and help of two Redemptorist priests, St. John Neumann and Thaddeus Anwander, saved the Oblates. Neumann, the Redemptorist superior, promised Eccleston that he would guarantee the support of the Oblates; meanwhile, Anwander, who would become the Oblates' priest-director in 1847, begged house to house in Baltimore for money and students for the Oblates' academy. Their efforts succeeded. By 1849 the Oblates had regained financial solvency and were able to expand their work. Enrollment grew at St. Frances Academy, reaching three hundred by 1855, and a boys' school was added. Graduates of St. Frances founded additional schools for blacks, including several in Washington, D.C. In the fifteen years following the Civil

28. John T. Gillard, S.S.J., *The Catholic Church and the American Negro* (1929; rpr. New York, 1968), 135–36; Cyprian Davis, O.S.B., "Black Catholics in Nineteenth Century America," *U.S. Catholic Historian*, V, No. 1 (1986), 4–6; Kauffman, *Tradition and Transformation*, 113–14; McNally, "A Minority of a Minority," 262–64, 265.

War, Oblate sisters staffed Catholic schools for black children in Washington, D.C., New Orleans, and St. Louis, as well as in Baltimore.[29]

In New Orleans, after two futile attempts to form an interracial community, both thwarted by the law, Henriette Delille and Juliette Gaudin, two free women of color, in 1842 founded the second permanent religious congregation of black women in the United States: the Sisters of the Holy Family. Their choice of the religious life represented a dramatic rejection of conventional expectations, which assumed that attractive free women of color would become the concubines of wealthy white Creoles. In their venture, Delille and Gaudin received the assistance of the Reverend Etienne Rousselon and Marie Jeanne Aliquot, a French woman who devoted her life to the religious instruction of slaves. The Sisters of the Holy Family taught catechism to slaves and later to poor free blacks. They also cared for the sick and opened a home for the aged called the Hospice of the Holy Family. In 1852, the first year in which they were permitted to make public vows, they established St. Augustine School; two years later, they opened an orphanage. After the Civil War, the Holy Family sisters expanded beyond New Orleans, providing many teachers for black Catholic schools in the South.[30]

The Oblate Sisters of Providence and the Sisters of the Holy Family encountered opposition from non-Catholics and Catholics alike. During 1856 in Baltimore, Know-Nothings twice allegedly broke into the Oblates' St. Joseph's School, forcing the suspension of classes. At a time when Catholic postulants in the South often brought slaves with them to convents as part of their dowries, many white Catholics could not accept the idea of black sisters. The black sisters hesitated to wear distinctive garb because of anticipated opposition; not until 1872 were the Holy Family sisters allowed to wear a religious habit in public. After they donned their

29. McNally, "A Minority of a Minority," 265–66; Sr. Jerome Francis Woods, C.D.P., "Congregations of Religious Women in the Old South," in Randall M. Miller and Jon L. Wakelyn (eds.), *Catholics in the Old South: Essays on Church and Culture* (Macon, 1983), 111; M. Reginald Gerdes, O.S.P., "To Educate and Evangelize: Black Catholic Schools of the Oblate Sisters of Providence (1828–1880)," *U.S. Catholic Historian*, Vol. VII, Nos. 2 and 3 (1988), 193–97. See also Grace Sherwood, *The Oblates' One Hundred and One Years* (New York, 1931).

30. Woods, "Congregations of Religious Women," 115–16; Sr. Audrey Marie Detiege, *Henriette Delille, Free Woman of Color: Foundress of the Sisters of the Holy Family* (New Orleans, 1976); Sr. Mary Borgia Hart, S.S.F., *Violets in the King's Garden* (N.p., 1976).

veils and wimples, black sisters endured insults, including being forced off sidewalks. Nevertheless, the black congregations of sisters persevered, aided by individual churchmen and white, women religious such as the Ursulines and the sisters of the Society of the Sacred Heart.[31]

The black sisters served as role models of Catholicism among blacks and as living proof that sanctity and religious vocations were perdurable in the black Catholic community. In addition to serving their people by educating them and caring for orphans and the elderly, black sisters also eventually provided the inspiration, guidance, and encouragement that often proved crucial in fostering vocations to the priesthood among black Catholic boys.

Throughout the nineteenth century, black priests were found even more rarely in the Catholic church in the United States than were black nuns. Between 1854 and 1864, only the three Healy brothers, sons of an Irish-born Georgia plantation owner and a mulatto slave woman, surmounted the formidable obstacles that blocked the path to ordination for most black men. James Augustine Healy and Alexander Sherwood Healy were ordained for the archdiocese of Boston, and Patrick Francis Healy became a Jesuit. Each studied for the priesthood in Canada or in Europe since no American seminary would accept black students; each was ordained in Europe because no bishop in the United States would ordain them. The Healys owed their ordinations and subsequent clerical advancement to the patronage and protection of Bishop John Fitzpatrick and Archbishop John Williams of Boston.[32]

Although they encountered racial prejudice, the Healys enjoyed considerable success in ministries devoted primarily to whites. After his ordination in Paris in 1854, James considered requesting a secretarial assignment whereby he could avoid the anticipated vilification from Boston's Irish Catholics. Healy confided to George Fenwick, a Jesuit friend at Holy Cross College, "The mercy of God has placed a poor outcast on a throne of glory that ill becomes him. . . . I should have desired never to show my face in Boston." Bishop Fitzpatrick, however, refused to allow his protégé to se-

31. Hennesey, *American Catholics,* 144; Woods, "Congregations of Religious Women," in Miller and Wakelyn (eds.), *Catholics in the Old South,* 116; Davis, "Black Catholics in Nineteenth Century America," 6; McNally, "A Minority of a Minority," 269.

32. Albert S. Foley, S.J., *God's Men of Color: The Colored Catholic Priests of the United States, 1854–1954* (1955; rpr. New York, 1969), 1–31.

quester himself and moved James into prestigious administrative and pastoral assignments over a twenty-one-year period. Fitzpatrick's unquestioned support of Healy did much to defuse any potential opposition: at various times, Healy served as personal secretary to the bishop, chancellor of the diocese, assistant at St. John's Church, rector of the cathedral, and pastor of St. James Church in Boston. In February, 1875, at Bishop Fitzpatrick's urging, the pope appointed James Augustine Healy bishop of the diocese of Portland, Maine. He remained bishop of Portland until his death in 1900.[33]

Although the Irish stevedores on the Portland docks reacted with astonishment at the news that the new bishop was a "Neegar," Healy won the loyalty of his Irish and French Canadian people. He comforted them in their hardships, worked tirelessly for Catholic orphans, defended the rights of Catholics from the attacks of the nativist American Protective Association, and extended charity to the poor of his diocese. He distinguished himself as an administrator, too, adding more than sixty parishes and eighteen schools to the diocese between 1875 and 1900. He moved easily among his fellow bishops, maintaining close friendships with Bishop Matthew Harkins of Providence and with Cardinal James Gibbons of Baltimore, who frequently visited Portland as his guest. Healy also achieved fame as a pulpit orator and made contributions to church law at the Third Plenary Council of Baltimore in 1884.[34]

Healy identified more with his Irish heritage and his French training than with his Afro-American background. His Maine diocese contained only about three hundred black Catholics; he made sure, though, that they received full and equal treatment in churches, schools, and other diocesan institutions. He was drafted at the Third Plenary Council to serve on the special subcommittee considering legislation for the black and Indian missions of the United States. For the next seven years, as a result of both his racial background and his experience with Indian missions in Maine, he served on the Commission for Catholic Missions Among the Colored People and the Indians that the council established. He did not participate in the Catholic Afro-American congresses, held between 1889 and 1894, though he wrote letters of recommendation for the congress agents who traveled through dioceses soliciting donations

33. Foley, God's Men, 57, 1–12; Osborne, "Freeman's Odyssey," 14.
34. Foley, God's Men, 6–12; Albert S. Foley, S.J., Bishop Healy: Beloved Outcaste (New York, 1954), 92–243.

and subscriptions to the *American Catholic Tribune,* a newspaper owned and edited by the leader of the congress movement, Daniel Rudd. The congresses became more aggressive in their insistence on an end to racial discrimination in the church, so Healy declined an invitation to speak at the 1892 gathering, explaining that he had "some apprehension about conventions which are held on such strictly racial lines." He insisted that "we are of the church where there is neither gentile nor Jew . . . slave or freeman, but Christ is in all." [35]

Following Alexander Sherwood Healy's ordination in Rome in 1858 and his reception of a canon law degree in 1860, Bishop Fitzpatrick considered him a possible candidate for rector of the new North American College in Rome, an elite seminary that educated only American students specifically chosen by their bishops and designated to serve as diocesan priests in the United States. In a letter to Archbishop Hughes of New York, however, Fitzpatrick concluded that he could not recommend Healy: "He has African blood and it shews [*sic*] distinctly. . . . This in a large number of American youths might lessen the respect they ought to feel for the first superior of the house." Fortunately, Healy never found out about this lost opportunity, and in 1864 Fitzpatrick arranged for his appointment to the faculty of the New York provincial seminary at Troy. Fitzpatrick's successor, Archbishop John Williams, took a liking to Healy and chose him as his theologian for the Second Plenary Council of Baltimore in 1866 and as his theological advisor for the First Vatican Council in Rome in 1869. During the Second Plenary Council, Healy refrained from participating in discussions about the church's missionary work among blacks. Like his brother before him, he served as rector of Holy Cross Cathedral and, for a few months before his death in 1875, as pastor of St. James Parish in Boston. [36]

Patrick Francis Healy received holy orders in the Society of Jesus in Brussels, Belgium, in August, 1864. He served successively as professor, prefect of studies, vice-rector, and, from 1874 to 1882, as rector of Georgetown University, where students referred to him as "the Spaniard," because of his swarthy appearance. At Georgetown

35. Albert S. Foley, S.J., "Bishop Healy and the Colored Catholic Congress," *Interracial Review,* XXVIII (May, 1954), 79–80.

36. Bishop John B. Fitzpatrick to Archbishop John Hughes, July 10, 1859, copy in Alexander Healy File, JFA; Foley, *God's Men,* 13–22; Misch, "American Bishops and the Negro," 206.

he modernized the curriculum and started the institution on the road to becoming a full-fledged university, organized an alumni association, and superintended the construction of the massive administration, classroom, and residential building that today bears his name. His efforts on behalf of the school earned him the sobriquet "Georgetown's Second Founder." The financial pressures associated with his building program, however, wore him down and damaged his health. He resigned from Georgetown in 1882 and remained in semiretirement until his death in 1910.[37]

Although each of the Healy brothers enjoyed considerable success in the predominantly white Catholic church, that success did not diminish the prevailing popular prejudice against the ordination of black men to the priesthood. The Healys' light skin, episcopal support, identification with white society and white ministries, and general silence on race questions led many whites to regard them as "near white" and not as "genuine Negroes." Many Catholics outside Massachusetts, Maine, and Washington, D.C., did not realize that the Catholic clergy in the United States included any black men among its members. Possessing only two black priests prior to the Civil War, the Catholic church simply had no counterparts to such activist black Protestant clergy in the North as Morris Brown, Samuel Cornish, Henry Highland Garnet, Leonard Grimes, Nathaniel and Thomas Paul, Daniel Payne, James W. C. Pennington, and Peter Williams, Jr. Whether African Baptist, African Methodist, Congregational, Episcopalian, or Presbyterian, they helped spearhead antebellum black protest and reform movements that resulted in new Afro-American institutions: churches and schools, newspapers, vigilance committees to aid fugitive slaves, petition campaigns, and the black convention movement.[38] For their part, the Healys functioned quietly in an American Catholic church that remained generally opposed to the notion of black clergy.

White Catholic hostility to the ordination of black priests helped kill the dreams of William Augustine Williams, a young Afro-American convert from Virginia. In 1853, Thaddeus Anwander recommended Williams for admission to the Propaganda's college in Rome. Since canon law required all seminarians to have a bishop

37. Foley, God's Men, 23–31.
38. David E. Swift, Black Prophets of Justice: Activist Clergy Before the Civil War (Baton Rouge, 1989), 1–18.

or religious congregation as a sponsor who would then assume responsibility for them upon ordination, Anwander convinced Bishop Louis A. Rappe of Cleveland and Archbishop Kenrick of Baltimore to sponsor Williams. When officials of the Propaganda solicited the opinion of Archbishop Hughes on the matter, he strongly recommended against sending Williams to Rome if the Propaganda and Rappe contemplated returning him to the United States upon ordination, for public opinion, Hughes claimed, violently opposed black priests. Despite that advice, the Propaganda accepted Williams for the academic year beginning in November, 1855. He was not the first black student admitted. Prior to Williams, black students from Africa had already matriculated at the Urban College and had returned to Guinea to take up missionary work among their people.[39]

Clerical skepticism about Williams' plans surfaced almost from the beginning of his seminary days. After meeting Williams on his way to Rome, Louis R. Deluol, professor at the Sulpician seminary at Issy, France, wrote in a letter to François Lhomme, president of St. Mary's Seminary in Baltimore, that, contrary to his expectations, he found Williams "very intelligent," but he wondered, "What will he do in Baltimore as a priest?" Three years later, Archbishop Kenrick provided an answer to Deluol's query. In a letter to the Propaganda, Kenrick urged the congregation to send Williams to Liberia, because virulent prejudice would make it nearly impossible for Williams to function as a priest in the United States. Williams' other sponsor, Bishop Rappe, gave a similar opinion. He wrote Williams that if the Propaganda asked his view, he would suggest Haiti as a possible alternative to the United States for the young man.[40] Neither bishop was willing to risk the ire of whites by introducing a black priest into his diocese.

39. Thaddeus Anwander, C.SS.R. to Propaganda, February 21, 1855, in 17, fol. 173r, Bishop Louis A. Rappe to Propaganda, November 24, 1854, in 16, fols. 1197r, 1198r, Anwander to Propaganda, February 21, 1855, in 17, fol. 173r, Propaganda note, n.d., in 16, fol. 1198v, all in Congressi, America Centrale, APF; Propaganda to Bishop Louis A. Rappe, January 24, 1855, in Lettere, 346, fols. 70v, 71r, APF; W. A. Williams to Propaganda, June 26, 1863, in Congressi, America Centrale, 20, fols. 333rv, 334v, APF.

40. Louis Deluol to François Lhomme, June 4, 1855, in RG 5, Box 11, SAB; Archbishop F. P. Kenrick to Propaganda, October 4, 1858, in 18, fols. 339rv, 340r, November 3, 1858, in 18, fols. 453rv, 456r, Bishop Louis A. Rappe to W. A. Williams, January 27, 1860, in 18, fol. 1188rv, all in Congressi, America Centrale, APF.

Williams understood his situation. Lacking the episcopal support that the Healys had enjoyed and never a strong student, he informed the prefect of the Propaganda on August 2, 1862, that he had decided "after mature deliberation and on the advice of his teachers" that he had no calling to the clerical state. Yet even after his return to Baltimore, Williams clung to his dream. He requested citizenship in the Papal States and informed the Propaganda that he was continuing to study privately in the hope that he would eventually become a priest—a hope that he entertained as late as May 1, 1867. Meanwhile, working with Jesuits Miller and O'Connor, he took charge of two schools for blacks and published a newspaper, *Clear Communicator*, on behalf of Baltimore's recently emancipated freedmen. In 1868, evidently recognizing that he would never become a priest, he gathered some associates together and tried unsuccessfully to establish a black male brotherhood. Some twenty years later, having failed to realize his life's ambition, Williams became the librarian at the Catholic University of America. In 1899, he left the university to work at the black parish of St. Benedict the Moor in New York City.[41]

While Williams futilely pursued his seminary studies in Rome, the American bishops attempted to deal with the growing sectional crisis in the United States by remaining aloof from the slavery issue. Since they viewed slavery as a political and social issue rather than a moral one and since they tried to avoid all purely political-social issues for fear of provoking nativist hysteria, they left the question of slavery up to politicians and individual Catholics. The Catholic church thus avoided the bitter division into northern and southern wings that had occurred in such Protestant denominations as the Methodists, the Baptists, and the Presbyterians.[42]

During the Civil War, Catholics in the North generally supported the Union, whereas their southern coreligionists rallied to the defense of the Confederacy. Some northern bishops vigorously

---

41. W. A. Williams to Propaganda, August 2, 1862, in Congressi, America Centrale, 19, fols. 872r, 873r; July 11, 1864, in Scritture, 20, fols. 892rv, 893r, September 4, 1865, in America Centrale, 20, fols. 1562rv, 1563rv, May 1, 1867, in Scritture, 12, fols. 949–950r, 949v, all in APF; A. J. Jourdan to Rev. Brother Athanasius, October 19, 1868, in Brothers of the Sacred Heart File, JFA; [John R. Slattery], "Biographie de J. R. Slattery" (MS in Papiers Houtin, *Oeuvres*, LIV, NAF 15741–42, Bibliothèque Nationale, Paris), XI, 21. Hereinafter, MS chapters are designated by Roman numerals and pages within chapters by arabic numbers.

42. Misch, "American Bishops and the Negro," 73.

promoted the Union cause. Archbishop Hughes, for example, flew the national flag from St. Patrick's Cathedral and in the autumn of 1861 at President Lincoln's request sailed to Paris and Rome to plead the Union cause. Bishop Patrick Lynch of Charleston performed a similar mission for the Confederate government in the spring of 1864.[43]

Although they were divided in their loyalties during the Civil War, most Catholics, north and south, could agree on opposition to immediate emancipation. Archbishop Hughes, writing to Secretary of War Simon Cameron, urged the Lincoln administration to continue to separate preservation of the Union from abolition. He warned that if Catholics "are to fight for the abolition of slavery, then, they will turn away in disgust from . . . patriotic duty." Privately, Hughes expressed fear of a "big Black beast" setting fire to his former master's property and engaging in violence and immorality. James McMaster's *Freeman's Journal*, a Catholic newspaper in New York, warned its Irish Catholic audience to look for houses in the West once "Massa Linkum" let loose the slaves.[44]

Only a few prominent Catholics, such as Cincinnati's archbishop John Purcell, his brother the Reverend Edward Purcell, who was editor of the *Catholic Telegraph*, and author Orestes Brownson, called for emancipation. The outspokenness of the Purcells provoked Martin John Spalding, bishop of Louisville, to forward an essay entitled "Dissertation on the American Civil War" to Alessandro Barnabo, cardinal prefect of the Propaganda, in May, 1863. Spalding wrote that immediate, as opposed to gradual, emancipation would ruin the country and cause serious injury to the slaves themselves. Spalding charged, moreover, that the Lincoln administration had converted the struggle from a war to preserve the Union into a war of confiscation, violent emancipation, destruction, desolation, and possible extermination of the South. The letter, signed "Alumnus of the S.C." so as not to compromise Spalding should it become public, received a sympathetic reading from Barnabo and Pope Pius IX and was published serially by the Vatican newspaper, *L'Osservatore Romano.*[45]

43. Hennesey, *American Catholics*, 147–48, 152.

44. *Ibid.*, 147–49; Connor, "The Northern Catholic Position on Slavery," 43–44.

45. Spalding, *Martin John Spalding*, 139–42; David [Thomas W.] Spalding, C.F.X. (ed.), "Martin Spalding's Dissertation on the American Civil War," *Catholic Historical Review*, LII (April, 1966), 66–85.

In a widely distributed sermon in 1861, Augustin Verot, vicar apostolic of Florida, defended slavery but called for significant reforms in the institution. Verot advocated legal recognition of a slave as a "man" and insisted on legislation to protect slave marriages and families, to promote religion, and to punish sexual violations of female slaves by white men. Charleston's widely respected Bishop Lynch expressed the racial views of most southern and many northern bishops in a pamphlet published in 1864 entitled *Letter of a Missionary on Domestic Slavery in the Confederate States of America.* Lynch described blacks "as a race very prone to excess; and who, unless restrained, plunge madly into the lowest depths of licentiousness." He acknowledged that a few black Catholics lived exemplary lives but considered their number insignificant in comparison with the majority of the race. He pointed to immorality as a defect of the race that made blacks unfit to rule themselves. When he described the actual workings of the slave system, Lynch painted a "magnolia scented" scene of benevolent paternalism. He concluded that emancipation would result in race war and that no working plan existed for an alternative to slavery.[46]

At war's end, however, Lynch and his fellow southern bishops had to deal with the realities of emancipation and the physical and human devastation caused by the war. Churches, schools, hospitals, convents, and rectories had been destroyed. Richmond and Charleston suffered the greatest physical damage. St. Finbar's Cathedral in Charleston, valued at $180,000, lay in ruins; Lynch confessed that he did not have a miter, crozier, or vestment with which to perform a single episcopal ceremony. In Galveston, Texas, the bishop could say mass in the cathedral only on days when it did not rain, because of the bullet-riddled roof. Twelve hundred Catholic war orphans in Louisiana depended on the church for care, and in Mississippi, Bishop William Elder and his handful of priests found themselves overwhelmed by thousands of black refugees, many of whom were facing death from starvation and disease. In men, money, and property the Catholic church in the South had suffered a blow it could ill afford.[47]

Southern bishops appealed to the North for help, but whereas Protestant missionary groups poured money, supplies, and people

46. Misch, "American Bishops and the Negro," 104–106, 111, 112–14.

47. Osborne, "Freeman's Odyssey," 13; Misch, "American Bishops and the Negro," 131–33, 146.

into the South to teach and proselytize the freedmen, the largely immigrant Catholics of the North sent relatively little. Only the archdiocese of Baltimore responded with any significant financial aid. Baltimore's Catholics sent $12,000, most of which went to help needy whites. Bishops Lynch, Elder, and Verot attempted to found schools and provide for Catholic freedmen, but only Verot succeeded to any extent. By 1873, he had established seven schools, a minuscule achievement compared with Protestant efforts.[48]

On the heels of emancipation, blacks left white-dominated churches in order to form their own. Alexander Crummel, the most prominent black Episcopalian priest of the late nineteenth century, explained that "when freedom came the emancipated class, by one impulse, rushed from the chapels provided by their masters,— deserted in multitudes . . . in search for a ministry of their own race." Between 1865 and 1870, three new black denominations— the Colored Primitive Baptists, the Colored Cumberland Presbyterian church, and the Colored Methodist Episcopal church— emerged. Indigenous black preachers who had ministered secretly to their people during slavery established numerous black congregations, mainly Baptist, throughout the South. Those churches, for the most part small, rural, and poor, served as centers of social, economic, educational, and political life for the former slaves. By 1870, black Baptist membership had soared to 500,000. Black Baptists created separate black state conventions, which eventually culminated in the establishment of the National Baptist Convention in 1895.[49]

Meanwhile, the two northern black Methodist churches established in the early nineteenth century in reaction to white Methodist discrimination, the African Methodist Episcopal (A.M.E.) and the African Methodist Episcopal Zion (A.M.E.Z.) churches, sent missionaries among the freedmen as Union armies moved through the South. The Reverend Theophilus G. Steward of the A.M.E. church found hundreds of thousands of blacks in the South without minis-

48. Misch, "American Bishops and the Negro," 149–59, 172–75; Hennesey, *American Catholics*, 162.

49. R. E. Hood, "From a Headstart to a Deadstart: The Historical Basis for Black Indifference Toward the Episcopal Church, 1800–1860," *Historical Magazine of the Protestant Episcopal Church*, LI (September, 1982), 284; Albert J. Raboteau, "Black Christianity in North America," in Charles H. Lippy and Peter W. Williams (eds.), *Encyclopedia of the American Religious Experience* (3 vols.; New York, 1988), I, 641; John Hope Franklin and Alfred A. Moss, Jr., *From Slavery to Freedom: A History of Negro Americans* (6th ed.; New York, 1988), 211.

ters to baptize, marry, or bury them. He wrote, "A ministry had to be created at once from the material at hand." The black Methodist churches commissioned as ministers those freedmen who felt a call from God. By 1876, A.M.E. church membership exceeded 200,000. Twenty years later, the church claimed 452,725 members, and the A.M.E.Z. church counted 349,788 communicants. By the 1890s, the A.M.E., A.M.E.Z., Colored Methodist Episcopal, and black Baptist churches claimed nine out of ten black Protestants.[50]

White northern churches refused to abdicate the missionary field of the South solely to black denominations. During and after the war, northern Protestants played a leading role in creating freedmen's aid societies. The largest and most famous of those societies was the American Missionary Association (AMA), which predated the war and, though technically nonsectarian, was financed chiefly by Congregationalists. Between 1861 and 1890, the AMA contributed approximately $7 million of the $20 million spent by benevolent societies and government agencies to help the former slaves. In 1866 alone, the association spent $253,000, furnished supplies worth $118,000, and dispatched 353 men and women to the South, the vast majority of whom helped to set up schools for the freedmen. Between 1866 and 1877, in addition to maintaining numerous elementary and secondary schools for the freedmen, the AMA opened seven institutions of higher learning to train a native black leadership: Atlanta, Fisk, and Straight universities, Hampton Institute, and Talladega, Tougaloo, and Tillotson colleges. By 1884, at the height of its work, the association supported fifty-seven schools and eight colleges.[51]

Realizing the opportunity for converts in the immediate postwar years and concerned for the plight of the freedmen, such predominantly white northern denominations as the Methodist Episcopal, Presbyterian, and Protestant Episcopal churches and the American

50. Sydney E. Ahlstrom, A Religious History of the American People (New Haven, 1972), 709; Clarence E. Walker, A Rock in a Weary Land: The African Methodist Episcopal Church During the Civil War and Reconstruction (Baton Rouge, 1982), 39–81; Misch, "American Bishops and the Negro," 341; Franklin and Moss, From Slavery to Freedom, 211; Robert A. Bennett, "Black Episcopalians: A History from the Colonial Period to the Present," Historical Magazine of the Protestant Episcopal Church, XLIII (September, 1974), 239–40.

51. Joe M. Richardson, Christian Reconstruction: The American Missionary Association and Southern Blacks, 1861–1890 (Athens, Ga., 1986), 105; H. Shelton Smith, In His Image, but . . . : Racism in Southern Religion, 1780–1910 (Durham, N.C., 1972), 220–21; Misch, "American Bishops and the Negro," 346–48.

Baptist convention formed their own commissions to evangelize and elevate freedmen, primarily through education. In 1869, for example, the Freedmen's Aid Society of the Methodist Episcopal church collected over $93,000 and supported 105 teachers in nine southern states; by 1873, it also financially maintained fifteen schools of higher learning. In the final year of the war, 68 missionaries of the Home Mission Society of the American Baptist convention worked among freedmen in twelve states. By the end of 1868, its third year in operation, the Freedmen's Commission of the Protestant Episcopal church could point to total collections of nearly $100,000, 65 missionary-teachers in the field, and the establishment of St. Augustine's Normal School in Raleigh, North Carolina, the forerunner of St. Augustine's College, the cradle of many black Episcopal priests.[52]

In their missionary endeavors, many Protestants, black and white, consistently overestimated the danger of competition from the Catholic church, believing that they needed to exert extraordinary efforts to block anticipated Catholic evangelization among the freedmen. The 1867 report of the AMA in Virginia warned that the Catholic church had discovered and entered the promising field and that its "splendors" would appeal to the "negro's love of display." The Methodist Episcopal church alerted its missionaries to Catholicism's "evil schemes" and urged Methodists to save blacks from the "wiles of Romanism." Speaking in 1872 before the Virginia conference of the A.M.E. church, the Reverend W. B. Derrick offered a resolution condemning the efforts and means used by the Catholic church to evangelize blacks.[53] The agitated Protestants, however, need not have worried.

Because the Catholic church did not offer blacks the opportunities for leadership and participation available to them in black Protestant churches, many black Catholics, emulating the exodus of blacks from white Protestant denominations, left the Catholic church following emancipation. To remain a Catholic often meant submitting to humiliating seating arrangements in church. The black Catholic sheriff of Natchez during Reconstruction, for example, though sending his children to what was designated as the

52. Smith, In His Image, 221–23; Arthur Ben Chitty, "St. Augustine's College, Raleigh, North Carolina," Historical Magazine of the Protestant Episcopal Church, XXXV (September, 1966), 216.

53. Walker, A Rock in a Weary Land, 90; Osborne, "Freeman's Odyssey," 12; Gillard, The Catholic Church and the Negro, 35–36.

"colored Catholic school," refused to attend mass at the local Catholic church because the church's rules required blacks to sit in the aisle. Neither did Catholic worship allow for the range of emotional expression that many freedmen found attractive in the Protestant churches. The less rigid church structure and educational requirements of many Protestant churches permitted gifted preachers with little formal education to assume authority in the church, which often meant leadership in the black community. The Methodist Episcopal Church North, for example, began ordaining blacks in 1866 and initially licensed thirty men to preach to the freedmen. Of the thirty, only four could read, and none could write. Even the Protestant Episcopal church, the denomination that was most similar to the Catholic church in liturgy, doctrine, and hierarchical structure and that also required extensive seminary education for its priests, still managed to raise eighty-six black men to the priesthood between 1866 and 1900, compared with only five in the Catholic church during the entire nineteenth century.[54]

Catholics further alienated blacks during Reconstruction by often allying themselves with the proponents of white supremacy. Thaddeus Stevens, leader of the Radical Republicans in the House of Representatives, lamented the white Catholic tendency to "support the pro-slavery party [the Democrats] and cry 'Down with the nigger.'" In 1863, after the Union forces had captured New Orleans, the Reverend Claude Maistre of St. Rose of Lima Parish in New Orleans incurred the wrath of Archbishop John Mary Odin when he publicly praised the the Emancipation Proclamation and advocated the elimination of racial discrimination. Odin, fearful of white southern reprisals against the church, accused Maistre of inciting blacks, warned him to stop, and eventually dismissed him from his parish. The "poet of the South," the Reverend Abraham Ryan, protested against the proposed Fifteenth Amendment in 1867, declaring in the pages of the Savannah diocesan newspaper, "This is a 'white man's government' and upon this doctrine future political contests must be fought." Eight years later, a Vincentian

54. Miller, "Failed Mission," in Miller and Wakelyn (eds.), *Catholics in the Old South*, 167; Peter Benoit Diary, April 13, 1875 (Typescript copy in JFA); Hennesey, *American Catholics*, 162; Misch, "American Bishops and the Negro," 351–53; Walker, *A Rock in a Weary Land*, 91; J. Carleton Hayden, "The Black Ministry of the Episcopal Church: An Historical Overview," in Franklin D. Turner (ed.), *Black Clergy in the Episcopal Church: Recruitment, Training, and Development* (New York, 1978), 7.

priest observed that hundreds of blacks "are drawn away by the Methodists, who take advantage of the present political turmoil, in which Archbishop and Priests side more or less openly against Republicans and hence against the Negroes."[55]

Some black Catholics attempted to secure full membership and greater autonomy within their church, whereas others found the struggle too difficult. Shortly after the war, black parishioners in St. Martinville, Louisiana, petitioned the state legislature to repeal an 1858 statute that allowed only whites to incorporate churches there. On January 23, 1866, colored Creole Catholics in New Orleans petitioned Archbishop Odin for their own separate parish church and for "a priest of the African race." Odin failed to respond to their petition. Unwilling to endure this racism in the church, many former slaves of Catholic masters, often only nominal Catholics at best, simply left it. One report claimed that in the years immediately following the Civil War, 65,000 blacks abandoned the church just in one section of Louisiana.[56] Although it exaggerated wildly, the report nevertheless accurately reflected the reality that many black Catholics had participated in an informal referendum on the church; the results indicated an overwhelming vote of no confidence.

Some in the Catholic church were aware of events, and one in particular worked to bestir the church to change course. Alarmed by the erosion occurring among black Catholics and anxious for the church to evangelize the nearly four million freedmen in the South, Archbishop Martin John Spalding attempted, in 1866, to organize a coordinated Catholic effort to reach Afro-Americans. A slaveholder's son who had become archbishop of Baltimore in 1864, Spalding had maintained public neutrality during the war, while privately opposing secession, deploring immediate emancipation, and embracing the Peace Democrats. At war's end, he sympathized with the freedmen's plight and viewed them as a potentially rich field for missionary labor. On June 14, 1865, he suggested to the Propaganda that it convene a Second Plenary Council of the Catholic hierarchy in the United States. Such a meeting had originally been scheduled for 1862, but it had been postponed because of the

55. Misch, "American Bishops and the Negro," 218, 126–29; Smith, *In His Image*, 253; anonymous Vincentian quoted in Benoit Diary, February 2, 1875.

56. Miller, "Failed Mission," in Miller and Wakelyn (eds.), *Catholics in the Old South*, 168; Misch, "American Bishops and the Negro," 166; Gillard, *The Catholic Church and the Negro*, 258.

war. Since the gathering of the First Plenary Council in 1852, the number of Catholics in the United States had increased from 1,980,000 to 3,842,000, the number of priests from 1,321 to 2,770, and the number of churches and mission stations from 2,092 to 5,067. A council could erect new dioceses, provide for greater unity in church government and discipline, organize contributions for the Holy Father, and offer public witness of American Catholic unity in contrast to some of the still-divided Protestant denominations. Spalding also suggested to Rome that the council address the problem of the freedmen. Writing about them to his friend Archbishop John McCloskey of New York, Spalding made his intentions clear: "Four million of these unfortunates are thrown on our charity. . . . It is a golden opportunity for reaping a harvest of souls, which neglected may not return."[57]

Rome approved a council for the autumn of 1866 and, at Spalding's suggestion, made Afro-Americans one of the topics for discussion. Spalding then prepared a thirty-six-page booklet for the archbishops, containing questions for consideration that represented his agenda for the council. He assigned several questions to each of the archbishops and asked them to prepare their responses in cooperation with the bishops of their ecclesiastical provinces. He distributed the questions dealing with "the best means of promoting the salvation of the Negro" to Archbishop Odin and the bishops of the province of New Orleans.[58]

Spalding's interrogatories embodied his proposals for the evangelization of blacks. He specifically requested the bishops of the New Orleans ecclesiastical province to consider the feasibility of establishing separate churches for blacks; the preparation of young blacks for the priesthood; and the preaching of missions, or Catholic revivals, to blacks. He asked the bishops furthermore, whether they should seek religious orders or found "Negro sisterhoods" to work among blacks and whether they should allow blacks to sing vernacular, as well as Latin, hymns at mass and vespers. Spalding's most controversial suggestion involved the possible appointment of prefects apostolic—priests possessing delegated authority and rights usually held by a resident bishop, except for that of bestowing holy orders—who would have special jurisdiction over black missionary work. Such prefects could devote their full energies to the black

57. Spalding, Martin John Spalding, 130–45, 194–95, 199–200.
58. Ibid., 202, 204–205.

missions and provide needed leadership and direction. Referring to his proposal in a May 24, 1866, letter to Archbishop Odin, Spalding wrote, "I incline to favor the idea as one most likely to do good."[59] He believed that bishops and prefects apostolic could avoid jurisdictional conflicts with one another, for they would have authority over different subjects. He cited Constantinople, where bishops for both Latin and Eastern rite Catholics resided, as a successful example of parallel episcopal jurisdictions.

The discussions among the bishops of the New Orleans province prior to the opening of the council indicated serious disagreements over Spalding's proposals. Bishop Elder of Natchez opposed the appointment of a prefect apostolic because he feared that it would only "cause much confusion" and tend "to widen and perpetuate the division of the two races." For Elder, "immorality" loomed as a great problem for the church in its work with Afro-Americans. Elder contended that the moral code of the Catholic church, with its emphasis on the sanctity of marriage and the avoidance of sexual impurity, had no currency among the former slaves. The assumption that there was a gulf between the "settled" morality of the church and what they saw as the "unsettled" morality of the freedmen led many white Catholics to regard the freedmen as hopeless semibarbarians. Ignoring the existence of strong black Catholic communities in Baltimore and New Orleans that could trace their Catholicism back several centuries and that had fostered religious vocations to the Oblate Sisters of Providence and the Sisters of the Holy Family, Elder voiced his opposition to a black clergy on the grounds of Afro-American immorality and ignorance. He argued, moreover, that black clergy would injure religion, for "they would not command the respect of the priesthood." Bishop Martin of Natchitoches simply insisted that the "Negro question" should have no place at all in the deliberations of the plenary council.[60]

When the bishops convened in Baltimore on October 7, 1866, they received the draft of the 566 proposed decrees that Spalding and his staff had prepared during the summer as the agenda for the council. The decrees were first divided into titles and then into chapters within the titles. The fourth chapter of Title X (*De Salute Animarum efficacius promovenda*) dealt with blacks. Spalding had dropped any reference to black priests but continued to recommend

59. *Ibid.*, 205; Misch, "American Bishops and the Negro," 202.
60. Misch, "American Bishops and the Negro," 204–207, 223.

the appointment of a priest administrator (*vir ecclesiasticus*) who would recruit missionaries, raise money, and generally attend to the needs of blacks. Spalding raised the prospect that the pope might consecrate the administrator a bishop, thus giving him greater prestige and effectiveness. Chapter Four further suggested the possibility of priest administrators charged with special responsibility for blacks in the ecclesiastical provinces of New Orleans, St. Louis, and Cincinnati, each of which contained large black populations. It also exhorted priests "through the bowels of the mercy of God" to devote their lives to "Negro work" and urged bishops to build separate churches, schools, and orphanages for blacks.[61]

The proceedings of the two-week-long council dragged on, forcing Spalding to schedule an extraordinary session for October 22, the day after the formal closing of the council, in order to deal with unfinished business, including discussion of the "Negro problem." At the beginning of what became a turbulent meeting, Spalding reminded the prelates that the Propaganda desired positive measures on behalf of blacks. The bishops responded by rejecting Spalding's proposals and opting for the status quo. Only Bishop Verot of St. Augustine and Bishop Whelan of Wheeling supported the concept of a priest administrator for work among blacks. The majority rejected it out of fear that jurisdictional disputes would arise between the priest administrator and bishops. The bishops jealously guarded their authority, in part because rebellious priests and laity habitually appealed disciplinary matters over their heads to Rome. Archbishop Peter Kenrick of St. Louis, brother of Archbishop Francis Kenrick, belligerently declared that the bishops' duty was to rule their dioceses, not to carry out instructions from the Propaganda. He went so far as to declare that if Rome forced a priest administrator for blacks on him, he would resign. Archbishop Odin insisted that blacks in New Orleans already received sufficient care and had no need for new programs. Archbishop McCloskey expressed the sentiments of most northern bishops, whose dioceses contained relatively few blacks, when he maintained that an obligation toward blacks did not weigh on the consciences of the bishops of the North.[62]

61. Spalding, *Martin John Spalding,* 215; Misch, "American Bishops and the Negro," 236–39; Edward J. Misch, "The Catholic Church and the Negro, 1865–1884," *Integratededucation,* XII (November–December, 1974), 37.

62. Spalding, *Martin John Spalding,* 222; Misch, "American Bishops and the Negro," 255–56; Misch, "The Catholic Church and the Negro," 37.

In the final decrees and accompanying pastoral letter addressed to the Catholics of the United States, the prelates substituted rhetoric for concrete action. They exhorted ecclesiastical provincial councils to discuss specific actions that might benefit Afro-Americans. They also urged zeal in bringing blacks into already existing parishes and in providing blacks with separate churches of their own. Bemoaning the limited means available for uplifting the race, the council appealed to bishops and religious superiors in the United States and Europe for missionary priests to work among blacks. The pastoral expressed regret that the freedmen had not been better prepared to use their freedom when they were suddenly emancipated, and it urged clergy and laity to give them moral training and Christian education. The bishops, however, left specific measures to the determination of each bishop in his own diocese, thus changing nothing.[63]

Two years after the Second Plenary Council, the Protestant Episcopal church met in general convention and considered its mission to black Americans, particularly the freedmen. Unlike the Roman Catholic bishops, who had assiduously avoided the issue, the Episcopalian general convention recommended "that every effort be made at once to prepare black clergy to minister to black people." Already, between 1804 and 1865, the church had ordained sixteen black Episcopalian priests, none of whom had served in any states south of Maryland. Although white Episcopalians, like Catholic bishops, remained suspicious of the moral capacity of blacks, they showed themselves more willing than Catholics to ordain black men, partly because in contrast to the situation of their celibate Roman Catholic counterparts, most Episcopalian clergy were married, thus providing them an outlet for carnal urges. Between 1866 and 1877, six blacks became Episcopalian priests. In 1878, the church established Payne Divinity School in Petersburg, Virginia, for the purpose of providing theological education for blacks. By 1900, eighty more black priests had been ordained, far outstripping the Catholic totals.[64]

63. Misch, "American Bishops and the Negro," 264, 268; Misch, "The Catholic Church and the Negro," 37.

64. J. Carleton Hayden, "After the War: The Mission and Growth of the Episcopal Church Among Blacks in the South, 1865–1877," *Historical Magazine of the Protestant Episcopal Church*, XLII (December, 1973), 420–21; Hayden, "The Black Ministry of the Episcopal Church," in Turner (ed.), *Black Clergy in the Episcopal Church*, 7, 11.

The meager results of the plenary council disappointed, but did not discourage, Spalding. He turned to Europe to secure help for the black missions. In July, 1867, while in Rome, he presented a set of petitions to the Propaganda in the name of the American bishops that requested the Holy Father to urge, or even command, the superiors general of several major religious communities to cooperate in every way possible with the American bishops on behalf of blacks in the United States. Spalding also used Jesuit Michael O'Connor as his unofficial agent in Europe. While traveling abroad, O'Connor contacted Herbert Vaughan, an English priest (later bishop of Salford and cardinal-archbishop of Westminster) who had founded St. Joseph's Society of the Sacred Heart for Foreign Missions in 1866 in the London suburb of Mill Hill.[65]

O'Connor spoke convincingly to Vaughan about the need for missionaries for the task of converting the nearly four million freedmen of the South and persuaded Vaughan to commit his fledgling society to America. In 1871, after receiving permission from Pope Pius IX and making arrangements with Archbishop Spalding, who agreed to assign St. Francis Xavier Church in Baltimore to the Mill Hill Fathers, Vaughan readied his band of missionaries to sail to the United States. In the coming of the Josephites, which represented the most promising development for the black missions up to that time, Spalding hoped he had found a solution to the nagging problems of organization and manpower that had hitherto crippled the black Catholic apostolate.[66]

Herbert Vaughan, the man in whom Spalding placed so much hope and trust, established his missionary society with the dream of converting the "heathens" of Africa and the East. His biographer claimed that "Africa pursued him like a shadow." Even after accepting the mission field among blacks in the United States, Vaughan kept the vision of Africa before his priests' eyes. At the departure ceremony, on November 17, 1871, for the first Josephite missionaries, Vaughan declared that they would go, not only "to labor among the Negroes of the South, but to found in America a Missionary College . . . in which the African population may there be

65. Spalding, *Martin John Spalding,* 231; Peter E. Hogan, S.S.J., "Historical Events Leading to the Development of the Josephites" (Typescript in Chapter of Renewal Papers, November, 1968–July, 1970, JFA), 182.

66. Hogan, "Historical Events," 182; Richard H. Steins, "The Mission of the Josephites to the Negro in America, 1871–1893" (M.A. thesis, Columbia University, 1966), 18.

trained to carry the faith into their own land." He added, "We are . . . acting not so much upon America as upon Africa." He also charged his missionaries in the United States to restrict their labor exclusively to blacks. Hence, from the beginning of the Josephite mission to the United States, Vaughan recognized the need for black leadership and participation in the evangelization of "Africans," whether in America or in Africa, if the effort was to be successful.[67]

Vaughan accompanied Cornelius Dowling, James Noonan, Joseph Gore, and Charles Vigneront, the first four Josephite missionaries, to their American headquarters in Baltimore and then set off on a tour of the South in order to judge the scope of the work and to raise money. What he saw of white Catholic treatment of blacks shocked him. Vaughan wrote to Lady Elizabeth Herbert of Lea, his friend and benefactor, that "the dislike of the Americans . . . to the negroes . . . far exceeds in intensity anything I had expected." He remarked in his diary that even priests regarded blacks as little better than dogs. As he traveled through Savannah, Vicksburg, Natchez, Memphis, Charleston, and New Orleans, he witnessed such scenes as a priest refusing communion to a black soldier in a cathedral and noted in Catholic churches the low, backless benches marked with signs that read "for Negroes." Reaching St. Louis in January, 1872, Vaughan endured a depressing interview with Archbishop Peter Kenrick, who told him that his plans would fail and denied him permission to beg for funds in the St. Louis archdiocese. Vaughan's tour strengthened his conviction that the Josephites should restrict their ministry exclusively to blacks and impressed upon him the desirability of separate parishes for blacks, where they would be free from the humiliations heaped upon them in white Catholic churches. After installing Dowling as the rector of St. Francis Xavier Church and the informal leader of the U.S. missions, Vaughan returned to England in June, 1872, leaving his priests with few guidelines and little formal administrative structure. Trouble began almost immediately.[68]

Between 1871 and 1878, administrative and philosophical difficulties, combined with the familiar problems of manpower and

67. J. G. Snead-Cox, *The Life of Cardinal Vaughan* (2 vols.; London, 1910), I, 105; Hogan, "Historical Events," 176.

68. Steins, "The Mission," 22; Osborne, *Segregated Covenant*, 23; Snead-Cox, *Cardinal Vaughan*, I, 169–79; Steins, "The Mission," 23; Hogan, "Historical Events," 183.

money, nearly destroyed the Josephites in the United States. No sooner had Vaughan returned to England than he received word that Pope Pius IX had named him bishop of Salford and also insisted that he remain as superior of St. Joseph's Society. As a result, Vaughan could no longer devote his full energies to the society and turned over its everyday operations to Canon Peter Benoit of the Salford Cathedral. Benoit, though, still felt compelled to clear matters of importance with Vaughan. Despite their working relationship, long-distance management of the U.S. missions through an assistant proved unsuccessful. The death of Archbishop Spalding in February, 1872, further deprived the Josephites in America of a guiding hand. His successor, Archbishop James Roosevelt Bayley, had little hope that the society could accomplish substantial good among blacks in America.[69]

The Josephites were forced to wrestle intimately with the difficult reality of race relations from their earliest days in America. Before returning to England, Vaughan had established an interracial brotherhood under the care of the Josephite Fathers. Lay brothers did not become priests but devoted themselves to the service of the religious community to which they belonged, often performing essential manual labor. Racial tension soon surfaced among the Josephite brothers. In July, 1872, Dowling reported to Mill Hill that Brother Gilligan from Cincinnati showed his dislike of blacks to his fellow brothers as well as to the congregation of the mission and that Brother Joseph displayed a bad temper and would not hear a single word against blacks. The quarreling, bickering, racial animosity, and lack of leadership that characterized the Josephite brotherhood resulted in its abolition and an early end to the experiment in interracial community.[70]

White people who chose to attend Josephite churches presented another sticky issue, involving not only race relations but also the missionary philosophy of the society. The problem first appeared in Baltimore in 1872 and subsequently perplexed Josephite missions in Louisville, Charleston, and Prince Georges County, Maryland. The Josephites disagreed among themselves about how best to deal with whites in their churches. There was a general feeling that the presence of whites would make blacks uncomfortable and fuel skepticism about where the real loyalties of the missionaries lay.

69. Steins, "The Mission," 24, 26; Benoit Diary, March 2, 1875.
70. Steins, "The Mission," 27–28.

However, even though the Josephites had taken a vow to labor exclusively among blacks and Vaughan had left strict orders against saying mass for whites, some Josephites, Francis Vigneront and James Noonan, for instance, relaxed the rule. The precarious financial condition of the Josephite missions induced them to welcome white attendance, since whites contributed more money to the church than did the generally impoverished blacks.

The issue came to a climax at the Marlboro missions in Prince Georges County—missions that included white Catholics. Financial considerations initially had convinced the Josephites to accept the mission complex. Misunderstandings with white parishioners soon arose, however, because they resented the amount of time that the priests devoted to blacks. The whites did not understand the nature of the Josephite mission, which was represented by the priests' vow to be "the fathers and servants of the colored people." The situation in Marlboro threatened to transform the Josephites into parish priests rather than missionaries. In 1879, only a year after they arrived there, they surrendered the Marlboro missions to the Baltimore archdiocese and recommitted themselves to work exclusively among blacks.[71]

In that work, the Josephites suffered poverty, isolation, and exhaustion, which eventually sapped the vitality of many. Death claimed three of the first four Josephites within four years of their arrival in the United States; frustration and despair drove the fourth, James Noonan, to leave the society. The Josephites received requests for missionaries from bishops throughout the South, and too often, Canon Benoit and Noonan, who replaced Dowling as rector of St. Francis Xavier and who became the first provincial of the American province, accepted missions without sufficient regard for the strain that the additional responsibilities would place on their limited resources. The Josephites took charge of St. Francis Xavier in Baltimore in 1872, opened St. Augustine's in Louisville and St. Peter's in Charleston in 1874, and accepted the four churches and schools of the Marlboro mission in 1878, even though within a few months only one priest remained to handle all of the duties there.

Schools constituted one of the most taxing responsibilities for the Josephite missionaries. Because schools were an essential part of

71. *Ibid.*, 27–29, 30–32, 39–41.

the mission—a potentially rich source of converts on which future growth depended—the Josephite priests found themselves scrambling to secure faculty, money, and facilities for them. Often they had to double as schoolmasters while they searched frantically for lay teachers who would accept the pittance they could pay. By December, 1878, the nine Josephite missionaries in the United States had fallen victim to fatigue, frustration, and dissatisfaction.[72]

As early as 1875, Vaughan and Benoit had tried to remedy the administrative and leadership problems and to ease the personnel crisis. On January 7, 1875, they brought over four new priests and a lay brother from England. Vaughan also convened the first society chapter, a canonical meeting of the superior and delegates selected by the members of the society. The chapter produced the first official body of rules for St. Joseph's Society and specified a hierarchical chain of command. The superior general of the society stood at the top of the pyramid. Under him were the provincials, the heads of the provinces of the society. The existence of a province required ten priests or three missions. Rectors, priests in charge of churches or institutions such as seminaries, constituted the third level of authority. The chapter also established the office of vicar of the society to assist the superior general and exercise authority in his name. Peter Benoit became the first vicar, and James Noonan received appointment from Vaughan as the first American provincial.[73]

On paper, St. Joseph's Society had a new structure and set of norms that would, it was hoped, rejuvenate the flagging spirits of the members. In reality, however, fundamental problems remained unsolved. Administratively, Vaughan continued as the superior general, but his duties as bishop required much of his time. Letters from America became lost in the paper shuffle between Benoit and Vaughan, and communications between England and America broke down. Then, in 1875, after Benoit's eager solicitation, St. Joseph's Society received Madras, India, as a mission field, resulting in the subordination of the American province. In the United States, Noonan was proving unequal to the task of provincial and had developed, in his own words, "a distaste for the work of being a priest for the colored people." Never a strong personality, he be-

72. *Ibid.*, 20–22, 29–30, 42, 86; [John R. Slattery], "John R. Slattery," *Colored Harvest*, III (March, 1902), 306–10.
73. Steins, "The Mission," 33–37.

came increasingly despondent and isolated from his men. Morale on the missions plunged, threatening the continued existence of St. Joseph's Society in the United States.[74]

After seven years of Josephite labor, Catholic mission work among blacks was still foundering. In many respects, the problems of the Josephites simply mirrored those of the Catholic church in the United States. Without sufficient men, money, organization, or leadership, neither the Josephites nor the church could expect to make significant headway among blacks. By 1878, the single most organized Catholic effort to evangelize Afro-Americans tottered, near collapse. In the crisis, Herbert Vaughan turned to a brilliant, dynamic, and headstrong young priest, John R. Slattery, to rescue the American missions. The new American provincial not only would revive the American missions but would eventually engineer the independence of the American province from Mill Hill, creating a new St. Joseph's Society in the United States, devoted exclusively to the black apostolate. He would also champion a bold new approach to evangelization, one that advocated the ordination of black men to the priesthood.

74. Ibid., 41–52.

Chapter II

JOHN R. SLATTERY: A NEW APPROACH, 1877–1893

There is, then, no chance to win the Negroes to the faith without priests of their own.

—JOHN R. SLATTERY, MARCH, 1891

During the last two decades of the nineteenth century, the cause of black priests in the Catholic church had no greater champion than the Reverend John R. Slattery. Convinced that the conversion of blacks to the church ultimately depended on black priests, Slattery advocated a "Negro clergy" in articles and speeches. He arranged seminary training for aspiring black candidates, established seminaries that accepted black men, and brought about the first ordination of a black Catholic priest in the United States. In addition, he engineered the independence of the American Josephites from their Mill Hill parent body, thus establishing an American missionary society solely devoted to the evangelization of blacks in the United States. For the few brief years between 1884 and 1894, Slattery and his clerical allies appeared to have infused a new spirit into the church's missionary efforts toward blacks, and his hopes for a black clergy appeared attainable.

Born in New York City on July 16, 1851, John Richard Slattery was the only surviving child of James and Marguerite Slattery, Irish immigrants who prospered in their adopted homeland. James Slattery acquired a considerable fortune in Boss Tweed's New York as a construction contractor and real estate speculator. The Slatterys belonged to St. Paul's Parish on Fifty-ninth Street in Manhattan, which was conducted by the Paulist Fathers, a community dedicated to the conversion of the largely Protestant United States. The young man's parents, particularly his mother, saw to his religious education and inculcated a strong sense of devotion in him through such family rituals as the recitation of the rosary during the month of May. He also served as a parish altar boy and made his first confession to Isaac Hecker, the founder of the Paulists.

Slattery attended New York City public schools for eight years before entering City College of New York, where he was one of only two Catholics in his class and thus became involved in "many a boy's fight" when he was called a "mick" or told to "kiss the Pope's toe." In 1865, during his junior year, he entered St. Charles College, a minor, or preparatory, seminary run by the Sulpicians and located in Ellicott City, Maryland. Eye trouble, however, forced him to withdraw; when he recovered, he entered Columbia Law School, a move that delighted his father.

In the spring of 1872, Slattery heard the Reverend Herbert Vaughan, superior of the Mill Hill Fathers, preach in St. Paul's Church on behalf of the black missions. The sermon made little apparent impression on Slattery, whose Republican politics presumably would have inclined him to listen sympathetically. Nine months later, however, as he waited for a column of parading black members of the Odd Fellows Society to pass on the street, Slattery underwent a conversion experience. The inspiration came to him, as it had to many evangelical Protestant missionary-teachers who flocked to the South during Reconstruction, to consecrate his life to the evangelization of blacks. Slattery returned home greatly troubled. That evening, after dinner, he sought the counsel of the Reverend William I. Dwyer, his Paulist confessor, who reassured and encouraged him. Dwyer arranged for Slattery's entrance into Vaughan's seminary in Mill Hill, and the two used a ruse to obtain the consent of Slattery's parents, telling them only that the young man wished to become a missionary priest and to study at the seminary in Mill Hill; they carefully refrained from specifying the mission field of the Mill Hill Fathers. Slattery's decision to become a priest overjoyed his mother but bitterly disappointed his father. James had dreamed of a brilliant career for his son and had planned to leave him his fortune. Not until two years later did Slattery's parents learn of his intention to become a missionary to American blacks, at which time they ordered him home. Displaying the determination that would become a trademark, he refused his parents' order and was ordained at St. Joseph's Missionary College, Mill Hill, on St. Patrick's Day in 1877, shortly after the inauguration of

President Rutherford B. Hayes, which signaled the end of Radical Reconstruction in the South.[1]

A solidly built man standing about five feet, ten inches tall, with a long face, prominent nose, large, deep-set eyes framed by rimless spectacles, and a high forehead topped by wavy black hair, Slattery presented a handsome appearance. He also excelled in the classroom, compiling a brilliant academic record, and as a result, Vaughan and Benoit assigned him to teach logic at St. Joseph's College in Mill Hill. Slattery protested vehemently against his first assignment, telling Benoit, "My whole soul is with the Negro." Not for the last time in their relationship, he refused to acquiesce humbly to his superiors' wishes. For eight months he relentlessly badgered Vaughan and Benoit until on October 28, 1877, they finally acceded to his demands and assigned him to Baltimore as rector of St. Francis Xavier Church. Slattery threw himself into his work, displaying considerable financial skill in reducing the $24,000 debt on the parish. He also collaborated with Elizabeth Herbert, a black woman, in the founding of St. Elizabeth's Home for Colored Foundlings in Baltimore.[2]

Slattery's success in Baltimore notwithstanding, the Josephite missions floundered. Slattery gloomily reported to Benoit that "the American bishops barely tolerate us." He added that most of the lay community opposed the Negro missions and expected them to fail. What was worse, Slattery claimed, was the low morale of the Josephites on the missions, which made united action impossible. Noonan's resignation as provincial brought matters to a head. Slattery's accurate and blunt reports, containing concrete suggestions for dealing with the malaise on the missions, impressed Vaughan. On December 13, 1878, in an attempt to instill new life into the American missions, Vaughan turned to Slattery, then twenty-seven years old and a priest for only eighteen months, and appointed him American provincial as well as rector of St. Francis Xavier.[3]

1. [John R. Slattery], "Biographie de J. R. Slattery" (MS in Papiers Houtin, *Oeuvres*, LIV, NAF 15741–42, Bibliothèque Nationale, Paris), I, 1–10; [John R. Slattery], "John R. Slattery," *Colored Harvest*, III (March, 1902), 306–10.

2. John R. Slattery to Canon Peter Benoit, May, 1877, copy in 7-B-8, JFA; [Slattery], "John R. Slattery," 306–10; [Slattery], "Biographie," II, 13–18, IV, 19; Richard H. Steins, "The Mission of the Josephites to the Negro in America, 1871–1893" (M.A. thesis, Columbia University, 1966), 52.

3. Steins, "The Mission," 53; membership rolls in CB-14-12, MHFP.

Slattery served as provincial from December 13, 1878, until February 28, 1883. He provided strong leadership, personally visited each of the missions, and secured the services of several teaching orders of sisters, thus providing a stable source of teachers for Josephite schools in Baltimore. He moved decisively in turning the troublesome Marlboro mission over to the archdiocese in 1879 so as to ensure that the Josephites would confine their labor exclusively to blacks. He won the confidence of James Gibbons, the new archbishop of Baltimore, and prevailed on the archbishop to provide space in a Catholic cemetery for Baltimore's deceased black Catholics, who had previously been excluded from all Catholic cemeteries. Through astute financial management, Slattery also reduced the debts of the society significantly.[4]

While in Baltimore as provincial and rector of St. Francis Xavier, Slattery began laying the groundwork for what became his most controversial plan: the development of a black clergy. He had many barriers to overcome, for racism permeated American society, and most white Catholics shared society's belief in the innate inferiority of the black race. Thus, they could not accept the idea of a black man serving as Christ's representative on earth, preaching the gospel and administering the sacraments. The ordination of black priests, moreover, implied a social equality generally considered dangerous. Robert L. Dabney, though a Presbyterian theologian, expressed the fears of many Catholics when he drew this scenario: "Do you tell me that after you have admitted this negro thus to your . . . pulpits . . . weddings and funerals, you will still exclude him from your parlours and tables? Of course not! . . . This doctrine . . . means ultimately amalgamation."[5]

Although not to be found in the United States for most of the nineteenth century, black seminarians were studying at a number of Catholic institutions throughout the world. The Healy brothers prepared for the priesthood in Canada and Europe, and William Williams at the Urban College in Rome. In 1862, when "cars for colored people" ran on Canal Street in New York City and slavery still existed in the American South, men of different races, including black Africans, gathered to study at the Urban College, where "no distinction was tolerated." All slept and ate together, and Americans served blacks at table when their turn came. The Con-

4. Steins, "The Mission," 54; [Slattery], "Biographie," IV, 18, 3.

5. H. Shelton Smith, In His Image, but . . . : Racism in Southern Religion, 1780–1910 (Durham, N.C., 1972), 239–40.

gregation of the Mission, or Vincentians, established a seminary in Ethiopia, from which they ordained fifteen native priests in 1852. The Congregation of the Holy Ghost, or Holy Ghost Fathers, ordained its first black priests in Paris in 1842 and assigned them to Senegal, Africa. Five years later, the society opened a junior seminary in Dakar, followed in 1857 by a major seminary that produced native priests, such as the Reverend Gabriel Sené. The Order of St. Benedict, or Benedictines, added the Reverend Pius Hadrian, another native African, to the ranks of its priests after his ordination in 1872.[6]

In England, Vaughan appeared willing to accept selected black American students into the society's minor and major seminaries. When St. Joseph's Missionary College opened in 1866, Vaughan defined its eventual task as providing every mission area served by Mill Hill with a good native clergy. His emphasis between 1871 and 1878 on training blacks in the American missions so that ultimately they would work to convert Africa certainly suggested black catechists, if not priests. Shortly before departing England for the United States with his first band of missionaries, Vaughan evidently asked Michael O'Connor about the feasibility of black priests. In his response of October 6, 1871, O'Connor urged Vaughan to train catechists as soon as possible but cautioned, "As to priests, it is another question which must be left to circumstances and the development that will take place under the influence of Providence." Within six months, however, Vaughan agreed to accept Medard Nelson, a young black man recommended by Archbishop Napoleon J. Perche of New Orleans, into the Mill Hill seminary but stipulated that the young man pay for his own passage and his first year's tuition, a total amount of approximately two hundred dollars. If he proved satisfactory, Vaughan would consider reducing the charges for the last two years. Nelson, perhaps for financial reasons, did not join Vaughan and the Josephites.[7]

---

6. Rev. Edward McSweeney, "Every Color Makes No Color in the Propaganda," *St. Joseph's Advocate,* II (October, 1891), 498–99; NCE, V, 585; Henry J. Koren, Archivist of the Holy Ghost Fathers, to Stephen J. Ochs, January 8, 1984, in possession of Stephen J. Ochs, Silver Spring, Md.; "Important Letter from Africa," *St. Joseph's Advocate,* II (April, 1890), 89–91; "Rev. Father Pius Hadrian," *St. Joseph's Advocate,* II (October, 1891), 291.

7. Lawrence Nemer, *Anglican and Roman Catholic Attitudes on Missions* (Steyl, Netherlands, 1981), 129–31; Bishop Herbert Vaughan to Rev. and Very Dear Fathers, November 14, 1878, copy, Michael O'Connor to Bishop Herbert Vaughan,

After his visit to the United States in 1875, Benoit evidenced caution on the question of black priests. He recorded in his diary a canard frequently repeated by whites: "All admit that a Negro-Priest w'd find no favor with his race." He also noted the apocryphal story about a black priest [perhaps Paddington?] who visited Charleston, South Carolina. Allegedly, Charleston's blacks would not accept him and forced him to leave. As he passed through New York, the servant at the white priest's home where he was staying, presuming him an impudent impostor, allowed him to say mass only in the basement. Benoit noted in his diary, "The Bishops, not we, are responsible for what should or sh'd not be done."[8]

On the day that Benoit made his diary entries, Theodore Wegmann, assistant pastor at the Franciscan parish of St. Boniface in Quincy, Illinois, wrote to James Noonan, then rector of St. Francis Xavier, recommending a twenty-year-old black man named Augustine Tolton and asking if the Mill Hill college would accept him. Tolton, according to Wegmann, was "very desirous of becoming a missionary for the people of his race." Noonan forwarded the letter to Benoit, who wrote cryptically on the last page of the letter, "1. Is he ready to remain a catechist? 2. If not, will he go to Borneo?" Evidently, Benoit would consider the young man for the seminary only if Tolton was willing to serve as a missionary priest outside the United States. Benoit assured Ignatius Brouwer, a Mill Hill missionary in India, of the society's willingness to admit native candidates to the seminary on the basis of Brouwer's recommendation and his guarantee that native clergy could work effectively on the missions. "We are guided by you," Benoit wrote. "If not in the way of usefulness, all might be for us."[9]

The guidance that Benoit received from the Josephites in the United States did not augur well for the cause of black priests. On July 15, 1878, in preparation for an upcoming Josephite chapter meeting, Benoit sent to the men in the United States a detailed

---

October 26, 1871, Archbishop N. J. Perche to Bishop Herbert Vaughan, April 6, 1872, Bishop Herbert Vaughan note, June 25, 1872, on the back of Perche-Vaughan letter, all in MHFP.

8. Canon Peter Benoit Diary, April 6, 1875 (Typescript copy in JFA).

9. Theodore Wegmann to James Noonan, April 6, 1875, Canon Peter Benoit note on last page of Wegmann-Noonan letter, both in MHFP; Albert S. Foley, S.J., *God's Men of Color: The Colored Catholic Priests of the United States, 1854–1954* (1955; rpr. New York, 1969), 36; Canon Peter Benoit to Ignatius Brouwer, April 15, 1880, in CB-2-55, MHFP.

questionnaire that covered five broad categories: the Negro race in the United States, means of conversion, obstacles to conversion, government of the society, and temporalities. Under the first heading, Benoit solicited the men's observations about black priests. Their responses were overwhelmingly negative: six of the eight missionaries dismissed the idea. John Crowley, serving in Marlboro, expressed their sentiments when he wrote that "certainly Negro priests for America are . . . altogether incapable—in consequence of the great drawbacks of ignorance, immorality, and instability of character." Only John H. Greene in Louisville expressed optimism about recruiting black priests, though he tempered his enthusiasm by warning that very few could be obtained "from the pure negro element fast disappearing."[10]

Ironically, given his later identification with the cause of black clergy, young Slattery, recently arrived from Mill Hill, described Benoit's query as "a scarcely practical question," one that "our successors may answer." Indeed, when he first returned to the United States, Slattery displayed a condescending attitude toward blacks. In correspondence, he referred derisively to his black parishioners as "Sambo and Deriah" and wrote in stereotypical fashion about their "placid" smiles, "rolling eyes," and love of music. Discussing his temptation to devote more time to mulattos than to "pure Negroes," Slattery confessed to Benoit that "it is hard to leave an agreeable and pleasing looking person to be friendly with a person as black as children regard the devil."[11]

Moreover, Slattery also clashed with the Oblate sisters, most of whom he justifiably regarded as unqualified to teach, given that they possessed only a smattering of grade school education at best, since all other Catholic schools and colleges remained closed to them. He urged the Oblates to open an industrial school and warned that the type of education offered at St. Frances Academy did not suit the social situation of most of the school's black students. He resigned as the Oblates' director and in 1881 replaced them at St. Francis Xavier School with Franciscan sisters from Mill Hill.[12]

Although he never completely shed his racial stereotypes, Slattery's daily contacts with blacks eroded his prejudices and con-

10. John Crowley to Canon Peter Benoit, August 22, 1878, John H. Greene to Canon Peter Benoit, August, 1878, both in MHFP.

11. John R. Slattery to Canon Peter Benoit, August 14, 1878, December 26, 1877, both in MHFP.

12. [Slattery], "Biographie," IV, 10–12, 18.

vinced him that blacks possessed intelligence and sanctity. By 1883 he had altered his earlier views about black priests; during that year, he took steps that eventually resulted in the initial ordination of a black man in the United States. The first step was his meeting Charles Randolph Uncles, a tall, bespectacled, young mulatto parishioner who expressed a desire to become a priest. Born in 1859, Uncles had attended St. Francis Xavier School, Baltimore public schools, and the Baltimore Normal School for Colored Teachers and had taught in Baltimore County public schools from 1880 to 1883. Struck by what he described as Uncles' "vivid intelligence," Slattery tutored him and Joseph Johnson (another black man who impressed him but who later decided not to enter the seminary) in rhetoric and logic, two prerequisites for the seminary. [13]

Initially Slattery attempted to secure an American bishop to sponsor Uncles at the Urban College, for Uncles indicated an unwillingness to become a Josephite, perhaps out of fear that he would be sent to the Far East. Unable to find an episcopal sponsor for Uncles or an American seminary that would accept him, Slattery arranged with the Sulpicians in Canada for his admission in 1883 to St. Hyacinth's College in Quebec. Despite those who criticized his plan as foolish, Slattery, who received generous grants from his wealthy father, personally paid for Uncles' seminary education. [14]

Meanwhile, however, conflict with Vaughan and Benoit and with his own men on the American missions marred Slattery's tenure as provincial. He castigated his Mill Hill superiors over the quality and number of men sent to the American missions and over Mill Hill's insistence that the American province pay the transportation expenses of American candidates sent to the seminary in England. Slattery also pressed Vaughan for a commitment to assign all Americans sent to Mill Hill to the black missions in the United States after their ordination. [15]

In 1879, Slattery's dissatisfaction led him to propose either the dissolution of the American province or its separation from Mill Hill. Vaughan sharply reprimanded Slattery for his proposal, at-

13. Foley, God's Men, 42–45; [Slattery], "Biographie," V, 3.
14. John R. Slattery to Canon Peter Benoit, October 14, 1885, in MHFP; Charles Uncles to John R. Slattery, June 7, 1887, in 10-N-4, John R. Slattery Papers, JFA; "Address of Father Slattery [to the first black Catholic congress, January 2, 1889]" (Printed copy in 9-K-16a, Slattery Papers); John R. Slattery to Cardinal James Gibbons, February 2, 1903, copy in Sulpician Papers, JFA.
15. Steins, "The Mission," 54–57.

tributing it to inexperience and a lack of humility before his superiors. Vaughan and Benoit regarded Slattery's stinging letters as intemperate. In one missive, Slattery virtually denounced Vaughan, called Benoit a liar, and condemned the charges paid by American students at Mill Hill as "monstrous." Regarding Slattery's letters, Vaughan lamented to Benoit, "I believe Father Slattery to be very undisciplined and that he speaks as he does from want of knowledge of what is common civility." [16]

In his dealings with the men on the missions, Slattery exhibited the impatience and arrogance often characteristic of talented young men suddenly thrust into leadership roles, though in many cases he certainly had reason for dissatisfaction. In August, 1882, Slattery complained to Benoit about many of the Josephites, who, "being European," ignored his recommendations to stay current with trends in education by reading such periodicals as the New York *Tablet* and *Catholic World.* He had no patience with priests who, he believed, neglected the preparation of their sermons and even less tolerance for those who failed to manage their mission finances effectively. Slattery caustically reproached the Reverend Michael Walsh, who struggled with a staggering $58,000 debt at St. Augustine's Parish in Washington, D.C., with the observation, "Your inability to handle money is natural to you as water to a duck." Walsh responded in kind: "You heap on us rebukes and reproaches. . . . Permit me to say that I so heartily hate your ways and manners." The other priests on the missions shared Walsh's opinion, and in balloting held in November, 1882, they overwhelmingly rejected Slattery and chose Alfred B. Leeson as the new provincial. Commenting on Slattery's defeat, Vaughan wrote to Benoit, "He will be a great loss in every way . . . except his temper with the men." [17]

Slattery felt humiliated and betrayed. "My removal was certainly a disgrace," he complained to Vaughan. "All Baltimore and Washington knew that the priests banded together against me." Leeson was also upset, but for a different reason: Slattery remained in Balti-

---

16. Bishop Herbert Vaughan to John R. Slattery, July 24, 1879, John R. Slattery to Bishop Herbert Vaughan, August 6, 1879, copies of both in "Biographie," IV, 5–10; John R. Slattery to Bernard Chevillion, March 31, 1881, in CB1-141-46, Slattery Papers; Bishop Herbert Vaughan to Canon Peter Benoit, May 3, 1881, in MHFP.

17. John R. Slattery to Canon Peter Benoit, August 29, 1882, in CB-13-9b, MHFP; Steins, "The Mission," 58; Bishop Herbert Vaughan to Canon Peter Benoit, October 24, 1883, in MHFP.

more. In order to relocate Slattery, and thus rid himself of a potential threat to his authority, Leeson accepted an invitation from Bishop John Keane to open a Josephite mission in Richmond and assigned Slattery to the post in early 1884. The speed with which Leeson accepted Keane's invitation and the embarrassing condition of the mission, which had a congregation of less than forty, no church, no rectory, and a small school with one teacher in the basement of the cathedral rectory, indicated Leeson's real motive in assigning Slattery to the mission.[18]

Although bitter about his new assignment, Slattery applied himself with his usual skill and energy, almost singlehandedly building up the Richmond mission. To construct the mission church, St. Joseph's, he appealed successfully to the children of the parochial schools in the United States, who sent him 800,000 pennies. Slattery also received invaluable help on these Virginia missions from Lydia O'Hare Nicholas and Wales Tyrrell, two black catechists. Relying on their assistance, he opened mission churches in Petersburg, Columbia, Keswick, and Union Mills and founded schools in Petersburg and Keswick between 1884 and 1888. In the process, he discovered an important new donor, Louise Drexel Morrell, an heiress and the wife of wealthy meat packer Edward V. Morrell. In 1891, Mrs. Morrell's sister, Katharine Drexel, founded a religious congregation, the Sisters of the Blessed Sacrament for Indians and Colored People. Using their personal fortunes, estimated in excess of $250 million in present-day dollars, Mother Katharine Drexel and Edward and Louise Morrell built schools and missions throughout the South, including Xavier University in New Orleans, America's only Catholic black university.[19]

During the four years of what he considered his exile in Virginia, Slattery wrote numerous articles for *Catholic World*, a publication of the Paulists, in an attempt to rally Catholic support for the Negro missions. In those articles, Slattery revealed how his ideas about blacks and about the nature of the race problem in the United States had developed. At a time when the emerging racial orthodoxy in most southern and many northern churches proclaimed the

18. John R. Slattery to Bishop Herbert Vaughan, May 31, 1883, in MHFP; Steins, "The Mission," 63–64; [Slattery], "John R. Slattery," 306–10.

19. Steins, "The Mission," 64; [Slattery], "John R. Slattery," 306–10; Peter E. Hogan, "Josephites in Virginia," *Josephite Harvest*, LXXXII (Spring, 1982), 9–10; Henry J. Koren, *The Serpent and the Dove: A History of the Congregation of the Holy Ghost in the United States, 1745–1984* (Pittsburgh, 1985), 155–56.

inherent inferiority of blacks to caucasians and denounced social intermingling between the races as sinful, Slattery maintained a relatively enlightened, albeit paternalistic, position. He denounced racial discrimination and blamed racial discord on whites who refused to treat blacks as their brothers and sisters in Christ. He denied that there was an inherent inequality of the races, though he did regard blacks as an immature, "slumbering race," in need of education and uplift as a result of the evil effects of slavery. He also viewed blacks as a problem for the nation—a problem that, left unsolved, could explode into race war.

Although Slattery considered blacks as a largely "frivolous and unreflecting people," he did not, like many of his contemporaries, attribute the alleged emotionalism, immorality, idleness, and ignorance of blacks to innate racial characteristics. Rather, Slattery viewed those weaknesses as the results of environmental and historical factors that the Catholic church could correct. He took as his own the statement of Archbishop William Elder that "Negroes as a race are less lustful than the whites, but because of external influences, [such] as . . . social life, respectability, and so forth, the whites control themselves better." Slattery insisted that only the Catholic church, "a mighty conservative force," could elevate the black race, keep it on the side of order, and produce real spiritual equality "without shock to true social distinctions." He scornfully attacked the "false conservatism" and prudence of those Catholics who "deprecate the colored race and say that our efforts would be wasted on them." He pointed to the thousands of youths enrolled in black colleges as evidence that blacks possess intellectual ability.[20]

During Slattery's first year in Richmond, the American hierarchy convened in the Third Plenary Council. The Propaganda, unhappy that the American bishops had failed to find a uniform method

20. Smith, *In His Image*, 239–40; [John R. Slattery], "The Catholic Church and the Colored People," *Catholic World*, XXXVIII (June, 1883), 374–84; [John R. Slattery], "Some Aspects of the Negro Problem," *Catholic World*, XXXVIII (February, 1884), 604–13; [John R. Slattery], "The Present and Future of the Negro in the United States," *Catholic World*, XL (December, 1884), 389–95; John R. Slattery, "Facts and Suggestions About the Colored People," *Catholic World*, XLI (April, 1885), 32–42; [John R. Slattery], "Is the Negro Problem Becoming Local?," *Catholic World*, XLIV (December, 1886), 309–16; [Slattery], "Biographie," IX, 2–3; John R. Slattery, "History of St. Joseph's Society of the Sacred Heart for Foreign Missions" (MS in Slattery Papers), 9.

for evangelizing and educating American blacks, insisted that the council, scheduled for the autumn of 1884, address the "Negro problem." Because the vast majority of blacks resided in the South, only about twenty of the seventy-six bishops and archbishops at the council perceived a direct responsibility for them.[21] Vaughan considered making some recommendations to the council through Gibbons, whom the Holy See had appointed apostolic delegate, or presiding officer. First, though, Vaughan sought information from his man on the scene. At Benoit's request, Slattery prepared a long memorandum for Vaughan on the council and on the needs of the black apostolate.

In the memorandum, Slattery claimed that Bishop Keane, with whom he had lived during his first year in Richmond, had told him that the Propaganda insisted the council establish a yearly collection in every diocese in the United States for the benefit of the Indian and Negro missions. Slattery advanced a plan based upon this annual collection—a plan that, if implemented, would have greatly increased the influence and power of the Josephites. He suggested that the proposed yearly collection be sent to and then distributed by the Lyon Society for the Propagation of the Faith, because it had "greater experience—would be more careful than the Bishops." He recommended, moreover, that Vaughan urge the bishops to establish American branches of the Society for the Propagation of the Faith in every part of the country. Since the Josephites "are the only part of the missionary work in the country, the management of these Societies might be secured for us," he argued. He also encouraged Vaughan to offer a Josephite to serve as the bishops' agent to publicize the missions and gather funds.

Slattery made a number of suggestions for more effective evangelization of blacks. He called for the establishment of churches in cities as opposed to rural areas, to serve as centers from which "missionaries might radiate up to a distance say of 200 miles." He also stressed the importance of admitting blacks to higher, middle, common, and industrial schools, pointing out that in 1880, 169 black youths, not one of whom was Catholic, attended sixty-nine predominantly white, northern colleges, and 14,000 attended institutions of higher learning, from normal to medical and theological schools, that were conducted by members of their own race.

21. Edward J. Misch, "The Catholic Church and the Negro, 1865–1884," *Integratededucation*, XII (November–December, 1974), 37.

60

Slattery emphasized the need for a Josephite seminary in Baltimore to train priests for the Negro missions and to provide the skeptical American bishops with some concrete evidence of Mill Hill's commitment to the American missions. In point twelve of the memorandum, Slattery raised "the question of negro boys for the priesthood." Reflecting on the sensitive nature of the topic, he advised, "Upon this there are many opinions. . . . Should you conclude to mention it, it must be done *cum maxima cautela* [with the greatest caution]." [22]

Even as he warned Vaughan about raising the subject, Slattery pushed ahead with a project that would increase the number of black priests. An American seminary to prepare priests for the Negro missions became his overriding goal. Slattery viewed the seminary as essential for the rejuvenation of both the Josephite missions and his own reputation. He presented a prospectus for the seminary in a memorandum to Vaughan, dated March 7, 1884, copies of which he sent to Cardinal Gibbons and Bishop Keane. Slattery clearly included blacks in his seminary plans; he stipulated in the prospectus that "no white student should be received under twenty five years of age; no Negro under thirty." [23]

Others publicly urged the council to move positively on the question of black priests. Edited by John H. Greene, the American supplement of *St. Joseph's Advocate*, the monthly Mill Hill mission magazine, implored the bishops to aid the Josephite efforts by opening their seminaries to "colored vocations." The *Advocate* argued that this action would present the highest inducement for the cultivation of virtue and letters among black students in Catholic schools. To the objection that a number of Afro-American candidates "have already been tried and found wanting," the *Advocate* answered, "One or two have failed, but where was the number from which they were selected?" It pointed out that even among whites, the failure rate in the seminary was two of every three. The article concluded with a reference to Augustine Tolton, then enrolled at the Urban College, and pointedly asked the council to "do as Rome does." [24]

22. John R. Slattery to Canon Peter Benoit, January, 1884 (although dated January, internal evidence in the memo indicates that Slattery wrote it in March), in MHFP.

23. John R. Slattery to Bishop Herbert Vaughan, March 7, 1884, in MHFP.

24. "A Great Work for the Council," *St. Joseph's Advocate*, I (October, 1884), 57.

A small group of liberal priests in New York also lent support to the cause of a black clergy. Those priests, including Edward McGlynn and Richard Burtsell, belonged to an informal group called the "Accademia." Many of them had received their training at either the Urban or the North American college. They prided themselves on their progressive views, believing that the Catholic church should abandon its "prudent" silence on social questions and take the lead in reform. Earlier, they had supported emancipation and Radical Reconstruction. The controversial McGlynn championed the Knights of Labor and the social theories of Henry George; he was excommunicated in 1887 and then reconciled in 1893. The efforts of Burtsell and Thomas Farrell, another member of the Accademia, led to the establishment of St. Benedict the Moor, the first black parish in New York City. At the dedication vespers for the church, McGlynn insisted that the black race "should be represented amongst God's ministry" and expressed the hope that the congregation "might one day have priests of their own race," drawn perhaps from among the acolytes who, for the first time, appeared around the altar in New York City.[25]

The bishops who met at the Third Plenary Council from November 9 through December 7, 1884, did not even consider the option of black priests. Despite its shortcomings, however, the council signaled increased Catholic missionary efforts among blacks. It recommended the use of black catechists (but no bishop acted on the recommendation following the council's adjournment). At the Propaganda's insistence, the council decreed, as Slattery had predicted, an annual collection in all dioceses for the Negro and Indian missions. It further established the Commission for Catholic Missions Among the Colored People and the Indians (Negro and Indian Commission), composed of two bishops and presided over by the archbishop of Baltimore. In addition, the bishops selected a priest-secretary to report to them on both the amount received from the collection and its use. The council also strongly recommended separate churches for blacks, wherever possible, because of the discrimination they encountered in white Catholic churches. Construction of churches and schools thus became a key part of the

25. Robert Emmett Curran, "Prelude to 'Americanism': The New York Accademia and Clerical Radicalism in the Late Nineteenth Century," *Church History*, XLVII (March, 1978), 49–50, 54; John R. Slattery to Edward McGlynn, November 21, 1881, in CB-1, Slattery Papers; "Rev. Edward McGlynn, D.D.," *St. Joseph's Advocate*, I (January, 1884), 12.

Catholic approach to evangelizing blacks. Bishop Keane, clearly influenced by Slattery, proposed a special American college for missionaries to Afro-Americans and Indians. The bishops looked with some favor on the idea and suggested that an episcopal committee examine its feasibility.[26]

Slattery regarded the establishment of an annual collection for the Negro missions as a promising development, especially since the Josephites could count on receiving some of its funds. The collection freed black missions from total dependence on local financing, though final decisions on the disposition of money and the fate of individual missions still rested with the local bishop in whose diocese the mission functioned. The commission conducted its first collection in 1887. Donations for the first five years totaled about $361,000; on a per capita basis, this sum amounted to less than one cent per Catholic per year.[27]

In an article in *Catholic World* in 1885, Slattery contrasted the paltry Catholic missionary efforts to those of Protestant sects, pointing out that the Freedmen's Aid Society, the child of the Methodist Episcopal Church North, had expended $893,918 between 1865 and 1879, just for black education. Its Church Extension Society had also provided nearly $250,000 for black churches during that same period. The American Baptist Home Mission of New York had contributed over $1,000,000 for theological and normal instruction among the freedmen. The AMA conducted 8 chartered institutions of higher learning, 12 high schools and normal schools, and 24 common schools for blacks in the South, whereas no Catholic college in the United States accepted blacks. Slattery ended his indictment by pointing out that in the southern states in 1880, 16,793 public and private schools, most of them Protestant at least in spirit, existed for black children, with a total enrollment of 800,113. At the same time, Catholics conducted 35 schools for blacks, enrolling 2,609 students.[28] These statistics made the need for increased Catholic missionary activity startlingly apparent.

26. Edward J. Misch, "The American Bishops and the Negro from the Civil War to the Third Plenary Council of Baltimore, 1865–1884" (Ph.D. dissertation, Pontifical Gregorian University, 1968), 530, 533–35, 540–41.

27. Steins, "The Mission," 71; Misch, "The Catholic Church and the Negro," 37.

28. Slattery, "Facts and Suggestions About the Colored People," 35.

Although the Third Plenary Council had not faced the issue of black priests, its small gestures toward blacks had made the climate for Afro-American priests more favorable. Also beneficial were Slattery's efforts in behalf of a black clergy. These efforts and the impending ordination of Augustine Tolton in Rome led Benoit, in February, 1886, to ask Slattery for an article addressing the question of "the moral and intellectual fitness of the Negro for the priesthood" and "of expediency, *viz.* would Negroes listen to him." Benoit also wanted him to indicate whether black priests would shock the southern aristocrat "so as to lower the Priesthood and the Church in his eyes."[29]

On the occasion of Tolton's ordination and return to the United States, an unsigned article, perhaps authored by Slattery but certainly echoing his views, entitled "Father Tolton—The Very First," appeared in the October issue of *St. Joseph's Advocate.* The article described Tolton's ordination on April 24, 1886, and the enthusiastic reception that he received from both whites and blacks when he arrived in Quincy, Illinois, to take up his assignment at St. Joseph's Church. The article claimed that Tolton's ordination belied the notion that blacks deserved degradation and that they lacked intellectual and moral capabilities. It praised Tolton as "the genuine article, a typical Afro-American—not your Episcopalian ideal, octoroon if possible, quadroon at most, Caucasian in chiseling." It also noted the salutary effect of a black priest on racial prejudice, observing that as Tolton passed through the streets of Quincy, "white gentlemen raise their hats." The article proclaimed, "We have seen it, not once or twice, but almost every time—MANHOOD!" An accompanying piece, reprinted from the Washington, D.C., *People's Advocate,* concluded that the arrival of Tolton represented the advance guard of many more Afro-American priests and marked a new era in Catholic evangelization of the black race. Tolton's ordination provided graphic evidence that Rome "has planted its foot firmly against caste in the priesthood." Rector of the North American College, Monsignor Denis J. O'Connell, who had attended St. Charles College and lived with Slattery at the Richmond cathedral rectory, assured him that Tolton's reception in the United States "opens the door wider here for colored candidates."[30]

29. Canon Peter Benoit to John R. Slattery, February 18, 1886, in CB-4, MHFP.

30. [John R. Slattery?], "Father Tolton—The Very First," *St. Joseph's Advocate,* I (October, 1886), 185–86; Denis O'Connell to John R. Slattery, September 18, 1886, in 10-K-17, Slattery Papers.

Slattery's own "colored candidate" at St. Hyacinth's, however, caused him some worry in 1886. Slattery regarded Uncles as his test case and monitored his progress closely. Alluding to opponents of black priests who claimed that blacks could not master such sophisticated courses as philosophy, Slattery expressed concern about Uncles' philosophy grade. Somewhat defensively, Uncles explained that his mark in philosophy stemmed not from a lack of understanding but rather from his difficulty in expressing himself in Latin. He assured Slattery that white doubts about the intellectual capacity of blacks stemmed from prejudice rather than fair trial. Referring to his own teaching experience as well as to his time at St. Hyacinth's, he told Slattery, "Other things being equal, colored boys learn as readily as whites. . . . Faculty and students of this college will admit that there is one colored young man able to grasp philosophy and reasoning." He then added, "O bosh! What's the use of my writing this to you! You know." Uncles finished the term solidly with four "tres biens" and three "biens," one of which included philosophy. The next year, out of a class of thirty-three, he placed third in history, first in math, and fifth in philosophy.[31]

A more troublesome issue, one that would plague their relationship for many years, surfaced in the autumn of 1886. Uncles thanked Slattery for financial and emotional support but informed him that he faced a dilemma in choosing between the Josephites or the diocesan priesthood. Uncles confided to Slattery that though he preferred to become a Josephite, he worried about the financial support of his parents. As a secular priest, he could earn money and hold property so as to support his parents in their old age. He assured Slattery that he would join the Josephites without a second thought if he could get enough money to ensure his parents' comfort.[32]

As early as September, 1886, Slattery asked his friend O'Connell to consult with the rector of the Propaganda's college about sending Uncles there to finish his seminary studies. After discussing the matter with the proper authorities, O'Connell scotched the idea, reminding Slattery that students at the Urban College had to have a bishop as a sponsor and could not enter the college with the intention of becoming a Josephite. He advised Slattery to leave

31. Charles Uncles to John R. Slattery, November 8, 1886, in 10-N-2, Charles Uncles' report card from St. Hyacinth's, December 30, 1886, in 10-N-4, Charles Uncles to John R. Slattery, June 28, 1887, in 10-N-9, all in Slattery Papers.

32. Charles Uncles to John R. Slattery, November 8, 1886, in 10-N-2, Slattery Papers.

Uncles at St. Hyacinth's since he was so far advanced in his studies.[33] Slattery's reasons for exploring this option for Uncles remain unclear. The move might have stemmed from his second thoughts about Uncles' suitability for the Josephites, from some dissatisfaction with St. Hyacinth's, from his desire to find a major seminary for Uncles, who had only two years left at the college, from a desire to give Uncles a more cosmopolitan education, or from a combination of the above. Whatever his motivation, Slattery followed O'Connell's advice, and Uncles remained in Canada.

Slattery evidently let the issue rest for the moment, but early in 1887 the two men exchanged sharp letters about Uncles' future and the plight of his parents. Slattery questioned Uncles' sincerity, which occasioned an emotional response from the sensitive seminarian. Uncles told Slattery that his mother had "often besought me with tears in her eyes not to become a priest because she would then lose all hope of any aid from me in her old age." He added that his father had "heaped reproaches and curses upon me because of what he says is my ingratitude and unfilial conduct." He promised Slattery that he would ignore his parents' criticism if Slattery advised him that he could do so prudently. Uncles also asked Slattery to speak to his parents about the matter when his patron visited Baltimore.[34] At least for the time being, Slattery succeeded in calming the fears of both son and parents.

Meanwhile, Slattery worked quietly at the Richmond mission on grooming several more black men for the seminary. By 1886, after nearly ten years of missionary experience, he summarized for Benoit what he characterized as his two basic convictions about blacks: "Catholics must do everything the Protestants do" and "White men will never convert them." Slattery regarded the schools that he had established on the Virginia missions as a potential source of vocations and a testing ground for the fitness of black candidates for the priesthood. He encouraged the priestly aspirations of such students as James Brown and Joseph Griffin and of Wales Tyrrell, a public school teacher in Keswick, Virginia, who also taught catechism on Sundays. In the fall of 1886, Slattery recommended Tyrrell for St. Peter's, the society's preparatory seminary at Freshfield, near Liver-

33. Denis O'Connell to John R. Slattery, September 18, 1886, in 10-K-17, Slattery Papers.

34. Charles Uncles to John R. Slattery, March 3, 1887, in 10-N-7, Slattery Papers.

pool. Canon Benoit, however, suggested a year's delay in order to test his vocation.[35]

Slattery's articles and letters also encouraged bishops to confront forthrightly the problems associated with black evangelization. Responding to a Slattery letter in December, 1886, Bishop Thomas Becker of Savannah informed him that several southern bishops had talked informally about "what may, can, or ought to be done" for blacks. Becker acknowledged that the bishops held differing views but assured Slattery that "all agreed something practical should be done." Some suggested one, large, Catholic industrial or normal school that would equal the Baptist or Methodist universities. Others, however, believed that "certain bigotry . . . would be brought to bear against the church here" as a result, and they also pointed out that the church had few resources in the South with which to support such a school. Still others argued that the bishops should commit the whole work to a prefect apostolic or a religious order. Becker favored the latter approach, though he believed that the Josephites had not succeeded in their task in the United States up to that time. Schools for the young seemed to offer some hope for success. "Your plan of gradually making them work for themselves is undoubtedly best," wrote the bishop. He added, "Bishop Janssens wants me to write some articles on the subject"; but then, voicing the sentiments of so many of the southern bishops, he confessed, "I am simply afraid to do it. It would not do any good; it would stir up prejudice."[36]

Slattery agreed with the bishop that the Josephites had not succeeded and laid the blame for lack of progress on the training at Mill Hill. According to Slattery, Mill Hill did not adequately prepare missionaries for America; instead, it produced a preponderance of foreigners who understood neither the United States nor the Negro missions. He reiterated the need for an American college to train Americans for these missions. Addressing Becker's fears about possibly exciting white opposition, Slattery admitted that his own actions and words had offended some white southerners. Still, he argued, such antagonism might actually benefit the church

35. John R. Slattery to Canon Peter Benoit, March 4, 1886, in MHFP; John R. Slattery, "The Seminary for the Colored Missions," *Catholic World*, XLVI (January, 1888), 547–49; Canon Peter Benoit to John R. Slattery, November 10, 1886, in 10-G-2, Slattery Papers.

36. Bishop Thomas Becker to John R. Slattery, December 11, 1886, in 10-G-7, Slattery Papers.

by encouraging more black converts, since blacks responded favorably to those churches whose ministers openly condemned racism. Charging that race prejudice tainted North and South, Catholic and Protestant, Slattery declared, "I can't still my pen."[37] Fortunately for him, neither could Janssens, the important southern bishop that Becker had mentioned.

In March, 1887, Bishop Francis A. Janssens of Natchez, a native of Holland and future archbishop of New Orleans, issued the first public pronouncement of any American bishop in favor of "colored priests for the colored people." Writing in the March, 1887, issue of *Catholic World*, reprinted later in *St. Joseph's Advocate*, Janssens insisted that "the colored man himself" should "be the instrument in the hand of God to evangelize his colored brethren." He cited church tradition regarding indigenous clergy and pointed to successful native seminarians and priests in China, Japan, and Africa and at the Propaganda's college. He affirmed from his own experience that "there are numbers of bright colored boys that have more than sufficient intelligence to become priests" and argued that blacks wanted to manage their own educational and religious affairs and did not want white preachers. As to morality, he insisted that a "colored boy who received special religious training could rely on the grace of God to enable him to live a pure life"; once ordained, he would have the advantage of knowing the character and ways of his people. Janssens urged the bishops to use a special portion of the Indian and Negro fund to establish a normal school for young Afro-Americans in order to train teachers and teach Latin. If any of them showed signs of a vocation, they could receive separate training for the priesthood. Although the first part of Janssens' article included stereotypical references to alleged laziness, lack of civilization, reckless living, and indifference to politics, the second part gave a significant boost to Slattery's efforts on behalf of a "native colored clergy." In 1892, after he had become archbishop of New Orleans, Janssens himself sent two young black men to Slattery to study for the priesthood. The archbishop also opposed as unjust and as "an infringement on human and religious liberty" Louisiana House Bill #136, which would have forbidden intermarriage between whites and persons of color.[38]

37. John R. Slattery to Bishop Thomas Becker, January 3, 1887, in 10-G-7, Slattery Papers.

38. [Bishop Francis A. Janssens], "Colored Priests for the Colored People," *St. Joseph's Advocate*, I (April, 1887), 229–31; "An Unjust Law," *St. Joseph's Advocate*, III (October, 1892), 235.

Slattery's long-term hopes for black priests, though, ultimately rested on the creation of a Josephite seminary in the United States. Between 1884 and 1888, he campaigned persistently for such an institution. He also believed that an American seminary would eliminate the financial burden of sending students to England, ensure a steady supply of priests for the Negro missions, and better prepare seminarians for the realities of life in the United States. Slattery felt a special urgency about the project because the bishops at the Third Plenary Council had roundly criticized the Josephites for the lack of progress on the missions and because the seminary project promised personal vindication for him after his four-year exile in Richmond.[39]

When he had first presented his seminary prospectus in 1884, Slattery had secured Vaughan's permission for a seminary and had purchased a site in Baltimore, only to have the bishop change his mind and postpone the plan. For the next three years, in magazine articles and in letters to priests and bishops, Slattery emphasized the need for a seminary. He had already secured the important support of Gibbons and Keane. In the spring of 1887, with the first distribution of money from the Negro and Indian missions collection approaching, Gibbons stopped in England on his return from Rome and again raised the question of an American seminary with Vaughan. As a result, Vaughan agreed to the enterprise and gave his formal consent to Slattery on August 28, 1887.[40]

Slattery again drew up a prospectus for the new institution, which he intended to name St. Joseph's Seminary, and submitted it to the American bishops with an accompanying letter soliciting their approbation. According to the prospectus, St. Joseph's students would attend classes at St. Mary's, the Sulpician seminary in Baltimore. St. Joseph's would accept only advanced students in order to produce new Josephites as quickly as possible and would receive financial support from burses, donations, and the Negro and Indian missions collection. Slattery also recommended a college or preparatory seminary, for a later date, to serve as a feeder school for St. Joseph's.[41]

The most controversial point of the prospectus, however, in-

39. John R. Slattery to Canon Peter Benoit, November 16, 1885, in CB-2, Slattery Papers; Steins, "The Mission," 71–73.

40. Canon Peter Benoit to Bishop Herbert Vaughan, 1884, in MHFP; [Slattery], "Biographie," VI, 12–13; Slattery, "History of St. Joseph's Society," 11–13; Steins, "The Mission," 74.

41. Prospectus for St. Joseph's Seminary, 1887, in 3-H-12, Slattery Papers; Steins, "The Mission," 75.

volved the nature of St. Joseph's student body. Referring to the students of the proposed seminary, Slattery told the bishops, "It was also decided upon that no distinction of color should prevent an otherwise worthy subject from entering the ranks of the priesthood. St. Joseph's Seminary would receive the black as well as the white man." He deflected suggestions for a separate seminary for blacks, telling the Josephite provincial Leeson that such a question should be left to time. The prospectus, however, also reflected Slattery's suspicions about the ability of young black males to remain celibate. It attempted to provide some insurance that blacks accepted into the seminary would have demonstrated their ability to remain chaste during their most virile years by its requirements, which were similar to those he expressed to Vaughan in 1884: "no white student should be received under twenty years of age. No Negro under thirty."[42]

Bishop Janssens congratulated Slattery on his prospectus and informed him that the bishops of the New Orleans province had assembled during the first week of November, 1887, to discuss Slattery's proposal. Although conceding "the difficulty of starting with negro candidates" and acknowledging that "it could prejudice the scheme," Janssens expressed agreement with Alphonse Maignen, the superior of the American Sulpicians, president of St. Mary's Seminary, and Cardinal Gibbons' trusted adviser, who argued, "It will be sometime before colored youths arrive at philosophy and time will teach whether a separate seminary for colored candidates will be required."[43] Maignen had to face the problem much earlier than he expected.

The problem involved Charles Randolph Uncles. In June of 1887, Slattery asked Maignen to accept Uncles into St. Mary's, evidently as a resident student until St. Joseph's Seminary was a reality. Maignen apparently demurred, and Uncles remained at St. Hyacinth's for another year.[44] On October 19, 1887, Slattery purchased for $24,500 the former Western Maryland Hotel, a dreary, warehouse type of structure located on property abutting the grounds of

42. Slattery, "History of St. Joseph's Society," 23; John R. Slattery to the American bishops, October 20, 1887, copy, John R. Slattery to Alfred B. Leeson, November 19, 1887, in 3-H-11, Prospectus for St. Joseph's Seminary, 1887, in 3-H-12, Rules for St. Joseph's Seminary, 1887, in 10-S-7a, all in Slattery Papers.

43. Bishop Francis Janssens to John R. Slattery, November 11, 1887, in 7-D-2, Slattery Papers.

44. John R. Slattery to Bishop Herbert Vaughan, June 14, 1887, copy in 10-S-1, Slattery Papers.

St. Mary's Seminary, and renamed it St. Joseph's Seminary. Prior to the opening of the seminary, Slattery once again asked the Sulpicians to allow Uncles to attend classes at St. Mary's, this time as a day student, along with the other Josephite seminarians. Since at the time no blacks attended lectures at St. Mary's, the Sulpicians put the proposal to the students, who unanimously voted for his admission. When Slattery informed Gibbons of the result, the cardinal reportedly said that had any voted against admission, he would have bowed his head in sorrow.[45] Gibbons dedicated St. Joseph's Seminary, which opened on September 9, 1888, with four students, including Uncles. In 1889, at Gibbons' request, the Negro and Indian Commission awarded an annual grant of $5,000 to the seminary, which helped lessen the burden of debt. Meanwhile, Uncles impressed professors and fellow students at St. Mary's. At the end of his first semester, for example, he scored the third highest grade out of a class of fifty in his theology examination.[46]

That there was only a handful of students at St. Joseph's Seminary indicated to Slattery the need for a preparatory seminary to serve as a feeder for the major seminary. With the aid of a generous donation from the Morrells, Slattery purchased and renovated the old Highland Park Hotel in Walbrook, Maryland, a suburb of Baltimore. On September 9, 1889, Epiphany Apostolic College opened its doors. It offered a classical, high school course of study and two years of college. After its first year of operation, Slattery reported that the college had four black students out of a total enrollment of thirty-eight. Alarmed at signs of increased Catholic missionary activity, *Christian Recorder*, the journal of the AME church, warned its members that Catholic "newspapers . . . schools . . . missionaries . . . [and] black priests . . . are going to be brought to bear upon the masses of our people with irresistible force."[47] Although guilty of hyperbole, the *Recorder* correctly perceived a new energy in Catholic efforts.

Two of the four black students enrolled at Epiphany Apostolic

45. Steins, "The Mission," 75–76; [Slattery], "John R. Slattery," 306–10; "Address of Father Slattery." According to Slattery, the Sulpicians at St. Mary's adopted in 1851 the rule of not receiving any seminarians of color. Seminary records are silent on the subject. See [Slattery], "Biographie," VIII, 2.

46. Steins, "The Mission," 75–76; Michael Heffernan to Canon Peter Benoit, December 8, 1888, in MHFP.

47. [Slattery], "John R. Slattery," 306–10; Steins, "The Mission," 77; John R. Slattery to Cardinal James Gibbons, 1889, in CB-2, Slattery Papers; "Catholics and Colored Americans," *St. Joseph's Advocate*, I (October, 1887), 294.

College in 1889 had already had a year of preparatory training in England. In 1887, Slattery had approached Vaughan about sending up to four black students (one from Richmond, two from Norfolk, and the possible fourth from New York) to the society's preparatory seminary in Freshfield. Vaughan left the matter up to Francis Henry, the rector of St. Peter's. Slattery wrote to Henry, "I am thoroughly convinced that Negroes will best convert their race. . . . If you agree to receive them, it will be a great blessing for the Colored race." Slattery noted that St. Peter's students had earlier treated a Chinese student in a kindly fashion, and he expressed confidence that "they would also treat well the Negroes, who will be picked boys." Henry visited the United States and personally examined two of the black students from the Virginia missions: Joseph Griffin and Wales Tyrrell. Pleased by what he saw, he accepted the two black candidates; later, he also accepted a third black student, James Brown of Upper Marlboro, Maryland. By the summer of 1888, Slattery had arranged to send four white and three black students to Freshfield. Vaughan reportedly expressed delight at the prospect of blacks at St. Peter's. Procedural disputes between Slattery and Henry, however, marred some of the good will. After receiving a typical Slattery letter, Henry complained to Vaughan, "Father Slattery's very peculiar way of asking makes one almost afraid of having any dealings with him—he seems to delight in alienating . . . his friends and well wishers."[48]

Despite administrative bickering, the seven American students departed for England in August, 1888. Slattery instructed Henry "to simply bounce" any who "do not suit." The Americans adjusted well to the English college, except for Tyrrell, who suffered from ague and rheumatism in the damp climate. They studied English composition, church history, Bible history, Latin, and geography. Henry reported to Slattery that with the exception of Tyrrell, "all of your other boys—Nigs included are doing well." At the end of the Christmas term, Griffin ranked fifth and Brown ranked seventh out of a class of twelve. Tyrrell's health problems, however, forced him to return to the United States in January, 1889, after Slattery had unsuccessfully attempted through Bishop Keane, who was in Rome

48. John R. Slattery to Francis Henry, December 6, 1887, John R. Slattery to Bishop Herbert Vaughan, March 23, August 15, 1888, John R. Slattery to Francis Henry, June 16, 1888, all in MHFP; Mother Mary Agnes to John R. Slattery, April 4, 1888, in 4-B-4, Slattery Papers; Francis Henry to Bishop Herbert Vaughan, September 7, 1888, in MHFP.

at the time, to secure a place for him at Urban College, where two other black American students had already enrolled for the year. With the opening of Epiphany Apostolic College impending, Brown, Griffin, and the other American students at St. Peter's left England on August 1, 1889, for Baltimore.[49]

Between 1870 and 1900, the Catholic church experienced a period of enormous growth. The Catholic population of the United States increased from 4,504,000 to 12,041,000. Immigration accounted for over 3,000,000 of the increase. Although the United States remained technically a missionary country under the jurisdiction of the Propaganda until 1908, every decade saw the creation of new dioceses, churches, schools, seminaries, and other Catholic institutions.[50]

With progress, however, came tensions. Nativism once again emerged, embodied in the anti-Catholic American Protective Association.[51] The last two decades of the nineteenth century also witnessed internal conflict within the American church between liberal and conservative camps over two broad issues: nationality and the relationship of the church to modern American society. The two issues were intertwined and surfaced in specific controversies over parochial schools, secret societies, the Knights of Labor, and a Catholic university.

The liberals, or Americanists, led by John Ireland, the outspoken archbishop of St. Paul, John Keane, bishop of Richmond and first rector of the Catholic University of America, and Denis O'Connell, rector of the North American College and later of Catholic University, together with their Paulist and Sulpician allies, desired a thoroughly American Catholic church, in tune with the American way of life. Desperately anxious for acceptance by the American mainstream, they pushed for the Americanization of recent Catho-

49. Patrick Fahey to John R. Slattery, July 30, 1888, in 3-B-12, Slattery Papers; John R. Slattery to Francis Henry, August 15, 1888, in MHFP; Wales Tyrrell to John R. Slattery, October 24, 1888, in 9-T-8, September 5, 1888, in 9-T-7, Francis Henry to John R. Slattery, November 20, 1888, in 6-Y-10, January 8, 1888, in 6-Y-12, November 20, 1888, in 6-Y-10, Bishop John J. Keane to John R. Slattery, January 11, 1889, in 10-H-21, Francis Henry to John R. Slattery, August 1, 1889, in 6-Y-19, all in Slattery Papers.

50. NCE, XIV, 434; Robert D. Cross, *The Emergence of Liberal Catholicism in America* (Cambridge, Mass., 1958), 22.

51. John Higham, *Strangers in the Land: Patterns of American Nativism, 1860–1925* (New Brunswick, N.J., 1955), 28–30, 58–63, 77–87.

lic immigrants and for greater Catholic participation in American public life, particularly in the movements for economic and social reform. They argued that the church should embrace the best of American culture and celebrate the virtues of American democracy. "A free church in a free society" became their slogan, as they confidently sought to reconcile their church with what they perceived as a dawning new age of republican liberty throughout the world. A "progressive doctrine of providence" dominated their thinking, according to which the kingdom of God was becoming more fully realized in history in and through the Catholic church. Unabashedly Republican in politics and nationalistic in outlook, the Americanists regarded the emerging American church as a model for the universal church. Confident that a transformed Catholicism held the key to solving the political, economic, and social problems of the age, including the race problem, the liberals lent support to Slattery.[52]

The conservatives, led by Archbishop Michael Corrigan of New York, Bishop Bernard J. McQuaid of Rochester, and the German bishops of the Midwest, such as Milwaukee's Frederick X. Katzer, remained suspicious of American culture, viewing it as basically Protestant and infected with the liberalism condemned by Pope Pius IX in his 1864 Syllabus of Errors. They viewed the church as a perfect society, not only superior to other human societies but also immune to any change or cultural influence. Somewhat paradoxically, the German bishops identified their German culture and particularly their German schools with Catholicism and defended them from the Americanizing efforts of the liberals in the hierarchy, the majority of whom were Irish or of Irish descent. Cardinal Gibbons, the unofficial leader of the American church, sympathized with the Americanists but approached issues cautiously and attempted to keep peace between the two groups.[53]

Slattery enthusiastically embraced Americanism and counted the movement's leaders, who exercised considerable influence in

52. Jay P. Dolan, *The American Catholic Experience: A History from Colonial Times to the Present* (Garden City, N.Y., 1985), 294–95, 301–304; Cross, *Emergence of Liberal Catholicism*, 43, 50; David [Thomas W.] Spalding, C.F.X., "The Negro Catholic Congresss, 1889–1894," *Catholic Historical Review*, LV (October, 1969), 337, 340.

53. Dolan, *American Catholic Experience*, 295–304; James Hennesey, S.J., *American Catholics: A History of the Roman Catholic Community in the United States* (New York, 1981), 194–96.

the American Catholic church during the late 1880s and early 1890s, among his friends. Where he had arranged for his seminarians to take their classes, St. Mary's, had become a stronghold of Americanism and liberal biblical scholarship under the Sulpician superior Maignen. Slattery also admired the Paulists and their founder, Isaac Hecker, the spiritual father of Americanism. Hecker's own spirituality, with its emphasis on devotion to the Holy Spirit and discernment of the Spirit's movement in the individual and society, and his unabashed republicanism and calls for the church to adopt modern methods in dealing with the world profoundly influenced Slattery and other Americanists, particularly Bishop Keane. Walter Elliott, Hecker's Paulist biographer and the editor of *Catholic World*, enthusiastically supported Slattery's work among blacks and opened the pages of the journal to Slattery's articles; the two men became close friends. Slattery called Bishop Keane, with whom he had lived in Richmond, the embodiment of Hecker's Americanism. The Richmond cathedral rectory was also home to Denis O'Connell, whom Slattery knew from his days at St. Charles College. Their friendship, nurtured by long conversations and shared ideals, blossomed. After O'Connell's appointment as rector of the North American College in 1885, he and Slattery corresponded regularly, using the code names "Gilpin" and "Joseph," about the fortunes of the "liberal party."[54]

Slattery first met Ireland, the "consecrated blizzard of the Midwest," in April, 1888, in St. Paul, where Ireland had invited him to attend the opening of a church for blacks. Although the mission, or revival, held in conjunction with the opening of the church was only a "mediocre success," Slattery later claimed that he and Ireland had "connected" and become strong friends. Slattery admired Ireland and believed him destined for great things. He was dining with Ireland when news arrived in April, 1888, that St. Paul had been elevated to an archbishopric.[55]

The two men shared similar hopes for their church and their na-

54. [Slattery], "Biographie," XII, 17–18, V, 6–9, XIV, 9, VI, 2, 5, XVI, 11; Christopher J. Kauffman, *Tradition and Transformation in Catholic Culture: The Priests of Saint Sulpice in the United States from 1791 to the Present* (New York, 1988), 153–68, 179–98; John R. Slattery to Bishop John J. Keane, February 28, 1898, in 10-H-19, Slattery Papers; William L. Portier, "Modernism in the United States: The Case of John R. Slattery," in Ronald Burke, Gary Lease, and George Gilmore (eds.), *Varieties of Modernism* (Mobile, Ala., 1986), 78–80.

55. [Slattery], "Biographie," VII, 10–14.

tive land and a common sympathy for the plight of blacks in the United States. Ireland emphasized his common bond with Slattery on issues of race when he wrote, shortly after Slattery's departure from St. Paul, "Thank God you are a *Christian* and a *Republican!*" Later that year, he agreed to accept another of Slattery's black protégés, fourteen-year-old John Henry Dorsey of Baltimore, into the college department of St. Thomas Aquinas Seminary in St. Paul. Dorsey and four white students had been attending a classical day college at St. Joseph's Seminary, conducted by a teacher whom Slattery had hired. In October, 1888, when the teacher left, Slattery sent the four white students to St. Charles College and asked Ireland to take Dorsey until Epiphany Apostolic College opened. John Keane (not to be confused with Bishop Keane), the rector of St. Thomas, mirroring the progressive spirit of his archbishop, wrote Slattery, "I esteem the privilege of accepting to St. Thomas the first Negro applicant. . . . I assure you he will be treated kindly and we will give him every encouragement." Dorsey responded to the hospitality of St. Thomas College by scoring nothing lower than 90 percent in Christian doctrine, Latin, Greek, English, history, and arithmetic. Two years later, on May 4, 1890, in a widely reported sermon delivered at St. Augustine's, the first black Catholic parish church in Washington, D.C., Ireland publicly signaled his support for integrated seminaries and created a sensation when he scathingly attacked racial discrimination in the church and in American society.[56]

Richard Burtsell of New York, another liberal, sent messages of encouragement, along with money, for Slattery's new seminary, and Cardinal Gibbons, perhaps emboldened by his friend the archbishop of St. Paul, weighed in with a cautious message of support for black priests. Responding in the pages of *St. Joseph's Advocate* to a letter from Colonel E. M. Seabrook about a split among South Carolina Episcopalians over the issue of ordaining black priests, Gibbons wrote, "It is in accordance with the spirit of the Catho-

56. Archbishop John Ireland to John R. Slattery, April 4, 1888, in 7-B-9, Slattery Papers; John R. Slattery to Francis Henry, August 15, November 6, 1888, both in MHFP; John Keane, rector of St. Thomas Aquinas Seminary, to John R. Slattery, October 12, 1888, in 7-K-18, "Address of Father Slattery," St. Thomas Aquinas Seminary Semi-Annual Report, June, 1889, in 9-K-16a, all in Slattery Papers; "A Famous Sermon," *St. Joseph's Advocate*, II (July, 1890), 151–52; "Bishop Ireland Denounced," *St. Joseph's Advocate*, II (July, 1890), 166–68; "Archbishop Ireland Is Interviewed by the Boston Pilot," *St. Joseph's Advocate*, II (October, 1890), 241.

lic Church, and of her practice, wherever practicable, to ordain clergy of the race that is to be evangelized." Gibbons noted the presence of black priests at the First Vatican Council in 1869 and 1870 and at the Propaganda's college. He ended his letter with the hope that "the day is approaching when colored clergymen will be multiplied."[57]

Thomas Donovan, a Josephite working in Kentucky, had predicted to Slattery in 1888 that the acceptance of black youths into the seminary "will draw the attention of the colored folk . . . to the interest now being taken in the race by the Church." Certainly by 1889, black Catholics began to evidence a heightened awareness about their rightful place in the church. Black seminarians and one recently ordained black priest represented the advance guard of that awareness, but it manifested itself most visibly in a series of five annual Catholic Afro-American congresses. In those congresses, held between 1889 and 1894, black Catholics aired their grievances, voiced their aspirations, and pledged their cooperation in the task of converting and educating their race.[58]

Slattery played a significant role in the Catholic Afro-American congress movement, especially at its inception. Daniel Rudd, its organizer, sought advice from him about the location of the first congress, the topics for discussion, and the proposed resolutions. Slattery responded with recommendations and with money for the convention. He also agreed to address the congress on "the Negro in the priesthood."[59]

The first Catholic Afro-American Congress opened in Washington, D.C., on January 1, 1889, with a mass at St. Augustine's Church celebrated by Augustine Tolton. Speaking on the second day, Slattery reviewed his efforts on behalf of black priests. Maintaining that blacks "have as much right to be priests as I have," he insisted that Catholics would not succeed in evangelizing blacks "until we have hundreds and thousands of Colored priests." Slattery claimed that the enthusiastic response of blacks to Tolton had demonstrated the falseness of the contention that blacks did not want priests of their own race. He pointed to a good family life as the

---

57. Richard Burtsell to John R. Slattery, September 14, 1888, in 4-H-8, Slattery Papers; "Priests of Color," *St. Joseph's Advocate*, II (October, 1890), 373.

58. Thomas Donovan to John R. Slattery, August 24, 1888, in 5-R-4, Slattery Papers; Spalding, "Negro Catholic Congresses," 337, 340.

59. Daniel Rudd to John R. Slattery, May 8, 1888, in 9-K-8, August 21, 1888, in 9-K-11, October 30, 1888, in 9-K-13, all in Slattery Papers.

source of vocations and ended his presentation with the promise that "as soon as we have plenty of good colored priests, things will change across the Potomac [in the South]."[60]

Although the delegates at the congress chose to adopt a more activist set of resolutions than Slattery had prepared, in the eyes of black Catholics, he had become the champion of black priests and something of a hero. Slattery received letters from black lay men suggesting candidates for the priesthood or seeking his help for black youths who had been rejected by seminaries or who could not find bishops to sponsor them. Often, Slattery could do nothing, but sometimes, as in the case of William Reed, he succeeded in aiding a black aspirant. Reed's poor health had forced him to withdraw from the Urban College. He subsequently tried, without success, to convince several bishops to sponsor him at the Grand Seminaire in Issy, France. Several bishops advised Reed to apply instead to the Josephites, even though the young man apparently desired to become a diocesan priest. After Reed contacted him, Slattery arranged for Archbishop Ireland to sponsor Reed at Issy.[61]

Augustine Tolton also esteemed Slattery as a special friend and protector. Tolton had grown increasingly unhappy in Quincy after his triumphant arrival in 1886. As pastor of St. Joseph's, he had a black congregation of only thirty persons, and conversions among the Protestant blacks came very slowly. Whites constituted the bulk of his congregation on Sundays, which caused resentment among the priests in other parishes. Tolton yearned to do more work among his own people. He also tired of hearing the racist comments of Quincy's Catholics. Priests entertained every conceivable doubt about him. "When they see me and hear me," Tolton wrote, "they are struck, and ask if there is any white blood in me: if so then that is the reason why I can preach, if not then God is powerful." One German priest in particular took a special dislike to Tolton and conducted a campaign against him that, Tolton claimed, "offends me often and hurts me deeply." Bishop James Ryan of Alton, Illinois, explained to the Propaganda that Tolton's trouble in Quincy resulted because "he wants to establish a kind of society here that is not possible (integration)." In late 1889, when blacks in Chicago

60. "Address of Father Slattery."

61. Daniel Rudd to John R. Slattery, February 8, 1889, in 9-K-15, J. T. Whitson to John R. Slattery, July 1, 1888, in 9-K-9, August 10, 1888, in 10-B-31, William Reed to John R. Slattery, June 6, 1890, in 9-P-20, Augustine Tolton to John R. Slattery, January 4, 1891, in 9-S-17, all in Slattery Papers.

convinced Archbishop Patrick A. Feehan to invite Tolton to open a parish in the heart of a slum neighborhood, the black priest readily accepted, but he confided to Slattery that if the situation in Chicago became similar to the one in Quincy, "I will put all my books in the trunk and come right there to Baltimore. Then, I know that I will be protected." He also told Slattery that he would have joined the Josephites if the archbishop of Chicago had not agreed to his coming to Chicago. He promised to advise "every young colored aspirant" to join the Josephites "so as to have direct protection." Tolton declared: "You are the only priest that cares for us anyhow. . . . You are our own man and priest."[62]

Slattery also continued to provide financial assistance out of his own pocket for black students, such as Joseph Green, who prepared for entrance into Epiphany Apostolic College by attending school in Keswick, under the tutelage of Wales Tyrrell. When the college opened for its second year on September 1, 1890, *St. Joseph's Advocate* announced, "The colored race has six representatives; all bright, intelligent boys." It added, "Each student has his own sleeping room; but all study together in one large room."[63]

Slattery hammered on the theme of black priests in two articles that appeared during the winter of 1890 and the spring of 1891. In an address to the convention of the Catholic Young Men's National Union, which *Catholic World* reprinted in December of 1890, Slattery called for "competitive equality" for blacks in American society and sadly noted the distance between the genuine teachings of the church, which preached the fundamental unity of human beings and recognized no color line, and the "Negrophobia" of many white Catholics, who barred blacks from Catholic schools and trade unions and found fault with Archbishop Ireland's sermon at St. Augustine's. Slattery counseled "our black brethren" to "silently and

62. Augustine Tolton to Denis O'Connell, n.d., Augustine Tolton to the Propaganda, July 25, 1887, Bishop James Ryan to the Propaganda, August 20, 1889, Augustine Tolton to the Propaganda, October 7, 1889, copies of all in Augustine Tolton file, JFA; Mary C. Elmore to John R. Slattery, July 7, 1890, in 5-R-29, Slattery Papers; Foley, *God's Men*, 39; Augustine Tolton to John R. Slattery, January 29, 1890, in 9-S-16, January 4, 1891, in 9-S-17, both in Slattery Papers.

63. Wales Tyrrell to John R. Slattery, November 10, 1890, in 9-T-12, December 11, 1890, in 9-T-14, Joseph Green to John R. Slattery, February 23, 1891, in 6-E-10, John R. Slattery to Thomas Donovan, May 25, 1901, in 18-C-26, all in Slattery Papers; "Our Preparatory Seminary," *St. Joseph's Advocate*, II (October, 1890), 229.

patiently persevere until a better day dawns." He promised, however, that "the day is not far distant when . . . the Negroes will have free access to our churches . . . colleges and schools." Claiming that true growth for a race occurs from within, he cited the history of the early church in creating a native clergy and argued that the church had lost Japan for 250 years because the successors of St. Francis Xavier "would have no native priests or bishops." He warned that Protestants fully appreciated the value of black self-help. As examples, he cited the Baptists and Methodists, who had black ministers and whose churches served as the social, political, and religious centers of their communities. In addition, Protestant denominations supported over 130 schools of higher education, which produced teachers, lawyers, doctors, and preachers—the leaders of their race.[64]

A second article, published in the March, 1891, issue of *Catholic World*, rehearsed the history of a native clergy from apostolic times through the work of the Paris-based Société des Missions Etrangères, or Society of the Foreign Missions, which by 1883 claimed 434 native priests. The society also conducted a general college at the Penay Straits settlement in the Philippines, in which over one hundred boys from throughout Asia studied. Slattery concluded, "There is, then, no chance to win the Negroes to the Faith without priests of their own." To the old canard that blacks preferred white priests, Slattery responded, "True, some old 'mammies' . . . will tell fashionable ladies they prefer white priests. . . . But . . . the youth and manhood . . . will cry . . . 'We want our own priests.'"[65]

Yet even in the midst of his campaign for black priests, which included declarations of his faith in the moral capacity of blacks, Slattery displayed ambivalence about "black character." He believed that slavery and its effects had seriously weakened the black family, resulting in rampant immorality. In his address to the Catholic Young Men's National Union, he acknowledged that most blacks lacked "domestic training" and that "moral restraint is too often thrown off." Slattery was not nearly as pessimistic as Bishop Thomas Heslin of Natchez, who described the Afro-American character as "so unsteady," and immorality as so prevalent among them, that "it will require a miracle . . . to convert them"; but the

64. John R. Slattery, "The Catholic Negro's Complaint," *Catholic World*, LI (December, 1890), 347–53.

65. John R. Slattery, "Native Clergy," *Catholic World*, LII (March, 1891), 882–93.

persistence among Southern blacks of prenuptial intercourse, child-birth out of wedlock, and bridal pregnancy appalled Slattery. He observed to Vaughan that "lying and fornication are so common . . . among our best Catholic Negroes, it is no disgrace for an unmarried woman to have a child, and the whiter the bastard, the less the disgrace."[66] Unlike most white Catholics, however, Slattery believed that the church could teach blacks the morality and self-restraint that would keep them from moral degradation. Still, doubts persisted. Slattery's rule at St. Joseph's Seminary not to admit any black students under the age of thirty reflected his concern about the ability of virile black males to remain celibate. The issue of black moral capacity would loom larger at the seminary in the years ahead; it was already present at the seminary's inception.

In 1891, however, as Charles Uncles' ordination approached, Slattery's concerns about morality remained in the background. Black Catholics watched Uncles' progress with great excitement. Wales Tyrrell wrote Slattery: "We rejoice to see Mr. Uncles moving on so well. His ordination alone will work wonders for the southern missions. He in whose mind the Negro priesthood was conceived did surely catch a breath of heavenly inspiration." Louise Morrell, Slattery's major benefactor, hailed the "good news about the Colored Deacon," whereas Josephite John A. DeRuyter, anticipating the powerful impact of a black and a white priest working together, requested that Slattery assign the black priest to Wilmington, Delaware, "to work hand in hand with me to save souls."[67]

On December 19, 1891, the six-foot-two-inch-tall seminarian became the first black man ordained in the United States when Cardinal Gibbons administered holy orders to Uncles and twenty-five other deacons in the Baltimore cathedral. Slattery later claimed that the ordination marked the first time that blacks in any numbers had been allowed to come into the cathedral or to sit in good

66. Slattery, "Catholic Negro's Complaint," 352–53; *Mission Work Among the Negroes and Indians* (Baltimore, 1891), 16; Herbert Gutman, *The Black Family in Slavery and Freedom, 1750–1925* (New York, 1976), 64–65, 449. Gutman points out that the small number of unmarried black women aged thirty or over in the 1900 census indicates that marriage usually followed either pregnancy or the birth of a child. John R. Slattery to Bishop Herbert Vaughan, September 4, 1890, in CB-2, MHFP.

67. Wales Tyrrell to John R. Slattery, January 15, 1891, in 9-T-16, L. D. Morrell to John R. Slattery, December 2, 1891, in 8-H-42, both in Slattery Papers; J. A. DeRuyter, "St. Joseph's Colored Mission, Delaware and Eastern Shore of Maryland and Virginia," *Colored Harvest*, I (October, 1891), 14.

seats. That America's preeminent Catholic churchman performed the ceremony quieted opposition and gave official sanction to an Afro-American clergy. Commenting on the ordination, Slattery wrote, "To the whites it was a surprising innovation; to the colored, an evidence of the universality of the Church."[68]

Uncles celebrated his first solemn high mass on Christmas Day, 1891, at St. Francis Xavier Church. The crowd filled the church and spilled out into the street a full half-hour before the mass started. Slattery preached the sermon and called the celebration "the most unique event in the history of the Catholic Church in this country." He held up Uncles as a model of purity and morality, virtue and temperance, to the black race. Burtsell sent a donation of $1,500 for the Josephite college and seminary and congratulated Slattery on bringing "forth such ripe fruit so speedily, as was seen in the ordination of Father Uncles." Uncles' ordination also had a profound impact on some black youths. Joseph Bell told Slattery, "My heart rejoiced to see a colored man offering up the holy sacrifice of the Mass. . . . I have more inspiration now . . . to prepare myself to work among my black brothers."[69]

Although Uncles' ordination pleased Slattery and portended progress for the black apostolate, Slattery still considered another step necessary in order to infuse the Negro missions in the United States with the necessary vitality. On March 30, 1891, he sent a memorial to Vaughan proposing the independence of the American Josephites from Mill Hill and outlining the steps necessary to effect the separation.[70]

Developments during the 1880s and early 1890s moved the American province toward independence. As early as June 12, 1879, Vaughan had recognized that "it would be a natural and fitting thing that the great American Church should have its own missionary organization." Increasingly, the missions in the East occupied Mill Hill's attention and resources. In 1876, the cardinal prefect of the Propaganda had cautioned Benoit not to send many Mill Hill missionaries to the United States. His recommendation struck a responsive chord in Benoit, who believed that "India ought to be the field of labor of the Society." By the time of Slattery's me-

68. Slattery, "History of St. Joseph's Society," 30; Foley, *God's Men*, 46; [Slattery], "Biographie," XI, 1.

69. Newspaper clipping, n.d., in 8-C-15a, Richard Burtsell to John R. Slattery, December 23, 1891, in 4-H-9, Joseph Bell to John R. Slattery, April 6, 1892, in 4-E-8, all in Slattery Papers.

70. Steins, "The Mission," 79–80.

morial to Vaughan, Mill Hill had missions in Madras, Punjab, and the Northwest Frontier in India and in Borneo. Men stationed in the United States would find themselves suddenly transferred to Madras or Punjab. The American province thus received less attention from Vaughan, who had also become increasingly involved in the affairs of the English church. In 1892 he was named archbishop of Westminster, the primatial see of England, and the following year was made a cardinal. The founding of St. Joseph's Seminary and Epiphany Apostolic College in 1888 and 1889, respectively, freed the American province somewhat from its reliance on England for manpower, depriving Mill Hill of a powerful means of control.[71]

Slattery's personality and ambition also figured prominently in the factors leading to independence. He had succeeded in carving out a semiautonomous role for himself as rector of the seminary. In that capacity, he reported only to Vaughan; he went his own way, all but ignoring Leeson, the American provincial.[72] Never content in a secondary role, Slattery was a leader with vision who believed that the success of the Josephite apostolate to blacks demanded an independent society, one headed by him.

Slattery believed that the deplorable state of the American missions demanded radical action. In his memorial to Vaughan, he roundly condemned what he termed the "lukewarmness" and "irregular behavior" of the priests on the missions. He accused them of being hostile toward him, the seminary, and the college and of scandalizing the seminarians. He blamed his opponents for "the sterility" of the missions: "Baltimore and Washington are today as they were nine years ago," he charged, "while Louisville and Charleston, after sixteen years, have . . . yet to take their first missionary steps." Slattery identified the root cause of the troubles as the "'laissez-faire' principle of government adopted and followed out both at home and abroad." He advocated a new beginning, a fresh start, and assured Vaughan that Gibbons and other members of the American hierarchy supported his project.[73]

71. Bishop Herbert Vaughan to John R. Slattery, June 12, 1879, in CB2-23, Canon Peter Benoit to Cardinal Edward Howard, December 12, 1877, both in MHFP; Steins, "The Mission," 68–69, 70; John Rooney, M.H.M., "A Divorce of Sorts," *Millhilliana*, No. 4 (1985), 120–26.

72. Steins, "The Mission," 77.

73. John R. Slattery to Bishop Herbert Vaughan, May 19, 1891, John R. Slattery to Archbishop Herbert Vaughan, March 2, 1892, copies of both in Slattery, "History of St. Joseph's Society."

Vaughan discussed Slattery's proposal with Gibbons, who had to accept jurisdiction over the American Josephites if independence was to come. Vaughan fretted about his duty to Leeson and to the men under him who did not want to join with Slattery and about the fragility of Slattery's plans, because there were as yet no priests from St. Joseph's Seminary ready for mission work. Vaughan also worried about whether Slattery would "have the tact and good judgement to manage men . . . in spite of his splendid energy . . . and his good will." Gibbons helped assuage Vaughan's fears by assuring him that age and experience had mellowed Slattery. They had not mellowed him so much, however, as to prevent his vigorous protest at Vaughan's proposal to transfer the title of superior general to Gibbons. Such a move, Slattery argued, would make the Josephites a society "whose head would never belong to us." Evidencing his suspicion of the American bishops, Slattery acknowledged that Gibbons took "a discreet interest in the well being of the Negroes," but, he asked, "who knows how his successor may feel?" Slattery insisted that the Josephites "should be a breakwater to protect the blacks, who are sure to suffer unless their friends are in a position to protect them." [74]

Throughout 1892, Gibbons, Vaughan, and Slattery worked out the details of separation. Gibbons agreed to accept the new society as a diocesan institute whose members would select their own superior general. The Josephites would, therefore, retain internal autonomy while remaining technically under the authority of the archbishop of Baltimore. The Mill Hill missionaries in the United States could select one of three options: they could join a diocese, enlist in Slattery's new society, or remain with Mill Hill. Four opted to become diocesan priests, and three remained with Mill Hill. John A. DeRuyter, Dominic Manley, Lambert Welbers, and Charles Randolph Uncles elected to join with Slattery in the new St. Joseph's Society of the Sacred Heart, still known as the Josephites. By May 6, 1893, every priest had indicated his preference, and Gibbons informed Vaughan that the old society had ceased to exist in the United States. On May 30, 1893, Vaughan released the five men of the new society to Gibbons' jurisdiction. [75]

74. Bishop Herbert Vaughan to Cardinal James Gibbons, November 3, 1891, Cardinal James Gibbons to Archbishop Herbert Vaughan, March 12, 1892, copies of both in Slattery, "History of St. Joseph's Society"; John R. Slattery to Archbishop Herbert Vaughan, March 2, 1892, copy in 66-F, Slattery Papers.

75. Steins, "The Mission," 82–84; Cardinal James Gibbons to Cardinal Herbert Vaughan, May 6, 1893, in CB-2, Slattery Papers.

Independence dramatically reduced the number of Josephites available for the missions. In 1889, seventeen men tended to three churches in Baltimore and one each in Charleston, Louisville, Richmond, Washington, D.C., and Wilmington, Delaware. A number of the churches also had outlying missions attached. Approximately twelve thousand black Catholics depended on the ministrations of the Josephites. Now, in 1893, with only five men, two of whom worked full time with seminaries and administration, the Josephites had to retrench. They turned over the Kentucky and South Carolina missions to their respective dioceses and surrendered as well St. Augustine's in Washington, D.C., and St. Monica's in Baltimore to the Baltimore archdiocese. That still left two large congregations, St. Francis Xavier and St. Peter Claver, in Baltimore, St. Joseph's in Richmond, and a struggling mission in Wilmington. Despite the cutbacks, the eleven students at St. Joseph's Seminary and the sixty at Epiphany Apostolic College represented the promise of future growth. The founding of the Sisters of the Blessed Sacrament for Indians and Colored People in 1891 by Mother Katharine Drexel also ensured more sisters and more financial support for mission schools.[76]

In 1893, John Slattery could look back over the previous ten years with satisfaction. He had helped to rally the Catholic church to greater efforts in the black apostolate and had staked out a radically new position on the question of black priests. With the support of liberal clergy and black Catholics, he had brought black men into Catholic seminaries and had witnessed the ordination of one of them to the priesthood. He had also established a new American missionary society, one that promised a more energetic approach to black evangelization. As a dark period of race relations across the country began in the early 1890s, prospects for black priests in the Catholic church yet seemed brighter. The next ten years would determine the extent to which Slattery had succeeded in opening the Catholic priesthood to blacks.

76. Steins, "The Mission," 85; Slattery note, n.d., in 22-A-14, Slattery Papers; William A. Osborne, "A Freeman's Odyssey," *Jubilee* III (September, 1955), 17.

Chapter III

JOHN R. SLATTERY: FALLEN CHAMPION, 1894–1906

If anything in this world is certain, it is that the stand of the Catholic Church toward the negroes is sheer dishonesty.
—JOHN R. SLATTERY, SEPTEMBER, 1906

The cautious optimism that Slattery and his supporters felt in the early 1890s about the prospects for more black priests gave way to disappointment, frustration, and disillusionment by the first years of the twentieth century. Several factors accounted for the change. The 1890s witnessed the triumph of Anglo-Saxon chauvinism throughout the nation and segregation, disfranchisement, and lynching of blacks throughout the South. In 1896, the United States Supreme Court ratified the southern solution to the race problem in the case of *Plessy* v. *Ferguson*, with its infamous "separate but equal" dictum.

In the South, white Protestant religious leaders enunciated a racial creed that supported white supremacy, and black ministers, forced to accommodate to the racial status quo, embraced temperance and education, rather than politics, as the long-term means for uplifting their people. The basic tenets of the white racial creed asserted the inherent inequality of the Negro race to the caucasian and the immorality of racial amalgamation or social intermingling of the races. This racial orthodoxy was espoused by both extremists, such as Presbyterian minister and theologian Robert Dabney, and moderates, such as Edgar Gardner Murphy, an Episcopalian clergyman. Both types subscribed to the belief that blacks were inferior, but the moderates had more faith in the growth potential of the race, arguing that in the future blacks might be able to narrow the vast intellectual gulf between them and whites.

86

The moderate churchmen, along with their allies in politics and business, exercised some restraining influence on the uncompromising extremists. They campaigned against the wave of lynchings that began sweeping the South in the 1890s and that claimed the lives of 134 blacks in the year 1894 alone. They helped black schools obtain some funds through a formalized racial division of the educational tax fund. In addition, they called for cooperation between white and black leaders to improve race relations. Booker T. Washington, the principal of the Tuskegee Institute and apostle of industrial education, was their model of the moral and upright black leader with whom moderate and progressive southern whites might cooperate. They admired the great proponent of black self-help because he counseled blacks to accept, at least temporarily, their racial subordination and segregation, expressed a willingness to work with the "better class" of southern whites, and articulated a gradual program for racial progress based on converting whites to a more favorable view of black character and capacity. Even though the moderates played a secondary role to the extremists in the South, they succeeded in winning an articulate segment of northern opinion to their brand of racist paternalism by stressing the quasi-missionary goal of training a "child-like race" and by extolling the self-help, industrial education, and accommodationist philosophy of Washington.[1]

Although he did not accept their belief in the innate inferiority of blacks, Slattery shared many of the views of the moderate paternalists. He especially agreed with Washington's emphasis on hard work, personal morality, acquisition of property, and industrial education as the best means for "Negro uplift"; in 1895, Slattery authorized the founding of St. Joseph's Industrial School in Clayton, Delaware, to provide a Catholic "Tuskegee-like" education for black youths.[2]

Washington's willingness to forgo agitation for civil and political rights also appealed to Slattery. At the Fifth Catholic Afro-

1. H. Shelton Smith, *In His Image, but . . . : Racism in Southern Religion, 1780–1910* (Durham, N.C., 1972), 260–67, 271; Sydney E. Ahlstrom, *A Religious History of the American People* (New Haven, 1972), 712; Edward L. Wheeler, *Uplifting the Race: The Black Minister in the New South, 1865–1902* (Lanham, Md., 1986), vii–xviii, 127–30; George M. Fredrickson, *The Black Image in the White Mind: The Debate on Afro-American Character and Destiny, 1817–1914* (New York, 1971), 266, 292–93, 298, 304.

2. "Sermon at the Funeral of the Rev. J. A. DeRuyter," *Colored Harvest*, I (January, 1897), 146–49.

American Congress in 1894, Slattery advised blacks to trust to silence and time and leave "the questions which ebb and flow around the negro problem" to their friends. After all, he claimed, emancipation and all subsequent progress for blacks in such areas as education, religion, and civil and public life had come to them from others. Although admitting that "rights ought to be recognized," Slattery nevertheless cautioned patient forbearance, since blacks had to live among whites. He urged blacks to turn their attention to fostering among themselves such virtues as thrift, honesty, and pure family life. *Colored Harvest* praised Washington's speech at the Atlanta Exposition of 1895, in which he enunciated his ideas for racial accommodation. Late in 1896, Slattery arranged for Washington to address the students of Epiphany Apostolic College and St. Joseph's Seminary. Preaching at the funeral of the Reverend John DeRuyter, founder of St. Joseph's Industrial School, Slattery assured the congregation that whites of the country "wish well to our colored people" if they "leave politics alone and buy land."[3]

The demise of the Catholic Afro-American congress movement during this time illustrated the unwillingness of white Catholic church authorities to encourage or respond to black lay Catholic activism and mirrored the eroding position of blacks in the United States. Delegates to the congresses emphasized the need for Catholic schools for blacks, especially those offering industrial education. The congresses became increasingly outspoken in their opposition to caste restrictions in the church. In 1893, for example, the congress established a special committee on grievances that would document, by means of a questionnaire sent to all American bishops, acts of discrimination against blacks in the church. The committee traveled to Philadelphia in October of 1894 to lay its complaints before the annual meeting of the American archbishops. Little changed, however, including the segregated seating in Cardinal Gibbons' own cathedral. After 1894, no more congresses met, victims of both clerical uneasiness about the black delegates' outspokenness and independence and the "separate but equal" atmosphere that prevailed in American society and the American Catholic church.[4] The end of the Catholic Afro-American congress

3. "Hope of the Colored Race," *Catholic Mirror*, n.d., clipping in John R. Slattery Papers, JFA; "Sermon at the Funeral," 146–49.

4. David [Thomas W.] Spalding, C.F.X., "The Negro Catholic Congresses, 1889–1894," *Catholic Historical Review*, LV (October, 1969), 337–57.

movement portended trouble for the even more controversial efforts of Slattery to create a black clergy.

The collapse of the movement also coincided with the beginning of the Americanist crisis, which resulted in a gradual decline in the power and influence of Slattery's liberal allies among the American hierarchy—allies such as Archbishop John Ireland, Bishop John Keane, and their agent in Rome, Monsignor Denis O'Connell. The crisis, which had little to do with racial issues in the United States, culminated in *Testem Benevolentiae*, the 1899 encyclical of Pope Leo XIII that condemned Americanism.[5]

Although not directly related to the question of race, the defeat of the liberals damaged the cause of reform in general. Prelates like Ireland and Keane continued to back Slattery's efforts on behalf of blacks, but their power and influence began waning. In 1895, for example, when Catholic University opened its schools of philosophy and social sciences to all qualified male applicants, three black men enrolled. Keane, the university's first rector, said of the black students, "They stand on exactly the same footing as other students of equal calibre and requirements."[6] By the end of the decade, however, Keane had been replaced as rector, and the liberals no longer possessed the prestige and authority they had once enjoyed in the American church. Slattery and the Josephites felt far more vulnerable on the sensitive issue of black priests than they had in 1891.

Compounding his problems, Slattery's joy over the ordination of Charles Uncles in 1891 soon gave way to disappointment and exasperation. At the time of the ordination, the Reverend Michael Heffernan, a priest in Philadelphia whose parish Uncles had visited, warned Slattery that Uncles had "got conceited as a peacock," and within six months Slattery found himself receiving complaints about Uncles' lack of prayer and zeal. When he made worried inquiries about Uncles to Dominic Manley, the rector of Epiphany Apostolic College, where Uncles taught Greek and Latin, Manley blamed Slattery for the situation, charging that Slattery had allowed Uncles "to do as he pleased since his ordination." Manley protested

5. Gerald P. Fogarty, *The Vatican and the American Hierarchy from 1870 to 1965* (Stuttgart, 1982), 134–42, 177–80.

6. *Inauguration of the Schools of Philosophy and the Social Sciences and Dedication of McMahon Hall, Catholic University of America, October 1, 1895* (Washington, D.C., 1895), 8.

that he could not discipline Uncles because Slattery allowed him so little authority.[7]

Alarmed by the reports, Slattery corresponded with Uncles about his alleged lukewarmness. "Your failure in chief seems to be," Slattery wrote, "a disposition to shirk, boil down, and quibble over work, duties, and obligations." He admitted that he had tolerated a certain amount of Uncles' indifference during the winter because of the black priest's work load and his bout with the grippe. Slattery assured Uncles that he meant his letter to "encourage and enlighten" the priest, since he believed that Uncles sincerely wanted to labor for God's glory. Reflecting his personal stake in Uncles' success, Slattery ended, "No one is so anxious for your sanctification . . . as myself: as no one is going to suffer more in case you do not fill all expectations."[8]

Uncles certainly failed to meet Slattery's expectations as to the kind of work he would do after ordination. Slattery had intended that Uncles, taking advantage of his notoriety as the first black priest ordained in the United States, would go on speaking tours throughout the North and Midwest to promote the missions. He confided to Charles Butler, a prominent figure in the Catholic Afro-American congresses, his belief that Uncles far surpassed Washington in mind and education and had excellent opportunities to do good by accepting some of the scores of speaking invitations that he had received. Much to Slattery's chagrin, however, the proud and sensitive Uncles spurned his superior's public relations plans for him, insisting that he would not be "trotted out before the public gaze" to become "a show priest" like Augustine Tolton. Uncles' aversion to missionary work in the South, owing to his hatred of segregation, also disappointed Slattery, though long acquaintance with Uncles certainly should have prepared him for the black priest's negative reaction to a proposed southern assignment in the spring of 1893.[9]

The financial plight of Uncles' parents, an issue that had surfaced before Uncles' ordination, further strained relations between the two

7. Michael Heffernan to John R. Slattery, n.d. [clearly 1891], in 6-W-7, Dominic Manley to John R. Slattery, May 16, 1892, in 7-W-13, both in Slattery Papers.

8. John R. Slattery to Charles Uncles, May 30, 1892, in CB-2, Slattery Papers.

9. Louis B. Pastorelli to Albert S. Foley, May 19, 1952, in Albert S. Foley Papers, JFA; John R. Slattery to Charles Butler, December 2, 1896, in LPB-2,

men. The Josephite rule limited each priest to six personal stipends for the masses he said throughout the year; those stipends, each of which often amounted to one dollar or less, provided Josephites with money for their personal use. Uncles found this limitation ex- cessive in light of his obligations to his parents. Slattery urged him to bring up the issue at the general chapter scheduled for the sum- mer but insisted that until then he abide by the rule. Meanwhile, Slattery tried to help him by appealing to the public through letters for funds on behalf of "a colored priest deserving of charity because of the poverty of his parents." The letters pointed out that Uncles' father, a mechanic, could not secure work because of discrimina- tion practiced by trade unions. The appeals brought in some contri- butions, which Slattery passed on to the priest. Uncles resented his embarrassing financial dependency on Slattery, made all the more difficult by his tardiness in thanking benefactors and by Slattery's persistent reminders to do so. On July 2, 1894, at the general chap- ter of the society, Uncles suffered further humiliation when, after a discussion from which he absented himself, the assembled Josephites unanimously rejected his petition for an extra allowance of money to go for his parents' support, on the grounds that "its recognition could prove a vital blow to the Society."[10]

Uncles became so discouraged in 1893 and 1894 that he twice submitted to Slattery letters of resignation from the Josephites. Slattery called Uncles' first letter, written in the summer of 1893, "illegal and uncanonical." In the second, dated May, 1894, Uncles informed Slattery that he had no desire to remain a member of any religious society, protested his deep friendship for Slattery, and assured his patron that his determination to resign resulted from "sad experience, prayerful reflection, and disinterested counsel."[11]

Slattery Papers; Albert S. Foley, S.J., *God's Men of Color: The Colored Catholic Priests of the United States, 1854–1954* (1955; rpr. New York, 1969), 48; interviews of Vincent D. Warren, S.S.J., by Peter E. Hogan, S.S.J., 1965 (Typescript in JFA), 45–46; John R. Slattery to J. A. DeRuyter, May 15, 1893, in LPB-1-142, Slattery Papers.

10. John R. Slattery to Charles Uncles, January 21, 1894, in LPB-1-355, Sr. M. Joseph to John R. Slattery, February 24, 1894, in 14-C-24, Charles Uncles to John R. Slattery, March 15, 1894, in 16-D-4, John R. Slattery to Charles Uncles, March 13, 1894, in LPB-1-404, Charles Uncles to John R. Slattery, November 3, 1894, in 16-D-8, July 26, 1897, in 16-D-19, all in Slattery Papers; minutes of the general chapters, July 2, 1894, in JFA.

11. John R. Slattery to Charles Uncles, April 23, 1894, in LPB-1-431, Charles Uncles to John R. Slattery, May 5, 1894, in 16-D-10, both in Slattery Papers.

Whether Uncles seriously intended to leave the Josephites and simply could not find a bishop to adopt him or whether he only attempted to use the threats of resignation to pressure Slattery for more money for his parents remains unclear. Uncles did not receive an increase in allowance, nor did he leave St. Joseph's Society.

By the spring of 1894, Slattery's disappointment with Uncles, his dissatisfaction with several black students at Epiphany Apostolic College and St. Joseph's Seminary, his fear of scandal, his own stereotyped views of black moral weakness, and his need to placate skeptical bishops and clergy led him to adopt a more cautious approach to the training of blacks for the priesthood, one designed to test their vocations. On June 9, 1894, he circulated to all the Josephites a memo containing six questions about black students that he wanted the general chapter to consider in July. Slattery reiterated the "hearty accord" of the Josephites with the principles laid down by the Propaganda in a letter of November 23, 1845, which stressed the need for seminaries to train native clergy. He indicated, however, that both he and Lambert Welbers, the rectors of St. Joseph's and Epiphany College, respectively, felt bound to submit the question of the status of black students to the members of the society because "of those now with us, we shall have to dismiss three this summer because of defects which portend future trouble." He evidently discounted the performance of such black students as George W. Cheese, who had "graduated with great honors" from the college in June of 1893, as less representative than the actions of those who had caused trouble.[12]

Slattery phrased the six questions that he wanted the general chapter to consider in such a way as to indicate the answers that he both preferred and expected. The third question, for example, asked, "Should not the colored students have their studies interrupted either after Rhetoric, or philosophy?" The reconsideration of black students at the college and the seminary upset Uncles, who maintained a special interest in them. He asked for and received permission to absent himself from the meeting that considered the standing of black students, pleading that "some points of discussion were of too delicate a nature" for him to deal with. As a gesture of protest, he proposed to read the rules of St. Joseph's Society to the

12. John R. Slattery memorandum, June 9, 1894, in 23-C-3, Slattery Papers; EAC Student file, 1890–1914, p. 76, in JFA.

assembled chapter, but according to the minutes of the meeting, "no action was taken" on his proposal.[13]

On July 3, 1894, the general chapter, composed of six of the seven Josephite priests, adopted by a majority vote six resolutions "governing the requisites of colored students for admission into the college or Seminary and their promotion to holy orders." The first resolution stated that neither institution would admit "Negro converts." The second, clearly based on the experience with Uncles' predicament, forbade admission of any black student who could not give a satisfactory guarantee that his parents would not depend on him for support. The remaining resolutions required that black students have their studies interrupted, either after graduation from Epiphany Apostolic College or after completion of their second year of philosophy at St. Joseph's Seminary, according to the discretion of the rectors, for a period of not longer than two years. During that time, priests on the missions would employ them "in teaching, catechizing, or otherwise." They would be readmitted after their two-year probation and promoted to higher studies only if they could ensure that their parents would not become economically dependent on them and if they could furnish letters of good conduct from the Josephites under whom they had served. Neither rector, of the college or of the seminary, could deviate from the new regulations without bringing the case before the superior general and his consultors. J. A. St. Laurent, the secretary of the chapter and rector of Epiphany College, marked the new rules "secret" in the minutes, probably for fear that word of them might provoke an outcry both from the black students at the seminary and the college and from black Catholics in general.[14]

The new regulations, which did not apply to white students or seminarians despite Slattery's experience with some rebellious and scandalous white seminarians and priests, clearly discriminated against blacks. Slattery later claimed that he instituted the new policy to mollify bishops and other clergy who maintained that blacks could not observe priestly celibacy. But from its inception, St. Joseph's Seminary had maintained a double standard in admissions,

13. Slattery memorandum, June 9, 1894, in 23-C-3, Slattery Papers; minutes of the general chapters, July 3, 1894, in JFA. The minutes of the July 3, 1894, meeting are incorrectly dated 1895.

14. Minutes of the general chapters, July 3, 1894.

requiring black applicants to have reached the age of thirty, in contrast to whites, who needed only to have attained the age of twenty—a standard that reflected Slattery's concern about black chastity. The 1894 regulations carried that discrimination one step further. Slattery's address to the Fifth Catholic Afro-American Congress that same year, in which he said, "Neither by nature, nor by traditional training can the colored people, taken as a body, stand as yet on the same footing of moral independence as their white brethren," indicated that he shared, at least to some extent, the concerns voiced by the bishops.[15]

That Roman Catholics were not unique in their doubts about black moral capabilities can be seen in the experience of the Protestant Episcopal church, most of whose clergy, black and white, were married. Writing in his diary in 1890, Charles Todd Quintard, Episcopalian bishop of Tennessee, expressed the desire to ordain black men to the priesthood, but feared "not their mental capacity . . . but that they will fail in morals." He thought they lacked "the true moral fiber." White Episcopalians generally regarded the diaconate, a major order one step below the priesthood, as the most suitable ministry for blacks, with the priesthood limited to the truly exceptional. Prior to their ordination as priests, black Episcopal clergy often spent years as deacons, preaching, baptizing, and assisting at liturgies.[16]

Fear that scandal involving black priests might fatally damage his fragile experiment reinforced Slattery's determination to proceed cautiously with their seminary training. When he learned that Augustine Tolton had left St. Monica's Parish in Chicago, he suspected the worst and inquired confidentially from Father McGuire, an acquaintance in Chicago, whether the archbishop had removed Tolton "because of some scandal or other." Slattery observed to his friend that Tolton's departure from St. Monica's "is a serious bit of

15. John R. Slattery to Charles Uncles, May 21, 1897, in LPB-2-512, John R. Slattery to Lambert Welbers, December 30, 1897, in LPB-2-576, Lambert Welbers to John R. Slattery, December 15, 1897, in 20-S-77, all in Slattery Papers; [John R. Slattery], "Biographie de J. R. Slattery" (MS in Papiers Houtin, Oeuvres, LIV, NAF 15741–42, Bibliothèque Nationale, Paris), XVI, 15; Rules for St. Joseph's Seminary, 1887, in 10-S-7a, in Slattery Papers; "Hope of the Colored Race," in John R. Slattery File, JFA.

16. J. Carleton Hayden, "The Black Ministry of the Episcopal Church: An Historical Overview," in Franklin D. Turner (ed.), Black Clergy in the Episcopal Church: Recruitment, Training, and Development (New York, 1978), 6–7.

news for those of us who are engaged in training a few colored boys for the altar," and he confessed that he had had "some trouble with our own man—Uncles" and had taken some steps at the annual meeting "in regard to our own Colored boys, interrupting their studies after rhetoric." When McGuire reported that the bishop had replaced Tolton because of illness, Slattery wrote, "Deo Gratias that his trouble is physical and not moral."[17]

The black students at Epiphany College and the seminarians at St. Joseph's soon felt the impact of Slattery's new policy. James Brooks, John Henry Bell, and Frederick Johnson were dismissed from the college in June, 1894, for reasons that included "want of proper qualifications and unwholesome influence upon other students"; Philip Dufan, one of Archbishop Janssens' protégés, also left. Brooks applied to St. Thomas Aquinas Seminary in St. Paul, whereupon Archbishop Ireland requested Slattery's opinion of the young man and indicated that "for the purpose of a solemn protest against color prejudice, I would take a negro into theology, provided he be solidly good and intelligent, fit to be a leader of his people." Revealing his low estimation of Tolton, Ireland added, "I want no Tolton's." Slattery advised the archbishop to have nothing to do with Brooks, since he was "a chip of the same block . . . as Tolton."[18]

Slattery also counseled John Henry Dorsey, the black student whom he had sent to St. Thomas Seminary for one year in 1888, to take up a calling other than the priesthood. Slattery's decision unnerved Dorsey, and after a tearful interview, he suggested that the young man teach at the mission school at Keswick, Virginia, for $10 a month. Slattery confided to Welbers that he hoped "a couple of years at Keswick" would "sober him up" and develop him into a good subject. The dismissals and suspensions left five black students at the college and only one at the seminary in the autumn of 1894. Ironically, just as Slattery imposed the new rules on black students, *Colored Harvest* trumpeted the interracial character of St. Joseph's Seminary and Epiphany Apostolic College, claiming that at St.

17. EAC faculty minutes, June 26, 1894, p. 45, in JFA; John R. Slattery to Fr. McGuire, July 4, 1894, in LPB-1-456, July 14, 1894, LPB-1-458, both in Slattery Papers.

18. EAC Student file, 1890–1914, pp. 2, 148, 260, in JFA; Archbishop John Ireland to John R. Slattery, August 25, 1894, in 16-T-19, John R. Slattery to Archbishop John Ireland, August 29, 1894, in LPB-1-476, both in Slattery Papers.

Joseph's "no distinction as to color is shown" and that at Epiphany College "white and black . . . enjoy the same rights."[19]

Joseph Griffin's experience further belied the lofty claims of *Colored Harvest* and exemplified the shattered dreams of many of the suspended seminarians. Griffin had known Slattery for twelve of his twenty-four years. As his pastor and confessor in Richmond, Slattery had advised Griffin to study for the priesthood and had sent him to St. Peter's in Freshfield in 1888, prior to the opening of Epiphany Apostolic College. In January, 1893, Griffin had the honor of delivering a Latin address to the newly appointed apostolic delegate, Archbishop Francisco Satolli, the pope's personal representative to the church in the United States, when that delegate visited Epiphany College. Griffin graduated from the college and entered St. Joseph's in September, 1893, where after two years of study he ranked seventh out of forty in philosophy and sixteenth out of fifty in sacred scripture. He also enjoyed a special standing in the eyes of black students. Dorsey turned to him for advice in July, 1894, following the news of his suspension, and Griffin wrote to Edward R. Dyer, the Sulpician secretary of the Negro and Indian Commission on Dorsey's behalf, but to no avail.[20] Since the Josephite general chapter kept the policy of enforced leave secret, Griffin evidently did not realize that Dorsey's fate also awaited him. In June of 1895, while in Richmond at the beginning of summer vacation, Griffin learned from Welbers that Slattery intended to interrupt his seminary studies for two years and to have him serve as DeRuyter's secretary in either Wilmington or Clayton, Delaware, "to see," as Griffin put it, "if I have a vocation."

The decision baffled Griffin, especially since Slattery admitted that he had no charge against him. Griffin protested again to Dyer, asking him to intercede on his behalf with Slattery. The seminarian

19. John R. Slattery to John H. Dorsey, July 19, 1894, in LPB-1-464, Slattery Papers; John H. Dorsey to Joseph Griffin, July 23, 1894, Joseph Griffin to Edward R. Dyer, July 25, 1894, both in RG 39, Box 1, SAB; John R. Slattery to Lambert Welbers, July 20, 1894, in LPB-1-467, John R. Slattery to the Hon. Wilson S. Bissell, Otober 22, 1894, in LPB-3-386, John R. Slattery to Hoffman Brothers, November 17, 1894, in LPB-3-405, all in Slattery Papers; "An Appeal to Noble Youths," *Colored Harvest*, I (March, 1895), 9; "The Apostolate," *Colored Harvest*, I (October, 1895), 39.

20. John R. Slattery to Albert Lightheart, January 3, 1893, in LPB-1-60, Slattery Papers; St. Joseph's Seminary Records, n.d., 149, in JFA; EAC Student file, 1890–1914, p. 171, in JFA; John H. Dorsey to Joseph Griffin, July 23, 1894, Joseph Griffin to Edward R. Dyer, July 25, 1894, both in RG 39, Box 1, SAB.

acknowledged that "on account of national prejudice it might not be prudent to give a colored man orders just yet." He also realized, he told Dyer, that "Fr. Uncles's case demands of Fr. Slattery more than ordinary prudence." Griffin pointed out that he would not receive holy orders for another three years, however, and further argued that to judge him on the basis of Uncles assumed incorrectly that "from one you can tell all." He also resented hearing about the impending suspension indirectly from Welbers rather than from Slattery. He insisted, too, that if he went to do a man's job for DeRuyter, he expected a man's pay, not the $10 per month that Dorsey had received for teaching. Dyer advised Griffin to follow Slattery's wishes; as a result, Griffin agreed to go to Clayton. St. Joseph's Seminary records for September 13, 1895, state that after a review of the case, Joseph Griffin, "being colored . . . was suspended." [21]

Because of objections from DeRuyter and disagreements with Slattery over wages, Griffin did not report to Clayton. He eventually made his way to Cherryvale in the Indian Territory, where he taught black children whose parents worked in the mines. The Reverend B. Murphy, pastor of St. Joseph's Church in the neighboring town of Krebs, reported that Griffin attended mass and the sacraments faithfully, even though he lived five miles from the church. Three years later, Slattery finally agreed to accept Griffin back into the seminary. Financial difficulties, however, prevented his return. [22]

Slattery's "go slow" policy failed to mollify critics of black priests and succeeded only in delaying, or in some cases thwarting, the hopes of black seminarians for ordination. Prospects for black Josephites further darkened as Slattery faced not only external but also internal opposition to them. In particular, new difficulties involving Uncles eroded support for black priests within the society and provided additional ammunition to opponents of the ordination of blacks.

Writing to J. A. St. Laurent in the autumn of 1894, Slattery la-

21. Joseph Griffin to Edward R. Dyer, July 18, 1895, in RG 31, Box 1, SAB; Consultors' Minutes Book—1 (hereinafter cited as CMB), August 28, 1895, St. Joseph's Seminary Records, September 13, 1895, both in JFA.

22. John R. Slattery to B. Murphy, April 22, 1897, copy in 15-B-31, Joseph Griffin to John R. Slattery, April 6, 1898, in 22-B-20, December 19, 1899, in 13-M-18, John R. Slattery to Joseph Griffin, December 30, 1899, copy in 13-M-19, all in Slattery Papers.

mented, "As for Uncles, there is nothing left for us but patience and prayer. No one knows better than myself his shortcomings, and none have to suffer more for them." The illness of a Josephite priest in Baltimore in early 1895, however, necessitated the transfer of Gerardus Wiersma from Norfolk and left only Uncles to fill the gap created in Virginia. According to canon law, only the ordinary of a diocese, the bishop, could grant faculties to a priest. These were necessary for the licit administration of the sacraments and for the exercise of any ecclesiastical authority. Thus, whenever Slattery wanted to assign a man to a particular diocese, he had to request faculties from the bishop. Usually the bishop granted them on request, but if he did not want a certain priest to function in his diocese, he could simply refuse to grant faculties or withdraw them from him, thus preventing his entry or necessitating his removal. Bishop Joseph Rademacher of Nashville, for example, made it clear to Slattery that he did not want black priests assigned to his diocese when he wrote, "Whenever you have any good student (white) to spare, you would do me a favor by assigning him to this diocese." [23] Obtaining faculties for a black priest, therefore, could prove tricky.

Because of Wiersma's transfer, Slattery sought permission to assign Uncles to Norfolk from Bishop Augustine Van de Vyver of Richmond, an old acquaintance. Slattery recognized the ticklish nature of the assignment and assured Van de Vyver that because of the medical emergency, he had only Uncles to send. "The one objection, of course," he added, "is his color—he is a quadroon and it is but proper that I write you beforehand." Slattery described Uncles as "well educated and competent," explained that since he had been raised in Baltimore, "it would not do to put him in charge here," and promised that the black priest would give satisfaction. Slattery added, "If the whites get mad and stay away from the Church, so much the better." Because of their long-standing friendship, Van de Vyver acceded, though reluctantly, to Slattery's request but granted faculties to Uncles only until November, 1895. During that time, the bishop observed, "he can . . . show what he is made of." [24]

23. John R. Slattery to J. A. St. Laurent, September 13, 1894, in LPB-1-483, Bishop Joseph Rademacher to John R. Slattery, September 30, 1893, in 9-H-2, both in Slattery Papers.

24. John R. Slattery to Bishop Augustine Van de Vyver, February 2, 1895, in LPB-2-163, Bishop Augustine Van de Vyver to John R. Slattery, February 3, 1895, in 16-G-10, both in Slattery Papers.

Slattery's triumph in convincing the ordinary of a southern diocese to accept a black priest proved short-lived, however. On hearing the news of his imminent assignment to the South, Uncles left
Epiphany College on February 9, 1895, without permission and
took up residence at his parents' home for almost three months.
During that time, he apparently tried without success to convince
a bishop to incardinate, or adopt, him into his diocesan clergy.
Uncles' abhorrence of the racial conditions in the South and his
concern about the care of his poverty-stricken parents evidently lay
behind his break. Slattery and DeRuyter agreed that if Uncles returned to the Josephites, he would have to return "on the same
money basis as before he left." Slattery eventually offered, though,
to allow Uncles' parents to have the house in which they lived in
Baltimore and to give Uncles $20 per month. The errant priest
thereupon apologized to Slattery and, after spending the summer at
St. Joseph's Industrial School in Clayton, returned to teach his
popular Latin classes at the college in the fall.[25]

In the wake of the Uncles problem, and in the midst of the de-
teriorating racial atmosphere of the mid-1890s, some Josephites
soured on the idea of black priests. In 1895, John DeRuyter, the
priest who had originally requested that Uncles be assigned to assist
him in Wilmington, expressed his disenchantment when he advised Slattery "to have Cardinal Gibbons give you an order that no
more Colored priests should be ordained for the next twenty years."
DeRuyter insisted that black priests would spell disaster for St.
Joseph's Society in its weak state, creating discord and the possibility of a break-up. He argued that the priests working with blacks
had to endure heartache, misery, and disappointment enough without black priests adding more "combustible to burn up what we are
giving our lives to." DeRuyter reminded Slattery that he had had
his "hands burned with Uncles" and urged him not to "bother with
any colored students at the seminary or Epiphany." Referring to
black students, he claimed that it would take years to establish

25. J. A. St. Laurent to John R. Slattery, February 6, 1895, in 19-Y-5, John R.
Slattery to Cardinal James Gibbons, February 11, 1895, in LPB-2-168, Lambert
Welbers to John R. Slattery, March 13, 1895, in 20-S-20, Charles Uncles to J. A.
DeRuyter, May 2, 1895, in 16-D-15, April 26, 1895, in 16-D-12, John R. Slattery
to J. A. DeRuyter, April 28, 1895, in LPB-2-223, J. A. DeRuyter to John R. Slat-
tery, May 3, 1895, in 16-D-14, Charles Uncles to John R. Slattery, May 2, 1895,
in 16-D-13, John R. Slattery to J. A. DeRuyter, May 9, 1895, in LPB-2-229, all in
Slattery Papers; CMB, April 3, 1895, in JFA.

solid, industrious habits in them and concluded, "They are just unfit for the priesthood." He expressed admiration for the Methodists,
who had established separate white and black conferences, and
speculated about the possibility of a similar arrangement in the
Catholic church that would thus allow for black priests. "And yet,"
DeRuyter added condescendingly, "the good colored people trained
by whites—do not want colored priests."[26]

DeRuyter's disillusionment indicated a potentially serious problem within the society—a problem that Slattery attempted to defuse. In what was probably a ploy to gain time, he indicated a
willingness for the general chapter, scheduled for the following
summer, to discuss the question of black students and to "let the
majority vote carry it pro or con." (Contrary to his assurances, the
1896 general chapter did not consider the question.) Attempting
to calm DeRuyter's fears about the future of the society, Slattery
pointed out that as of the autumn of 1895, the seminary had no
black students and the college counted only four. While conceding
that the outlook for black priests appeared bad, he told DeRuyter
that he nevertheless remained "thoroughly convinced that they are
a necessity." He added, however, that he did not see any reason
why black priests should be the special province of the Josephites.
In an obvious slap at such prelates as Archbishop William Elder of
Cincinnati and Bishop Thomas S. Byrne of Nashville, who viewed
the Josephite institutions as the "Negro seminaries" and recommended "intelligent negro boys" to the Josephites but did not accept them into their own seminaries, Slattery added, "Let them become diocesan priests." Slattery also promised to send DeRuyter a
book on ethnic characteristics that he hoped would help correct
some of DeRuyter's misconceptions about blacks.[27]

The internal problems that the issue of black priests created for
the Josephites gave some clerics the impression that the society had
forsaken its policy of developing black priests. Repeated entreaties
from the recently suspended John Henry Dorsey for admission into

26. J. A. DeRuyter to John R. Slattery, September 4, 1895, in 17-H-22, Sep-
tember 21, 1895, in 17-H-25, both in Slattery Papers.
27. John R. Slattery to J. A. DeRuyter, September 20, 1895, in LPB-2-264,
Slattery Papers. For examples of black students recommended by the archbishop of
Cincinnati and the bishop of Nashville, see Archbishop William Elder to John R.
Slattery, October 27, 1893, in 5-S-1, John B. Morris, chancellor, to John R. Slat-
tery, December 11, 1895, in 11-N-8, Bishop Thomas S. Byrne to John R. Slattery,
January 3, 1896, in 11-H-36, all in Slattery Papers.

Archbishop Ireland's seminary in St. Paul led a concerned Ireland to ask Slattery, "To what degree have you abandoned the idea of preparing Negroes for the priesthood and what are the grounds for which you are abandoning it?" Slattery assured Ireland that the Josephites had made no changes in principle but needed rather to go more slowly, not only because of the blacks "but because of my confreres, who may have to live with them when ordained." He explained that Dorsey possessed a violent temper, which, he admitted, the young man was "trying to overcome." Slattery claimed that during a drunken bout, one of Dorsey's brothers (probably C. Marcellus) had drawn a pistol on a Josephite. "Of course," he concluded, "taking the Colored people as they are, this militates against Harry."[28]

Even though he doubted John Dorsey's suitability for the Josephites, Slattery nevertheless attempted to salvage the black man's hopes for the priesthood. He explored the possibility of sending Dorsey to the Mill Hill Fathers' seminary in England for future service with Bishop Henry O'Hanlon, the vicar apostolic of the upper Nile in Africa. Dorsey, a native of Baltimore who wished to work among his own people in the United States, rejected Slattery's proposal that he join a foreign missionary society such as Mill Hill. As a result, Slattery dropped the scheme; two years later, he readmitted Dorsey to St. Joseph's Seminary.[29]

Although Slattery had not abandoned his hopes for a black clergy, evidence of increased resistance to black priests in the Catholic church continued to mount. Walter Elliott and Alexander P. Doyle, the liberal Paulists who published the *Catholic World*, warned Slattery about damaging rumors concerning black priests and urged him to write some articles in defense of a black clergy. Doyle told Slattery, "There is an impression gone abroad . . . heard in more than one quarter, that even Cardinal Gibbons does not favor native negro vocations." Slattery denied that the cardinal opposed black vocations but sadly acknowledged that those rumors abounded and that there was "fresh opposition to negro priests." He reiterated his belief that "the black man has every right to be a priest" and that such men would be needed "to plant the seed, work the crop, and

28. Archbishop John Ireland to John R. Slattery, January 18, 1896, in 25-G-1, John R. Slattery to Archbishop John Ireland, January 24, 1896, copy in 25-G-2, both in Slattery Papers.

29. John R. Slattery to Bishop Henry O'Hanlon, April 4, 1896, in LPB-2-362, Slattery Papers; St. Joseph's Seminary Student Journal, September, 1900, in JFA.

garner the harvest for Christ." Admitting that neither Tolton nor Uncles had "been conspicuous successes," he implied that the former suffered from emotional instability and conceded that the latter's troubles, though "nothing serious," nonetheless had provided opponents with evidence to support the "hue and cry against black priests." Slattery found it difficult to confront these critics because, as he complained to Elliott, the opposition "is not open and above board" but rather "is heard in the parlor; it follows the back door direction; it offers no argument, save a shilly-shally sentiment." The death, on June 9, 1897, of Archbishop Janssens of New Orleans, deprived Slattery of a strong episcopal champion of black priests and underscored his vulnerability.[30]

In addition to dealing with the thorny issues and personalities connected with his efforts on behalf of black priests, Slattery also had to attend to the institutional demands of St. Joseph's Society, one of which was providing a proper place to educate his seminarians. On April 23, 1893, Cardinal Gibbons laid the cornerstone for a new St. Joseph's Seminary, a four-story building costing $80,000. The first story housed a library, a chapel, and lecture, reception, and work rooms; the other three stories contained forty-five rooms for the seminarians, each furnished modestly with a bed and bedstead, chair and table, bookshelves, washstand, and wardrobe. In their studies, the seminarians followed a traditional Catholic curriculum. They took the divinity course at St. Mary's Seminary, attending lectures in philosophy, theology, natural sciences, liturgy, canon law, and sacred scripture. Although *Colored Harvest* claimed that St. Joseph's students studied "the traits of their black brethren, to fit themselves for their life work," that study did not occur in the classroom. What contact the seminarians had with blacks came from the catechism classes that they conducted for children on Sundays or from their Wednesday afternoon visits to comfort and encourage the sick and poor, in hospitals or in slums.[31]

The formal curriculum at Epiphany College was virtually indistinguishable from the curricula of most other Catholic colleges and

30. A. P. Doyle to John R. Slattery, June 1, 1897, in 12-N-21, John R. Slattery to A. P. Doyle, June 2, 1897, in LPB-2-525, John R. Slattery to Walter Elliott, May 29, 1897, in LPB-2-517, all in Slattery Papers; Dolores Egger Labbe, *Jim Crow Comes to Church: The Establishment of Segregated Catholic Parishes in South Louisiana* (2nd ed.; Lafayette, La., 1971), 30, 58.

31. "St. Joseph's Seminary," *Colored Harvest*, I (October, 1893), 2, 4; "An Appeal to Noble Youths," 9; [Slattery], "Biographie," VII, 9–10.

minor seminaries throughout the country and contained little that explicitly pertained to blacks. In 1895, the approximately sixty students taking the five-year classics course studied Virgil and Horace, Cicero and Demosthenes, St. John Chrysostom and Lactanius, along with history, English, science, and mathematics. Their religious training included prayer, meditation, mass, and devotions such as reciting the rosary and reading the lives of the saints.[32] It was assumed that the combination of a classical education and proper spiritual formation constituted the best training for future missionaries.

Slattery faced considerable financial burdens in running the institutions and missions of St. Joseph's Society. He found it necessary to provide some monetary assistance to struggling missionaries whose poverty-stricken parishioners could not support them, though he judged that he could afford to send individual missionaries no more than $300 per year. Unlike diocesan seminaries, the Josephite institutions had no bishop on whom they could rely for special collections; they depended entirely on charity. The operating expenses of St. Joseph's Seminary and Epiphany Apostolic College exceeded $30,000 yearly. It cost $250 per year to pay for the support, education, and clothing of a seminarian and about $150 per year for a student at the college. The Josephites received $5,000 a year from the Negro and Indian Commission, though many clergy mistakenly assumed that the Josephites received the bulk of the commission's funds. Receipts from the annual collection for the Negro and Indian missions were unsure and after 1890 declined. In 1891, for example, the collection garnered over $18,000 less than in 1887, its first year. One historian observed, "The collection remained a haphazard method of mission support. The money collected was barely sufficient to maintain existing missions, and never enough to improve radically the previous mission work." The society also received important help from Edward and Louise Morrell, who contributed over $4,000 annually to the support of the seminary and the college. This sum paid the yearly interest on the seminary loan, the salaries of the sisters at St. Peter Claver (a parish closely connected with the seminary), and the salaries of the professors and the operating expenses at Epiphany College for the scholastic year. Subscriptions to *Colored Harvest*, costing twenty-five cents per year,

32. "Holy Communion," *Colored Harvest*, I (October, 1895), 38; "Epiphany Apostolic College," *Colored Harvest*, I (October, 1893), 15.

however, provided the chief means of support for the two institutions, and Slattery also succeeded in securing donations for seminary burses, interest from which supported seminarians.[33]

Financial pressures notwithstanding, increasing numbers of priests ordained from St. Joseph's Seminary allowed the Josephites to expand their mission field. During the summer of 1897, Slattery made his first visitation of the southern missions since the opening of St. Joseph's Seminary in 1888. As a result of the trip, the Josephites established new missions in the diocese of Richmond and the archdiocese of New Orleans and received invitations to open missions in five other southern dioceses.[34]

The task of beginning the first Josephite mission in the Deep South fell to a remarkable young native Louisianian, Pierre LeBeau. LeBeau arrived in Bayou Petite Prairie, a primitive, rural area located approximately 100 miles northwest of New Orleans, to minister to the 500 colored Creole Catholic families scattered among the area's plantations. Palmetto, Louisiana, a train stop located 8 miles from Petite Prairie, was the nearest town. The crude chapel in Petite Prairie, an old, converted country store, measured only forty by twenty by ten feet. A loose board in the roof that worshippers could remove provided ventilation. The mission of Petite Prairie served a 60-square-mile region interlaced with swamps and forests and teeming with alligators, lynx, raccoons, and flamingos. The flat, alluvial farm land produced crops of cotton, rice, sweet potatoes, and watermelons. LeBeau traversed his domain by buggy or horseback.

The people of Petite Prairie appeared delighted to have a resident priest and on the day of his arrival welcomed him enthusiastically in "good old Creole fashion," shouting in their patois, "Nos content vous vini [We are glad you have come]." Two old women stood at the church door with rosary beads hanging from their uplifted hands, uttering words of thanksgiving. Many of the inhabitants, however, expressed fear that he would not stay at Pe-

33. "Where Do We Stand?," *Colored Harvest*, II (March, 1898), 1–2; "Our Benefactors," *Colored Harvest*, I (October, 1895), 62; Edward J. Misch, "The American Bishops and the Negro from the Civil War to the Third Plenary Council of Baltimore, 1865–1884" (Ph.D. dissertation, Pontifical Gregorian University, 1968), 569, 583; John R. Slattery to Cardinal James Gibbons, June 20, 1903, copy in 25-D-32, Slattery Papers; "An Appeal to Noble Youths," 3.

34. "A Southern Trip," *Colored Harvest*, I (October, 1897), 225–26; "Père of the Bayous," *Catholic Action of the South* (New Orleans), May 13, 1943, clipping in Pierre LeBeau file, JFA.

tite Prairie for any length of time because they were people of color.[35]

LeBeau soon convinced his new congregation of his commitment to them. He slept in their homes until parishioners raised $300 to build him a house, a two-story structure, "boarded inside and out, and quite innocent of plaster." During one of his periodic visits, Slattery awoke one night during a thunderstorm to find that his bed "had turned into a miniature bayou." LeBeau broke the power of dishonest storekeepers who had cheated the people on their bills and, in the process, had reduced many to a state of credit slavery. He and his parishioners felled cypress logs in the swamps and constructed a new church. In 1900, long before public schools became available, LeBeau, with the help of three lay teachers and later of the Sisters of the Holy Family, established the first school in Petite Prairie, which 45 black children attended. He also succeeded in reclaiming many fallen-away black Catholics who had left the church because white Catholics in the nearby communities would not allow them to attend mass in their churches. Many of his parishioners traveled 5 miles to get to Sunday mass at Petite Prairie; some came from as far as 15 miles. Writing to Slattery, LeBeau told his mentor that his experiences in the Louisiana mission had convinced him of the need for more separate black churches and "for colored priests . . . to do the best work among the colored people."[36]

Like LeBeau, other Josephite priests faced formidable difficulties on the missions. Every month, the priests at St. Joseph's in Richmond ranged throughout the state to such places as Lynchburg, 140 miles away, for brief visits to say mass, administer the sacraments, and preach. In Jarratt, Virginia, located in southern Sussex County, the priests spoke in a dimly lit hall from a soap box on top of a barrel, which served as their rostrum. Before departing the next morning, the missionaries left Catholic pamphlets in the grocery store of the village. The school in Norfolk, staffed by Franciscan sisters, boasted 115 students (most of them non-Catholic) in three overcrowded, poorly ventilated, and dimly lit rooms. The boards and beams of the roof "were eaten by dryrot and the plaster had fallen away, admitting the wind and rain from every side." In 1898, Lambert Welbers, describing the privations at St. Joseph's Home

35. "Père of the Bayous," in LeBeau file.

36. "St. Joseph's Work Among the Negroes," *Colored Harvest*, II (October, 1899), 115–22; "Père of the Bayous," in LeBeau file; "Immaculate Conception Church, Palmetto P.O., Louisiana," *Colored Harvest*, II (October, 1898), 50.

for Orphans in Wilmington, Delaware, and at St. Joseph's Industrial School in Clayton, told the Negro and Indian Commission, "Only by practicing the most rigid economy have we been able to keep alive at all. We are obliged to refuse any application for the home, because we have not enough food for them." He lamented that St. Joseph's Industrial School "has been an industrial school in name only as we have been unable to pay for instructors; indeed, many of our boys have to go bare-footed and in rags."[37]

Despite the hardships, however, the society and its missions continued to grow, thanks to the heroic efforts of the priests in the field and to Slattery's skillful overall direction. By October, 1898, St. Joseph's Society had grown to nineteen priests. At Epiphany Apostolic College there were 65 students, and at St. Joseph's Seminary 29 seminarians. The first Josephite mission in the Deep South had been opened, as well as an orphanage and an industrial school in Delaware. Josephites ministered to over 6,500 black Catholic parishioners and, with the indispensable help of communities of women religious, such as the Franciscan sisters of Glen Riddle, Pennsylvania, maintained schools for over 1,100 students, many of whom were non-Catholics. In addition, Slattery hoped to supply priests within two years for five southern bishops from whom he had received invitations to open missions in their dioceses.[38] Meanwhile, he turned his attention to a new venture, one that employed not only a more indirect but also a "separate but equal" approach to the education of black candidates for the priesthood.

This new venture involved the establishment of a Josephite college to train black catechists, an old idea that had first surfaced at the Third Plenary Council in 1884. Catechists, as lay people who gave instruction in Catholic doctrine, especially in mission lands or among the unbaptized, fit well with Slattery's two-fold objective. He would develop catechists in order to relieve manpower shortages on the missions and, in addition, to prepare selected black men for the priesthood, albeit in a segregated setting. He believed the two goals to be further related because the work of the catechists would strengthen the faith of blacks and thereby produce more priestly vocations.

37. "A Few Words from the Richmond Mission," *Colored Harvest,* I (March, 1896), 88; "Five-fold Mission of Richmond, Virginia," *St. Joseph's Advocate,* II (January, 1891), 295–96; *Mission Work Among the Negroes and Indians* (Baltimore, 1898), 23.

38. "Sisters of St. Francis, Glen Riddle, Pa.," *Colored Harvest,* II (October, 1898), 55, 58–59; "Where Do We Stand?," 1.

Slattery's experience with catechists stretched back to his first assignment in Baltimore, when he used a band of eight women he called "guardian angels" to catechize prospective converts and to look after people whenever he had to leave Baltimore to visit the missions. Later, after his assignment to Richmond, he employed Wales Tyrrell as a paid catechist. In 1894, the resolves adopted by the Josephite general chapter urged Josephite priests on the missions to employ black students and seminarians, who had been forced to take a leave from Epiphany College or St. Joseph's Seminary, as teachers and catechists.[39]

During 1897 and early 1898, Slattery received inquiries from five different Josephites about the possibility of using black catechists on the missions. In April of 1898, he solicited the views of his men on this topic and then broached the idea to his friend Archbishop Ireland, calling it "a growth in our work among the Negroes." Slattery hoped that Cardinal Gibbons would more readily accept his concept for using black catechists if he could cite the support of the archbishop of St. Paul, whose opinions carried considerable weight with the cardinal. He also gathered information about catechists from missionaries who had extensive experience with them, such as Albert Lightheart, the Mill Hill provincial in New Zealand. Lightheart praised the contributions of catechists in his country but cautioned Slattery that though he "felt the great necessity of ordaining Colored clergy, it is nevertheless wise to be prudent and to give the young aspirants a fair trial that they may be thoroughly grounded in the virtue of humility."[40]

In early 1899, after convincing Cardinals Gibbons and Vaughan to support his project, Slattery traveled to Rome for a meeting with officials of the Propaganda. En route, he consulted with the superiors of several missionary societies, including the Society of Foreign Missions, the Society of African Missions, and the Society of Missionaries of Africa, or White Fathers, whose legendary founder, Cardinal Charles M. A. Lavigérie, archbishop of Algiers and primate of Africa, had effectively employed catechists and had long inspired Slattery. These consultations reinforced his conviction that he had chosen the right plan. He then met with Cardinal

39. John R. Slattery to Walter Elliott," November 16, 1893, in LPB-1-276, Slattery Papers; minutes of the general chapters, July 3, 1894, in JFA.

40. John R. Slattery to Archbishop John Ireland, May 10, 1898, copy in 25-G-4, Thomas Plunkett to John R. Slattery, May 1, 1898, in 19-K-18, Albert Lightheart to John R. Slattery, October 10, 1898, in 12-G-9, all in Slattery Papers.

Miescylaw H. Ledóchowski and Archbishop Agostino Ciasca, prefect and secretary, respectively, of the Propaganda, who recommended that Slattery embody his plan in a memorial.

In that document, Slattery pointed to the growth of St. Joseph's Society, which at the time had twenty-one priests laboring in seven states and thirty-one seminarians, including three blacks, at St. Joseph's Seminary. Slattery explained that the growth of the missions produced a need for helpers who would live in the various missions and take the place of the missionaries, as far as possible, when they had to travel. The common experience of the missionaries of St. Joseph's Society, he argued, showed that blacks themselves, serving as priests and catechists, were indispensable to the conversion of their race. Black catechists, he insisted, would sustain the faith of black Catholics scattered throughout the South. Most important, they would meet and offset the influence of the black Protestant preachers, elders, class-leaders, and exhorters. Slattery believed that officially appointed Catholic catechists would, in the eyes of many blacks, assume an importance equal to that enjoyed by black ministers.

In addition to providing black catechists, however, Slattery also envisaged the new institution as a setting in which to nurture priestly vocations in a "separate but equal" environment. Explaining his thinking in an article that appeared in *Catholic World*, he noted that "colored boys, very few in number, are at once introduced among a disproportionate number of whites" at Epiphany College and St. Joseph's Seminary. Although acknowledging that "some of them rise to the occasion and equal and even outrank whites," as with the black student at St. Mary's who had carried off prizes for two successive years in philosophy, Slattery clearly implied that most blacks could not succeed in such circumstances. The new college would afford the means of training the bulk of black youths apart from the white. "In this matter," Slattery said, "we have before us the example of the Protestant sects, which . . . have . . . almost all of their negro students in separate institutes."

Slattery's tentative plan for the college for black catechists anticipated an eventual enrollment of one hundred students. Black candidates for the college would live for a while under the watchful eye and in the care of Josephite missionaries, who would send selected ones to the school. The course of studies at the college would include English, mathematics, Christian doctrine, and Latin for three years, philosophy during the third year, followed by a three-year course of theology and sacred scripture, using as texts the cate-chism of the Council of Trent, originally prepared as a manual for parish priests, and the Douay-Rheims Bible, the translation most widely used by Catholics in English-speaking countries. The pro-posed curriculum also required two hours of manual labor daily and made students responsible for all necessary work about the house and property. In addition, the college would acquire a few hundred acres of land from which it could support the students. Slattery em-phasized the need for plain, simple buildings so as not to create in the students tastes ill-suited to the plantation and share-cropper en-vironment in which they would ultimately work. Upon graduation from the college, those qualified would be commissioned as cate-chists in an appropriate ceremony and then sent to the missions to work as salaried teachers. Those who married would remain cate-chists, whereas those who stayed single and, according to Slattery, "persevered" would advance step by step to the priesthood. He did not make it clear whether black candidates would receive all of their seminary education at the college or whether they would also attend St. Joseph's Seminary in Baltimore.[41] Slattery, nevertheless, intended to institutionalize at the college for catechists the two-year mandatory suspension policy for black priestly candidates that he had earlier imposed at Epiphany Apostolic College and St. Joseph's Seminary.

Once the Propaganda approved his memorial, Slattery moved swiftly to execute it. On June 29, 1899, the seventh general chap-ter of St. Joseph's Society authorized Slattery to proceed with the foundation of St. Joseph's College for Negro Catechists (later known as St. Joseph's Catechetical College). Bishop Edward P. Allen of Mobile agreed to allow the establishment of the college within his diocese. Estimating that he would need $10,000 for the initial costs, and $3,000 to $4,000 yearly for its maintenance, Slattery ap-pealed to Edward Dyer of the Negro and Indian Commission for fi-nancial assistance for the new institution. At first, Dyer expressed optimism about a substantial donation, but in October of 1899 he informed Slattery that the commission could not increase its dona-tion to the Josephites and added, "This is rather a work for some well-to-do Catholics." Through appeals in honor of St. Anthony,

41. John R. Slattery, "Lavigerie, the New St. Paul," *Catholic World*, LVI (Feb-ruary, 1893), 593–608; "What the Bishops Say," *Colored Harvest*, I (October, 1893), 5; J. R. Slattery, "A Catholic College for Negro Catechists," *Catholic World*, LXX (October, 1899), 1–12.

Slattery managed, in early 1900, to raise enough money to purchase the Browder place, a two-story, wooden-frame house situated on 210 acres approximately six miles from Montgomery, Alabama.[42]

As plans went forth for the new college during what Slattery called "the hardest and busiest" year of his life, two black graduates of Epiphany College, Wallace O'Hare and John Green, aspiring seminarians beginning their two years of enforced leave on the Virginia missions, provided Slattery with a graphic example of effective catechetical work. The two men traveled to Jarratt, located sixty miles south of Richmond in the heart of the "Black Belt," to open a Catholic school. The township was populated by five hundred blacks, all Protestants, and not more than thirty whites. Many of the black people in the area practiced a trade or owned their own farms. Reports that the two men would open a Catholic school upset the town's black ministers, who convoked a series of protest meetings in their churches. Included among the charges hurled during those assemblies was a warning that the Catholic church wished to reintroduce slavery. O'Hare and Green confronted the ministers' challenge directly, attending two of the protest meetings and effectively refuting the preachers' charges. Thereafter, they recruited sixty students, ranging in age from six to twenty-eight, for the school. Ten of the students came a distance of eight miles and had to board in the neighborhood. The others had to drive to school in mule carts and wagons. O'Hare and Green also conducted a school two nights a week, which was attended by twenty adults, all of them Protestant. Through their work, the two catechists soon won the confidence of many of the people of the town. One old lady remarked that she "never thought any good would come from the school or church, but now they have sent us just what we wanted."[43]

Every Sunday, the catechists held services in the chapel that adjoined the schoolhouse. They opened with a hymn, moved to a prayer, read the epistle and gospel of the day, gave a set of instructions from Goffine's catechetical text, and closed the service with a

42. Minutes of the general chapters, June 29, 1899, in JFA; John R. Slattery to Cardinal James Gibbons, September 1, 1899, copy in 13-H-6, Edward R. Dyer to John R. Slattery, July 25, 1899, in 12-R-8, Edward R. Dyer to John R. Slattery, October 16, 1899, in 12-R-9, John R. Slattery to Louis B. Pastorelli, January 8, 1900, copy in 19-G-11, Louis B. Pastorelli to John R. Slattery, March 18, 1900, in 19-G-22, all in Slattery Papers.

43. "Work of Catechists," *Colored Harvest*, II (October, 1900), 197–99; Wallace O'Hare to John R. Slattery, September 13, 1899, in 17-S-12, Slattery Papers.

hymn. Attendance averaged between fifty and seventy. Sunday school followed in the schoolhouse, with thirty in attendance, all preparing for baptism. At 2 P.M., O'Hare and Green closed the day's religious services by leading the stations of the cross devotion. Slattery publicized their work in the pages of *Colored Harvest* to illustrate the potential of catechists and to encourage contributions for St. Joseph's Catechetical College.[44]

His requests for donations, however, brought Slattery criticism from two very different sources, revealing the tightrope he walked on the issue of black priests. E. W. J. Lindesmith of Doylestown, Ohio, a priest for forty-five years, sent $100 for the new college but complained that Slattery had too few black seminarians. "There must be something wrong somewhere," Lindesmith observed. "I had intended to send . . . boys to you. But I always felt they were not wanted." He assured Slattery that "if the Negroes were the big majority, I would send you $1,000" and added that "the worst national prejudices are found among Bishops, Priests, seminarians, and Nuns." Expressing a much more generally held, if opposite, opinion, Nannie B. Younger of Lynchburg, Virginia, urged Slattery "to keep the negro out of the priesthood." Claiming that northerners did not know blacks as well as southerners did, Younger warned, "We have scandals now but it would be infinitely worse with negro priests. Protestants have a great respect for the priesthood now, but put the negro in it, and they will very naturally conclude it is not much."[45]

In his reply to Younger, Slattery rehearsed the historical precedents of the church's use of native clergy and then reminded her, "Priesthood never goes to a race. It is a gift to the individual." Younger's worries about scandal elicited a straightforward and logical reply from Slattery, one that masked some of his own doubts. He claimed that he knew of many good "Negro boys," and cited the "hundreds of Negro priests in Africa," as well as Bishop James Augustine Healy of Portland and Blessed Martin de Porres, as examples of holy black men. He did not, however, mention his own Father Uncles. While acknowledging the danger and difficulty of scandal, Slattery pointed out that the church had had to fight con-

44. "Work of Catechists," 197–99.
45. E. W. J. Lindesmith to John R. Slattery, April 27, 1900, in 14-H-23, Nannie B. Younger to John R. Slattery, September 22, 1900, in 16-R-10, both in Slattery Papers.

cubinage in Europe for over a thousand years during the Middle Ages "yet had never stopped ordaining Europeans."[46]

Four months earlier, in May, 1900, Slattery had defended the cause of black priests from a podium in the heart of the South. Slattery had accepted an invitation from the Reverend Edgar Murphy of Montgomery, one of the leaders of the Southern Society for the Promotion of the Study of Race Conditions in the South, to speak at a session of the Southwide conference on black-white relations held in that city. Slattery agreed to speak on the subject "Should We Advise the Raising of the Standard of Ordination of Negro Clergy?" He viewed the topic "as quite in line" with the college he proposed to open in Montgomery and saw the conference as an opportunity to explain its mission. He promised Murphy that he "would avoid controversy and speak to the point."[47]

Virtually every paper presented during the three-day conference assumed black inferiority; this attitude was particularly evident in the address by Paul Barringer of the University of Virginia—an address that Booker T. Washington considered "the most discouraging" he had ever heard. Thus, Slattery's speech, which affirmed the capabilities of blacks for ministry, called for a recognition of their manliness, and proclaimed their moral equality with whites, did not inspire a warm reception from the predominantly white audience. He reminded his listeners that "the 'Our Father' ascends from the lips of black men to the same God to whom that universal prayer goes from those of white." While admitting the existence of some "bad Negro leaders," Slattery argued that these did not justify denying blacks the right of priesthood. He contended that "those who fall away from the high standards of the Christian priesthood do not hurt those standards or their race; rather, they drop out of sight." Slattery then informed the conference that he had six or seven black students studying in Baltimore either at St. Joseph's Seminary or at Epiphany College and explained the purposes of the new college for black catechists, emphasizing its potentially uplifting influence on the morals of black youth.[48]

46. John R. Slattery to Nannie B. Younger, September 27, 1900, in 16-R-11, Slattery Papers.

47. John R. Slattery to E. G. Murphy, March 30, 1900, copy in 14-T-25, Slattery Papers.

48. Smith, *In His Image,* 286; New Bedford, Massachusetts, *Evening Standard,* May 26, 1900, clipping in Slattery Papers; John R. Slattery, "Should We Advise the Raising of the Standard of Ordination of Negro Clergy?," in *Race Problems of*

Black leaders appreciated Slattery's speech. Washington thanked him for his "brave, wise, and statesmanlike address" and characterized it as "the finest thing that was delivered on the platform." He offered to help the new college in any way that he could. T. Thomas Fortune, the publisher of the Afro-American newspaper New York *Age*, also thanked Slattery, not only for his speech at Montgomery but also for the positions he had "always taken on the race question, in word and act." J. E. Wallace, another black man who had observed the conference, congratulated Slattery for possessing "the manhood to stand up before that vast audience and to plead eloquently for the Negro."[49]

Even as Slattery publicly rebutted objections to black priests on the score of morality, he had to deal with potentially damaging scandals involving Father Uncles. In January, 1900, Sister Mary Claire, a white Franciscan sister working at Epiphany College as a domestic, accused Uncles of allowing "himself freedom" with her "entirely contrary to his and my vocation" when they were alone. The mother superior of the Franciscans promptly removed Sister Mary Claire from the college; later that year, the young woman left the order. Whether Uncles indeed made romantic advances to the sister remains unclear. Nevertheless, Slattery went to considerable lengths to keep the embarrassing incident quiet. The scandal that he had dreaded had been narrowly averted.[50]

Further trouble involving Uncles ensued in the summer of 1901 when a warrant for his arrest was issued in Baltimore. Uncles fled the city for St. Joseph's Industrial School, where he stayed until the following summer, when Slattery succeeded in getting the warrant withdrawn. The circumstances surrounding the issuance of the warrant remain a mystery, and since the warrant was quashed, no record of it survives. Thereafter, Uncles spent his life teaching classics at Epiphany College. A very popular teacher whom the students nicknamed "Daddy," he settled into the relative obscurity of

the South: Report of the First Annual Conference Held Under the Auspices of the Southern Society for the Promotion of the Study of Race Conditions and Problems in the South (New York, 1900), 131–41.

49. Booker T. Washington to John R. Slattery, May 14, 1900, in 16-K-5, T. Thomas Fortune to John R. Slattery, May 18, 1900, in B-6-35, J. E. Wallace to John R. Slattery, May 23, 1900, in 16-P-12, all in Slattery Papers.

50. Sr. M. Claire to John R. Slattery, January 1, 1900, Sr. Mary Adele Francis Gorman to Peter E. Hogan, August 24, 1981, both in Special File, JFA; Lambert Welbers to John R. Slattery, November 10, 1900, in 21-B-24, Slattery Papers.

the classroom, emerging only occasionally for public appearances to celebrate mass for black Catholic organizations. As a respected and popular teacher, however, Uncles performed valuable work, influencing generations of young Josephites and dispelling, at least to some extent, preconceived notions about the intellectual inferiority of blacks.[51]

Over time, Uncles' bitterness concerning the treatment of blacks in the society apparently grew. In his later years, he refused to celebrate St. Patrick's Day because other ethnic groups did not receive similar recognition. He also developed the habit of flinging open the windows when he walked into a room of white priests. Although he possessed a well-known passion for fresh air, many of his fellow Josephites suspected that Uncles also meant to communicate a need to "clean out the white smell in the room." He died in July, 1933, protesting that he did not belong to St. Joseph's Society.[52]

From its earliest days, confusion and disagreement over its purpose dogged St. Joseph's College for Negro Catechists. Although not always clear and consistent in his thinking about it, Slattery conceived of the college both as a training center for catechists and as an incubator for priestly vocations. In its latter role, he apparently hoped to develop it into an all-black minor and major seminary that would be less academically rigorous than Epiphany College and St. Joseph's Seminary. The rectors of St. Joseph's College, however, regarded it more as a Catholic Tuskegee, a much narrower view that did not include the education of future priests. Personality conflicts between Slattery and Thomas B. Donovan, the first rector, added to the difficulties. As a result, St. Joseph's College for Negro Catechists produced no black Josephites and fell far short of Slattery's original goals.

Initially, Slattery intended to appoint P. J. McCaffrey to head the new college in Montgomery, but McCaffrey's illness forced a change in plans. In his place, Slattery chose Donovan, a strong, practical man from St. Joseph's Industrial School, to serve as rector of the college. Slattery expected Donovan to handle the financial

51. John R. Slattery to Louis B. Pastorelli, June 19, 1902, copy in 19-H-29, June 21, 1902, copy in 19-H-31, John R. Slattery to Charles Uncles, June 21, 1902, copy in 20-R-17, Charles Uncles to John R. Slattery, June 24, 1902, in 23-W-1, all in Slattery Papers; Foley, God's Men, 47–51.

52. Warren interviews, 52; Charles Carroll to Joseph Hanley, July 24, 1933, in 53-C, JFA.

and agricultural aspects of the operation and McCaffrey, a deeply religious man, to "put the proper spirit among the boys." Since they could not take possession of the property until November 1, 1900, and since the property needed extensive repairs, Slattery advised Donovan to restrict the number of students to twelve during the first year. Slattery emphasized the importance of the enterprise to Donovan, saying, "Its success means a great advancement for the Negro by incorporating them in the work of evangelization. Its failure will throw us back twenty or thirty years." [53]

Almost as soon as Donovan arrived at the Browder place in late October of 1899, however, he and Slattery began to quarrel. Donovan found a dilapidated house, missing sashes and windows in some places, which had been vacant since October 1. He had to cook in the fireplace because the house had no stove and had to spend his "little means" buying furnishings. Donovan and McCaffrey had to rely on their legs to get into town, for they possessed neither horse nor buggy. Into this situation, Slattery encouraged the Reverend Joseph W. Kellogg to send a student. His arrival on November 2 occasioned a furious telegram from Donovan to Slattery that screamed, "Outrage to send boy. Do not repeat." In a subsequent letter, Donovan admonished Slattery, "So use a little judgement and common sense . . . we expect more consideration from one of your age and experience." [54]

Serious disagreement between the two men also surfaced over the proposed assignment of John Green and Louis Bouldin, two Epiphany Apostolic College graduates, to the catechetical college. Slattery wanted Green, who had worked so successfully as a catechist in Jarratt, both "to teach and study logic." Donovan informed Slattery that he preferred "no northern fry or city fry as subjects"; rather, he favored "bright colored lads" who would live contentedly in the country and "would be apt to do our bidding." He protested against Green teaching any classes, arguing that priests should run all the educational features of the school. Donovan's real objection, however, stemmed from his distrust of "the spirit of the EAC

53. John R. Slattery to Bishop Edward P. Allen, September 25, 1900, in Bishop Edward P. Allen Papers, AAM; John R. Slattery to P. J. McCaffrey, June 19, 1900, copy in 18-Y-19, John R. Slattery to Thomas Donovan, September 12, 1900, in 17-Y-1, all in Slattery Papers.

54. Thomas Donovan to John R. Slattery, October 29, 1900, in 17-Y-9, November 2, 1900, in 18-B-5, November 2, 1900 (telegram), in 18-B-4, November 2, 1900, in 18-B-5, all in Slattery Papers.

Negro." Green and Bouldin, according to him, were too urban and too puffed up by their education at Epiphany College "to help foster the spirit we would like the institution to have." He feared that they would object to performing household chores like bed making, house cleaning, and dish washing. In short, they would lack docility, a quality he wanted and one that he believed did not prevail at the college in Baltimore. Donovan urged a fresh start at Montgomery "with entirely new material." [55]

Donovan's letter angered Slattery and clearly illustrated the very different conceptions of the college that the two men held. Slattery upbraided Donovan because his letterhead read, "St. Joseph's College for Colored Youth," implying a Catholic Tuskegee-like institution, rather than "St. Joseph's College for Negro Catechists." Slattery pointed out that the college had a specific catechetical purpose, approved by the Propaganda. He accused Donovan of attempting to alter the nature and purpose of the institution and forbade "any publication or circular to go forth from [him] with the heading, 'St. Joseph's College for Colored Youth.'" Several weeks later, Slattery took issue with Donovan for his reluctance to accept Green and indicated that Donovan's refusal to do so would cause the superior the "very deepest pain." He suggested that McCaffrey instruct Green for two hours each day in the catechism of the Council of Trent, and in that way, Green would cover moral and dogmatic theology. After that, said Slattery, "we shall have him ordained." Slattery went on to explain, "Had he been white, I would have put him through at St. Joseph's Seminary, but because he is colored and would have been unable to reach the minimum mark, we must try to help him along at Montgomery." He indicated that Green should receive room and board and should spend his free time as a teacher or prefect of the boys. [56]

Slattery correctly perceived Donovan's lack of enthusiasm for using St. Joseph's Catechetical College to foster black vocations to the priesthood, though Donovan denied that he had intended to change or alter the purpose of the institution. In replying to Slattery, Donovan bitterly observed, "At times I don't know what

55. John R. Slattery to Thomas Donovan, September 2, 1900, copy in 17-Y-1, Thomas Donovan to John R. Slattery, November 21, 1900, in 18-B-7, both in Slattery Papers.
56. John R. Slattery to Thomas Donovan, November 24, 1900, in 18-B-8, December 10, 1900, in 18-B-21, December 17, 1900, in 18-B-24, copies of all in Slattery Papers.

shape your brain gets in anyway." Donovan's earlier letter, however, had emphasized the possibilities of expanding the college to include Protestant as well as Catholic youth, a clear departure from the original concept and one inimical to priestly training according to the standards of the day. Whereas Slattery's letters and reports always mentioned his intention to advance worthy catechists by degree to the priesthood, Donovan's remained strikingly silent on the topic.[57]

Actually, Donovan had already concluded, as indicated by his actions toward Green, that black men in the United States lacked the qualities necessary for priesthood. In the spring of 1901, he sent Green away from St. Joseph's Catechetical College and then used his absence as a pretext for denying him readmittance for the autumn term. When Green protested that Donovan had not dealt fairly with him, the rector cited Green's protests as evidence of arrogance and pride. The rules of St. Joseph's Society, which prohibited Green's entrance into any Josephite institution if he had been dismissed from another belonging to the society, tied Slattery's hands. A defensive Donovan told a skeptical Slattery that "it does not seem probable that . . . all . . . our men could be wrong and you alone right about Mr. Green." Further, he accused Green of laziness and warned that "a number of those applying have the notion of priesthood in their heads," which would, he thought, portend trouble for the school. He also suggested dropping Latin, a prerequisite for any seminary training, from the curriculum for at least two years, a suggestion Slattery quickly vetoed.[58]

Donovan believed that any black priests in the near future should come from "South America," by which he meant the Caribbean. Some West Indian and what he called "South American" blacks had impressed Donovan while he was a student at both Fordham University and St. Joseph's Seminary. He suggested that Slattery secure "a few Cuban Negroes" through the archbishop of Havana to enter the seminary in Baltimore and prepare for work in the South, especially in the diocese of St. Augustine, where many "Cuban

57. Thomas Donovan to John R. Slattery, November 28, 1900, in 18-B-14, Thomas Donovan circular letter, January 1, 1901, in 18-C-1, both in Slattery Papers; *Mission Work Among the Negroes and Indians* (Baltimore, 1901), 13.

58. Joseph Green to Thomas Donovan, May 16, 1901, in 18-C-25, Thomas Donovan to John R. Slattery, May 23, 1901, in 18-C-23, Joseph Green to Thomas Donovan, June 11, 1901, in 18-C-37, Thomas Donovan to John R. Slattery, June 14, 1901, in 18-C-35, all in Slattery Papers.

people of Negro blood" lived. Donovan argued that, unlike American blacks, the South American of "Negro blood has backbone, ambition, and all that go to make good groundwork." Possibly displaying some of his own ambivalence about American black men and perhaps seeking to mollify Donovan, Slattery responded, "With all you wrote about the 'SA' Negroes, I heartily agree." He told the rector that he planned to visit Havana, in U.S.-administered Cuba, in the winter of 1901 to discuss the matter with Archbishop Donato Sbaretti.[59]

Donovan, meanwhile, busied himself with raising money, refurbishing the physical plant of the college, and supervising the farm. By the end of 1901, he had solicited $16,284 through a letter campaign and had deposited $3,500 in the bank. By the spring of 1902, Donovan, with the aid of hired craftsmen, had overhauled the old mansion (reflooring, reroofing, and repainting it) and had constructed a one-story chapel, a refectory, and a two-story combination dormitory and classroom building, all of which were wooden frame and none of which had indoor plumbing; he had also added a barn. In his annual report for 1902, Donovan could indicate an enrollment of thirty-five students, a significant increase over the twelve who had attended during the previous year.[60]

As formal and informal racial segregation intensified throughout the country, Slattery backed away from the concept of integrated seminary education in favor of a seminary exclusively for blacks. Although he had not worked out all the details, by 1902 Slattery had come to view St. Joseph's College for Negro Catechists as his future black seminary. In Maryland, where the college and seminary were located, racist sentiment increased during the first years of the twentieth century. In 1902, the Maryland legislature considered two bills requiring racial segregation on steamships and railroads. Although they failed to pass, the Democratic victory in the 1903 statewide election gave the segregationists their opportunity,

59. Thomas Donovan to John R. Slattery, June 27, 1901, in 18-C-41, John R. Slattery to Thomas Donovan, July 1, 1901, copy in 18-D-1, both in Slattery Papers.

60. Thomas Donovan to John R. Slattery, December 26, 1901, in 18-D-30, February 18, 1902, in 18-E-7, 1902 Annual Report for St. Joseph's College for Negro Catechists, in 2-H-17, all in Slattery Papers; Warren interviews, 53; *Mission Work Among the Negroes and Indians* (Baltimore, 1901), 13; Donovan to Slattery, December 26, 1901, in 18-D-30, February 18, 1902, in 18-E-7, April 14, 1902, in 18-E-16, October 14, 1901, in 18-D-5, 1902 Annual Report for St. Joseph's College for Negro Catechists, in 2-H-17, all in Slattery Papers.

and the ensuing session of the state legislature placed more dis-
criminatory legislation on the books than any previous or subsequent legislature.[61]

Thomas Hennessy, a diocesan priest and the pastor of Annuncia-
tion Parish in Houston, who believed that black priests represented
the best hope for success on the missions, struck a responsive chord
in Slattery, therefore, when he suggested that "white and black students cannot abide under the same roof" and proposed Montgomery as the "seminary for blacks only." Slattery replied, "You hit
the nail on the head in stating that Montgomery should be the
Black Seminary. That is just my idea." He explained that if catechists remained single after graduation and a stint on the missions,
he intended to "have them priested." He also hoped that in the
future, catechists in the college could receive minor orders—the
first four orders, following tonsure, through which all aspirants to
the priesthood had to pass—thus acquiring "a qualified clerical
status . . . giving them a higher degree of respect among blacks."
Despite Slattery's hopes, however, St. Joseph's College for Negro
Catechists never became the black seminary. It reached its peak enrollment in 1914, when it claimed sixty-six students, but developed
into something of a junior high school before its demise in 1922.[62]
Long before that time, though, John R. Slattery had given up the
fight. In 1902 the explosive issues of black priests and modernism
fused in him, precipitating a crisis that resulted in his eventual
resignation from the Josephites and repudiation of the Catholic
church.

The roots of Slattery's crisis of faith trace back to 1885, when he
was stationed in Richmond. During the first half of that year, he
carried on a spirited correspondence about theories of evolution with
a well-read female benefactress, identified as Madame Pvormann.
Pvormann attacked the church and cited contemporary scientists
and philosophers, such as Charles Darwin, Thomas H. Huxley, and
John Tyndall, to buttress her arguments. When Slattery persisted
in arguing that "theistic evolution" and belief in divine creation
were compatible, a liberal position in Catholic circles, Pvormann
broke off the correspondence with the patronizing observation that

61. Margaret Law Calcott, *The Negro in Maryland Politics, 1870–1912* (Baltimore, 1969), 133–34.

62. Thomas Hennessy to John R. Slattery, March 23, 1903, in 23-T-5, John
R. Slattery to Thomas Hennessy, March 27, 1903, copy in 23-T-51, both in Slattery Papers; Warren interviews, 58.

Slattery, as a Catholic priest, could not think freely. The short period of correspondence with Pvormann, however, proved unsettling for Slattery. It raised many questions about the church in his mind and plunged him into an anguishing crisis of faith, which was exacerbated by the absence of his close friend Denis O'Connell and by his resentment at being exiled to Richmond. True to form, Slattery attempted to resolve his doubts by immersing himself in study. He possessed an optimistic faith in science, or what he called "the conclusions of the higher criticism"—a faith characteristic of the late nineteenth century. Science for Slattery meant an inductive, as opposed to a deductive, approach to the study of the natural world, history, dogma, theology, and scripture. His crisis eased within the year, but his curiosity remained unquenched. Although science appeared to contradict his faith on many points, for the next fifteen years Slattery clung to the belief that they could be harmonized, hence, his passionate attachment to the Americanist camp, which, for him, held out hope for the reconciliation of the church with the modern world.[63]

After engineering the erection of St. Joseph's Seminary and Epiphany Apostolic College and becoming the superior general of the American Josephites, Slattery moved into the first ranks of the Baltimore clergy. From 1890 until 1902, he assisted Gibbons as the deacon of honor at all ordinations, and he occupied a distinguished place at celebrations of the archdiocese or St. Mary's Seminary. Nearly every year Gibbons invited Slattery to spend several days with him during his holiday, and almost every week he asked Slattery to join him on one of his daily walks. Slattery ghostwrote the chapter on congregational singing that appeared in Gibbons' book *The Ambassador of Christ*. At the suggestion of John Ireland, Slattery edited a collection of Archbishop Satolli's speeches, published under the title *Loyalty to Church and State*, which appeared to place Satolli squarely in the liberal camp. Only later did Slattery and his Americanist confreres realize how badly they had erred in their initial estimations of Satolli, as the delegate increasingly sided with the conservatives. For the moment, though, a delighted Slattery found the speeches liberal and American; they ratified his idea that the church should adapt itself to scientific and social conditions of the new generation.[64]

63. [Slattery], "Biographie," VI, 13–19.
64. *Ibid.*, XII, 1–2, 7–14.

The last five years of the nineteenth century were pivotal for Slattery. He accompanied Gibbons on a trip to Rome beginning on May 18, 1895. In Pisa, they met O'Connell, who briefed them on curial developments. Rome scandalized Slattery. He came away convinced that ecclesiastical authorities at the Vatican were simply ambitious, power-hungry politicians who were determined to exert their control over the American church. He judged the Curia indifferent to the conversion of Americans and even more apathetic about the conversion of blacks. While traveling in Europe after his departure from Rome, Slattery heard the news that the conservatives had succeeded in having O'Connell removed as rector of the North American College; the following year, Keane lost his job as rector of Catholic University. In July, Slattery confided to a Sulpician retreat director in Issy that his study of church history and reading of scholarly journals, both Catholic and Protestant, had greatly modified his ideas about the origins of the church. He had begun to view doctrine, church structure, and worship as historically developed rather than divinely originated. He found himself drawn increasingly into the orbit of such modernists as Alfred Loisy, who sought to reexamine traditional Catholic teachings— the nature of revelation, biblical inspiration, and Church authority, for example—in light of the modern disciplines of philosophy, history, and biblical criticism. Although a diverse group, modernists shared a commitment to historical and critical methods, an aversion to Scholasticism and Thomism, an abhorrence of ecclesiastical authoritarianism, and something of a positivistic approach to reality.[65]

Back in the United States, Slattery also had to contend with the daily scandal of the church's treatment of blacks. Despite his personal high standing among the clergy in Baltimore, he felt increasingly isolated and powerless in the face of racism in the church. "A thousand incidents," particularly clerical opposition to black priests, assaulted his spirit, tempting him to regard the church not as a society of divine origin but as "a human institution . . . the product of a particular evolution of the white race." The scandal of

65. Ibid., XIII, 1–18; Jay P. Dolan, The American Catholic Experience: A History from Colonial Times to the Present (Garden City, N.Y., 1985), 317; William L. Portier, "Modernism in the United States: The Case of John R. Slattery," in Ronald Burke, Gary Lease, and George Gilmore (eds.), Varieties of Modernism (Mobile, Ala., 1986), 77–97; Thomas Bokenkotter, A Concise History of the Catholic Church (Rev. ed.; New York, 1979), Chap. 29.

racial prejudice and discrimination in the church, combined with his critical study of philosophy, church history, and theology, eroded his faith. Still, Slattery clung to the hope that the eventual triumph of liberal ideas in the church would transform the institution and redound to his own work among blacks. The condemnation of Americanism in 1899 by Leo XIII in *Testem Benevolentiae* crushed that hope.[66]

For Slattery, the early years of the new century constituted a "long goodbye" to the Josephites and the church. After reading *Testem,* which he called "the condemnation of all my ideas and of all my experiences," he resolved to go to Rome to learn firsthand what was happening. He used the presentation of his memorandum to the Propaganda for the foundation of St. Joseph's Catechetical College as a pretext for meeting Ireland, Keane, and O'Connell on March 26, 1899, in the Eternal City, where they spent a Saturday morning discussing the fate of Americanism. On April 23, Slattery met Ireland and O'Connell in Geneva, and after dinner, the three had a long informal discussion and walk. Slattery later claimed that all three voiced skepticism about fundamental points of religion. At the end of the evening, Ireland reportedly asked, "What is left to us?" and Slattery replied, "Extreme Unction [the sacrament of the dying]."

After his return from Europe, Slattery recommenced his work among blacks but distanced himself from the ecclesiastical world. The condemnation of Americanism had wounded his friends Ireland, Keane, Maignen, and O'Connell. In their private conversations, they bitterly criticized the Curia and the pope, yet when they mounted the pulpit, they exalted the papacy. Slattery regarded their behavior as dishonest, self-seeking, and ultimately political. He resolved to throw himself into his work on behalf of blacks and to take his vacations in Europe, to which continent he returned in the summers of 1900 and 1901. He devoted much of his spare time in those two years to studying the work of John Cardinal Newman, whom many Catholic liberals regarded as a great apologist and theologian. He found Newman's developmentalist approach to doctrine unconvincing, however, and later described the year 1901 as "the most unhappy of my life."

In 1902, Slattery decided that the only honest recourse left to him was to leave active ministry, if not the church. That decision

66. [Slattery], "Biographie," XI, 23, 25–27, XVI, 1. The translations are mine.

arrived at, he first sought to resign as superior of the seminary. He had already turned over to another priest his authority to decide on the fitness of candidates for holy orders two years earlier. Slattery resolved to use the occasion of the ordination and first mass of John Henry Dorsey, the Josephites' second black priest, who had returned to the seminary in September, 1898, after having taught on the missions, to create a scene that would force Cardinal Gibbons to accept his resignation. He chose as his point of attack the church's woeful treatment of blacks and, more particularly, its resistance to ordaining black priests.[67]

Paradoxically, the year 1902 seemed to hold great promise for Slattery and the Josephites and gave no hint of impending disaster. It marked Slattery's twenty-fifth anniversary as a priest and witnessed the continued growth of St. Joseph's Society, including the ordination of a second black Josephite. The Reverend Charles Hannigan in Richmond urged Slattery to assign Dorsey to Keswick or Columbia, Virginia, following his ordination in order to show "the rabid opponents of your negroid policy" what a bright black priest could do to win black converts for the church. Hannigan told Slattery, "I hear so much . . . as to the inopportuneness of ordaining colored men to the priesthood. You have it in your power to shove a fact in the face of their theories!" On Dorsey's ordination day, June 21, Slattery assigned him to St. Joseph's College for Negro Catechists, in hopes that his presence would inspire priestly vocations in the students and in the others to whom he would minister.[68]

On June 22, 1902, showing little consideration for the trouble it might cause the newly ordained black priest sitting in the sanctuary, Slattery delivered at Dorsey's first mass a scathing sermon he later termed his "farewell to the Church." Fully expecting an explosive response, Slattery gave vent to the frustration and disillusionment of twenty-five years spent as a "Nigger priest." In the sermon, he claimed that the early church had never drawn any ethnic lines in the priesthood and pointed to Origen, Tertullian, Cyprian, and Augustine, all Africans, as proof. He repeated his oft-stated conviction that the church would never make significant inroads among blacks until it sent them catechists, nuns, and priests of

67. *Ibid.*, XVI, 1–14.
68. St. Joseph's Seminary Student Journal, June 12, 1902, p. 7, in JFA; EAC Student file, 1890–1914, p. 104, in JFA; Charles Hannigan to John R. Slattery, June 2, 1902, in 18-H-29, John R. Slattery to Thomas Donovan, June 21, 1902, copy in 18-E-26, both in Slattery Papers.

their own race, and he condemned European missionaries in other lands who ignored the wishes of Rome by failing to develop native clergies. Showing the influence of Loisy on his thought, Slattery unfavorably contrasted the complicated dogmas and hierarchical structure of the contemporary Catholic church with the simplicity of the apostolic church and urged a simpler catechetical approach to blacks.

Referring to the efforts of the Democratic party in Maryland to disfranchise blacks, Slattery alleged that the spirit of that party, which was inimical to the interests of blacks, dominated many Catholics. "Perhaps it is the wisest policy," he added, "to admit frankly that because a man enters the sanctuary or a woman the cloister, he or she . . . carries along the . . . prejudices of his or her part of the country." He concluded, "The fact is clear that many Catholics are prejudiced against the Negro." Slattery claimed that "it is this uncatholic sentiment which looks askance at Negro priests."

Despite some of his own somewhat contradictory actions at the college and seminary, Slattery ridiculed the commonly voiced opinion of many white Catholics that blacks should not receive holy orders for fear that they might fall away from the church or prove incapable of celibacy. He charged that whites could ill afford to throw stones on the question of morality, sarcastically noting that mulattos and quadroons did not "drop from the skies."

Slattery claimed that the countless letters he received from black men and women expressing their joy at Dorsey's ordination and the sea of black faces in the crowded church that day offered striking evidence that "every race naturally loves to see its own sons at the altar." He called Dorsey "a light set on a candlestick" and warned him that "no man is so little watched by his superior as a priest, and no man is more under the public eye." In what may have been a slap at Uncles, Slattery urged Dorsey to model himself not "after your brother priest who is colored" but after Blessed Martin de Porres, the Oblate Sisters of Providence, or St. Benedict the Moor.[69]

The next day, Slattery sent Gibbons a short report on the progress of St. Joseph's Society in which he repeated his conviction that "Negro priests must do the work" and reiterated his aim of creating

69. Rev. John Henry Dorsey, A Colored Man, Was Ordained by His Eminence, Cardinal Gibbons (Baltimore, n.d.), in John H. Dorsey file, JFA. Slattery had a thousand copies of this sermon printed. See also Walter Yates to Thomas Donovan, April 27, 1906, in 18-E-20, JFA, and [Slattery], "Biographie," XVI, 17.

a large body of catechists from St. Joseph's Catechetical College who, "after a long trial in that function," would become priests. Then, after appointing Justin McCarthy to administer the society in his absence, Slattery put his papers and affairs in order as if he had quit the seminary and the Josephites and left Baltimore for a six-month stay in Europe. On June 24, he wrote to O'Connell that he had burned his bridges, and he arranged to meet his friend in Geneva on August 5.[70]

Slattery's sermon, which was published in the Baltimore *Sun*, provoked just the storm of controversy he had anticipated. Requests for copies poured into St. Joseph's Seminary; one thousand printed copies disappeared within two days. On the one hand, blacks commented favorably on the sermon. The Reverend O. D. Robinson of the Mt. Zion A.M.E. Church of Baltimore, for example, commended Slattery for his "humane and Christ-like utterances," and Dr. R. M. Hall of Baltimore assured him that "every colored man who has read your sermon feels prouder today of his race."[71] Many white Catholic clergy, on the other hand, found the sermon outrageous. Their spokesman, the Reverend William E. Starr of Corpus Christi Parish in Baltimore, circulated a response to Slattery among the city's clergy that was eventually published in the July 25 issue of the *Sun*. Starr excoriated Slattery for what he called "the most incendiary pronouncement which I can recall as coming from a Catholic priest" and claimed that most of the clergy regarded it with "disgust and indignation." Professing a knowledge of blacks rooted in his southern background, Starr accused Slattery of playing on their simplicity by making "altogether false and unsubstantial claims of past racial glory" and of "filling their minds with incendiary notions of their rights and their wrongs."

Starr took greatest exception, however, to what he regarded as Slattery's public vilification of the church. He declared that Slattery had "wrought irreparable harm" to his own cause and had succeeded in pleasing only the bigots who would use his charges to attack the church. Starr also scolded Slattery for placing Cardinal Gibbons in a difficult position: "If . . . he call you to account . . .

---

70. John R. Slattery to Cardinal James Gibbons, June 23, 1902, copy in Slattery file; [Slattery], "Biographie," XVI, 17.

71. O. D. Robinson to John R. Slattery, June 28, 1902, in 24-T-21, Hugh M. Browne to Robert S. Brady, July 11, 1902, in 27-B-12, John R. Slattery to Morton L. Griffin, February 6, 1903, in 13-P-20, R. M. Hall to John R. Slattery, June 24, 1902, in 24-N-6, all in Slattery Papers.

the unreasoning . . . colored people would see in you a champion of their rights, made to suffer for having had the courage to speak"; however, "if he keep silent he is held responsible for every absurd statement you see fit to make." Three months later, Gibbons appointed Starr to his archdiocesan board of consultors, thus making him one of the cardinal's official advisors.[72]

On August 27, 1902, Joseph Anciaux, a Belgian priest working with the Josephites in Virginia, also jumped into the fray. A dedicated, outspoken man who formally became a Josephite in 1904, Anciaux boasted of influence in the Roman Curia, claiming Cardinal Willem van Rossum, who was consultor of the Congregation of the Holy Office and who later, in 1918, became the cardinal prefect of the Propaganda, as his uncle. Anciaux wrote a letter entitled "Plain Facts for Fair Minds," which he sent to the Propaganda and to each member of the American hierarchy. In it, he charged that the American Catholic clergy had not done its duty toward blacks because "the Protestant idea of a radical and unchristian separation of the races" had invaded the Catholic church and because American priests had adopted the idea that "nothing can nor ought to be done for the Negroes." Anciaux scornfully pointed to the pittance donated by American Catholics to the yearly collection for the black missions as an indication of white Catholic apathy toward this cause. He defended Slattery as "almost the only one who always courageously raises his voice against the wrong done the unfortunate Negro" and accused Cardinal Gibbons and Bishop Van de Vyver of Richmond of excessive timidity in the face of "negro-haters." Further, Anciaux explained that opposition to black priests did not stem, as claimed, from fears of immorality or of the lessened honor of the priesthood. It came instead "from . . . unchristian negro-phobia; from the horror of thinking that a colored seminarian will sit beside a white seminarian . . . and . . . being a priest . . . will consecrate and bless as any other priest," and "because that hurts the feelings of the Southerners, they cry, 'Down with colored priests.'" Anciaux included a thinly veiled warning that he would publish his letter "if compelled by circumstances."[73]

72. William E. Starr, *A Letter to the Very Rev. John R. Slattery, Superior of St. Joseph's Society for the Colored Missions* (Baltimore, n.d.), in Dorsey file; *Baltimore Sun*, January 18, 1903, clipping in Slattery file; William E. Starr to Cardinal James Gibbons, February 13, 1913, in 111-Q-9, AAB.

73. "Obituary," *Colored Harvest*, XIX (February, 1931), 7; Joseph Anciaux, "Plain Facts for Fair Minds" (Typescript in 31-G-16, Slattery Papers).

Anciaux's missive brought a swift response from American bishops. Archbishop Ireland applauded him, declaring, "I make every one of your words my own. The situation as it is, is a disgrace and a shame." Cardinal Gibbons, however, always concerned to avoid public controversy regarding the church, directed his chancellor to communicate his regret to Anciaux over the "sad controversy" that had grown out of Slattery's sermon and to beg him to give it no additional publicity, since "no good can possibly come from further agitation." Bishop Van de Vyver reacted more punitively. On October 28, 1902, he withdrew Anciaux's faculties, thereby forcing him to leave the Richmond diocese.[74]

Slattery, meanwhile, had arrived in Paris on July 17. Two days later, he visited Loisy, the controversial French modernist whom he had first met in 1895; the two men discussed French politics and religious questions. On August 6, Slattery joined O'Connell in Geneva. There, he learned firsthand about the flap following his sermon from Dennis J. Stafford, rector of St. Patrick's Church in Washington, D.C. Slattery spoke openly about leaving the priesthood in front of Stafford, who warned the Josephite: if Slattery really meant to carry through on his plans, Stafford would inform Slattery's liberal friends of his intentions so that the move would not compromise them. After touring Switzerland and Germany, O'Connell and Slattery parted in September, with Slattery traveling to Berlin. There, he studied German, read theology, wrote an unsigned article entitled "The Root Trouble in Catholicism" for the *Independent*, a New York weekly published under the auspices of the Congregational church, and attended lectures on church history given by German modernist Adolph Harnack. Slattery relished news about the continuing uproar caused by his sermon and kept abreast of developments through his correspondence with Robert S. Brady, his secretary back in Baltimore.[75]

Throughout the autumn of 1902, the shock waves from Slattery's sermon and from his prolonged absence continued to spread. True to his word, on his return to the United States Father Stafford began to inform Slattery's episcopal friends and allies about his

74. Archbishop John Ireland to Joseph Anciaux, September 8, 1902, in 31-G-18, P. C. Gavan, chancellor, to Joseph Anciaux, August 31, 1902, in 31-G-17, Bishop Augustine Van de Vyver to Joseph Anciaux, October 28, 1902, in 31-G-20, all in Slattery Papers.
75. [Slattery], "Biographie," XVII, 1–7.

pending apostasy. Ireland immediately penned a frantic warning to O'Connell: "One dense cloud now hangs over the horizon— Slattery. The reports . . . are that he has thrown everything to the wind. If he does not turn up soon, the press will talk and the sensation will be dreadful,—all his friends suffering." Ireland implored O'Connell to write Slattery at once to "beg him to quickly silence reports." He added, "The Cardinal is affrighted."[76]

Slattery's sermon had also disturbed the Josephites' most important benefactors, Edward and Louise Morrell, who considered voicing such sentiments inappropriate for the "head of an order." Slattery's continued absence, moreover, and persistent rumors that he would not return and that the Josephites verged on disintegration further alarmed the Morrells. They, in turn, communicated their concern to Gibbons.[77] The dwindling enrollment at Epiphany Apostolic College, which had shrunk to a little over twenty students, and reports of administrative disarray led Mrs. Morrell to arrange a meeting with Lambert Welbers, the rector of the college, at her home on October 16, 1902, to discuss the Josephites and their management of the Negro missions.

The meeting went badly. Mrs. Morrell obviously had an ax to grind and demanded to know why the Josephites had not made greater progress in the conversion of blacks, given the amount of time and money already spent. Welbers attributed the relatively slow progress to "the surroundings of the Colored People and the distrust of the Catholic Church which they shared with white protestants." He emphasized the need for "a Negro clergy" to achieve greater results and then made a controversial suggestion that shocked the Morrells and cost him his post at the college. He suggested that the church consider the possibility of allowing black candidates for the priesthood to marry, just as it allowed priests of the Eastern rites to do. He had earlier mentioned this idea to Slattery, but Slattery had wisely enjoined him never to discuss it. Welbers' argument began with stating that many Catholics had registered their opposition to black priests "on the score of morality" and that "the colored man is *weaker* than his *white* brethren." These two facts created a problem, he believed, since the church needed black priests

76. *Ibid.*, 7–8.
77. Edward Morrell to Cardinal James Gibbons, January 5, 1903, copy in 31-G-14, Edward Morrell to John R. Slattery, January 21, 1903, in 31-G-32, both in Slattery Papers.

to spread the faith but also wanted to avoid scandal. His solution to the dilemma safeguarded morality by channeling what he considered the black man's weakness into an acceptable form, marriage.[78]

His suggestion, however, coupled with their other concerns about the Josephites, led the Morrells to complain to Gibbons about heresy at Epiphany College and to suspend their annual contributions to the Josephites "until after a thorough investigation has been made and some definite plan of action decided upon." The loss of the Morrells' annual contributions posed a serious danger to the Josephites. To make matters worse, after meeting with his consultors about the society's future, Gibbons added to the Josephites' financial woes by deciding to withhold the annual $5,000 appropriation from the Negro and Indian Commission until Slattery returned from Europe.[79]

After sending letters of reassurance to O'Connell, Ireland, and Gibbons on December 17, 1902, Slattery decided to return to Baltimore. Writing in his diary en route to New York on New Year's Eve, he described the year as "one of the most fateful, tragic years of my life." He noted, "It includes my first attempt to break away from the past of 30 years, which enchains me, but yet the chains hang on me." Slattery may have delayed making a clean break with the church out of consideration for his father, who, though never happy about Slattery's decision to become a priest, most likely would have been embarrassed by any action that would have resulted in his son's excommunication. Slattery, moreover, still saw in the church's philanthropic activities the potential for accomplishing good. Instead of a formal break, he decided to take a new step to recover his "intellectual and moral liberty."[80]

Slattery dealt with the uproar that he found in Baltimore on his return in January, 1903, by taking the offensive. He quickly contacted the Morrells and denounced the "gossip mongers" who had

78. Lambert Welbers to Cardinal James Gibbons, December 12, 1902, in 31-G-26, Edward Morrell to John R. Slattery, January 21, 1903, in 31-G-32, both in Slattery Papers; [Slattery], "Biographie," XVII, 14.

79. Edward Morrell to Cardinal James Gibbons, January 5, 1903, copy in 31-G-14, Cardinal James Gibbons to Edward Morrell, December 10, 1902, copy in 31-G-23, Edward Morrell to Cardinal James Gibbons, January 5, 1903, copy in 31-G-14, Edward Morrell to John R. Slattery, January 21, 1903, in 31-G-32, all in Slattery Papers.

80. [Slattery], "Biographie," XVII, 9, XIX, 4.

spread "villainous reports" about him. On Gibbons' orders, he removed Welbers from the rectorship of Epiphany College but defended him to the Morrells as "a pure and good man," blaming
Welbers' indiscretion on fatigue and illness. As for his own sermon at Dorsey's first mass, Slattery offered no apologies to Edward
Morrell, claiming that "there was nothing startling except in its
truthfulness." Slattery insisted that the real question involved
whether the public should know "the true status of the Catholic
Hierarchy toward *Negro priests* and the Negro missions." Acknowledging that most Catholics would say that publicity about the issue
created scandal and gossip, Slattery asked rhetorically, "Is it right to
ask men to devote their lives to the Negro missions when . . . they
meet the steady opposition of sanctuary and cloister?" He charged
that though the church publicly boasted about its fairness and justice to blacks, "privately, every obstacle imaginable is put in the
way of the Negro missions." To the Morrells' complaints that enrollment at Epiphany College had dropped, he explained that "our
best efforts have been turned toward the College for Negro Catechists," where thirty-five black boys "are studying for the catechist
work and afterwards the priesthood."[81]

While he responded aggressively to his critics, Slattery pursued a
plan for obtaining his freedom. The day after his arrival in New
York, he sent two letters to Gibbons, one administrative and public, announcing that he would resume his post on January 15 and
remain there until the midsummer vacation, the other confidential.
Slattery had originally been ordained *ad titulum missiones*, or as a
missionary. In his private letter to Gibbons, he now requested a
change *ad titulum patrimonii*, which would have ended his membership in St. Joseph's Society, making him thus responsible for his
own support and allowing him to live as a priest outside the framework of the active ministry and the supervision of a bishop.[82]

On January 15, 1903, Slattery met with Gibbons to discuss his
request for the transfer. Ironically, his request came in the midst of
a triumphant tour of northern cities and southern missions by Father Dorsey, which apparently confirmed Slattery's oft-stated con-

81. John R. Slattery to Edward Morrell, January 16, 1903, copy in 31-G-30,
Slattery Papers; [Slattery], "Biographie," XVII, 15; John R. Slattery to Edward
Morrell, January 23, 1903, copy in 31-G-34, Slattery Papers.
82. John R. Slattery to Cardinal James Gibbons, January 5, 1903, in 100-F-3,
AAB; [Slattery], "Biographie," XVII, 9–10.

tention that black people desired their own priests. Slattery, nevertheless, explained to Gibbons that after twenty-five years spent on the black missions, he wished to devote the rest of his days to himself and study. He told the cardinal that his family wished him to leave the Josephites, that his father had always opposed the priesthood for him and now claimed that Slattery's continued association with the Josephites had made his life "a failure."[83]

Gibbons bade Slattery to apply to the Propaganda for the transfer and agreed to endorse it. In March, the Propaganda consented to the transfer on the condition that Slattery find a bishop to incardinate him for a diocese. Gibbons had already indicated to Slattery his unwillingness to do so, and Slattery, who had become a clerical pariah, knew that no bishop would touch him. Slattery had already taken steps both to recover some of the $56,000 of his father's money that he had spent on society expenses between 1877 and 1902 and, paradoxically, to protect the Josephites from dissolution by encumbering the seminary with a $40,000 mortgage. He told Gibbons that he would resign as Josephite superior general and that the Josephites would probably name him superior emeritus. After his meeting with Gibbons, he decided to dispense with the formality of an application to the Propaganda and resolved never to see Gibbons again.[84]

Slattery's intention to resign from the Josephites set off a debate in ecclesiastical circles about the future of the society. True to his character, Gibbons approached the problem cautiously, soliciting opinions and keeping his options open. On June 16, 1903, Slattery obtained a year's leave of absence and returned to Europe in July, after a brief visit with his father. Justin McCarthy, the rector of the seminary, assumed direction of the society as vicar.[85]

Shortly thereafter, Archbishop Patrick Ryan of Philadelphia suggested to Gibbons that the Josephites merge with the Holy Ghost Fathers, or Spiritans, a French-based congregation of missionaries noted for their work in Africa, who also maintained missions for

83. [Slattery], "Biographie," XVII, 10–13; "Fr. Dorsey in Louisiana," *Colored Harvest*, III (January, 1903), 381; Pierre LeBeau to John R. Slattery, September 29, 1902, copy in LeBeau file; [Slattery], "Biographie," XVII, 15; John R. Slattery to Cardinal James Gibbons, February 2, 1903, copy in Slattery file, January 5, 1903, in 100-F-3, AAB.

84. [Slattery], "Biographie," XVII, 17–18, 20–24.

85. *Ibid.*, XVIII, 15, XIX, 1–2; CMB, June 16, 1903, in JFA.

blacks in Philadelphia, Pittsburgh, and Arkansas. When that plan proved unfeasible because the Josephites were secular priests living in community under promise, whereas since 1855 the Holy Ghost Fathers had been a community of religious living under vows of poverty, chastity, and obedience, Cardinal Gibbons, Archbishop Ryan, Mother Katharine Drexel, Bishop Alexandre Le Roy, the superior of the Holy Ghost Fathers, a representative of the Sulpicians, and several other bishops discussed the possible dissolution of the Josephites and the assumption of their missions and seminary by the Holy Ghost Fathers. The $40,000 mortgage on St. Joseph's Seminary, however, which no one wanted to assume, helped serve as an incentive for keeping the Josephites afloat. After consulting with the Sulpicians of St. Mary's Seminary, Gibbons gave the Josephites a chance to reorganize. In March of 1904, Slattery informed the members of St. Joseph's Society of his intention to retire as superior general. In June, 1904, Thomas B. Donovan was elected as the new superior general of the shaken society; and evidently with Gibbons' approval, the Josephites designated Slattery "Superior Emeritus," a fuzzy title that left to Slattery, albeit tenuously, some clerical respectability. "Let us hope," wrote Anthony Zielenbach, the provincial of the Holy Ghost Fathers, "that this will be the end of their troubles."[86]

Unfortunately for the Josephites, their troubles did not end with the election of Donovan, for two years later, in July of 1906, in the pages of a publication called the *Converted Catholic*, Slattery, whose father had died in the winter of 1905, declared, "There is no hope of reforming the Catholic Church. . . . It will fall by its own weight." In September, Slattery used the pages of the *Independent* to renounce the Catholic church publicly and to announce that he had married. In conversations with Walter Yates, a Josephite traveling in Europe in 1906, Slattery explained that he had become convinced that the church "was all a fraud" long before the Dorsey sermon and had waited to repudiate it publicly until after his father's death. In the article in the *Independent*, however, he pointed

86. Henry J. Koren, *The Serpent and the Dove: A History of the Congregation of the Holy Ghost in the United States, 1745–1894* (Pittsburgh, 1985), 175–76; Charles Bonaparte to Edward Morrell, October 27, 1903, copy in 31-H-23, Slattery Papers; "Very Rev. J. R. Slattery, Superior Emeritus of St. Joseph's Society for the Colored Missions," *Colored Harvest*, IV (January, 1905), 532; Koren, *Serpent and Dove*, 177.

to his work among blacks as "the rake which finished the sloughing off" of his priesthood. "If anything in this world is certain," he wrote, "it is that the stand of the Catholic Church toward the negro is sheer dishonesty." Slattery's old friend Archbishop Ireland expressed the feelings of many of Slattery's former clerical associates when he wrote to Denis O'Connell, then the rector of the Catholic University of America, "Well, Slattery has gone to the devil for good—and is acting the devil."[87]

The following year, Pope Pius X condemned modernism in his encyclical *Pascendi dominici gregis*. Much to the embarrassment of the Josephites, Slattery continued to blast the church in books and articles for several years after his defection. By 1910, he had abandoned religious polemic as well as Christianity. He was admitted to the California bar in 1916 and died in Monte Carlo in 1926. The bulk of his $1.5 million estate went to the New York Public Library.[88]

John R. Slattery suffered the fate of many pioneers. He broke new ground in the face of great difficulties but paid a tremendous price for his efforts. He managed to shepherd two black men to ordination but could not overcome the obstacles to black priests created by racism in American society, in the Catholic church, or, ultimately, in himself. As a result of his experiences with Charles Randolph Uncles, the first black Josephite, his own stereotypical views of black moral weakness, and his recognition of increasing opposition to black priests in the Catholic church, Slattery opted for more cautious approaches after 1893, but this caution slowed the ordination process for a few and ended it for many. Slattery never realized the part that he himself played in thwarting his treasured goal. Frustrated and scandalized by the indifference and hostility to blacks that he continually experienced in the church and increasingly skeptical about the authenticity of its dogma and authority, he finally decided to forsake the crusade he had waged for twenty-five years. His defection from the church embarrassed and

87. John R. Slattery to Jeremiah Crowley, April 14, 1906, in *Converted Catholic*, VII (July, 1906), 111–12; John R. Slattery, "How My Priesthood Dropped from Me," *Independent*, LXI (September 6, 1906), 565–71; Walter Yates to Thomas Donovan, August 27, 1906, in 29-T-9, JFA; Baltimore *American*, September 6, 1906, p. 9; Archbishop John Ireland to Denis O'Connell, October 29, 1906, copy in Slattery file.

88. Portier, "Modernism in the United States," in Burke, Lease, and Gilmore (eds.), *Varieties of Modernism*, 89–91; New York *Times*, June 15, 1927, p. 48.

weakened the Josephites, who barely avoided dissolution and found themselves suspect and vulnerable because of the apostasy of their founder, and discredited the cause of black priests, who found a more hostile atmosphere in the church toward them. The champion of black priests had fallen. For John Henry Dorsey and the handful of black priests and seminarians who remained after Slattery's departure, the time on the cross had just begun.

Chapter IV

TRIAL AND TRANSITION, 1904–1918

From . . . my ordination till the present, my life has been one heavy cross.
—JOHN HENRY DORSEY, AUGUST 7, 1907

The fifteen troubled years following Slattery's resignation marked a period of trial and transition for the Josephites as resistance to black priests became more overt. During that period, black Josephites John Henry Dorsey and John J. Plantevigne suffered rejection and humiliation at the hands of bishops of the South. Feeling themselves powerless in the face of episcopal opposition to black priests and still reeling from Slattery's defection, his beleaguered successors as superior general, Thomas B. Donovan, from 1904 to 1908, and Justin McCarthy, from 1908 to 1918, who possessed neither his zeal for a black clergy nor his leadership ability, began the long retreat from Slattery's advanced position on the issue of black priests that would characterize the direction of St. Joseph's Society for the next forty years. Groping their way toward a new policy, they gradually and quietly began to reject most black candidates for Epiphany Apostolic College and St. Joseph's Seminary, thereby accommodating the bishops but sacrificing, in the process, a key element of their society's identity and damaging its credibility among segments of the black community. Keenly aware of the Josephites' vulnerability vis-à-vis the American bishops but also convinced of the need for black priests and cognizant of new concern about the issue shown by the Holy See, Josephite missionary John J. Albert sought to salvage hopes for a black clergy by proposing a new plan for their education and assignment, one that did not involve the society. Albert attempted to enlist the support of the Holy See through the person of the apostolic delegate and urged missionaries of the Society of the Divine Word to implement his proposal.

The Josephite retreat on the issue of black priests reflected a continuing deterioration in the status of blacks in the Catholic church. It also coincided with the failure of progressivism on the national scene to effect significant racial reforms. During this era, blacks in the South continued to suffer disfranchisement, segregation, and lynching; between 1900 and 1917, more than 1,100 blacks were lynched in the United States. Black migration to urban areas in both the North and the South, moreover, sparked race riots in cities as diverse as Atlanta, in 1906, and Springfield, Illinois, in 1908. Beginning in 1914, officials at Catholic University in the nation's capital began to deny admission to black students, thus mirroring the segregation imposed in the federal government by the progressive Wilson administration and symbolizing the triumph of racism in church as well as state. Catholics, like most other Americans, viewed the National Association for the Advancement of Colored People (NAACP), founded in 1910 by a racially mixed group of liberals to combat racial discrimination, as a dangerous and radical organization.[1]

As conditions for blacks were worsening between 1904 and 1918, the Catholic church was attaining a measure of maturity and respect in the United States. In 1908, Pope Pius X terminated the mission status of the American church, removing it from the jurisdiction of the Propaganda and placing the bishops under the Sacred Consistorial Congregation. By 1910, overall Catholic population in the United States had grown to 16,363,000 and by 1920 to 19,828,000. Immigration after 1900, largely from southern and eastern Europe, accounted for 3,500,000 of the latter total and taxed the resources of already overburdened bishops. Descendants of earlier Catholic immigrants began to take their places in business

1. John Hope Franklin and Alfred A. Moss, Jr., *From Slavery to Freedom: A History of Negro Americans* (6th ed.; New York, 1988), 244–50, 282–86; Blase Dixon, T.O.R., "The Catholic University and the Racial Question, 1914–1948," *Records of the American Catholic Historical Society of Philadelphia*, LXXXIV (December, 1973), 221–24; C. Joseph Neusse, "Loss and Recovery of Interracial Virtue: Desegregation at The Catholic University of America" (Paper presented at the annual meeting of the American Catholic Historical Association, Washington, D.C., December 28–30, 1987), 5–6; Rev. Francis J. Weber, "A Catholic Bishop Meets the Racial Problem," *Records of the American Catholic Historical Society of Philadelphia*, LXXXIV (December, 1973), 217–20.

and especially politics, with men like Charles Bonaparte serving in President Theodore Roosevelt's cabinet, first as secretary of the navy in 1905 and then as attorney general from 1906 to 1908. On the municipal level, Irish Catholic political machines, usually identified with the Democratic party, dominated the great cities in the Northeast and Midwest, such as New York, Boston, and Chicago. While muckrakers and other reformers took aim at Irish machine politics, some individual Catholics, both lay and cleric—for example, the Reverend John A. Ryan, state senator and later United States senator from New York Robert Wagner, and Mary Harris ("Mother") Jones—made significant contributions to labor reform, though Catholics in general did not figure prominently in Progressive Era reform movements.

During the first two decades of the twentieth century, Cardinal James Gibbons of Baltimore continued to enjoy preeminence in the American Catholic church, a church still largely controlled by the Irish clergy, except in the German dioceses of the Midwest. Despite its monolithic appearance to outsiders, however, the American Catholic church remained remarkably decentralized during this period, with annual archbishops' meetings providing what little unofficial coordination existed. Ethnic conflict among Catholics, which often centered on control of the burgeoning parochial schools or appointment of priests or bishops for various nationalities, testified to the heterogeneous composition of church membership and illustrated the difficulties of maintaining church unity. Pius X's attempt to ensure unity through theological orthodoxy for the worldwide church by his condemnation of modernism in 1907 had the additional effect of stifling American theological thought for the succeeding half-century

Although Catholics achieved greater acceptance and respectability in urban areas, many Americans still viewed them and their church as foreign. Between 1910 and 1917, in the strongholds of WASP America, the rural South and Midwest, where it was weakest, the church was beset by yet another wave of anti-Catholicism, making bishops and priests even more wary about disturbing social or racial taboos.[2]

2. Gerald P. Fogarty, *The Vatican and the American Hierarchy from 1870 to 1965* (Stuttgart, 1982), 204; James Hennesey, S.J., *American Catholics: A History of the Roman Catholic Community in the United States* (New York, 1981), 207–17, 221–22.

In the midst of the Slattery scandal, Justin McCarthy and Thomas Donovan, the temporary administrators of the Josephites, undoubtedly wanted to avoid further controversy for their embarrassed and weakened society. The irrepressible Joseph Anciaux, however, kept the Josephites in the forefront of debate about the status of blacks in the church and the future of black priests. On August 19, 1903, Anciaux, who became a Josephite the following year and whose criticisms of the American clergy's indifference and racism were as sharp as the nose that dominated his broad face, sent to the Holy See a forty-six-page pamphlet he had written, entitled *de miserabili conditione catholicorum nigrorum in America [Concerning the Wretched Condition of Negro Catholics in America]*. Dubbed the "red book" because of its binding, Anciaux's booklet briefly described the appalling political, civil, social, and legal barriers confronting blacks in American society. He devoted most of his attention, though, to "The Religious Status of the Negroes." Anciaux detailed how the segregation in Catholic churches and schools humiliated blacks and, in many cases, prevented their children from receiving a Catholic education. He reproached the vast majority of American priests for ignoring blacks, either because of racism or fear of negative white reaction. Turning to the hierarchy, he claimed that, with only a few exceptions, American bishops failed to defend and protect the rights of blacks, because they, like their priests, feared white backlash.

Although he tempered his charges with protestations that the bishops eagerly desired the salvation of all souls, Anciaux left no doubt that he believed the American clergy suffered not only from the sins of timidity and respecting human opinion over divine law but also from racism. He specifically fingered Bishop Benjamin J. Keiley of Savannah, a veteran of the Confederate army, who had publicly denounced President Theodore Roosevelt for having lunched with Booker T. Washington. Anciaux attributed the dearth of black priests to white clerical opposition and cited a private conversation with Monsignor J. M. Laval, the vicar general, or archbishop's deputized assistant, of the archdiocese of New Orleans, to illustrate his claim. According to Anciaux, Laval told him that "in America, no Negro should be ordained," that just as illegitimacy constituted an impediment to holy orders under canon law, so, too, the church should declare all blacks "irregular" because whites held them in such contempt. Anciaux noted that Laval, displaying more honesty than most, had framed his objections in terms of race rather than in terms of the commonly used pretext of immorality. He contended that most priests in the United States shared Laval's opinion and even included the respected Cardinal Gibbons in his critique. Anciaux insisted that Gibbons knew the truth of his charges but, "weighed down by difficulties," did nothing for fear of what might happen if "anyone rush headlong in opposition to the present state of affairs." He faulted Gibbons for believing, along with many other whites, that blacks should "stay in their place like good Negroes of the past." Such patronizing attitudes on the part of Catholic prelates constituted, in Anciaux's opinion, their greatest error and gravely injured the standing of the church in the eyes of many blacks.

In order to help remedy the terrible condition of blacks in the church, Anciaux resurrected an old idea, first associated with Archbishop Martin John Spalding and later promoted unsuccessfully by Slattery. Anciaux proposed the creation of a central office for all "colored work" in the United States—an office similar to the Bureau of Catholic Missions, which had been created in 1874 to protect and advance missionary work among the Indians. He also called for the appointment of a prelate who would be attached to the Apostolic Delegation in Washington, D.C., and who would head the central office and have charge of blacks and mission work among them. This prelate, though having no authority "either above or opposed to" the bishops, could prudently investigate the condition of blacks and submit reports or proposals either to Gibbons or, preferably, to the Propaganda through the apostolic delegate. Anciaux assured the Holy See that the new bureau could obtain funds from the annual Negro and Indian collection or from Mother Katharine Drexel.[3]

To press his case in Rome, Anciaux relied not only on the strength of his booklet but also on the help of his Belgian cousin, the Reverend Alfred Le Grand. Le Grand had spent six years in Rome and maintained contact with such high-ranking prelates as Secretary of State Raffaele Cardinal Merry del Val and Prefect of the Propaganda Girolamo Cardinal Gotti. In addition to relying on Anciaux's red book, Le Grand also used information about the condition of blacks in the American church he obtained from Arch-

3. Joseph Anciaux, *de miserabili conditione catholicorum nigrorum in America* (N.p., 1903), in Joseph Anciaux file, JFA; John R. Slattery to Joseph Anciaux, April 21, 1903, in 27-E-2, John R. Slattery Papers, JFA.

bishop Le Roy, the superior general of the Spiritans, who had toured the United States in 1903. In early 1904, Le Grand secured two audiences with Pope Pius X, during which he stressed the inertia of the American bishops and the necessity of intervention by the Holy See on behalf of American blacks. Pius X promised prompt action.

As a result of Anciaux's letter and Le Grand's audiences with the pope, the curial congregations began to pressure the bishops about the treatment of black Catholics in the United States. A few days after Le Grand's audience with the pope, several cardinals informed him that the Propaganda had taken action: the apostolic delegate had been instructed to obtain a commitment from the American hierarchy that it would create a bureau to organize and direct the black apostolate in the United States. On January 18, 1904, Cardinal Gotti wrote to Archbishop Sebastiano Martinelli, the apostolic delegate, advising him the Propaganda had received disturbing information that in some dioceses in the United States the condition of black Catholics "not only in respect to other faithful but also in respect to their priests and bishops is very humiliating and entirely different from that of whites." Gotti asked the delegate to call Gibbons' attention to the matter so that at their next meeting the archbishops could take steps to lessen and gradually remove the diversity of treatment.[4]

On April 14, 1904, at the archbishops' meeting, Gibbons communicated Gotti's concerns, but the archbishops, defensive about Roman meddling in the delicate area of race relations, responded to Gotti's letter with rhetoric rather than with substantive actions. Deciding that "this is a matter depending on local circumstances," the archbishops sent a copy of Gotti's letter to each of the bishops of the United States, requesting that any abuse be corrected. During their meeting, they admitted that Indians received more attention from the church than did blacks and urged "more efficient efforts and means for the conversion of the colored race among us." Believing themselves unfairly maligned by Anciaux's pamphlet, however, the prelates asked Gibbons to present to the Propaganda "a correct account of the action of the Church in America concerning the colored race." Gibbons reported the results of the meeting

4. Henry J. Koren, *The Serpent and the Dove: A History of the Congregation of the Holy Ghost in the United States, 1745–1984* (Pittsburgh, 1985), 178–79; Cardinal Girolamo Gotti to Apostolic Delegation, January 18, 1904, copy in 101-G-6, AAB.

to Rome and, ignoring the reality of segregated seating in his own cathedral in Baltimore, praised the clergy of his diocese, and by implication the clergy of the United States, for their "zealous work" on behalf of blacks. He declared that they showed blacks no less charity than the rest of the faithful. Anciaux's accusations against priests and bishops also displeased Theophile Meerschaert, the bishop under whose jurisdiction he labored in the Oklahoma Territory. Although he retained his personal affection for Anciaux, Meerschaert, like the archbishops, believed that the missionary had exaggerated in his letter to Rome. Anciaux, therefore, left Oklahoma in the summer of 1905.[5]

Gibbons' assurances notwithstanding, the Holy See maintained pressure on the American bishops throughout the spring of 1904 to demonstrate "more efficient efforts and means" for the conversion of blacks. On April 25, 1904, newspapers reported a message sent from Pius X through Cardinal Merry del Val to Nick Charles, editor of the Topeka Plain Dealer, an Afro-American newspaper. Merry del Val assured Charles that the pope both extended "his loving care to every race without exception" and urged "all Catholics to be friendly to Negroes, who are called no less than other men to share in all the great benefits of the Redemption." In mid-May, newspapers announced the creation of a provisional committee of the archbishops, composed of John Ireland, Patrick Ryan of Philadelphia, and John J. Glennon of St. Louis, to examine the church's efforts on behalf of blacks. "All that remains to be done," a jubilant Anciaux wrote to Le Roy, "is to make the committee permanent and add a delegate from the Holy See to it." Anciaux's sources told him that Rome had plainly advised the American hierarchy to do something about the evangelization of blacks and was now watching to see what would happen. American Spiritan provincial Anthony Zielenbach, who closely followed developments, remained more skeptical. "I don't expect much," he wrote. "All he got was a letter from the Holy Father on the Negro question in very general terms."[6]

Zielenbach's skepticism proved well-founded, despite the efforts

5. Minutes of the meeting of archbishops at The Catholic University of America, April 14, 1904, in 101-G-2, Cardinal James Gibbons to Cardinal Girolamo Gotti, May 14, 1904, copy in 101-J-3, both in AAB; Joseph Anciaux to Thomas Donovan, January 5, 1905, in 24-A-18, JFA.

6. "Pope Pius Writes on Negro Question," Colored Harvest, IV (October, 1904), 506; Joseph Anciaux to Justin McCarthy, May 18, 1904, in 24-A-7, JFA; Koren, Serpent and Dove, 179.

of his superior general, Archbishop Le Roy, who submitted to the Propaganda an ambitious outline for a permanent central Negro bureau that would collect money, gather information, and have the power to intervene against bishops who refused to grant faculties to missionaries registered with it. Months dragged by, however, with little apparent progress in implementing the proposal. Anciaux prevailed on Mother Katharine Drexel to speak on behalf of the bureau to her close friend Archbishop Ryan. Assured of a respectful hearing from the archbishops because of her immense wealth and personal sanctity, Mother Katharine bombarded Ryan and the other archbishops with letters and personal appeals.[7]

As a result of her entreaties, on April 26, 1906, the archbishops created the Catholic Board for Mission Work Among the Colored People. Sitting on the board were Cardinal Gibbons, Archbishops Ryan of Philadelphia and John Farley of New York, and Bishops Thomas Byrne of Nashville and Edward Allen of Mobile. Eight months later, they appointed John E. Burke, the pastor of St. Benedict the Moor Parish in New York City and an advocate of black clergy, as their secretary general.[8]

Although its title was impressive, the Catholic Board for Mission Work Among the Colored People never provided the central direction, coordination, and protection for the black apostolate that Anciaux and his allies had envisioned. During the first years of the board's existence, the relationship between it and the older Negro and Indian Commission, though frequently discussed, remained unclear, leading to unnecessary duplication and confusion. The archbishops, moreover, limited Burke's job to publicity, fund raising, and distribution of proceeds. Each bishop retained full control over priests and missionaries in his own diocese; thus, the board had no real power. Dubbed the "Gold Dust Twins," Burke and his assistant, the Reverend D. J. Bustin, collected money for the board by begging in northern dioceses. An incident in one parish illustrates both the relative obscurity of the board and the indifference that its appeals encountered: the pastor read a letter to his parishioners from their bishop recommending the Catholic Board's work and then casually remarked, "I do not know about this collec-

7. Koren, *Serpent and Dove*, 181; Sr. M. Georgiana Rockwell, S.B.S., "The Influence of Mother M. Katharine Drexel on the Formation of the Catholic Board for Mission Work Among the Colored People" (Typescript in JFA), 8–9, 11–12.

8. Minutes of the annual meeting of archbishops, April 10, 1907, in 103-L-5, AAB.

tion. . . . You will find a box down there at the door and if you wish to put anything in it . . . you can do so." Under Burke, the board paid the salaries of sisters teaching in the black mission schools and provided small allowances of fifteen dollars per month to the neediest priests on those missions. By 1913, Burke was dividing approximately $1,500 per month among sixty-five teachers.[9] Through financial assistance to beleaguered teachers in the black mission schools and especially through the pages of *Our Colored Missions,* the organ of the Catholic Board, he became a spokesman on a whole range of issues affecting black missionary work, including the ordination of black priests. Denied substantive authority, however, he had to rely instead on persuasion and personal influence. In the case of the Catholic Board for Mission Work Among the Colored People, the American hierarchy had once again frustrated efforts to secure more effective coordination and centralization of missionary efforts among blacks. Left to the care of their bishops, black Catholics often experienced neglect and discrimination. The traumatic experiences of two black Josephites at the hands of southern bishops during the first two decades of the twentieth century exemplified the marginality of black Catholics within their own church and raised serious doubts about the viability of black clergy in the United States.

In the midst of the gathering storm, as Joseph Anciaux played the role of firebrand, his new superior general, Thomas Donovan, adopted a more conservative approach. Donovan, a pudgy, bald, round-faced Kentuckian who succeeded Slattery in 1904, looked more like a farmhand than the superior of a religious community. The forty-eight-year-old Donovan, however, had held a series of important posts during the preceding ten years, including professor at Epiphany Apostolic College, pastor of St. Peter Claver and St. Francis Xavier parishes in Baltimore and St. Joseph's in Richmond, and rector of St. Joseph's Industrial School, St. Joseph's College for Negro Catechists, and Epiphany Apostolic College. During

9. Monsignor John E. Burke Diary, May 15, 1907 (Typescript in JFA); Joseph F. Martino, "A Study of Certain Aspects of the Episcopate of Patrick J. Ryan, Archbishop of Philadelphia, 1884–1911" (Ph.D. dissertation, Pontifical Gregorian University, 1982), 83; Koren, *Serpent and Dove,* 185; *The Great American Catholic Missionary Congress* (Chicago, 1913), 112–18; William A. Osborne, *Segregated Covenant: Race Relations and American Catholics* (New York, 1967), 31; John E. Burke to Bishop John E. Gunn, November 20, 1912, in Bishop John E. Gunn Papers, ADJ.

Slattery's leave of absence, Donovan also served as visitor of the missions. In 1904, he took command of a society whose membership had grown to thirty-five priests, with eighty students preparing for the priesthood and with missions in the archdioceses of Baltimore and New Orleans, the dioceses of Wilmington, Richmond, Mobile, Natchez, Galveston, San Antonio, and Nashville, and the vicariate of the Oklahoma Territory. *Colored Harvest* described Donovan's attitude toward blacks as that of a "moral benefactor" and claimed that whereas his predecessor's pleas for the uplift of blacks had aroused disfavor in the South, Donovan's work had elicited more appreciation.[10]

Although he had recommended black American candidates for the seminary in the 1880s, by 1900, when he became rector of St. Joseph's College for Negro Catechists, Donovan had soured on the idea and pinned his slim hopes for black priests instead on candidates from the Caribbean. While rector, he repeatedly clashed with Slattery over the latter's intention of transforming St. Joseph's College into a black seminary. On becoming superior general, therefore, he did not encourage black applicants to Epiphany Apostolic College or St. Joseph's Seminary. In 1906, he allowed George Chisholme Knight, a West Indian black from Georgetown, British Guiana, to take classes and teach at St. Joseph's College for Negro Catechists. Two black lay teachers there, aware of the difference in attitude between Donovan and Slattery, warned Knight that though he might get to the seminary, the Josephites would never ordain him. Knight, nevertheless, persevered in his study of Latin and entered Epiphany Apostolic College in July, 1907, just as a crisis involving John Henry Dorsey reached its climax.[11]

Dorsey's priestly career began in 1902 amid the controversy of Slattery's stinging indictment of Catholic clergy for their opposition to black priests. The second black parishioner from St. Francis Xavier Parish to be ordained to the priesthood, Dorsey held A.B, A.M., and S.T.B. degrees from St. Mary's Seminary and possessed

10. Information sheet in Thomas B. Donovan file, JFA; "Very Rev. J. R. Slattery, Superior Emeritus of St. Joseph's Society for the Colored Missions," *Colored Harvest*, IV (January, 1905), 530, 532; "January 13," *Colored Harvest* (n.d.), in Donovan file.

11. Walter Elliott to Justin McCarthy, December 5, 1904, in 26-G-3, EAC Student file, 1890–1914, p. 274, Jeremiah McNamara to Thomas Donovan, August 30, 1906, in 27-N-10, Joseph Butsch to Thomas Donovan, November 10, 1906, in 27-N-11, all in JFA.

a "sonorous voice" and "elegant and flowing diction." Standing five feet, eight inches tall and with arching, heavy eyebrows, intense eyes, a strong chin, and a missionary's cross hung around his neck and stuck into the sash of his cassock, he projected an air of authority.[12] Dorsey, however, was repeatedly rejected and humiliated by white bishops and priests. Eventually, the strain of racial prejudice wore him down, leaving him a shell of his former self.

Initially, his public ministry seemed to promise success and acceptance. Unlike Uncles, he enjoyed conducting parish missions. In the nine months following his ordination and before his taking up his assignment at the catechetical college, he toured major cities of the North and most of the Josephite missions in the South. In the North, he attempted to enlist white support for the Josephite missions by showing them a "real black priest." White ladies of Boston knelt before him to receive his blessing and to take Holy Communion; in doing so, Dorsey pointed out, they reverenced the priestly character that he represented rather than any particular race.[13] Elated by this reception, young Dorsey did not yet realize that reverential acts like those rendered to him by the Boston ladies would engender hostility and fear in many other whites.

In the South, Dorsey hoped that his presence would convince blacks that the Catholic church valued them. At places like Palmetto, Louisiana, and San Antonio and Houston, crowds of blacks packed the churches where he preached. Pierre LeBeau, pastor in Palmetto, reported the emotions the people of his parish displayed when they heard Dorsey say mass and preach: "Their enthusiasm knew no bounds. Some wept openly." Dorsey heard confessions as well, giving lie to the rumor that blacks would not go to confession to black priests. LeBeau's parishioners begged him to keep Dorsey at Palmetto. "If we had colored priests," LeBeau observed, "I feel confident we should soon convert the South." For Dorsey's visit countered the effective Protestant gibe that Catholics had only white priests whereas black Protestants had ministers of their own. During his southern tour, Dorsey dined with the bishops of Nash-

12. "Rev. J. H. Dorsey's Recent Mission Trip," *Colored Harvest*, III (October, 1903), 421; unidentified New Orleans newspaper clipping, June, 1903, in Dorsey family scrapbook, in the possession of Olga Dorsey, Baltimore, Md., and copy in John Henry Dorsey file. For an account of Dorsey's life as a priest, see Stephen J. Ochs, "The Ordeal of the Black Priest," *U.S. Catholic Historian*, V, No. 1 (1986), 45–66.

13. "Rev. Dorsey's Recent Mission Trip," 421.

ville and San Antonio and received visits during his parish missions from a number of white priests; those in San Antonio even tendered him a reception. Slattery congratulated Dorsey on his success and assured him that his experiences on the retreats and the contacts he made with whites would serve him well. But, Slattery added prophetically, "you have a hard life ahead of you if you attempt to work." He advised Dorsey to keep the examples of Booker T. Washington and W. E. B. Du Bois before his eyes.[14]

Despite the triumphant appearance of his tour, a dark cloud hung over Dorsey's head as he made his way slowly toward Montgomery. He had learned that some priests and lay people in Montgomery opposed his coming and that Slattery had not cleared his appointment with Bishop Allen but rather had simply presented Allen with a fait accompli and then departed for Europe. As early as July 25, 1902, eight months before Dorsey would arrive at St. Joseph's College, the Reverend Hugh O'Brien, assistant pastor of St. Peter's Church in Montgomery, wrote to Bishop Allen on behalf of his incapacitated pastor and "several prominent Catholic laymen," asking him to do whatever he could to prevent Dorsey's appointment to the college, no matter how distant from whites Dorsey might keep himself. O'Brien claimed that Catholics and Protestants believed strongly that Slattery "is purposely ignoring the opinions and sentiments of the southern people on the Negro question," that "he is rubbing it in."[15]

Dorsey confided to Slattery that prior to his ordination he had realized he would have a hard life as a priest. He confessed, however, that when bishops and priests, "from whom encouragement ought to come," considered him persona non grata, he felt drained of all energy in soul and body. "We are human," he told Slattery, "and cannot stop the flood of thought that rushes in upon us." Convinced that the conversion of his people depended on black priests, he declared himself willing to suffer for the cause but described the outlook as discouraging because of the opposition of many priests

14. "Fr. Dorsey in Louisiana," *Colored Harvest*, III (January, 1903), 381; "Notes," *Colored Harvest*, III (June, 1903), 414; John H. Dorsey to John R. Slattery, January 13, 1903, in 23-N-39, Slattery Papers; unidentified New Orleans newspaper clipping, June, 1903, in Dorsey family scrapbook; "Rev. Dorsey's Recent Mission Trip," 421; John R. Slattery to John H. Dorsey, March 18, 1903, copy in 23-M-41, Slattery Papers.

15. John H. Dorsey to Thomas Donovan, August 13, 1907, in 25-P-8, JFA; Hugh A. O'Brien to Bishop Edward P. Allen, July 23, 1902, in Bishop Edward P. Allen Papers, AAM.

"to a colored man being raised to the dignity of the priesthood." He pleaded with Slattery not to station him at Montgomery but promised obedience to what Slattery thought best. On his part, Slattery advised the black priest to "play possum," do his duty, and pay no attention to outsiders, despite feeling keenly the opposition. He tried to encourage Dorsey by reminding him that "every graduate [of St. Joseph's College] stands for a large number whom you will reach through him." Then, in a well-intentioned but insensitive closing, Slattery told him, "We all suffer from race prejudice, myself just as you." [16]

Dorsey stayed at St. Joseph's College for seventeen months. During his fortnightly visits to say mass for the Catholic students at Tuskegee Institute, he charmed Booker T. Washington, who, in May, 1903, invited him to commencement exercises. Dorsey also accepted invitations to say mass and preach at black parishes in Atlanta and New Orleans. He lost his strongest defender, however, when Slattery resigned. Shortly thereafter, relations between Dorsey and Francis Tobin, the rector of St. Joseph's College, deteriorated. In September, 1904, therefore, Dorsey was assigned as assistant pastor to J. J. Ferdinand at St. Peter's Church in Pine Bluff, Arkansas, a city with a population of 12,000, half of whom were black, located fifty miles southeast of Little Rock in the heart of Arkansas' black belt. After Dorsey had taken up residence, Donovan warily observed to Justin McCarthy, "So Colored Priest, Colored Church, and Colored Sisters at Pine Bluff. Let us pray and hope that this move will be blessed." [17] It was not.

Dorsey found himself in an environment not only marked by tense race relations between blacks and whites and by the implacable hostility of black Protestant ministers toward the Catholic church but dominated by the sometimes difficult J. M. Lucey, pastor of St. Joseph's Parish, founder of the Colored Industrial Institute, and self-proclaimed expert on black people. Lucey had vexed the Josephites since their arrival at St. Peter's in 1898, finding fault

16. John H. Dorsey to John R. Slattery, March 21, 1903, in 23-M-42, John R. Slattery to John H. Dorsey, March 27, 1903, copy in 23-M-43, both in Slattery Papers.

17. John R. Slattery to Thomas Donovan, June 21, 1902, copy in 18-E-26, Slattery Papers; Booker T. Washington to Thomas Donovan, May 15, 1903, in 23-M-21, JFA; unidentified New Orleans newspaper clipping, June, 1903, in Dorsey family scrapbook; "Diocese of Little Rock," *St. Joseph's Advocate*, II (April, 1890), 87; Francis Tobin to Bishop Edward P. Allen, September 18, 1904, in Allen Papers; John H. Dorsey to Thomas Donovan, August 13, 1907, in 25-P-8, Thomas Donovan to Justin McCarthy, January 13, 1905, in 24-B-34, both in JFA.

with Josephite pastors over the slow pace of conversions, parish finances, and relations with the sisters teaching at the Colored Industrial Institute and at the parochial school attached to St. Peter's. He particularly objected to what he termed the scandalous behavior of Josephite pastors in "walking with colored people," a practice he thought smacked of "social equality," likely to inflame white opinion. Although he had publicly denounced attempts by some state legislators in 1890 and 1891 to enact a segregation law governing railroads and though he would later become a vocal foe of lynching, Lucey, at the time of Dorsey's arrival, perceived the need to tread carefully with respect to the opinions of whites, owing to the steadily worsening racial climate throughout the state. He believed that "one of the most important points of the education of colored youth is their bearing and conduct towards the whites." He therefore made sure that in addition to its sewing, literary, music, and woodwork programs, his Colored Industrial Institute also stressed deportment for its male and female students.[18]

Lucey furthermore cultivated the support of influential non-Catholic whites in Pine Bluff who valued the respect for authority, discipline, and purity that they believed the Catholic church could instill in blacks. By 1898, when Thomas Plunkett, the first Josephite pastor of St. Peter's, arrived to take charge of his congregation of six, the Colored Industrial Institute, staffed by six Sisters of Charity, had increased its enrollment to 235 students and had moved from a two-story, wood-frame building into a modern, three-story, brick structure. Lucey envisioned the institute as a central mission headquarters for Arkansas, western Mississippi, northern Louisiana, eastern Texas, and the western Indian Territory. Plunkett therefore became, at least in Lucey's eyes, responsible for a vast area that reportedly included five hundred lapsed black Catholics. Lucey pressed the Josephites for conversions. Plunkett responded with thirty-seven baptisms during his first two years as pastor. The congregation at St. Peter's remained small.[19]

18. William Murphy to Justin McCarthy, November 27, 1907, in 27-N-34, JFA; John William Graves, "Jim Crow in Arkansas: A Reconsideration of Urban Race Relations in the Post Reconstruction South," *Journal of Southern History*, LV (August, 1989), 448; "Diocese of Little Rock," 87; "Our Work," *Colored Harvest*, III (October, 1901), 272–73.

19. "The Colored Industrial Institute and Mission of Pine Bluff, Arkansas," *Colored Harvest*, II (October, 1898), 43–44; "Pine Bluff Mission," *Colored Harvest*, II (January, 1901), 212.

In 1901, in an attempt to encourage more converts, Lucey brought in the black Sisters of the Holy Family to conduct both the Colored Industrial Institute and that part of the institute constituting the parochial school of St. Peter's. Shortly after the arrival of the Holy Family sisters, Lucey and J. J. Ferdinand, the new Josephite pastor, clashed over whether the sisters should provide Ferdinand with his meals as part of his compensation for serving as their chaplain. Lucey opposed such an arrangement, fearing that a young white priest taking his meals with the black sisters might cause a scandal or "troubles of a worse character." He also bridled at Ferdinand's habit of walking with his black parishioners. By the end of 1901, Lucey regretted ever having invited the Josephites to Arkansas.[20]

In October, 1901, *Colored Harvest* reported a congregation of fifty at St. Peter's, with 40 children attending catechism classes and 135 enrolled in the parochial school. Ferdinand attributed the poor state of the church in Arkansas to the lack of priests, especially black priests. For once, Lucey appeared to agree with him, and in his report to the Negro and Indian Commission, he declared that two black priests giving missions could accomplish great good, "provided that they would be as good morally and intellectually as white priests and that people could be convinced of this fact and the absolute trustworthiness of colored priests."[21] Clearly, Lucey had his doubts on both scores, but he acceded to Dorsey's appointment as assistant pastor of St. Peter's.

The glow from the jubilant public welcome accorded to Dorsey on his arrival in Pine Bluff, which featured a speech by the white mayor, quickly faded as the young priest found himself enmeshed in the complexities of the little southern parish. Within three months, Dorsey and Ferdinand quarreled, with Ferdinand complaining to Donovan that Dorsey did nothing but spend all of his time "from early morning till late at night with the sisters." Soon

20. J. M. Lucey to Sisters of the Holy Family, July 10, 1900, J. M. Lucey, "Relations of the Pastor of St. Peter's Church, Pine Bluff, Arkansas and the Sisters of the Holy Family in Charge of the Colored Industrial Institute," Memorandum to the Sisters of the Holy Family, n.d., both in ASHF; *Mission Work Among the Negroes and Indians* (Baltimore, 1902), 18; William Murphy to Justin McCarthy, November 27, 1907, in 27-N-34, JFA; J. M. Lucey to Mother Austin, May 17, 1902, in ASHF.

21. "Our Work," 272–73; "Rev. J. J. Ferdinand," *Colored Harvest*, III (October, 1903), 436–37; *Mission Work Among the Negroes and Indians* (Baltimore, 1902), 18.

after, Ferdinand abruptly left St. Peter's for the Ft. Smith mission without telling anyone. Ferdinand's housekeeper harassed Dorsey by controlling the mail and by refusing to cook for him or to show him the financial records of the mission. Dorsey appealed to the Reverend M. Kraemer, O.S.B., the vicar general of the diocese, who praised his conduct in the matter and recommended Ferdinand's transfer. On January 27, 1905, Donovan reassigned Ferdinand to Dallas, thus making Dorsey the only black pastor in the United States. Lucey asked Donovan to impress upon Dorsey his great responsibility and warned that if Dorsey failed, no other black priest would be tried for years. In March, 1905, Lucey indicated a favorable first impression but added cautiously, "Time will tell."[22]

By the end of the year, Lucey began to find fault with Dorsey. He complained the black priest did little work because of a stomach ailment that, according to Lucey, barely allowed Dorsey to say mass and prevented him from giving any missions. Lucey suggested that Dorsey seek treatment at the infirmary in Little Rock or possibly even Baltimore. He attempted to justify the paltry share of the Negro and Indian fund collection given by the diocese of Little Rock to St. Peter's by telling Donovan that Dorsey's ill health seemed to forbode his early departure and implying that in such a situation of uncertainty and drift, the funds would not be used effectively. The appointment in 1906 of John B. Morris as coadjutor, or assistant, bishop to the incapacitated Edward Fitzgerald did not augur well for Dorsey. While serving as vicar general of the diocese of Nashville, Morris reportedly had objected to and refused to attend a dinner hosted by Bishop Byrne for Dorsey during the latter's postordination tour.[23] Morris succeeded to the see of Little Rock when Fitzgerald died on February 21, 1907.

Trouble between Dorsey and the Sisters of the Holy Family soon gave Lucey further ammunition against Dorsey. Part of the difficulty apparently stemmed from the Creole backgound of the sisters.

22. J. M. Lucey, "The Matter of J. H. Dorsey, Pastor of St. Peter's Church (colored), Pine Bluff, Arkansas" (Report to John B. Morris, bishop of Little Rock), November 18, 1907, in Bishop John B. Morris Papers, ADLR; J. J. Ferdinand to Thomas Donovan, December 2, 1904, in 24-C-14, M. Kraemer to Thomas Donovan, January 23, 1905, in 26-A-26, Thomas Donovan to J. J. Ferdinand, January 27, 1905, copy in 25-P-6, Thomas Donovan to John H. Dorsey, January 27, 1905, in 25-P-7, all in JFA; Lucey, "The Matter of J. H. Dorsey," in Morris Papers; J. M. Lucey to Thomas Donovan, September 6, 1907, in 25-P-14, JFA.

23. J. M. Lucey to Thomas Donovan, December 18, 1905, in 26-B-7a, JFA; Burke Diary, May 17, 1907.

Some of them looked down on American blacks and felt insulted at the prospect of receiving the sacraments from a black, rather than a white, priest. Differences of opinion about Dorsey, coupled with personality conflicts, split the community of sisters at Pine Bluff.[24] In addition, the familiar bugaboo of immorality further complicated matters. According to Lucey, in August, 1906, Mother Mary Austin, the mother general of the Holy Family sisters, informed him that she feared criminal intimacy between Dorsey and one of her sisters at Pine Bluff. She requested that Lucey ask Bishop Morris for authority to replace Dorsey as the sisters' regular confessor with Lucey's white assistant. The bishop granted the request. Mother Austin subsequently reassigned all the sisters at Pine Bluff, bringing in a new contingent who were suspicious of Dorsey. Lucey told Mother Austin that if Donovan insisted on Dorsey as the sisters' confessor (since Dorsey remained pastor of St. Peter's and thus, according to the agreement between the Josephites and the diocese, entitled to serve as the sisters' confessor), he would recommend that the Josephite superior name a white priest as pastor and make Dorsey the assistant, reasoning that "there would be less danger on moral grounds."

Lucey became increasingly concerned about possible immorality and scandal involving Dorsey. Unaccountably, however, he failed to communicate his concern to Donovan. Instead, Lucey suggested to Mother Austin that she lay down strict rules governing the relations of the sisters and their pupils with Dorsey. He insisted that Dorsey not visit the sisters after nightfall and noted disapprovingly that several small girls visited the priest quite frequently. Although according to Lucey the girls were so young that "no harm to them can be done," still, he added, it did not look good, and besides, "the little girls at the Colored School are so untidy in dress that they excite thoughts."[25]

During the next year, both Bishop Morris and Lucey, who had become monsignor as well as the new vicar general of the diocese, sought to remove Dorsey from St. Peter's and the Josephites from Arkansas. Morris explored the possibility of entrusting all the black missions in Arkansas, beginning with Pine Bluff, to the Holy Ghost Fathers. At a meeting in May of 1907 with John T. Murphy, the

---

24. Adaline Robinson to Thomas Donovan, August 19, 1907, in 25-P-13, JFA.
25. Lucey, "The Matter of J. H. Dorsey," in Morris Papers; J. M. Lucey to Mother Austin, August 31, 1906, in ASHF.

American provincial of the Spiritans, Morris expressed dissatisfaction with Dorsey and with the Josephites in general. According to Murphy, the Arkansas prelate emphasized the need for racial segregation until prejudices diminished. While acknowledging the need to use blacks themselves in missionary work, Morris observed that prevailing circumstances in the South allowed for only white priests. He therefore suggested that the church should restore the permanent diaconate. Under such a plan, black men would be ordained as deacons, one step below the priesthood. They would preach, baptize, distribute the Eucharist, yet remain free to marry. A married black diaconate would keep black deacons subordinate to white priests, an important consideration in the South, and would alleviate the burden of priestly celibacy for blacks—a burden that Morris doubted Dorsey could bear. Morris finally asked Donovan to remove Dorsey from Pine Bluff, in July, 1907, alleging concern for Dorsey's happiness in view of southern racial norms, which isolated him from the white clergy. But when Donovan checked with Dorsey about whether he wished to leave St. Peter's, the black priest indicated his desire to remain at the parish. Donovan informed Morris of Dorsey's preference, expressed his confidence that the "regrettable problem" between Dorsey and the sisters "can be arranged satisfactorily," and left the priest in place.[26]

Dorsey's illness in July, 1907, however, began a chain of events that resulted in his removal from St. Peter's. Suffering from chronic appendicitis, which apparently had plagued him for years, he traveled to Mercy Hospital in Chicago for an operation. His distrust of southern doctors and institutions was apparent when he explained to Donovan, "They wanted to butcher me in Pine Bluff but I politely refused." Dorsey assured Donovan that he would return to Pine Bluff in approximately three weeks, since the doctors promised that all his stomach problems would cease as a result of the operation. He also told Donovan that he had asked Lucey to look after the church in his absence and that no replacement for him was needed, because so few attended the church after the school closed for the summer.[27]

26. John T. Murphy to Archbishop Alexandre Le Roy, May 25, 1907, copy in 2C-07-8, SPAUSA; Bishop John B. Morris to Thomas Donovan, July 20, 1907, in 26-B-31, Thomas Donovan to Bishop John B. Morris, July 25, 1907, copy in 26-B-32, both in JFA.

27. John H. Dorsey to Thomas Donovan, July 18, 1907, in 25-P-4, JFA.

Two days later, Donovan received a letter from Bishop Morris expressing surprise that Donovan had not yet removed Dorsey from Pine Bluff and insisting that if he did not, the Sisters of the Holy Family, with whom Dorsey was again feuding, would not return to the Colored Industrial Institute. Dorsey remained a source of division within the community of sisters in Pine Bluff. Sister Regina, the local superior, and Sister Colombe both opposed Dorsey, whereas four other sisters supported him. According to one parishioner, Sisters Regina and Colombe, "Creole ladies from head to toe," disliked "real colored people" and wanted Dorsey removed so that they could have a white priest. The situation had reportedly become so polarized that one of the sisters walked out of church every time Dorsey gave a sermon. Sister Regina, moreover, refused to allow two of the sisters to attend to Dorsey when he became ill with typhoid fever. The hostility between Dorsey and some of the sisters, in addition to Dorsey's ill health, adversely affected the parish, which failed to record a single baptism or First Holy Communion in 1907.[28] Morris viewed Dorsey as the culprit in the conflict.

On the heels of Morris' letter, Donovan also received one from Lucey. The monsignor accused Dorsey of leaving for Chicago without securing a priest to look after his parish or informing Lucey or Morris of his departure. Lucey complained that Dorsey failed to show proper respect to the bishop and warned that Morris would no longer tolerate "the way that Fr. Dorsey has of leaving without his permission in the independent manner that he does." Lucey closed his letter with a telling observation: "Fr. Dorsey is about like colored people generally, he needs someone to be over him if any work is to be done."[29]

Donovan bowed to the pressure and on August 5, 1907, notified the still hospitalized Dorsey that he should report in mid-August to St. Peter Claver Church in San Antonio, Texas, to take up his new duties as the assistant to Lambert Welbers. Hoping for no difficulties, Donovan assured Bishop John Anthony Forest that Dorsey would do well in his diocese. He suggested, however, that in order

28. Bishop John B. Morris to Thomas Donovan, July 20, 1907, in 26-B-31, Adaline Robinson to Thomas Donovan, August 19, 1907, in 25-P-13, both in JFA; interview of Sr. Audrey Marie Detiege, S.S.F., by Stephen J. Ochs, December 22, 1983.

29. J. M. Lucey to Thomas Donovan, August 1, 1907, in 26-B-8, JFA.

to avoid offending the white sisters at the school, the bishop might appoint Welbers, the white Josephite, as their confessor.[30]

Dorsey exploded at the news of his transfer, claiming that Donovan's action threw a damper over his whole life. He flatly refused to go to San Antonio and declared himself tired of the constant hounding he had endured. "From . . . my ordination till the present," he wrote, "my life has been one heavy cross." He demanded to be allowed to remain in Pine Bluff until after Christmas and warned, "If I am to be dogged about, I prefer to leave the priesthood out of my life. . . . Change me and I do not care for the consequences." Donovan, nevertheless, insisted that Dorsey report to San Antonio by August 18.[31]

The vicar general of the diocese of San Antonio confounded Donovan's plans, however, by wiring Dorsey and telling him not to come to San Antonio. "Now this is another awful situation. Another insult offered me," a miserable Dorsey complained to Donovan. The situation so upset him that his doctor ordered him to remain in the hospital for an additional week. Dorsey chided Donovan for failing to protect his priests, for sacrificing them unjustly, and for having neglected to consult sufficiently with Bishop Forest prior to assigning him to San Antonio. "I have been kicked about enough!" Dorsey cried. "I will not be the victim."[32]

An embarrassed Donovan, citing Dorsey's recent attack of appendicitis, lamely suggested Epiphany Apostolic College to Dorsey as a less rigorous assignment than parish work. Perhaps Donovan hoped that putting Dorsey into a teaching position like the Josephites did with Uncles would eliminate the disconcerting problem of trying to place him in a diocese. Dorsey, however, insisted on Pine Bluff or nothing. Assuring Donovan that he considered him a friend and did not wish to impugn his motives, he yet observed, "The men in the priesthood and even the bishops are not what people think they are. Fr. Slattery has written the truth." Dorsey said he would leave the hospital in a few days but did not know what he would do. "I don't want to give scandal," he assured Donovan but then added,

30. Thomas Donovan to John H. Dorsey, August 5, 1907, in 27-H-39, Thomas Donovan to Joseph Waering, August 6, 1907, in 26-C-45, Thomas Donovan to Bishop John Anthony Forest, August 6, 1907, in 25-R-9, copies of all in JFA.

31. John H. Dorsey to Thomas Donovan, August 7, 1907, in 25-P-7, Thomas Donovan to John H. Dorsey, August 9, 1907, in 27-H-40, both in JFA.

32. John H. Dorsey to Thomas Donovan, August 7, 1907, in 25-P-7, August 13, 1907, in 25-P-8, both in JFA.

"If there be scandal, the fault will not be mine." Donovan finally acquiesced to the black priest's demand and consented to his return to Pine Bluff, telling Bishop Morris that manpower shortages necessitated Dorsey's return until after ordinations. By the end of August, Dorsey was back at St. Peter's, apparently having won his battle.[33]

Morris reacted with pique at Dorsey's return. "You are aware," he lectured Donovan, "that he is, has been, and will be, a failure at Pine Bluff." The bishop repeated his desire for Dorsey's removal on the grounds of constant friction between Dorsey and the sisters, an average attendance of only twelve to fourteen persons for Sunday mass, and the priest's absences from the diocese without permission. Morris told Donovan that he would not accept Dorsey's assignment without a protest and warned, "You must not think my diocese a dumping ground for your incapable missionaries."[34]

Within a week, Morris and Lucey raised another charge, more serious but very familiar, in their campaign to rid themselves of Dorsey. Writing on behalf of the bishop, Lucey accused Dorsey of illicit sexual relations with Adaline Robinson, a woman he described as a public school teacher, a recent convert, and a morphine addict. Lucey contended that Dorsey's affair with the woman had scandalized parishioners and accounted for the small attendance at Sunday mass. He further claimed that, according to the "unimpeachable testimony" of Dr. G. W. Bell and a Mrs. Perry (allegedly Robinson's sister), Adaline Robinson had frequently spent the night at Dorsey's rectory, had been thrown out of the Perry home by Mr. Perry when she refused to stop seeing Dorsey, had attempted suicide when confronted by her sister about the affair, and had revealed, in the delirium following her suicide attempt, that Dorsey had impregnated her and that she had subsequently had an abortion. Lucey also cited Mother Austin's fears about Dorsey's supposed criminal relations with some of the sisters at the Colored Industrial Institute, which had led her to replace the whole community. For good measure, he threw in charges about dereliction of duty, unexcused absences, and leaving "the Blessed Sacrament for

33. Thomas Donovan to John H. Dorsey, August 13, 1907, in 25-P-10, John H. Dorsey to Thomas Donovan, August 18, 1907, in 25-P-11, Thomas Donovan to Bishop John B. Morris, August 19, 1907, copy in 26-B-35, John H. Dorsey to Thomas Donovan, August 22, 1907, in 25-P-14, all in JFA.

34. Bishop John B. Morris to Thomas Donovan, August 31, 1907, in 26-B-36, JFA.

nearly a month with an irregular [altar] light."[35] Lucey did not explain why he had waited so long to act on the alleged Dorsey-Robinson affair, rumors of which reputedly had circulated for over a year, or why he had failed to mention it to Donovan in their earlier exchanges about Dorsey's tenure.

In a meeting with Morris and Lucey, Dorsey denied the allegations. Lucey insisted on the truth of the charges, though he admitted that he did not care to go into a detailed investigation of them. The bishop and vicar general agreed to allow Dorsey to remain at St. Peter's for thirty days because of insurance problems if they left the church unattended. Morris, however, decided to withhold the parish's share of money from the Negro and Indian collection until after Dorsey's departure. The mother general of the Holy Family sisters reported that she had replaced the faction at Pine Bluff supporting Dorsey and therefore had no objection to Dorsey's remaining for another month. (The Sisters of the Holy Family themselves would only stay in Pine Bluff for three more years; in 1910, at Lucey's insistence, they left the Colored Industrial Institute, for its attendance had fallen to less than fifty.)[36]

Dorsey explained his version of events in a letter to Donovan. He claimed that the main reason for his removal lay in Morris' opposition to black priests in his diocese. Dorsey quoted the bishop as saying during their interview that the time was not ripe for black priests and would not be for fifty years. He maintained that the rumors about Adaline Robinson had originated with one who hoped to secure her teaching position, which paid forty dollars per month. Robinson's brother-in-law Mr. Perry, a "narrow bigoted Baptist" in Dorsey's words, persecuted her when she became a Catholic and originated several of the charges against her. Dorsey reminded Donovan that the superior had known about Robinson preparing his meals because Lucey would not permit the sisters to do so. Dorsey also admitted that, because the sisters refused to nurse him, Robinson had attended him when he suffered from typhoid, occasionally even spending the night in the rectory. He added, however, that two teenage boys, one of whom was nineteen, had always been present. Dorsey attributed Dr. Bell's accusations about Robinson's purported dalliances with him to a personal vendetta. Bell had

35. J. M. Lucey to Thomas Donovan, September 6, 1907, in 25-P-14, JFA; Lucey, "The Matter of J. H. Dorsey," in Morris Papers.

36. J. M. Lucey to Thomas Donovan, September 16, 1907, in 25-P-17, JFA; J. M. Lucey to Mother Elizabeth, October 18, 1910, in ASHF.

tried, according to Dorsey, to overcharge the priest for drugs during his bout with typhoid and had himself made immoral advances to Robinson, which she rebuffed. In retaliation, Bell had manufactured his charges against the two. "Once again," Dorsey concluded, "I am the victim of southern prejudice. . . . Where are we drifting?"

In order to avoid the appearance of guilt, Dorsey insisted on staying at Pine Bluff until Christmas. He invited Donovan to come down to investigate matters for himself and assured the superior of his own willingness to stand trial in any ecclesiastical or civil court. In his discouragement, Dorsey then unwittingly made a recommendation that would become unofficial Josephite policy: "If colored priests must forever suffer and be outcasts, better not ordain them, or if you ordain them, get them places in northern cities." He quickly recovered his spirits, however, and urged a fight. While admitting that he would eventually have to acquiesce in a transfer, he nevertheless advised Donovan to take a different attitude: "A good public fight would help the cause immensely. One must not live supinely on our backs. If we do we shall never gain anything. What is worth having is worth fighting for."[37]

Leading black citizens of Pine Bluff rallied to Dorsey's defense. In October, 1907, they drew up a petition of support for Dorsey and sent it to Lucey. They also addressed a copy to Donovan, urging him to keep Dorsey at Pine Bluff for the good of the community. The petition included the names of two of the directors of the Colored Industrial Institute, the former and current principals of the black normal college, every black physician except for Dr. Bell, five black attorneys, the black teachers in all of the city's public schools, and numerous black Protestant ministers—forty-six names in all. The petition praised Dorsey's intelligence, high moral character, and labors for his people. It also enraged Lucey, who charged that Dorsey had encouraged the black people of Pine Bluff, had taken advantage of their ignorance, and had increased the danger that the scandal would become public, a curious charge given his earlier contention that public knowledge of the affair had already caused a decline in church attendance at St. Peter's. Accusing Donovan and Dorsey of dilatory tactics, Lucey denied Donovan's request to extend Dorsey's faculties past October 16, 1907. Faced with the inevitable, Donovan transferred Dorsey back to St. Joseph's College for Negro Catechists in Montgomery. Then, perhaps with a touch

---

37. John H. Dorsey to Thomas Donovan, September 16, 1907, in 25-P-18, JFA.

of perverseness, he informed Morris that he intended to replace Dorsey with Joseph Anciaux. Not surprisingly, Morris telegraphed that he refused to accept the outspoken Anciaux "for reasons known to myself."[38]

Justin McCarthy, acting on behalf of Donovan, who had become ill and would die the following January, then assigned William Murphy to Pine Bluff. The new pastor, after talking with Dorsey, St. Peter's parishioners, and Lucey, concluded that "Dorsey's crime was a black skin" and attributed the trouble at Pine Bluff to Lucey's "evil, suspicious mind." Murphy advised McCarthy to give up the mission in Pine Bluff, reasoning that in light of the treatment accorded to Dorsey and Anciaux "it is now high time that we . . . take an independent stand."[39] Despite Murphy's advice, the Josephites remained at St. Peter's until 1928.

The beleaguered Josephite administrators had few options available for making a stand against the bishops. Ultimately, a bishop could refuse faculties to any priest in his diocese, thus forcing his removal. The society could retaliate against such behavior by closing its missions in the offending bishop's diocese. Such a move, however, would result in abandoning blacks to the care of local churches, which often neglected or discriminated against them. Josephite administrators, still attempting to stabilize their shaky community and technically subject, as a diocesan institute, to the archbishop of Baltimore, had little confidence in appeals to a distant and slow-moving Holy See. As if to illustrate Josephite vulnerability to episcopal prerogative, Bishop Allen of Mobile advised Donovan that he did not favor Dorsey's return to Montgomery, "because of certain local circumstances." Instead of reporting directly to Montgomery, therefore, Dorsey went on leave for two months. Although he finally consented to grant faculties to Dorsey, Allen advised the Josephites not to accept any black candidates unless they could show that their families had been Catholics for three

38. John Albert to Bishop John B. Morris, January 24, 1915, in Morris Papers; L. R. Jones et al., petition to Thomas Donovan, October 2, 1907, in 25-P-20, J. M. Lucey to Thomas Donovan, October 3, 1907, in 25-P-21, Thomas Donovan to John H. Dorsey, October 10, 1907, copy in 25-P-22, Bishop John B. Morris to Thomas Donovan, October 12, 1907 (telegram), in 25-N-11, all in JFA.

39. William Murphy to Thomas Donovan, October 21, 1907, in 26-B-29, William Murphy to Justin McCarthy, November 27, 1907, in 27-N-34, both in JFA.

generations.[40] Applying such criteria to whites would have disqualified from the priesthood such luminaries as James Roosevelt Bayley, archbishop of Baltimore from 1872 to 1877, and John Cardinal Newman of England.

Further complicating Josephite relations with bishops, the volatile Joseph Anciaux, on learning of Morris' refusal to approve his appointment to Pine Bluff, again took up his pen and let fly a stinging letter to the bishop of Little Rock. In his patois, Anciaux called Morris the "Son of Irish immigrant . . . of a tramp of a slaveholder." He implicitly accused the bishop of heresy for objecting to holy orders for black men and charged that the bishop valued southern customs more than he did the priesthood. Anciaux, who claimed descent from "the royal blood of Orleans," invited Morris to black his boots, since according to the social rank that Morris seemed to prize, that was all the bishop was fit to do. Anciaux predicted that they would meet at the Last Judgment, when Morris and other southern bishops and priests would have to answer for the loss of millions of black souls because of their neglect.[41]

After receiving a copy of Anciaux's letter, with an accompanying protest from Morris, Archbishop Diomede Falconio, the apostolic delegate from 1902 to 1911, demanded that Donovan secure an apology from Anciaux for his "grievous insult" to the bishop. Anciaux subsequently apologized, but Louis B. Pastorelli, the increasingly influential rector of St. Joseph's Industrial School in Clayton and a trusted confidant of McCarthy, advised his friend to try to convince Anciaux to leave the Josephites and return to Belgium. Then, Pastorelli suggested to him, "notify the bishops. . . . It will be the whitest and most diplomatic feather—should you succeed—that will adorn your cap."[42] Anciaux did return to Belgium in 1908, because of ill health. However, he remained a Josephite until his death in 1931.

Dorsey, meanwhile, reported to St. Joseph's College for Negro

40. Bishop Edward P. Allen to Thomas Donovan, October 22, 1907, in 25-N-1, Thomas Donovan to M. H. Wiltzius Co., November 26, 1907, copy in 32-C-36, both in JFA.

41. Joseph Anciaux to Bishop John B. Morris, November 12, 1907, in 25-C-12, JFA.

42. Archbishop Diomede Falconio to Thomas Donovan, November 28, 1907, in 25-N-10, Joseph Anciaux to Justin McCarthy, December 11, 1907, in 27-E-12a, Louis B. Pastorelli to Justin McCarthy, May 5, 1908, in 26-M-22, all in JFA.

Catechists in December, 1907, assuming charge of the boys as chief prefect and visiting the Catholic students at nearby Tuskegee Institute every two weeks. Jeremiah McNamara, the rector of St. Joseph's, expressed complete satisfaction with Dorsey's work. Nevertheless, the black priest's trials continued. Probably in deference to the bishop's fears about local conditions, McNamara initially assigned mission work in the city of Montgomery itself to the Reverend Daniel J. Rice instead of to Dorsey, who had requested it. In addition, Walter A. Yates, a Josephite priest prone to gossip who was stationed at the college, criticized Dorsey to McCarthy, implying that Dorsey, who possessed a strong temper, beat students. Yates also complained that Dorsey failed to recite his office, talked modernism at the supper table, and mysteriously locked himself in his room because of exhaustion. Dorsey's tribulations, however, appeared to ease in March, 1908, when McNamara decided to use him for missions in Montgomery. The rector reported that Bishop Allen appeared pleased by the opening night of one of Dorsey's two-week missions in Montgomery; he speculated that the bishop had perhaps changed his mind about Dorsey.[43]

In the wake of Dorsey's ordeal with southern bishops and in the midst of mounting racial tensions in Baltimore and throughout much of the state of Maryland, a new Josephite superior general retrenched further on the issue of black priests, informally deciding to accept almost no new black students into Epiphany Apostolic College. Justin McCarthy, the fifty-year-old former president of St. Joseph's Seminary and the man ultimately responsible for the more restrictive Josephite policy toward black applicants, was elected as the third Josephite superior general in March, 1908, following the death of Thomas Donovan. About McCarthy, an acid-tongued critic observed, "He belongs to that rather large class of numbskulls who plum themselves on their stupidity and who measure a man's godliness as if it were mathematically proportionate to his intellectual vacuity." Although this critic probably judged him too severely, McCarthy did not distinguish himself either as a leader or as an administrator during the ten years that he served as superior general. A thin, sad-eyed, amiable man, McCarthy preferred working on the farm or in his workshop to running St. Joseph's Society and

43. Jeremiah McNamara to Justin McCarthy, January 17, 1908, in 26-K-34, January 29, 1908, in 26-K-33, Walter Yates to Justin McCarthy, January 27, 1908, in 27-T-15, Jeremiah McNamara to Justin McCarthy, March 16, 1908, in 26-K-37, November 10, 1908, in 26-K-43, all in JFA.

was ill-suited to deal with the explosive issue of black priests. The priests themselves were aware of his shortcomings, as is apparent in a report from Pastorelli to McCarthy in which he bluntly reported that the "men on the missions say that they wished the Superior manifested more interest in the missions and less on the farm."[44] McCarthy inherited a society consisting of forty-nine priests, known for their individualism and described by one Josephite wag as "an organized band of lawless men." Administratively, McCarthy did nothing to curb the rampant individualism that at times bordered on insubordination; instead, he adopted a policy of well-intentioned benign neglect that continued the period of drift and indecision for St. Joseph's Society.

Just as McCarthy assumed his new post, a wave of negrophobia struck the state of Maryland, adding to the difficulties of conducting integrated seminaries. Democrats pushed for a state constitutional amendment to disfranchise blacks, a move publicly condemned by Cardinal Gibbons. Although the disfranchisement amendment failed in 1909, the campaign surrounding it led to the passage of additional jim-crow legislation in 1908 and also to a sharp increase in informal segregation of the races. When white Epiphany College students took walks through Druid Hill Park with John C. Teureaud, one of their few remaining black classmates, white youngsters taunted them with cries of "Nigger lovers." Such experiences took an emotional toll on both blacks and whites at the college and seminary. The Baltimore *Afro-American* reported that a wave of segregation and segregationist sentiment had engulfed the city of Baltimore. It culminated in 1911 with the passage of a city ordinance (later declared unconstitutional by the Supreme Court) mandating residential segregation of the races.[45] Even though it exempted areas already racially mixed, the law did not provide a climate conducive to integrated seminary training, especially since Josephite students also attended classes at St. Mary's Seminary.

In light of Dorsey's ordeal and the hostile atmosphere in both

44. Joseph M. Kellogg to Edward R. Dyer, March 2, 1904, in RG 39, Box 1, SAB; Louis B. Pastorelli, report to Justin McCarthy on missions east of the Mississippi, September, 1916, in 33-B, JFA.

45. Margaret Law Calcott, *The Negro in Maryland Politics, 1870–1912* (Baltimore, 1969), 129–36; John T. Ellis, *James Cardinal Gibbons, 1834–1921* (2 vols.; Milwaukee, 1952), II, 400–401; interviews of Vincent D. Warren, S.S.J., by Peter E. Hogan, S.S.J., 1965 (Typescript in JFA), 45–46; Calcott, *The Negro in Maryland Politics,* 137.

church and society, Justin McCarthy and his advisors informally decided against accepting any more black candidates for the Josephites. In the summer of 1908, McCarthy refused to admit Joseph A. John to Epiphany Apostolic College. On hearing this news, Jeremiah McNamara wrote him, "If you intend to take in any more of them, I think he is one of the best you will find." McNamara praised John's "remarkably fine character" and his fine, old, Catholic family in Grenada, British West Indies, a family that boasted two aunts and a sister who had all become nuns. A few weeks later, McNamara assured McCarthy that he did not blame his superior for rejecting John since McCarthy had to deal with the bishops and could not dictate to them. He nevertheless emphasized once again the need for a black clergy and insisted that he knew at least five morally upright and gifted black students who possessed God-given vocations. McNamara warned that God would hold bishops and priests accountable for their failure to allow blacks to follow their vocations. "Of course," he lamented, "we few Josephites can do nothing, only our little best."[46]

Reports about the fate of Joseph John and other unsuccessful black applicants for the Josephites upset black Catholics in Baltimore. Led by Father Dorsey's sister-in-law, Mary Dorsey, some black Catholic women formed a society for the support of black students at Epiphany College and St. Joseph's Seminary. On July 28, 1908, the group communicated to McCarthy its alarm about the rejection of black applicants to both institutions for no apparent reason. Father Dorsey himself complained publicly in the pages of the *Freeman's Journal* about the small number of black Catholic priests, and the following year Charles Marcellus Dorsey, Father Dorsey's outspoken, fiery younger brother, who operated a printing business in Baltimore, founded the newspaper *Colored Catholic* to fight against discrimination in the Catholic church and to promote the ordination of blacks to the priesthood.[47]

Buoyed by support from Baltimore's black Catholic community, Joseph John persisted in his efforts to gain admission to a seminary.

46. Jeremiah McNamara to Justin McCarthy, July 5, 1908, in 26-K-40, July 28, 1908, in 26-K-41, both in JFA.

47. Rebecca Parker and Mary Dorsey to Justin McCarthy, July 28, 1908, in 28-B-14, A. P. Doyle to Justin McCarthy, July 28, 1908, in 28-B-15, both in JFA; Penelope L. Bullock, *Afro-American Periodical Press, 1838–1909* (Baton Rouge, 1981), 164.

The major seminary of the Society of African Missions in Canada indicated a willingness to accept him on completion of his classical and philosophical studies. John appealed for help to Mother Katharine Drexel, who advised him to reapply to McCarthy. McCarthy relented and agreed to allow John to enter Epiphany College, but only on the condition that he obtain a written guarantee from the Dominicans, with whom he resided and for whom he worked as a gardener, that they would ordain him after his studies at the college. The Dominicans agreed, and in September, 1908, Joseph John joined Teureaud, the only other black student at Epiphany Apostolic College; he had entered in September, 1907, just as the Dorsey crisis was reaching its climax. George Knight was the sole black candidate at St. Joseph's Seminary.[48]

The Josephite dilemma alarmed the Holy Ghost Fathers, who in 1905 had opened an integrated preparatory seminary in Cornwells, Pennsylvania, to educate not only aspirants for their congregation but also those who might prefer to join the secular clergy or other communities. In 1907 in France, the Spiritans had ordained Joseph C. Burgess, a black native of Washington, D.C., and a former student at Epiphany College, to the priesthood. Dorsey's situation, however, led the Spiritans to reappraise their policy. On July 2, 1908, the Spiritan American provincial council met to discuss the admission of black candidates to their junior seminary and unanimously agreed that prudence dictated against accepting any more of them. Calling the situation unfortunate, the council nevertheless concluded that prejudice in the South rendered the use of black priests there practically impossible and noted that as a result of sad experiences in that region, the Josephites no longer accepted black candidates. John Murphy, the Holy Ghost provincial, transmitted the observations of the council to the generalate, or headquarters, in France. The Holy Ghost Fathers in the United States thus made the Josephite policy their own. In 1910, the same year that witnessed the ordination of Stephen L. Theobald, a black diocesan priest, for the racially liberal archdiocese of St. Paul, Murphy considered a foreign assignment for Burgess, his lone Afro-American priest, because of difficulty in finding him a position in the United

48. Joseph John to Justin McCarthy, August 28, 1908, in 24-N-28, Justin McCarthy to Joseph John, September 4, 1908, copy in 24-N-29, Joseph John to Justin McCarthy, September 14, 1908, in 24-N-30, EAC Student file, 1890–1914, pp. 261, 276, 526, all in JFA.

States. (Burgess, however, remained in the United States except for a brief stint in Haiti in 1919.)[49] Murphy, no doubt, hoped to protect Burgess from the fate that had befallen John Plantevigne, the third black Josephite priest, who had been ordained in 1907.

Plantevigne, a Catholic colored Creole, was born on October 22, 1871, on a small farm near Chenel, Louisiana, in Pointe Coupee Parish, about one hundred miles upriver from New Orleans, near the Mississippi border. After attending public schools and working on a farm for six years, John and his brother Albert enrolled at Straight University in New Orleans. Albert remained at Straight, became a Congregational minister, and in 1901 returned to the vicinity of New Roads, Louisiana, about twelve miles from his birthplace, to open a church and to conduct a school for blacks. John, encouraged by the attitudes of Archbishop Janssens and Father Slattery and undeterred by his Protestant friends at Straight who warned him that the white Catholic clergy would place insurmountable obstacles in his path, entered Epiphany Apostolic College on August 24, 1898. He graduated to St. Joseph's Seminary in 1901.[50]

A stocky, powerfully built man with a round, chubby face, large, deep-set eyes, and tight black hair parted on the left side, Plantevigne impressed teachers, fellow students, and visitors with his maturity, intelligence, and piety. One Josephite described him as the "perfect gentleman." Monsignor John Burke spoke of him as a thoughtful, informed, observant man, "still harping on the grievances of the colored Catholics in the South, but with reason." Plantevigne had already experienced the racism of the South in a deeply personal way. While he was in the seminary, he received word that his brother, who had regularly visited him in Baltimore and who had opened a high school for blacks in New Roads despite white opposition, had been ambushed by two white gunmen, who shot off the back of his head and left his body lying in the road to terrorize blacks in the vicinity.[51]

49. Koren, *Serpent and Dove*, 183–84, 186–89; Albert S. Foley, S.J., *God's Men of Color: The Colored Catholic Priests of the United States, 1854–1954* (1955; rpr. New York, 1969), 97.

50. Foley, *God's Men*, 82–83; EAC Student Journal, 1890–1914, p. 419, in JFA; John Plantevigne to Archbishop James H. Blenk, March 23, 1909, copy in Archives of the Archdiocese of New Orleans (AANO) file, JFA.

51. Foley, *God's Men*, 83; Warren interviews, 49; Burke Diary, August 20, 1907; EAC Student Journal, 1890–1914, p. 231, in JFA; Burke Diary, May 15, 1907; Foley, *God's Men*, 83.

Deeply shaken by the tragedy, Plantevigne nevertheless persevered in his studies and was ordained, along with his white classmate, John Albert, on September 21, 1907, just at the height of the Dorsey imbroglio in Pine Bluff. As if to illustrate the growing isolation of the few black priests in the Catholic church, Plantevigne and Albert received holy orders in the chapel of St. Joseph's Seminary instead of at the cathedral with the other ordinandi from the archdiocese. The ordaining prelate, moreover, was Bishop Alfred Curtis of Wilmington rather than Cardinal Gibbons, who had ordained the first two black Josephites. Monsignor John Burke, who had come from New York to preach at Plantevigne's first mass at St. Francis Xavier Parish in Baltimore, noted the changed atmosphere in his diary: "No priests outside 'Josephites' attended the Mass. Strange!"[52]

Ignoring the warnings of friends and relatives that he stay away for his own safety, Plantevigne set off for his home parish in Chenel. He stopped in New Orleans and offered mass at St. Katherine's Church, the first black church in that city; he then entrained for Chenel. The Reverend Louis Savouré, his old pastor who had regularly sent him funds for seminary expenses but who had also introduced rigid segregation into the parish church, greeted him. Plantevigne celebrated mass in the middle of the week in an attempt to avoid publicity, but the occasion still attracted many whites, including three state legislators. He did not say mass at New Roads, nor did he attend a benefit given by friends in the town, but he did visit and bless his brother's simple grave on the grounds of the abandoned school. On his way back to Baltimore, Plantevigne stopped once again in New Orleans, where the delighted parishioners of St. Katherine's asked him to remain as their pastor.[53]

In the autumn of 1907, Plantevigne and John Albert enrolled at the Apostolic Mission House in Washington, D.C., where the Paulist fathers trained priests to conduct parish missions. They both studied pastoral homiletics and methods of evangelization. During the fall semester, they concentrated on missions among Catholics and during the spring, on missions among non-Catholics, with particular emphasis on the use of the question box, a popular technique that afforded non-Catholics the opportunity to obtain an-

52. Burke Diary, September 22, 1907.
53. Burke Diary, May 15, August 22, 1907; Foley, God's Men, 84; Pierre LeBeau to Thomas Donovan, October 8, 1907, in 26-B-4, JFA.

swers to questions they had about the Catholic church. In February, 1908, under the watchful eye of Alexander Doyle, one of the directors of the mission house, Plantevigne and Albert conducted a successful mission at St. Barnabas Church in Baltimore, netting 50 converts and bringing many lapsed Catholics back into the fold.[54]

McCarthy decided that Plantevigne and Albert should form a mission band and give missions near Baltimore in the fall of 1908. If they met no opposition, the two would travel down to Scranton (later renamed Pascagoula), Mississippi, despite McCarthy's fears that Plantevigne's color might create difficulties for the two priests that far south. Using St. Peter the Apostle Parish in Scranton as a headquarters, they would conduct missions "in any place they could procure." They would stay at a site from three to eight weeks, encourage the construction of a mission church, and then either arrange to have another priest follow up to care for the converts or return themselves to make sure converts did not fall away after the initial fervor of the mission had ebbed.[55]

During the summer of 1908, while he prepared to move south on the mission band, Plantevigne threw himself into a project he called "the great wish of my life": a Catholic school for the black children of his hometown, Chenel. The black people of the town had selected the site and raised the money to buy the land for the school. Plantevigne asked Mother Katharine Drexel to provide the funds necessary for the school building and the teacher's salary. He assured both her and McCarthy that Pierre LeBeau, residing in Palmetto, about a hundred miles away, could watch over the school and provide any needed assistance. Plantevigne also wrote to Archbishop James H. Blenk of New Orleans for permission to build the school, for the archdiocese of New Orleans required that the archbishop have title to all church property. Plantevigne evidently expected the archbishop's approval of the project.[56]

54. EAC Student file, 1890–1914, pp. 261, 276, 526, in JFA; notes on John Plantevigne, in Albert S. Foley Papers, JFA; Thomas Donovan to M. H. Wiltzius Co., November 5, 1907, copy in 32-C-35, JFA; Burke Diary, May 17, 1907; "The Mission at St. Barnabas Church," *Colored Harvest*, V (June, 1908), 115–17; Foley, *God's Men*, 85.

55. Justin McCarthy to Mother Katharine Drexel, March 20, 1908, in SBSA; John Plantevigne to Justin McCarthy, September 21, 1908, in 26-M-15, M. M. James to Justin McCarthy, September 26, 1908, in 26-G-52, both in JFA; Justin McCarthy to Mother Katharine Drexel, March 20, April 7, 1908, both in SBSA.

56. John Plantevigne to Mother Katharine Drexel, two letters, both dated June, 1908, in SBSA.

McCarthy explored the possibility of stationing Plantevigne at a mission among the black people of Chenel or at least somewhere in the archdiocese of New Orleans, so that he could look after the school. He doubted, however, that Blenk would consent to such an assignment, "on account of the opposition to color." McCarthy proved prescient. Father Savouré, the parish priest in Chenel, disapproving of education for blacks, allegedly convinced Blenk to deny permission for the school. Blenk expressed the hope to a disappointed Plantevigne that "later on, under more favorable circumstances," he might undertake such a project.[57]

Plantevigne received news of the archbishop's decision in the midst of a triumphant mission tour that had begun the previous October at St. Joseph's Church in Wilmington, Delaware. The Wilmington *Standard and Times* approvingly noted "the presence of Father Plantevigne, the colored missionary, who won the admiration of his auditors by his prepossessing appearance and his forceful eloquence." As he traveled south, Plantevigne continued to receive enthusiastic reviews, but he also inspired some apprehension among his fellow Josephites at the catechetical college in Montgomery, who worried about his outspokenness. Jeremiah McNamara urged McCarthy to instruct Plantevigne to "leave the discussing of Race issues to others whose usefulness will not be thereby jeopardized." Plantevigne exercised discretion in his public talks during missions, but his sensitivity to racial discrimination increased during his tour of the South because jim-crow laws sometimes prevented him from sitting with his good friend and partner, John Albert, as they moved from one mission to another.[58]

December found Albert and Plantevigne at St. Peter's in Scranton, a city the Josephites intended to use as their base for missions along the Gulf coast between Mobile, Alabama, and Bay St. Louis, Mississippi. Plantevigne's presence in Scranton elicited much comment from both blacks and whites, since most had never seen a black priest. Some, considering the possibility of a black priest so remote, wagered that Plantevigne "was not the real thing" and that the church had sent him to bluff the black folks and kidnap them

57. Justin McCarthy to Mother Katharine Drexel, September 18, November 26, 1908, both in SBSA; Archbishop James H. Blenk to John Plantevigne, January 13, 1909, copy in AANO file, JFA.

58. "Missionary Report," *Colored Harvest,* V (January, 1909), 162–63; Jeremiah McNamara to Justin McCarthy, October 9, 1908, in 26-K-42, JFA; Warren interviews, 66.

into the Catholic church. Others contended that Plantevigne, though a priest, did not possess all the powers of a white priest.[59]

From January to March, 1909, Albert and Plantevigne preached missions throughout Alabama, finishing at the Most Pure Heart of Mary Church in Mobile. Prior to the Mobile mission, Albert reported to McCarthy that he and Plantevigne had worked together admirably. He described Plantevigne as a fine missionary who "takes well wherever he goes—preaches magnificently—and is always on the job," and he assured McCarthy that "given a square deal and some encouragement . . . splendid results [from Plantevigne] are obtainable." He noted that the "spectacle of white and black priests working together" gave black people a more favorable impression of the Catholic church.

Albert also noticed, however, that colored Creoles and American blacks differed in their responses to Plantevigne. Skin color and hair texture counted heavily to both groups. Creoles prized light skin and fine, straight hair, whereas American blacks favored darker skin and tightly curled hair. Despite his Creole background, Plantevigne elicited a warm response from American blacks, especially non-Catholics in Baltimore, Richmond, Norfolk, and Chastang, Alabama, in part because his skin was darker and his hair was more woolly than that of most colored Creoles. In distinctly Creole congregations, such as Bellefontaine, Mon Louis, and Scranton, Mississippi, the lighter skinned Creoles reacted more coolly. During the mission at Mobile, nevertheless, both blacks and Creoles enthusiastically flocked to hear him. Hundreds of people, including even some whites, packed the church every night, some spilling out onto the street, leading Conrad Rebesher, the pastor, to exclaim that he had "never witnessed anything equal to this." As a result of the mission, more than 230 people returned to the sacraments and 30 converted to Catholicism. As the exhausted missionaries returned to Scranton from Mobile, they made plans for a two-week mission, scheduled to begin on March 28, that they would preach for Pierre LeBeau to help launch St. Dominic's, the first Josephite parish in New Orleans. John Plantevigne looked forward to the mission as a kind of homecoming.[60]

59. John Albert, "Mission Work in the Gulf States," *Colored Harvest*, V (March, 1909), 178.

60. John Albert to Justin McCarthy, March 8, 1909, in 28-A-1, March 29, 1909, in 28-K-1, Conrad Rebesher to Justin McCarthy, March 25, 1909, in 28-R-2, all in JFA; Foley, *God's Men*, 86; John Albert to Justin McCarthy,

Arriving back in Scranton, Plantevigne found a letter from Arch-bishop Blenk that contained, in Plantevigne's words, "a thunder-bolt which I never expected." Afraid that the black priest's presence in New Orleans would provoke a negative reaction from whites, Blenk informed Plantevigne that he would not allow him to con-duct the scheduled mission at St. Dominic's. "Death would have been more welcome to me than such news," a shocked and de-spondent Plantevigne wrote to the archbishop. He cited the success of his previous missions and the cordial receptions he had received from bishops, priests, and black and white laymen. "Surely," he im-plored, "New Orleans, a city where there are so many Catholics ought not be the exception." He warned Blenk that because his friends in New Orleans already expected him, news of the arch-bishop's refusal would do untold harm to the Catholic church among blacks. He pleaded for at least a trial mission in the city and begged Blenk to relieve him from "this agony of spirit."[61]

As in Dorsey's case, so too in Plantevigne's, bishops' rejections not only wreaked havoc in the private lives of black Josephites but also strained their relationships with Josephite superiors general, whom the priests blamed for failing to protect them. On learning from John Albert that McCarthy had expected Blenk's decision, for example, Plantevigne angrily reproached his superior general for having failed to warn him about "this awful blow." He described his life as a "perfect wreck" and demanded that McCarthy immediately relieve him from the mission band and station him in a parish, where he could work alone. Plantevigne suggested either Florida, "where the bishop has no objection to me," or Chastang, where the congregations had been so responsive to him.[62]

In a letter dated March 31, 1909, Blenk wrote Plantevigne that the priest had put "an entirely wrong construction" on the arch-bishop's motives for "advising" him to refrain from taking part in the mission at New Orleans. Blenk denied bearing any ill will to-ward Plantevigne or "the colored race" and explained that he did not want to expose himself and the work already in hand to any risk

[February, 1909?], in 26-D-12, Pierre LeBeau to Justin McCarthy, February 28, 1909, in 28-N-17, March 12, 1909, in 28-N-19, John Plantevigne to Archbishop James H. Blenk, March 23, 1909, copy in AANO file, all in JFA.

61. John Plantevigne to Justin McCarthy, March 29, 1909, in 28-P-27, John Plantevigne to Archbishop James H. Blenk, March 23, 1909, copy in AANO file, both in JFA.

62. John Plantevigne to Justin McCarthy, March 29, 1909, in 28-P-27, JFA.

"that might be run by over-zeal or any action that might stir up prejudice and suspicions calculated to endanger the real progress that I have, just as much at heart as you have." Blenk expressed confidence that in the not-too-distant future, Plantevigne would be able to do excellent work in the archdiocese. He urged Christian resignation and a spirit of humble obedience until then. John Albert characterized Blenk's letter as "very diplomatic," that is, meaning "much or nothing" and quite useful in his favor should the missionary appeal to the apostolic delegate.[63]

Contrary to Blenk's urging, Plantevigne refused to resign himself to the archbishop's decision. Informing McCarthy that he meant "to see this thing through," he appealed his case to Archbishop Falconio, who, as the apostolic delegate, wielded influence but had no direct power over the American hierarchy. In addition, Plantevigne's friends in New Orleans threatened to expose Blenk's actions in the public press. On April 13, 1909, Plantevigne personally responded to Blenk's letter of March 31. After reviewing his previous mission successes, he pointed out to the archbishop that his earlier visits to New Orleans had resulted in no unpleasantness and had instead occasioned much favorable comment; he had even said mass without incident before a mixed congregation in Pointe Coupee, "where the devil's own imps are." He assured Blenk that he did not seek social equality with whites but explained that "to be put off, under any pretense, from working for my own people is the thing that is tearing my very vitals away."[64]

Plantevigne also feared that his rejection by Blenk would give impetus to the growing tendency of the Josephites to refuse admission to any more black students at Epiphany College or St. Joseph's Seminary. He argued vigorously for continued acceptance of black candidates, reasoning that "if there is only one bishop who will take them there is already room enough for more than you will ordain in the next twenty years, so there is no reason to worry about that." He exhorted McCarthy to have enough backbone "to hold our ground and stand for the right."[65]

When Falconio requested information from McCarthy about

63. Archbishop James H. Blenk to John Plantevigne, March 31, 1909, copy in AANO file, John Albert to Justin McCarthy, April, 1909, in 28-K-3, both in JFA.
64. John Plantevigne to Justin McCarthy, April 1, 1909, in 27-R-1, April 2, 1909, in 28-P-8, John Plantevigne to Archbishop James H. Blenk, April 13, 1909, copy in AANO file, all in JFA.
65. John Plantevigne to Justin McCarthy, April 2, 1909, in 28-P-8, JFA.

Plantevigne's charges that Blenk had refused him because of his race, the Josephite superior found himself in a difficult position. He wanted to support Plantevigne, yet he also wished to avoid alienating Blenk, whose backing and approval he would need if he hoped to open more Josephite parishes in New Orleans, with its large population of black and Creole Catholics. McCarthy was tactful, but he clearly sided with his own priest. He gave the delegate a brief description of Plantevigne's good work on the mission band and a copy of Blenk's letter of March 31 to Plantevigne, which, he observed, "purports to be an answer." He added, "This letter speaks for itself. All we can say is, that we presume his Grace the Archbishop had some good reason for his action."[66] McCarthy obviously intended to cast doubt on the archbishop's explanation. It is not clear what additional steps, if any, the apostolic delegate took in the matter. Plantevigne, though, did not go to New Orleans; it appeared that he, and by extension other black priests and their religious congregations, could not rely on the Holy See for protection against bishops in the South. They stood alone.

News of Blenk's treatment of Plantevigne aroused black Catholics along the Gulf coast. The Reverend Samuel J. Kelly in Scranton described the "crash at New Orleans" as "the last straw to break the camel's back" and indicated it had "caused hell around here." He estimated it would take two generations to restore respect for church authority. John Albert termed the incident "an unfortunate occurrence" and feared that when it became widely known, it would lead to increased defections from the church. Albert sadly noted, "The tragedy of the Negro priest is no joke. He needs all our sympathy and fraternal consideration." Kelly and Albert proceeded to New Orleans, attempting to "pull off the mission . . . before the stink comes." The action, however, angered Plantevigne and many of his supporters along the Gulf, who believed that the two Josephites should have made a stand against Blenk by refusing to preach the mission.[67]

McCarthy, meanwhile, scrambled to find Plantevigne an assignment. Plantevigne himself wrote Archbishop James Quigley of Chi-

66. J. A. St. Laurent to Justin McCarthy, November 3, 1909, in 28-S-2, November 18, 1909, in 28-S-3, Archbishop Diomede Falconio to Justin McCarthy, April 6, 1909, in 25-C-16, Justin McCarthy to Archbishop Diomede Falconio, April 8, 1909, copy in 25-C-17, all in JFA.

67. Sam Kelly to Justin McCarthy, April 12, 1909, in 28-N-2, John Albert to McCarthy, March 29, 1909, in 28-K-1, both in JFA.

cago, offering to take over Augustine Tolton's old mission, which had not had a black pastor since Tolton's death in 1897. Quigley informed the black priest that he preferred to continue the mission under the direction of one of his own priests. McCarthy tried but failed to convince Blenk to accept Plantevigne as pastor in the heavily Catholic, black town of Palmetto. The minutes of a meeting of McCarthy's consultors note succinctly that the proposed appointment failed "through the refusal of Archbishop Blenk to allow a Colored Priest to take up work in his diocese." [68] McCarthy considered keeping Plantevigne at St. Peter's in Scranton or sending him to Houston, but Plantevigne refused the former, and Albert advised against the latter. McCarthy then asked Bishop William J. Kenny of St. Augustine to allow Plantevigne to take charge of the new church for black Catholics in that city. Kenny replied that he "could never think of placing a colored priest," because "both white and colored Catholics would be up in arms at such a proposition." Having exhausted his other options, McCarthy then assigned Plantevigne to St. Francis Xavier Parish in Baltimore as an assistant pastor. [69]

Some parishioners of St. Peter's in Scranton erroneously believed that the Josephites had moved Plantevigne from their church because of the imminent arrival of the bishop for confirmations. In order to correct that impression, Father Kelly invited Father Dorsey to assist at the bishop's solemn mass. Kelly reported that Dorsey preached a "beautiful sermon" and that the bishop and Dorsey "sat down together like true priests in God's Church," thus helping to restore the shaken confidence of the parishioners. As Plantevigne made his way back to Baltimore, Kelly expressed relief at his departure, blaming him for "not fitting in" and accusing him of a lack of discretion for discussing with the parishioners his recent troubles. [70]

En route to his new assignment, Plantevigne continued to speak out. He accepted an invitation from Walter Elliott to address the Catholic Missionary Congress, which was meeting at the Catholic

68. Notes on Plantevigne, in Foley Papers; John Plantevigne to Justin McCarthy, April 22, 1909, in 28-P-30, CMB, April 3, 1909, both in JFA.

69. John Plantevigne to Justin McCarthy, April 22, 1909, in 28-P-30, John Albert to Justin McCarthy, April 22, 1909, in 28-K-5, both in JFA; Justin McCarthy to Bishop William Kenny, May 3, 1909, in ADSA; Bishop William Kenny to Justin McCarthy, May 8, 1909, in 25-H-8, CMB, May 3, 1909, both in JFA; Foley, God's Men, 89.

70. John Albert to Justin McCarthy, May, 1909, in 28-K-13, Sam Kelly to Justin McCarthy, June 7, 1909, in 28-N-5, May 30, 1909, in 28-N-3, all in JFA.

University of America. There, he delivered what some regarded as the strongest speech on behalf of black Catholics since Slattery's controversial 1902 sermon. Plantevigne described the resentment blacks felt toward the jim-crow system in the Catholic church, reiterated the need for black priests, urged the opening of seminaries to black Catholics, and asserted the moral and intellectual equality of blacks and whites. He condemned compromise with racism in society, which alienated blacks from the church. He declared bluntly that any white seminarian who objected to the ordination of blacks thereby revealed his lack of a priestly vocation. Northern priests at the congress applauded his speech, but some southern priests argued that Plantevigne should include a disclaimer of social equality between the races. The absence of such a disclaimer, they insisted, would ruin mission work among southern, white non-Catholics.[71]

Plantevigne's trials, coming on the heels of Dorsey's nightmare, had a traumatic effect on the Josephites. In September, 1909, George Knight, the single remaining black seminarian at St. Joseph's, informed McCarthy that in light of the obstacles faced by black priests in trying to work for their people in the United States, he would leave the Josephites to enroll in the Belgian seminary conducted by the Society of African Missions. Anxious that no one blame the Josephites for his departure, Knight authorized McCarthy to tell any skeptics that "it was my free choice to leave, owing to the present conditions in the South." Although individual Josephites still occasionally suggested candidates for Epiphany College or St. Joseph's Seminary, the suggestions invariably received negative responses from either McCarthy or the rectors of the respective institutions. A frustrated John Albert, convinced that the church would "*never* gather in these hordes of Baptists" without a black clergy, nevertheless voiced the sentiments of most of his confreres when he concluded, "This is too big a nut for the Josephites (as a Society) to crack and the good God only knows when a too conservative hierarchy will learn this lesson."[72]

Plantevigne's health seemed to mirror the declining fortunes of black priests in the Josephites and the Catholic church. While serv-

71. "Fr. Plantevigne Talks Out Plainly," Baltimore *Afro-American Ledger*, June 26, 1909, clipping in the John Plantevigne file, JFA; Baltimore *Afro-American*, March 16, 1912, p. 1; "Death of Fr. Plantevigne," *Colored Harvest*, VII (March, 1913), 9–10.

72. George Knight to Justin McCarthy, September 9, 1909, in 28-D-26, John Albert to Justin McCarthy, January 31, 1910, in 29-A-3, both in JFA.

ing as assistant pastor at St. Francis Xavier's, he contracted tuberculosis and subsequently suffered a nervous breakdown in March, 1912. On January 27, 1913, at the age of forty-two, he died. The medical diagnosis notwithstanding, many Josephites and black Catholics attributed the cause of death to "a broken heart." The Baltimore *Afro-American* called his passing "a genuine loss to the race." Cardinal Gibbons pronounced the final absolution at the funeral mass and delivered a eulogy. He praised Plantevigne's zeal for souls and uncommon intellectual attainments. Exhibiting an increasingly conservative attitude on racial issues, however, Gibbons stressed the superiority of moral freedom over civil freedom and ended with an admonition to the black assembly to prove themselves "worthy of the love and respect" of their fellow citizens. "If you do," Gibbons assured them, "civil rights will never be denied you."[73] Given the ordeal of the worthy John Plantevigne, who lay prematurely dead in his coffin in the sanctuary, the cardinal's words had a hollow ring to them.

Plantevigne's family did not want the body returned either to Chenel, his hometown, or to Baton Rouge, where they resided, for fear of racial incidents. Archbishop Blenk, with his characteristic prudence, would not provide a burial plot in New Orleans. Plantevigne, therefore, was laid to rest in Baltimore, where the faithful of St. Francis Xavier Parish erected a plaque in the church to his memory. Some opponents of black priests ascribed Plantevigne's breakdown to racial weakness and argued that it clearly demonstrated the unsuitability of blacks for ordination. Almost two years later, in December, 1914, the mental collapse and subsequent death of another black Josephite, seminarian John Teureaud, who had graduated from Epiphany College and entered St. Joseph's Seminary, appeared to lend credence to that allegation.[74]

Even before Teureaud's death, by 1913, prospects for black priests in the Josephites and the American Catholic church appeared grim. Convinced that their dependence on southern bishops made it im-

73. "A Protestant Tribute to Fr. Plantevigne," *Colored Harvest*, VII (June, 1913), 10–11; Foley, *God's Men*, 91; "Death of Plantevigne," 9–10.

74. Dolores Egger Labbe, *Jim Crow Comes to Church: The Establishment of Segregated Catholic Parishes in South Louisiana* (2nd ed.; Lafayette, La., 1971), 67; Foley, *God's Men*, 91–92; notes on Plantevigne, in Foley Papers; Sr. M. Magdalene to Joseph Butsch, March 23, July 5, 1912, both in 30-M-26, JFA; Warren interviews, 45–46; Eugene Teureaud to Louis B. Pastorelli, December 14, 1914, in 34-E, JFA. Eugene Teureaud, John's father, reported that his son kept trying to pick nonexistent bugs off the walls.

possible for them either to protect their black priests or to fight the hierarchy on the issue, Justin McCarthy and his confidant, Louis B. Pastorelli, the rector of St. Joseph's Seminary and by 1912 the de facto manager of the society, decided to leave the development of a black clergy to others. They therefore continued a policy almost totally exclusionary toward black applicants to Epiphany Apostolic College. In 1912, for example, just prior to Plantevigne's death, a total of fifteen black youths applied to the college; all were rejected.[75]

Despite the bleak outlook, John Albert, Plantevigne's seminary classmate and partner on the mission band, refused to abandon hope for a black clergy. Sympathetic to the plight of black priests yet also sensitive to the difficulties faced by his Josephite superiors, Albert searched for a new approach that would rescue the dream of a black clergy and, at the same time, remove the Josephites from the firing line. He drew encouragement from renewed interest on the part of the Roman Curia.

The unfortunate experiences of black priests in the United States may have helped spark the new concern evidenced in Rome about the black apostolate in the United States. The perceived failings of the American hierarchy in this respect particularly vexed Cardinal Gaetano De Lai, the doctrinally arch-conservative secretary of the Sacred Consistorial Congregation, the curial congregation that wielded jurisdiction over the American bishops. De Lai pressed Archbishop Giovanni Bonzano, the apostolic delegate from 1911 to 1922, for a report on the black apostolate in the United States in preparation for a thorough discussion of the topic by the Consistorial Congregation.[76]

Since De Lai had ordered him to consult Americans for information, in October, 1912, Bonzano asked John Burke of the Catholic Board for Mission Work Among the Colored People for a report on missionary efforts among blacks. Burke, in turn, solicited the views of a number of priests engaged in this work, especially John Albert, and forwarded a comprehensive report to Bonzano. Burke attributed the segregation in Catholic churches to existing social conditions in the South, "before which the Catholic Church in the South, on account of its small numbers there . . . seems powerless." He

75. Warren interviews, 45–46; John Albert to Archbishop Giovanni Bonzano, September 1, 1913, copy in SPA.

76. Cyprian Davis, O.S.B., "The Holy See and American Black Catholics: A Forgotten Chapter in the History of the American Church," U.S. Catholic Historian, VII, Nos. 2 and 3 (1988), 173.

claimed that a shortage of priests for black work and the absence of a black clergy constituted the chief obstacles to the conversion of Afro-Americans. With forty-nine priests on the missions, caring for 11,721 souls in their churches and providing education for 2,895 students in schools staffed largely by 82 sisters, 10 of whom were black, the Josephites, he pointed out, carried the greater part of the mission burden. But he noted that other religious communities were also involved in the work: the Society of African Missions, with nine priests working in Georgia; the Society of the Divine Word, with four priests working in Arkansas and Mississippi; and the Congregation of the Holy Ghost, with ten men working in Pennsylvania, Louisiana, New York, and Detroit. Several other communities and thirty-one diocesan priests supplied the remaining manpower.

Burke identified *"the absence of its own clergy"* as one of the main obstacles to the conversion of blacks and proposed a "separate college and finally a Seminary for the training of a colored clergy."[77] In this latter recommendation he reflected the influence of John Albert. To his report to the apostolic delegate, Burke attached an appendix prepared by Albert and entitled "How to Convert the Colored Race." In this appendix, Albert proposed a separate college and seminary for the education of black priests, separate black churches for the preservation of "the colored man's Catholicity," and the creation of a black ordinariate, that is, the appointment of a special bishop, initially white but later black, with jurisdiction over black missionary work. Albert acknowledged that "this solution is all the way through a Jim Crow measure" and could, therefore, provoke objections. He defended his plan, however, as "so practical and so absolutely necessary under present conditions" that it made sentimental objections look "puerile" when compared to "the immense good resulting from it."

Albert professed adherence to what he called the "be careful— go slowly—do not ordain unfit subjects" approach, but he insisted that the church could not justifiably deny priesthood to a whole race simply on the basis of the argument that "the time is not ripe." He claimed that he knew black Catholics who possessed all the qualifications needed for priesthood and argued that "a colored priesthood would sweep the [Protestant] preachers off their feet."

According to Albert, the basic opposition to black priests had its

77. John E. Burke to Archbishop Giovanni Bonzano, March 8, 1913, copy in Bishop Thomas S. Byrne Papers, ADN.

roots in the ticklish issue of social equality. He maintained that bishops objected to ordaining black men and having jurisdiction over them because "the South denies social equality, but this colored man is a priest and under these circumstances, must be accorded social consideration." He suggested that his proposal for a separate college and seminary to train black clergy would dispose of this weighty objection to the ordination of black men. "It is a mistake," he claimed, "in light of existing circumstances to train black students in company with white students." In that situation, the black student received an overdose of adulation from one direction and an overdose of humiliation from another, thus spoiling his character, to the detriment of hopes for a black priesthood. In a racially mixed setting, moreover, "the number of colored students is depressingly small on account of inside and outside opposition to the idea."

Albert advanced the idea of a black ordinariate precisely in order to avoid the problem of bishops refusing to accept black priests into their dioceses. He suggested the elevation to the episcopacy of a white priest who would then have jurisdiction over the training, ordaining, and placing of black priests. This new bishop would also have the privilege of forming a black parish in any diocese, thus relieving the ordinary of all responsibility in the matter and easing the friction and animosity long felt in many mixed parishes. In time, when a sufficient number of black priests warranted it, a black bishop could be consecrated for the purpose of directing the black apostolate. Such a bishop, he argued, would delight the black race and satisfy the mind of the southern white man, "who hates to see even a white priest working for the colored people." The Reverend James Wendel, a Divine Word missionary working on the black missions in Mississippi, described the problems he encountered with the southern sensibility. If he invited a black priest to preach at his church, the black parishioners responded enthusiastically. The whites in the town, however, would ask, "Are you taking the colored priest into your rooms?" If he replied, "Yes," then he could count on receiving scorn and even threats from whites. Albert's plan would obviate this problem. Additionally, the black bishop would assume responsibility for any scandals involving black priests.[78]

78. John Albert, "How to Convert the Colored Race," appendix attached to Burke to Bonzano, March 8, 1913, in Byrne Papers; James Wendel, "Our Negro Missions, a Short Historical Sketch" (Typescript in Foley Papers).

On September 1, 1913, Albert expanded on some of the ideas that he had put forth in his appendix with a direct plea of his own to Bonzano. He bemoaned the rejection during the preceding six months of all fifteen black applicants to Epiphany Apostolic College and questioned how such action could represent the will of God. Instead of advocating a change in Josephite policy, however, Albert, acting on a suggestion from a member of the hierarchy, urged the establishment of a new society of black priests, governed for the present by a white abbot. He called for a conscious accommodation with the southern social system, saying, "In the training of these priests the idea of social uplift through the priesthood would be discouraged and the idea of converting their race would be made ever present." He expressed confidence that a majority of the southern bishops would approve his idea and revealed that Bishop Morris of Little Rock had gone so far as to offer ten thousand dollars if the motherhouse of this new society would be located within the confines of his diocese.

Albert also advanced another plan, one that he considered as important to black evangelization as black clergy: the revival in the church of the permanent married diaconate. Deacons would exercise all of the functions given to deacons in the early church, including preaching, teaching, baptizing in the absence of the priest, though Albert had some reservations about their distributing the Eucharist. His suggestions for a married diaconate, of course, resembled Slattery's older plan for black catechists and, paradoxically, accorded with suggestions advanced by Bishop Morris, Dorsey's old nemesis.[79]

Bonzano, who lacked sympathy for black priests as a result of his earlier experiences with Zulu seminarians at the Urban College, received Burke's and Albert's recommendations, but he prepared his own, more negative, report, which he submitted to De Lai in May, 1914. In it, he insisted that blacks preferred white priests and that "few blacks would succeed in being good priests" because of defects in their character, intellect, and morals.[80]

De Lai, meanwhile, continued to gather information from various sources and to exert subtle pressure on American church authorities. On February 13, 1914, he sent Cardinal Gibbons a copy of a report he had received from an "African prelate" (probably

79. John Albert to Archbishop Giovanni Bonzano, September 1, 1913, copy in SPA.
80. Davis, "The Holy See," 176.

Archbishop Le Roy) criticizing the efforts of the American bishops and proposing remedies for the problems that existed. De Lai asked Gibbons for his opinion about the report. Gibbons responded with a long letter in which he claimed that the American bishops had already carefully considered and applied, as far as was practicable, every recommendation contained in the report. He repeated his familiar refrain that "the Bishops of the South are devoting all their energy to the spiritual welfare of the Negro." Gibbons acknowledged that blacks desired priests of their own race and admitted that the presence of black priests would inspire greater trust in the Catholic church among black people, but he cautioned that the issue required "delicate handling" because of obstacles that were "seemingly unique" to the United States and that the church had no control over. Gibbons maintained that black priests would have to possess "extraordinary tact, prudence, and self-denial"; they would have to accept education in their own segregated schools and seminaries and, after ordination, content themselves with their own conferences, retreats, and meetings. "In a word," Gibbons said, "they would have to submit to all the rigors of the caste system just as do the Methodist, Baptist, Episcopalian, and other Negro ministers of the sects." [81]

In a plenary session held in June, 1914, the members of the Consistorial Congregation discussed the black apostolate in the United States. In his report of the meeting to Bonzano, De Lai called on American bishops to train black catechists and to establish more schools, hospitals, and other institutions for blacks. He did not mention the issue of black priests and indicated that matters involving blacks were to be left to the "vigilance and exclusive direction and surveillance of the Ordinary." [82] There matters stood as the Holy See's attention became absorbed in the conflagration that engulfed Europe in August of 1914.

While the cardinals were meeting, the energetic Albert was urging the priests of the Society of the Divine Word, whose Mississippi parishes he visited in order to conduct missions, to undertake his black seminary project. Albert believed that the predominantly

81. Archbishop Alexandre Le Roy, "L'évangelization des États-Unis d'Amerique," memorandum to the Propaganda, February 5, 1914, copy in SPAUSA; Cardinal Gaetano De Lai to Cardinal James Gibbons, February 13, 1914, in 113-D-2, Cardinal James Gibbons to Cardinal Gaetano De Lai, March 28, 1914, copy 2, in 113-G-1, AAB.
82. Davis, "The Holy See," 176.

German Divine Word missionaries—members of a worldwide missionary order that included one bishop, three prefects apostolic, more than six hundred priests, and almost seven hundred lay brothers, headquartered in Steyl, Holland—possessed more strength and resources for such a project than the Josephites, who remained a diocesan institute with a total membership of approximately fifty men. At their Christmas meeting in December, 1914, the six Divine Word priests on the Mississippi missions, through their superior, the Reverend Alois Heick, unanimously recommended to their provincial, the Reverend Adolph Burgmer, "to try as soon as possible to educate some of our boys to the *status sacerdotalis*, whatever difficulties might be against the undertaking." Matthew Christman, only twenty-seven at the time, personally volunteered to devote himself to the work. At the same time, Heick wrote to John E. Gunn, the Bishop of Natchez, requesting permission to open a black seminary.[83]

The Divine Word missionaries initially received little positive encouragement. Burgmer replied that he wanted more time to study the question. Gunn answered that he did not think "that a colored priesthood is necessary or even advisable," though he did not oppose it in theory. He alluded to the Josephite experience with black priests as a failure and suggested that if the attempt were made again, it should be done under the supervision of a religious community in "an exclusively colored mission preferably in Africa." Black priests would form a quasi-religious community whose houses could be extended to the United States. "I do not think that a colored secular priesthood would ever be a success," Gunn declared. Instead of a black seminary, he proposed an apostolic school for the training of a married black diaconate. The Divine Word missionaries considered and then rejected Gunn's idea, for they considered it unlikely that Rome would approve the extraordinary privilege of marriage for deacons and they believed that the time had come for black priests.[84]

83. Interview of John Albert, S.S.J., by Albert S. Foley, S.J., notes in Foley Papers; Wendel, "Our Negro Missions"; statistics on the Society of the Divine Word provided by Kathie Till, Department of Archives and Records, Society of the Divine Word, Chicago Province, to Stephen J. Ochs, April 19, 1988; Alois Heick to Adolph Burgmer, January 1, 1915, Alois Heick to Bishop John E. Gunn, December 8, 1914, copies of both in SASA.

84. Bishop John E. Gunn to Alois Heick, January 2, 1915, in SASA; Matthew Christman, "St. Augustine's Mission House" (Typescript in SASA), 5.

During Easter, 1915, Burgmer and Heick attended a meeting of prominent missionaries engaged in black evangelization and found opinion there "quite unfavorable" to a black priesthood because of "past experience." The strong opposition they encountered convinced the Divine Word men to refrain from trying to force the seminary through. Instead, they opted to study the reasons behind the previous failed efforts—a study that was taken up especially by thirty-four-year-old James Wendel, who became a passionate advocate of a black clergy in the pages of *Colored Messenger*, a quarterly magazine that he published. In 1916, Christman, also with an eye to a future seminary, opened a high school for black boys in Greenville, Mississippi. Wendel confided to Thomas Wyatt Turner, a professor at Howard University and an emerging black Catholic leader, that "we find almost insurmountable difficulties, whose nature I cannot explain in a few words." He urged black Catholics to exert pressure of their own in favor of the project.[85]

While prelates and missionaries discussed the future of black priests, John Henry Dorsey continued his work in the South, enduring the daily humiliations of the jim-crow system. Unlike the white priests at St. Joseph's College for Negro Catechists, for example, he did not receive an invitation from the bishop to attend the annual clergy retreat, scheduled for July 5, 1909. In an attempt to avoid embarrassment both for Dorsey and for himself, Dan Rice asked Justin McCarthy to furnish an excuse to the bishop to exempt Rice from attendance. "This is the South," Rice told McCarthy, "and you and I can't change it. Can we?" Dorsey also had to contend with harassment from the assistant postmaster, who circulated rumors that the black priest mistreated the boys at the college, charges that nearly led to Dorsey's removal, until an investigation by Rice revealed that the assistant postmaster had fabricated them.[86]

In the summer of 1909, McCarthy, attempting to repair the damage caused by the Plantevigne affair, assigned Dorsey to give missions along the Gulf coast. Both Albert and Kelly applauded the move, which they had earlier recommended after Dorsey's successful missions in the midst of the uproar surrounding Plantevigne in

85. Christman, "St. Augustine's Mission House," 5–6; James Wendel to Thomas Wyatt Turner, November 16, 1915, in Thomas Wyatt Turner Papers, MSRC.

86. Dan Rice to Justin McCarthy, June 4, 1909, in 28-R-26, June 15, 1909, in 28-R-27, July 29, 1909, in 28-R-28, April 4, 1909, in 28-R-30, all in JFA.

the spring of 1909. They described Dorsey as "level-headed," "well-equipped," and "able to stand patiently under the fire of prejudice." Endeavoring to calm the parishioners of newly established St. Dominic's in New Orleans, where Plantevigne was to have conducted the opening mission, Dorsey visited the parish in August, 1909, at the invitation of LeBeau and with the consent of Archbishop Blenk. In October of that year, Dorsey also played an important role in the preliminary meetings that eventually resulted in the foundation of the Knights of Peter Claver, a Catholic fraternal association for black men similar to the all-white Knights of Columbus and established in Mobile, Alabama, by another Josephite, Conrad Rebesher. Dorsey served as the national chaplain of the knights from 1909 to 1923 and often sided with lay leaders of the organization in their not-infrequent disagreements with Josephite fathers Rebesher and Kelly.[87]

In June, 1913, the Josephite consultors moved Dorsey from the catechetical college to St. Peter's Church in Pascagoula, Mississippi, and assigned him full-time to the mission band. From 1913 to 1917, Dorsey, billed as the "Great Pulpit Orator," conducted missions before large, enthusiastic audiences throughout the South. The missions had a twofold purpose: to offer special opportunities for Catholics to renew their faith or return to the sacraments and to give non-Catholics a chance to hear the Catholic faith explained. Dorsey's lectures during those missions included such topics as "Why Am I a Catholic?," "Bible Reading," "Marriage and Divorce," "Heaven, Hell and Purgatory," and "Is One Religion as Good as Another?" He also effectively used the question box to answer non-Catholics' questions about the Catholic church.[88]

Dorsey appealed effectively to black Protestants. One of his con-

87. Sam Kelly to Justin McCarthy, June 7, 1909, in 28-N-5, John Albert to Justin McCarthy, June 13, 1909, in 28-K-10, Pierre LeBeau to Justin McCarthy, August 24, 1909, in 29-D-15, Conrad Rebesher to Justin McCarthy, September 16, 1909, in 28-R-5, all in JFA; *Colored Harvest*, VI (March, 1910), 18–19; Bishop John E. Gunn to John E. Burke, October 2, 1912, copy in Gunn Papers; Foley, *God's Men*, 57.

88. CMB, June 16, 1913, in JFA; "Mission Work in the Gulf States," *Colored Harvest*, V (March, 1909), 178; "Non-Catholic Missions," *Colored Harvest*, VII (June, 1914), 3–4; "From Mission to Mission," *Colored Harvest*, VII (June, 1914), 6–7; "More Non-Catholic Missions," *Colored Harvest*, VII (October, 1914), 3–4; "The Non-Catholic Missions," *Colored Harvest*, VIII (June, 1915), 2–4; "Non-Catholic Work," *Colored Harvest*, VIII (October, 1916), 4; Foley, *God's Men*, 58–60; *Mission Work Among the Negroes and Indians* (Baltimore, 1918), 21–22.

verts later described the experience of seeing a black priest for the first time: "I came out of curiosity to see the unbelievable and when I saw him I was struck. He . . . looked as good as any other Black minister . . . but he impressed me more. . . . I was impressed by what appeared to be culture." During his travels, Dorsey drew generally favorable notices from black newspapers like the Memphis *Sun.* Realizing that many Protestants would never come to a Catholic church, he employed innovative and unique methods to reach people, such as lecturing at meeting halls, Protestant churches, and black college campuses and surrounding himself on lecture platforms with local black preachers and politicians. In Memphis, he secured the services of Handy's Band, a famous black musical organization known throughout the South for its interpretation of the most modern forms of Afro-American music; most Catholics would not have recognized the hymns sung at the mission. In that same city in 1915, leading black citizens held a luncheon for Father Dorsey, the first time in the city's history that any representative body of non-Catholic church, social, or business leaders had so honored a Catholic priest.[89]

Not all black Protestants reacted favorably to Dorsey. During a 1916 mission in Mobile, Baptist and Methodist preachers brought their congregations to the vicinity of the Catholic church where Dorsey was conducting his mission and staged competing revival meetings. "Every night," said Dorsey, "when our bell peals forth, all the bells of the Protestant churches ring out in a melody of discord." In many areas of the South, some who might have converted as a result of hearing Dorsey hesitated for fear of social ostracism and possible loss of employment. As one woman in Dallas explained to Dorsey, "Why, if I were to become a Catholic, I would simply have to leave Texas."[90]

Dorsey's visits became annual fixtures in the life of southern black Catholic communities, which responded to him with affection and devotion. In 1914, at St. Dominic's in New Orleans, he gathered in 152 converts and 250 fallen-away Catholics and created such a good impression among both whites and blacks in New Or-

89. Interview of John Clouser by Peter E. Hogan, S.S.J., January 2, 1978 (Typescript in JFA), 4; "Non-Catholic Missions," 3–4; "Father Dorsey's Mission at Memphis," *Colored Harvest,* VIII (March, 1917), 5–6; "The Non-Catholic Missions," 2; *Mission Work Among the Negroes and Indians* (Baltimore, 1918), 21–22.

90. "Non-Catholic Work," 4; "The Non-Catholic Missions," 2–4.

leans that the vicar general of the archdiocese even offered some grudging praise. Following the death of Pierre LeBeau in 1916, a number of St. Dominic's parishioners petitioned McCarthy to give them "good Fr. Dorsey" as their pastor. They argued that a black priest would stem the exodus of blacks in New Orleans from the Catholic church. After a Dorsey mission at Most Pure Heart of Mary Church in Mobile in 1915, the Josephite pastor noted that "a large number of careless Catholics were brought back to their duties, some of whom had neglected the sacraments for as long as forty-three years." Dorsey also gave missions in non-Josephite black Catholic parishes. His missions at Divine Word parishes in Jackson and Meridian, Mississippi, helped convince those priests of the value and feasibility of black priests.[91]

Unfortunately for Dorsey, even during his successful mission tours, he could not escape the burden of racial prejudice. He became a target of the scurrilous anti-Catholic attacks launched by Tom Watson, Populist hero turned negrophobe and religious bigot. No issue of Watson's weekly or monthly publications was complete without an exposure of the "papal menace to America." Anti-Catholic articles in *Watson's Jeffersonian Weekly* included "The Sinister Portent of Negro Priests," and the periodical also carried a cartoon depicting Dorsey as a big ape, with a stole around his neck, sitting and hearing the confession of a very beautiful, young, virginal, white girl.[92]

Watson's attacks deeply concerned Catholic bishops in the South, especially since his ravings helped inspire convent inspection bills in Alabama and Georgia and a law in Florida making it illegal for whites to teach blacks. In 1916, several sisters at St. Peter Claver Parish in Tampa were arrested for instructing black students in the parish school. Fortunately for the sisters, a higher court ruled that the law did not apply to private schools and dismissed the charges. Dorsey's presence in the South afforded anti-Catholic bigots a chance to appeal to both racial and religious prejudice and therefore made many priests and bishops nervous. When a Divine

91. "More Non-Catholic Missions," 3–4; F. L. Gassler to Justin McCarthy, September 10, 1914, in AANO file, JFA; Foley, *God's Men*, 58–60; A. J. Bell *et al.* to Justin McCarthy, January 3, 1916, in 32-K-12, JFA; "The Non-Catholic Missions," 2–4; John H. Dorsey to Justin McCarthy, November 29, 1915, in 32-K-10, Alois Heick to Justin McCarthy, January 4, 1916, in 32-D-18, both in JFA.

92. C. Van Woodward, *Tom Watson: Agrarian Rebel* (New York, 1938), 419, 421; Warren interviews, 165.

Word priest in Vicksburg, Mississippi, invited Dorsey to give a mission there in early 1915, the diocesan priests objected, advising him to secure another priest because of the danger of adverse comment.[93]

Dorsey once again raised the hackles of his nemesis, Bishop Morris of Little Rock, when he accepted an invitation from John Albert, the pastor of St. Peter's in Pine Bluff, to give a lecture at the parish one evening when he was traveling between Memphis and Dallas. Albert had invited the black priest because parishioners could not understand why Dorsey never stopped in Pine Bluff during the course of his missionary work. He extended the invitation without informing the bishop, and Dorsey stayed only one night, leaving the next morning without even saying mass. When Morris rebuked Albert for the visit, the Josephite responded with a spirited defense both of his own actions and of Dorsey's reputation. This response further angered the bishop, who demanded, and received, an apology from Albert.[94]

Loneliness, prejudice, and overwork finally took their toll on Dorsey. He lost control of his weight, swelling to an eighteen and a half collar size on a five-foot, eight-inch frame. In June, 1916, he could not tolerate the 100° temperatures in San Antonio and wrote to McCarthy, "Really, I do not feel able to do any more missionary work just now." Alcohol further exacerbated his health problems. Despite the danger signals, Dorsey set up an ambitious itinerary in 1917, including Galveston, Memphis, Vicksburg, San Antonio, Walter (Mississippi), and Baltimore. Although he had first publicly exhibited evidence of heavy drinking in Mobile, by the time he arrived in Galveston in March, 1917, Charles Gately, the Josephite pastor, could report with satisfaction that Dorsey "was on the water wagon the whole time." John Albert also sprang to Dorsey's defense. Writing to Louis Pastorelli, Albert urged the Josephites "to stand behind Dorsey and do all we can to help him make good, because we must be careful not to give the Colored priest a black eye, even though he might be instrumental in earning one." Albert then attempted to place Dorsey's lapses in context: "His life is naturally a

93. James Albert (younger brother of John Albert) to Justin McCarthy, April 25, 1916, in 32-D-4, May 9, 1916, in 32-D-5, May 18, 1916, in 32-D-6, May 20, 1916, in 32-D-7, all in JFA; John Albert to Justin McCarthy, March 25, 1915, in 32-D-18, JFA.

94. John Albert to Bishop John B. Morris, January 24, 1915, in Morris Papers; John Albert to Justin McCarthy, February 18, 1915, in 32-D-16, JFA.

hard one and the loneliness which we cannot feel might at time be productive of temporary lapses of sobriety."[95]

Dorsey's health finally forced him to give up active missionary work and to return to St. Joseph's Seminary in Baltimore in 1917. Yet episcopal snubs still followed him. When illness and death among the Josephites in the autumn of 1917 forced Pastorelli to assign Dorsey temporarily to Nashville, Bishop Thomas Byrne professed fear that Dorsey was "not a man fitted for this place" and would encounter failure. Byrne suggested that Memphis might suit Dorsey better than Nashville. Taking the bishop at his word, Pastorelli temporarily assigned Dorsey to Memphis in December. Byrne, however, curtly informed Pastorelli that "Fr. Dorsey will not do in Memphis." He added petulantly, "You will remember that you are not allowed to send a Priest into a Diocese without first asking the Ordinary's leave to do so and whether or not he will be received." Pastorelli withdrew the appointment after reminding the bishop that it was he who had suggested Memphis. Dorsey settled into a sullen and embittered residence at St. Joseph's Seminary.[96]

In June, 1918, Louis B. Pastorelli, who for several years had unofficially filled the leadership vacuum created by the ineffectual McCarthy, won election as superior of St. Joseph's Society. He focused his attention on centralizing the society and systematizing mission work. The fifteen years between Joseph Anciaux's red book and Pastorelli's election witnessed a profound transformation of the Josephites. Bereft of Slattery's charismatic leadership, confronted by episcopal opposition to black Josephites, and shaken by the sufferings of their black confreres, the three Josephite leaders, Donovan, McCarthy, and Pastorelli, felt constrained to accommodate the bishops. They also attempted to leave the development of black priests to others. That issue, so intimately linked to the origins of St. Joseph's Society, would not disappear, however; black Catholics refused to allow Pastorelli or his Josephites to leave the field of battle quietly.

95. Interview of Olga Dorsey and Earl Counters by Stephen J. Ochs, November 2, 1983; John H. Dorsey to Justin McCarthy, June 13, 1916, in 32-K-14, Charles Gately to John Albert, March 22, 1917, in 32-D-30a, John Albert to Louis B. Pastorelli, April, [1917], in 32-D-30, all in JFA.

96. Bishop Thomas S. Byrne to Louis B. Pastorelli, September 17, December 4, 1917, Justin McCarthy to Bishop Thomas S. Byrne, all in 67-A, JFA.

Cardinal Herbert Vaughan (1832–1903), founder in 1866 of St. Joseph's Society of the Foreign Missions, or Mill Hill Josephites. Five years later, Vaughan sent four Mill Hill missionaries to work among blacks in the United States.

John R. Slattery (1851–1926), first superior general of St. Joseph's Society of the Sacred Heart, or Josephites, and in the late nineteenth and early twentieth centuries the foremost advocate of a black Catholic clergy. Slattery's resignation from the Josephites and his apostasy from the church hurt the cause of black priests.

Courtesy Josephite Fathers Archives

St. Joseph's Seminary, Baltimore, founded by John R. Slattery in 1888. In 1932, the Josephites moved the seminary to a site located near the campus of the Catholic University of America in Washington, D.C.

Courtesy Josephite Fathers Archives

Epiphany Apostolic College, Walbrook, Maryland, which opened in 1889. The college moved to Newburgh, New York, in 1926.

Courtesy Josephite Fathers Archives

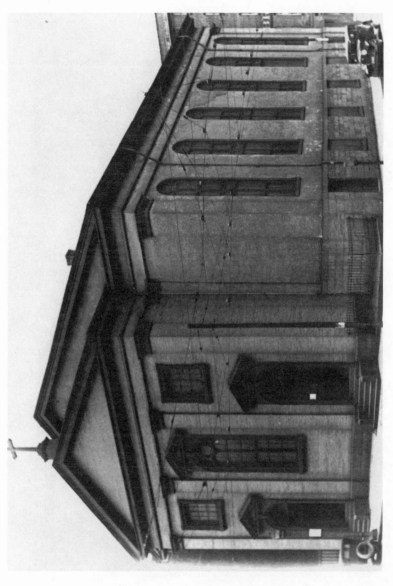

St. Francis Xavier Church, Baltimore. Formerly a Protestant church and a convention hall, this building at the corner of Calvert and Pleasant streets became the first black Catholic parish church in the United States in 1863. The building was also the site of Slattery's controversial sermon at the first mass of John H. Dorsey in 1902.

Courtesy Josephite Fathers Archives

James Augustine Healy (1830–1900), first Afro-American priest, ordained in 1854. James Healy was consecrated bishop of Portland, Maine,
in 1875. Like his two brothers, he identified more with his Irish than his
Afro-American heritage.

Alexander Sherwood Healy (1836–1875), ordained in 1858. Alexander
Healy later became rector of Holy Cross Cathedral, Boston.

Patrick Francis Healy (1834–1910), Jesuit and rector of Georgetown University from 1874 to 1882.

Augustine Tolton (1854–1897), born a slave. Tolton received holy orders in Rome in 1886 and returned to the United States to labor in Quincy, Illinois, and later Chicago.

Charles Randolph Uncles (1891–1933), one of the original five members of the American Josephites. Ordained in 1891, Uncles was the first Afro-American priest to receive holy orders in the United States.

Courtesy Josephite Fathers Archives

John H. Dorsey (1873–1926), second black Josephite priest, ordained in 1902. After being removed from St. Peter's Parish, Pine Bluff, Arkansas, at the insistence of Bishop John B. Morris, Dorsey spent the period between 1910 and 1917 conducting parish missions throughout the South.

Courtesy Josephite Fathers Archives

John J. Plantevigne (1871–1913), ordained a Josephite in 1907. Plantevigne's life was shattered when Archbishop James H. Blenk of New Orleans refused to allow him to conduct a mission scheduled there.

Courtesy Josephite Fathers Archives

Louis B. Pastorelli, Josephite superior general from 1918 to 1942. Pastorelli rebuilt St. Joseph's Society in the wake of Slattery's apostasy and the ineffectual efforts of two succeeding superiors general, but he felt constrained to restrict admissions of Afro-Americans to the society's college and seminary to only an occasional mulatto.

Courtesy Josephite Fathers Archives

Thomas Wyatt Turner (1877–1978), founder of the Federated Colored
Catholics in 1925. Turner regarded black priests as essential for the attainment of equal rights by black Catholics in the church and was un-
sparing in his criticism of Pastorelli's admissions policy.

John Joseph Albert (1875–1968), peripatetic Josephite missionary and classmate of John J. Plantevigne. Albert's letter to the Holy See in 1913 helped alert Rome to the need for more black clergy.

Courtesy Josephite Fathers Archives

James Wendel (1881–1920), Divine Word missionary. Wendel first proposed a seminary for blacks during meetings held by the Divine Word Missionaries in Jackson, Mississippi, during December, 1914.

Matthew Christman (1887–1929), Divine Word missionary who founded
Sacred Heart College, Greenville, Mississippi. The college was relocated
to Bay St. Louis, Mississippi, in 1923 and was renamed St. Augustine's
Seminary.

Courtesy Southern Province Archives of the Society of the Divine Word

One of the early structures on the campus of St. Augustine's Seminary, Bay St. Louis, Mississippi. A later view of the church and seminary building.

Both photographs courtesy Southern Province Archives of the Society of the Divine Word

John H. Dorsey, Charles Randolph Uncles, and Joseph A. John, between 1923 and 1926.

Courtesy Josephite Fathers Archives

Anthony Bourges, Maurice Rousseve, Francis G. Wade, and Vincent Smith, the first four black Divine Word priests ordained from St. Augustine's Seminary, in 1934.

Courtesy Josephite Fathers Archives

John LaFarge (1880–1963), Jesuit missionary, editor, and founder of the
Catholic Interracial Council of New York. LaFarge became the most
prominent Catholic spokesman in behalf of interracial justice and urged
Louis B. Pastorelli to admit more blacks into Josephite seminaries.

Jules B. Jeanmard (1879–1957), first bishop of the diocese of Lafayette, Louisiana. Jeanmard created Mary Immaculate Parish in Lafayette for the first four black priests from St. Augustine's Seminary. In 1952, he became the first bishop of the Deep South to ordain a black priest for his diocesan clergy.

Richard O. Gerow (1885–1976), bishop of Natchez, with William Henry Adams, of the Society of the Divine Word, after Adams' ordination on September 29, 1945. Gerow personally ordained most of the black priests from St. Augustine's Seminary between 1934 and 1955.

Courtesy Mississippi Today

Charles Chester L. E. Ball (1913–1970), ordained a Josephite in 1941, thirty-four years after John J. Plantevigne.

Courtesy Josephite Fathers Archives

Edward V. Casserly (1896–1982), Josephite superior general between 1942 and 1948. Casserly reopened Epiphany Apostolic College to significant numbers of black students, thus reclaiming John R. Slattery's legacy for St. Joseph's Society.

Cardinal Samuel A. Stritch (1887–1958), archbishop of Chicago from 1939 to 1958. In the capacity of president of the American Board of Catholic Missions, Stritch obtained a pledge from southern bishops in 1946 to accept black candidates for their diocesan clergy.

Courtesy Archives of the Archdiocese of Chicago

Joseph F. Rummel, archbishop of New Orleans from 1935 to 1964. Rummel publicly defended the cause of black priests in the Jesuit Bend incident in 1955.

New Orleans Clarion Herald

Joseph C. Verrett, ordained a Josephite in 1955. Verrett's assignment to
St. Augustine's High School in New Orleans marked the return of black
Josephite priests to the Deep South.

Chapter V

LOUIS B. PASTORELLI: CIRCLING THE WAGONS, 1918–1924

This element does not represent the race as a whole but are following in the footsteps of the agitators of their race who during and since the war are clamoring for all sorts of things and rights.
—LOUIS B. PASTORELLI, APRIL 5, 1920

Louis B. Pastorelli served officially as the superior general of the Josephites from 1918 to 1942. During his long tenure, he brought order and stability to St. Joseph's Society by centralizing authority, improving standards and discipline, and systematizing missionary efforts. Deeply influenced by what he characterized as the "living martyrdom" endured by the society's three black priests; convinced that bishops in the South simply would not accept black priests into their dioceses; handicapped by his own paternalism toward blacks; and possessing an almost slavish reverence for bishops, on whose sufferance the Josephites, and therefore the bulk of black Catholic missions, depended, Pastorelli maintained a restrictive policy toward blacks at Epiphany Apostolic College and St. Joseph's Seminary. With the exception of a few mulattos, whose presence in the college or seminary over the years he offered as evidence of the society's support for the goal of a black clergy in the United States and as proof that he had not closed the doors of Josephite seminaries to blacks, Pastorelli rejected almost all Afro-American applicants. Black Catholics, however, did not accept Pastorelli's seminary policy passively.

Between 1918 and 1924, Pastorelli and black Catholics became polarized over the issue of black priests. In the years following World War I, lay black Catholics in Baltimore and Washington,

D.C., were inspired by the democratic idealism of the war and by their faith in the universality of the Catholic church. Led by men such as Professor Thomas Wyatt Turner, they organized and waged a determined, sometimes bitter, campaign to force Pastorelli to open the college and the seminary to more black candidates. The virulence and persistence of black Catholic protest surprised and angered Pastorelli. He nevertheless believed that the bishops had left him no other practical alternative and he therefore steadfastly refused to change course at either the college or the seminary. He used a combination of stonewalling, half-truths, and carefully planned counterattacks to fend off the challenges of black Catholic dissidents, whom he regarded as reckless agitators. By 1924, black Catholic protest against the Josephites eased as Turner and his associates modified their tactics and organization and as attention shifted to the efforts of two European missionary societies to establish seminaries for blacks in the United States. Pastorelli had apparently steered the Josephites safely through the turbulent postwar years. He believed that he had strengthened St. Joseph's Society; black Catholic leaders believed that he had abandoned one of the society's most important missions.

Louis B. Pastorelli, the major figure in the drama, was born in Genoa, Italy, in 1874, and while still a young boy, he immigrated with his family to the United States, settling in Boston, Massachusetts. He entered Epiphany Apostolic College in 1889 with the first class and was ordained a priest in September, 1898. Throughout his years as a Josephite, he distinguished himself in a series of difficult assignments. From 1899 to 1902, he was stationed at St. Anthony's Parish (later renamed Most Pure Heart of Mary) in Mobile; he also served attached missions in remote rural settlements like Fish River, Bon Secour, and Bellefontaine. Pastorelli's work in Mobile earned him the respect and friendship of Bishop Edward P. Allen and the priests at the cathedral rectory, where he took his meals for a time. According to Bishop Allen, the young priest also earned the good will of the people and made himself "master of the situation." Indeed, Pastorelli appeared to thrive in the primitive Alabama setting. During one two-week stretch, for example, he covered ninety-seven miles by buggy, forty-five by rail, and about thirty by water; yet he could still write Slattery, "I enjoy this wild romantic life. Nothing suits me better." Pastorelli particularly came to love the light-skinned, Catholic colored Creoles, who kept aloof from the largely Protestant American blacks. Writing again to Slattery, he expressed the hope that the Creoles would "ever . . . continue" their splendid isolation.[1]

In 1902, Slattery, needing a firm hand at St. Joseph's Industrial School in Clayton, called Pastorelli away from his rugged missionary life in Alabama and appointed him rector of the Delaware school. Thus began a fifty-year administrative career for Pastorelli. He remained at St. Joseph's Industrial School until he became rector of St. Joseph's Seminary in 1912, a post he held for six years. Beginning in 1910, he also started to exert increasing influence in society councils, both as a consultor and as secretary to Justin McCarthy, the superior general. For all practical purposes, he operated as the de facto superior general of the society during McCarthy's last years in office. In June, 1918, Pastorelli formally became the fourth superior general of St. Joseph's Society. The society included seventy-one priests; had charge of thirty-nine black parishes and twenty-eight attached missions; cared for a total of 28,177 souls, about one-quarter of all black Catholics; operated forty-nine schools, with an enrollment of 6,080 children; and counted thirty seminarians at St. Joseph's Seminary and fifty students at Epiphany Apostolic College.[2]

A diminutive, bald-headed man with a classic Roman nose and dark, piercing eyes, Pastorelli was a strong, demanding administrator who brought order, centralization, and businesslike management to the Josephites, a priest of a mold similar to such "consolidating, urban bishops" as Cardinals William O'Connell of Boston, Dennis Dougherty of Philadelphia, George Mundelein of Chicago, and, later, Francis J. Spellman of New York. Under Pastorelli, for example, the Josephites adopted a more systematic approach for establishing missions. He insisted on approving all new missions and making all arrangements with bishops, thus ending the free-lance activities of some of his missionaries, Sam Kelly, for instance,

1. See list of Louis B. Pastorelli's assignments, in 45-M, JFA; Bishop Edward P. Allen to John R. Slattery, December 18, 1899, in 25-A-12, February 17, 1902, in 25-A-23, Louis B. Pastorelli to John R. Slattery, February 2, 1900, in 19-G-15a, May 27, 1900, in 19-G-25, all in John R. Slattery Papers, JFA.

2. John R. Slattery to Bishop Edward P. Allen, February 19, 1902, copy in 25-A-24, Slattery Papers; list of Pastorelli's assignments, in 45-M, Edward V. Casserly to Joseph Lally, July 8, 1944, in Joseph Lally file, Justin McCarthy to Josephite Fathers, February 24, 1910, copy in 61-H, Louis B. Pastorelli to Thomas Foley, December 2, 1931, in 51-D, all in JFA; interview of Peter E. Hogan, S.S.J., by Stephen J. Ochs, July 25, 1983; Louis B. Pastorelli to Bishop Peter Muldoon, [Summer, 1919?], in NCWC-USCC Records, ACUA.

who first erected churches and schools and only later informed his Josephite superiors general. Conscious of manpower constraints and also of the need to impress the bishops, Pastorelli de-emphasized missions in rural, heavily Protestant areas, which yielded relatively few converts, and concentrated on conserving the faith of black Catholics through parish work in urban centers such as Baltimore and New Orleans—cities that had significant black Catholic populations and promised greater results.[3]

In contrast to Justin McCarthy, Pastorelli closely supervised the men on the missions through frequent letters and visits. Few details, however small, escaped his notice. He filled his letters with questions, instructions, advice, encouragement, and admonitions. For example, when P. J. McConnell, a Josephite priest in New Orleans, nagged Pastorelli for a transfer, he received a stinging reply that read in part, "I am doing my level best to spur you on to act as a man, with some backbone, and as a priest, with some sense of your priestly character and obligations. But you insist upon playing the role of a child." Despite the sometimes lecturing, even scolding, nature of his letters, however, most of the Josephites appreciated the interest Pastorelli showed in their work. On a personal level, he could be a genial, charming back slapper, especially to young seminarians. Yet around many of his fellow Josephites, he tried to maintain an aura of authority and control by keeping them off balance with petty criticism of their work or personal habits.[4]

During his years as superior general, financial concerns weighed heavily on Pastorelli. He found it necessary to raise funds not only to meet operating expenses at the college and the seminary but also to provide regular subsidies for missions whose weekly collections (sometimes no more than two dollars) could not support them and whose pastors spent considerable amounts of their time thinking up begging schemes and planning fund raisers to keep themselves afloat. He also needed funds to respond to emergency appeals from

3. Edward R. Kantowicz, *Corporation Sole: Cardinal Mundelein and Chicago Catholicism* (Notre Dame, 1983), 2; Louis B. Pastorelli, report to Justin McCarthy on missions east of the Mississippi, September, 1916, in 33-B, John Albert to Louis B. Pastorelli, [1918?], in 36-A, both in JFA; "Exodus," *Colored Harvest*, VIII (March, 1918), 4–5; Louis B. Pastorelli to Bishop Peter Muldoon, [Summer, 1919?], in NCWC-USCC Records, ACUA.

4. Louis B. Pastorelli to P. J. McConnell, September 3, 1919, in 37-M, JFA; interview of James F. Didas, S.S.J., by Stephen J. Ochs, November 3, 1983; Hogan interview, July 25, 1983.

desperately poor Josephite missionaries who had simply run out of money. Although he ordinarily sent a check in response to an urgent plea from one of his missionaries, Pastorelli usually accompanied it with a warning that "it is of course out of the question to keep up such allowances," followed by concrete suggestions for raising more revenue or by exhortations for greater efficiency and creativity in financial management.[5]

Pastorelli depended on several sources of revenue for his hard-pressed society, including the annual collection of the Negro and Indian Commission, the American Board of Catholic Missions (created in 1924 by the American hierarchy to collect and distribute funds to missions in the United States), the Catholic Board for Mission Work Among the Colored People, individual donors, such as Mother Katharine Drexel and her sister, Louise Morrell, the subscribers to *Colored Harvest*, and occasional bank loans. Through resourceful and ingenious financial management, Pastorelli managed to sustain and expand Josephite missions, to relocate and construct a new Epiphany Apostolic College in Newburgh, New York, in 1925, and to lay plans for a new St. Joseph's Seminary in Washington, D.C.[6]

In English, the name *Pastorelli* means "little shepherd," a particularly apt description of Pastorelli's stance toward blacks. He viewed Afro-Americans as a childlike race, suffering from the damaging effects of hundreds of years of slavery and racial discrimination and desperately in need of education and moral uplift from the Catholic church. He had little confidence in blacks as leaders and approached the black apostolate in terms of what white men could do *for* blacks. Although he acknowledged that the conversion of blacks in the United States would ultimately depend on the efforts of blacks themselves, he believed that for the present white men should educate and lead blacks to a higher level of civilization. Regarding social conditions in the South, where most Josephite missionaries worked, he insisted on prudence and accommodation. While Pastorelli applauded priests who prevented "the ravages of an unscrupulous police court or blocked the greed of swindling employers," he did not want his priests to become agitators for social

5. See, for example, Louis B. Pastorelli to Matthew A. Donahue, October 16, 1918, [?] to Louis B. Pastorelli, November 14, 1918, both in 36-D, John Brodie to Louis B. Pastorelli, October 31, 1918, in 36-B, all in JFA.

6. Louis B. Pastorelli to Bishop Christopher Byrne, June 18, 1925, in 68-D, Louis B. Pastorelli to Father Will [?], September 20, 1925, in 43-M, both in JFA.

equality. If they did so, he feared, they would lose influence among "the better element of colored people" and "become personally obnoxious to the white members of the community," including the bishop, thus jeopardizing the very existence of the black mission. He urged his missionaries to seek the constant guidance of the bishop in touchy racial matters and to ally themselves with southern liberals—"fair-minded southerners" and "reputable southern editors"—who could help Josephite missionaries attain their ends without requiring direct action by the priest.[7]

Pastorelli's personal experiences with black Josephites significantly influenced his later policies concerning the admission of blacks to the preparatory and major seminaries of St. Joseph's Society. In 1902, he had hosted Charles Uncles at St. Joseph's Industrial School while the latter eluded the outstanding warrant for his arrest in Baltimore. Between 1910 and 1918, in his capacities as secretary to the superior general, consultor, rector of the seminary, and de facto superior general, he had participated in the unsuccessful efforts to secure assignments outside the Baltimore archdiocese for Fathers Plantevigne and Dorsey and had witnessed firsthand their suffering and torment. It was Pastorelli who officiated at Plantevigne's funeral mass and who pronounced the final "requiéscat in pace" over the coffin of the young priest. The difficulties of the early black priests convinced him that for the good of St. Joseph's Society and of the black seminarians and priests themselves, the Josephites had to restrict their admissions of Afro-Americans to the college and seminary to only an occasional light-skinned mulatto. Between 1910 and 1918, Pastorelli helped McCarthy to implement that policy; as superior general after 1918, he continued it.

Pastorelli succeeded Justin McCarthy as superior general of the Josephites six months before the armistice that ended World War I. The war dramatically spurred black migration to cities in the North, creating new opportunities and problems for Afro-Americans and beginning the transformation of the race question from a purely southern into a national issue. With its democratic slogans and evi-

7. Louis B. Pastorelli to Bishop Peter Muldoon, [Summer, 1919?], in NCWC-USCC Records, ACUA; George K. Hunton, *All of Which I Saw, Part of Which I Was: The Autobiography of George K. Hunton, as Told to Gary MacEoin* (Garden City, N.Y., 1967), 16–17; Louis B. Pastorelli to Bishop Peter Muldoon, [1919?], in NCWC-USCC Records, ACUA; John T. Kneebone, *Southern Liberal Journalists and the Issue of Race, 1920–1944* (Chapel Hill, 1986); Morton Sosna, *In Search of the Silent South: Southern Liberals and the Race Issue* (New York, 1977).

dence of black valor in the trenches of France, the war also raised hopes among blacks that they would achieve greater opportunity and true democracy at home after Germany's surrender. Instead, at war's end they encountered a virulent white reaction, marked by the rebirth of the Ku Klux Klan, the resurgence of lynchings (seventy alone during the first postwar year), and the widespread urban race riots of the "Red Summer" of 1919.

Blacks responded to white reaction with an assertiveness nurtured by wartime experiences in France and by dreams of a world made "safe for democracy." They fought back during the race riots of 1919 and attempted, through organizations such as the NAACP, to combat racial discrimination by instituting challenges in the courts, lobbying for federal antilynching legislation, and publicizing racial atrocities in the pages of *Crisis*, the association's official journal. Urban blacks on the lower socioeconomic levels, feeling alienated from the middle- and upper-class blacks and white liberals of the NAACP, registered their own protest against the antiblack reaction of the postwar period by responding enthusiastically to Marcus Garvey and his appeals to race pride.[8]

Black Catholics shared the hopes of many in the wider Afro-American community that World War I would usher in a new era of opportunity and justice. Gilbert S. Faustina, supreme knight of the Knights of Peter Claver, for example, declared that the war, which had "created a world interest in human justice—has given the Negro an opportunity to demonstrate his worth as a soldier and his value as a man and a citizen."[9] Thomas Wyatt Turner, a biology professor and a member of St. Augustine's Parish in Washington, D.C., combined his democratic idealism with his fervent Catholicism and demanded greater justice for blacks within the Catholic church. For the next twenty years, his was the leading voice of black Catholic activism.

Turner was born on March 16, 1877 (one day before John Slattery's ordination to the priesthood), in Hughesville, a small town located in Charles County, Maryland. Baptized a Catholic as an infant, he attended county black schools and then graduated in 1892 from Charlotte Hall, a black Episcopalian institution in St. Mary's County, but he declined a scholarship from Lincoln Univer-

8. John Hope Franklin and Alfred A. Moss, Jr., *From Slavery to Freedom: A History of Negro Americans* (6th ed.; New York, 1988), 304–23.

9. *Official Bulletin: Minutes of the National Board of Directors, Knights of Peter Claver, August 20–21, 1919,* in T-34, JFA.

sity because it would have required him to become an Episcopalian. Possessing a passion for education, Turner made his way to Howard University in Washington, D.C., where, while supporting himself by part-time jobs, he earned his B.A. degree in 1901. After graduation from Howard, he took science courses at Catholic University until his funds ran out, taught at Tuskegee Institute for a year, and then joined the faculty of the Baltimore High and Training School, where he taught for ten years, broken only by a one-year stint at St. Louis High School. While he was teaching high school, Turner also earned his M.A. from Howard University in 1905, to which institution he returned as a professor of biology in 1913. Eight years later, he received his Ph.D. in botany from Cornell University, and he moved to Hampton Institute in 1924.[10]

A civil rights activist as well as a devoted Catholic, Turner, in 1910, became the first secretary of the Baltimore branch of the NAACP; when he moved to Washington, D.C., in 1913, Turner helped recruit members for the Washington chapter of the organization. Turner's opposition to racism had a deeply religious dimension. He believed that *true* Catholicism proclaimed the universality of redemption and the common brotherhood and sisterhood of all human beings in Jesus Christ and was, therefore, incompatible with racial prejudice and discrimination.[11]

Beginning in 1913, Turner increasingly focused his attention on racism in the Catholic church. In that year, he asked Cardinal Gibbons to write to President Woodrow Wilson as part of a campaign to secure civil justice for blacks. Gibbons, whose relations with the Wilson administration were strained over Mexican persecution of the church and other issues, declined to write the president, explaining that he did not feel well enough acquainted with him to warrant a letter that "would mean a criticism of his administration." Gibbons assured Turner, however, that he would not hesitate to raise the subject in conversation with the president if the opportunity presented itself. Turner also tried to enlist Catholic clergymen to support the opening of Catholic schools and seminaries to black students, but without much success. In a reply to

10. Marilyn W. Nickels, "Thomas Wyatt Turner and the Federated Colored Catholics," *U.S. Catholic Historian*, VII, Nos. 2 and 3 (1988), 216–17, 226.

11. Marilyn W. Nickels, "The Federated Colored Catholics: A Study of Three Variant Perspectives on Racial Justice as Represented by John LaFarge, William Markoe, and Thomas Turner" (Ph.D. dissertation, The Catholic University of America, 1975), 21–22.

one Turner appeal, for example, Walter Elliott, the liberal Paulist who had trained John Plantevigne for the mission band, described as impossible the mixing of black and white students, even in schools in the North, because if schools or colleges admitted black students, "they would have to close their doors." Elliott advised Turner to accept the facts of the situation and turn his thoughts to practical solutions, such as more, exclusively black, Catholic schools.[12]

Unlike many of his lay contemporaries, Turner showed no reticence on the issue of racism in the church. In his reply to Elliott, he asserted that if priests and other authorities dealt with racial prejudice as they did other violations of the Ten Commandments, "the monstrous falsehood would soon die" and black students could gain entrance into all Catholic institutions. Turner declared that racism "is too flagrant and positive a wrong to be tolerated for a moment by the Church after its attention has been sufficiently called to it." Unfortunately, Turner concluded, many pastors allowed racial prejudice to develop without a word of rebuke.[13] His definition of racism as sinful anticipated later developments in Catholic moral theology. In 1920, most Catholic moral theologians did not recognize racism as sinful but rather regarded it as a sociopolitical question. Until the 1950s, theology and philosophy books used in U.S. Catholic seminaries, colleges, and universities did not address racism or discrimination against blacks.[14]

Turner refused to allow church authorities to dodge the issue of racism. In February, 1916, he complained to Owen Corrigan, the auxiliary bishop of Baltimore and spiritual director of the archdiocesan Holy Name Union, about diocesan newspaper accounts of the local Holy Name parade that referred to black boys as pickaninnies. The Holy Name Society, a confraternity of men, had a twofold purpose: to promote love and reverence for the name of God and to discourage profanity, blasphemy, perjury, and all improper language. Its members, usually organized into parish units,

12. Cardinal James Gibbons to Thomas Wyatt Turner, September 17, 1913, Walter Elliott to Thomas Wyatt Turner, September 8, 1914, both in Thomas Wyatt Turner Papers, MSRC.

13. Thomas Wyatt Turner to Walter Elliott, August 28, 1915, copy in Turner Papers.

14. See Edward S. Stanton, S.J., "John LaFarge's Understanding of the Unifying Mission of the Church, Especially in the Area of Race Relations" (Ph.D. dissertation, St. Paul University, 1972), 49–52.

held processions in honor of the Holy Name. It seemed improper, therefore, for members of such an organization to be abused in this way. A few months later, Turner once again protested to Corrigan, this time about the "jim-crowing" of his Holy Name group at Corpus Christi Parish in Baltimore during a special archdiocesan Holy Name mass.

Corrigan and others viewed Turner as a pest, a complainer, and a troublemaker. Much to their chagrin, they soon discovered that his letter-writing campaign was only a prelude to more formal, organized action. In 1917, Turner invited a few friends to his home to discuss the situation of blacks in the Catholic church. Out of the meetings emerged the Committee Against the Extension of Race Prejudice in the Catholic Church, or the Committee of Fifteen. Clearly modeled on the NAACP, the committee proposed to combat racism in the church through investigation, publicity, and appeals to lawful authority. As it stated in one of its earliest public releases, the committee sought to bring about a better feeling and closer union among all Catholics, to eradicate any and every obstacle that prevented black men and women from participating fully in the activities of the church, to raise the status of black Catholics within the church, to cooperate with all efforts within the church to promote the spiritual welfare of all Catholics, and to collect and keep records of all unchristian acts committed in the jurisdiction of the church and to bring notice of them to proper authorities. The Committee of Fifteen insisted that only black Catholics themselves could articulate their needs, and it respectfully asked the American hierarchy to help black Catholics secure equal opportunities for educational, economic, and spiritual uplift.

Shortly thereafter, the committee turned its attention to the plight of black Catholic troops in the U.S. army. During World War I, black troops served in segregated units, and the Protestant-affiliated YMCA and YWCA provided services such as reading classes, libraries, and canteens in segregated cantonments for black troops. The war forced the Catholic church to coordinate its various agencies so it could minister effectively to Catholics among the troops, and under the leadership of John J. Burke, C.S.P., the National Catholic War Council emerged. The council represented a major organizational step for the heretofore loosely organized church in this country. An administrative committee of bishops, headed by Peter Muldoon of Rockford, Illinois, oversaw the council's activities. Under the auspices of the war council, the Knights of Columbus operated canteens for white Catholic troops; they did not, however, provide any facilities or personnel for black Catholic troops. When Turner learned of the problem, he and a small committee met with Cardinal Gibbons. At Gibbons' suggestion, the group contacted Colonel P. H. Callahan, the director of welfare services for the Knights of Columbus, who agreed to provide black Catholic workers for cantonments at several camps in the United States. One month after the armistice, the Committee of Fifteen wrote to Gibbons, applying for recognition and inclusion into what they regarded as the two most powerful organizations within the church: the Knights of Columbus and the National Catholic War Council. Years of experience had convinced him, Gibbons replied, that separate societies for blacks best served the interests of black Americans.[15] Gibbons' attitude, held by most enlightened clergy in 1919, did not augur well for black Catholic dreams of greater justice and opportunity in the postwar church in the United States.

Neither did the Josephites remain immune from the racial discord that racked the United States after World War I. Indeed, the bitter relations between Pastorelli and Dorsey, one of the two remaining black Josephites, seemed to mirror the racial turmoil of the postwar years and soon became entangled in a public controversy over Josephite policy regarding the admission of blacks into the society's college and seminary. Pastorelli recalled Dorsey from the mission band in 1917, charging him with "drink, laziness . . . old sermons," refusal to go to rural areas, and keeping money without submitting returns or accounts to the superior general. To support the charges of drunkenness, Pastorelli cited complaints about Dorsey's drinking from Conrad Rebesher in Mobile and John A. Clarke in New Orleans.

During the general chapter meeting in June, 1918, Dorsey, together with the Reverends John J. Glancy and James J. Nally, bitterly attacked Pastorelli. Dorsey also opposed making unanimous Pastorelli's election as superior general on the strength of thirteen proxy votes. Four days after the conclusion of the chapter, Pastorelli and his consultors decided "for reasons of policy and in the interests

15. Nickels, "Federated Colored Catholics," 2–3, 28–29, 31–32; Christopher J. Kauffman, *Faith and Fraternalism: The History of the Knights of Columbus, 1882–1982* (New York, 1982), 190–227; Thomas Wyatt Turner *et al.* to Cardinal James Gibbons, December 23, 1918, in 124-C-4, Cardinal James Gibbons to Thomas Wyatt Turner, January 7, 1919, copy in 124-G-4, both in AAB.

of the Society and the welfare of the subject" to remove Dorsey from the mission band. They appointed him pastor of St. Monica's, a poor, rundown, black parish in south Baltimore, whose weekly collection rarely exceeded three dollars. His assignment to St. Monica's upset members of the Dorsey family, who believed that the Josephites should have rewarded Father Dorsey's years of service on the missions with an appointment to a more prosperous parish.[16]

Relations between Pastorelli and the black priest deteriorated further after Dorsey took up his post. He angered Pastorelli by accepting, without the superior's prior permission, the chairmanship of a committee seeking to raise fifteen thousand dollars for the Oblate Sisters of Providence. In February, 1918, Pastorelli accused Dorsey of neglecting his duties at St. Monica's and told him to inaugurate Sunday evening services and to end his involvement with the sisters' campaign so that he could devote his time to the work assigned him by his superior. Pastorelli also rebuked Dorsey for failing to gather an accurate census of his parish; he ordered him to recanvass St. Monica's because he did not want to shame Dorsey before the public, he said, "by putting down the figures you give as the number of Catholics for a parish here in Baltimore."[17]

Dorsey heatedly denied Pastorelli's allegations. He claimed that he had worked himself "like a slave" both on the missions and at St. Monica's and had suffered two nervous breakdowns as a result of overwork. He disputed the accuracy of previous census reports for St. Monica's, pointed out that he had given only one speech on behalf of the Oblate sisters, blamed Cardinal Gibbons and Pastorelli for seven years of prior neglect at St. Monica's, and accused Pastorelli of expecting miracles from him.[18]

One month later, the bitterness between Pastorelli and the Dorseys burst into public view. On March 10, 1919, the campaign for the Oblate sisters ended with a program at a Baltimore theater. C. Marcellus Dorsey, whom Pastorelli regarded as an agitator and as the mouthpiece for his brother, read a paper in which he publicly attacked the Josephites for mistreating his brother and living off

16. Private data book, June, 1918, pp. 9, 45, minutes of the general chapters, June 26, 1918, CMB, August 29, 1918, John H. Dorsey to Louis B. Pastorelli, February 5, 1919, in 36-D, all in JFA; interview of Olga Dorsey and Earl Counters by Stephen J. Ochs, November 2, 1983.

17. Private data book, October, 1918, p. 45, Louis B. Pastorelli to John H. Dorsey, February 4, 1919, copy in 36-D, both in JFA.

18. John H. Dorsey to Louis B. Pastorelli, February 5, 1919, in 36-D, JFA.

black people while doing nothing for them. Father Dorsey, seated on the stage, spoke immediately after his brother but in no way challenged the latter's remarks. The incident upset many of the Catholics in the audience and outraged Pastorelli, who believed that the Dorsey brothers had caused great scandal, especially to the many Protestants who attended the function.[19]

Marcellus Dorsey's public attack on the Josephites in March, 1919, signaled the beginning of a campaign by a small group of black Catholics in Baltimore, closely identified with the Dorsey family and concentrated in the Dorseys' home parish of St. Peter Claver, to force the Josephites to open their college and seminary to more black students. In September, 1919, the Baltimore black Catholic dissidents formed a branch of Turner's Washington organization, which by then had changed its name to the Committee for the Advancement of Colored Catholics. The Dorseys apparently served as the link between the Baltimore and Washington groups, evidently having become acquainted with Turner when he taught in Baltimore. The members of the Baltimore branch became known as the "insurgents" and chose Charles Woodland as president and Royal G. Addison as secretary; Marcellus Dorsey also played a key role, as publicist and firebrand. Whereas the Washington committee focused on lobbying the hierarchy, the Baltimore insurgents adopted the more controversial tactic of publicizing their grievances against the Josephites and the Catholic church in the pages of the *Afro-American*.[20]

Turner and his Committee for the Advancement of Colored Catholics viewed the first annual meeting of the American hierarchy, scheduled for September, 1919, and mandated by the National Catholic Welfare Council (changed in 1922 to National Catholic Welfare Conference), the postwar successor of the National Catholic War Council, as a splendid opportunity to present their case. Probably at Rome's insistence, Cardinal Gibbons had asked the organizing committee of bishops to include the black apostolate on the agenda and to reflect about "whether our methods were at fault or zeal lacking." Turner's committee addressed an ap-

19. Private data book, March 10, 1919, pp. 45–46, in JFA.
20. Louis B. Pastorelli to C. W. Wallace, April 12, 1920, in PMC; Committee for the Advancement of Colored Catholics to Most Reverend Archbishop, 1919, copy, John H. Dorsey to Thomas Wyatt Turner, August 14, 1919, both in Turner Papers; Olga Dorsey and Earl Counters interview, November 2, 1983.

peal to the hierarchy, calling attention to the growing practice of discrimination against black Catholics in the church, as illustrated by the policy of refusing admission to black students at Catholic University. It deplored the inadequate elementary and high school facilities provided by the Catholic church for black children and also asked for representation for black laymen on all boards of the church that dealt with their welfare. Emphasizing the need for more black priests, which they regarded as essential for the protection and expansion of black rights within the church, the committee claimed that ample facilities existed for the education of a black clergy at the Josephites' seminary and respectfully asked why St. Joseph's Society had "adopted a policy against admitting colored candidates for the priesthood," a policy the committee described as "without justification." The committee requested the privilege of presenting its case in person before the hierarchy at the September meeting.[21]

The approaching bishops' meeting in Washington D.C., and the departure of William E. Floyd, the only black Josephite seminarian, from St. Joseph's Seminary in September, 1919, at the end of two years of theology, prompted Marcellus Dorsey to pen a strong attack in the *Afro-American* against racism in the Catholic church. Dorsey denounced what he described as "white priests and ecclesiastical tyranny." He noted that the forthcoming meeting of the Catholic bishops had inspired more interest in the Catholic church among members of the black community than had any event since John Slattery's repudiation of the church. Dorsey repeated Slattery's statement that "the Catholic Church's attitude toward the Colored people is one of sheer dishonesty" and cited the alleged rejection of William Floyd at St. Mary's Seminary, where Josephite seminarians attended classes, as evidence of church hypocrisy. Declaring that "white priests are not angels" and that discrimination existed in nearly every white Catholic church in Baltimore, he demanded "Catholicity without conditions." His article caused a stir among Baltimore's black Catholics, some of whom did not approve of public criticism of the church.

The *Afro-American*, nevertheless, claimed that Dorsey's article illustrated general unrest among black Catholics over intolerable

21. Cardinal James Gibbons to Bishop Peter Muldoon *et al.*, May 5, 1919, copy in 126-D-6, AAB; Committee for the Advancement of Colored Catholics to Most Reverend Archbishop, 1919, copy in Turner Papers.

conditions in their church.[22] In an editorial on September 25, 1919, the newspaper explained that its articles on the Catholic church were part of an effort to bring all black Catholics into the fight for equal and just treatment. It likened the struggle for black Catholic priests to concurrent struggles in the Protestant Episcopal and Methodist Episcopal churches for black bishops. "Longer than every other denomination," the editorial writer claimed, "the Catholic Church has kept its white priests and it stands alone today as the single American Church where practically all of its parish heads are white and all of the communicants colored."[23]

The bishops' meeting in September, so long awaited by black Catholics and held in the wake of the summer's numerous race riots, produced few concrete results. On September 24, 1919, Turner and members of his committee met informally with a number of bishops on the campus of Catholic University to discuss the issues that the committee had raised in the brief they sent earlier. Members of the committee, however, were not permitted to address the assembled bishops. The bishops did issue a pastoral letter in which they deprecated "all attempts at stirring up racial hatred." In making this statement they were responding to an urgent request from Pietro Gasparri, the cardinal secretary of state, that they consider the "Negro problem" and condemn the lynching of blacks. They also affirmed their belief that "education is the practical means" of bettering the condition of blacks, but they did not address the problem of discrimination in the church.[24]

Despite the lack of dramatic results, black Catholic activists felt encouraged after their meetings with the bishops. They had, after

22. "Catholic Church Good to Die In," Baltimore *Afro-American*, September 18, 1919, clipping in PMC; Louis B. Pastorelli to Ignatius Lissner, September 20, 1919, copy in PMC.

23. "The Catholic Agitation," Baltimore *Afro-American*, September 25, 1919, clipping in PMC. On the struggle for black bishops in the Protestant Episcopal and Methodist Episcopal churches, see David C. Reimers, *White Protestantism and the Negro* (New York, 1965), 66–75.

24. Committee for the Advancement of Colored Catholics to Most Reverend Archbishop, 1919, copy, Peter J. O'Callaghan to Thomas Wyatt Turner, October 21, 1919, both in Turner Papers; Nickels, "Federated Colored Catholics," 3; Thomas Wyatt Turner *et al.* to Cardinal James Gibbons, March 1, 1920, in 131-H, AAB; Aluigi Cossio to Archbishop George Mundelein, September 15, 1919, in Menceslaus Madaj Collection, AAC; Raphael M. Huber (ed.), *Our Bishops Speak, National Pastorals and Annual Statements of the Hierarchy of the United States* (Milwaukee, 1952), 20.

all, presented their case to members of the hierarchy and had sent a copy of their brief to the apostolic delegate. Turner and his committee hoped that the information and testimony they had given would move the prelates in the near future to take more decisive action against racism in the church. They also regarded the publication, on November 30, 1919, of Pope Benedict XV's encyclical *Maximum illud*, which called for native clergy and seminaries in mission areas, as a positive development that would increase pressure on the American bishops to provide for more black priests.[25]

Turner and the Committee for the Advancement of Colored Catholics did not sit back and leave the initiative to the American bishops or the Holy See; they continued to press their campaign for black priests and against discrimination within the church. Attempting to discover the extent to which racial prejudice had figured in the case of William Floyd at St. Mary's and St. Joseph's seminaries, Turner addressed a letter to the Reverend Edward Dyer, vicar general of the Sulpicians in the United States, rector of St. Mary's Seminary, and executive secretary of the Negro and Indian Commission. Turner quizzed Dyer about the truth of rumors and press reports that St. Mary's Seminary refused to accept applicants if they were dark enough to be identified as "Negro." Dyer answered that the authorities at St. Mary's Seminary would receive black students and that a black Josephite student, William Floyd, had attended courses during the previous two years. He added, however, that the seminary had to take into consideration "conditions which are not at all of our making or of our choice." Dyer insisted that St. Mary's could not admit black students to live as members of the seminary community, because that would make it impossible for the seminary to serve the many bishops who depended upon St. Mary's for the education of their clergy; the bishops simply would not enroll their students at St. Mary's if it accepted black students to live there. Reaffirming his belief in the desirability and necessity of black priests, Dyer proposed preparatory clerical colleges and seminaries specifically for black men; under existing circumstances, he said, "distinction without any sense of inferiority on either side" should govern relations between the races. Dyer further argued that

25. Cyprian Davis, O.S.B., "The Holy See and American Black Catholics: A Forgotten Chapter in the History of the American Church," *U.S. Catholic Historian*, VII, Nos. 2 and 3 (1988), 178; Stephen Neill, *A History of Christian Missions*, (Rev. ed.; Harmondsworth, Eng., 1986), 388; J. Derek Holmes, *The Papacy in the Modern World, 1914–1978* (New York, 1981), 23–25.

black racial pride should keep blacks from wishing to mingle with those who in any way objected to associating with them.[26]

Turner refused to accept Dyer's arguments. He told him that blacks had suspected the trouble lay higher up with the bishops, and he declared that black Catholics would have less respect for bishops who turned the church into a sociopolitical institution simply to appease "the unreasoned prejudice of a locality." Turner promised, however, that black Catholics would continue to "cling to the banner of the Lord Jesus Christ," despite the unchristian behavior of clerics. Calling racism the "paramount evil of the age," he insisted that true followers of Jesus should challenge and change prejudice, not accommodate to it by declaring it beyond the power of individuals to alter. He accused Dyer of having swallowed southern propaganda and argued that separate black seminaries would make a mockery of the declared all-inclusiveness of the church. Turner warned Dyer that black Catholics would cease to confide in any spiritual director who counseled against their taking possession of every civil and religious privilege.[27]

Turner also questioned Pastorelli about the truth of reports that the Josephites had "put up a bar against the further admission or ordination of colored men."[28] Turner's query placed Pastorelli in a difficult position and initiated a twenty-year conflict between the two men. Paternalistic by nature, Pastorelli resented the temerity of Turner and other lay black Catholics in questioning Josephite policies. More important, he could not reveal to Turner that the opposition of bishops to black priests had forced the Josephites to adopt a restrictive policy at Epiphany Apostolic College and St. Joseph's Seminary. Such an admission would have enraged the bishops and would also have confirmed the charges of discrimination leveled against the Josephites by the Baltimore and Washington branches of the Committee for the Advancement of Colored Catholics. Nor could Pastorelli disclose his own dissatisfaction with the two remaining black Josephite priests or his doubts about the leadership capabilities of black men, since to do so would surely have alienated additional numbers of black Catholics.

In his patronizing response to Turner, therefore, Pastorelli re-

26. Edward R. Dyer to Thomas Wyatt Turner, October 14, 1919, in Turner Papers.

27. Thomas Wyatt Turner to Edward R. Dyer, October 18, 1919, copy in Turner Papers.

28. Thomas Wyatt Turner to Louis B. Pastorelli, October 15, 1919, in PMC.

sorted to tactics that would mark his dealings with black activists over the years: evasions, half-truths, and stonewalling. He acknowledged that "certain agitation" had erupted in a number of places and had even found its way into the pages of the *Afro-American*, but he hoped that "men of your intelligence and judgment would be able to discriminate between facts and unreasoning sentiment." After reviewing the service of the Josephites to the black community over the years, he asked rhetorically, "What conceivable object could the Fathers of St. Joseph's Society have in attempting to establish as a principle that no colored men shall be admitted to the priesthood? May I not appeal to your common sense?" As to William Floyd, who had become the center of public controversy, Pastorelli claimed that the black seminarian had been judged by the same standards as white seminarians. He further explained that Floyd had come "under influences that we sincerely regret . . . expressing views that we considered incompatible for work on our missions." Pastorelli indicated that he had provided Floyd with a good recommendation and the opportunity to pursue his priestly studies with another religious society. He closed by declaring, "The Josephite Society has never said that there should not be a priesthood for the Colored race, and while I am at its head it will never say so."[29]

Not surprisingly, Pastorelli's circuitous response failed to satisfy Turner, who bluntly accused Pastorelli of having failed to answer his question about Josephite admissions policy and of having insulted him by gratuitously attributing his inquiry to sentiment. "You know as well as I do," Turner lectured the Josephite superior general, "that the rankest kind of discriminations are being practiced even from the sanctuary." Turner questioned Pastorelli's fitness to handle the "Negro's case" in the church when he could so casually dismiss inquiries about whether the Josephites "are shutting the door to our sons." He called on Pastorelli to explain his "silence in the midst of the wholesale discrimination practiced in and out of the Catholic Church upon the Colored Catholic."[30]

Expressing regret at the tone and the "rather extreme view" of Turner's letter, Pastorelli defended the church's efforts among blacks. He explained that he had intended the statement in his earlier letter to apply to the Josephite admissions policy toward black

29. Louis B. Pastorelli to Thomas Wyatt Turner, October 18, 1919, copy in PMC.
30. Thomas Wyatt Turner to Louis B. Pastorelli, October 24, 1919, in PMC.

students and then asserted that the Josephites "have not closed Epiphany's or St. Joseph's doors to them." He left himself an escape route, though, by adding that "the right to determine their fitness to continue in their studies when admitted is ours," fitness being a highly subjective judgment. For a statement on the Josephites' position vis-à-vis black priests, Pastorelli referred Turner to forthcoming articles in the *Ecclesiastical Review* by Timothy B. Moroney, the rector of St. Joseph's Seminary. In the January, 1920, issue of the journal, Moroney wrote, "A native clergy is, of course, inevitable, and the question is at present an absorbing topic of thought for those who are charged with the practical administration of the colored missions."[31] The article, remarkable only for its ambiguity, could be interpreted several ways. Turner did not find in it a satisfactory explanation of Josephite policy.

Pastorelli's disingenuous denials of discrimination at Epiphany College and St. Joseph's Seminary only served to anger the insurgents, who could see for themselves the dearth of black students at both institutions. Father Dorsey fueled their skepticism by charging that as early as 1917 the Josephites had attempted to keep Floyd from advancing to St. Joseph's by lying to him that the Sulpicians at St. Mary's, where the Josephite seminarians took their theology classes, opposed black students. According to Dorsey, on learning of the lie, the Sulpicians informed the Josephites and Floyd that they had no objection to his attending classes, and the young man advanced to the seminary. Dorsey charged that two years later Josephite oppositon forced Floyd out of the seminary.[32]

In November, 1919, at a smoker-buffet sponsored by the Baltimore branch of the Committee for the Advancement of Colored Catholics and held at the hall of the Knights of St. John in St. Peter Claver Parish, several speakers condemned the Josephites for their alleged opposition to black Catholic priests. Marcellus Dorsey cited several examples of how racial prejudice had prevented otherwise qualified black men from studying for the priesthood. At the end of the meeting, a collection netted $55 for William Floyd, by then a seminarian studying for the Society of African Missions at St. Paul's Seminary in the archdiocese of St. Paul.

31. Louis B. Pastorelli to Thomas Wyatt Turner, October 31, 1919, copy in PMC; T. B. Moroney, "Catholic Activity in Behalf of the Negro," *Ecclesiastical Review*, LXII (January, 1920), 53.

32. "Negro Priests Urged," Baltimore *Afro-American*, November 21, 1919, clipping in PMC; John H. Dorsey to James Wendel, January 3, 1920, in SASA.

Tension between the insurgents and the Josephites led to a confrontation after Sunday mass at St. Barnabas Parish in Baltimore
between Conrad Rebesher, the pastor, and Charles Woodland,
president of the insurgents. During the face off, Rebesher reportedly
threatened Woodland with personal violence. Following the incident, Royal Addison and Marcellus Dorsey stridently attacked
Rebesher and the Josephites in the *Afro-American*. Addison charged
that Rebesher and "his clique" had no sympathy for the progress of
blacks, from whom they drew their bread and salary. He accused
the Josephites of having done nothing for black education during
the previous fifty years and of having established segregation wherever they went. "It is time," he declared, "for them to get off the
job and give it to someone who will put it over." Marcellus Dorsey
also denounced the Josephites for operating "backward" schools and
for failing to provide any schools for higher training, high school,
or college. He repeated the charge that "the present directors and
the clique in charge of the headquarters of the Josephite Fathers . . .
are prejudiced and after years among the colored people . . . are mis-
erably incompetent and hostile to the religious and educational developments of colored Catholics." Although black Catholics such
as Gustave Aldrich, a former student at Epiphany College, urged
on the insurgents, many of their fellow black Catholics, raised in
the tradition of never questioning the parish priest, disapproved of
their actions.[33]

While the Baltimore insurgents waged their campaign against
the Josephites in the black press, Thomas Turner and his branch of
the Committee for the Advancement of Colored Catholics continued to lobby church authorities. On Monday, December 1,
1919, Turner and several members of his committee met in Washington, D.C., for two hours with Archbishop Giovanni Bonzano.
In addition to recounting their personal experiences of discrimination in the church, the members of Turner's delegation also discussed the creation of black courts in the Knights of Columbus, admission of blacks to all Catholic institutions, including Catholic
University, and promotion of a black clergy. Writing in the *Afro-
American* about the meeting, Marcellus Dorsey, clearly unaware of
Bonzano's private views of blacks, judged it a success and indicated

33. "Negro Priests Urged," Baltimore *Afro-American*, November 21, 1919,
clipping in PMC; "Former Student at Epiphany College in Walbrook, Urges Insurgents to Fight On," Baltimore *Afro-American*, November 28, 1919, clipping in
PMC; Olga Dorsey and Earl Counters interview, November 2, 1983.

that the committee left the apostolic delegate convinced it had a friend in court who held the same interests as they did. Dorsey predicted that Rome would intervene on behalf of American black Catholics and would satisfy their grievances.[34]

Bonzano, however, in describing his meeting with the Turner committee to the Reverend Peter Janser, provincial of the Divine Word Missionaries, sounded a far more cautious note. He remained noncommittal on the issue of black priests, telling Janser that he had spoken to many bishops and received but one answer about black Catholic priests: "The time had not yet arrived, they could not be relied upon, etc." Janser quoted Bonzano as saying, "The fact that the Jospehites have discontinued taking candidates undoubtedly strengthened [the bishops'] view."[35]

The barrage of criticism that he received about Josephite policy naturally weighed heavily on Pastorelli. Individual Josephites tried to encourage and console him. Charles Hannigan, writing from Richmond, urged him to remember that "the Society has certainly been the friendliest friend the colored people have had in this country, and we know the facts will bear out this statement." He recommended that Pastorelli ignore the attackers. Harry Kane in San Antonio reassured his worried superior that he had not heard the "first word . . . or read of propaganda for a colored priesthood" in his parish of St. Peter Claver's.[36] That soon changed.

In January, 1920, *Crisis* published an article by George Joseph MacWilliam of Philadelphia entitled "The Catholic Church and the Negro Priest"—an article that sent shock waves through the black Catholic community. MacWilliam alleged that the Josephites had agreed to accept him into Epiphany Apostolic College but had insisted that he pay $250 in tuition, unlike white students, who, he mistakenly asserted, attended free. When he agreed to that condition, MacWilliam claimed, the Josephites reneged on their promise and revoked his acceptance. He further charged that the Holy Ghost Fathers had rejected his application to their preparatory seminary and that their American provincial, whom he incorrectly identified in the article as the "Rev. J. Griffin," had made insulting

34. "Catholic Insurgents Take Fight to Papal Delegate," Baltimore *Afro-American*, December 11, 1919, clipping in PMC.

35. Peter Janser to James Wendel, February 20, 1920, copy in Albert S. Foley Papers, JFA.

36. Charles Hannigan to Louis B. Pastorelli, December 22, 1919, in 37-H, Harry Kane to Louis B. Pastorelli, December 16, 1919, in 37-K, both in JFA.

remarks about Joseph Burgess, the lone black American Spiritan. According to MacWilliam, the provincial had declared his unwillingness to accept black students for three reasons: because God did not want black men as priests, because black men were absolutely unfit for the priesthood, and because black people did not want them. MacWilliam claimed in the article that he had sought admission to Catholic seminaries for eight years and that his story illustrated the sad fate of many worthy young black men who desired holy orders. "We are," he declared, "governed by the most prejudiced men on this continent, who impose their conditions on us and tell us it is God's will."[37]

His story, appearing as it did in the widely read *Crisis* and in the midst of the feud between the Josephites and the Committee for the Advancement of Colored Catholics, created a furor among Catholic and non-Catholic blacks. MacWilliam's tale appeared so similar to the experiences of many other black aspirants to the priesthood that many blacks overlooked its glaring inaccuracies. The Indianapolis *Ledger*, only one of a number of black newspapers to voice outrage, declared in an editorial, "If these statements are true, it is time that every self-respecting person of Color who is identified with the Roman Church, should get up, brush the dust of shame from off his garments, and walk out of a so-called Christian Church that would dare thus insult a developing race." A. A. Steer, a black Catholic resident of the Panama Canal Zone, informed Cardinal Gibbons that the *Crisis* article had caused discussion among the black Catholic converts there, and he asked the cardinal for the church's version of the case.[38]

Monsignor John Burke, of the Catholic Board for Mission Work Among the Colored People, describing black Catholics as stunned by the MacWilliam article, urged Eugene Phelan, the Holy Ghost provincial, to reply to *Crisis*. Burke worried that since "*Crisis* is read by very many of the better class of Colored Protestants . . . great harm will come to our Missionary work if the complainant is not satisfactorily answered." Although Phelan at first believed he should simply ignore the flap, he subsequently allowed T. J. Park, MacWilliam's pastor in Philadelphia and the man who, according to MacWilliam, had related the provincial's comments about black

37. George Joseph MacWilliam, "The Catholic Church and the Negro Priest," *Crisis*, XIX (January, 1920), 122–23.
38. "The Negro and Romanism," Indianapolis *Ledger*, [1920?], clipping in PMC; A. A. Steer to Cardinal James Gibbons, February 1, 1920, in PMC.

priests, to deny categorically the statements attributed to him by MacWilliam. The next month Joseph Hanley, the Josephite rector of Epiphany College, explained in a letter to *Crisis* that the Josephites had indeed rejected MacWilliam but had done so because he had misrepresented himself and had been caught in untruths and inaccuracies that manifested character defects undesirable in a candidate for the priesthood. Hanley indicated that "at the time of Mr. McWilliams' [*sic*] application, there was a colored student in the college, and at the same time two other colored candidates had been accepted."[39]

The Baltimore insurgents viewed the MacWilliam story as further evidence of Josephite perfidy and maintained their pressure on Pastorelli. In early February, 1920, when the pastorate of St. Peter Claver Parish in Baltimore became vacant, Royal Addison, writing as commander of the St. Peter Claver post of the fraternal organization the Knights of St. John and claiming to represent more than half of the parish membership, requested that Pastorelli name Father Dorsey to succeed the Reverend James Nally, an old ally of the Dorseys. After informing Addison that such an appointment would violate established procedures and the rights of men who had more seniority than Dorsey, Pastorelli appointed Justin McCarthy, the former Josephite superior general, as pastor. The *Afro-American* concluded, with good reason as it turned out, that Pastorelli had appointed McCarthy in order to curb those at St. Peter Claver's who criticized the Josephites and the church. The paper indicated its distaste for the new pastor by identifying him as the Josephite superior who had refused to admit MacWilliam and who had "formulated the policy by which colored candidates are virtually excluded from St. Joseph's Seminary." It quoted a parishioner as saying about McCarthy, "We are tired of supporting broken down hacks and Negro haters." For his part, McCarthy wasted no time in challenging the insurgents. In his first sermon, he attacked those who had openly criticized the church and the Josephites and warned his congregation that "the devil was among them."[40]

39. John E. Burke to Eugene Phelan, February 8, 1920, Eugene Phelan to John E. Burke, February 19, 1920, copy, both in 6D-12-6, SPAUSA; Albert S. Foley, S.J., *God's Men of Color: The Colored Catholic Priests of the United States, 1854–1954* (1955; rpr. New York, 1969), 77.

40. "From Janitor to Priesthood," Baltimore *Afro-American*, February [12?], 1920, clipping in PMC.

Disillusionment with the Josephites finally led Turner to write on behalf of his committee to Cardinal Gibbons on March 1, 1920, to call his attention once again to its charge, voiced at the September, 1919, meeting of the hierarchy, that the Josephites refused to accept black candidates for the priesthood. Turner protested against the further expansion of St. Joseph's Society in the black community "so long as it maintains this pernicious and un-Catholic discrimination against our boys." It grieved him to make such a protest, he wrote, since he knew that some of the Josephites "are fine Christian spirits and do not believe in these anti-Christian practices of the latter-day superiors of the Order in stifling the priestly vocation of . . . colored boys." Turner accused the two superiors, McCarthy and Pastorelli, of patronizing blacks, of assuming "that white men can interpret the feelings and aspirations of colored men" without allowing them a voice in matters that affected them. He viewed the Josephite failure to "provide a single school beyond the elementary grade" as part of an approach designed to keep black Catholics in subordinate positions. After all, Turner pointed out, if black youth could not obtain decent educations, they could never qualify for seminaries. In the absence of a black priesthood, he declared, black Catholics would prefer white diocesan priests to a Josephite society that failed to understand their needs and aspirations. Charging that the Josephites tried to shift blame onto diocesan priests and bishops, Turner said, "Many facts lead us to feel that this is not wholly the case."[41]

Gibbons passed Turner's letter on to Pastorelli, who prepared a lengthy, clever memo for the cardinal. Pastorelli denied that either he or McCarthy had inaugurated a policy of refusing black candidates for the priesthood and pointed out that during the previous six years, two black seminarians, John Teureaud and William Floyd, had attended St. Joseph's Seminary. John Teureaud had died in 1915 but, according to Pastorelli, "would have been ordained had he lived," whereas Floyd had been "urged to discontinue" because of "traits judged not in the best interests of the Society." Still, Pastorelli reported, he had helped Floyd find a seminary where he could continue his studies. Pastorelli maintained that 75 percent of the letters of application to Epiphany College on file from black stu-

41. Thomas Wyatt Turner *et al.* to Cardinal James Gibbons, March 1, 1920, in 131-H, AAB.

dents indicated that the applicants exceeded the acceptable age limit or lacked the necessary education to take up college studies. Although failing to explain adequately what had happened to the other 25 percent, Pastorelli claimed that during the previous two years, Epiphany had accepted two black candidates, neither of whom had enrolled when classes began. As further proof of his support for black priests, he also disclosed that, on his instructions, Father Manley, the rector of Epiphany College, had written to some of the applicants deemed unsuited for Josephite community life and had offered to educate them at the college if they could find bishops who would adopt them.

Pastorelli denied that Josephite authorities had blamed the bishops for the small number of black priests; he countercharged that some blacks confused a vocation with race advancement. Pointing out that normally only 10 percent of white seminarians persevered to ordination, Pastorelli argued that blacks could not realistically expect many priests from among their people, since Catholics constituted such a small percentage of the race—a race only a half-century removed from slavery. As for Turner's charges about inadequate schools, he pointed to high school departments at parish schools in Mobile, Pine Bluff, and Baltimore and to plans for a high school as part of the new St. Peter Claver parish school in Baltimore. He reminded Gibbons of the key role played by two Josephites, Pierre LeBeau and Justin McCarthy, in the founding of Xavier University in New Orleans, the only black Catholic college. Pastorelli blamed the inadequacies found in Josephite educational institutions on shortages of priests, sisters, and money.[42]

Gibbons used Pastorelli's memo as the basis for his reply to Turner. In addition, the cardinal appealed to Turner to use his influence to make blacks realize and appreciate the efforts the church, with limited funds and personnel, had made on their behalf. He closed with his familiar assertion that "there is not a bishop in the United States but what is concerned with the spiritual progress of the Colored Race and doing all in his power along the line."[43] Thus certain that the Josephites clearly enjoyed the cardinal's confidence despite the attacks of the small coterie of black Catholics in Baltimore and Washington, Pastorelli then took the offensive.

42. Louis B. Pastorelli memorandum to Cardinal James Gibbons, March 6, 1920, copy in PMC.

43. Cardinal James Gibbons to Thomas Wyatt Turner, March 15, 1920, copy in 131-P-2, AAB.

He had laid the groundwork for his counterattack against the insurgents by naming McCarthy as pastor of St. Peter Claver's and by cultivating the favor of the bishops. In the March 12, 1920, edition of the *Afro-American,* Royal Addison unwittingly provided Pastorelli with an excuse to move against the insurgents when he published an insulting personal attack against several Josephites that exceeded in stridency and bitterness any of his previous articles. Addison savaged Joseph Butsch, a Josephite who had written to the *Afro-American* to complain about articles that he believed unjustly criticized the Josephites and the Catholic church. Addison called Butsch "a miserable failure as a pastor" and a member "of the headquarters clique which barred Negroes from the seminary" and accused the Josephites of instituting segregated churches in order to create "desirable berths for inefficient and incapacitated priests to live by and at the expense of their propaganda." Addison also took exception to the articles Moroney published in the *Ecclesiastical Review,* which described blacks as irreligious and implied that they lacked the capacity for proper moral family relationships. "Such types of men as McCarthy, Moroney, Butsch, Rebesher, and Pastorelli are lamentable accidents to the priesthood," Addison declared, "self-styled benefactors . . . who pretend they are making such great self-sacrifice . . . who put stumbling blocks in the way of the pious progressive Negro." Addison and the insurgents also published a pamphlet that repeated many of their standard charges against the Josephites and the church in general; it also included a copy of MacWilliam's article from *Crisis.*[44]

After obtaining a copy of the pamphlet and reading Addison's broadside, Pastorelli took steps to silence the insurgents. He ordered McCarthy to refuse to recommend any candidates or sign any more applications for Commandery #4 of the Knights of St. John in St. Peter Claver Parish, the organization that Addison headed. He also showed a copy of the insurgent pamphlet to Gibbons, who agreed that the Josephite superior should take punitive action against Addison. Pastorelli subsequently wrote to C. W. Wallace, supreme secretary of the Knights of St. John, charging Addison and his compatriots with attacking priests and bishops in articles, letters, and

---

44. "Mr. Addison Adds Another Chapter to Discussion in Reference to Colored Catholic's Fight for Just Recognition," Baltimore *Afro-American,* March 12, 1920, clipping, Louis B. Pastorelli to C. W. Wallace, April 12, 1920, copies of both in PMC.

pamphlets "of the most abusive kind," spreading false statements and twisting the meaning of words and events, fostering disloyalty to their pastors, and generally disturbing the body of black Catholics and scandalizing Protestants. At Wallace's urging, Addison and Pastorelli met at the seminary to discuss their differences. The black leader, however, stood by what he had written and told the Josephite that he believed he had done nothing for which he should make amends. Pastorelli advised Gibbons that Addison remained obdurate; the cardinal insisted that he could not tolerate Addison's conduct. Pastorelli then informed the Supreme Board of the Knights of St. John about the unsatisfactory results of his meeting with Addison and also about Gibbons' insistence that Addison be punished. Thereupon, the board brought charges against Addison. The leaders of Commandery #4, displeased with Addison over his public dispute with clergy, first demanded his resignation; when it was not forthcoming, they removed him from office.[45]

Pastorelli interpreted the removal of Addison by the members of Commandery #4 as proof that the majority of black Catholics supported the Josephites and disapproved of the tactics of the "radical insurgents." Expanding on his views about the insurgents to his good friend Archbishop John W. Shaw of New Orleans, Pastorelli wrote that no one denied blacks deserved to have some of their sons raised to the priesthood. But he thought the means used by the insurgents against the Josephites, who for years had labored for the uplift of the black race without thought of remuneration, to be "dastardly" and "the limit." Pastorelli wrote that "fortunately" the insurgents did not represent the majority of blacks but rather followed in the footsteps of black agitators who, during and since the war, had clamored "for all sorts of things and rights, social equality, inter-marriage, etc." He blamed "godless education" and "the untiring labors of . . . educated agitators" for the changes that had occurred in the race during the previous ten years. Shaw, who had written Pastorelli to complain about Josephites such as Sam Kelly, who allegedly advocated social equality between the races, sadly agreed with Pastorelli that agitation and propaganda for the ideal of

45. Louis B. Pastorelli to Archbishop John W. Shaw, April 5, 1920, C. W. Wallace to Royal G. Addison, April 14, 1920, Louis B. Pastorelli to C. W. Wallace, April 26, 1920, C. W. Wallace to Robert Hicks, May 3, 1920, Robert Hicks to C. W. Wallace, May 4, 1920, C. W. Wallace to Robert Hicks, May 13, 1920, copies of all in PMC.

social equality—an ideal that he "as a southerner" did not believe that God ever intended—had created "a discontented and rebellious spirit" among black Catholics.[46]

Pastorelli attempted to extinguish the "rebellious spirit" in Baltimore by depriving the activists of their propaganda forum. In April, 1920, with the blessing of Cardinal Gibbons, Pastorelli and Conrad Rebesher met with Dr. M. B. Rhetta of the *Afro-American* and assured him that St. Joseph's Seminary remained open to properly qualified black men. The interview satisfied the concerns of Carl Murphy, the publisher and editor of the *Afro-American* and an admirer of Gibbons for "the sledge hammer blows" the cardinal had struck against segregation laws and disfranchisement amendments in Maryland. Murphy wrote Gibbons that when the Josephite policy became generally known, "there will be no further need for the kind of articles that have been recently contributed to this paper by men who ardently stood for a colored priesthood." Gibbons accepted Murphy's letter as an apology for the appearance "of many misleading and at times abusive letters in the pages of the paper" and averred that the Catholic church did not draw any color line or refuse admittance to her priesthood solely because of color.[47] Gibbons did not, however, exclude social conditions, or even a partial consideration of color, as possible reasons for refusing a black student.

Despite the apparent accommodation between the *Afro-American* and the Josephites, Father Dorsey encouraged Turner to continue pressuring the society. "Constant judicious agitation is bound to bring good results," Dorsey wrote. He urged Turner to "Agitate! Agitate!" Dorsey accused the Catholic church in the United States of doing nothing to stem the tide of race prejudice; to the contrary, he claimed, "prejudice in the Church has kept pace with prejudice in the state." Dorsey also confessed to Turner that while on the mission band, he had defended the church by falsely claiming that prejudice did not exist within it. "I knew I was not telling the truth and my inner self rebelled. It is a God-given mission to rid the church of race prejudice."[48]

46. Louis B. Pastorelli to Archbishop John W. Shaw, April 5, 1920, copy, Archbishop John W. Shaw to Louis B. Pastorelli, April 12, 1920, both in PMC.
47. Carl Murphy to Cardinal James Gibbons, April 24, 1920, Cardinal James Gibbons to Carl Murphy, handwritten draft, both in 68-H, JFA.
48. John H. Dorsey to Thomas Wyatt Turner, May 22, 1920, in Turner Papers.

Constant agitation, however, created a backlash among more conservative black Catholics. In August, by a vote of fifty-seven to four, with sixteen abstentions, the Knights of Peter Claver, meeting in New Orleans for their tenth annual national convention, expelled Marcellus Dorsey for refusing to sign a retraction of the articles he had published criticizing priests and hierarchy. Stunned by his repudiation, he reportedly required the aid of two men as he staggered from the room. There was further talk and much consternation over the actions of his brother. Father Dorsey, who served as the national chaplain of the knights and who was in the city for the convention, publicly manifested his alienation from many of his fellow Josephites when he refused Joseph A. Lally's offer of hospitality and stayed instead at a house not belonging to St. Joseph's Society, thus creating the impression that the Josephites would not receive him.[49]

The installation of the Irish-born Michael Curley as the archbishop of Baltimore on November 30, 1921, following Cardinal Gibbons' death the previous March, further strengthened Pastorelli's hand in dealing with Turner and the insurgents. Curley had come to Baltimore after seven years as bishop of the diocese of St. Augustine, where he had led the fight against the Florida law that prohibited white sisters from teaching black children. While in Florida, he had apparently also absorbed a paternalistic racism that viewed blacks as little more than children in need of supervision from whites. Curley knew firsthand the vulnerability of the church and the depth of racial animosity in both the lower and upper South. As archbishop of Baltimore from 1921 to 1947, he feared the possibility of a race riot (one had occurred in Washington, D.C., which was part of the archdiocese, in 1919) and sought to avoid any action by the church that might inflame racial passions. Thus, when Monsignor Aluigi Cossio of the Apostolic Delegation queried him regarding segregation in the archdiocese, Curley recommended that the church "leave well enough alone." He explained that "it would be the height of imprudence" for any priest or bishop in the South even to suggest that blacks and whites should mingle in Catholic churches. "It would mean," he con-

49. Minutes of the Tenth Convention, National Council of the Knights of Peter Claver, in A. P. Tureaud Papers, ARC; Joseph Lally to Louis B. Pastorelli, n.d., in 38-K, JFA.

tinued, "if not a race riot, at least a kind of inconvenience which might lead in a moment of passion to unforeseen results."[50]

Although he occasionally met with Turner and other members of the Committee for the Advancement of Colored Catholics, Curley had little understanding of or sympathy for black Catholic activists and their causes. On March 15, 1922, for example, during one of their meetings, he listened to Turner express dissatisfaction with the Josephites for thwarting the ambitions of young black men for the priesthood. Turner also asked for better black Catholic schools and for an explanation of why Catholic University refused admission to black students. Following the meeting, Curley discussed Turner's concerns with Bishop Thomas J. Shahan, the rector of Catholic University, and Edward Dyer, the president of St. Mary's Seminary. When both men assured the archbishop that the health of their respective institutions depended on the maintenance of the racial status quo, that settled matters for Curley.[51]

A few months later, writing again to Cossio, Curley referred to Turner's call for black priests and told the monsignor that the vast majority of black people did not want black priests but wished rather to retain their bond with white priests. "Besides," the testy archbishop continued, "we can't give them what we have not, namely colored priests. There are only a few in the country." Alluding to Father Dorsey, Curley said, "We have one of them in Baltimore and I cannot say that he is a success." Obviously convinced that Rome did not appreciate the difficulties faced by the church in the United States, Curley closed by appealing to the delegation to explain to the Holy See the "keen race distinction which the Catholic Church in America has not made and cannot solve."[52]

Not surprisingly, Curley sympathized with the Josephites in their struggle with the Committee for the Advancement of Colored Catholics. He was not favorably disposed, therefore, when on December 30, 1922, he received yet another complaint from the

50. Peter Janser to Alois Heick, June 6, 1922, in SASA; Peter E. Hogan, S.S.J., "Archbishop Curley and the Blacks" (Paper presented at the spring meeting of the American Catholic Historical Society, Louisville, April 16, 1983); Archbishop Michael Curley to Aluigi Cossio, December 12, 1922, copy in Roman file, AAB.

51. CMB, March 15, 1922, in AAB.

52. Archbishop Michael Curley to Aluigi Cossio, December 12, 1922, copy in Roman file, AAB.

committee about the Josephites. The complaint sprang from an incident at Holy Redeemer Church in Washington, D.C. On November 3, 1922, in the church basement during a meeting of a group of black laymen and several white priests working to raise funds and arouse enthusiasm for Cardinal Gibbons Institute, a proposed national Catholic high school for black Catholics in Ridge, Maryland, Francis Tobin, the Josephite pastor, "took violent exception" to some of the comments made about the part that Catholic blacks should play in their education. He allegedly went up to vespers and denounced those meeting in the basement as "enemies of the Church." He then reportedly returned to the basement and shut off the lights on them. As a result of that episode, characterized by J. Arthur Henson, secretary of the Committee for the Advancement of Colored Catholics, as indicative of "an absolute lack of appreciation of the aspirations and desires of the Colored," Turner's committee asked Archbishop Curley to withdraw the Josephites from Holy Redeemer Parish and from the black apostolate in general. They requested that he replace the Josephites with such diocesan clergy as he might choose. Henson, writing on behalf of the committee, closed his letter to the archbishop by stating, "We cannot have advancement of the Negro in the Church with the Josephite methods of dealing with our problems."[53]

Curley vigorously defended the Josephites, calling them "the best and sincerest friends of our colored people"; he adamantly refused to consider withdrawing them from Holy Redeemer Parish or from the black apostolate. The archbishop scolded Henson, telling him that "we are going to advance the welfare of the colored people but little by an agitation that will mean disintegration of unity of purpose."[54]

Pastorelli had thus withstood attempts by black Catholic activists to force a change in his policy at the college and seminary. He enjoyed the confidence of the archbishop of Baltimore and could draw comfort from the knowledge that Curley would not pressure him to embark on any new, "dangerous experiments" with black students at Epiphany Apostolic College or St. Joseph's Seminary. As a way of attempting to deflect black Catholic criticism and to manifest Josephite support for the concept of a black clergy, Pasto-

53. J. Arthur Henson to Archbishop Michael Curley, December 30, 1922, in H-792, AAB.

54. Archbishop Michael Curley to J. Arthur Henson, January 5, 1923, copy in H-791, AAB.

relli tried, in succeeding years, to keep at least one light-skinned Afro-American student at either one of the institutions.[55]

It is difficult to judge the effects of the controversy between the Josephites and the Baltimore and Washington branches of the Committee for the Advancement of Colored Catholics on the mass of black Catholics served by the society. The Josephites' own statistics, not always reliable before 1929, indicated that between 1918 and 1922, the years of bitterest contention, yearly adult conversions dropped by 40 percent, from approximately 775 in 1918 to 475 in 1922. After 1922, they began gradually to increase. Other factors, such as the dislocation caused by black migration to northern cities, might also explain the dramatic five-year decline in conversions. Nevertheless, the public attacks on the Josephites in the black press certainly did not help Josephite efforts to evangelize the black community.[56]

Attacks on the Josephites by lay black Catholics abated somewhat after 1922, in part because black Catholic protest had borne fruit. Despite their failure to effect a change in Josephite policy, the persistence of black Catholics kept the issue of black priests before church authorities, both in the United States and in Rome. As a result, even as Turner and his allies battled with Pastorelli, two missionary societies—the Society of the Divine Word and the Society of African Missions—with significant support from the Holy See, moved to establish seminaries that would educate black men for the priesthood.

55. Louis B. Pastorelli to Archbishop John W. Shaw, September, 1930, copy in 70-R, JFA.

56. John T. Gillard, S.S.J., *The Catholic Church and the American Negro* (1929; rpr. New York, 1968), 65–66.

Chapter VI

WATCHFUL WAITING, 1918–1924

*It is our wish to wait upon the guidance of the Bishops, as we believe
ourselves ancillary to the Bishops and not so much an independent group
working by and for ourselves.*
—LOUIS B. PASTORELLI, FEBRUARY 25, 1920

While Louis Pastorelli and his Josephites fended off the challenges
of black Catholic activists, two European missionary communities,
the Society of the Divine Word and the Society of African Missions, headquartered respectively in Steyl, Holland, and Lyon,
France, responded to the need for black clergy by opening seminaries in Mississippi and New Jersey to educate black priests. Their
efforts drew support from the pope and from powerful congregations
of the Roman Curia, whose proposals for reinvigorating the black
apostolate alarmed American bishops. Anxious to placate Rome
and to avoid radical intervention by the Holy See, the bishops became more willing to tolerate a black seminary. Pastorelli, who regarded the missionaries of both European communities as naïve
about racial conditions in the United States and about future prospects for black priests, skeptically watched the progress of the new
seminaries. He refused to alter Josephite policy without a clear
signal that American bishops would accept black priests into their
dioceses. The painful experiences of the few black priests and seminarians in the United States during the early 1920s confirmed
Pastorelli's belief that a conservative approach to the issue best
served the interests of St. Joseph's Society.

   As noted earlier, the Divine Word Missionaries in 1915 temporarily shelved plans for a black seminary after they encountered opposition to their initial proposal. During the next four years, they
studied the problems connected with opening such a seminary and

laid the groundwork for another attempt. The Reverend James Wendel attempted to enlist public support for a black seminary through articles that appeared in *Colored Messenger*, a quarterly magazine he had founded, and through correspondence with white clergy and black laymen. For his part, the Reverend Matthew Christman founded a high school for blacks in Greenville, Mississippi. The curriculum of the school, which included four years of Latin, a prerequisite for seminaries, went far beyond the rudimentary education advocated by Bishop John Gunn and demonstrated the intellectual capacity of blacks for "a higher literary education." Following the conclusion of World War I, therefore, the predominantly German Divine Word Missionaries, sensing a crisis among blacks in the church and feeling "much better prepared for the great work," subsequently resurrected their plan for a black seminary.[1]

In April, 1919, following a tour of the North by Wendel during which he sampled lay and clerical opinion about the Negro problem, the five Divine Word missionaries of the southern missions assembled at their Easter meeting and petitioned Father Burgmer, their provincial, to approve a seminary for black students. Shortly thereafter, Peter T. Janser replaced Burgmer as provincial. A number of months passed, while he became familiar with his new office, without Janser's taking any formal action on the Easter resolution. Wendel, meanwhile, remained busy. He persuaded Gunn to grant informal permission for a black seminary in the Natchez diocese, on the conditions that the future black priests form a religious community and that the Divine Word Missionaries control and direct that community. Wendel also raised the idea of a black seminary with Nicholas Blum, the acting Divine Word superior general, who applauded his efforts and encouraged him to make a formal proposal through Janser to the general council, or generalate.[2]

The Divine Word Missionaries also took heart from the publica-

1. James Wendel to Thomas Wyatt Turner, November 16, 1915, in Thomas Wyatt Turner Papers, MSRC; "Site of First Divine Word Seminary," *Catholic Action of the South* (New Orleans), October 11, 1945, clipping in Black Priests file, JFA; Matthew Christman, "St. Augustine's Mission House" (Typescript in SASA), 6–8.

2. Charles W. Malin, S.V.D., "Integration of the Catholic Clergy in the United States, The Divine Word Missionaries' Chapter" (M.A. thesis, Marquette University, 1964), 25; Christman, "St. Augustine's Mission House," 8; Bishop John E. Gunn to James Wendel, August 23, 1919, January 5, 1920, Nicholas Blum to James Wendel, October 21, 1919, all in Albert S. Foley Papers, JFA.

tion of Benedict XV's encyclical *Maximum illud.* Following the war, Benedict began a major reorganization of missionary activity, emphasizing the recruitment of indigenous clergy and the formation of native hierarchies. The encyclical was a major step in that reorganization, for in it he recommended the development of native clergies and the creation of native seminaries in centers of Catholic missionary activity. Some American clergy argued that the pope had not intended his encyclical to apply to the United States, with its "unique race conditions."[3] The Divine Word Missionaries claimed otherwise, however, and cited the papal letter to strengthen their arguments for a black seminary in Mississippi.

In January, 1920, Janser traveled to Baltimore and Washington, D.C., to test the reactions of key individuals, among them Archbishop Bonzano, John Dorsey, Cardinal Gibbons, and Mother Katharine Drexel, to the proposed seminary. He missed Pastorelli, who was out of town when he arrived in Baltimore. Janser found Bonzano unwilling to commit himself. The delegate referred to his November meeting with Turner and told Janser that he had polled the bishops on the subject of black priests: all to whom he had spoken argued that the time was not yet suitable for black clergy because of unfavorable social conditions and also because the few blacks who had previously been ordained priests had proven unreliable. Janser believed that "the fact that the Josephites have discontinued taking candidates . . . undoubtedly strengthened this view." Bonzano did not overtly object to the plans of the Divine Word Missionaries to establish a religious community of black priests, but he warned of potential difficulties should a black priest wish to leave the community but be unable to find a bishop to accept him into a diocese. Unlike the apostolic delegate, John Dorsey minced no words with Janser. He bitterly assailed the notion of a segregated seminary. "A most bitter fight is on," he declared in an earlier letter to Wendel, referring to the conflict that raged between Pastorelli and the Committee for the Advancement of Colored Catholics. He warned that "if the Josephites do not open the doors of their college and seminary to colored students, they will lose out in their missionary endeavors." Dorsey insisted that the Catholic church in America should countenance no segregation and deplored what he termed the "weak kneed and spineless priests and bishops!"

3. J. Derek Holmes, *The Papacy in the Modern World, 1914–1978* (New York, 1981), 23–25; A. F. Isenberg to Bishop Jules Jeanmard, September 12, 1920, in Bishop Jules B. Jeanmard Papers, ADL.

Gibbons expressed sympathy for the project, but, Janser noted, "he is a man of the past, whose views may be quoted on paper, but whose voice will not carry far with the hierarchy." Mother Katharine Drexel demonstrated her support for the seminary in a concrete way by pledging two thousand dollars if the Divine Word Missionaries opened it that year.[4]

Janser did not receive so encouraging a response on February 9, 1920, when he met with Archbishop George Mundelein of Chicago, whose archdiocese included the Divine Word provincial headquarters in Techny, Illinois. Mundelein opposed a "colored priesthood at this time" and insisted that he would not accept black students into his seminary. "Right or wrong," Janser told Wendel, "we cannot change him." Mundelein showed interest, though, in a plan for a black religious community of teaching brothers; he even volunteered to issue a special letter on its behalf. Janser demurred, however, insisting on preparing young men for the priesthood. He tried to allay Mundelein's fears by pointing out that if black candidates came from good Catholic families, the normal twelve- to thirteen-year span of time between entrance into a minor seminary and ordination would surely reveal their true character and vocation.[5]

Janser also crossed swords, albeit courteously, with Louis Pastorelli. During the provincial's absence, someone had included a reference to the infamous MacWilliam article in a publication sent out from Techny. Pastorelli thereupon wrote to Janser urging caution and discretion. Janser assured Pastorelli that he would instruct his priests to show greater reserve and prudence and "not aid a movement which is more or less radical." However, he firmly told Pastorelli that "we must give the Negro an education and must provide for Negro priests." The war had aroused their consciousness about racial justice, Janser observed, and though it might not include social equality, "it does include political, economic, and religious equality." Declaring that he had no doubt that the Holy Father had American blacks in mind when he wrote his recent encyclical, Janser insisted that blacks should have a priesthood of their own and warned, "It is almost too late to establish institutions for negroes only. There is no taste for segregation now." Janser then contacted Wendel, and, though congratulating him for his strong

4. Peter Janser to James Wendel, February 10, 1920, copy in Foley Papers; John H. Dorsey to James Wendel, January 3, 1920, in SASA.
5. Peter Janser to James Wendel, February 10, 1920, copy in Foley Papers.

advocacy of black priests in the latest issue of *Colored Messenger,* he nonetheless advised his friend to use discretion, "since there is still too much opposition in official quarters."[6]

Pastorelli's correspondence with two southern prelates illustrates the nature of the opposition faced by the Divine Word Missionaries. When Bishop John Morris of Little Rock solicited his confidential opinion about the missionaries' plans to create a community of black priests—a plan that Morris had once suggested to John Albert but now opposed—Pastorelli responded with a revealing exposition of his own views. He told Morris that most Josephites agreed the ultimate conversion of blacks would depend on blacks themselves. "Our hesitancy," he explained, "falls only on questions of immediate policy." Pastorelli claimed that the Josephites intended to draw "what young men we shall have raised to the priesthood" from black youth in Louisiana who had several generations of Catholic blood and traditions behind them. He dismissed the other element, which was made up, he claimed, mostly of converts who reflected "the Negro journals of the day" and who regarded the priesthood not so much as a sacred vocation but as an issue of "race advancement." Pastorelli flatly stated that "a Negro clergy must come" but added, "How and when it is to be brought about is the problem." Displaying a wariness born of personal experience in dealing with bishops on the issue, he suggested that before any religious community tried to develop black priests, the bishops of the South should meet to discuss the problem and "formulate a plan acceptable to all of us to follow." He continued, "It is our wish to wait upon the guidance of the Bishops as we believe ourselves ancillary to the Bishops and not so much an independent group working by and for ourselves."

Pastorelli attributed the apparent determination of the Divine Word Missionaries to proceed with their plan for a black seminary to their "German tenacity" and to their ignorance of conditions in the South. He warned that, before proceeding, the Divine Word Missionaries should obtain the bishops' assurances that they would allow black priests into their dioceses. Otherwise, "it would be a sort of martyrdom for those poor colored men raised to the priesthood." Referring to his experiences with the three black Josephite priests, Pastorelli told Morris that the Josephites could find no per-

6. Peter Janser to Louis B. Pastorelli, February 6, 1929, in PMC; Peter Janser to James Wendel, February 10, 1920, copy in Foley Papers.

manent place for them outside the Baltimore archdiocese and confided that "the three we had ordained have been a source of worry to us and we would gladly give them over to take part in the proposed work." In an attempt to promote discussion among southern bishops that might result in guidelines about black priests for religious communities, Pastorelli sent Archbishop Shaw a copy of his letter to Morris.[7]

The guidance provided by Morris and Shaw in response to his request only served to fuel Pastorelli's skepticism about the ultimate success of the Divine Word project. Morris thanked Pastorelli for his ideas and informed him that he had decided to discourage any proposal for a black seminary until the southern bishops as a group could meet and make recommendations. He indicated that he would suggest such a meeting to Archbishop Shaw. Morris pronounced earlier experiments with black priests failures and implied that the future promised little better. Shaw, though protesting his great sympathy for a race that he had "known since childhood," deemed the time inopportune to make the venture. He expressed no desire or need to discuss the issue with his suffragans.[8]

Despite Pastorelli's skepticism and the less-than-enthusiastic support of most bishops, however, the tenacious Germans persisted in their efforts. On February 24, 1920, the day that Wendel died, the Divine Word Missionaries received word from John Boden, the acting general administrator of the society, that the general council, pending more definite information regarding location, curriculum, funding, and the attitudes of bishops and a formal recommendation from the American provincial council, favored, at least in principle, the "Negro Minor seminary," as did Pope Benedict XV.[9]

Apparently, though, the generalate had not yet abandoned the idea that the Divine Word Missionaries might be able to educate the black seminarians for the diocesan clergy. Matthew Christman even suggested that the young black men become members, without vows, of the new religious community directed by the mission-

7. Bishop John B. Morris to Louis B. Pastorelli, February 12, 1920, in 69-M, Louis B. Pastorelli to Bishop John B. Morris, February 25, 1920, copy in 69-M, Louis B. Pastorelli to Archbishop John W. Shaw, April 5, 1920, copy in 69-S, all in JFA.

8. Bishop John B. Morris to Louis B. Pastorelli, March 4, 1920, copy in Bishop John B. Morris Papers, ADLR; Archbishop John W. Shaw to Louis B. Pastorelli, April 12, 1920, in 69-S, JFA.

9. John Boden to James Wendel, February 24, 1920, copy in Foley Papers.

aries, thereby making it easier for those already ordained to become diocesan priests if they so wished and if racial conditions improved to the point where they could find a bishop to incardinate them. On February 23, 1920, however, the provincial council, declaring that "no race has ever been converted except by its own priesthood" and citing the opposition of the American hierarchy to black diocesan clergy, supplied the requisite recommendation formally requesting the generalate to approve the creation of a religious community for blacks with a black preparatory seminary under the direction of Father Christman, to be located temporarily in Greenville, Mississippi. In May, 1920, the general council of the Society of the Divine Word approved the founding of Sacred Heart College in Greenville, Mississippi, for the special purpose of raising black priests.[10]

That same month, Janser met with Bishop Gunn in his official capacity as ordinary of the diocese to secure his permission to open the seminary. Gunn confirmed what he had earlier promised to Wendel. Although expressing himself as "entirely opposed to a secular colored priesthood," he expressed his approval of a religious community of black priests formed and directed by the Divine Word Missionaries. He promised to welcome black priests of this community into his diocese and to give them faculties so that they might work in missions among their people. He also approved the location of the preparatory seminary in Greenville, but he added that he "would like to be sure that the idea of forming a religious colored community of priests got the sanction of the proper Ecclesiastical superiors." Janser also called on Archbishop Shaw to explain his plans. Despite Shaw's earlier negative statements to Pastorelli, he gave Janser his verbal endorsement, which he promised to put in writing—a promise he never kept.[11]

Cognizant of the delicateness of his position in relation to the American hierarchy, Janser attempted to secure the support of the Holy See for the black seminary. To that end, he enlisted the help of Carl Friedrich, the Divine Word procurator general, or agent to the Roman Curia. Friedrich found Camillus Cardinal Laurenti, the

10. Malin, "Integration of Catholic Clergy," 33; resolutions of the provincial council meeting between February 19 and 23, 1920, copy in Foley Papers; Matthew Christman to Bishop John E. Gunn, June 19, 1920, in Bishop John E. Gunn Papers, ADJ.

11. Bishop John E. Gunn to Alois Heick, June 28, 1920, Peter Janser to Archbishop John W. Shaw, May 28, 1920, Peter Janser to Bruno Hagspiel, June 29, 1934, copies of all in SASA.

secretary of the Propaganda, Theodore Cardinal Valfre die Donzo, prefect of the Congregation of Religious, and Willem Cardinal van Rossum, prefect of the Propaganda, particularly supportive of a seminary for blacks. Laurenti even arranged a private audience for Friedrich with Pope Benedict XV, who applauded the plan and asked Friedrich to tell Janser he should pursue the work. When Friedrich referred to the possible opposition of some American bishops to the project, Benedict observed that it made no difference whether they objected, since he, the pope, supported the plan and "above the bishops stands the Pope." If Janser experienced difficulties with bishops, the pope instructed Friedrich, Janser should appeal directly to the Holy Father.[12]

Buoyed by knowledge of papal support, Christman proceeded with plans to open the seminary in the autumn. Janser suggested that he construct only temporary quarters until the seminary passed the experimental stage. Christman estimated that he would need twenty thousand dollars for a two-story building measuring fifty by forty-five feet. On July 1, 1920, Janser sent a letter to all priests in the United States advising them of plans for a separate black community of religious priests under the full control of the Society of the Divine Word. He noted that church authorities would decide at some future time whether the new community would affiliate with the Society of the Divine Word or become an independent organization. The Divine Word provincial attempted to wrap the seminary in the pope's mantle by claiming that his society had undertaken the project "at the request of Rome." Janser solicited advice, funds, and cooperation, asking priests to direct black young men who showed signs of a vocation to the Divine Word Missionaries. The letter indicated that Sacred Heart College would ordinarily accept only the children of Catholic parents. Janser's appeal to the largely indifferent or hostile clergy produced little in the way of donations for the seminary.[13]

12. Carl Friedrich to Alois Heick, December 22, 1921, in SASA. Attached to the letter was a typed, two-page essay in German entitled "Der Einfluss der römischen Kurie beim Werke des Priesterseminars in Bay Saint Louis" ["The Influence of the Roman Curia in the Erection of the Seminary in Bay St. Louis"]. See also Peter Janser to Archbishop George W. Mundelein, March 13, 1922, in Menceslaus Madaj Collection, AAC.

13. Christman, "St. Augustine's Mission House," 10; Peter Janser to Rev. and Dear Father, July 1, 1920, copy in SASA; M. Christman, "Pro Memoria: Financial Struggles and Conditions of St. Augustine [sic] Mission House, 1920–1928" (Typescript in SASA).

In September, 1920, Sacred Heart College accepted its first two students. Three separate gifts of two thousand dollars each from Monsignor Burke, Mother Katharine Drexel, and a northern donor by the name of Mr. Murphy gave the seminary its financial start. Christman erected a small, two-story, frame building, containing classrooms, a dining room, and a kitchen, on the spacious grounds of Sacred Heart Mission and also remodeled the attic of the high school building to serve as a dormitory for the prospective seminarians. The energetic Christman, aided by the Reverend Anthony Jacobs, served as rector, prefect, and teacher in the seminary, while still remaining pastor of Sacred Heart Parish. By the close of the first school year, the college had fourteen students.[14]

The new seminary drew mixed reactions from the Josephites. Many enthusiastically applauded and supported the venture. Stephen G. Sweeney, for example, the pastor of St. Philomena Parish in Pass Christian, Mississippi, assured Christman, "It will be one of my greatest joys if I can secure for you some candidates for your school." Joseph Lally, at Holy Redeemer Parish in New Orleans, bested Sweeney by proudly sending four youths to Christman during the seminary's first year of operation, including Maurice Rousseve, who was later ordained a priest. Lambert Welbers, a veteran of earlier controversies at Epiphany Apostolic College during the Slattery era and at the time stationed at Holy Redeemer in San Antonio, reacted more guardedly, asking Pastorelli to advise him on the proper Josephite attitude. Welbers suggested that "if it . . . has the sanctions of the hierarchy, we ought to support it." Pastorelli recommended that he simply "look on and mark the result for future use."[15]

John Albert, however, expressed no reservations about the Divine Word seminary; he welcomed it as the culmination of the proposal he had made back in 1913. He offered Christman his services as a field agent, whereby he would give parish missions and preach vocation sermons to generate support and recruit students for Sacred Heart College. He also suggested the possibility of the Divine

14. Christman, "St. Augustine's Mission House," 10; Albert S. Foley, S.J., *God's Men of Color: The Colored Catholic Priests of the United States, 1854–1954* (1955; rpr. New York, 1969), 126.

15. Stephen Sweeney to Matthew Christman, November 2, 1920, in SASA; Joseph Lally to Louis B. Pastorelli, November 10, 1920, in 38-K, JFA; Foley, *God's Men*, 126, 135; Lambert Welbers to Louis B. Pastorelli, November 4, 1920, in 38-W, JFA.

Word Missionaries taking over the 216-acre campus of the failing St. Joseph's College for Negro Catechists in Montgomery as a permanent site for Sacred Heart College.[16] Further, Albert urged Pastorelli to make a public gesture of support for Sacred Heart College as a diplomatic way of countering the impression that the Josephites did not favor black priests. Opposing this seminary, he told Pastorelli, would be unfair and would win little support for the Josephites. "They have the field," he advised him. "Let us not be jealous but enter heart and soul in the movement." Albert warned that the episodes with the insurgents in Baltimore had placed the Josephites "in a most unfavorable light in the North" and had created the impression, even at the Catholic Board for Mission Work Among the Colored People, that the society opposed "the Colored clergy idea." Such an impression, he cautioned, would eventually harm Josephite finances, vocations, and credibility among blacks.

Albert spelled out his interpretation of the Josephite stand on black priests. It was essentially that the Josephites rejected the notion, prevalent among many diocesan clergy, that St. Joseph's Society "is the receptacle for the trying out of all Colored vocations." Rather, the Josephites wanted bishops and other religious communities to assume their own responsibilities for accepting and developing whatever vocations came to their notice. The Josephites felt themselves limited by their society's constitutions, which defined them as a diocesan institute subject to the authority of the archbishop of Baltimore. The Society of the Divine Word, because of its status as a pontifical institute subject to the Sacred Congregation of Religious and because of its larger membership and connections in Rome, could more effectively promote the special seminary for black vocations.

Albert followed up on his tentative offers to Christman by suggesting that Pastorelli tender the property of St. Joseph's College for Negro Catechists to the Divine Word Missionaries. Such an overture, even if rejected, would make for good public relations in the black community and would signal Josephite willingness to give every assistance to Sacred Heart College. Albert also asked Pastorelli to allow him to serve as an advance agent for the new seminary, even to the extent of his being loaned by the Josephites to the Divine Word fathers so he could give missions, preach vocation sermons, and recruit students for the college. Albert assured Pasto-

16. John Albert to Matthew Christman, October 20, 1920, in SASA.

relli that approving such a move would go far toward placing the Josephites in a "proper and acceptable light" before the rest of the country.[17]

With manpower and financial worries of his own, however, Pastorelli showed no willingness to consider donating St. Joseph's College land or loaning Albert to the Divine Word Missionaries. Albert, nevertheless, continued to entreat his superior to make some concrete gesture of support for Sacred Heart College, perhaps a monetary donation through Monsignor Burke's office, with an accompanying letter expressing Josephite good will. "This could hardly do any harm," Albert wrote, "and in the event that my surmises are correct, this gift and letter would check hostile opinions."[18] Once again, however, Pastorelli ignored Albert's suggestion and maintained his distance from the seminary.

Besides urging Pastorelli to support Sacred Heart College, Albert also offered advice and encouragement to Christman during the trying first months of the institution's operation. When Christman grew impatient and discouraged over the small number of black students who had come there, Albert counseled patience and persistence and explained that some priests were reluctant to recommend candidates because they did not know what the bishops had decided on the matter and did not want to begin something they could not finish. He reassured Christman that missions and vocation sermons would eventually encourage applicants, though he did not hold out much hope for Greenville as the permanent site for the seminary.[19]

Albert also consoled Christman when some black Catholics objected to the segregated nature of Sacred Heart College and insisted that black students receive their education along with whites at the major Divine Word seminary in Techny. The annual convention of the Knights of Peter Claver, for example, quashed a motion to commend and support the work of the Divine Word Missionaries after listening to speeches by Marcellus Dorsey and John Clouser that characterized Sacred Heart Seminary as "a Jim Crow School for the purpose of educating Jim Crow Priests to work in Jim Crow Catholic Churches." Marcellus Dorsey and Royal Addison, locked in their conflict with Pastorelli, subsequently published articles in the *Afro-American* describing the seminary as "destined to defeat the very object for which we are now contending." In addition, John

17. John Albert to Louis B. Pastorelli, October 28, 1920, in 38-A, JFA.
18. *Ibid.*, October 29, 1920, in 38-A, JFA.
19. John Albert to Matthew Christman, October 23, 1920, in SASA.

Henry Dorsey and Stephen Theobald, two well-known black priests, also publicly criticized segregated seminary education. Despite the disapproval registered by some black Catholics, however, Albert reassured Christman that a separate seminary for black students represented the only practical approach to the development of black priests. He predicted that the "loud mouthed Colored fellows" clamoring for black priests and motivated by "pride rather than zeal" would not have a long-lasting effect on the opinions of most black Catholics.[20]

Bishop Gunn did not share Albert's optimism about the future of Sacred Heart College. Writing to Edward Dyer of the Negro and Indian Commission, Gunn portrayed the Divine Word attempt to establish a "Negro religious priesthood" as a compromise, for he had always opposed a black secular clergy as unworkable given the social conditions in the South. Although admitting that reports about the preparatory school at Greenville seemed satisfactory, he confided that the plan "is hoping against hope and without much chance of doing any good or pleasing anybody."[21]

During the same period, the Society of African Missions, or S.M.A. Fathers, which conducted missions for blacks in Georgia, joined the Society of the Divine Word in attempting to provide seminary education for blacks. The efforts of their mission superior in Georgia, the Reverend Ignatius Lissner, resulted not only in a fledgling integrated seminary in New Jersey but also in dramatic curial initiatives on behalf of the black apostolate—initiatives that alarmed American prelates.

In 1906, at the invitation of Bishop Benjamin Keiley, who had entrusted all black missions in his diocese to the S.M.A. Fathers, Lissner arrived in Savannah to begin his ministry to Georgia's blacks. After almost ten years of work there, Lissner, whose long, flowing beard and intense eyes gave him a prophetlike appearance, wrote to the Negro and Indian Commission that "the future of the mission to the Negro lies in the colored sisters, brothers, and priests."[22] Lissner felt an urgent need for black sisters because of bills introduced into the Georgia legislature. In 1915, that body

20. *Ibid.*; Malin, "Integration of Catholic Clergy," 37–38; John Albert to Matthew Christman, October 23, 1920, in SASA.

21. Bishop John E. Gunn to Edward R. Dyer, December 20, 1920, January 26, 1921, copies of both in Gunn Papers.

22. Jean-Marie Chabert, "Foundations—Report on the Colored Missions in Georgia, 1921–1922" (Typescript in SMAA); *Mission Work Among the Negroes and Indians* (Baltimore, 1916), 22.

considered a bill that would have prohibited white teachers from instructing black students. Lissner feared that such a law would deprive black students in his mission school of the services of the white Francisan sisters who taught there. In 1916, therefore, in collaboration with Elizabeth Williams, a black woman who took the name Mother Mary Theodore, he secured Keiley's approval for a new congregation of black sisters known as the Franciscan Handmaids of the Most Pure Heart of Mary. Mother Mary Theodore became the Handmaids' first mother general.[23]

In order to secure black priests, a more difficult task than obtaining approval for black sisters, Lissner settled on a more comprehensive approach. He prevailed for help on Jean-Marie Chabert, the superior general of his society, who submitted a proposal to the Propaganda on November 22, 1919, that called for the consecration of one of the S.M.A. Fathers as an auxiliary bishop to act as Keiley's vicar for blacks in Georgia. Chabert also proposed the establishment of a seminary for blacks in Savannah. The cardinal-prefect of the Propaganda, van Rossum, approved the plan, assuring Chabert that the Propaganda "is in truth animated by the very keenest regard for the poor Negroes of America, whose abandoned condition we appreciate." A cold and formidable man, accustomed to overcoming opposition through "patience and obstinate labor," the cardinal promised to watch the progress of the seminary with keen interest, certain that "the formation of priests of that race will be the easiest way to redeem those people."[24]

In February, 1920, van Rossum informed Keiley of the Propaganda's plans for both a seminary and an auxiliary bishop possessing ordinary jurisdiction over blacks in his diocese. Van Rossum explained that since Protestants had already established a clergy and episcopate for blacks, "only the Catholics . . . will be left without a special bishop of their own to be zealous for the training of a native clergy, to add to the solemnity of sacred functions . . . to collect offerings for the Negroes, and to show them the other attentions which become the episcopal dignity." Van Rossum invited Keiley's opinion about the plan.[25]

23. "SMA Presence in the United States" (MS in SMAA); see also *Mission Work Among the Negroes and the Indians* (Baltimore, 1917), 35–36.

24. Cardinal Willem van Rossum to Jean-Marie Chabert, January 30, 1920, copy in SMAA; Stephen Neill, *A History of Christian Missions* (Rev. ed.; Harmondsworth, Eng., 1986), 388.

25. Cardinal Willem van Rossum to Bishop Benjamin Keiley, January 30, 1920, in Bishop Benjamin Keiley Papers, ADS.

Van Rossum's proposal alarmed and angered Keiley, who regarded it as a grave threat to the church in Georgia. A feisty Irishman and Confederate army veteran, Keiley served as bishop of Savannah from 1900 until his death in 1922. Throughout that period, he was forced to contend with virulent anti-Catholicism, which was endemic to Georgia and which had been whipped to a fever pitch by Tom Watson. Describing the atmosphere to Gibbons in September, 1916, Keiley wrote, "I am becoming quite an issue in this benighted state of Georgia. I have been publicly assailed in the Senate . . . denounced by a candidate for the U.S. House . . . accused by Mr. Watson of a great desire to murder him, and a host of little politicians have made me a campaign card." He added with relish, "And I am really enjoying it."[26]

Keiley complained bitterly to Gibbons about the Propaganda's proposals, characterizing them as "a sort of 'African Cahenslyism,'" a reference to the efforts of Peter Paul Cahensly and other Germans in the 1890s to secure the appointment of bishops for Catholics of each nationality group, especially Germans, in the United States. Keiley blamed Lissner, whose Jewish ancestry he disparaged, for the Propaganda's initiative. Keiley believed that a Catholic seminary in Georgia that accepted black youths would only provide additional ammunition for Tom Watson and the resurgent Ku Klux Klan and would spell disaster for the church in Georgia and throughout the region. He bemoaned the difficulty of getting Rome to understand conditions in the South and advised Gibbons that his diocesan consultors had unanimously condemned the recommendation of the Propaganda. Keiley urged Gibbons to send a communication on the subject to Rome.[27]

The diplomatic Gibbons, cognizant of Benedict XV's desire for native clergy, framed a careful response to Keiley. He told the bishop that he favored the establishment of a seminary for training black youths for the priesthood and advised him to interpose no objection to it. Gibbons suggested that if such a seminary would harm the interests of white Catholics in Georgia, perhaps Lissner could find another location, such as Catholic University, though Gibbons would have to consult the rector and faculty. The cardinal did indi-

26. Bishop Benjamin Keiley to Cardinal James Gibbons, September 11, 1916, in 117-K, AAB.

27. Bishop Benjamin Keiley to Cardinal James Gibbons, February 26, 1920, copy in Keiley Papers. For an account of the "Cahensly episode," see Gerald P. Fogarty, *The Vatican and the American Hierarchy from 1870 to 1965* (Stuttgart, 1982), 55–61.

cate, however, that he shared Keiley's objections to the naming of an episcopal vicar for blacks, with its implications for the possible creation of a black ordinariate in the United States. Under such a plan, the Holy See would designate a bishop with ordinary juris- diction over all blacks and black missionary work in the country. Gibbons branded such a move "entirely premature," for in his judg- ment, the existing ordinaries of dioceses were quite capable of ade- quately caring for the relatively small number of black Catholics under their charge. As for writing to Rome, Gibbons demurred, suggesting instead that Keiley communicate his own views to the Propaganda and inform the congregation that he had consulted with Gibbons.[28]

There matters stood until the summer of 1920. Just as the Divine Word Missionaries announced their decision to open Sacred Heart College, Lissner, recently returned from a visit to Rome, met with Gibbons and recounted for him his conversation with Pope Bene- dict XV about the plight of blacks in the United States. According to Lissner, Benedict had expressed his desire to see seminaries, and "possibly bishops," for blacks in the United States. Lissner then produced a letter from the Propaganda approving a seminary for blacks in Georgia. The conference with Lissner, along with the document from the Propaganda, convinced Gibbons that Rome wanted action and that the time had come for the American bish- ops to consider thoroughly the evangelization and education of blacks, "particularly the education of colored boys and young men for the priesthood." Gibbons therefore asked Bishop Peter Muldoon, the vice-chairman of the administrative committee of the National Catholic Welfare Council, to place the topic on the agenda of the hierarchy's September meeting. Muldoon granted his request.

In order to prepare for the discussion, Gibbons asked each mem- ber of the hierarchy to consider several points, some of which, he noted, had come from the Holy Father himself. Gibbons acknowl- edged that a lack of black priests helped explain the meager results of Catholic evangelization among blacks. After reminding the bish- ops that Benedict XV's encyclical on the missions had strongly re- affirmed the church's policy of fostering a native clergy, he re- quested the bishops to consider whether black candidates should prepare for the priesthood alongside white candidates in the same seminaries. Acknowledging that integrated seminary education

28. Cardinal James Gibbons to Bishop Benjamin Keiley, February 29, 1920, copy in 131-G-12, AAB.

represented the ideal, Gibbons yet questioned whether "results justify a preference for that policy"; he suggested that wisdom required segregated preparatory and major seminaries. The cardinal also invited the bishops' opinions about whether black priests should serve under the current ordinaries or whether another arrangement might prove preferable.[29]

After receiving Gibbons' questions, Bishop Jules B. Jeanmard of Lafayette, Louisiana, whose newly created diocese lay northwest of New Orleans and, by 1928, contained about one-fourth of the nation's 200,000 black Catholics—the largest number of black Catholics of any diocese in the country—solicited the views of three of his most prominent clergy.[30] The three priests, J. M. Langlois, pastor of St. Peter's Church in New Iberia and the vicar general of the diocese, Philip Keller, founder of the Holy Rosary Institute in Lafayette, and I. F. Isenberg, pastor of St. Michael's in Crowley, Louisiana, agreed that the church should attempt to secure priestly vocations from the black race. In Langlois' words, to exclude blacks from the priesthood would "be against the spirit of God." All three endorsed segregated seminaries and membership for black priests in a black religious community, along the lines proposed by the Divine Word Missionaries.

The reasoning that lay behind the recommendations of the three priests provides a revealing glimpse of what was enlightened southern Catholic thought on the issue of black priests. Keller opted for a separate religious community of black priests because he feared that black diocesan priests could cause a bishop much unpleasantness. A segregated black religious community of priests appealed to Langlois because he believed it would provide much needed control and supervision of black priests, thus reducing the danger of their giving scandal. Isenberg explained that a separate religious institute would furnish community and companionship for black priests, who otherwise would find themselves isolated and friendless among hostile or indifferent white clergy. He cautioned, though, that the appointment of a black priest to a black parish might lower the

29. Cardinal James Gibbons to Bishop Peter Muldoon, July 10, 1920, copy in SMAA.

30. John T. Gillard, S.S.J., *The Catholic Church and the American Negro* (1929; rpr. New York, 1968), 48–49. The first official national census of black Catholics was not conducted until 1928. According to that census, the three archdioceses or dioceses containing the largest numbers of black Catholics were the diocese of Lafayette with 60,000 and the archdioceses of New Orleans and Baltimore, with 35,000 and 22,000, respectively.

prestige of the Catholic priesthood in the eyes of some non-Catholic southerners and thus embarrass some white Catholics. He also pointed out that in some areas, blacks, long accustomed to inferiority, would probably prefer white priests. Reservations notwithstanding, Isenberg expressed the consensus of the three Louisiana priests when he acknowledged that he could imagine conditions and localities where "a colored pastor at the head of a colored parish would do well."[31]

J. A. St. Laurent, at St. Dominic's in New Orleans, took the pulse of the southern bishops and kept Pastorelli informed about their reactions to Gibbons' questions. Writing about a recent meeting with Jeanmard, he described the bishop as convinced that blacks had to receive greater recognition from the church but noncommittal on the question of black priests. St. Laurent speculated that the time had come for the bishops to take a stand on the matter. He regarded Gibbons' memo to the bishops, which, after all, had originated in Rome, as "almost like an ultimatum." St. Laurent wagered that the southern bishops would accept the Divine Word plan, thus easing Roman pressure about the issue, but he warned, "It will not settle it." He advised Pastorelli to venture no opinion, "for Rome is decidedly in favor of a native clergy"; he counseled Pastorelli instead to pledge the cooperation of St. Joseph's Society, as heretofore, and allow the bishops to decide for themselves how they should answer Rome.[32] His advice accorded well with Pastorelli's own inclinations.

The bishops' meeting, however, again proved anticlimactic. The Negro question was only one of six topics on the agenda and by no means constituted the most important item in the eyes of most bishops. Despite migration between 1910 and 1920 that increased the black population living outside the South by almost 50 percent, to a total of 1,550,900, most bishops continued to regard the race problem as a southern concern, especially since the South still remained home to 8,912,231 blacks.[33]

Gibbons introduced the subject of the black apostolate to the meeting on September 22, 1920, by reading a copy of his original

31. J. M. Langlois to Bishop Jules Jeanmard, September 8, 1920, Philip Keller to Bishop Jules Jeanmard, September, 1920, I. F. Isenberg to Bishop Jules Jeanmard, September 12, 1920, all in Jeanmard Papers.

32. J. A. St. Laurent to Louis B. Pastorelli, September 15, 1920, copy in J. A. St. Laurent correspondence, JFA.

33. Minutes of the administrative board of the NCWC, July 28, 1920, in AUSCC; Gillard, *The Catholic Church and the Negro*, 97.

letter to Muldoon and apprising the bishops of the pope's wish, communicated to him by Lissner, for seminaries and perhaps even separate bishops for blacks. He spoke against the idea of a black ordinariate and expressed anxiety about the seminaries. Archbishop Mundelein, ignoring the Divine Word Missionaries' decision to begin a seminary to train black priests, spoke only of the plan that he favored: the formation, under white superiors, of separate religious communities of black brothers and sisters who would teach in black vocational schools in the South. Bishop William T. Russell of Charleston moved that the bishops accept Mundelein's recommendation for black teaching sisters and brothers. Gibbons explained that the bishops needed only to give the project their blessing, that they need not commit themselves to anything or touch the financial issue. The prelates then referred the matter to the committee on missions, effectively burying it.[34]

Father Chabert, meanwhile, continued to press the Holy See on the need for a seminary to prepare black priests both for the Society of African Missions and for the diocesan clergy. He also emphasized the crucial importance of a black ordinariate to the ultimate success of the seminary and its future priests. As a result of Lissner's erroneous reports, he mistakenly believed Gibbons supported this notion of a black ordinariate. Chabert painted a grim picture for van Rossum of conditions in Georgia under Keiley. What he reported van Rossum knew only too well: Keiley would refuse the help of a vicar apostolic or an episcopal vicar general for blacks in his diocese and would never accept black priests into his diocesan clergy. Such resistance, Chabert explained to the cardinal, created special difficulties. For example, Keiley's refusal to accept black diocesan priests had forced the Society of African Missions to accept William Floyd and Joseph John. Both were students at St. Paul's Seminary in the archdiocese of St. Paul when the rector advised Lissner that he could not keep the two men at the seminary unless each had an ecclesiastical superior in the person of a bishop or a religious community. Without a bishop wielding special jurisdiction over black work, Chabert claimed, black priests, regardless of their diocesan or religious status, would have no place to go, since southern bishops such as Keiley would not allow them to work in their dioceses.[35]

34. Minutes of the annual meeting of the bishops of the United States, September 22, 1920, in AUSCC.
35. Jean-Marie Chabert to Cardinal Willem van Rossum, November 12, 1920, copy in SMAA; Chabert, "Foundations—Report on the Colored Missions."

In early December, 1920, Keiley received a letter from Cardinal Gaetano De Lai, secretary of the Consistorial Congregation, who had obviously been in contact with van Rossum. De Lai asked for reasons the congregation should not recommend that the pope appoint a missionary priest, most likely Lissner, as Keiley's vicar general and then consecrate him a bishop with special jurisdiction over blacks. Keiley believed that he had many reasonable objections to such an appointment and tried once again to enlist Gibbons' aid. Fuming about Lissner, "the grandson of a Jewish convert" with "all of the objectionable traits of the race," Keiley claimed that his appointment would displease the people of the diocese and that "every priest in the diocese would sign a letter of protest against the unpopular priest." He was right at least in part: on December 10, 1920, Keiley received a petition, signed by all sixteen of his diocesan priests, protesting the plan to make Lissner the episcopal vicar for blacks. Keiley promised Gibbons that if Rome forced Lissner on him, he would resign; he implored the cardinal to inform De Lai of the incalculable harm that such an appointment would do to the church in Georgia.[36]

The idea of creating a black ordinariate or episcopal vicars with ordinary jurisdiction over blacks did not occur in a vacuum. The issue of bishops for various ethnic groups, including Eastern rite Catholics in the United States, had bedeviled the American hierarchy since the 1880s. In 1907, as a result of pressure from the Austro-Hungarian ambassador to the Holy See, Soter Stephan Ortynsky had been appointed bishop for Ruthenian Catholics living in the United States. Ortynsky was subject to the Holy See through the Apostolic Delegation and received delegated powers from the Latin rite bishops in whose dioceses Ruthenians resided. In 1913, Ortynsky was named ordinary for all Ruthenian Catholics in the United States. In 1907, Pope Pius X elevated Joseph M. Koudelka, a Bohemian pastor in Cleveland, to auxiliary bishop with jurisdiction over Slavic peoples of the diocese. Six months later, at the request of Archbishop James Quigley, Polish-born Paul Rhode was appointed auxiliary bishop for the archdiocese of Chicago. Rhode was regarded as the spokesman and mediator for Polish Catholics

36. Cardinal Gaetano De Lai to Bishop Benjamin Keiley, November 18, 1920, Bishop Benjamin Keiley to Cardinal James Gibbons, December 7, 1920, copy, petition to Bishop Benjamin Keiley from priests of the diocese, December 10, 1920, all in Keiley Papers; Bishop Benjamin Keiley to Cardinal James Gibbons, December 30, 1920, in 139-B-11, AAB.

throughout the nation. Most American dioceses with large ethnic concentrations had several vicars, each assigned to a separate
nationality.[37]

After the war, the issue of ethnic bishops resurfaced. Only about
a month before Keiley sought his aid against the De Lai plan,
Gibbons sent a letter in the name of the entire American hierarchy
to the cardinal secretary of state, Pietro Gasparri. Drafted by a committee composed of Cardinal Dennis Dougherty of Philadelphia
and Archbishops George Mundelein and Sebastian Messmer of
Milwaukee, it strongly denounced attempts by a group of Polish-
American priests to enlist the Polish legation at the Vatican to help
them secure more Polish auxiliary bishops in the archdioceses of
Philadelphia, Chicago, and Milwaukee and better treatment generally from American bishops. In the draft of his section of the letter,
Dougherty warned that if the Poles succeeded in obtaining more
bishops for themselves, they would set a precedent for appointing
bishops for every other national and racial group, resulting in "confusion which would surpass any discord recorded in history."[38]

Always sensitive to what he perceived as threats to the unity of
the church in the United States or to legitimate episcopal autonomy, Gibbons fired off a strong letter of protest to De Lai about the
Consistorial Congregation's plans for Savannah. He told De Lai
that Lissner, and by implication the Holy See, did not understand
the tense racial situation in the United States following the return
of black soldiers from the war in Europe. He warned that the church
would suffer great harm in Georgia if the pope or one of the curial
congregations insisted on executing Lissner's plans. Echoing the arguments that he had used in his letter to Gasparri about Polish attempts to secure more Polish bishops, Gibbons raised the specter of
an American church riven into distinct ethnic and racial groups,
each with its own bishop. (He inconsistently overlooked, however,
the existing racial divisions within the church in the United States
wrought by discrimination and segregation.) Gibbons argued, moreover, that immediately after ordination, young black priests showed
an aversion to working among their own people and often asked for
the same social status as white priests, thereby creating problems for

37. Fogarty, *The Vatican and the American Hierarchy*, 61–64, 184–85; Richard
M. Linkh, *American Catholicism and European Immigrants (1900–1924)* (New
York, 1975), 116; Anthony J. Kuzniewski, *Faith and Fatherland: The Polish Church
War in Wisconsin, 1896–1918* (Notre Dame, 1980), 75–76.

38. Fogarty, *The Vatican and the American Hierarchy*, 211–13.

bishops. He also maintained that black people always preferred white, as opposed to black, priests. He urged Rome to leave the care of black people to the local ordinaries.[39]

The following February, Archbishop Giovanni Bonzano delivered a report on the black apostolate in which he, too, indicated the opposition of the American hierarchy to either the appointment of episcopal vicars for blacks or the creation of a black ordinariate. Bonzano explained that most bishops still remained opposed to black priests because of social divisions in the South and because of continuing concerns about the inferior intelligence and morality of blacks. He noted, however, that movement toward a "clergy of color" had begun in the United States.[40]

In the face of overwhelming opposition from the American bishops, the Propaganda and the Consistorial Congregation abandoned their plans for a bishop with special jurisdiction over work among blacks. Van Rossum, however, wanted Bonzano to recommend to the American bishops that they "do as much as possible to clear away the difficulties that hinder the reception of Blacks into seminaries." Bonzano pledged that he would "seek to encourage and to favor the progress of the formation of an indigenous clergy."[41]

Despite the defeat of his proposal for an episcopal vicar, Lissner pressed on with his plans for a seminary. When Keiley's opposition forced him to find a new site, Lissner asked Bishop John J. O'Connor of Newark for permission to open a major seminary in Highwood, New Jersey. Aware of the wishes of Benedict XV and Cardinal van Rossum in the matter, O'Connor gave his approval. On November 16, 1921, Joseph John arrived at St. Anthony's Mission House, a simple, white, frame structure situated on twelve acres of land, to complete his studies.[42] Unlike the Divine Word seminary in Mississippi, however, St. Anthony's was an integrated institution.

At the same time adverse conditions forced Lissner to relocate his seminary, the Divine Word Missionaries also decided to move Sacred Heart College from Greenville, Mississippi, to a more hospi-

39. Cardinal James Gibbons to Cardinal Gaetano De Lai, December 13, 1920, copy in Keiley Papers.

40. Cyprian Davis, O.S.B., "The Holy See and American Black Catholics: A Forgotten Chapter in the History of the American Church," U.S. Catholic Historian, VII, Nos. 2 and 3 (1988), 177.

41. Ibid., 178.

42. Ignatius Lissner press release, 1921, Edward Lacqueyrie to Bishop John O'Connor, December 7, 1921, copy, both in SMAA.

table location. In February, 1921, the missionaries and Bishop Gunn began to explore the possibility of moving the seminary in order to separate it from the high school in Greenville and to place it nearer a Catholic population center. John Albert suggested New Orleans in the South or New York or Chicago in the North because of their proximity to potential financial donors.[43]

The Divine Word Missionaries, however, favored the Gulf coast of Mississippi. The area boasted a larger Catholic population than the interior of the state, featured a warm climate, and afforded opportunities for the missionaries to bring in extra money by assisting priests in neighboring parishes on Sundays. After some initial misgivings, Gunn agreed to the Gulf coast and suggested Bay St. Louis, Mississippi. He put the Divine Word Missionaries in contact with a sympathetic parish priest, A. J. Gmelch, and a Mr. Korndoffer, a wealthy benefactor. The missionaries found some available property, and Gunn advanced them six thousand dollars from the bequest of a Monsignor Zimmerman for the purchase. The bishop also wrote letters of recommendation for the Reverend John Hoenderop, a Divine Word priest who toured the East and returned with a donation of ten thousand dollars and a promise from Father Dyer of a larger donation from the Negro and Indian Commission.[44]

Although still skeptical about its ultimate fate, Gunn tried to ensure that the seminary would not fail because of a lack of funds. Throughout the summer of 1921, he peppered the Negro and Indian Commission with appeals for financial help for the struggling institution. He believed that if the Divine Word Missionaries did not succeed in "raising a colored priesthood in the South," the bishops could justifiably leave the work to "the theoretical advocates of the clerical brunettes." In effect, he told Cardinal Dougherty, the president of the Negro and Indian Commission, that northern clergy who criticized southern bishops for failing to develop black priests should now support financially what they said they believed in. Gunn insisted to Dyer that if northern clergy did not want to provide the financial assistance, southern bishops would "not be tormented any longer about our unChristian color line." He pre-

43. Michael J. O'Neil to Louis B. Pastorelli, February 23, 1921, in 39-N, JFA; John Albert to Matthew Christman, October 23, 1920, in SASA.
44. Alois Heick to Bishop John E. Gunn, March 2, 1921, Bishop John E. Gunn to Edward R. Dyer, April 9, 1921, copy, both in Gunn Papers; Matthew Christman to Bishop John E. Gunn, April 14, 1921, copy in SASA.

dicted that the seminary would never secure southern sympathy and speculated that more clergy would oppose it outright except for their reluctance to hurt his feelings. According to him, they were "hopeful that the thing [would] die for want of support." Gunn confessed that he never supposed that any religious order would have the bravery to attempt a black seminary and admiringly attributed the effort of the Society of the Divine Word to their "invincible ignorance" of southern conditions—an ignorance, he suggested, that just might "bring these good SVD men to save themselves and . . . their brunettes."[45]

That same month, the superior general of the society ended two years of internal debate about the relationship between the society and its new black seminarians. He informed the American province that the Sacred Congregation of Religious wished the Divine Word Missionaries to accept the black candidates into their society with the aim of eventually creating a separate black southern province. Cardinal Valfre die Donzo judged that both canonically and practically a separate province was preferable to founding a new religious community for blacks, who were judged not sufficiently mature for such a society. A separate province, initially with a white provincial and white superiors, would minimize areas of conflict between black and white and would make easier the separation of blacks from the society if, in the future, their presence threatened its unity. Black students and seminarians would take the same vows and follow the same exercises, rules, and orders as the white students and seminarians at the society's preparatory and major seminaries in Techny.[46]

On hearing of the decision, Bishop Gunn asked for a guarantee in writing from either Janser or the superior general that the young men would become members of the Society of the Divine Word. Gunn explained, "This will make it easier for myself or any other bishop to ordain them as members in a canonically erected religious community that would supply the ordination title required for sacred orders." Janser responded with a long letter in which he as-

45. Matthew Christman to Bishop John E. Gunn, April 14, 1921, copy in SASA; Bishop John E. Gunn to Cardinal Dennis Dougherty, June 17, 1921, Bishop John E. Gunn to Edward R. Dyer, June 29, 1921, copies of both in Gunn Papers.
46. Matthew Christman to Alois Heick, June 13, 1921, Peter Janser to Bruno Hagspiel, September 27, 1931, copy, both in SASA; Carl Friedrich, "Promemoria," [December, 1921?] (Typescript in SASA).

sured the bishop that the Society of the Divine Word would accept the black students as candidates. Black seminarians would receive their training in a separate institution and, when ordained, would eventually form an autonomous province under the superior general. For the foreseeable future, they would remain under the authority of white Divine Word Missionaries until such time as their numbers and experience made it safe to allow them into the government of the society. Janser promised to proceed cautiously so as not to arouse the "antagonism of hostile elements." He hoped to employ the ordained black men for work not only among blacks in the United States but eventually also for the Divine Word foreign missions, especially in Africa.[47]

Janser's statement relieved Gunn "of a kind of dread" about the future of the seminarians. A religious community had its own subjects and gave its priests a canonical title that made them a family party, thus enabling Gunn or his successors to ordain them for the Society of the Divine Word rather than for the diocese of Natchez. The bishop assured Janser that he would not hesitate to ordain any candidate presented to him by the Divine Word Missionaries or to allow the black Divine Word missionaries to work among the diocese's one million black people. A black priest "need never come in social contact with either white priests or white laymen," the relieved bishop concluded. Gunn also probably felt freer in making his promises to the society because the first black candidates would not reach ordination for thirteen more years. He pointed out to Janser that should difficulties occur, well-trained Divine Word men could "always find a field for usefulness in Africa." The African option, not available to the Josephites, provided the Divine Word Missionaries with an important backup in case American bishops would not accept their black priests. Janser emphasized the potential importance of the international mission field to the success of this experiment when he wrote to Christman, "No doubt, even if there were no room for colored priests in the States, the various islands and Africa would offer ample opportunity."[48]

In October, 1921, Janser sent a letter to the hierarchy of the United States notifying them of plans to move the seminary, grown to twenty-eight students, to Bay St. Louis. Janser quoted Benedict

47. Bishop John E. Gunn to Peter Janser, June 29, 1921, copy in Foley Papers; Peter Janser to Bishop John E. Gunn, October 19, 1921, in Gunn Papers.
48. Peter Janser to Matthew Christman, February 23, 1924, in SASA.

XV on the need for a native clergy but also stressed the basically conservative objectives of the Divine Word Missionaries. He reassured the hierarchy that though the Divine Word Missionaries believed that conversion of blacks to Catholicism would provide the ultimate solution to the race problem, they did not seek immediate resolution of the present political, social, or economic aspects of the problem. Janser expressed the hope that his letter would dispel rumors that the missionaries sought radical remedies to racial issues. He served notice, however, that the Divine Word Missionaries would "not be deterred by the opposition and clamor of the few that are non-Catholic in their utterances."[49]

Janser's circular brought in some funds. An appropriation from the Negro and Indian Commission allowed for the purchase of the new property in Bay St. Louis, and an additional gift of twenty-two thousand dollars from the commission enabled the Divine Word Missionaries to erect the brick structure that became the permanent home of the seminary. Bishop Allen sent one hundred dollars, and Cardinal William O'Connell of Boston dispatched one thousand dollars, along with the message that "you Germans are the only ones who can do it." Bishop Gunn donated ten thousand dollars, and the Knights of Peter Claver, overcoming their initial misgivings, also sent a donation. Mother Katharine Drexel promised two thousand dollars. In all, the bishops of the United States donated thirty-five thousand dollars, either directly or indirectly through the Negro and Indian Commission.[50] For many bishops, a modest donation for a seminary stuck down in Mississippi was a small price to pay to defuse the issue and to forestall more drastic action by the Holy See.

The promises of financial support for the new seminary were fortuitous: trouble with the Ku Klux Klan underscored the need to relocate the black seminarians. In the spring of 1922, issues of the *Rail-Splitter*, a Klan newspaper published in Ft. Worth, Texas, appeared on the streets of Greenville. Boxcar headlines across the top of the paper, clearly designed to engender bitter feeling and possibly to incite to violence, screamed, "White Women Act as Scullery Maids for Young Negroes at Greenville, Mississippi." The accom-

---

49. Peter Janser to Archbishop John W. Shaw, November 25, 1921, copy in Archives of the Archdiocese of New Orleans (AANO) File, JFA.

50. Christman, "Pro Memoria: St. Augustine Mission House"; Matthew Christman to Alois Heick, December 6, 1921, Matthew Christman to Gilbert Faustina, March 28, 1923, copies of both in SASA; "Greenville Site of First Divine Word Seminary," *Catholic Action of the South* (New Orleans), October 11, 1945, clipping in SASA.

panying story also claimed that blacks and whites mingled freely at the school. Other KKK papers pressed these charges, too, alleging that the existence of the seminary meant that soon white women would have to kneel down to confess their sins to black priests. Even some Catholic papers carried the inaccurate reports about life at Sacred Heart College. At the request of the superiors of the seminary, a civic committee, composed of an Episcopalian priest, the mayor of Greenville, and a former mayor who was a Baptist and a Freemason, investigated the institution, in the end issuing a report denying that white women served black students. The committee even noted the similarities between the practices at Sacred Heart College and non-Catholic bible institutes. The committee's report calmed the atmosphere, but the young black students still had to endure the taunts of some townspeople who called them "little nigger priests." As a precaution following the KKK newspaper attack, a black Catholic man always accompanied the seminarians on their outings in the country, conspicuously displaying a loaded gun to let the local Klan know that he intended to defend the students.[51]

In June, 1923, the seminary, renamed St. Augustine's, moved to Bay St. Louis, located approximately forty miles east of New Orleans. On September 16, 1923, before a crowd of over eight hundred people, many of whom had arrived on a sixteen-coach train from New Orleans and had marched behind three brass bands of the Knights of Peter Claver from the station to the seminary, Bishop Gunn dedicated the new seminary building, a large brick structure capable of accommodating over one hundred students. Harry Kane, a Josephite from New Orleans, preached the sermon at the dedication mass. St. Augustine's Seminary offered a six-year, combined high school–college program and a six-year seminary course interspersed with a year's novitiate (a period of spiritual training during which the novice was prepared for taking temporary vows in a religious community) in Techny. A faculty of four priests instructed twenty-two students during the 1923–1924 academic year.[52]

51. Emmet Harty to Harry Sylvester, April 28, 1941, Matthew Christman to Alois Heick, April 27, 1922, both in SASA; Peter Janser to Bishop John E. Gunn, June 30, 1922, Mayor J. A. Hunt to the Hon. William H. Clark, July 20, 1922, copy, Matthew Christman to Bishop John E. Gunn, September 26, 1922, all in Gunn Papers; Foley, God's Men, 128–29.

52. Foley, God's Men, 128–29; Malin, "Integration of Catholic Clergy," 51; Matthew Christman to Alois Heick, September 26, 1923, "Greenville Site of First Divine Word Seminary," Catholic Action of the South (New Orleans), October 11, 1945, clipping, both in SASA.

On April 5, 1923, Pope Pius XI, who had succeeded Benedict XV in 1922, gave an unmistakable signal of his support for St. Augustine's Seminary and for the efforts of the Divine Word Missionaries to develop a black clergy when he addressed a public letter of congratulations thus: "To His Son, William Gier, Superior General of the Society of the Divine Word," on the occasion of the transfer of the seminary to Bay St. Louis. The Divine Word Missionaries had been maneuvering for an official letter of support from the Holy See for several years. The pope declared that the seminary accorded with the ideals of the society, with God's admonition to the church to teach all nations, and with the precepts of the Apostolic See. It is indispensable, the pope declared, that black priests should make it their life's work to lead their people to Christian faith and a higher level of culture. Pius XI praised the Divine Word Missionaries for adhering to the guidance of Benedict XV's *Maximum illud* by planning to ordain black men as members of their society. He closed by expressing his willingness to do everything he could to promote the undertaking.[53]

Although St. Augustine's Seminary had the potential of transforming the Society of the Divine Word into a formidable rival to the Josephites for the black missions, especially if it managed to produce significant numbers of black priests, its existence also inadvertently helped ease the pressure on Pastorelli and St. Joseph's Society. The segregated nature of St. Augustine's seemed to confirm the commonly held opinion among whites that integrated seminary education, such as had existed at St. Joseph's Seminary under John R. Slattery, had failed. Now, clergy and laity would regard St. Augustine's, rather than St. Joseph's, as the black seminary. Pastorelli could refer black applicants to St. Augustine's, thus allowing him to maintain his support for black vocations while avoiding risks to St. Joseph's Society. Pastorelli had been wary and cautious on the issue of black priests; now he waited and watched the fate of the black seminarians at Bay St. Louis.

Unlike St. Augustine's Seminary, which, despite financial difficulties and deprivation, expanded its enrollment and received papal approbation, Lissner's seminary, St. Anthony's Mission House, languished and eventually closed. Its first black alumnus, the Reverend Joseph John, endured many of the same kinds of indignities visited

53. Carl Friedrich to Alois Heick, December 22, 1921, Pope Pius XI to William Gier, April 5, 1923, copy, both in SASA.

on earlier black priests, including the refusal of bishops to allow him to work in their dioceses. As a result, the S.M.A. Fathers, like the Josephites and Spiritans before them, decided to discontinue the education of black seminary students. The sorry fate of Lissner's venture reinforced Pastorelli in his view that conditions did not yet allow for a significant increase in the number of black priests and that any new undertaking or change in his own policy should await clear signals from the bishops that they would allow black priests to function in their dioceses.

St. Anthony's Mission House, which had only six students and four faculty members in 1922, suffered from a host of problems. It lacked adequate financial support, which Lissner blamed on episcopal prejudice against his foreign background. Internal conflicts between Lissner and the superior of the seminary further crippled the institution. The European model of education that the seminary faculty adopted made little provision for recreation other than yard work and failed to appeal to American youth; black students were alienated by the African orientation of the faculty and by Lissner's own reported preference for simple African natives over American blacks. In addition, friction between white and black seminarians soon became apparent. The three white seminarians avoided walking with the black students and admitted to the Reverend Joseph Werle, the superior, that they had lost their sympathy for blacks and had serious doubts about continuing at the mission house. All three eventually left.[54]

Difficulties at the seminary notwithstanding, Joseph John persevered, entered the Society of African Missions, and was ordained by Bishop John J. Collins, S.J., on June 13, 1923, before a joyous throng at St. Benedict the Moor Church in New York City. Uncertainty clouded the festivities for Lissner and John, however, because Lissner could not secure a pastoral assignment for his new priest. The New York *Catholic News* reported what most black Catholics assumed: John would labor at one of the six black missions in Georgia conducted by the S.M.A. Fathers. But when Lissner proposed John as pastor of St. Anthony's Mission in West Savannah, Bishop Michael J. Keyes, Keiley's successor, objected

54. Ignatius Lissner, "African Missions in the United States—Colored Vocations" (Typescript in SMAA); Jean-Marie Chabert memorandum, "Historical Summary of Our Missions for the Colored in America," to Cardinal Willem van Rossum, n.d., in SMAA; Foley, *God's Men*, 198; Joseph Werle to Ignatius Lissner, March 2, 1923, in SMAA.

because he feared that the appointment of a black priest might provoke opposition from whites, which would harm the church in Georgia. Keyes told Lissner that for the time being, he wanted mission work among blacks left solely to white S.M.A. Fathers.[55]

Writing from Savannah, Mother Mary Theodore, mother general of the black Franciscan Handmaids of the Most Pure Heart of Mary, who had accepted an invitation to relocate her community in the archdiocese of New York, reported to Lissner that whites had stopped her on the street to voice their displeasure over the prospect of Father John's assignment to their city. "Now we meet the Colored Sister," more than one remarked scornfully. "Next we will be meeting the colored priest." Even some of the white Franciscan sisters complained that it was enough to have black sisters in Savannah without bringing in a black priest. Mother Mary Theodore suggested, however, that whites were not the only angry people in Savannah; many black Catholics were furious with the bishop when they learned that he had rejected Father John. She worried that these people would leave the Catholic church as a result. "The Japanese . . . Italians . . . Chinese . . . Africans have priests," she plaintively wrote to Lissner. "Why can't the American Negroes?"[56]

Unable to station Father John in Georgia but hoping to enable blacks in the state to see the newly ordained priest, Lissner and the Reverend Alfred Laubé of Augusta, with the bishop's permission, arranged for John to officiate at a high mass in Augusta on December 8, 1923, and to attend a series of receptions in his honor in Macon, Savannah, and Atlanta. News about preparations for the celebrations, however, gave Bishop Keyes second thoughts. He wrote to Lissner that he feared the church in Georgia might suffer great damage unless the S.M.A. Fathers handled John's visit with care. Keyes reminded Lissner that white people in the state would not accept a black man, priest or layman, as their equal. The bishop worried that white southerners would view a solemn high mass with John as the celebrant assisted by a deacon and a subdeacon as "two white men waiting on a colored man." The bishop also warned that a high mass necessitated "that intimacy between white and colored which is as yet practically impossible in Georgia." The bishop suggested instead a *missa cantata*, a mass celebrated by a

55. *Catholic News* (New York), June 23 1923, p. 1; Ignatius Lissner to Bishop Michael Keyes, August 30, 1927, copy in SMAA.

56. Mother Mary Theodore to Ignatius Lissner, July 27, 1923, in SMAA.

priest without a deacon or subdeacon. As for the receptions in Macon, Savannah, and Atlanta, the bishop fretted that white Protestants would view them as an attempt by the hated Catholics to force social equality between the races, so he cautioned against too much display. He hoped that John would arrive and depart quietly, since the celebrations would necessarily involve white priests, and great trouble would result if white men rode around with a black man, held celebrations in his honor, and dined with him. After reminding Keyes that the bishop had earlier granted permission for the high mass in Augusta and asserting that the receptions planned for the cities outside Augusta were meant to be "all black affairs," Lissner informed the bishop that John would have to cancel appearances other than in Augusta because of "engagements in St. Mary's County, Maryland."[57]

The bishops' refusals to allow Lissner to station John in their dioceses doomed Lissner's hopes of developing black priests. He appointed John to the faculty of St. Anthony's Mission House as professor of English, literature, Latin, and homiletics for the seminary's nine students. When he informed Chabert about the difficulties of getting bishops to accept John and about the grim prospects for any future black priests, the superior general ordered him "not to form Negro priests for the present time."[58]

For five years after his ordination, Joseph John searched unsuccessfully for a pastorate. A brief trial period of several months in late 1924 and early 1925 at St. Augustine's Parish in Louisville, Kentucky, ended unhappily. John returned to teaching in the seminary (which had moved to Tenafly, New Jersey), with which job Lissner urged him to satisfy himself. John, however, longed for an assignment in a parish. His prayers were finally answered when Bishop Emmanuel Ledvina of Corpus Christi issued a desperate call for a priest to staff Holy Cross (black) Church. The Reverend Edward C. Kramer, who had succeeded Monsignor Burke as the director of the Catholic Board for Mission Work Among the Colored People, arranged for black sisters to staff the school and for Father John to become pastor in September, 1926. Pastorelli congratulated Bishop Ledvina for taking John and giving him a chance, since "the

57. Bishop Michael Keyes to Ignatius Lissner, December 1, 1923, Ignatius Lissner to Bishop Michael Keyes, December 4, 1923, copy, both in SMAA.
58. Foley, God's Men, 108; Jean-Marie Chabert to Ignatius Lissner, September 30, 1927, Ignatius Lissner memorandum, n.d., both in SMAA.

poor fellow has been going from pillar to post ever since his ordination as nobody wanted him."[59]

After only two years, conflict between John, whose Caribbean background and personal aloofness added to his difficulties, and the Sisters of the Holy Family resulted in the sisters withdrawing from the parish. Since the bishop could only secure white sisters as replacements and since he believed that white southerners would never tolerate a black priest and white sisters in the same parish, Ledvina felt compelled to ask John to leave. Finally, in 1929, John accepted the invitation of Bishop Pius Dowling to work in the diocese of Trinidad; ten years later Dowling incardinated him into that diocese.[60]

Other black priests in the United States endured their own purgatories during the early 1920s. Joseph Burgess, the Spiritan seminary professor who, like Father John, spent much of his priestly life fruitlessly searching for a parish, died prematurely on December 4, 1923, while serving as an assistant pastor at the French-Canadian parish of St. Joachim's in Detroit, where, according to Stephen Theobald, Burgess passed for a Spaniard. The outspoken Theobald, Archbishop Ireland's protégé and pastor of St. Peter Claver Parish in St. Paul, felt constrained by his clerical superiors and told Thomas Wyatt Turner that he doubted he could help Turner and his organization as much as the professor might wish. "As a priest," Theobald confessed, "I would be in constant danger of being 'beheaded' if I dared associate myself with any lay movement calculated to head off the theories of the men directing the destinies of the Church amongst our people."[61]

The most tragic misfortune befell John Henry Dorsey. In September, 1924, during a dispute over disciplinary action Dorsey took toward one of the school children at St. Monica's, the father of the child, an ex-convict, seized a heavy block of wood and struck Dorsey over the head, knocking him down and fracturing his skull. Dorsey never recovered from the blow, suffering progressive paraly-

59. Foley, *God's Men*, 109–11; Bishop Emmanuel Ledvina to Louis B. Pastorelli, September 22, 1926, Louis B. Pastorelli to Bishop Emmanuel Ledvina, October 2, 1926, copy, both in 69-K, JFA.

60. Foley, *God's Men*, 110; Bishop Emmanuel Ledvina to Louis B. Pastorelli, August 3, 1928, in 72-L, JFA.

61. Foley, *God's Men*, 78–79; Stephen Theobald to Thomas Wyatt Turner, May 23, 1924, in Turner Papers.

sis and several strokes. He died at Mt. Hope Sanitarium on June 30, 1926, the same year his old patron, John R. Slattery, passed away.[62]

The Reverends Joseph John and A. Norman DuKette, the latter a newly ordained black priest from the diocese of Detroit, served as deacon and subdeacon, respectively, at the funeral mass that was celebrated by Dorsey's old friend Charles Randolph Uncles before three thousand mourners. The Baltimore *Afro-American* eulogized "Our Father Harry Dorsey," but some white clergy viewed his death as the end of a problem. Welbers and Pastorelli believed that Dorsey had at last found peace and that his death "would likely quiet an unpleasant commotion"; and Archbishop Shaw of New Orleans wrote to Pastorelli, "All things considered, the death of Fr. Dorsey seems providential, as I believe that he was not much consolation." Rumors and gossip led many whites to regard the attack that led to Dorsey's infirmity as evidence of a full-scale rejection of the black priesthood by black Catholics. The rumor circuit in the South twisted the story into the alleged lynching of Dorsey by his black congregation.[63]

The failure of St. Anthony's Mission House and the misfortunes of Joseph John, Joseph Burgess, and John Henry Dorsey indicated to Pastorelli that nothing had substantially changed for black priests in the United States. Thomas Wyatt Turner's protests notwithstanding, the Josephites, with almost all of their missions located in the South, simply could not risk accepting more than a token black seminarian, for they could not hope to place these priests in southern dioceses after ordination. Even Roman pressure on the bishops failed to impress or reassure Pastorelli; he had seen the bishops finesse the Holy See on the issue too often.

The members of St. Joseph's Society signaled their approval of Pastorelli's leadership and policies at the general chapter held in 1924. On June 25, they overwhelmingly reelected him superior

62. Foley, *God's Men*, 61; Francis Tobin to Louis B. Pastorelli, September 13, 1924, in 42-D, James S. Cobb to Louis B. Pastorelli, December 1, 1924, in 42-C, C. M. Dorsey to Louis B. Pastorelli, May 3, 1926, in 44-C, Matt Morrissey to Louis B. Pastorelli, July 8, 1926, in 44-L, all in JFA; biographical sketch in John H. Dorsey file, JFA.

63. "Death of Father Dorsey, Colored Priest, After Lingering Illness," *Colored Harvest*, XIV (September–October, 1926), 10; "Our Father Harry Dorsey," Baltimore *Afro-American*, July 10, 1926, clipping in PMC; Lambert Welbers to Louis B. Pastorelli, August 4, 1926, in 44-U, Archbishop John W. Shaw to Louis B. Pastorelli, August 10, 1926, in 69-S, both in JFA; Foley, *God's Men*, 61.

general of St. Joseph's Society, despite the bitter opposition of a small minority led by Sam Kelly, who accused Pastorelli of ignoring the Holy Father's wishes for native vocations.[64] The voting for superior general, however, showed that Pastorelli's approach to the question of black priests reflected the consensus of opinion in the society.

The same general chapter that reelected Pastorelli also heard him appeal for a change in the Josephite constitutions. He proposed to drop the promise that bound the Josephites to work exclusively for blacks, because he was concerned that the Josephites not restrict their future activities. "A Negro clergy is bound to come," he argued. "They will increase and so will their activities. We must have a field for our future labors."[65]

Pastorelli's suggested constitutional change reflected his basic view of the nature of St. Joseph's Society and its relationship to black priests. He implicitly defined *Josephite* as white and regarded black priests as necessarily other. He could not even envisage a future St. Joseph's Society that would include a significant number of black priests. Existing conditions in the South made it impossible for white and black priests to live together, and even the Divine Word Missionaries planned a separate province for their black members. In Pastorelli's view, another religious society would have to develop black priests, and when they did, the Josephites, bound by the restrictions of southern life and unable to join them in an interracial effort to bring black Americans into the church, would surrender the field to them.

As he looked back over the turbulent and difficult years of his first term as superior general, Pastorelli could feel reasonably satisfied. He believed that he had brought badly needed order, consolidation, and leadership to his society. His careful and adroit management of money had allowed him to begin strengthening society institutions, through construction of a new Epiphany Apostolic College, for example. He had cultivated the friendship of American bishops and had skillfully and convincingly represented his society before them at a series of missionary conferences in 1919 and 1920, winning increased respect, prestige, and financial support for the Josephites. He believed that his emphasis on consolidating mis-

64. Sam Kelly to Louis B. Pastorelli, June 9, 19, 1922, both in 40-H, JFA.
65. Minutes of the general chapters, June 25, 1924, in JFA.

sions and conserving the faith of existing black Catholics, especially in urban areas such as Baltimore and New Orleans, would provide a solid base for more effective efforts to reclaim lapsed black Catholics and convert Protestant or unchurched blacks. In 1924, Pastorelli could proudly count seventy-six Josephites in black work, sixty of whom attended to forty-nine churches and twenty-two attached missions. Sixteen other priests administered or worked in society institutions, such as Epiphany Apostolic College, St. Joseph's Seminary, St. Joseph's Industrial School, and St. Joseph's Home for Orphans. Studying at St. Joseph's were 31 seminarians, and at Epiphany College 103 students.[66]

In his stand on the question of black priests, Pastorelli seemed also to have been successful. His restrictive policies toward black students at the college and seminary had involved him in a bitter conflict with articulate black Catholic leaders who denounced restrictions on black vocations as un-Catholic. In the end, though, they could not force him to open the doors of Epiphany College and St. Joseph's Seminary to more black students. Finding himself caught between activist black Catholics on the one hand and bishops who would not accept black priests into their dioceses on the other and ensnared by his own paternalism, which gave short shrift to black leadership, Pastorelli basically evaded the issue, resorting to half-truths and deceptions in dealing with black Catholic leaders. By 1924, the campaign waged by black Catholics had subsided, and the Holy See appeared mollified by the establishment of the seminaries for blacks in Mississippi and New Jersey. The pressure had eased on Pastorelli and the Josephites; they appeared to have weathered the storm of postwar discontent.

66. [Louis B. Pastorelli], "Our Yearly Report," *Colored Harvest*, XII (March–April, 1924), 3.

Chapter VII

THE LETTER OF THE LAW, 1926–1932

Rome now demands action and we cannot stand by idly simply looking on. . . . Just how is the great question.
—LOUIS B. PASTORELLI, OCTOBER 12, 1928

During the decade of the 1920s, the black apostolate remained a low priority for the Catholic church in the United States. Bishops and priests, given a respite from the flood of European immigration that had required so much of their attention, energy, and resources during the first two decades of the century, focused on institutional development and consolidation. They introduced modern business management techniques into the administration of dioceses and parishes and built churches and schools to improve the self-image, skills, and prestige of their people. Lay Catholics, who numbered twenty million by the end of the decade, remained painfully aware of the persistence of anti-Catholicism among some of their fellow countrymen. Still, they maintained their optimistic faith in the basic compatibility of Catholicism and American democracy and, like other Americans, shared in the economic prosperity of the Republican New Era.

For a few years after 1923, it appeared that the establishment of St. Augustine's Seminary in Bay St. Louis had defused the issue of black priests, placated the Holy See, and taken the pressure off the Josephites. By the midtwenties, however, the situation had changed. Advances in transatlantic communication and transportation and the diffusion of leadership within the American hierarchy following the death of Cardinal James Gibbons enabled the strong-willed Pope Pius XI and the Roman congregations, operating usually through the Apostolic Delegation, to exert a more immediate and consistent influence on the church in the United States, including its missionary efforts among blacks, than had been possible during previous generations.[1]

The publication of Pius XI's encyclical *Rerum Ecclesiae* in 1926 signaled the renewal of subtle, yet steady pressure by the Holy See on the American hierarchy to increase its missionary work among black Americans. Pius XI, an outspoken champion of indigenous clergy in mission lands, believed that the eventual conversion of Afro-Americans depended on the development of a black clergy. In addition to his encyclical, the pontiff used his apostolic delegate in the United States, Archbishop Pietro Fumasoni-Biondi, who served in this capacity from 1922 to 1933, to prod northern bishops into giving more serious consideration to the fostering of black vocations for the diocesan clergy. As a result, Archbishop John T. McNicholas of Cincinnati and Bishops Joseph Schrembs of Cleveland and John J. Cantwell of Los Angeles-Monterey agreed either to accept a few black candidates into their seminaries or at least to sponsor them in seminaries conducted by others. Within a couple of years, however, McNicholas and Schrembs soured on their black seminarians, forcing several to leave the United States in order to complete their studies, secure ordination, and find a diocese in which to work. By the early 1930s, prospects for black diocesan clergy appeared as grim as prospects for the depression-ridden economy.

For Pastorelli and the Josephites, the issue of black priests, like some Shakespearian specter, would not disappear, in part because of the persistence of black Catholics. Throughout the second half of the decade, the Josephites sparred defensively with their old nemesis, Thomas Wyatt Turner, and his newly formed Federated Colored Catholics, and with the federation's Jesuit allies, John LaFarge and William M. Markoe. Aware of Pius XI's desire for native clergy, Pastorelli discussed the issue of black priests with the pontiff in 1926 during a twenty-minute private audience. As a loyal son of the Holy Father, he searched for ways to satisfy the pope's desire for indigenous clergy, at the same time taking care to safeguard the interests of his beloved society. Three Josephite general chapters, held toward the end of the decade, reviewed and wrestled with the question of admitting blacks to Epiphany Apostolic College and St. Joseph's Seminary. The actions of a few northern bish-

1. James Hennesey, S.J., *American Catholics: A History of the Roman Catholic Community in the United States* (New York, 1981), 237–43.

ops in accepting or sponsoring a handful of black seminarians on an experimental basis tempted even Pastorelli to conjecture that prospects for black priests had brightened somewhat. The subsequent disillusionment of the prelates with their black seminarians and the difficulties endured by those young men, however, reconfirmed Pastorelli's judgment that conditions in the church still required a cautious, conservative approach. With the support of the vast majority of the members of St. Joseph's Society, he attempted to honor the letter, if not the spirit, of Pius XI's pronouncements by continuing to admit an occasional, usually light-skinned Afro-American to Epiphany Apostolic College or St. Joseph's Seminary.

In January, 1926, Pastorelli discussed the subject of black priests with Pius XI himself. He had arranged for a personal audience with the pontiff through a fellow Bostonian, Monsignor Francis J. Spellman, a rising clerical star, the first American to serve in the Vatican Secretariat of State, and the future cardinal-archbishop of New York. Pastorelli requested the audience in order to begin proceedings to transform St. Joseph's Society from a diocesan into a pontifical institute. Such a change would place the society under the authority of one of the congregations of the Curia, the Congregation of Religious, thereby giving the Josephites a direct line to Rome and, theoretically at least, greater independence from the bishops. On January 7, 1926, prior to the papal audience, Pastorelli submitted a report on St. Joseph's Society to Cardinal Gaetano De Lai, secretary of the Sacred Consistorial Congregation. The report sounded many of Pastorelli's familiar themes, stressing the difficult social situation confronting the church in the South and calling any marked improvement in race relations, at least for the short term, "nearly morally impossible." In a swipe at white and black Catholic activists in the North who criticized the Josephites for failing to speak out more forthrightly against the southern caste system, Pastorelli advised that the church in the South should follow "that line of action . . . deemed best suited to the times and circumstances" by prudent bishops and clergy "acquainted with the true situation." As if to demonstrate the validity of Pastorelli's assessment, later that year the Ku Klux Klan kidnapped and almost lynched Vincent Warren, the Josephite pastor of St. Joseph's Church in Norfolk, Virginia.[2]

2. "Report Presented by Very Rev. L. B. Pastorelli, S.S.J., to our Holy Father, His Holiness, Pope Pius XI, January, 1926," insert in Copy Book 2, pp. 6–8, JFA; Albert S. Foley, S.J., *God's Men of Color: The Colored Catholic Priests of the United States, 1854–1954* (1955; rpr. New York, 1969), 194–95.

On January 26, 1926, Pastorelli met with Pius XI for twenty-two minutes in the pope's study. The Holy Father referred almost immediately to the report and then, according to Pastorelli, went over the Negro question, especially the black clergy question, "from every angle" with him. Implying that the pontiff approved of his approach to the problem, he later claimed that the pope recognized the difficulties for black priests posed by the "the bi-racial set up in the United States."[3] Unfortunately, Pastorelli left no minutes of the meeting. The pope probably told him of his desire for more black priests in the United States, encouraged him to do what he could under existing circumstances to promote black vocations, and left the timing and manner of implementation up to him.

The visit to Rome strengthened Pastorelli's resolve to seek a new status for St. Joseph's Society. After his return to Baltimore, the Josephite consultors decided to take steps to secure the *Decretum Laudis*, or formal approbation of the Holy See, that would remove the society from the jurisdiction of the archbishop of Baltimore and place it under the Congregation of Religious. J. A. St. Laurent expressed the hopes of many Josephites when he wrote to Pastorelli: "When we have secured an independent status . . . we shall be in a better position to demand reasonable terms. . . . I hope that Rome will give us what we need so that we can take the stand that we consider as necessary to our self-respect."[4]

On February 28, 1926, a month after his meeting with Pastorelli, Pius XI issued the encyclical *Rerum Ecclesiae*, in which he called for the formation and systematic training of native clergies in mission lands. The pope said: "Let Us recall to your attention how important it is that you build up an indigenous clergy. If you do not work with all of your might to accomplish this . . . your apostolate will not only be crippled, but it will become an obstacle and an impediment to the establishment . . . of the Church." Pius XI felt compelled to issue the encyclical because missionaries had generally ignored *Maximum illud*, his predecessor's apostolic letter on the same subject. To dramatize his commitment to indigenous clergies, notwithstanding considerable opposition, Pius XI consecrated the first six Chinese bishops in St. Peter's Basilica on October 28, 1926. Be-

3. Introduction to Louis B. Pastorelli report submitted to Pius XI, January, 1926, in PMC; Louis B. Pastorelli, "The Late Pope Pius XI," *Colored Harvest*, XXVII (April–May, 1939), 10–12; Louis B. Pastorelli to Edward Knight, October 12, 1928, copy in 51-H, JFA.

4. CMB, March 4, 1926, in JFA; J. A. St. Laurent to Louis B. Pastorelli, June 8, 1929, in 48-S, JFA.

tween 1922 and 1939, the term of Pius XI's papacy, the number of native priests in mission lands rose from 2,670 to more than 7,000, and the number of mission dioceses headed by native clergymen increased from zero to forty.[5] The spirit and logic of the pope's message clearly lent support and encouragement to champions of a black priesthood in the United States.

The issuance of *Rerum Ecclesiae,* however, appeared to have little immediate effect on Pastorelli's policies toward black students, partly because he believed that the encyclical applied only to *foreign* missions, not those in the United States. Harry Kane, the rector of Epiphany Apostolic College, which had just relocated from Walbrook to Newburgh, New York, thought he understood Pastorelli's expectations regarding black applicants and indicated so when he corresponded with Pastorelli in April, 1926, about a black man named Steel. "I did not think that you wanted to handle any more of them," Kane wrote. He then added a disclaimer: "I do not think that it will be good for the cause in these parts to have them around. But if you say so, I will take him." Pastorelli seemed to confirm Kane's perception of current policy, informing the rector that he wanted Steel only as a groundskeeper, not as a seminarian.[6]

Nonetheless, a week later Pastorelli signaled Kane that he had not completely closed the doors to black applicants. Kane received a copy of a will with a bequest for "the education of a colored student at EAC." Expressing regret to Pastorelli that the benefactor had attached that particular condition, Kane advised Pastorelli to write the lawyer and explain the situation, hoping that "he may let it pass." On April 14, 1926, Pastorelli instructed Kane to accept the legacy, because "we shall always have one at least of the colored."[7] Kane thereupon suggested that Pastorelli might consider Clarence Howard, one of Vincent Warren's parishioners from St. Joseph's in Norfolk, "who made application long since." Warren had earlier seen both Kane and Pastorelli in an attempt to get Howard into Epiphany. Pastorelli, however, preferred fair-skinned candidates and advised Warren that, in light of previous Josephite experi-

5. NCE, XI, 412, III, 946–47; Stephen Neill, A History of Christian Missions (Rev. ed.; Harmondsworth, Eng., 1986), 388–89; J. Derek Holmes, The Papacy in the Modern World, 1914–1978 (New York, 1981), 24–25.

6. Harry Kane to Louis B. Pastorelli, April 13, 1926, Louis B. Pastorelli note written on Kane-Pastorelli letter, April 13, 1926, both in 44-K, JFA.

7. Harry Kane to Louis B. Pastorelli, April 17, 1926, in 44-K, JFA. A copy of Pastorelli's reply to Kane, dated April 20, 1926, is scrawled at the top of Kane's letter of April 17, 1926, in 44-K, JFA.

ences with black priests, prudence dictated that they wait a few years before accepting such applicants as Howard. Howard enrolled at St. Augustine's Seminary in Bay St. Louis, where he was ordained in 1937.[8]

Unlike Pastorelli, Thomas Wyatt Turner and his newly founded Federated Colored Catholics, the successor to the Committee for the Advancement of Colored Catholics, interpreted *Rerum Ecclesiae* as a clarion call for action. They renewed their appeals to the American hierarchy and to Rome for more black priests. Turner intended that the Federated Colored Catholics, founded on December 29, 1925, would affiliate every black Catholic organization in the country, act as a clearinghouse for black Catholic opinion, and serve as a conduit for black Catholic protest to the American hierarchy and the Holy See. The federation made Catholic education and black priests its two priorities. Turner and the federation viewed the two issues as interrelated, for if Catholic schools remained closed to black youth, they would never secure the education they needed to enter the seminary. Turner persistently demanded more black priests because he believed that in the cleric-dominated Catholic church, significant numbers of black priests would prove more effective than black laymen in calling the attention of church authorities to the problems of black Catholics. Referring to black priests, Turner explained, "As they multiply, they will be able to carry the Catholic Negroes' cause to places now inaccessible to laymen."[9]

Attempting to capitalize on the momentum created by the pope's encyclical, in October, 1926, the federation sent a letter, probably written by Turner, to the bishops of the United States. The letter described the plight of black Catholics and asked the hierarchy to take steps to eliminate discrimination in the church. The first three sections of the letter focused on prejudice and discrimination in Catholic churches and schools, especially in areas of the North un-

---

8. Harry Kane to Louis B. Pastorelli, May 18, 1926, in 44-K, JFA; Foley, *God's Men*, 197.

9. Federated Colored Catholics to the Hierarchy of the Roman Catholic Church in the United States, October, 1926, copy in Thomas Wyatt Turner Papers, MSRC; Marilyn W. Nickels, "The Federated Colored Catholics: A Study of Three Variant Perspectives on Racial Justice as Represented by John LaFarge, William Markoe, and Thomas Turner" (Ph.D. dissertation, The Catholic University of America, 1975), 42–43; Thomas Wyatt Turner to Francis G. Wade, December 27, 1938, copy in Turner Papers.

hindered by formal jim-crow laws. The fourth section dealt with a native clergy. As evidence of the scandal that Catholic racism created among non-Catholic blacks, the letter approvingly quoted an editorial in *Crisis*, in which the writer accurately pointed out that only "in lawless Mississippi was there a seminary where Colored Catholics were urged and permitted to become priests." Nowhere else, the editorial claimed, "is it possible, without extraordinary effort, influence, and pressure, for a Colored man to be educated for the Catholic priesthood." *Crisis* blamed the "Irish hierarchy" for creating the situation and for ignoring the wishes of the pope and apostolic delegate on the issue.[10]

The federation acknowledged some progress in the years since the first letter to the hierarchy from the Committee for the Advancement of Colored Catholics in 1919. It praised, for example, the founding of St. Augustine's Seminary and the graduation of its first college class. It also applauded the ordinations to the priesthood of Joseph John and Norman DuKette and the willingness of the seminaries of the archdiocese of St. Paul and the diocese of Detroit to admit some black candidates. The federation letter noted, however, that "neither of the ordinands came from that Society from whose fields of labor we would logically expect vocations . . . the Society of St. Joseph." The federation declared that black Catholics still wanted to know "whether or not this Society is continuing its policy of discouragement of a colored priesthood, which we brought to your attention in 1919." It insisted that the "only convincing argument that priests and bishops can make that they are friendly and looking out for the interests of the colored people will be found in their attitude and activity in preparing the men and women of these respective races to serve their people in the fullest way." It expressed the hope that the bishops would not view its letter as overly critical, and assured the bishops of its constructive aims. "Long-suffering," the letter explained, "makes for impassioned speech!"[11]

The letter drew praise from Jesuit John LaFarge, a fifteen-year veteran of black missionary work in eastern Maryland; founder of Cardinal Gibbons Institute, an industrial school for blacks in Ridge, Maryland, that opened in 1923; associate editor of *America* magazine; advisor to Turner, whom he had met in connection with

10. Federated Colored Catholics to Catholic Hierarchy, October, 1926, copy in Turner Papers.
11. *Ibid.*

the campaign for the institute; and arguably the foremost American Catholic spokesman for racial justice. LaFarge informed Turner that he had given a copy of the letter to a prelate visiting New York who "is very close to the Holy Father" and that it had deeply moved the prelate and all to whom LaFarge had shown it. He promised Turner that the letter "will have its effect, even though that effect may not be at once apparent." [12]

Two months later, following their December convention in Washington, D.C., the Federated Colored Catholics sent a committee of twelve delegates to meet with Archbishop Fumasoni-Biondi to press their case and to enlist his help in bringing pressure to bear on the hierarchy. Fumasoni-Biondi, who had recently completed a tour of the black missions in the South and who was much more sympathetic to their cause than his predecessor, received the committee cordially. He revealed a wide knowledge of the difficulties faced by black Catholics, assured the committee that the Holy Father knew of their problems, and led them to believe that efforts were underway to eliminate the racial discrimination faced by black Catholics in the church. The publication of the resolutions of the national convention of the federation in the December 30, 1926, issue of L'Osservatore Romano bestowed an added degree of legitimacy to federation demands and confirmed that Rome was at least aware of the grievances of black American Catholics. [13]

More concretely, between 1926 and 1930, the Holy See, working through the apostolic delegate, responded to black Catholic entreaties by persuading some northern archbishops and bishops to experiment with a few black seminarians for the diocesan priesthood. Archbishop Michael Curley, no friend of black priests (LaFarge described him as a "frank reactionary" on the subject), lamented his situtation: "The colored question is becoming a keen one. . . . It is a very difficult matter just to know how to handle them." [14]

12. Nickels, "Federated Colored Catholics," 210–14, 226–36; George K. Hunton, *All of Which I Saw, Part of Which I Was: The Autobiography of George K. Hunton, as Told to Gary MacEoin* (Garden City, N.Y., 1967), 47, 55–56; John LaFarge to Thomas Wyatt Turner, October 3, 1926, in Turner Papers.

13. Charles Hannigan to Louis B. Pastorelli, November 8, 1926, 44–6, JFA; report of committee on visit to papal delegate, in minutes of the first session of the Federated Colored Catholics, December 5, 1926, Thomas Wyatt Turner to Matthew Christman, April 2, 1927, copy, both in Turner Papers.

14. John LaFarge to Father Provincial, May 20, 1934, in Box 12-11, John LaFarge Papers, GUA; Archbishop Michael Curley to Cornelius Dacey, October 21, 1927, in D-6, AAB.

As Fumasoni-Biondi toured the southern missions following the publication of *Rerum Ecclesiae* in early 1926, he quizzed bishops there, and later throughout the country, about their attitudes toward black priests. Under both canon law and the terms of his appointment, the delegate could not order bishops or superiors of religious communities to accept black candidates into their seminaries. As the pope's personal representative, however, and as a key figure in recommending bishops for vacant dioceses in the United States, the delegate wielded considerable influence. During his visit to San Antonio, he summoned Lambert Welbers, the Josephite pastor of Holy Redeemer parish. According to Welbers, the delegate told him that Pius XI had strictly charged Fumasoni-Biondi to report any injustice shown black people. The delegate, therefore, requested that Welbers do the same for him so that he could duly inform the pope.[15]

The next year, perhaps as a result of the federation campaign and the apostolic delegate's quizzing, the issue of black priests surfaced during a special two-day conference of the bishops of the South and Southwest on the "Mexican and Colored Problem," called by the American Board of Catholic Missions, a body created by the bishops and approved by the pope in 1924 to collect and distribute funds for missions in the United States and its territories. Pastorelli attended at least one of the meetings, explaining the work of St. Joseph's Society and pleading for more aid to seminaries of religious communities working among blacks. During the discussions, Archbishop Shaw, responding to a paper prepared by Bishop Morris on recruiting priests for the southern Negro missions, argued that black priests "were not a proven success" and still in the experimental stage, because of social conditions over which the church had no control.

George Mundelein, who had become both a cardinal and the chairman of the American Board of Catholic Missions in 1924 and who was one of the most prominent members of the American hierarchy, reversed his earlier opposition and now endorsed the plan of the Divine Word Missionaries for a community of black priests wherein each would sustain the morale of the other. He warned his fellow bishops that the American Catholic church had to make a beginning with black priests "for the Church had been reproved with the charge that Colored people were not welcome to the ranks

15. Louis B. Pastorelli to Edward Knight, October 12, 1928, copy in 51-H, Lambert Welbers to Thomas A. Carney, October 28, 1936, in 56-W, both in JFA.

of her clergy." Bishop Richard O. Gerow, Gunn's successor in Natchez, declared St. Augustine's Seminary a success thus far and argued that its financial difficulties "should be worked out, as it was decidedly worth the trial." He appealed to the board for special consideration on its behalf.[16]

Other than St. Augustine's, however, most seminaries remained closed to black aspirants during the late 1920s. Even such liberal northern bishops as Archbishop Austin Dowling of St. Paul, whose seminary accepted black students from other dioceses and religious communities and who counted Stephen Theobald among his diocesan clergy, refused to sponsor black seminarians of his own. He could foresee no way to use them, since he had so few blacks in his archdiocese and since his progressivism never included the radical idea of black priests ministering to white congregations.[17]

Seminaries conducted by religious orders often proved as reluctant as diocesan seminaries to accept black applicants. On July 27, 1927, for example, Bishop Hugh C. Boyle of Pittsburgh asked Archabbot Aurelius Stehle, O.S.B., of St. Vincent Archabbey whether he would admit William L. Grau and William L. Lane, a black student and a black seminarian, to the archabbey's minor and major seminaries, respectively, if the bishop promised to adopt them. Boyle wrote, "I can see reasons for and against. . . . The Catholic thing would seem to be to open to them." He assured Stehle, however, that he would not quarrel with whatever decision the archabbot made. Stehle consulted with Ambrose Kohlbeck, the rector of the seminary, who responded that if the bishop wanted to adopt the black youths, he could send them to another seminary and not "impose a lonely Negro on St. Vincent Seminary at the present time until we shall open our special negro department some future day." Expressing a sentiment held by many Catholic clergy, he added, "I sincerely hope that I will have nothing to do with the seminary when that day shall come." Archabbot Stehle informed Boyle that "we deem it inexpedient at the present time to accept colored men who prefer to be in a place where they are at least numerically stronger."[18]

16. "The American Board of Catholic Missions, Minutes of the Meetings of January Third and Fourth, Nineteen Twenty Seven, in Consultation with Bishops of the South and Southwest, Subject: Mexican and Colored Problems," 13, 18–19, in American Board of Catholic Missions file, AUSCC.

17. Archbishop Austin Dowling to Max Murphy, July 10, 1928, in SMAA.

18. Bishop Hugh C. Boyle to Archabbot Aurelius Stehle, July 23, 1927, Ambrose Kohlbeck to Archabbot Aurelius Stehle, July 29, 1927, Archabbot Aurelius Stehle to Bishop Hugh C. Boyle, July 30, 1927, copy, all in SVAA.

Despite the generally inhospitable atmosphere, a few blacks managed to edge their way into the ranks of the priesthood. On February 7, 1926, Norman DuKette, from St. Augustine's Parish in Washington, D.C., was ordained for the diocese of Detroit. DuKette had been deeply influenced as a teenager by his friendship with John Plantevigne and had briefly attended the Josephites' St. Joseph's College for Negro Catechists. Taking advantage of the relatively tolerant racial atmosphere created in the archdiocese of Dubuque by John J. Keane, from 1900 to 1911, and his successor, James J. Keane, from 1911 to 1929, and in St. Paul, Minnesota, by John Ireland, from 1888 to 1918, and his successor, Austin Dowling, from 1919 to 1930, DuKette completed three years at Loras College in Dubuque and then entered St. Paul Seminary in St. Paul, Minnesota. Following his ordination, DuKette toured the country for a year, filling speaking engagements and spending a month with J. A. St. Laurent, pastor of St. Peter Claver Parish in New Orleans and an old friend from DuKette's days at the catechetical college. In 1927, Bishop Michael Gallagher of Detroit commissioned DuKette to found a new black parish, St. Benedict the Moor, in Detroit.[19]

In that same year, on June 11, 1927, Archibald Augustine Derricks, a native of Santo Domingo who had converted to Catholicism in 1905 while attending the high school department of Howard University and who, like DuKette, also belonged to Washington's St. Augustine's Parish, received holy orders in Rome, Italy, as a member of the Order of the Most Holy Trinity for the Redemption of Captives, or Trinitarians. After he spent a year of advanced study in Rome, the Trinitarians missioned Derricks to the United States, where he served as an assistant pastor at St. Ann's, an Italian parish in Bristol, Pennsylvania. There, however, he had few opportunities to work among blacks. The Reverend V. A. Devers, a veteran of black missionary work in the Philadelphia archdiocese, presented Cardinal Dennis Dougherty with a plan for Derricks to work among black people as he desired, but Derricks died of complications from appendicitis on October 22, 1929, before the plan could be implemented.[20]

19. Norman DuKette to Cardinal James Gibbons, June 7, 1919, in 126-P-4, AAB; Foley, *God's Men*, 116–19; John T. Gillard, S.S.J., *The Catholic Church and the American Negro* (1929; rpr. New York, 1968), 86.

20. Foley, *God's Men*, 111–14; *Standard and Times* (Philadelphia), November 2, 1929, clipping in Black Priests file, JFA.

A handful of black applicants, several from Josephite parishes, also found the doors of several seminaries opened to them. In 1927, Bishop Cantwell of Los Angeles-Monterey, a liberal on race questions and one of the few Catholic prelates to maintain friendly relations with the NAACP, secured the admission of Charles Logan of Los Angeles to St. Patrick's, the major seminary of the archdiocese of San Francisco, located in Menlo Park, California. Cantwell agreed to incardinate Logan after his ordination and also arranged for Max Murphy, a protégé of Josephite Tim Sullivan at St. Peter's Parish in Dallas, to enroll at St. Patrick's Seminary while he searched for a sponsoring bishop.[21] Bishop Schrembs of Cleveland, meanwhile, came to the rescue of William Grau and William Lane, both rejected a year earlier by St. Vincent Archabbey Seminary. Schrembs accepted Grau into the Cleveland diocesan seminary of Our Lady of the Lake and consented to sponsor Lane at St. Vincent Archabbey Seminary. The Benedictines at St. Vincent reversed their earlier decision on Lane as a result of several factors: the election of a new archabbot, Lane's appeals to the apostolic delegate, and Schrembs' willingness to sponsor the young man. Lane entered St. Vincent Seminary in September, 1928. John T. McNicholas, the archbishop of Cincinnati, also admitted a black student, Theldon F. Jones, who came from the Josephite parish of St. Peter Claver in San Antonio, into Mount St. Mary of the West, the major seminary for the Cincinnati archdiocese.[22]

Pastorelli knew about the experiments that Archbishop McNicholas and Bishop Schrembs had initiated with black seminarians; indeed, those developments accorded with his view that bishops should meet their obligations in accepting black candidates for the diocesan priesthood and not regard blacks as fit only for those religious communities that worked among them. The actions of McNicholas and Schrembs also provided Pastorelli with additional seminaries, besides St. Augustine's, to which he could refer black correspondents.[23] Furthermore, though the more liberal poli-

21. Rev. Francis J. Weber, "A Catholic Bishop Meets the Racial Problem," Records of the American Catholic Historical Society of Philadelphia, LXXXIV (December, 1973), 217–20; Foley, God's Men, 123, 168. See also Rev. Francis J. Weber's Documents of California Catholic History (Los Angeles, 1965), 255–60, and his The Pilgrim Church in California (Los Angeles, 1973), 63–64.

22. William Lane to Archabbot Alfred Koch, November 13, 1929, Ambrose Kohlbeck to Whom It May Concern, March 28, 1931, copy, both in SVAA; Foley, God's Men, 170, 174–84.

23. Louis B. Pastorelli to Henry Armstrong, April 15, 1929, copy in PMC.

cies of Cantwell, Gallagher, McNicholas, and Schrembs did offer some hope for the future of black priests, they also gave Pastorelli one more excuse for his "go slow" approach. He could argue that he should not embark on significant new departures for his society until the bishops in the more tolerant North demonstrated their general willingness to accept and ordain black seminarians. But their liberal policies worked the other way, too: the greater flexibility shown by the northern prelates helped encourage some of the same in Pastorelli, especially since he believed that Rome lay behind the bishops' newly found readiness to consider black applicants.

During the second half of the decade, many Josephite missionaries demonstrated their support for the cause of black priests not only in reviewing Josephite policy regarding the admission of black students and seminarians, which they did in three different general chapters, but through specific actions. Vincent Warren, for example, attempted to convince Pastorelli to accept Clarence Howard into Epiphany College in 1926, but he was unsuccessful. When Pastorelli balked, Warren subsequently sent Howard, and a number of other youths from his Norfolk parish, to St. Augustine's Seminary. Other Josephites, such as Joseph Lally, John Albert, and Edward Brunner, also sent promising young men from their missions to Bay St. Louis. J. A. St. Laurent and Tim Sullivan encouraged the eventually successful efforts of Norman DuKette and Max Murphy to secure ordination as diocesan priests. Charles Evers and Francis P. Linton preached retreats to students at St. Augustine's Seminary and sent glowing reports about its programs and students to Pastorelli.[24]

Support among the rank and file for the cause of black priests did not necessarily translate into accepting significantly greater numbers of black candidates for St. Joseph's Society. Although they sometimes bridled under his authoritarian yoke, most Josephites gratefully regarded Pastorelli as the man who earlier had saved their society from collapse. They regarded him as indispensable and trusted his judgment. For example, when the July, 1927, general chapter, which had been called to consider new society constitutions, also discussed the question of black students, it ended by

24. Harry Kane to Louis B. Pastorelli, May 18, 1926, in 44-K, JFA; interviews of Vincent D. Warren, S.S.J., by Peter E. Hogan, S.S.J., 1965 (typescript in JFA), 174; Foley, God's Men, 119, 168, 170; Charles Evers to Louis B. Pastorelli, August 22, 1925, in 43-D, Francis P. Linton to Louis B. Pastorelli, August 4, 1926, in 44-L, both in JFA.

simply reaffirming what it called "the old regulation," which was "that colored candidates should be selected only from our missions and cases should be referred to the Superior General."[25] In effect, the chapter gave Pastorelli a vote of confidence and left decisions regarding black students in his hands.

In those decisions, Pastorelli showed himself far more willing to consider mulatto candidates for Epiphany College and St. Joseph's Seminary than candidates who possessed clearly negroid features. He probably believed that bishops, priests, and seminarians would more readily accept blacks who were light skinned, or he may even have hoped that they might actually pass for white. His partiality toward mulatto candidates may also have stemmed from his early years as a missionary in the Mobile area, where he experienced success among the colored Creoles but frustration among American blacks.

The case of Louis A. Clemente, a young man recommended by the Reverend Mariano Vassalo, secretary to the bishop of Puerto Rico, illustrates Pastorelli's preference for mulatto candidates. Vassalo enthusiastically recommended Clemente to Pastorelli, describing him as "pious and intelligent . . . possessing a winning personality." Vassalo noted that Clemente, "while black, has fine features and a well-formed body." Pastorelli informed Vassalo that he could not take Clemente, explaining, "If he were light, so as to pass almost for a white boy, I would accept him." Under the circumstances, however, he feared that Josephite "students might object to [Clemente's] presence, as has been our experience in the past; then the problem of placing him is one that one must consider." He assured Vassalo that the young man would have no trouble gaining admission to St. Augustine's Seminary.[26]

Despite his wariness about accepting black students, once Pastorelli admitted a mulatto candidate, he genuinely tried to help him successfully complete his studies for the priesthood. In December, 1927, for instance, Pastorelli applied to the apostolic delegate for a dispensation from illegitimacy (which constituted an impediment to ordination) for Augustine McCarthy, the son of a black father and a white mother. McCarthy evidently had entered Epiphany College in 1919 or 1920 and by 1927 attended classes at St. Mary's Semi-

25. Minutes of the general chapters, July 19, 1927, in JFA.
26. Mariano Vassalo to Louis B. Pastorelli, May 2, 1928, Louis B. Pastorelli to Mariano Vassalo, copy, May 14, 1928, in PMC.

nary along with all the other Josephite seminarians. The Reverend James Hickey, one of his professors, spoke highly of McCarthy's ability and the quality of his work. In his letter to Fumasoni-Biondi on behalf of the young seminarian, Pastorelli told the delegate that he had "no doubts about his making a very good priest." Fumasoni-Biondi granted the dispensation, but McCarthy withdrew from the seminary the following year, discouraged by the trials that most likely awaited him as a black priest.[27]

In January, 1928, just as Archbishop McNicholas and Bishop Schrembs began to admit a few black students into their seminaries, Pastorelli also attempted to find a few acceptable black prospects for Epiphany College, which had experienced a gradual, but steady, drop in enrollment. He asked Edward Brunner, pastor of Blessed Sacrament Parish in New Orleans, if he had any likely candidates for the college. Brunner replied in the negative since he, like other Josephites, had sent his prospective vocations to Bay St. Louis. He reminded Pastorelli that "likely vocations are not plentiful" but promised to keep an eye open for any. Pastorelli finally located an acceptable black candidate at Cathedral College in New York City, though the young man did not come from a Josephite parish. Demonstrating that he alone determined the criteria for admission to the minor and major seminaries, the Josephite superior simply ignored the general chapter provision that black students "be selected only from our missions" and admitted Marcus Glover, a young man who had spent his whole life among whites, to Epiphany College in September, 1928.[28]

Pastorelli's efforts to find a black student for Epiphany evidently related to pressure he felt from Rome and from some of his own men to comply with the pope's desire for more black priests. The 1928 general chapter, meeting in July, discussed black priests in light of the pope's encyclical. Several months after the chapter, Edward A. Knight, pastor of St. Benedict the Moor Parish in St. Augustine, Florida, complained to Pastorelli that Rome remained ignorant

27. Louis B. Pastorelli to Archbishop Pietro Fumasoni-Biondi, December 5, 1927, copy in 68-B, Archbishop Pietro Fumasoni-Biondi to Louis B. Pastorelli, March 24, 1928, in 70-A, [Augustine] Gus McCarthy to Louis B. Pastorelli, October 3, November 12, 20, 1928, in PMC, all in JFA.

28. Louis B. Pastorelli to Harry Kane, January 7, 1928, copy in 46-K, Edward Brunner to Louis B. Pastorelli, January 26, 1928, in 46-A, minutes of the general chapters, July 19, 1927, Marcus Glover transcript, Cathedral College, June 30, 1928, Marcus Glover transcript, Epiphany Apostolic College, June, 1930, copies of both in Marcus Glover file, all in JFA.

about many of the difficulties under which the Josephites labored and about the real status of blacks in America. "We appreciate Rome's wishes about the ordination of foreign priests . . . but a colored man is unlike a Chin in China or a Japanese' in Japan," Knight wrote. "Rome ought to be made aware of conditions here." He suggested sending a secret representative to Rome to place the matter before the Holy See—secret because "we cannot jeopardize our position with any one bishop here." Pastorelli responded that Rome was well informed about a Negro clergy and that he had personally covered the question with the pope from every possible angle. He observed that Rome had quizzed the American bishops, that the apostolic delegate had toured all the southern missions, and that the Josephites could add no new information. "Rome now demands action," Pastorelli wrote to Knight, "and we cannot stand by idly, simply looking on. We must meet the situation as most of our Fathers feel and know." But he let slip some of his own frustration and uncertainty over the seemingly insoluble problem when he added, "Just *how* is the great question." [29]

At the last general chapter held at the old seminary in Baltimore in July, 1929, two delegates, John Albert and Dan Rice, proposed a solution to Pastorelli's dilemma. According to Edward Brunner, Albert and Rice arrived at the chapter with a "crusading spirit" and passionately urged the opening of a preparatory school for black Josephite candidates in Clayton, Delaware. During the ensuing discussion, Brunner expressed himself "willing and anxious" to accept the Albert-Rice plan but raised the question that haunted the Josephites: "Where would we put them once ordained?" For the welfare of both the society and the men involved, Brunner countered the Albert-Rice plan with his own. He recommended that the Josephites accept and educate black candidates free of charge at Epiphany College and St. Joseph's Seminary, on the condition that they come from a bishop who would agree in advance to sponsor, ordain, and incardinate them. Brunner argued that the Josephites should place the burden where it belonged—on the bishops. Sam Kelly, however, disagreed with Brunner over where properly to lay the blame for the scarcity of black Josephites. [30]

29. Edward Knight to Louis B. Pastorelli, October 4, 1928, in 46-K, Louis B. Pastorelli to Edward Knight, October 12, 1928, copy in 51-H, both in JFA.

30. Edward Brunner to Edward V. Casserly, July 26, 1944, in Edward V. Casserly-Thomas P. McNamara Papers, JFA.

Kelly, a zealous but emotionally unstable missionary who, during the course of his career, had managed to alienate most of his Josephite colleagues, refused to point the finger at bishops for the dearth of black Josephites. Instead, he placed the blame closer to home. In a strident, rambling paper prepared for the chapter, he bitterly denounced Pastorelli for a host of sins, including unfairly persecuting him and cheating him out of money. More important, Kelly accused Pastorelli of purposely ignoring *Rerum Ecclesiae* and of conspiring with Archbishop Curley to change the pope's mind about a native clergy in the United States.[31]

The shrillness and obvious paranoia of much of Kelly's diatribe obscured whatever elements of truth his paper contained and created a backlash of sympathy for Pastorelli. The intemperate paper also discredited Pastorelli's other critics among the delegates by appearing to associate them with an unstable man. An abashed Vincent Warren, a strong advocate of black priests and the candidate some of the younger men preferred to succeed Pastorelli as superior general in 1930, tried to dissociate himself from Kelly. Writing to Pastorelli, he expressed his "utter contempt" for Kelly's statements and pledged his own loyalty and obedience to the superior general.[32]

Although the general chapter minutes do not record any action on the Albert-Rice proposal, Pastorelli appears to have adopted it, at least rhetorically, as a long-range, even if not carefully formulated, goal. He spelled out his thinking to George Foster Peabody, a prominent banker, philanthropist, and Episcopalian layman who had added his voice to the chorus calling for a reassessment of Josephite policy. Two weeks after the general chapter, Peabody wrote to Pastorelli and expressed his puzzlement "at the rather definite refusal" of the Josephites "to encourage the entrance of the Negroes into the priesthood in any numbers." Peabody recalled that his own experience in education (he was a trustee of Hampton Institute) had convinced him that blacks ultimately needed to control work among their people. He warned Pastorelli that it would certainly prove a hindrance to the rapid spread of Catholicism among blacks if "there shall not be a large contingent of Negro priests to further the work." Peabody assured Pastorelli that he did not mean

31. Sam Kelly, paper read at the general chapter, July 2, 1929 (Typescript in PMC).
32. Vincent Warren to Louis B. Pastorelli, July 9, 1929, in 48-T, JFA.

to criticize but only to help him "realize the thought in the minds of friends of the Negroes who are observing you from the outside."[33]

In his reply, Pastorelli contended that the outlook for more black priests had recently improved. Acknowledging that the Josephites had "been rather slow in the development of this phase of the work," he assured Peabody that "there is no definite refusal to encourage their elevation to the priesthood." Instead, Pastorelli attributed the slow pace to the need "of educating them to an idea of its dignity and the required fitness." Pastorelli nevertheless claimed that the Josephites had established the groundwork and that prospects "look bright today for an increase in the number of colored ecclesiastical students." After repeating his standard defense of the Josephite record, which included reference to the three black Josephite priests, the two other black seminarians who would have received holy orders had they not died, and the presence of two black students at Epiphany College, Pastorelli enunciated a new goal for the Josephites. "This number we intend to increase year by year," he explained, "our purpose being to prepare a colored faculty for a preparatory school for colored students studying for the priesthood." He ruled out integrated seminary education on a wide scale, claiming that the earlier Josephite policy of educating black students together with whites unsuited them for their work in the South, "where . . . the social lines are tightly drawn." The priests, he continued, "crave for past equality and do not care to be sent where they find themselves ostracized." Pastorelli suggested that hope for black priests in the South lay in "a larger number of colored priests," along the lines envisaged by the Divine Word Missionaries, who would form "a social centre of their own," thus enabling them to endure the color bar.

Pastorelli further justified his selectivity in regard to black students by raising the old bugbear, the alleged inability of blacks to remain celibate. Although he blamed historical and social factors rather than inherent racial characteristics for the supposed lack of chastity among blacks, he nevertheless contended that "it again compels us to be most careful and cautious for so much harm would result from a clergy weak in this respect." Despite his characterization of blacks, Pastorelli closed his letter to Peabody with the observation that, problems notwithstanding, "a change of sentiment is evident in the minds of the Bishops of our land and I know

33. George F. Peabody to Louis B. Pastorelli, July 18, 1929, in PMC.

within the next decade or two many more . . . will be raised to the priesthood."[34]

Encouraged by that "change in sentiment," Pastorelli went to great lengths to help Marcus Glover, who graduated from Epiphany College in June, 1930, and prepared to enter the major seminary. The Sulpician decision to relocate the theology department of St. Mary's Seminary from Paca Street, next door to St. Joseph's Seminary, to Roland Park in the Baltimore suburbs, complicated matters for Glover and Pastorelli. Since Josephite seminarians still studied philosophy and theology at St. Mary's, the Sulpician move forced the Josephites to construct a new seminary building of their own. Pastorelli and his council, or consultors, chose a location near Catholic University as the site of the new St. Joseph's Seminary so as to enable the Josephite seminarians to take their classes at the university's seminary. The new St. Joseph's Seminary building, begun in 1929 and finished in 1930 at a cost of $500,000, imposed a heavy financial burden on Pastorelli and his society just as the Great Depression began. The site, moreover, posed two serious problems for black Josephite seminarians: Catholic University did not admit black seminarians, and St. Joseph's Seminary was located in a "restricted residential district" where, according to Pastorelli, "no colored are allowed." John LaFarge expressed the desire of some of the Catholic clergy when he wrote that he hoped the presence of the Josephite seminary at Catholic University would dramatically expose some of the anomalies of the jim-crow situation at the university "and hasten their abolition."[35]

Pastorelli, meanwhile, had to decide what to do about Glover. In April, 1930, he appealed to his friend and fellow Bostonian Francis Spellman to find a seminary for Glover in Rome. Pastorelli promised to pay whatever fee was required, adding, "He is a good student and I would like to see him become one of our priests." Spellman attempted to enroll him in the Urban College, but found all of the places taken. Pastorelli then turned to Emile Filion, rector of the Sulpician Seminary of Philosophy in Montreal, and asked Filion to accept Glover, describing him as a "good, model student, whom we would like to do all in our power to see become a priest

34. Louis B. Pastorelli to George F. Peabody, August 12, 1929, copy in PMC.

35. CMB, June 21, 1929, in JFA; Louis B. Pastorelli to Joseph E. McKee, September 15, 1930, Louis B. Pastorelli to Francis J. Spellman, April 30, 1930, copies of both in PMC; John LaFarge to Thomas Wyatt Turner, November 28, 1930, in Turner Papers.

of our Society." On July 28, J. S. Moreau, the superior, informed Pastorelli that the seminary would "be pleased to receive . . . the seminarian." Filion told Pastorelli that after two years of philosophy, new arrangements for theology would have to be made with the Grand Seminaire.[36]

On September 18, Glover entered the Seminary of Philosophy. He described the reactions of faculty and students as "most wonderful and agreeable." Filion reported that after some initial bashfulness, Glover adjusted, seemed happy, and performed well academically. Although Pastorelli realized that the Sulpicians "are doing us a great favor," he wrote to Glover expressing his sorrow "that conditions over which we have no control forbid you the pleasure of being with us in Washington." He added, "Let us hope that at no distant date this obstacle will be removed and . . . no student of ours will be compelled to make his course of studies elsewhere than in our own seminary."[37]

Despite Pastorelli's efforts on behalf of Marcus Glover, however, Thomas Wyatt Turner and his associates continued to press the Josephites to accept more black students and seminarians. Pastorelli resisted their pressure, defending Josephite policy through spokesmen such as John T. Gillard, an able young Josephite scholar whose book and private correspondence sparked additional controversy between the Josephites and their critics.

The defensiveness that characterized the Josephites' dealings with their critics surfaced dramatically at the fifth annual convention of the Federated Colored Catholics in Baltimore on September 1, 1929. Prior to the convention, Pastorelli had heard rumors that the leaders of the convention invited him to preside at one of the sessions in order to "force his hand and that of the Josephites on the question of colored priests." Pastorelli was wary of traps. He believed that more than once blacks had applied to the Josephites not from a sincere desire to join the society but for the purpose of discovering whether the Josephites welcomed black students. Rather than attend the convention himself, he sent his per-

36. Louis B. Pastorelli to Francis J. Spellman, April 30, 1930, copy, Francis J. Spellman to Louis B. Pastorelli, June 28, 1930, Louis B. Pastorelli to Emile Filion, July 24, 1930, copy, J. S. Moreau to Louis B. Pastorelli, July 28, 1930, Emile Filion to Louis B. Pastorelli, August 2, 1930, all in PMC.

37. Marcus Glover to Louis B. Pastorelli, October 9, 1930, Emile Filion to Louis B. Pastorelli, October 19, 1930, Louis B. Pastorelli to Marcus Glover, October 11, 1930, copies of all in PMC.

sonal representative, Thomas Duffy, who delivered a lengthy and defensive policy statement. Duffy declared: "What the Church desires, we desire. . . . St. Joseph's Society believes absolutely and unqualifiedly in colored priests." At the same time, he added, "St. Joseph's Society reserves the right to say who shall be admitted into membership, just as every other Society."

Duffy then reviewed the pioneering role played by the Josephites in developing black priests such as Fathers Uncles, Dorsey, and Plantevigne. He further pointed out that Fathers Burgess, John, and DuKette had all received at least part of their training from the Josephites and ticked off a list of seventeen black students who had studied at Epiphany Apostolic College or St. Joseph's Seminary, conveniently failing to mention, however, that most of the black students named had attended those institutions around the turn of the century. Reacting to what he perceived to be a lack of gratitude and understanding on the part of federation members, he complained that despite all that the Josephites had done to foster black vocations, "there are some who seem to think that we do not favor a colored clergy." He steadfastly maintained that the society had no apologies to make for its stand on the question of black priests and that its work had "met the approval of the episcopate and the Holy Father himself." He claimed, moreover, that few black young men came forward when they were offered the opportunity to study for the priesthood. He built up the good that the society had done, for through their mission schools, each involving expenses beyond the power of the people to bear, he pointed out, the Josephites had "paved the way for that higher education necessary for the priesthood and the professions."

In a slap at John LaFarge, William Markoe, and other clerical allies of the federation, Duffy belittled "armchair missionaries" who criticized and condemned the Josephites without having firsthand experience of conditions in the South. To those impatient to know Josephite plans for the future, he huffed, "They are ours and ours only until we see fit to divulge them." He closed by urging those in his audience to raise the issue of black priests "openly and above board" rather than through trickery or deceit.[38]

Because of the constraints they felt from bishops, the Josephites' defense of their own policies was lacking in openness and honesty,

38. "Address delivered by Rev. Thomas J. Duffy at the Convention of the Federated Colored Catholics, September 1, 1929" (Typescript in John T. Gillard Papers, JFA).

the very qualities they asked for from others. Presentations such as Duffy's revealed an almost contemptuous disregard for the intelligence of black Catholic audiences and assumed a high level of gullibility. Although Duffy's aggressive defense caught Turner and the federation by surprise, it failed to dispel their dissatisfaction with the Josephites.

The reaction to Duffy's speech, however, was as nothing compared to the uproar that greeted the 1930 publication of John T. Gillard's *The Catholic Church and the American Negro*. Gillard, a native of Scranton, Pennsylvania, was ordained a priest in 1928 and became the editor of *Colored Harvest* and Pastorelli's personal secretary. The two men enjoyed a close personal and professional relationship built on mutual esteem and respect. The scholarly Gillard, who earned his doctorate from Catholic University in 1929 and who pioneered in the study of the relationship between the Catholic church and blacks, wrote prolifically for many Catholic publications and, for more than a decade, served as the chief spokesman for Pastorelli and the Josephites.[39]

Gillard's book, a revision of his doctoral dissertation, contained six sections. In the first five, he presented a ground-breaking historical and statistical analysis of Catholic missionary efforts among blacks in the United States. In the final section, he ventured into a discussion of contemporary issues, including the topic of black priests. Gillard later claimed he had based the hypotheses in his concluding section on conversations with and letters from Josephites and priests of other societies who had worked among blacks for many years. Unfortunately, he absorbed and repeated some of their common and demeaning stereotypical assumptions about blacks, including a claim that they possessed "a child-like mentality." Although he acknowledged the need for and the theoretical feasibility of black priests in the United States, he hedged his statements throughout the book with so many qualifications that he conveyed a largely negative message, one that manifested the ambivalence the Josephite administration felt over both the issue of black priests and the related question of the potential for black leadership in the church.[40]

39. Obituary in John T. Gillard file, JFA; Paul E. Czuchlewski includes a discussion of Gillard's writing in his "Liberal Catholicism and American Racism, 1924–1960," *Records of the American Catholic Historical Society of Philadelphia,* LXXXV (March–June, 1974), 144–62.

40. John LaFarge to John T. Gillard, July 1, 1930, in Gillard Papers; Gillard, *The Catholic Church and the Negro,* 85–93, 255, 284, 286.

Gillard claimed that the feasibility and advisability of a black clergy was inextricably bound up with the race question and that he could draw no empirical conclusions about black priests because of the paucity of their numbers. He denied that the church had prevented blacks from studying for the Catholic priesthood, citing the Josephite record of having enrolled thirty-five black students over the years and pointing to the ten or twelve black students in diocesan seminaries and the thirty-nine students, novices, and scholastics at St. Augustine's Seminary in Bay St. Louis.

Conceding that "a native priesthood is the general desire of the Holy Father," Gillard warned that an adequate solution required due regard "to the matter of fact difficulties" in American society and concluded that therefore the pope had not intended *Rerum Ecclesiae* to apply to the United States "with its unique race conditions." Besides, he contended, the church could not draw on a very large pool of potential black seminarians, because a majority of the race would not qualify on moral and intellectual grounds. He insisted that the few black priests there were had proven no more effective in gaining converts than white priests and further implied that many blacks did not want black priests. "Will the Negro receive, respect, and obey a colored pastor?" Gillard asked. "Some will: some will not. Perhaps the future will be kinder than the past."

Gillard maintained that black leaders who "insistently and loudly" clamored for black priests allowed their zeal to blind them to "difficulties which are not lightly ignored," particularly the emotional and psychological toll on black priests and the problem of placing them in a diocese. He declared, "It is not without a certain significance that those missionary societies that have experimented with colored priests have learned to be conservative in considering Negro applicants."

Gillard attempted to shift the responsibility for developing black priests away from religious communities such as the Josephites and onto the bishops in the North. Pointing out that the only black priests in the country worked in northern dioceses, Gillard wrote, "The problem of the Negro clergy will find satisfactory solution in the secular ranks of the northern clergy . . . where prejudice is not so all pervading or fatal." Only after bishops, priests, and laity in the more tolerant North accepted black priests, he averred, would the idea pervade the South. If a black priest belonged to a diocese, that would also solve the problem of placement, since a bishop would have already adopted him. To that end, Gillard pro-

posed the establishment in the United States of a pontifical seminary for black priests on the model of the Josephenium Seminary,
which was established by the Holy See in Ohio in 1892 for the
training of German-speaking aspirants to the diocesan priesthood.
The seminary would be maintained by the hierarchy or by the likely
diocesan beneficiaries. Assignment from the seminary would be
made on request by the bishops or through the apostolic delegate.
Eventually, Gillard predicted, the time would come when white
priests on the black missions would gradually withdraw from the
work and leave to a black clergy the spiritual concerns of the race. [41]

Not surprisingly, Gillard's book provoked a storm of unfavorable
criticism. John LaFarge published a critical review in the *Chronicle*,
the official organ of the Federated Colored Catholics. Although
LaFarge praised the historical and statistical information contained
in the first five sections of the book, he took exception to what he
called the "sweeping statements" and "half truths" found in the last
part, which, in his view, conveyed "an impression of distrust, almost pessimism concerning the race." LaFarge especially faulted
Gillard for asserting that blacks possessed "a childlike mentality"
and for denying that Pius XI had intended *Rerum Ecclesiae* to apply
to the black priesthood in the United States. [42]

Gillard was shaken by LaFarge's review. In a letter to the Jesuit,
he described the review as "devastating," complained that it dwelt
disproportionately on part six, and charged that it seemed calculated to place him "in a very unfavorable light" with blacks. He
fretted that if blacks got the impression that he distrusted them, he
"might as well abandon the work." [43]

LaFarge attempted to explain his criticisms in a long reply. He
pointedly told the young Josephite that if Gillard believed that
public controversy would destroy his effectiveness among blacks,
then he should have confined himself to noncontroversial topics.
LaFarge claimed that he had written his review in the *Chronicle* to
prevent readers from forming the impression that Gillard's statements represented the general opinion of Catholic priests or the
official attitude of the Catholic church. The harm that he saw in
many passages, LaFarge said, "lay in that of placing the emphasis
precisely in the direction contrary to what the true interests of the

41. Gillard, *The Catholic Church and the Negro*, 87–92, 284–87.
42. John LaFarge to John T. Gillard, July 1, 1930, in Gillard Papers.
43. John T. Gillard to John LaFarge, June 30, 1930, copy in Gillard Papers.

Negro Catholic demand." He further charged that a great number of Gillard's statements simply fed the racial stereotypes that many white Catholics, including quite a few priests and sisters, already held about blacks; he expressed puzzlement that anyone who had the interests of black Catholics at heart would take up "with those stock phrases or overworked notions which have a sinister connotation to Negroes." He found Gillard's statements about *Rerum Ecclesiae* particularly deplorable since opponents of black priests would seize upon them "as an excuse to disregard the spirit of the encyclical, which spirit . . . is one of the Negro's chief hopes."[44]

Gillard's worry that LaFarge's review would encourage "a certain group among the more intellectual Negroes, who are only too willing to take down the pants of the Josephites" soon proved well founded. Writing in the July, 1930, issue of the *Journal of Negro History*, Carter G. Woodson, its editor, leveled a withering critique at both Gillard's book and the Josephites. Like LaFarge, Woodson scored Gillard for uncritically accepting negative stereotypes about blacks; he also faulted him for "failing ingloriously to face courageously such questions as the need for a Negro clergy, race distinctions, and segregation." Woodson unfavorably contrasted Gillard and the Josephites with LaFarge and his outspoken Jesuit colleague William Markoe, editor of the *Chronicle*, pastor of St. Elizabeth's (black) Parish in St. Louis, and fiery advocate of black priests. He claimed that the two Jesuits had won a place in the hearts of the black people whom they served, "while the Josephite Fathers, with a different policy are all but hated by the very Negroes among whom they toiled for generations."[45]

The controversy over Gillard's book continued into the autumn of 1930, igniting a lively debate over the issue of black clergy between Gillard and his fellow Josephite, Edward Brunner, pastor of St. Joan of Arc Parish in New Orleans, on the one side, and their more activist Jesuit critics, LaFarge and Markoe, on the other. Their disagreements stemmed in large part from different perspectives: the two Josephites spoke for a small society, many of whose missions lay in the Deep South, whereas the two Jesuits, members of one of the Catholic church's most prestigious and powerful reli-

44. John LaFarge to John T. Gillard, July 1, 1930, in Gillard Papers.
45. John T. Gillard to John LaFarge, July 3, 1930, copy in Gillard Papers; Carter Woodson, Review of John T. Gillard's *The Catholic Church and the American Negro*, in *Journal of Negro History*, XV (July, 1930), 106–107.

gious orders, drew on their missionary experiences in the border states of Maryland and Missouri.

In addition, LaFarge possessed the confidence and certitude of a man born to the purple. His ancestors included Benjamin Franklin and Oliver Hazard Perry on his mother's side; his father, John, was one of America's most distinguished mural painters. Intellectual, urbane, diplomatic, deeply spiritual, and utterly committed to interracial justice, LaFarge had acumen, social position, influence as an associate editor of *America*, and numerous contacts within the church, eventually including even Pius XI—all of which gave him extraordinary independence and breadth of view.[46]

William M. Markoe, LaFarge's Jesuit colleague and pastor from 1927 to 1941 of St. Elizabeth's (black) Parish in St. Louis, was much more the firebrand and maverick. Between June 19, 1920, and May 2, 1925, he contributed twenty-four articles to *America* on the race issue and consistently supported a black clergy. In 1930, he offered his monthly parish bulletin, *St. Elizabeth's Chronicle*, to the Federated Colored Catholics for use as its official organ. Turner accepted, Markoe remained as editor and publisher, and the name was shortened to the *Chronicle*.[47]

Edward Brunner initiated the exchanges between Josephites and Jesuits by complaining to Markoe about "offending things" appearing in the *Chronicle* and by describing the Josephites as victims of "misrepresentation—as well as slander" on the question of a black clergy. He explained that the Josephites, as a result, had become "rather sensitive and resentful of criticism" based on either a lack of knowledge or, in some cases, ill will. Brunner particularly took exception to criticism from Jesuits, whose order in the United States did not accept black candidates. He needled Markoe by telling him that he prayed daily for "one of the more powerful societies to take

46. Nickels, "Federated Colored Catholics," 210–14, 226–36; Edward S. Stanton, S.J., "John LaFarge's Understanding of the Unifying Mission of the Church, Especially in the Area of Race Relations" (Ph.D. dissertation, St. Paul University, 1972), 168–99.

47. Markoe specifically addressed the issue of black priests in "Catholics, the Negro, and a Native Clergy," *America*, September 24, 1921, pp. 535–36, and in "Negro Morality and a Colored Clergy," *America*, November 12, 1921, pp. 79–80. For more information on Markoe's crusading career on behalf of interracial justice in the church, see Nickels, "Federated Colored Catholics," 61–135, 136–209, 266–85, 319–21, and William M. Markoe, "An Interracial Role, Memoirs of William Markoe, 1900–1906" (Typescript copy in JFA).

up this question of a colored clergy and force it to a conclusion," since the Josephites, a small and weak community, "were too easily squelched." Brunner asked pointedly, "Is it possible for a colored student to aspire to become a Jesuit?"[48]

Markoe attempted to calm the indignant Josephite by assuring him that if Markoe could meet more frequently with the Josephites, they would probably discover that "we are standing on pretty much the same platform even as regards most accidental details." Acknowledging that many in the Catholic church regarded him as an extremist and an eccentric because of his frank espousal of racial justice and his association with the Federated Colored Catholics, Markoe reassured Brunner that those who knew him did not regard him as such. He advised Brunner that the Josephites had misjudged Thomas Wyatt Turner and the Federated Colored Catholics; he described the federation and its journal as effective agents for combating the inroads of communism among blacks and for promoting Catholic social action. Markoe promised that if the Josephites displayed less sensitivity and suspicion and more cooperation toward the federation, they could transform what had seemed like a radical movement into a powerful ally.[49]

Markoe's letter neither reassured nor mollified Brunner, who told the Jesuit that he expected him to let the leaders of the federation know the true Josephite attitude toward a black clergy, namely their willingness to create such a clergy "IF THEY GET ASSURANCE THEY CAN PLACE THEM" (Brunner's emphasis). Brunner then explained the rationale behind the Josephites' general unwillingness to speak out publicly for change in the South. He said that they had learned from experience that to have any positive effect at all, they had to confine their activities in the South to bringing religion to blacks. "Their social, economic, and political difficulties would have to wait for a better attitude on the part of those among whom they are forced to live," Brunner declared. Displaying the myopia and misplaced optimism that characterized many Catholic commentators on race relations in the 1930s, Brunner professed to see a better attitude slowly developing in the South and claimed that "our present method has contributed somewhat to this change." He admitted

48. Edward Brunner to William Markoe, September 17, 1930, copy in Gillard Papers.

49. William Markoe to Edward Brunner, September 20, 1930, in Gillard Papers.

that the strategy would not set the world on fire but insisted that it would produce the best results over the long run.[50]

Markoe admitted that he had not personally contended with the race problem in the Deep South, though he thought St. Louis, where he labored, to be "practically speaking a southern city." He claimed, however, that he would emphasize the same ideas in Georgia as in St. Louis. Indeed, speaking at Okmulgee, Oklahoma, to the Knights of Peter Claver convention the previous August, Markoe had provoked a storm of protest from priests on black missions by emphasizing the grievances of black Catholics and calling on priests laboring for blacks to "work tooth and nail" to correct injustices. He insisted to Brunner that the greatest obstacle to the conversion of blacks was the "uncatholicity" of white Catholics. "If the priests engaged in Negro work would become known to the race throughout the country as champions in behalf of the cause of justice," Markoe argued, and "more publicly insist that the Negroes be accorded their inalienable rights, the results would soon be the conversion of the Negro race in this country."[51]

LaFarge, more genteel and diplomatic than Markoe, nevertheless agreed with the basic thrust of his colleague's arguments. He attempted to persuade Gillard that a more aggressive stance would serve the interests of both the Josephites and the black apostolate. To Gillard's fear, voiced during a conversation between the two men in New York, that the Josephites would incur the wrath of the bishops if they spoke the plain truth, he responded that "the Bishops seem . . . far more dependent on you than you are on them." Ignoring the Josephites' reliance on crucial funds from the episcopally controlled Negro and Indian Commission and the American Board of Catholic Missions, LaFarge quoted one bishop as saying that without the aid of the Josephites in his diocese, "I should be at my wits' end." LaFarge argued that in other situations undue fear of possible consequences from higher authority had hindered good men, when they actually controlled the situation. "Bishops, too, will be encouraged to come out for the right if priests and intelligent laity voice their opinion," he insisted. "It is no longer prudence," he declared, "but a grave imprudence, to be too timid in

50. Edward Brunner to William Markoe, September 22, 1930, copy in Gillard Papers.
51. Markoe, "An Interracial Role," 58; William Markoe to Edward Brunner, September 24, 1930, in Gillard Papers.

stating boldly and clearly the essential right of the Negro as a human being; both in the natural order and in the . . . Church."

In reply to Gillard's objection that he and LaFarge should talk privately about the issues, not before "unlettered Negroes" who would become unnecessarily agitated, LaFarge pointed out that both educated and uneducated blacks discussed those issues and that "we can't put them off when they ask us about matters of essential human rights." Besides, LaFarge added, the widely read Afro-American press covered all of those topics. He insisted that all friends of black Americans ought to unite "on a fundamental platform of basic human rights, which we shall proclaim without fear, in the name of Christ." Brunner, Gillard, and Pastorelli, however, remained unconvinced by the arguments of Markoe and LaFarge, suspecting, as Brunner put it, that "there is very little good will toward us in that quarter."[52]

Actually, evidence suggests that LaFarge and Markoe possessed more good will toward the Josephites than Brunner, Gillard, or Pastorelli supposed. Following the letter debate, the two Jesuits evidently heeded Brunner's admonition and passed the word to black Catholics of the federation that the Josephites did not oppose black priests in principle but were the victims, at least in part, of circumstances. In a letter to the *Chronicle* on November 6, 1930, shortly after the exchanges between the Josephites and the Jesuits ended, Turner made a conciliatory gesture to the society. Despite his having published his own stinging review of Gillard's book earlier in the pages of the *Chronicle*, Turner nevertheless disputed Woodson's claim that black Catholics hated the Josephites. He pointed out that many Josephites "are as fondly loved as any priests among our people." He added that though "certain practices of the Order have been subjects of criticism by thinking colored men and women . . . My impression is that a fuller understanding is maturing between the Josephites and the thoughtful of the group."[53]

Privately, Turner remarked that Gillard's book accurately reflected "the policies of the Order" and constituted "possibly the greatest reproach to the Negro that has come from the pen of any

52. John LaFarge to John T. Gillard, September 30, 1930, in Gillard Papers; Edward Brunner to John T. Gillard, October 8, 1930, in 49-A, JFA.

53. John LaFarge to Thomas Wyatt Turner, November 28, 1930, in Turner Papers; Brunner to Gillard, October 8, 1930, in 49-A, JFA; Thomas Wyatt Turner to Alan C. J. M. Bates, November 18, 1930, Thomas Wyatt Turner to the editor of the *Chronicle*, November 6, 1930, copies of both in Turner Papers.

Catholic writer." Still, he expressed only the highest personal regard for Pastorelli, who in the summer of 1930 had been reelected
superior general. Turner believed that, Gillard's book notwithstanding, he detected signs that St. Joseph's Society had recently
begun "more and more to return to its original moorings and to develop a policy that will meet the approval of intelligent colored
people."[54]

To help the society to return to its original goal, the Federated
Colored Catholics attempted to encourage movement on the issue
of black clergy through a steady stream of remonstrances and petitions directed to the American hierarchy and the apostolic delegate. As Turner explained, "The question of a Race clergy is so vital
to our efforts . . . that we might say it is part and parcel of our
aims." In November, 1930, LaFarge persuaded *L'Osservatore Romano*
to print on its front page, "where everybody from the Holy Father
himself down could and undoubtedly would read it," a statement
from the Federated Colored Catholics asking for the opportunity to
educate black youth in Catholic schools, colleges, universities, and
seminaries in the United States. The next year, the federation appointed a committee to make a formal presentation before the
American hierarchy at its annual meeting, on November 11 and
12, 1931, at Catholic University. Before the conference, Turner, in
the name of the federation, wrote to the Catholic archbishops and
bishops asking that they "take such steps as are needed to open to
our Colored Catholics our elementary schools, high schools, colleges, universities, and seminaries." In his proposed meetings with
the bishops, he planned to focus on education and also hoped to
discuss with southern bishops the outlook for black clergy.[55]

Although the rules governing the meeting prevented Turner and
his committee from formally addressing the assembled prelates, the
persistent black Catholics buttonholed as many of them as they
could during the episcopal gathering. Turner expressed particular
satisfaction over conversations with Cardinal William O'Connell of

54. Thomas Wyatt Turner to Alan C. J. M. Bates, November 18, 1930, copy
in Turner Papers.
55. Thomas Wyatt Turner to Archbishop Pietro Fumasoni-Biondi, February
20, 1932, John LaFarge to Thomas Wyatt Turner, November 28, 1930, Thomas
W. Turner, "Statement of the Federated Colored Catholics," *Chronicle*, November, 1930, Thomas Wyatt Turner to H. M. Smith, September 21, 1931, Thomas
Wyatt Turner to Stephen Theobald, October 8, 1931, Thomas Wyatt Turner to
the Hierarchy of the United States, October 20, 1931, Thomas Wyatt Turner to
Edward Kramer, November 4, 1931, copies of all in Turner Papers.

Boston about desegregating Catholic University and with Bishop William J. Hafey of Raleigh, North Carolina, regarding "the often quoted statement that the southern Bishops won't have Negro priests." His talk with Hafey convinced him that "the position of the Bishops is not being put before the Catholic Negro group in the proper light."[56]

In early 1932, the Reverend Stephen Theobald presented a report, prepared in conjunction with Edward Kramer and John LaFarge and black laymen H. M. Smith, Elmo Anderson, and Thomas Turner, to the administrative committee of the National Catholic Welfare Conference (NCWC). Claiming that close contact with Catholic priests in Catholic schools provided the initial incentive for many youths to aspire to the priesthood, Theobald urged the hierarchy to ensure that capable black Catholics had the opportunity for Catholic education. He cited the predicament of the Josephites at Catholic University to dramatize his plea for the desegregation of the university. Arguing that black seminarians should have the opportunity for the best possible training at Catholic University and obviously alluding to the plight of Marcus Glover, Theobald pointed out that the exclusion of blacks from the university had created an unfortunate situation in St. Joseph's Society, which could not "give all of its candidates for the priesthood the advantage of training which their residence at the University affords." Such a condition, he maintained, would cause "undeniable psychological effect" on Josephites, who, though theoretically equal among themselves, knew of the inequalities forced on some of their members.[57]

Once again, though, black Catholics received little satisfaction from the American hierarchy. In May, 1932, the executive committee of the Board of Trustees of Catholic University, composed entirely of archbishops and bishops and chaired by Cardinal O'Connell, who, the previous year, had led Turner to believe that he would take action on the federation's request to end segregation by exclusion at Catholic University, decided that "without prejudice to the case, the time is not ripe to admit colored students."[58]

56. Thomas Wyatt Turner to John LaFarge, November 16, 1931, copy in Turner Papers.

57. Stephen Theobald to administrative committee of the NCWC, January 8, 1932, copy in Turner Papers.

58. Thomas Wyatt Turner to John LaFarge, November 16, 1931, James H. Ryan, rector of The Catholic University of America, to Eugene A. Clark, president of Miner Teachers' College, May 27, 1932, copies of both in Turner Papers.

In August, the federation followed up Theobald's presentation and the unsatisfactory decision of the university's board of trustees with a petition to Pius XI asking for his help in opening Catholic University to black students. It also sent another appeal to the American bishops in November, 1932, asking them to remove any color bar in their dioceses that civil law did not require. In response, the administrative committee of the NCWC agreed to conduct a survey of the problems of black Catholics and to appoint a liaison official between the federation and the conference. Despite their smiles and apparent willingness to listen to committees from the federation, however, the American hierarchy did little to address the problems pointed out by Turner and his group.[59] With Catholics only beginning to enjoy a modest amount of respectability and acceptance in American society and with anti-Catholic feeling still strong, especially in the South, the bishops insisted on the need for prudence and patience in dealing with racial questions.

Archbishop McNicholas, writing to George B. Conrad, a prominent member of the federation, expressed the conservative spirit of the hierarchy when he promised that the church would "always proceed with great prudence," since "all cannot be gained at once and much can be lost by immoderate zeal and an impudent crusading spirit." He told Conrad that blacks should learn from the church "how to be patient and forbearing, yet steadfast in . . . their purpose to do away ultimately with injustice." The *Afro-American* offered a contrasting analysis when, in an editorial entitled "Do You Call That Religion?," it claimed that the Catholic church, like the U.S. army, exhibited by its actions the belief that "white men are ordained to lead Negroes."[60]

John Gillard, manifesting both the clericalism and paternalism common in the church during that period, certainly believed that black laity should follow the lead of their white clergy. The audacity of the Federated Colored Catholics in petitioning pope and bishops, therefore, particularly rankled him; in the October, 1931, issue of *Colored Harvest,* he had attacked the federation as unCatholic precisely because it pursued that avenue. Several months later, when Archbishop Curley asked him to help Anite Williams reorganize the federation in Baltimore, Gillard refused, describing

59. Thomas Wyatt Turner to the Hierarchy of the United States, November 14, 1932, copy in Turner Papers; minutes of the administrative board of the NCWC, November 14, 1932, in AUSCC.

60. Markoe, "An Interracial Role," 108; "Do You Call That Religion?," Baltimore *Afro-American*, n.d., clipping in PMC.

the organization as dominated by a group that "sets its face against matter of fact difficulties, refuses to recognize . . . existing agencies in the field, and is seemingly set on a program of coercing the Hierarchy." Gillard sniffed, "I always thought the Catholic Church was directed from the Head down, not the feet up."[61]

Gillard, consequently, shed few tears when between 1931 and 1933 the Federated Colored Catholics split into two factions as a result of a dispute between William Markoe and Thomas Turner over the essential character of the organization. Markoe insisted that the federation should transform itself into an interracial organization that would educate white Catholics about the race problem and thereby enlist their support and aid in eradicating discrimination in the church. Turner, while inviting white clerical and lay help, wanted to maintain the lay, black identity of the organization. Remembering the fate of the earlier black Catholic congress movement, Turner feared that white domination would transform the federation from an activist organization into a discussion group. He also bridled at what he perceived as the high-handed white clericalism of Markoe and LaFarge.[62]

Markoe and his supporters subsequently formed a short-lived midwestern alliance called the National Catholic Interracial Federation. LaFarge, though agreeing with Markoe's interracial thrust, remained largely silent during the controversy, diminishing his ties with the federation and devoting more of his attention to the Catholic Laymen's Union, a group of twenty-five black professionals and businessmen he had formed in New York in 1928 that eventually evolved into the Catholic Interracial Council of New York. Turner's eastern faction of the old federation functioned until 1952, whereas the new Catholic Interracial Federation of the Midwest lost its initial momentum and disappeared relatively quickly. The Catholic Interracial Council of New York and a parallel clerical organization, the Northeast Clergy Conference on Negro Welfare, however, became increasingly active during the thirties and made black priests a key part of their programs for racial justice in the church.[63]

61. "An Ill-Timed Comparison," Chronicle, October 13, 1931, clipping, John LaFarge to Thomas Wyatt Turner, October 16, 1931, both in Turner Papers; John T. Gillard to Archbishop Michael Curley, April 13, 1932, in G-848, AAB.

62. For a thorough analysis of the controversy that split the Federated Colored Catholics, see Nickels, "Federated Colored Catholics," 61–135, 175–209, 266–85, 286–315.

63. Ibid., 281–86; NCE, XVII, 670–71; Hunton, All of Which I Saw, 55–61, 86–89, 100–101, 114–17, 147–53.

Gillard doubtless expressed the sentiments of many Josephites over the break-up of the Federated Colored Catholics when he described himself to Archbishop Curley as "delighted to learn that thieves are falling out," though he did worry that Turner's group might leave the church. Apparently vindicated by events, Gillard vented his spleen on his tormentors. He characterized Turner as "only half a Catholic with a messianic complex and an inadequate mental machinery" and sarcastically referred to Markoe as "cracked wide open . . . the Moses sent by God to deliver the Negroes from hierarchical bondage." He depicted LaFarge as a "dreamer" whose creature, Turner, had turned on him, and he accused both Jesuits of having manufactured "many radicals these past years."[64] Gillard clearly hoped that radicalism had been dealt a mortal blow.

Curley shared Gillard's abhorrence of radicalism. On May 10, 1932, he expressed his sentiments to the Reverend Henry Wiesmann of Jefferson City, Missouri, who had written the archbishop recommending a twenty-nine-year-old black man as a potential candidate for the Baltimore archdiocesan clergy. Curley protested to Wiesmann that the Baltimore archdiocese lay south of the Mason-Dixon Line and claimed that "whatever we may think about it, the fact is that the color line is drawn everywhere." He went on to warn that "any talk of social intermingling or equality would cause a riot." Curley alluded to Father Dorsey's career as evidence that black priests had not been successful in the archdiocese. Having refused to consider Wiesmann's candidate for his own clergy, Curley did suggest that Wiesmann contact the Josephites, whom he erroneously assumed to have no blacks among their students or seminarians. When Wiesmann communicated with Pastorelli, the Josephite superior advised him to direct the young black man to Archbishop McNicholas, who still had a black seminarian studying for the archdiocese of Cincinnati and might be willing to take another.[65]

Archbishop Curley adopted a conservative, narrow view on the issues of black clergy and of equality between the races. LaFarge, representative of the other, more liberal, pole of opinion, deplored Curley's attitude toward blacks, which he attributed to the seventeen years Curley spent as a priest and bishop in Florida prior to his

64. John T. Gillard to Archbishiop Michael Curley, October 10, 1932, in G-849, AAB.

65. Henry W. Wiesmann to Archbishop Michael Curley, May 7, 1932, copy in PMC; Archbishop Michael Curley to Henry W. Weismann, May 10, 1932, in W-773, AAB; Louis B. Pastorelli to Henry W. Weismann, May 13, 1932, in PMC.

coming to Baltimore. LaFarge claimed that Curley had told him frankly of his absolute opposition, on principle, to black priests, whom he believed to be unworthy of the high ideals of the clergy. According to LaFarge, Curley had declared that the Propaganda had erred seriously in educating young Africans for the priesthood. In a memo to his provincial, LaFarge described Curley as a "frank reactionary" who lived by the slogan "Avoid trouble! All is well when all is quiet." Curley believed that trouble lurked very close to the surface of everyday life. As evidence of the volatility of race relations in certain parts of his see, he could point to an incident that occurred in late October, 1933, in Princess Anne, Maryland, a hideous lynching during which a crowd of two thousand whites watched as a black man was doused with gasoline, set afire, and hanged in front of a warehouse. According to the Baltimore *Afro-American*, men, women, and children passed by to gaze on the naked, tortured body.[66]

In addition to the splintering of the Federated Colored Catholics and the continued opposition of prelates like Curley, who sat on both the Negro and Indian Commission and the Catholic Board for Mission Work Among the Colored People, the cause of black priests suffered another setback when Archbishop McNicholas and Bishop Schrembs decided to abandon their experiments with black seminarians. Difficulties began in May, 1929, when Norman DuKette, Detroit's only black priest, went out late at night looking for a drugstore where he could buy some medicine for a severe headache. A policeman, mistaking DuKette for a prowler, stopped him and announced his intention of taking him into the station for questioning. Fearing that his reputation might suffer if it became known that the police had detained him, DuKette fled from the officer, who gave chase and shot him in the leg. Although the police filed no charges when they learned DuKette's identity, the incident damaged the priest's standing with Bishop Gallagher. The next year, Gallagher sent him to Flint, Michigan, to minister to black automobile workers.[67]

In June of 1929, Bishop Schrembs, reportedly disturbed by rumors surrounding DuKette's run-in with the police and alarmed by William Lane's outspoken opposition to racial discrimination, noti-

66. John LaFarge to Father Provincial, May 20, 1934, copy in Box 12-11, Baltimore *Afro-American*, October 28, 1933, clipping, both in LaFarge Papers.
67. Foley, *God's Men*, 119–20.

fied Lane that he would not need him for work in the Cleveland diocese. Claiming that he had transferred the black parish in the diocese to a religious order, he assured Lane that he would continue to pay his board and tuition at St. Vincent Seminary until another bishop adopted him. Schrembs also dismissed William Grau from Our Lady of the Lake Seminary, attributing his decision to "conditions in the Diocese" that made it "inadvisable . . . to adopt a colored student." He confided to Edward Kramer, "Personally, I feel that a religious community would offer far better chances to a colored student than the diocesan priesthood." At the annual meeting of the hierarchy in Washington, D.C., Schrembs offered to educate Lane and Grau free of charge in Cleveland if one of the other bishops would adopt them. There were no takers.[68]

In January, 1930, Schrembs informed Lane that he would give his case additional consideration, but finally, on October 24, 1930, the chancery office notified the seminarian that the diocese of Cleveland would not accept him. Lane wrote to Pastorelli about continuing his studies with the Josephites, and Pastorelli later claimed that he had advised Lane he would consider him. Lane, however, wanted to become a diocesan priest and did not follow up his inquiry to Pastorelli.[69]

Lane instead appealed for help to the apostolic delegate, and his case became something of a cause célèbre among black Catholics after he asked Thomas Turner to write on his behalf to Archbishop Pietro Fumasoni-Biondi. The uproar led the apostolic delegate, on November 18, 1932, to exert subtle pressure on Archbishop McNicholas by requesting his help in resolving the problem. Acknowledging that Schrembs had never incardinated Lane into the diocese of Cleveland, Fumasoni-Biondi argued that nevertheless Lane "has been treated most unfairly by the good bishop, who has vacillated until the young man is on the very threshold of the priesthood." The delegate claimed that he "could insist on his ordination for the Diocese of Cleveland" but refrained from doing so in the interests of Lane. He asked McNicholas to consider accepting Lane for the archdiocese of Cincinnati, though, he assured the

68. Bishop Joseph Schrembs to Edward Kramer, September 20, 1930, copy in Bishop Joseph Schrembs Papers, ADC; minutes of the annual meeting of the hierarchy, November 6, 1929, in AUSCC.

69. Archbishop Pietro Fumasoni-Biondi to Archbishop John T. McNicholas, November 22, 1930, in Archbishop John T. McNicholas Papers, AACi; Louis B. Pastorelli to Michael Gumbleton, November 27, 1937, copy in 57-G, JFA.

archbishop, "Your Grace must consider yourself absolutely free in this matter."[70]

McNicholas' reply revealed his ambivalence about black priests. He claimed that he had no objection to ordaining blacks for his archdiocese "provided I can be reasonably sure that I am not taking too great risks for our clergy and people." To that purpose, he informed the delegate, he had inquired about all the black priests so far ordained in the United States and had concluded that "the trouble with nearly all has been, not moral weakness but rather a breaking down of their mental powers." McNicholas further complained that in most cases he found it almost impossible "to make any satisfactory inquiry" into the family histories of black applicants, even though seminary procedures required a thorough investigation of family background to check for evidence of stability, legitimacy, and Catholicity. Therefore, he concluded, he should scrutinize black seminarians for a longer period of time than he did their white counterparts. McNicholas disclosed to Fumasoni-Biondi that he had decided to interrupt the theological course of black students (as Slattery had done) "and put them out in Negro parishes to do the work of catechists for two or three years, or whatever period seems necessary to test them thoroughly." In keeping with that policy, he had sent Theldon Jones, after his second year of theology, to live and work with one of the diocesan priests engaged in the black apostolate. McNicholas observed that if Jones were not black, "perhaps . . . we would already have counselled him to leave"; he added, however, that he and the seminary professors wanted to give Jones further opportunities "in order to be most just to him."

As for William Lane, McNicholas expressed his willingness to put him in the archdiocesan seminary for at least two years so that he would have some friends among the younger clergy, "provided he will stand the test that I shall demand of every Negro seminarian." McNicholas insisted that he should demand much more of the black seminarians than he did of the others, "considering the history of their families and that many are likely to be converts (Mr. Jones . . . is a convert), and considering also the rather sad experience we have had with several of our Negro priests."[71]

70. Thomas Wyatt Turner to Archbishop Pietro Fumasoni-Biondi, February 20, 1932, copy in Turner Papers; Archbishop Pietro Fumasoni-Biondi to Archbishop John T. McNicholas, November 22, 1930, in McNicholas Papers.

71. Archbishop John T. McNicholas to Archbishop Pietro Fumasoni-Biondi, December 14, 1930, copy in McNicholas Papers.

Two years later, McNicholas dismissed Theldon Jones from Mount St. Mary's Seminary. Lambert Welbers, pastor of Holy Redeemer Parish in Jones's hometown of San Antonio, appealed to St. Laurent and Pastorelli to accept the young man, who had only two years of study left, into St. Joseph's Seminary. Welbers advised Pastorelli that Archbishop Pius Dowling of Trinidad would adopt Jones and pay his board at the seminary and his passage to Trinidad. Welbers added, "It seems to me that the seminary would lose nothing; rather the contrary." Pastorelli replied that he could not admit Jones, since Josephite seminarians took their classes at Catholic University and the seminary building itself was located within a restricted residential area; he did not want to raise an issue at Catholic University "with a student not our own."[72]

Theldon Jones, William Lane, William Grau, and Max Murphy eventually had to leave the United States in order to salvage their hopes for attaining the priesthood. Through the efforts of Father Kramer, Murphy and Jones completed their theological studies at the Charles University Seminary in Prague, Czechoslovakia, and were ordained in Prague in 1934 and 1935, respectively. Archbishop Pius Dowling then adopted them for his island archdiocese.[73]

Dowling also came to the rescue of William Lane. In response to the pleas of Ignatius Lissner, Dowling agreed to adopt Lane, thus enabling him to complete his studies at St. Vincent Seminary. Lane was ordained in New York, on December 30, 1933. In 1930, Kramer convinced Bishop Bernard J. Mahoney of Sioux Falls, South Dakota, to sponsor William Grau, for seminary studies only, at the Gregorian University in Rome. Grau received holy orders in Rome in 1934, but failing to find a bishop willing to incardinate him, he continued his studies there, where he obtained his licentiate in sacred theology. In 1938, Grau returned to the United States after Bishop John A. Duffy of Buffalo agreed to accept him for a five-year probationary period. Only Charles Logan of Los Angeles was able both to complete his seminary education in the United States and to secure adoption by an American bishop: he was ordained on June 10, 1933, and was appointed as an assistant pastor in a Los Angeles parish by Bishop Cantwell.[74]

72. Lambert Welbers to Louis B. Pastorelli, February 3, 1932, in 52-T, Louis B. Pastorelli's handwritten note on the back of Welbers-Pastorelli letter, February 3, 1932, both in JFA.

73. Foley, God's Men, 167–69, 170–71.

74. Ambrose Kohlbeck to Whom It May Concern, March 28, 1931, copy, John N. Hruza, rector, to Cardinal Patrick Hayes, March 22, 1933, copy, March

The death of Stephen Theobald on July 8, 1932, from appendicitis deprived black Catholics of an articulate spokesman and served to dramatize the depressing prospects for black diocesan clergy in the early 1930s. Problems involving black diocesan clergy and seminarians, moreover, had a serious impact on the Josephites. On July 1, 1932, as if taking his cue from McNicholas and Schrembs, Pastorelli advised Marcus Glover, who had completed his philosophy course in Montreal and expected to attend the Grand Seminaire in theology in the fall, that the general council had decided to dismiss him so that he could seek admission to a community more given to the contemplative life. Pastorelli explained to Glover that the council had reached its decision because, according to the Josephite superior, Glover had voiced doubts the previous summer about spending his life laboring among blacks. Claiming that Pastorelli had misunderstood him and that he harbored no reluctance about working in the black apostolate, Glover asked for reinstatement and a probation period of one year. Pastorelli remained adamant, however, and Glover subsequently applied to the White Fathers, to whom Pastorelli recommended Glover without hesitation. In a letter to Father Filion, Pastorelli revealed what was probably his primary reason for dismissing Glover: "To become a priest in his case, being a colored man, would have meant endless hardships and heartbreaks here in the states. The feeling against the Colored amongst the whites is growing stronger. Two of the colored students we had ordained priests led a martyrs life." [75]

The year 1933 witnessed further diminution in the number of black priests and marked the end of an era for the Josephites. On July 21, 1933, Charles Randolph Uncles, the first black priest ordained in the United States, died at Epiphany Apostolic College in Newburgh, New York, at the age of seventy-four, after forty-two years as a priest. For the first time in its history as an American community, St. Joseph's Society included no black priests among its members. Pointing out that Uncles' death left Norman DuKette

---

22, 1938, copy, Bishop John J. Swint to John N. Hruza, December 7, 1933, list of William Lane's assignments, all in SVAA; Foley, God's Men, 173–74; Bishop Bernard Mahoney to Bishop Joseph Schrembs, April 8, 1933, in Schrembs Papers; Foley, God's Men, 184–85, 123.

75. Louis B. Pastorelli to Michael Gumbleton, July 1, 1932, copy in 52-G, JFA; Louis B. Pastorelli to Marcus Glover, July 1, 1932, copy, Marcus Glover to Louis B. Pastorelli, July 13, 1932, Louis B. Pastorelli to Emile Filion, July 27, 1932, copy, all in PMC.

and Charles Logan as the only two black priests active in the United States, the *Afro-American* editorialized that "there must be something wrong with the present administration of the Church which is unwilling to train young black men for the priesthood." The editorial concluded, "If tragedy entered Uncles's life . . . it was because his college talked Christianity and practiced it not."[76]

Pastorelli found a successor to Uncles that same summer in the person of Charles Chester L. E. Ball, who preferred to be known as Chester, of Washington, D.C.; eight years later, he became the first black man ordained a Josephite priest since 1907. Ironically, in light of Pastorelli's many rejections of prospective black applicants on the grounds that they did not come from Josephite schools, the nineteen-year-old Ball, who had completed four years of high school and two years of college at Miner Teachers' College, belonged not to a Josephite parish but to Washington's venerable St. Augustine's Parish, where Monsignor Alonzo Olds, the pastor, encouraged numerous black vocations. Prior to writing Pastorelli inquiring about the Josephites, Ball had unsuccessfully applied to the archdiocese of Baltimore and at least six other dioceses. On receiving Ball's letter of inquiry, Pastorelli advised him to call on Thomas Duffy of Holy Redeemer Parish for an interview. He cautioned Ball, however, that difficult economic times might force the Josephites "to put off all students who could not pay tuition."[77]

The meeting on February 26, 1933, between Ball and Duffy went well, with the latter reporting to Pastorelli that Ball "presented a good appearance and would pass for white . . . and spoke with no trace of a dialect." Duffy also pointed out that Ball had studied Greek and Latin, attended daily mass, and served as secretary of the parish Holy Name Society. Duffy reassured Pastorelli that Ball had applied out of a sincere desire to become a Josephite, not to test Josephite policy toward blacks, and despite the advice of some of his friends, who had objected to his decision, telling him that the Josephites had mistreated their black priests. "If there were any question of accepting a colored student," Duffy advised, "this one seems the best prospect I have seen in many years." Pastorelli agreed

76. John J. Dunn to Louis B. Pastorelli, July 22, 1933, in 70-D, JFA; Foley, *God's Men*, 50; Baltimore *Afro-American*, n.d., clipping in Box 8-20, LaFarge Papers.

77. Foley, *God's Men*, 230–31; Chester Ball to Louis B. Pastorelli, February 23, 1933, Louis B. Pastorelli to Chester Ball, February 24, 1933, copy, both in PMC.

with Duffy's evaluation, and Ball entered Epiphany Apostolic College in September, 1933.[78]

Two significant changes within St. Joseph's Society probably helped make Pastorelli more receptive to Ball's admission. On May 6, 1932, the Holy See approved and confirmed the new Josephite constitutions and granted the *Decretum Laudis* that elevated St. Joseph's Society to the status of a pontifical institute, subject to the jurisdiction of the Congregation of Religious rather than to Archbishop Michael Curley of Baltimore. The following May, Pastorelli, citing economic conditions, informed Monsignor James Ryan, the rector of Catholic University, that beginning in September the Josephites would remove their seminarians from Catholic University and would conduct classes, taught by their own faculty, at St. Joseph's Seminary.[79] Although motivated by economic considerations, Pastorelli's decision to remove Josephite theologians from the segregated Catholic University eliminated a serious obstacle to future black Josephite seminarians.

Nevertheless, Pastorelli showed no signs of significantly expanding the number of black Josephite students. The comments of Archbishop John Shaw of New Orleans, whose archdiocese contained the largest number of Josephite parishes in the country and who claimed that black Catholics in New Orleans did not want black priests, reinforced his caution. Pastorelli informed Shaw that he had "a very fine colored student entering EAC this year." Whether from conviction or from a desire to placate the bishop or both, Pastorelli added a justification for accepting Ball: "Being in the Colored work we feel that we should have at least one or two of the colored to keep the race from crying out against us. Since Bay St. Louis started operations, we direct all applicants there." Shaw applauded Pastorelli's tokenism.[80] Within two years, however, the reactionary Shaw was dead, and events in Mississippi and Louisiana signaled a new day for black seminarians and priests in the United States.

78. Thomas Duffy to Louis B. Pastorelli, February 27, 1933, in PMC; Louis B. Pastorelli to Archbishop John W. Shaw, September, 1933, copy in 69-S, JFA; Foley, *God's Men*, 231.

79. Minutes of the general chapters, July, 1936, in JFA; James Ryan to Louis B. Pastorelli, March 9, 1933, Louis B. Pastorelli to James Ryan, May 5, 1933, copy, both in PMC.

80. Note penned by Archbishop John W. Shaw to Louis B. Pastorelli on a letter from Brother Francis Xavier that he forwarded to Pastorelli, September 11, 1933, in 70-R, Louis B. Pastorelli to Archbishop John W. Shaw, September, 1933, copy, in 70-R, Archbishop John W. Shaw to Louis B. Pastorelli, September 11, 1933, in 70-R, all in JFA.

Chapter VIII

WINDS OF CHANGE, 1933–1942

We might as well face the cold fact that we will be compelled to staff our southern parishes little by little with colored priests of our own Society. . . . We have allowed feeling, yes even . . . prejudice to blind us to our own best interests.

—LOUIS B. PASTORELLI, APRIL 30, 1936

During his last two terms as superior general of the Josephites, from 1930 to 1942, Louis B. Pastorelli remained a prisoner of the fear and ambivalence that had determined his policy toward black students at Epiphany Apostolic College and St. Joseph's Seminary since 1912. Developments during the 1930s—most notably the historic ordinations of the first 4 black priests from St. Augustine's Seminary and their subsequent enthusiastic reception by black Catholics throughout the South and a directive to the bishops of the United States from the Holy See—forced him to a belated recognition that his society's long-term self-interest would require the development of black Josephite priests. He moved carefully, however, following a painfully slow timetable. The ordination in 1941 of the first new black Josephite priest in thirty-four years, while an important event for the society in that it marked the return of a black priest to its ranks after the eight-year hiatus following Charles Uncles' death, did not signal a radical new departure. Rather, it was consistent with Pastorelli's long-held objective of maintaining at least a token black presence in St. Joseph's Society. Although he no longer dismissed black applicants out of hand, he found only 2 suitable black candidates for Epiphany Apostolic College between 1933 and 1942. He left to his successor the task of accommodating St. Joseph's Society to the winds of change that swirled around it.

Those winds had begun to blow more noticeably through both American society and the Catholic church in the United States during the New Deal years. As a result of black migration to northern cities, urban blacks began to command some political attention. The Harlem Renaissance and Marcus Garvey's ill-fated yet influential popular movement during the 1920s awakened the pride of Afro-Americans and raised their consciousness about the possibilities of change. Despite frequent setbacks, the NAACP repeatedly attacked racism in American society, gradually gaining adherents among blacks and whites in northern cities and eroding the myth that blacks were happy with the status quo. In the 1930s, the proponents of civil rights fought alongside radicals, labor leaders, ethnic and political minorities, and liberals. A new ideological consensus in the academic community undermined racism and threw white supremacy on the defensive by emphasizing the primacy of environment over innate racial characteristics in determining behavior and achievement. Most of all, the New Deal's substantive and symbolic aid to blacks stimulated hope for racial change. The support of such prominent white citizens as Eleanor Roosevelt for a wide variety of racial issues legitimated the aspirations of blacks. Although disfranchisement, segregation, and poverty remained the rule for most blacks, civil rights began to emerge as a major national concern. Conditions created by World War II further emboldened blacks to demand greater justice.[1]

Movements within the Catholic church paralleled those in secular society. The church gained recognition as a major force in American life from Franklin D. Roosevelt and the New Deal. Working-class, ethnic Catholics constituted an important bloc in Roosevelt's electoral coalition and, for the most part, enthusiastically supported his programs. Catholic clergymen—for example, Monsignors Francis J. Haas and John A. Ryan and the Reverend John J. Burke—cooperated with New Deal agencies and boards and articulated a Catholic social philosophy compatible with the newly emerging welfare state. Roosevelt publicly courted such Catholic leaders as Cardinal Mundelein and appointed priests to labor mediation boards. With this recognition from the political sphere and having achieved institutional stability and consolidation, the Catholic church during the 1930s was able to give more attention

1. John Hope Franklin and Alfred A. Moss, Jr., *From Slavery to Freedom: A History of Negro Americans* (6th ed.; New York, 1988), 338–59; Harvard Sitkoff, *A New Deal for Blacks: The Emergence of Civil Rights as a National Issue: The Depression Decade* (Oxford, 1978); Richard M. Dalfiume, "The Forgotten Years of the Negro Revolution," *Journal of American History*, LV (June, 1968), 90–106.

to the black apostolate. Although segregation persisted in many Catholic schools, hospitals, and churches, the great migration of blacks to the cities of the North, which included black Catholics from Louisiana and the Alabama and Mississippi Gulf coasts, began to transform the Negro problem in the eyes of church leaders from a purely southern concern into a national one. White Catholic priests, such as John LaFarge, William Markoe, and John Gillard, though sometimes differing in their emphases and tactics, shared a thirst for justice and a fear of communist inroads among American blacks. As an antidote to the twin poisons of racism and communism, they promoted interracial justice in church and society through Catholic publications, clergy conferences, Catholic interracial organizations, and Catholic student groups.[2]

Just as blacks in secular society looked expectantly to Franklin and Eleanor Roosevelt and their New Deal, black Catholics, as they had done for years, continued to regard the Holy See as an ally in their struggle for equality within the church. Although the movement was weakened by the rupture of the Federated Colored Catholics, black Catholics, by persisting in sending their sons to St. Augustine's Seminary and by according black priests enthusiastic receptions, doggedly maintained pressure on the institutional church for clergy of their own race. The Holy See responded decisively: the apostolic delegate enabled the first 4 black priests ordained from St. Augustine's Seminary to secure a field of labor in a southern diocese, and the Consistorial Congregation took action to open more diocesan and religious seminaries to black candidates.

The ordinations of the first 4 black Divine Word missionaries from St. Augustine's Seminary in 1934 represented a watershed event in the history of black priests in the United States. Unlike earlier efforts by the Josephites, other religious communities, or individual bishops, the Society of the Divine Word did not thrust individual black priests into isolated situations; rather, it provided for a community of black priests to sustain and cushion its members

2. See George Q. Flynn, *American Catholics and the Roosevelt Presidency, 1932–1936* (Lexington, 1968). For Catholic preoccupation with the communist menace among blacks, see John T. Gillard's *Christ, Color, and Communism* (Baltimore, 1937) and his *Colored Catholics in the United States* (Baltimore, 1941), 221, 253; Paul E. Czuchlewski, "Liberal Catholicism and American Racism, 1924–1960," *Records of the American Catholic Historical Society of Philadelphia*, LXXXV (March–June, 1974), 146; Edward S. Stanton, S.J., "John LaFarge's Understanding of the Unifying Mission of the Church, Especially in the Area of Race Relations" (Ph.D. dissertation, St. Paul University, 1972), 98–111.

against the racism they would inevitably encounter. The venture in Bay St. Louis enjoyed the backing of its parent international missionary society, which by 1933 included 8 bishops, 1,210 priests, and 1,390 brothers; St. Augustine's Seminary also had the support of the Holy See.[3] Nevertheless, it took several years of complicated and tortuous negotiations involving the Divine Word Missionaries, the cardinal-archbishop of Chicago, several southern bishops, and the apostolic delegate to ensure that the black priests would have somewhere to go after the holy oils of ordination on their hands had dried.

During the 1920s, despite daunting financial problems, St. Augustine's Seminary managed to survive and even to expand. Students and seminarians worked as janitors and gardeners each day in order to cut down on maintenance expenses. The parents of most of the students barely eked out their own existences and consequently could contribute little or no money for their sons' educations. Some students could not leave the seminary, even during summer vacations, because their parents could not afford their train fare home. Each year between 1923 and 1929, Father Christman, the rector, requested $10,000 from the Negro and Indian Commission and received only $5,000. As a result, in 1929, he not only had to shorten the school year by one month in order to save on operating costs but also had to borrow $2,000 to help cover the yearly expenses of $25,000. By September, 1929, the Divine Word Missionaries had erected a separate major seminary building: a humble, temporary, frame structure that cost $7,500 and housed the 6 major seminarians. That same year, 4 students went to the Divine Word novitiate in East Troy, Wisconsin, and total enrollment in the minor seminary college reached 36. The entire teaching staff of both the major and minor seminaries consisted of 6 Divine Word priests and 2 lay teachers.[4]

Spartan conditions notwithstanding, visitors to St. Augustine's Seminary came away favorably impressed by the quality of the religious and academic programs and by the students themselves. On April 30, 1925, Richard Gerow, the prim, gentle bishop of

3. "St. Augustine's Seminary," 3–4, article in Box 8-20, John LaFarge Papers, GUA.

4. Louis Carter to the General Council of the Pontificum Opus a Sancto Pietro, January 18, 1934, A. G. Stieg to J. B. Tennelly, July 3, 1929, Gerard Heffels to Archbishop Pietro Fumasoni-Biondi, September 18, 1929, copies of all in SASA.

Natchez, visited the seminary. After an informal entertainment, he quizzed some students in algebra, placing on the board a difficult problem that few students in other schools of the diocese had managed to solve. Francis Wade rose from his seat and quickly unraveled it, much to the bishop's delight. That same year, Archbishop Pietro Fumasoni-Biondi, who closely monitored the progress of St. Augustine's, sent a glowing report about the seminary to the Sacred Consistorial Congregation following his apostolic visitation. Cardinal Carlo Perosi, pro-secretary of the congregation, expressed his pleasure over developments in Bay St. Louis to Gerow and encouraged him to rally support among his diocesan clergy for the work of the seminary.[5]

Each step in the process of training the black seminarians, however, seemed to generate problems and controversy within the Society of the Divine Word. After the first black students graduated from the college division of St. Augustine's in 1926 and completed their novitiate in East Troy the following year, the question arose as to where they should pursue their major seminary studies. One proposal, advanced in 1928 by William Gier, the superior general, who worried lest the black seminarians receive too parochial an education, would have had them study in Rome rather than in Bay St. Louis. Christman and Bruno Hagspiel, the provincial who had replaced Janser, opposed Gier's idea. They believed that the black seminarians, or scholastics (seminarians were referred to as scholastics after completing the novitiate), should take all of their philosophy and theology classes at St. Augustine's Seminary. They worried that these black scholastics, having studied abroad and experienced equality in Europe, would become dissatisfied on their return with conditions in the South.[6]

Educating the black seminarians with the white seminarians at the major seminary in Techny, another alternative, remained out of the question because of Cardinal Mundelein's expressed opposition

5. Bishop Richard O. Gerow Diary, April 30, 1925 (Typescript in Richard O. Gerow Papers, ADJ); index to diocesan archives, Natchez, 1837–1941, Vol. 1, p. 66, "Apostolic Delegate," copy, in Natchez-Jackson file, both in JFA; Cardinal Carlo Perosi to Bishop Richard O. Gerow, June 26, 1928, in Gerow Papers.

6. Matthew Christman to Alois Heick, October 3, 1928, in SASA; Charles W. Malin, S.V.D., "Integration of the Catholic Clergy in the United States, The Divine Word Missionaries' Chapter" (M.A. thesis, Marquette University, 1964), 53.

to such a plan. Mundelein, a prelate known as something of a New Deal liberal, nonetheless held conventional racial views. He remembered the terrible race riot of 1919 and knew well the ethnic patchwork of the Catholic church in Chicago, with its bitter and potentially explosive racial antagonisms. Moreover, he disliked what he described to the apostolic delegate as "a new species of negro" in the North who, unlike southern blacks, stepped out of his place: "a so-called 'sassy nigger,' who is constantly agitating for social equality with the whites." Mundelein expressed his hope and prayer "that the Catholic Church will never commit itself on this question of racial equality," which he regarded as "loaded with dynamite."[7] He had no trouble supporting the Divine Word plan for educating black priests as long as they remained in the South, away from his archdiocese.

The black scholastics themselves wished to remain in Bay St. Louis. On hearing rumors that they might be required to attend the major seminary in Techny, they requested they be allowed to pursue their seminary studies at St. Augustine's. Although characterizing as "friendly and brotherly" the atmosphere of their year-long novitiate with white novices in East Troy, the black students expressed skepticism about successful long-term integration within the seminary context, which would involve daily contact and academic competition between blacks and whites, an environment quite different from the intense spiritual atmosphere of the novitiate. They also argued that Techny was geared to the foreign missions, whereas Bay St. Louis was focused on the black missions in the United States. Gerard Steig, the black seminarians' prefect, agreed that they should not go north for their major seminary training. He insisted that such a move would engender racial conflict in the society because northern Negroes would implant "race pride and race hatred in the minds of . . . southern students." Integration would not work because "the colored of this country are too sensitive, too touchy."[8]

As late as June, 1929, however, Gier remained unconvinced by Hagspiel's recommendation that the black candidates receive all of

7. Bruno Hagspiel to Bishop Richard O. Gerow, June 24, 1929, copy in SASA; Cardinal George Mundelein to Archbishop Amleto Cicognani, August 17, 1933, copy in Menceslaus Madaj Collection, AAC; see also Edward R. Kantowicz, *Corporation Sole: Cardinal Mundelein and Chicago Catholicism* (Notre Dame, 1983), 212–15.

8. Malin, "Integration of Catholic Clergy," 54–56.

their education (except for the novitiate) in, as Gier put it, "that one little spot of St. Augustine's." He worried that they would become narrow-minded and short-sighted and that such training would "represent a crying injustice to the men and an utter disregard of the Colored race." He suggested to Hagspiel that the six scholastics attend St. Gabriel's, the Divine Word seminary near Vienna, Austria, where they would study philosophy and theology in German.[9]

Hagspiel enlisted the help of Bishop Gerow, pleading with him to meet with the superior general or his consultors and to defend the existing plans for educating the black candidates when Gerow visited Rome that fall. Sounding very much like John Gillard, Hagspiel complained to Gerow: "If only our men in Europe could be brought to realize what a delicate matter this Negro question is . . . to stand upon the broadest Catholic principles here, without careful qualifications to meet temporal necessities . . . will never do." Gerow agreed with Hagspiel and promised to have "a good heart to heart talk" with Gier. Hagspiel and Gerow eventually prevailed; the black seminarians remained at Bay St. Louis for the course of their studies. On November 1, 1930, Bishop Gerow conferred tonsure, the first clerical degree, on six of them.[10]

As the black seminarians moved toward taking the perpetual, or final, vows that would make them permanent members of the Society of the Divine Word, an extended debate arose within the society over whether to admit them into full membership. One last time, in a four-hour meeting with the apostolic delegate, Hagspiel explored the possibility of the black seminarians' having at least the option of becoming diocesan priests. An agitated Fumasoni-Biondi made it clear to the provincial that both he and the Holy See would consider "any digression from the original plan . . . as a breach of promise and a . . . 'Blamage' [sic] for the entire Society." He was particularly vexed that Hagspiel should raise the issue just after he had made a report to the Holy See concerning the future work of the black priests.

Meanwhile, the superior general, having learned of the opposition in some quarters of the society to admitting the black semi-

9. Bruno Hagspiel to Bishop Richard O. Gerow, June 24, 1929, copy in SASA.

10. Bruno Hagspiel to Bishop Richard O. Gerow, September 17, 1929, Bishop Richard O. Gerow to Bruno Hagspiel, June 27, 1929, copy, both in Gerow Papers; Bishop Richard O. Gerow to Gerard Heffels, October 10, 1930, in SASA; index to diocesan archives, vol. I-8, p. 196, in ADJ.

narians into full membership, asked for recommendations from the rector and consultors of St. Augustine's Seminary and from the provincial council. Their responses revealed a split, pitting Rector Gerard J. Heffels and a majority of the seminary faculty, all opposed to admitting the black seminarians to full membership, against Hagspiel, the provincial council, Peter Janser, and Herman J. Patzelt, all favoring admission. Heffels and his consultors resurrected the old proposal that the Society of the Divine Word create and superintend a new religious congregation of black priests. He argued that blacks should not become full-fledged members of the society for two major reasons: the impossibility of combining two different races in a religious community and the difficulty of creating a separate black province in the South. Heffels also cited defects he saw in blacks that made them unsuitable for the society, including their lack of cleanliness, diligence, order, tact, uprightness, sincerity, and morality; their lesser intellectual talents and will power; and a growing self-assurance, "which forces them into . . . stronger opposition toward the whites." He also warned of difficulties that would ensue from customary as well as de jure segregation in the South.

The proponents of full membership countered Heffels with the argument that simple justice required the black seminarians, who had already been admitted to temporary vows and who had always operated under the assumption that they would become Divine Word Missionaries, be admitted fully into the society. To answer Heffels' warning, they maintained that prudence and circumspection in community life would avoid problems involving the southern racial code. Most important from the point of view of the provincial council was that in 1921 the society had promised Bishop Gunn and the rest of the American episcopate that the black seminarians would become religious as members of the Society of the Divine Word. To back down now would break faith with the American hierarchy. As a compromise, the council did propose the immediate establishment of a southern province as a first step toward an autonomous black province. It further proposed that the next general chapter of the society alter the constitutions so as to allow for a purely black province.

Divine Word authorities in Rome mulled over the problem for over a year before they reached a decision. Finally, on July 7, 1933, Joseph Grendel, the new superior general, announced that the Society of the Divine Word would accept the black seminarians as full members. The generalate postponed creation of a separate southern province until conditions were more favorable, and it vetoed the notion of a strictly black province.[11]

As debate continued over the eventual status of the seminarians within the society, Hagspiel and his confreres wrestled with the question of where the black men could be stationed should they be accepted into the society and ordained as priests. The question had arisen as early as October 19, 1931, during a visit to Techny by Bishop Gerow. After dinner, he conferred with Hagspiel and the society's consultors about the future of St. Augustine's Seminary and the Negro priests. Gerow got the impression from the assembled Divine Word missionaries that they wanted his guidance, especially when the conversation turned to the ticklish question of where to assign the black priests. (Gerow and Hagspiel discussed the placement of six priests, since six seminarians had received tonsure and were proceeding toward ordination. One would subsequently leave the seminary, and another would be held back several years.) Gerow suggested placing two of them at St. Rose's Parish in Bay St. Louis, "where they could do parish work under the eyes of the Fathers of the Seminary." He recommended employing two others as prefects over one of the departments at the seminary. As for the two remaining priests, Hagspiel proposed that they study in Rome to prepare for work as professors at St. Augustine's. Unfortunately from Hagspiel's point of view, these plans all envisaged the black priests remaining tied, in one way or another, to St. Augustine's and raised the specter of a solely institutional future for them. At the end of the discussion, Gerow agreed to a timetable whereby the six who received tonsure the previous year would progress through the minor and major orders between 1931 and 1933 and receive holy orders in 1934, the last year of their theological studies.[12]

Once the generalate had settled the question of admitting the black seminarians to full membership, Hagspiel devoted himself to finding an appropriate assignment for them after ordination. To that end, throughout 1933 and into 1934 he became involved in a series of delicate negotiations involving the cardinal-archbishop of Chicago, the apostolic delegate, and several bishops of the South.

11. Malin, "Integration of Catholic Clergy," 59–60, 61–63, 67–69.
12. Gerow Diary, October 19, 1931; Albert S. Foley, S.J., *God's Men of Color: The Colored Catholic Priests of the United States, 1854–1954* (1955; rpr. New York, 1969), 177; Bishop Richard O. Gerow to Gerard Heffels, October 31, 1931, in SASA.

In March, 1933, he met with Mundelein, in whose archdiocese the Divine Word provincialate was located and whose chairmanship of the American Board of Catholic Missions made him a crucial figure. Hagspiel found the cardinal anxious to talk about the black priests, who were scheduled to be ordained in May, 1934; he therefore raised the thorny question of finding suitable work for them. Both Hagspiel and Mundelein agreed that the men should not be scattered around the diocese of Natchez for several reasons: they would have little contact with one another, and the difficult task of making converts among black southern Baptists might discourage and dishearten them. In addition, they would not receive the close supervision from white priests that Hagspiel and Mundelein considered essential. Finally, because all the schools conducted by the Divine Word Missionaries in Mississippi had white teachers, to place the black priests in a school would require the construction of a new parish or parishes, which Bishop Gerow simply could not afford.

Hagspiel proposed another alternative to Mundelein. Since the cardinal agreed on the need for white supervision of the newly ordained men, the provincial raised the possibility of assigning them as assistants to either St. Elizabeth's or St. Anselm's, two Divine Word parishes in Chicago's black belt. Three of the black Divine Word missionaries could work for a year or two under the supervision of the white pastors before returning to the South for their life's work. Mundelein, however, rejected the suggestion as impractical, arguing that Chicago's black Catholics would not accept it and that one or two years of city life would make it impossible for the men to return to isolated country places. He insisted that the black priests should remain in the South throughout their priestly careers and claimed that Archbishop Fumasoni-Biondi, the former apostolic delegate and newly appointed prefect of the Propaganda, had always held that the black priests should never go north of the Mason-Dixon Line.

Since neither Natchez nor Chicago appeared acceptable, Hagspiel suggested to Mundelein that the black priests should go to a diocese containing large numbers of black Catholics: either the diocese of Lafayette or the archdiocese of New Orleans. There, the black priests could work among black Catholics, gain confidence, and sharpen the skills necessary for some eventual missionary work in Mississippi. Mundelein reacted enthusiastically to Hagspiel's idea and advised him to "have a good talk" with Daniel Desmond, the newly consecrated bishop of Alexandria, Louisiana, who had, the cardinal believed, a great interest in the black apostolate.

Hagspiel's conversation with Mundelein convinced him that the only way out of his dilemma lay in persuading one of the bishops in Louisiana to give the Divine Word Missionaries a cluster of black parishes near one another. Such an arrangement would enable the black priests to engage in pastoral work and to attend in proper manner to their own religious life. Hagspiel directed Heffels to discuss the matter with Gerow and to pass the word through him to the other southern bishops that if they "are helpless in giving us some practical, definite advice . . . and are unwilling to come across and make a definite, practical proposal or offer in their respective dioceses," then the Divine Word Missionaries would have no recourse but to lay the whole matter before Archbishop Amleto Giovanni Cicognani, the recently appointed apostolic delegate, and ask him to take the whole problem in his hands. Hagspiel also instructed Heffels to take up the question particularly with Archbishop Shaw, Bishop Desmond, and Bishop Jules Jeanmard of Lafayette, noting carefully what each man said in case Hagspiel felt compelled to refer the matter to the apostolic delegate. "We have done . . . our share," he declared. "Now let the bishops of the United States do their bit also toward carrying out the Holy Father's desires with regard to native priests." [13]

Hagspiel's Divine Word emissaries in the South, including Herman Patzelt, the chaplain of Holy Rosary Institute in Lafayette, explored various alternatives for placing the black priests. These included the creation of a *Praelature Nullius*, a territory under the supervision of a delegate appointed by the Holy See, in Mississippi or Louisiana for the black priests; the appointment of a coadjutor bishop for all black Catholics in the Lafayette diocese; the naming of a Divine Word missionary as bishop of Lafayette; or the erection in Louisiana of a diocese composed solely of the state's black parishes. When Hagspiel's men approached Jeanmard, the soft-spoken Cajun bishop of Lafayette, he indicated his desire to allow the black priests into his diocese but claimed he could not do so. He feared he could not do justice to the black priests without offending the white clergy and laity in his diocese. [14]

In July, Hagspiel turned to Cicognani, a tactful and discreet diplomat, who suggested the erection of a deanery (a group of parishes

13. Gerard Heffels to Bruno Hagspiel, January 9, 1932, copy, Bruno Hagspiel to Gerard Heffels, March 23, 1933, both in SASA.

14. Herman Patzelt to Bruno Hagspiel, June 14, 19, 1933, copies of both in SASA; interview of Bishop Joseph G. Vath by Stephen J. Ochs, July 12, 1983; Malin, "Integration of Catholic Clergy," 74–75.

within a diocese that are put under the supervision of a senior priest, called a dean, who then reports to the bishop) in the Lafayette diocese. This deanery would be turned over to the Divine Word Missionaries but would remain under Jeanmard's jurisdiction. Cicognani told the provincial that he would discuss the matter with Mundelein and Jeanmard at the next bishops' meeting, scheduled for November. He counseled strict confidentiality meanwhile and a thorough survey of possible locations in the Lafayette diocese. The house council of St. Augustine's Seminary endorsed the idea of a deanery in the Lafayette diocese, which would allow the black priests to live together in a house under the supervision of a white Divine Word missionary and to minister to the whole district from the central location. The council emphasized the need for the black priests to do parish work, as both they and black Catholics expected, in order to familiarize the country with black priests and to demonstrate their feasibility in pastoral work.[15]

On learning of the plan, Jeanmard objected, however, on practical as well as social grounds. Hagspiel then appealed to Cicognani for help in resolving "the delicate problem." On November 9, 1933, Hagspiel informed Heffels that the American Board of Catholic Missions would meet in Chicago during the third week of November and that Cicognani would attend and discuss the disposition of the black priests with Mundelein and Gerow. He hoped that the Chicago meeting would finally produce a solution to the predicament that had vexed him for so long.[16]

When he announced the adjournment of the morning session of the mission board meeting shortly before noon on November 21, 1933, Cardinal Mundelein requested Bishops Desmond, Jeanmard, and Gerow to remain behind. A half-hour conference ensued, with Mundelein presiding and Cicognani in attendance. Mundelein pointed out that the imminent ordinations of the black scholastics from St. Augustine's Seminary required a definite plan for placing them. He left no doubts that he expected one of the assembled bishops to agree to accept the black priests into his diocese before the meeting ended. Cicognani applied additional pressure by speaking of the keen interest of the Holy Father in this work.

Jeanmard begged off, arguing that the introduction of black priests into his diocese would involve too much trouble. Gerow ex-

15. Malin, "Integration of Catholic Clergy," 75–76; House Council Minutes Book, October 23, 1933, in SASA.
16. Bruno Hagspiel to Gerard Heffels, November 9, 1933, in SASA.

pressed his willingness to undertake the work, but both Mundelein and Cicognani insisted that an area with a larger Catholic population would provide a more hospitable setting. Having listened to the discussion for fifteen or twenty minutes, Desmond, a native Bostonian and Yankee intruder in the poor diocese of Alexandria, which comprised the northern half of the state, enthusiastically volunteered to begin the work in the Avoyelles district of his diocese. Mundelein had considered Desmond a likely candidate to receive the black priests, and he quickly accepted the bishop's offer. Shortly after the meeting, Mundelein informed the incredulous Hagspiel that Desmond had applied for the black priests; the cardinal suggested that the provincial contact Desmond for the particulars. An equally flabbergasted Archbishop Shaw told Desmond that if he succeeded with "those colored priests in your diocese, you will be canonized before you . . . depart from this life."[17]

On December 8, 1933, Desmond spelled out his plans in a long letter to Hagspiel. He clearly indicated, however, that their implementation hinged on financial help from the American Board of Catholic Missions. Desmond proposed to erect a three-room school, a community house for the black priests, and a black church in Mansura, a town in Avoyelles civil parish approximately 40 miles southeast of Alexandria and 150 miles northwest of New Orleans. In addition to running the school, the black priests would also service chapels that Desmond intended to build for black Catholics in the nearby communities of Bunkie and Thoreauville. Finally, Desmond offered to turn over to the Divine Word Missionaries St. Theresa's Church in Evergreen, 12 miles from Mansura, to serve as the headquarters for the white Divine Word priest who would supervise the black priests.

According to Desmond, the entire project, independent of Evergreen, would require approximately $13,000. He promised to put Evergreen on a clear financial footing with an outlay of $3,000 from his own pocket, and he further pledged to raise $2,000 of the $13,000 needed for Mansura—pledges particularly generous since his own cathedral parish had received several notices of foreclosure and carried a debt in excess of $100,000 on which no interest had been paid for eighteen months. The bishop urged Hagspiel to prevail on Mundelein to allocate $11,000 from the mission board.

17. Bishop Daniel F. Desmond Diary, November 21, December 5, 1933 (Typescript in Daniel F. Desmond Papers, ADAS); Archbishop Amleto Cicognani to Bruno Hagspiel, November 24, 1933, copy, Bruno Hagspiel to Herman Patzelt, March 27, 1934, both in Provincial's Correspondence, SPA.

Somewhat misleadingly, Desmond assured Hagspiel that "there has not been one disheartening reaction among the elder priests and prominent lay folks to whom I have confided my plan." He also reported that a crowd of twelve hundred blacks, 70 percent of them non-Catholic, received his news about the Mansura project "with surprise and pleasure."[18]

Hagspiel thanked Desmond for his generosity. Privately, though, he expressed his disappointment that Jeanmard had not volunteered to accept the black priests into the Lafayette diocese, which had fifty thousand black Catholics as opposed to four thousand in Alexandria. In the hope of convincing Jeanmard to change his mind, Hagspiel inundated him with entreaties and petitions and authorized Patzelt to visit the bishop frequently to discuss the matter. He did not, therefore, accept Desmond's offer outright, pleading instead the need for consultations with the superior general and also with the Divine Word missionaries on the southern missions.[19]

Desmond foresaw no problems from Hagspiel's letter and forged ahead with his plans for the black priests, attempting to preempt or suppress any opposition in his diocese. He took pains to make it appear that higher authorities had made him accept the black priests. Despite warnings he received at the Chicago meeting to keep all news about preparations secret, he announced the imminent arrival of the black priests in the December 15, 1933, edition of the diocesan newspaper, *Catholic Herald*. Above the name plate of the paper a headline proclaimed, "Bishop Desmond Asked To Lead New Project," and the second-deck headline for one of the stories on the front page read, "American Mission Board Names His Excellency to Initiate Steps for Negro Clergy Work." The bishop also published correspondence between himself and Hagspiel and included in the paper an open letter to the clergy and laity of his diocese, filling it with references to the "will of the Holy Father." Desmond later reassured Hagspiel, "If my statements have left the people under the impression that I have been acting under orders, so much the better for the cause."[20]

18. Bishop Daniel Desmond to Bruno Hagspiel, December 8, 1933, copy in Desmond Diary.

19. Bruno Hagspiel to Bishop Daniel Desmond, December 18, 1933, copy in SASA, June 18, 1934, in Desmond Papers.

20. *Catholic Herald* (Alexandria, La.), December 15, 1933, clipping in Provincial's Correspondence, SPA; Bishop Daniel Desmond to Bruno Hagspiel, February 10, 1934, copy in Desmond Papers.

Desmond failed, however, to stifle opposition, which had arisen in Mansura almost from the moment he announced his plans for the black priests. The bishop hinted at trouble on January 10, 1934, when he informed Hagspiel that he would have to go over the whole project with his consultors at the end of the month, since "there is a feeling among some of the older priests that the proposed program should be altered in some little details." He neglected to tell the provincial until later that he had also received a visit from several prominent Mansura laymen, who characterized his project as an "importation from the North . . . foreign to the spirit of Louisiana." Desmond told them that he had no choice in the matter because the apostolic delegate and the mission board had compelled him to take the black priests.[21]

Hagspiel's apprehension increased as he learned more about the climate of opinion in the Alexandria diocese. After an inspection of Mansura in January, Patzelt reported back what the pastor of St. Paul's Parish had told him: that white Catholics had sent a petition to Desmond asking him to refrain from sending the black priests and threatening trouble if he persisted. A letter that Hagspiel received from Lawrence Coco, a parishioner at St. Paul's, confirmed his suspicion that Desmond had seriously underestimated the depth of hostility in the Alexandria diocese toward black priests. Coco, a white man, wrote, "We are a rather prejudiced people here in Louisiana and have never accepted Negroes on an equal social standing, which . . . might be more or less expected as to priests." He advised Hagspiel, "It is the firm belief of every leading layman in the congregation that the bringing of colored Priests to this community will degrade the Catholic religion, here as well as in the surrounding territory." Hagspiel sent a copy of Coco's letter to Desmond, remarking simply but tellingly, "It is quite interesting."[22]

When Desmond met with his consultors on January 29, 1934, the Reverend M. P. Nothofer of Mansura expressed apprehension about having black priests in the diocese and, according to Desmond's diary, "seemed disposed to convert the consultors to his opinion that the project was a mistake." Desmond stood firm, however, telling Nothofer that the time for second-guessing had

21. Bishop Daniel Desmond to Bruno Hagspiel, January 10, February 10, 1934, copies of both in Desmond Papers.
22. Malin, "Integration of Catholic Clergy," 78–79; Lawrence M. Coco to Bruno Hagspiel, January 27, 1934, copy in Desmond Papers.

passed and that they now needed to address the question of making the plan succeed. Nevertheless, the consultors managed to persuade Desmond that the best hope for success lay in making as unostentatious a beginning as possible. They convinced him to begin the work in Marksville, 5 miles from Mansura, by arguing that Marksville would require little new construction. Desmond thereupon asked the Holy Ghost Fathers to exchange Holy Ghost Parish in Marksville for St. Theresa's Parish in Evergreen.[23]

Desmond explained the change in plans to Hagspiel and admitted for the first time the existence of opposition in Mansura. He proposed limiting the black priests to teaching in the black schools in Marksville and Mansura. They would live in the rectory of Holy Ghost Church in Marksville, while their white director would reside just across the fence at St. Joseph's Church with Father Van der Putter, the pastor, whom he would help with parochial duties.[24]

Desmond's revision of the original plan only added to Hagspiel's misgivings about sending the black priests to the Alexandria diocese. A visit to Alexandria and the towns of Mansura, Bunkie, Cottonport, and Marksville on March 22 and 23, 1934, confirmed his worst fears. At Bunkie and Cottonport, he questioned the pastors about sentiment in Avoyelles Parish. Much to Desmond's chagrin, the Reverend F. X. Kronemeyer told Hagspiel that he would do the bishop a big favor by assigning the black priests to some other diocese. Hagspiel returned to Techny determined to do so, not only because of Kronemeyer's warning but because he had learned that Jeanmard had yielded at last to his and Patzelt's pleas and had agreed to allow at least two black priests to work in the Lafayette diocese. The Divine Word missionaries had convinced Jeanmard that his diocese offered the best environment for the development of a black clergy, one that would feature relatively little opposition to the black priests from clergy or laity. Jeanmard made his agreement to take the black priests conditional on approval from the apostolic delegate. He also insisted, at least for a while, on secrecy.[25]

23. Desmond Diary, January 29, 1934; Bishop Daniel Desmond to C. J. Plunkett, February 2, 1934, copy in Desmond Papers.

24. Bishop Daniel Desmond to Bruno Hagspiel, February 10, 1934, copy in Desmond Papers.

25. Bruno Hagspiel to Herman Patzelt, March 27, 1934, Herman Patzelt to Bruno Hagspiel, February 2, 1934, copy, both in Provincial's Correspondence; Bruno Hagspiel to Bishop Daniel Desmond, June 18, 1934, in Desmond Papers.

When the Divine Word provincial returned to Techny on the evening of March 26, he immediately summoned his provincial council to a ninety-minute meeting. All agreed that they could not make an outright refusal of Desmond's generous offer, especially in light of Jeanmard's earlier unwillingness to take the black priests. Describing Jeanmard's behavior at the mission board meeting in Chicago as "a regrettable mistake," Hagspiel ruefully observed that if the bishop had simply asked for time to think matters over, "the whole situation might have been saved without trouble." Hagspiel and his council unanimously agreed to propose to the superior general in Rome a compromise whereby two of the newly ordained men would go to Alexandria and the other two to Lafayette. The council additionally recommended making Lafayette a training center for future black priests of the Society of the Divine Word. The presence in the city of Holy Rosary Institute, with its Divine Word chaplain, ensured a residence for the white priest needed to supervise the black priests and thereby added to Lafayette's appeal.[26]

Hagspiel informed Desmond that the council had made its recommendations to the generalate in Rome and now awaited final approval. Hinting at his proposed compromise, Hagspiel wrote: "From all indications I take it for granted that our Generalate in Rome will put its final O.K. to Alexandria taking in our colored priests. Just how many of them will be assigned to the diocese . . . will depend on the Roman decision." In a gesture of appreciation, he invited Desmond to preach the sermon at the first mass celebration in Bay St. Louis on May 24, the day following the ordinations of the black priests by Bishop Gerow.[27]

During the succeeding two months, Hagspiel maneuvered carefully to guarantee that the black priests would end up in Lafayette. After a meeting with Cicognani in Chicago on April 26, he led Jeanmard to believe that the apostolic delegate not only approved of the bishop's taking two of the black Divine Word missionaries but actually desired it. On May 6, Mundelein talked with Desmond and broached the idea of a compromise whereby the diocese of Lafayette would start the work concomitantly with the diocese of Alexandria.[28]

26. Bruno Hagspiel to Herman Patzelt, March 27, 1934, in Provincial's Correspondence; Bruno Hagspiel to Bishop Daniel Desmond, June 18, 1934, in Desmond Papers.

27. Bruno Hagspiel to Bishop Daniel Desmond, April 10, 1934, in Desmond Papers.

28. Bishop Jules Jeanmard to Archbishop Amleto Cicognani, June 13, 1934

Meanwhile, unbeknown to Desmond, Jeanmard began preparations to receive black priests into his diocese. His consultors expressed their unanimous approval and agreed to create a new parish for the black priests. Located in north Lafayette and named Immaculate Heart of Mary, the new parish was formed by dividing St. Paul's (black) Parish at the railroad tracks that split the city. When he wrote to T. A. Wrenn, the Spiritan pastor of St. Paul's, Jeanmard put the onus for the division of the parish on Cicognani, saying, "His Excellency, the Apostolic Delegate, has let it be known that he would wish to see a parish in the diocese of Lafayette entrusted to the care of two of the young priests to be ordained at St. Augustine's Seminary." He also secured pledges of financial assistance for construction of a church, community house, and school in the new parish. Mother Katharine Drexel promised five thousand dollars for the church, and Mundelein, noting that the Holy See wanted the project "fostered and encouraged," promised three thousand dollars per year for several years from the American Board of Catholic Missions.[29]

On May 23, 1934, in the midst of the planning and maneuvering, Bishop Gerow ordained Anthony Bourges, Maurice Rousseve, Vincent Smith, and Francis Wade. Since the small seminary chapel could not accommodate the throng of two thousand that gathered for the event, the ceremony took place outdoors under a large tent that served as a sanctuary. The next day, still waiting for final word on their disposition, Bishop Desmond preached at the first masses of the four new priests, which were celebrated simultaneously.[30]

The ordinations thrilled black Catholics throughout the country. Gilbert Faustina, former supreme knight of the Knights of Peter Claver, expressed the joy felt by many when he called the ordinations "one of the greatest . . . occasions" he had ever attended. The *Claverite*, the official organ of the knights, proclaimed that the event had brought "inspiration to Catholic youth and rejoicing to Catholic parents" everywhere.[31]

(telegram), copy in Bishop Jules Jeanmard Papers, ADL; Archbishop Amleto Cicognani to Bishop Daniel Desmond, June 23, 1934, in Desmond Papers; Desmond Diary, May 6, 7, 1934.

29. Consultors Minutes, May 2, 1934, in ADL; Bishop Jules Jeanmard to T. A. Wrenn, May 9, 1934, copy, Bishop Jules Jeanmard to Cardinal George Mundelein, May 11, 1934, copy, Cardinal George Mundelein to Bishop Jules Jeanmard, May 19, 1934, all in Jeanmard Papers.

30. Desmond Diary, May 24, 1934; Malin, "Integration of Catholic Clergy," 84.

31. *Claverite*, August, 1934, pp. 1, 19, in 50–13, Miscellaneous file, JFA.

By late May, after he received a preliminary report from Jeanmard on the bishop's preparations to receive two of the black priests, it became evident to Cicognani that there was a serious misunderstanding about the ultimate destination of the four new Divine Word priests. Informing Hagspiel that he would accept any plan agreed to by Jeanmard and Desmond, Cicognani urged Hagspiel to end the confusion by communicating with Bishop Desmond.[32] In a blunt, sharply worded letter, Hagspiel finally explained to Desmond "the reasons why . . . in conscience" the Divine Word Missionaries felt obliged to decline his offer to take all of the black priests: he confessed that both he and his advisers had preferred Lafayette from the start but that Jeanmard's initial refusal in Chicago had thwarted their original plans. Only after repeated entreaties had Jeanmard agreed to change his mind. Hagspiel frankly told the bishop that opposition in Avoyelles to the black priests far exceeded anything that the bishop had acknowledged. In addition, he objected to Desmond's plan for using the priests almost exclusively as teachers. "That they would be assigned for years to practically grammar school teaching," he wrote, "and be expected to be exceedingly cautious and reserved in doing pastoral work among the adult Negro population of the town . . . must be utterly discouraging for the new priests." If conditions in Avoyelles necessitated such extreme precaution, he argued, it was just one more proof that Alexandria "is not the ideal district for beginners." Hagspiel also complained about inadequate arrangements for the white Divine Word priest who would act as the "guardian angel" of his black confreres.

Hagspiel expressed his society's appreciation for Desmond's readiness, before all the other bishops in the South, to take black priests into his diocese, but he believed the diocese of Lafayette offered a less risky and more promising field. Out of consideration for Desmond, Hagspiel offered to send two of the newly ordained priests, along with a white priest as their superior, to the diocese of Alexandria at the same time that he assigned the other two to Lafayette, where the Divine Word Missionaries would also construct a community house for future black priests. Anticipating a negative reaction, Hagspiel warned that if, for any reason, Desmond found the compromise plan unsatisfactory, then the Divine Word Missionaries

32. Archbishop Amleto Cicognani to Bishop Jules Jeanmard, June 13, 1934, Bishop Jules Jeanmard to Archbishop Amleto Cicognani, June 13, 1934 (telegram), copy, both in Jeanmard Papers; Archbishop Amleto Cicognani to Bishop Daniel Desmond, June 23, 1934, in Desmond Papers.

would be compelled to assign all four black priests to Lafayette, with the possibility of giving Desmond some black priests the next year or in future years, when conditions proved more favorable.[33]

Desmond described Hagspiel's letter as breathing "an acrimonious tone." He acknowledged that Hagspiel ostensibly offered a compromise, but he concluded that "it is obvious that the Society would prefer not to begin in Alexandria." Desmond therefore advised Hagspiel that he would not accept the compromise offer. Writing to Cicognani about the Divine Word Missionaries' preference for Lafayette over Alexandria, Desmond observed, "The reasons for this opinion are set down with such finality that I am led to concur . . . on the relative merit of the two dioceses in question."[34]

Lafayette's black Catholics reacted with "unrestrained enthusiasm" when Bishop Jeanmard announced at the graduation exercises of Holy Rosary Institute that he would erect Immaculate Heart of Mary Parish for the four black priests who would arrive in the fall of 1934. Thanks to an emergency gift of three thousand dollars for the construction of the new black church from the Extension Society (a pontifical society that had been established in 1905 to serve the needs of the home missions but that did not normally give money to black missions) and the money from Mother Katharine Drexel and the mission board, construction of the concrete-block church, school, and rectory of Immaculate Heart of Mary Parish was finished by late autumn.[35]

Fathers Bourges and Smith assumed their duties on September 20, 1934; Fathers Rousseve and Wade arrived on November 1, after completing a series of missions throughout the South. The four black priests technically served at Immaculate Heart as assistants to Patzelt, the nominal pastor and their white superior, who lived two miles away at Holy Rosary Institute. During the five years of his tenure as official pastor, he never once celebrated mass at Immaculate Heart of Mary. He did take charge, however, of hiring

33. Bruno Hagspiel to Bishop Daniel Desmond, June 18, 1934, in Desmond Papers.

34. Bishop Daniel Desmond to Archbishop Amleto Cicognani, June 21, 1934, copy in Desmond Papers.

35. "Negro Priests Assume Duties in New Colored Parish. Lafayette sets precedent for the South," September 20, 1934, newspaper clipping in Jeanmard Papers; Foley, God's Men, 168; Bishop Jules Jeanmard to E. McGuinness, June 25, 1934, Bishop Jules Jeanmard to Cardinal George Mundelein, November 8, 1934, copies of both in Jeanmard Papers; minutes of the ABCM meeting, November 21, 1934, in AUSCC.

all parish employees, handling parish funds, and even picking up the mail.[36]

The cautious Patzelt's insistence that the black priests strictly observe the racial code of the Lafayette diocese, including never offering a hand to shake on meeting white priests, eventually resulted in strained relations between him and his black assistants. Vincent Smith, in particular, resented Patzelt's absentee pastorate and his treatment of the black priests, but all of them came to regard Patzelt's suzerainty as a sign that the society lacked confidence in black priests.[37] As a result, the young black clerics began to defy both their white superior and the customary practices of segregation. Anthony Bourges, for example, a diminutive, cheerful man who possessed a sweet smile and a will of iron, listened attentively to whatever Patzelt had to say and then did what he thought best. He persistently offered his hand whenever he met a white priest. Happily for him, his assignment in 1935 as resident missionary in Duson, about fifteen miles from Lafayette, kept him at a distance from Patzelt, though he officially remained an assistant at Immaculate Heart of Mary.

Bourges' most dramatic gesture of independence from Patzelt and from southern racial codes occurred in 1939, when he accepted a general invitation from Jeanmard extended to the clergy of the diocese to attend a memorial service at the cathedral for the recently deceased Pope Pius XI. Black priests never attended functions at the cathedral, which they understood to be off limits to them. Bourges, nevertheless, was determined to go to the cathedral to pray for the soul of the pope, whom he greatly admired. Unable to persuade Francis Wade to accompany him, he went alone. As he passed through the receiving line, Monsignor I. F. Isenberg, the rector of the cathedral, greeted him coolly. That evening, a Sunday, Isenberg dined with Patzelt, as was his custom, and the following morning, Patzelt informed Bourges that Isenberg wished to see him. When Bourges met with Isenberg later in the day, the monsignor accused him of having taken advantage of his light skin and his priesthood in attending the memorial service. When Bourges explained that Jeanmard had invited him, Isenberg responded that he understood but still advised the black priest that it was "best not to come" to functions that would result in mixing white and black

36. Interview of Anthony Bourges, S.V.D., by Stephen J. Ochs, July 11, 1983.
37. *Ibid.*; Malin, "Integration of Catholic Clergy," 87–88.

clergy. Bourges calmly told Isenberg that he intended to take up the matter with the bishop. The next morning he called on Jeanmard and recounted the previous day's conversation with the cathedral rector. Jeanmard claimed that he had heard no complaints about the black priests and dismissed Isenberg's comments with the remark that "some old crank must have said that." Isenberg gave Bourges no further trouble.[38]

In 1939, relations between Patzelt and his black assistants degenerated to such a point that the intervention of Provincial Hugo Aubry was required. Friction between Patzelt and Vincent Smith had already led to the latter's transfer the previous year. Aubry listened to each of the black priests individually and counseled greater prudence in dealing with southern racial etiquette. In recognition of their sincerity and to demonstrate his confidence in them, however, Aubry replaced Patzelt with Bourges, who became administrator and, shortly thereafter, pastor of Immaculate Heart of Mary Parish.[39]

Despite their struggles with Patzelt and Jim Crow, the black priests in Lafayette enjoyed considerable success in their pastoral work, winning the respect and admiration of Bishop Jeanmard, of their parishioners, and of many of the white priests in Lafayette for their devoted, selfless work. Their days usually began about 5 A.M. with morning prayers. At 6 A.M. they said mass, which was followed by breakfast. They divided their two-thousand-member parish in half and then paired up to make visits to their parishioners: Bourges with Smith and Rousseve with Wade, for Bourges and Rousseve spoke French as well as English. On Sundays, the priests celebrated three well-attended masses at Immaculate Heart of Mary Church and taught catechism classes as well. During the week, they also taught in the parish school. In addition, Bourges ranged outside the city of Lafayette, tending to missions at Scott, Duson, and Mouton Switch; following his move to Duson as resident missionary, more than four hundred families returned to the practice of their Catholic faith. In 1937, Wade succeeded Bourges as resident missionary of the one-hundred-square-mile mission at Duson. The apostolic delegate followed the work of the four black

38. Bourges interview, July 11, 1983.
39. Malin, "Integration of Catholic Clergy," 88–89; Foley, *God's Men*, 143–44; Albert S. Foley to William C. Bauer, May 1, 1953, copy in Albert S. Foley Papers, JFA; Bourges interview, July 11, 1983.

Divine Word missionaries closely, asking for and receiving periodic progress reports from the rector of St. Augustine's Seminary and from Bishop Jeanmard. Cicognani included the sterling evaluations that he received in his reports to the Holy See.[40]

Between 1920 and 1934, Pastorelli had warily kept his distance from St. Augustine's Seminary, referring most of the blacks who applied to the Josephites there but half-expecting the enterprise to fail. The ordinations and successful ministries of the black Divine Word priests and the likelihood of even more black Divine Word priests in the near future, however, generated great excitement in the black Catholic community and posed, according to Pastorelli, a significant challenge for the Josephites.

Many Josephite missionaries viewed the events of 1934 not as a potential problem but as an answer to their prayers. In February of 1934, when Joseph Lally, pastor of Sacred Heart Parish in Port Arthur, Texas, learned that Bishop Daniel Desmond had agreed to accept the black priests into his diocese, he congratulated the bishop and informed him that news of his action had elated the parishioners of Sacred Heart. He predicted that Desmond's courageous decision would lay to rest the stock argument used to deny blacks admission to so many seminaries, that ordinaries would not accept them. For years, such Josephites as Lally, John and James Albert, Edward Murphy, Vincent Warren, and Dan Rice had sent young men from their parishes to St. Augustine's. They maintained contact with the young men and, despite their own meager resources, provided some with financial aid—aid gratefully acknowledged by seminary officials. Lally pointed with pride to Maurice Rousseve as one of his boys and even offered Sacred Heart Parish as a vacation spot for the black seminarians in 1931 when they had nowhere else to go. Josephites visited St. Augustine's frequently, saying mass and giving retreats to the students.[41]

Josephite pastors, attuned to the sentiments of their parishioners and themselves enthusiastic over the advent of more black priests,

40. Bourges interview, July 11, 1983; Foley, God's Men, 153, 161; Archbishop Amleto Cicognani to Gerard Esser, November 16, 1935, Gerard Esser to Archbishop Amleto Cicognani, May 17, 1935, copy, Gerard Esser to Brother Thomas Aquinas, January 12, 1936, copy, all in SASA.

41. Joseph Lally to Bishop Daniel Desmond, February 8, 1934, in Desmond Papers; John Albert to Gerard Esser, September 10, 1934, Gerard Esser to Louis B. Pastorelli, February 13, 1936, copy, both in SASA; A. G. Steig to Vincent Warren, May 7, 1929, copy in SASA; CMB, 1931, in JFA.

extended their courtesy and support to the new priests from St. Augustine's Seminary. John Lundrigan of Holy Redeemer Parish in New Orleans heartily welcomed Maurice Rousseve back to his home parish for his first mass there and preached a glowing sermon. In late May and early June of 1934, both Stephen Boysko, of St. Luke's in Thibodaux, Louisiana, and Joseph Van Baast, of St. Catherine of Sienna in Donaldsonville, Louisiana, invited one of the black Divine Word missionaries to celebrate Sunday mass in their parishes. Boysko reported to Pastorelli that "all the people were more than pleased at both places."[42]

Recognizing the powerful appeal of the black priests to their own parishioners, Josephite pastors also invited black Divine Word missionaries to conduct missions in their parishes. In March, 1935, for example, Michael J. Flaherty in Houston informed Pastorelli that he had secured Father Wade to conduct a two-week mission at Our Mother of Mercy Parish. Flaherty explained his reasoning: "The folks of the parish have been asking that I invite one of the Colored Padres for a visit here since they were ordained. The mission offered me a real opportunity so I took advantage of it." Joseph Lally found the black Divine Word missionaries useful in combatting Protestant propaganda in Port Arthur. For years black ministers had effectively hurled the charge that the Catholic church refused to allow black youths to become priests. Now, Lally enthused, "by having the S.V.D. [Divine Word] colored priests here on occasions, I have done a lot to make Protestants feel better toward the Church."[43]

Josephites throughout the South also provided the black priests with an invaluable assist: the hospitality of their rectories. As Father Bourges' experience at the Lafayette cathedral illustrates, southern white clergy expected the black Divine Word missionaries to remain invisible and to absent themselves from ceremonies, celebrations, parties, banquets, retreats, and clergy conferences, in short, from any functions not held in black facilities. The Josephites, often snubbed, ridiculed, and insulted by other white clergy because they worked among blacks, empathized with the plight of the black missionaries and attempted to help them. Josephites in New Orleans, for example, opened their rectories to visiting black Divine Word priests, affording them a place to stay and the oppor-

42. Foley, God's Men, 136–37; Stephen Boysko to Louis B. Pastorelli, June 8, 1934, in PMC.

43. Michael Flaherty to Louis B. Pastorelli, March 13, 1935, in 55-D, Joseph Lally to Louis B. Pastorelli, February 18, 1937, in 57-K, JFA.

tunity for a holiday in the city away from the isolation and rigors of mission work. The black priests deeply appreciated those gestures of Josephite generosity and kindness.[44]

Pastorelli and Gillard did not share the enthusiasm of their men on the missions for the black missionaries. They feared that Josephite parishioners would make unfavorable comparisons between the Josephites and the Divine Word Missionaries and begin to demand black Josephite priests of their own. When Clarence Howard, Vincent Warren's prize student from St. Joseph's Parish in Norfolk, asked Gillard to preach at his first mass in the Virginia port city on June 13, 1937, Gillard confided to Pastorelli that "my opinion is to refuse because I don't like to get into a spot like that." He asked for Pastorelli's advice and then made the following observation: "I can see where it might be wise not to appear opposed to the colored priests. It sort of puts us on the spot either way." On another occasion, Flaherty drew a rebuke from Pastorelli after he arranged with Patzelt for a black Divine Word priest to substitute for him during his vacation the first week of August and two succeeding Sundays. "I must tell you in confidence," Pastorelli wrote, "that we do not approve of the getting of Colored Priests to relieve our men. . . . Bringing Colored priests to one's place is but inviting future trouble in the parish." He ordered Flaherty to avoid such situations in the future and stick to white priests for replacements.[45]

The second half of the decade of the thirties witnessed increased Catholic missionary activity on behalf of blacks and an improving climate for black priests. The four ordinandi from St. Augustine's Seminary broke the ice. In addition, the work of the Northeast Clergy Conference on Negro Welfare and of the Catholic Interracial Council of New York, combined with a strong directive from the Holy See to the American bishops, gave added impetus to the campaign for a black clergy. Pastorelli, ever distrustful of northern racial liberals, regarded both organizations with suspicion.

In November of 1933, a handful of priests involved in the black

44. Interviews of Vincent D. Warren, S.S.J., by Peter E. Hogan, S.S.J., 1965 (Typescript in JFA), 194; interview of Rawlin B. Enette, S.S.J., by Peter E. Hogan, S.S.J., March 9, 1971 (Typescript in JFA), 146; Bourges interview, July 11, 1983.

45. John T. Gillard to Louis B. Pastorelli, April, 1937, in 57-G, Michael Flaherty to Louis B. Pastorelli, July 17, 1937, in 57-D, Louis B. Pastorelli to Michael Flaherty, July 19, 1937, copy, in 57-D, all in JFA.

apostolate from several dioceses and religious communities in the northeast, including John LaFarge, Cornelius J. Ahern, pastor of Queen of Angels Parish in Newark, New Jersey, and Harold Purcell, C.P., editor of *Sign* magazine, met in Torresdale, Pennsylvania, to discuss how best to educate the clergy on their duty to their black fellow citizens. From that meeting arose the Northeast Clergy Conference on Negro Welfare. Members of the conference met three times a year from 1934 until the war forced its suspension in 1942. They strove, in the words of one member, "to make our priests and nuns colored conscious" so that they would recognize their opportunity and obligation to win the souls of America's blacks. The meetings of the clergy conference were always off-the-record in order to encourage frankness of discussion. The gatherings convinced participants that they needed to conduct an intensive propaganda campaign among the clergy in order to change attitudes about blacks and to enlist those important opinion molders in the cause of racial justice.[46]

The members of the conference did most of their work by word of mouth at clergy meetings, informal discussions in rectories, and articles in religious publications. They also used pamphlets, the secular press, the Paulist-owned WLWL radio station in New York City, and a series of mailings to priests and nuns. One such mailing in 1934 to ten thousand priests bore on its cover the slogan "Keep the Negro in his Place." Inside, the flier explained that the Negro's place was in the Catholic church. Clergy conference members organized themselves into committees, including one on seminaries and colleges. In their discussions with bishops, they set black clergy as one of the topics. By 1938, the Northeast Clergy Conference had spawned similar organizations centered in the archdiocese of Cincinnati and in the dioceses of Mobile, Richmond, and Raleigh.[47]

In October, 1936, the conference invited the participation of Michael O'Neil, the Josephite rector of Epiphany Apostolic Col-

46. George K. Hunton, *All of Which I Saw, Part of Which I Was: The Autobiography of George K. Hunton, as Told to Gary MacEoin* (Garden City, N.Y., 1967), 147–50; William A. Osborne, *Segregated Covenant, Race Relations and American Catholics* (New York, 1967), 37.

47. Hunton, *All of Which I Saw,* 147–53; agenda for Conference Group for Catholic Action Toward Negroes, in Box 20-1, LaFarge Papers; William J. Walsh, "Organization of the Propaganda of the Clergy Negro Welfare Conference, February 1, 1938," in Papers of the Catholic Interracial Council of New York, ACUA; William J. Walsh, "The Clergy Conference is Growing," *Interracial Review,* XI (November, 1938), 172–73.

lege. Privately, he expressed the familiar Josephite apprehension about Negro champions from the Northeast. He concluded, however, that "it may be best to play ball with them." Within two years, Francis Schmutz, who had replaced O'Neil at Epiphany, complained that the members of the conference, about twenty-five in number, "seemed to be stealing the show from the Josephites: we doing the work and they in on the publicity campaign."[48] The Josephites' wounded pride notwithstanding, membership in the clergy conference exposed them to diverse opinions and approaches, thus challenging their tendency toward parochialism and isolation. By the end of the decade, the Northeast Clergy Conference had effected some change in clerical attitudes toward blacks, including making some white priests more receptive to their black counterparts.

Another of LaFarge's organizations, the Catholic Interracial Council of New York, also helped create a more hospitable atmosphere within the church for black priests. Although he devoted considerable time and energy to working with clergy, LaFarge believed that racial justice would be achieved finally through the efforts of the Catholic laity. The Catholic Interracial Council emerged from the Catholic Laymen's Union, the group of twenty-five black professional men that LaFarge founded in 1928. His experience with the laymen's union led him to formulate an interracial approach to the race problem, based on the idea that the fight for racial justice demanded blacks and whites work together, not separately. William Markoe's insistence on transforming the Federated Colored Catholics into just such an interracial organization (with LaFarge's tacit approval) precipitated the rift with Thomas Turner in 1932.[49]

On Pentecost Sunday, 1934, the laymen's union sponsored a mass meeting, attended by approximately eight hundred people, in New York City's Town Hall. The town meeting led to the formation of the Catholic Interracial Council of New York, with George K.

48. Michael J. O'Neil to Louis B. Pastorelli, October 8, 1936, in 56-N, Francis Schmutz to Louis B. Pastorelli, February 9, 1938, in 58-S, both in JFA.

49. Osborne, *Segregated Covenant,* 37–38; Hunton, *All of Which I Saw,* 60–61; *NCE,* III, 269–70; Marilyn W. Nickels, "The Federated Colored Catholics: A Study of Three Variant Perspectives on Racial Justice as Represented by John LaFarge, William Markoe, and Thomas Turner" (Ph.D. dissertation, Catholic University of America, 1975). See also LaFarge's own books, *The Manner Is Ordinary* (New York, 1954), 340–42, and *The Race Question and the Negro: A Study of the Catholic Doctrine on Interracial Justice* (New York, 1944), 256–57.

Hunton, a white Catholic lawyer who had participated in the joint defense of the Scottsboro boys, as executive secretary and John LaFarge as chaplain. Convinced that all persons shared a common dignity and equality as children of God and concluding that white prejudice based on ignorance had created the race problem, the council embarked on a broad educational campaign directed toward white Catholics to teach and publicize moral, scientific, and democratic principles concerning race. The Catholic Interracial Council took over publication of the *Interracial Review* from Markoe in October of 1934, sponsored the "Interracial Hour" on WLWL, and sent lecturers to address numerous Catholic groups. It also attempted to give wide circulation to the works of such theologians as the Reverend Francis J. Gilligan of St. Thomas Seminary, who in his Catholic University doctoral dissertation, published under the title *The Morality of the Color Line*, argued the immorality of discrimination against blacks in the United States. The council strove to eliminate racial discrimination in Catholic churches, schools, seminaries, hospitals and other institutions, and societies through quiet appeals to episcopal and lay authorities. Finally, anticipating the ecumenical movement that later became so powerful in the church, it collaborated with existing groups, Protestant, Catholic, Jewish, black, and sectarian, that worked for interracial justice. Over the next thirty years, sixty Catholic interracial councils were established in cities throughout the country.[50]

As part of its campaign for interracial justice, the council strongly supported the cause of black priests. Aware of the high esteem priests enjoyed in the eyes of most Catholic laity, Hunton and LaFarge viewed black priests as potentially effective agents for breaking down racial stereotypes. They believed that exposure to black priests would improve the image of blacks in the minds of average white Catholics. The Catholic Interracial Council went out of its way to help black priests who visited New York and attempted to give them publicity through speaking engagements, radio spots, or articles in the *Interracial Review* that would create a favorable impression among white Catholics.[51]

Although the cause of black priests benefited from the more favorable climate of opinion among clergy and laity generated

50. Osborne, *Segregated Covenant*, 37–38; Hunton, *All of Which I Saw*, 72–75, 86–89; Francis J. Gilligan, *The Morality of the Color Line* (Washington, D.C., 1929).

51. Hunton, *All of Which I Saw*, 86–89, 112.

by the Northeast Clergy Conference and the Catholic Interracial Council, an even more important boost to the cause came from the Holy See. In May, 1935, Archbishop Cicognani, writing to Joseh F. Rummel, the newly installed archbishop of New Orleans, apparently invited the response of the southern bishops to five recommendations from the Consistorial Congregation concerning the black apostolate, including one on racially mixed schools and seminaries. The very fact that the Consistory had submitted the recommendations indicated that Rome contemplated taking new action. Rummel, recently arrived from New York and regarded suspiciously by many in his archdiocese as a Yankee, sincerely wanted to expand the church's efforts on behalf of blacks and to achieve progress on the race question, but he wanted to do so in ways that would not alienate the white majority of his see. He solicited the views of his suffragan bishops and then sent a report to Cicognani, which he claimed described categorically the attitudes of the bishops.[52]

In the report, Rummel basically suggested maintenance of the racial status quo. He stated that the bishops saw no possibility at that time of establishing "racially mixed grade or high schools," because state laws prohibited such schools in the state of Louisiana. Any attempt at violation or circumvention of the law would result in disaster for white and black parochial schools. The southern bishops agreed with the Consistory on the need to expand the church's work for blacks in the North as well as in the South and urged the establishment of black parishes in northern cities, for many black Catholics had lost their faith when they migrated to the North.

Rummel insisted that the same arguments that applied to mixed Catholic elementary schools and secondary schools in the South applied equally to seminaries. He predicted disaster if blacks were admitted into diocesan seminaries. Rummel assured Cicognani, however, of the bishops' continued support for St. Augustine's Seminary in Bay St. Louis and St. Joseph's Seminary in Washington, D.C., which he characterized as "the established institutions for the education of a colored priesthood." Rummel also described the work of the recently ordained black alumni of St. Augustine's as "very successful." He emphasized to Cicognani and the Consistory the bishops' solicitous concern for the spiritual welfare of blacks

52. Vath interview, July 12, 1983; Edward Murphy to Louis B. Pastorelli, June 26, 1935, in 55-M, JFA; Archbishop Joseph Rummell to Archbishop Amleto Cicognani, November 11, 1935, copy in Archbishop Thomas J. Toolen Papers, AAM.

in their jurisdictions and claimed considerable progress in increasing the number of black churches and schools. In that regard, he also praised the "splendid cooperation" that southern bishops had received from the Josephites.[53]

In the same report that contained his summary of the bishops' responses to the May inquiry from the Consistorial Congregation, Rummel also included the bishops' answers, gathered during a meeting on November 5, to five questions advanced by Cicognani. The bishops unanimously agreed that the Holy See should address a letter about the Negro problem to the American episcopate. They suggested that Rome release one letter for publication and send another to the bishops "regarding the more intimate details of the question." The southern bishops also strongly recommended that the Holy See publicly laud the annual collection for blacks and Indians as a way of increasing dwindling receipts. Although they expressed their preference for confining black work to the Josephites, Holy Ghost Fathers, Divine Word Missionaries, and priests and female religious already engaged in the work, Rummel informed Cicognani that they would not object should the Holy See urge additional communities of religious to establish schools and missions in the South "in accord with the bishop of the place," provided that they properly selected the missionaries from groups of volunteers.

Addressing the larger question of race relations in the South, the bishops recommended that "this should be permitted to work out itself." They warned that public discussions at meetings or over the radio "of this delicate problem . . . are apt to do more harm than good," since tradition and state law would not admit of the issue being forced. Echoing a theme advanced by many southern and Catholic liberals, the bishops professed to see evidence of progress in the South, particularly in education, and to detect "a kindlier, more sympathetic attitude" toward blacks, particularly in areas where a major portion of the population, black and white, professed Catholicism.[54]

Pastorelli knew that Rome was once again tightening the screws on the southern bishops, for they, in turn, began pressing the Josephites for greater numbers of adult converts. In a letter dated March 28, 1935, he advised his missionaries that other religious

53. Archbishop Joseph Rummel to Archbishop Amleto Cicognani, November 11, 1935, copy in Toolen Papers.

54. *Ibid.*; Czuchlewski, "Liberal Catholicism and Racism," 144–62.

communities were becoming involved in the black missions; he urged every priest to do his utmost to increase conversions in order to avoid being compared unfavorably to the newcomers. "The day has passed," he warned, "when we may rest satisfied with routine attention to . . . a well organized congregation; its numbers must be augmented by the reclamation . . . of fallen-aways . . . and by an increase in the number of conversions, particularly adults." He also encouraged his men to keep themselves conversant with all phases of the so-called Negro question. He claimed that the aspirations and outlook of blacks had changed dramatically over the course of a generation and advised his missionaries, "if for no other reason than that of self protection," to "acquaint themselves with the present day situation in Negro circles" by purchasing for rectory libraries up-to-date books on and by blacks. Arguing that Josephites could "no longer confine our knowledge merely to the spiritual realm," he called on his men to take the initiative and advise, direct, and lead their people; if they did not, he predicted, others would, "with possible disaster" to the Josephites.[55]

Concerns about increased competition from other communities of religious, the apparent success of the black Divine Word missionaries, the obvious desire of Josephite parishioners for black priests of their own, and the apparent intention of the Holy See to address once again the issue of a black clergy all led the consultors of St. Joseph's Society, at their meeting of February 4, 1936, to decide "to accept a few black students for Epiphany Apostolic College." Pastorelli inadvertently revealed the reasoning that lay behind their decision in a note he scrawled at the bottom of a copy of a letter he sent to a Josephite brother on April 30, 1936. He reminded himself to bring a plan for a "Colored Priesthood and Brotherhood" to the attention of the fathers. "We might as well face the cold fact," he wrote, "that we will be compelled to staff our southern parishes little by little with colored priests of our own Society—else the people will clamor for Colored priests not of our own Society." He observed that "even bishops will eventually reach this conclusion," and he then confessed: "We have allowed feeling, yes even I will say prejudice to blind us to our own best interests. Time to arise and to wake up to the needs and present and coming conditions."[56]

55. Louis B. Pastorelli to Reverend and Dear Father, March 28, 1935, copy in PMC.

56. CMB, February 4, 1936, note scrawled by Louis B. Pastorelli on the bottom of copy of letter he sent to Brother George S. Tobin, April 30, 1936, in 56-G, both in JFA.

Pastorelli and the Josephites were not alone in reevaluating their position on the admission of black students and seminarians. The day after Pastorelli wrote his memorandum, the Benedictine monks at St. Vincent Archabbey in Latrobe, Pennsylvania, met in their chapter to discuss "whether or not Colored young men should be admitted into the institution." The archabbey had admitted several blacks since 1929, including William Lane, but had not encouraged their attendance. The Reverend Benno Brink, a monk of the archabbey who had promoted Catholic work among blacks for years, addressed the chapter on "the present movements in the country." He described both Cardinal Dougherty of Philadelphia and Archbishop Cicognani as "very anxious to place Negro youth in institutions," and he informed the monks that, at that moment, seven young black men wanted to attend St. Vincent Seminary. The chapter rephrased the question under discussion to read, "Shall St. Vincent continue its past policy of not restricting the admission of negroes for the institution?," and all present acclaimed it. Archabbot Alfred Koch, recognizing the importance of the decision for other institutions, issued a formal statement declaring that at no time and under no circumstances would officials of St. Vincent consider the question of race in admitting applicants to any branch of the archabbey.[57]

In early September, 1936, the Holy See climaxed a decade of subtle, but increasing pressure on the American episcopate. Cardinal Rafaello Rossi, pro-secretary of the Consistorial Congregation, acting with the knowledge and approval of Pius XI, who formally headed the congregation, used the occasion of the fiftieth anniversary of the Negro and Indian collection to issue what amounted to a directive on the black apostolate to the American hierarchy. In a covering letter, dated September 9, 1936, Cicognani emphasized the importance of the missive by telling the bishops that the pope had spoken "very earnestly" to him during an audience on August 22, expressing the hope that "the enclosed letter would be regarded as a personal appeal from him to the Bishops and religious institutes." The delegate summarized the appeal with the phrase "More schools, More churches, More Apostles for the Negroes." He advised against publishing the letter in toto but indicated that the bishops could make excerpts public from time to time "in order to show the mind of the Holy See and its recommendations in regard to the Negro apostolate." Cicognani also suggested that bish-

57. Chapter minutes, May 1, 1936, in SVAA.

ops in specific regions of the country consult among themselves as to the best means of putting into effect these recommendations. Promising the bishops that the Consistorial Congregation, which was ultimately in charge of the government of dioceses and which also named bishops to vacant sees, would "follow this apostolate with interest," Cicognani indicated that the Holy See wished also to receive reports from the bishops on their progress in implementing the proposals contained in the letter.[58] Translated, the arcane language of the Vatican meant that the pope, who was the official prefect of the Consistorial Congregation, wanted to see action and results!

In his communication, addressed "To their Eminences, the Cardinals, and To their Excellencies, the Archbishops and Bishops of the United States of America," Rossi congratulated religious institutes, male and female, that had dedicated themselves to work among blacks. He noted, however, that only 250,000 out of 13,000,000 blacks in the United States professed Catholicism. As a result, because of "their simple nature," they stood exposed to the dangers of atheism and communism. Stressing that he wrote "with the full approval of the Holy Father," Rossi made "a pressing recommendation" to the American hierarchy "that they more and more intensify this apostolate."

While taking special care to recognize and praise the work of the Josephites, the Holy Ghost Fathers, and the Divine Word Missionaries, Rossi underscored the need for more churches and schools for blacks and for greater numbers of priests to undertake the work. The Consistorial Congregation, accordingly, called on religious institutes, especially the larger ones, "to undertake . . . particularly in the South . . . some mission or schools for the colored." In order to increase the number of priests for the black apostolate, the Consistory directed that "ecclesiastical vocations among the Negroes," for diocesan as well as religious clergy, "are to be cultivated with particular care and effort." Rossi stated that Pius XI's 1923 letter to William Gier, the superior general of the Divine Word Missionaries, clearly expressed the pope's approval of and desire for black vocations in the United States. Consequently, the Consistory urged the bishops, especially those in the North and "in areas where Negroes have been Catholics for generations," to give great atten-

58. Archbishop Amleto Cicognani to Your Excellency, September 9, 1936, copy in 71-C, JFA.

tion and care to fostering vocations to the diocesan clergy and to accept "carefully chosen youths" into diocesan seminaries "to be promoted to the priesthood and employed in the sacred ministry for the benefit of their own people."[59]

Cicognani tried to contact Pastorelli by telephone on September 15, 1936, to discuss both his own letter and Rossi's. Since Pastorelli had already left for Newburgh, the delegate forwarded copies to him, asking him to call at the delegation at his earliest convenience, and the two conferred shortly thereafter. Later, Pastorelli commented that Rossi's message "stands out stronger and stronger with each reading" and predicted that it would "do much good for the Negro mission cause."[60]

Even the normally suspicious NAACP applauded Rossi's letter, which was published by, among others, Colored Harvest and St. Augustine's Messenger (a monthly magazine produced by St. Augustine's Seminary), welcoming it as an indication of changing church policy and growing interest in blacks. Some NAACP board members, Dr. Algernon Black and Walter White, for instance, were outspokenly anti-Catholic. Roy Wilkins, however, who was married to a Catholic woman, was cordial and helpful to the Catholic Interracial Council. On their part, many Catholics, convinced that communists had infiltrated the organization, distrusted the NAACP. Despite wariness on both sides, the NAACP greeted this new step from Rome as a straightforward and sincere effort on behalf of blacks. In a December 26, 1936, news release, the NAACP declared that though the letter concerned itself primarily with winning more blacks to the Catholic church, "its powerful but indirect effect is expected to be the enlistment of the Catholic Church in the fight for citizenship rights for Colored Americans." The news release claimed that already numerous Catholic clergy, newspapers, and magazines had spoken out freely and forthrightly in support of full civil rights for black people. It also noted with particular satisfaction that Catholic weekly papers had come to the front in the fight against lynching, a fight that Pastorelli ardently supported.[61]

59. Cardinal Rafaello C. Rossi to their Eminences, the Cardinals, and to their Excellencies, the Archbishops and Bishops of the United States of America, August 24, 1936, copy in SASA.

60. Archbishop Amleto Cicognani to Louis B. Pastorelli, September 15, 1936, Louis B. Pastorelli to Archbishop Amleto Cicognani, September 23, 1936, copy, both in PMC.

61. "Bishops and Lynching," Colored Harvest, XXIII (April–May, 1935), 2; Hunton, All of Which I Saw, 176–77; News release, "Pope Urges U.S. Catholics to Work for Negroes," December 26, 1936, in Catholic Interracial Council Papers.

The upsurge in Catholic activism, coinciding with and following the issuance of the Consistorial Congregation's letter, appeared to confirm the NAACP's optimism. The autumn of 1936 saw the Catholic Interracial Council and the Northeast Clergy Conference continuing to expand their work; it also witnessed the reopening of Catholic University, which for many blacks represented the Catholic church, to black students for the first time in twenty years. Thereafter, an increasing number of Catholic colleges and universities in the North began to admit at least token numbers of black students. Gillard, working through the Catholic Students' Mission Crusade, with its 800,000 members in three thousand Catholic educational institutions, could claim some credit for integration in Catholic schools. He conducted a vigorous educational program aimed at acquainting students with Catholic teachings about race and galvanizing them into concrete actions, such as raising money for black missions and signing petitions favoring the admission of qualified black students to their schools.[62]

Josephites in the South, particularly in New Orleans, also became more assertive. At Rummel's request, Edward Murphy, of Xavier University, arranged for meetings between leading white and black Catholics of the city in an effort to promote mutual understanding. Edward V. Casserly, of Corpus Christi Parish, protested to Rummel against the exclusion of black Catholics from religious functions and rallies, declaring that "the moral support of white Catholics in the South, especially in Catholic Louisiana, must be forthcoming if the Negro is to be brought . . . into the Church." When archdiocesan officials refused to allow black Catholics to participate on an equal footing with whites in the Holy Name rally on Palm Sunday, 1937, Joseph Van Baast and his assistant at St. Catherine's Parish in Donaldsonville boycotted the event, telling Monsignor Celestine Chambon, the chan-

62. William J. Walsh to John LaFarge, 1950, in Box 18-5, LaFarge Papers; Albert S. Foley, S.J., "The Catholic Church and the Washington Negro" (Ph.D. dissertation, University of North Carolina, 1950), 195–99; Roy J. Deferrari, *Memoirs of the Catholic University of America, 1918–1960* (Washington, D.C., 1960), 283–87; Louis B. Pastorelli to Mr. Chairman, Very Reverend and Right Reverend Fathers, [1937?], copy in PMC; C. Joseph Neusse, "Loss and Recovery of Interracial Virtue: Desegregation at The Catholic University of America" (Paper presented at the annual meeting of the American Catholic Historical Association, Washington, D.C., December 28–30, 1987), 10–22; Gillard, *Colored Catholics*, 246–48; Richard A. Lamanna and Jay J. Coakley, "The Catholic Church and the Negro," in Philip Gleason (ed.), *Contemporary Catholicism in the United States* (Notre Dame, 1969), 155.

cellor of the archdiocese, "If you do not want our people, you do not want us."[63]

The letter from the Consistorial Congregation also helped spark a great increase in the number of priests and sisters engaged in the black apostolate. In 1928, 196 priests, along with 829 sisters who constituted the backbone of the mission schools, worked exclusively with blacks; by 1940, the figures had risen to 486 priests and 1,670 sisters. By 1940, members of twenty-two religious communities of men, plus the diocesan clergy, and seventy-two communities of women labored on black missions, as opposed to only nine communities of men and thirty-two of women in 1928. Of the male religious communities in 1940, the 153 men of the Josephites maintained the largest number of missions: 102, or 30 percent of the total. The diocesan clergy ranked second, claiming 72 priests and 63 missions (though half of those missions represented only part-time responsibility). Next came the Holy Ghost Fathers, with 62 priests and 48 missions; the Divine Word Missionaries followed, counting 54 priests in charge of 19 missions. The Franciscans Minor counted 21 priests and 13 missions; the Jesuits, 16 priests and 15 missions; the Redemptorists, 16 priests and 11 missions; and the Society of African Missions, 19 priests and 10 missions. The others had 10 or fewer priests and missions. Not surprisingly, given the increased missionary activity during the decade of the thirties, the number of black Catholics increased from approximately 200,000 to about 250,000, up 25 percent. During that same period, the annual number of black converts jumped from roughly 3,000 to nearly 6,000.[64]

Competition with other religious communities entering the field remained a constant worry for Louis Pastorelli during the remainder of the decade. Addressing the 1936 general chapter following his reelection to a fourth term as superior general, he reviewed the previous six years, noting that the total of Josephite priests had jumped from 84 to 125, that half of all Josephites had been ordained since 1926, and that adult conversions had averaged 1,000 per year and

63. Edward Murphy to Louis B. Pastorelli, December 18, 1936, in 56-M, Edward V. Casserly to Archbishop Joseph Rummel, November 30, 1936, copy in 66-D, Joseph Van Baast to Louis B. Pastorelli, November 20, 1937, in 57-T, all in JFA.

64. Gillard, *Colored Catholics*, 180–82, 191. See also Lamanna and Coakley, "The Catholic Church and the Negro," in Gleason (ed.), *Contemporary Catholicism in the United States*, 169–74.

infant baptisms 3,289. Even so, Pastorelli warned, the Josephites could not rest on laurels from the past, when they had had the field practically to themselves, for a new group of bishops "knew not Joseph" and wanted only "results," in the form of conversions. "Rome as you know," he explained to one of his priests, "is and has been for the past decade, urging the bishops to greater activity with the Negro in mind," which accounted for bishops who seemed dissatisfied with the number of converts garnered by Josephites. Responding to yet another Pastorelli letter urging more converts, Joseph Lally attributed his lack of conversions to resentment against the Catholic church as "the white man's church" and wrote bluntly, "Until the Church gets liberal in her attitude towards the Colored Catholic priesthood, conversions will not be numerous here."[65]

Although Pastorelli recognized the truth of Lally's statement and privately acknowledged the need for St. Joseph's Society eventually to develop black priests of its own, he envisioned a slow and gradual process. During his last term as superior general, he showed a greater willingness to receive and consider applications from blacks, especially those recruited and recommended by the society vocation director, the rector of Epiphany Apostolic College, or Josephite pastors. Caucasian features, in addition to moral and intellectual attributes, remained an important consideration in any judgment on the suitability of prospective black students. After a vocation lecture at Boston College High School in April, 1938, for example, Arthur O'Leary, the master of novices and the vocation director, reported to Pastorelli that he had interviewed "a colored boy who was above the average Negro in intelligence" but who, unfortunately, "had more of the African in his make-up than of the Caucasian."[66]

Pastorelli oversaw every stage of the application process and made the final decision on all black applicants. In the end, for various and sundry reasons ranging from perceived academic deficiencies to the lack of a Catholic tradition in the family or failure to hail

65. Minutes of the general chapters, July 8, 1936, Louis B. Pastorelli to Edwin Youngkin, June 1, 1939, copy in 60-W, Joseph Lally to Louis B. Pastorelli, February 18, 1937, in 57-K, all in JFA.

66. Frank Robinson to Louis B. Pastorelli, October 5, 1938, in 58-N, Francis Schmutz to Louis B. Pastorelli, December 11, 1938, in 58-S, Michael J. O'Neil to Louis B. Pastorelli, February 16, 1939, in 60-N, Patrick Veale to Louis B. Pastorelli, December 9, 1939, in 60-T, Arthur O'Leary to Louis B. Pastorelli, April 30, 1938, in 58-N, all in JFA.

from a Josephite parish, Pastorelli judged all of the black applicants unsuitable. The lone exception was Percy Williams, a young man from a non-Josephite parish in Chicago, whom Pastorelli accepted into Epiphany College in August of 1941.[67]

Certain hopeful signs, however, seemed to indicate that Pastorelli could safely adopt a more liberal policy toward black students. As the nations lurched toward world war, Pope Pius XI and his successor, Pope Pius XII, challenged the barbarous racism of Nazi Germany and emphasized the essential unity of the human race in their respective encyclicals, *Mit brennender Sorge* in 1937 and *Summi Pontificatus* in 1940. A decree of the Sacred Congregation for Seminaries and Universities in 1938, which ordered a refutation of racism in seminary instruction, gave further evidence of papal hostility to this pernicious doctrine. In *Sertum Laetitiae*, his first letter to the American episcopate, written in 1939, Pius XII reaffirmed his "special paternal affection . . . for the Negro people" and gently prodded the bishops to give them "special care and comfort." On October 31, 1940, in a ceremony intended to emphasize the inclusiveness of the church and the divine unity of all races and the pope's personal commitment to indigenous clergy, Pius XII purposely selected representatives from twelve different national and racial groups for consecration as bishops.[68]

In the United States the number of black priests increased, as did the number of seminaries admitting Afro-Americans. The Divine Word Missionaries ordained 2 black priests in 1937 and 5 more in 1939. By January, 1941, the Society of the Divine Word in the United States counted 14 black priests among its members. In 1939, under Abbot Alcuin Deutsch, St. John's Abbey Seminary in Collegeville, Minnesota, began to accept black students to study for the Benedictine order. In addition, one of the abbey monks, Father Gregory, proposed establishing an interracial Benedictine monastery in the South. In that same year, the Jesuits welcomed Leslie Xavier Russell, a black man, into their society and educated

67. Francis Schmutz to Louis B. Pastorelli, April 12, 1939, in 60-S, August 6, 1941, in 64-S, both in JFA; Louis B. Pastorelli to J. W. Roddix, August 30, 1941, Louis B. Pastorelli to Charles Michael, December 9, 1941, copies of both in PMC.

68. NCE, XII, 56; Lamanna and Coakley, "The Catholic Church and the Negro," in Gleason (ed.), *Contemporary Catholicism in the United States*, 158; Stephen Neill, *A History of Christian Missions* (Rev. ed.; Harmondsworth, Eng., 1986), 389; Archbishop Samuel Stritch and Bishop Emmet Walsh to Thomas Wyatt Turner, November 29, 1939, copy in Thomas Wyatt Turner Papers, MSRC.

him at their theologate in Weston, Massachusetts, for service in the British West Indies. The following year, at the urging of LaFarge, the California province of the Jesuits accepted a black candidate for the brotherhood. Chicago's new archbishop Samuel A. Stritch, who succeeded Cardinal Mundelein in December, 1939, showed none of his predecessor's reluctance to accept black Divine Word missionaries into his archdiocese. Accordingly, when Vincent Smith was appointed assistant pastor at St. Elizabeth's Parish in the autumn of 1940, he became the first black priest to work in the archdiocese of Chicago since Augustine Tolton. Two years later, Stritch approved the admission of the first black student into the archdiocesan seminary.[69]

Despite the apparent progress on a number of fronts, Pastorelli remained fearful about Josephite vulnerability to the whims of the bishops. "We are outsiders," he never ceased telling his Josephites, "and hence must take care of ourselves, if we don't the diocese never will." He drew no particular consolation from the ordinations of Divine Word priests. He knew that the ordinations in 1937 and again in 1939 had necessitated the creation of new parishes in the Lafayette diocese to accommodate the black priests, and he believed that southern bishops had neither the money nor the inclination to continue creating new parishes in order to provide places to station black priests. Then, too, Jeanmard remained the only southern bishop to accept black clergy into his diocese. Although by 1941 the Divine Word Missionaries could boast of 14 black priests, 9 of the 10 priests assigned to mission churches in the United States found themselves in the Lafayette diocese.[70]

Moreover, Pastorelli, along with many others, suspected that the decision in 1939 of Hugo Aubry, the Divine Word provincial, to send two black priests to the new missions in the Gold Coast in

69. Report of St. Augustine's Seminary to the Commission for the Catholic Missions Among the Colored People, November 22, 1941, in SASA; John LaFarge to Abbot Alcuin Deutsch, October 8, 1940, in Abbot Alcuin Deutsch Papers, SJAA; Foley, *God's Men*, 256; *Pilot* (Boston), May 22, 1948, clipping, J. H. Dolan to John LaFarge, May 15, 1940, both in Box 12-9, Edward J. Whelan to Francis J. Seeliger, May 18, 1940, John LaFarge to Francis J. Seeliger, May 20, 1940, [?] to J. H. Dolan, June 7, 1940, copies of all three in Box 12-11, all in LaFarge Papers; Foley, *God's Men*, 144, 285; Archbishop Samuel Stritch to Edward Kramer, October 14, 1944, copy in Samuel Cardinal Stritch Papers, AAC.

70. Louis B. Pastorelli to Edward Murphy, September 15, 1940, copy in 62-M, JFA; Bishop Jules Jeanmard to Mother Katharine Drexel, December 29, 1936, December 10, April 20, 1938, Bishop Jules Jeanmard to Bishop William D. O'Brien,

Africa stemmed, at least in part, from difficulties in finding them places to minister in the United States. Archbishop John J. Glennon of St. Louis, for example, had ignored Aubry's offer to send two black priests to St. Nicholas Parish in St. Louis. In the spring of 1939, notices went up at St. Augustine's Seminary asking for volunteers for mission work in Africa. Joseph Bowers and John Dauphine volunteered. On hearing that Dauphine, a former parishioner, would go to Africa, Joseph Lally expressed the skepticism and ambivalence felt by many. "I am elated," he wrote to John H. Gaspar, the rector of St. Augustine's, "that he is worthy of the great grace of a foreign mission vocation." He also added his reservations about the matter: "I am a bit disturbed. The thought persists that there is a great need of Negro priests in our own land, and that maybe the bishops will not accept any more, hence the decision to send the Negro priests to Africa."[71]

The decision to send men to Africa alarmed many students at St. Augustine's. A number of them, realizing that membership in the Society of the Divine Word would make them liable to mission duty abroad and wishing to remain in the United States to work among their own people, withdrew from St. Augustine's and applied to dioceses or other religious communities, including the Josephites. Sermons like the one preached by the Reverend Philip Keller on August 5, 1939, at the first mass of Carmen Chachere, a black Divine Word priest, in which Keller proclaimed his desire to see Father Chachere and all the other black priests depart for Africa, deepened the suspicions of many black Catholics that assignments to Africa resulted from white opposition to black priests in the United States. That same year, the Knights of Peter Claver authorized a committee, including their national chaplain Joseph Lally, to begin "propaganda for the acceptance of Negro priests throughout America." Regardless of whether concern about placing the black priests motivated the decision to send some men to Africa, Aubry felt enough anxiety about the matter to consider issuing a general

---

March 6, 1937, Bishop Jules Jeanmard to Hugo Aubry, June 25, 1938, Bishop Jules Jeanmard to Bishop William D. O'Brien, December 9, 1938, Bishop Jules Jeanmard to Ovide de St. Aubin, February 23, 1939, copies of all in Jeanmard Papers; Foley, *God's Men*, 137, 161; Report of St. Augustine's Seminary to the Commission, November 22, 1941; Gillard, *Colored Catholics*, 191.

71. Foley, *God's Men*, 206, 216; William Barnaby Faherty, S.J., "Breaking the Color Barrier," *Universitas*, XIII (Autumn, 1987), 19; Joseph Lally to John H. Gaspar, April 27, 1939, in SASA.

letter to the bishops of the United States asking whether they would accept black priests into their dioceses.[72]

The attitude of Monsignor Joseph M. Nelligan, chancellor of the archdiocese of Baltimore-Washington, demonstrated the serious qualms that many bishops and diocesan officials still had about black seminarians and priests. Nelligan wrote to Pastorelli in February, 1941, about Melvin Richardson, a black man who had left St. Augustine's Seminary because of his aversion to possible mission work in Africa and who had met with Nelligan to discuss the possibility of entering the diocesan priesthood. The chancellor asked Pastorelli whether he believed "that such a possibility might be entertained" and hastened to add, "It would certainly not work out in this jurisdiction." Pastorelli observed that "it is a problem when it comes to deciding just what to do about Colored students" and claimed that he did not know of a diocese in the United States where the young man could look for adoption. He suggested that Richardson try Trinidad.[73]

Pastorelli's desire to avoid trouble made him extremely cautious in handling the ordination on June 10, 1941, of Chester Ball, the first black Josephite ordained a priest since John Plantevigne in 1907. A native of Washington, D.C., and the first black ordained in the capital city, Ball studied at Epiphany Apostolic College in 1933, made his novitiate at Newburgh in 1934, and began his seminary course at St. Joseph's Seminary in 1935. He graduated from the Preacher's Institute at Catholic University in 1940 at the age of twenty-seven. Ball stood approximately six feet tall and fought a losing battle with obesity throughout his lifetime. His light skin enabled him to pass for white whenever he chose. He received holy orders along with nine other Josephites at the hands of John M. McNamara, auxiliary bishop of Baltimore and Washington. Although his first mass at St. Augustine's Parish in Washington, D.C., attracted a great crowd and special attention from the arch-

72. Foley, *God's Men*, 210; Joseph M. Nelligan to Louis B. Pastorelli, February 12, 1941, Louis B. Pastorelli to Joseph M. Nelligan, February 18, 1941, copy, Joseph M. Nelligan to Louis B. Pastorelli, February 19, 1941, all in 73-D, JFA; Bourges interview, July 11, 1983; Foley, *God's Men*, 209; resolution passed by the Knights of Peter Claver, n.d., copy, minutes of the house council, August 22, 1939, both in SASA.

73. Joseph M. Nelligan to Louis B. Pastorelli, February 12, 1941, Louis B. Pastorelli to Joseph M. Nelligan, February 18, 1941, copy, Joseph M. Nelligan to Louis B. Pastorelli, February 19, 1941, all in 73-D, JFA.

diocesan newspaper, the *Catholic Review*, the Josephites' *Colored Harvest* played down the event, giving Ball no more attention than any of the other ordinandi.[74]

When Pastorelli assigned Ball to St. Joseph's Church in Wilmington, he went out of his way to reassure Bishop Edmond J. Fitzmaurice of Wilmington: "There is a slight strain of Colored blood in him, but one would have to be told this to be aware of the fact." He emphasized that Ball possessed a fine character and that the seminary faculty had judged him "the best all around member of his class." Pastorelli advised the bishop that Ball would serve as assistant pastor in Wilmington for only one year, after which he would tour the South on the mission band. Ball's auspicious debut as a preacher won him accolades and helped ease some of Pastorelli's anxieties. Michael O'Neil of St. Vincent De Paul Parish in Washington, D.C., also gave him a positive report: "The Rev. Chester preached at our three sessions of the Novena yesterday and brought down the house. He ought to make a fine missionary."[75]

During his last term as superior general, Pastorelli found the burdens of office increasingly onerous. In addition, the death of John Gillard on January 13, 1942, from a coronary thrombosis deprived him of his closest aide and the society of its most articulate spokesman. Pastorelli mourned the loss of his friend, telling the Reverend J. B. Tennelly, secretary of the Negro and Indian Commission, that "were he alive today, I think that he would have been chosen as our new Superior." Instead, the general chapter, meeting on July 8 and 9, 1942, chose as the fifth superior general of St. Joseph's Society Edward V. Casserly, a veteran missionary who had spent most of his time working in parishes in New Orleans. Pastorelli became a society consultor and later accepted the post of rector at St. Joseph's Seminary in Washington, D.C.[76]

74. "Rev. Charles C. Ball, Negro, Is Ordained" and "Negro Priest Says First Mass," *Catholic Review* (Baltimore), June 20, 1941, clippings in Chester Ball file, JFA; "Ordinations, Professions, and Reception Add to Josephites," *Colored Harvest*, XXIX (August–September, 1941), 1.

75. Louis B. Pastorelli to Bishop Edmond J. Fitzmaurice, July 12, 1941, copy in 73-G, Michael J. O'Neil to Louis B. Pastorelli, July 14, 1941, in 64-N, both in JFA.

76. Obituary of John T. Gillard, January 15, 1942, in 65-F, JFA; Louis B. Pastorelli to J. B. Tennelly, June 5, 1942, copy in PMC; Louis B. Pastorelli to Reverend and Dear Father, July 14, 1942, copy in 65-N, Priest Assignment Book, 58, both in JFA.

Pastorelli had accomplished much as superior general, including shepherding his small society through wars and the Great Depression. During his twenty-four-year tenure, the number of priests in the society increased from 65 to 165, the number of parishes from thirty-four to seventy-two, and the number of souls under Josephite care from 27,912 to 83,987.[77] He built a new Epiphany Apostolic College and established a novitiate in Newburgh, New York; he also constructed a new St. Joseph's Seminary in Washington, D.C. The Holy See recognized the growth and achievements of the Josephites under Pastorelli by raising the society to the status of a pontifical institute in 1932. Despite his many accomplishments, however, Pastorelli ended his tenure as a prisoner of his fears and ambivalence about black priests in St. Joseph's Society. He had neither the inclination nor the will to alter the course that he had set back in 1918. Times had begun to change, but he could not. He left the initiative to others. Try as they might in succeeding years, though, Pastorelli's successors could not regain for the Josephites the leadership in developing black clergy.

On receiving word of Pastorelli's imminent departure as superior general, Bishop Jules Jeanmard, reflecting the sentiments of many bishops, expressed his regret at seeing Pastorelli leave office and praised him for having "understood so well the problems and difficulties of the work in the deep-South." He thanked Pastorelli for his sympathetic cooperation and said frankly, "I cannot but be a little anxious about your retirement from office and the changes it may bring about as we are concerned down here."[78] With Edward V. Casserly as the new superior general of the Josephites, the bishop and the Josephites had good reason to expect great changes.

77. Newspaper clipping in Louis B. Pastorelli file, JFA.
78. Bishop Jules Jeanmard to Louis B. Pastorelli, July 11, 1942, in 73-I, JFA.

Chapter IX

EDWARD V. CASSERLY: RECLAIMING
THE LEGACY, 1942–1948

I am much more afraid to have to face God on the basis of injustice in handling the problem than I am in having to face men on the charge of not giving sufficient consideration to matters of expediency as dictated by social conditions.

—EDWARD V. CASSERLY, MARCH 23, 1945

Edward V. Casserly served as superior general of the Josephites for only six years, from 1942 to 1948. During that brief span, however, he reclaimed for St. Joseph's Society the legacy of John R. Slattery by opening wide the doors of Epiphany Apostolic College and St. Joseph's Seminary to black candidates. Personal conviction, changing social conditions, the willingness of key bishops in the South to accept black priests, and the support of new generations of Josephites who had not experienced such traumas of the early twentieth century as Slattery's defection and John Plantevigne's breakdown enabled Casserly to move decisively where Pastorelli had temporized. By freeing St. Joseph's Society from the cloud that had hung over it for more than thirty years, Casserly revitalized the Josephites, enabling them to become more effective collaborators with the black people whom they served and more effective spokesmen for racial justice in church and society. His abrasive personality cost him re-election as superior general in 1948, but Casserly's successors were able to continue and expand upon his policy of opening the society to black aspirants.

The return of substantial numbers of black students to Epiphany College and St. Joseph's Seminary after the midforties reflected, at least in part, the gains in status registered by Afro-Americans in the

United States as a result of World War II. The contradiction between fighting for the Four Freedoms against the Nazi master race and maintaining segregation in the United States became more apparent and helped to erode racism's respectability. During the war, the U.S. army integrated its officer training program; the marine corps and the U.S. navy enlisted blacks for duties other than messman. The wartime labor shortage and a threatened march on Washington organized by A. Philip Randolph in 1941 led to President Roosevelt's Executive Order 8802, which established the President's Committee on Fair Employment Practices. As a result, blacks made significant gains in employment and income throughout the war.

After the war, black organizations, most notably the NAACP, pressed more vigorously for full equality, in particular by launching an assault on segregation in the armed forces and in public education. In those efforts they were aided by political, civic, labor, and religious groups and, most important, by the executive and judicial branches of the United States government.

During the late forties, blacks breached the color barrier in numerous fields. Negro firsts included Jackie Robinson's desegregation of the National League in baseball and rise to stardom with the Brooklyn Dodgers and the integration of the U.S. armed forces as a result of Harry S. Truman's executive order. The number of black registered voters in the South jumped from 250,000 in 1940 to over 1,000,000 in 1950, and black leaders claimed that the black vote in the North swung the 1948 election to Truman. The number of blacks attending colleges soared from about 20,000 in 1930 to over 113,000 in 1950.

The spectacular growth of the Gross National Product in the postwar years made possible increasing income, entrance into some industries and labor unions previously closed to blacks, and gains in occupational status. The urbanization of blacks continued in both the North and the South. Over 1,000,000 blacks left the South in the 1940s, increasing the national scope of the race problem. The New Deal and World War II, moreover, weakened localism and decentralization, which had always stood as barriers to federal action on behalf of black civil rights or economic opportunity. Nazi brutality and the decline of the European colonial empires further discredited white supremacy, and racial egalitarianism became a major theme in the nation's media and schools.

The advent of the Cold War, which eventually involved competition with the Soviets for the hearts and minds of the people of the

Third World, underscored the danger that racism at home posed to U.S. security interests abroad. Many black leaders and their liberal allies, beguiled by the apparent advances of the decade, believed that continued and automatic progress to a new day of racial justice in the United States would require only a little more political pressure or legal action. Racial justice in American society, however, would prove more elusive and difficult to achieve than they had thought.[1]

World War II served as another rite of passage for American Catholics, as they once again demonstrated their patriotism. Educational, financial, and occupational mobility characterized many Catholics after the war, for they took advantage of the GI Bill and the financial and occupational gains made by organized labor during the New Deal and war years. Socially and politically more conservative than during the thirties, Catholics focused on such issues as anticommunism, Catholic education, and birth control; like their fellow white Americans, they paid relatively little attention to the problems of blacks. Following race riots in Detroit, the Catholic bishops, in their pastoral letter of 1943, emphasized the nation's obligation to recognize the political, educational, economic, and social rights of blacks. In most Catholic churches, though, blacks felt constrained to worship separately from whites.[2]

In spite of the persistence of apathy and racism, conceptions of the church as individualistic, which had been dominant throughout the nineteenth century and well into the twentieth, began to yield to a movement characterized by a new awareness of the corporate nature of the church as the Mystical Body of Christ, in which, in the Pauline phrase, "members were one of another." Especially after the issuance of Pius XII's encyclical *Mystici Corporis* in 1943, "the movement functioned as a quiet but effective leaven in the practical and intellectual life of the Church." It promoted a serious concern for the role of the laity in strengthening that body of Christ on earth—a concern that manifested itself in race relations, particularly in the activities of members of Catholic interracial coun-

1. Harvard Sitkoff, *The Struggle for Black Equality, 1954–1980* (New York, 1981), 11–15, 19; John Hope Franklin and Alfred A. Moss, Jr., *From Slavery to Freedom: A History of Negro Americans* (6th ed.; New York, 1988), 385–435; Richard M. Dalfiume, "The Forgotten Years of the Negro Revolution," *Journal of American History*, LV (June, 1968), 90–106.

2. James Hennesey, S.J., *American Catholics: A History of the Roman Catholic Community in the United States* (New York, 1981), 280, 283, 285–87, 304.

cils, the Catholic Worker and Friendship House movements, and the Catholic Committee of the South.[3]

Concerned clergy and laity waged successful campaigns against the color line at a number of Catholic institutions during the forties, one of the most widely publicized the desegregation of St. Louis University in 1944. Although the Catholic bishops as a body failed to follow the lead of the Federal Council of Churches, which in 1946 denounced segregation as a violation of the Christian gospel, individual prelates, such as Archbishops Joseph E. Ritter of St. Louis and Patrick O'Boyle of Washington, D.C., desegregated Catholic schools in their see cities in 1947 and 1948, respectively. Continuing a trend begun in the thirties, the number of clergy working in the black apostolate increased during the forties, as did the number of black seminarians, sisters, and priests. Still only a token few, nevertheless, the thirty-five black priests working in the United States in 1949 represented approximately a sixfold increase over the number in 1935.[4]

Casserly took advantage of the changes occurring within American society and the church. Unhindered by the fear that had gripped Pastorelli, convinced that justice demanded opening Epiphany College and St. Joseph's Seminary to blacks, and confident that bishops would accept black Josephites into their dioceses, he moved decisively to reclaim Slattery's heritage for St. Joseph's Society.

Forty-six years old at the time of his election as superior general, Edward Casserly differed markedly in appearance, background, and outlook from the society's godfather for the previous twenty-four

3. Sydney E. Ahlstrom, A Religious History of the American People (New Haven, 1972), 1014–15; Hennesey, American Catholics, 305; William A. Osborne, Segregated Covenant, Race Relations and American Catholics (New York, 1967), 38–39; Katherine Martensen, "Region, Religion, and Social Action: The Catholic Committee of the South, 1939–1956," Catholic Historical Review, LXVIII (April, 1982), 249–67.

4. Hennesey, American Catholics, 304–306; Barbara Jean Clay, "Desegregation of Catholic Schools in the District of Columbia from 1930 to 1950" (M.A. thesis, Howard University, 1961); William Barnaby Faherty, S.J., "Breaking the Color Barrier," Universitas, XIII (Autumn, 1987), 18–21; Donald J. Kemper, "Catholic Integration in St. Louis, 1935–1947," Missouri Historical Review, LXXIII (October, 1978), 1–22; "The Work of the Catholic Church Among the Negroes of the United States" (Report issued in Rome by the Fides Documentation Agency of the Society for the Propagation of the Faith), in Box 20-5, John LaFarge Papers, GUA.

years. The son of Irish immigrants, Casserly was tall and handsome, possessing finely chiseled features and a shock of thick, slightly graying hair, which he parted down the middle. He entered Epiphany Apostolic College in Baltimore in 1915, following graduation from high school in his hometown of Jersey City, New Jersey, and a three-year stint working for a manufacturing firm in New York City. By the time of his ordination in 1921, he had earned B.A., M.A., and Bachelor of Sacred Theology degrees from St. Mary's Seminary and University. After a series of temporary assignments as associate pastor in North Carolina, Tennessee, Louisiana, and Texas, he took up a teaching post at Epiphany from 1923 to 1925. In 1926, Pastorelli reassigned him to Josephite headquarters in Baltimore, where he taught at St. Joseph's Seminary and edited *Colored Harvest*.

A year later, Casserly traveled to New Orleans, where he was to spend the next fifteen years. He served first as chaplain and professor of philosophy and religion at Xavier University, where he remained for five years, during the last two of which he also served as pastor of Blessed Sacrament Parish. In 1934, he left Blessed Sacrament to become pastor of St. Peter Claver Parish in the same city; he also accepted a part-time teaching assignment at the Dominican St. Mary's College. From 1937 to 1942, he shepherded Corpus Christi, the largest of the Josephite parishes. While pastor there, he unsuccessfully pressed Archbishop Rummel to end the practice of requiring black parishes to march at the rear of the annual Holy Name parade. For his efforts, he drew a mild rebuke from Pastorelli, who accused the "lads down there" of trying "to put spokes in the wheel." In all of his parish assignments, Casserly displayed a talent for financial management. When he departed St. Peter Claver Parish in 1937, for example, he left a balance of $6,000 in the society's favor, no mean feat during the Great Depression. Amid all of his other duties and activities, he also helped found the New Orleans chapter of the National Urban League.[5]

Unlike Pastorelli, and many other Josephites for that matter, Casserly valued advanced education and believed strongly in gradu-

5. Biographical and assignment sheets, in Edward V. Casserly file, JFA; interview of Eugene P. McManus, S.S.J., by Stephen J. Ochs, September 9, 1983; Louis B. Pastorelli to Edward V. Casserly, December 8, 1941, copy, Edward V. Casserly to Louis B. Pastorelli, February 17, 1941, both in 63-C, obituary in Edward V. Casserly file, all in JFA.

ate training for the Josephites who staffed the society's educational institutions. An intensely inquisitive man who read voraciously and possessed a remarkable memory, Casserly had little patience with those whom he considered his intellectual inferiors. Commenting on the quality of Josephite seminarians in 1931 to Pastorelli, for example, Casserly made a characteristically blunt observation: "I knew them before you did when they started at Walbrook [Epiphany Apostolic College]. Positively, they were the dumbest set that ever entered to my knowledge." Casserly vehemently criticized the poor quality of teaching at Epiphany. He urged Pastorelli to encourage graduate studies for Josephites who had been designated to teach, in order to ensure quality faculties for Epiphany College and St. Joseph's Seminary and also to provide a pool of teachers for a high school and college for blacks that he hoped to see constructed in New Orleans. Burned by previous experiences with men he had sent to graduate school, one of whom had secretly married and fathered two children while still in the society, Pastorelli ignored Casserly's plea. Once Casserly became superior general, however, he realized his goal of sending men to graduate school.[6]

His undeniable intelligence, integrity, and talent notwithstanding, Casserly dealt with his Josephite subordinates highhandedly, barking out orders with no apparent consideration for their feelings. His men respected him, but many came to resent his gruff, domineering, autocratic style and his perceived lack of empathy for the difficulties faced by the men on the missions. To his female secretary and other women on the staff at Josephite headquarters, though, Casserly showed another side of his personality, blending high expectations with kindness and courtesy. Casserly also won the loyalty and admiration of George F. O'Dea, his young assistant and a future superior general, whose strong personality enabled him to stand up to his boss and establish a relationship of mutual trust and respect. Pastorelli cautioned Casserly about his hard-driving ways a year before Casserly's election to superior general. Hardly a soft touch himself, Pastorelli advised Casserly not to "drive but coax men under you to do their work" and to "forget the New York boss pattern." He continued, "Your heart is big but you do wish at

6. Interview of James F. Didas, S.S.J., by Stephen J. Ochs, October 7, 1983; Edward V. Casserly to Louis B. Pastorelli, July 2, 1931, June 25, 1930, copy, both in 51-C, JFA; interview of Peter E. Hogan, S.S.J., by Stephen J. Ochs, December 29, 1982.

times to throw fear into others, don't do it."[7] The "New York boss" served only a single six-year term as a result of his abrasiveness. Yet some of the very personality traits that angered his fellow Josephites also enabled him to stand up to southern bishops in a way that Pastorelli never could.

Casserly came from a different generation than Pastorelli. Entering the seminary in 1915, he did not experience firsthand, as had Pastorelli, the shock of Slattery's departure, the near destruction of the society, and the agonies of John Dorsey and John Plantevigne at the hands of southern bishops. As superior general, Casserly showed himself far more willing than Pastorelli had been to defend his increasingly outspoken missionaries against southern bishops. Of course, unlike Pastorelli, he had inherited a strong and healthy society from his predecessor. As of May, 1943, for example, the Josephites boasted 172 priests and 112 mission units distributed throughout the archdioceses of Boston, Baltimore, New Orleans, and San Antonio and the dioceses of Wilmington, Richmond, Raleigh, St. Augustine, Mobile, Natchez, Alexandria, Lafayette, Galveston, Dallas, and Nashville. The Josephites cared for over 80,000 parishioners and educated, in collaboration with 284 sisters and 54 lay teachers, 15,498 students in sixty-eight parochial schools. They could also point proudly to a "harvest" of 32,705 converts brought into the church during their fifty-year existence.[8]

No doubt many converts were impressed by how closely Josephites identified with their parishioners. Most black Catholics apparently respected the white Josephite priests who served them in their parishes. When they complained about whites, they usually exempted their priests and sisters from criticism. "They were different . . . from the people downtown," one black Catholic remembered, "because they lived among us . . . worked for us . . . and . . . educated us." At a time when towns such as Beaumont and Port Arthur provideded no recreational facilities for blacks,

7. Interview of Joseph L. Waters, S.S.J., by Stephen J. Ochs, August 10, 1983; Didas interview, October 7, 1983; interview of Agnes Rembus by Stephen J. Ochs, July 9, 1983; interview of George F. O'Dea, S.S.J., by Stephen J. Ochs, August 10, 1983; Louis B. Pastorelli to Edward V. Casserly, July 5, 1941, in Edward V. Casserly-Thomas P. McNamara Papers, JFA.

8. "Chronology of St. Joseph's Society," [prepared for Archbishop Amleto Cicognani in 1943?] (Typescript in Casserly-McNamara Papers); "Josephite Fathers to Hold Golden Jubilee," Baltimore Afro-American, October 9, 1943, clipping in Casserly-McNamara Papers.

Josephite parish basketball courts, bingo games, and dances answered a crying need in many black communities. Joseph Lally and other priests like him bailed men out of jail, interceded with local police on behalf of black youths arrested unfairly, and found jobs for unemployed parishioners.[9] Much to the annoyance of some southern bishops, Josephite missionaries in the 1940s became more vocal in their denunciations of the injustices that burdened the lives of their people.

In Casserly, activist Josephites found a sympathetic protector. For example, when Archbishop Rummel notified the superior general in November, 1942, that he had received complaints about Charles Morrissey at St. David's Parish in New Orleans, Casserly defended his man by describing to Rummel the dilemma that Josephites on the missions experienced. On the one hand, he pointed out, the Josephite had to "be an astute diplomat," trying to avoid offending neighboring pastors who served whites and to please not only the bishop under whom he worked but also his superior general. A white man, he had "to think colored," for if he said nothing about the injustices suffered by his people for fear of stirring them up, "he is accused by the Negro of being unsympathetic and unfaithful to the cause he is supposed to have espoused." On the other hand, Casserly noted, if the Josephite denounced segregation, "he is blacklisted as a 'troublemaker'" by other priests and by the bishops. Signaling his sympathy for a more activist approach by his priests, Casserly explained to Rummel that the Josephite should "be like his Master, who spoke not only the Beatitudes, but also denounced the Scribes and Pharisees."[10]

In early 1943, Joseph Hennessy's denunciation of racism in the diocese of Mobile led to a confrontation between Casserly and the imperious bishop Thomas J. Toolen that tested the Josephite superior's ability and resolve to defend his missionaries. A paternalist who regarded himself as an expert on blacks because of the many churches, schools, and hospitals he had built for them, Toolen insisted on maintaining segregation in diocesan institutions so as not to incur the hostility of white Alabamians. Hennessy, the Josephite pastor of St. John the Baptist Parish in Montgomery, angered

9. Interview of Rawlin B. Enette, S.S.J., by Peter E. Hogan, S.S.J., March 9, 1971 (Typescript in JFA), 1–3; interview of Bishop Eugene A. Marino, S.S.J., by Stephen J. Ochs, December 6, 1983.

10. Edward V. Casserly to Archbishop Joseph Rummel, October 24, 1942, copy in Casserly-McNamara Papers.

Toolen by taking the floor at a clerical conference in Birmingham and specifying to the gathered priests several easily correctable practices that hindered the conversion of blacks. He recommended that priests avoid using the word *nigger*, that they remove signs in their churches that read "For Colored," and that *Catholic Week*, the diocesan newspaper, change its editorial policy concerning blacks. The discussion that ensued focused on Hennessy's third point.

Subsequent to the clergy meeting, on January 23, 1943, Hennessy had written to Bishop Toolen, calling his attention to the lead editorial in the January 22 edition of *Catholic Week*. Entitled "A Platform for Racial Peace," it reprinted a speech given by Governor Charles P. Aycock of North Carolina in 1901 that called segregation essential for good will, mutual respect, friendship, and cooperation between the races. Hennessy condemned the reprint as heretical and also complained that the paper refused to capitalize the word *Negro* in its editorials, something that even the prejudiced Montgomery *Advertiser* did. Toolen responded with a blistering letter in which he accused Hennessy of lacking respect for his episcopal office and failing to appreciate his efforts to evangelize blacks. The bishop also told Hennessy that he wanted to replace him with a "more experienced man." Hennessy sent copies of the *Catholic Week* editorial and his correspondence with the bishop to Casserly.[11]

In marked contrast to his predecessor's almost abject servility to bishops' demands for the removal of Josephites from their dioceses, Casserly went on the offensive. Referring to Toolen, Casserly told Hennessy that he "was tempted to ignore the whole matter until such time as he wrote me but on second thought I decided to get in a whack first." He cautioned Hennessy, nonetheless: "If we lick this uprising, don't you fellows get the idea that I am always going to bat for you no matter what the charge is. I could make the Society very much *non grata* and we can't afford anything like that. We have to live with some folks in this world." He informed Toolen that he had learned from Hennessy that the bishop wanted the priest's removal. Casserly reviewed Hennessy's solid record, praised his sincerity, and pointed out that while Hennessy was serving successfully in the Natchez diocese, he had enjoyed the complete confidence of Bishop

11. Joseph Hennessy to Edward V. Casserly, January 29, 1943, Joseph Hennessy to Bishop Thomas Toolen, January 23, 28, 1943, copies, all in Casserly-McNamara Papers; "A Platform for Racial Peace," *Catholic Week* (Mobile), January 22, 1943, clipping in Casserly-McNamara Papers.

Richard Gerow. Casserly then came to the heart of the matter: "I don't think he is an agitator among the people. There are a number of priests I know who do not hesitate to speak openly before priests about what they regard as injustice. These same priests would be the last to agitate such things among the people they serve. . . . Fr. Hennessy is that kind." Casserly argued that Hennessy's removal would hurt the morale of both the mission and the man.[12]

Casserly won. On February 5, 1943, Toolen notified him of his willingness to allow Hennessy to remain at St. John's, "but only on the condition that there be no agitation." Toolen complained that Hennessy had expressed himself publicly on many occasions prior to the Birmingham clergy meeting about the unjust treatment of blacks in the South. He said Hennessy's comments at Birmingham were "uncalled for" and added that the FBI had investigated Hennessy because of his reputation as an agitator. Although he acknowledged that blacks suffered from injustice, Toolen yet decried agitation at that particular time. Claiming that no diocese in the country did more for blacks than Mobile, he warned that he would not allow agitators to upset the work.[13]

Casserly sent Hennessy a copy of Toolen's letter, cautioning him about probable FBI surveillance, since the bureau, bent on catching German spies attempting to foment race riots, had questioned and monitored the activities of other outspoken Josephites. "So for the time being," he advised, "you will have to confine your activities to bringing the Gospel to the Negro and the Negro to the Gospel." Casserly's stand against Toolen raised the morale of Josephites on the missions. Walter Mulroney, at Holy Family Parish in Natchez, for example, praised his superior for promoting Josephite unity and spirit and called his stand in the Hennessy case "splendid," though he also expressed fear that the willingness of such men as Hennessy to "slug it out with the bishops" might prove a problem.[14]

Casserly, however, exuded optimism. On the society's fiftieth anniversary in 1943, he wrote Lambert Welbers, the oldest surviving Josephite: "The work today is on a solid basis. It has attained a

12. Edward V. Casserly to Joseph Hennessy, February 2, 1943, Edward V. Casserly to Bishop Thomas Toolen, February 2, 1943, copies of both in Casserly-McNamara Papers.

13. Bishop Thomas Toolen to Edward V. Casserly, February 5, 1943, in Casserly-McNamara Papers.

14. Edward V. Casserly to Joseph Hennessy, February 11, 1943, Walter Mulroney to Edward V. Casserly, April 1, 1943, both in Casserly-McNamara Papers.

respect on all sides: from the people for whom we work—from the hierarchy and clergy—from those outside the fold. . . . I think the foundation is about completed, and we are now ready to begin the real work."[15] For Casserly, fostering black vocations for the Josephites lay at the heart of that real work.

In August, 1942, shortly after Casserly's election, Francis Schmutz, rector of Epiphany Apostolic College, informed him that Mike McCormack, the Josephite pastor of St. Theresa Parish in Orange, Texas, had recommended two black candidates from Texas for the college, one from Dayton and the other from Raywood. Schmutz noted that with seven new students going into first-year college or into the special Latin class reserved for those with weak Latin backgrounds and with ten students moving into the novitiate, only three students remained in the high school department of Epiphany from the previous year. The college would not even offer first or second year of high school for the approaching academic term. Schmutz commented, "It doesn't look so encouraging." That same month, Mulroney in Natchez also suggested a black candidate, this one with the enthusiastic backing of Bishop Gerow.[16]

Although Casserly wanted black students, he insisted that they possess the educational background required for success at the college. No doubt, he had in mind the case of Percy Williams, a black student Pastorelli had admitted who had only recently left Epiphany, at least partially because of educational deficiencies. Casserly hoped to avoid such situations in the future. Deciding that the students proposed by McCormack and Mulroney had "received insufficient education for admittance under our present conditions at the college," he turned down their applications. He hoped eventually to establish high schools staffed by Josephites in New Orleans, Baltimore, and Washington, D.C., to act as feeders for the college.[17]

Meanwhile, Casserly tried to find the qualified black candidates that he knew existed. In that effort, he relied for help on a new generation of Josephites, in the seminary and on the missions, who believed whole-heartedly in the desirability and necessity of black

15. Edward V. Casserly to Lambert Welbers, May 8, 1943, copy in Casserly-McNamara Papers.

16. Francis Schmutz to Edward V. Casserly, August 12, 1942, Walter Mulroney to Edward V. Casserly, August 26, 1942, both in Casserly-McNamara Papers.

17. Edward V. Casserly to Francis Schmutz, August 13, 1942, Edward V. Casserly to Joseph Hennessy, September 3, 1943, Edward V. Casserly to George Wilson, February 10, 1943, copies of all in Casserly-McNamara Papers.

Josephites. In February, 1943, Louis Jungman of Devine, Texas, sent a ten-dollar donation to the Josephites through Archbishop Robert E. Lucey of San Antonio "for the education of a Negro student." Casserly accepted the donation, explaining that though the Josephites had no black candidate in the seminary at the time, having ordained Chester Ball two years earlier, he expected that the Lord would "send us some in the future." Casserly did not have to wait long before he found some prospective black students. He placed the topic of a black student on the agenda of the April 8, 1943, meeting of the society consultors.[18] Several months later, another black applicant approached Casserly; he bore the familiar last name of Dorsey.

On July 16, 1943, Charles H. Dorsey, Jr., recently graduated from the eighth grade of St. Pius V School in Baltimore, asked Archbishop Michael Curley to sponsor him as a student at St. Charles College in Catonsville, Maryland, a preparatory seminary conducted by the Sulpicians that also served as the minor seminary for the archdiocese of Baltimore-Washington.[19] Dorsey was the grandnephew of the Reverend John Henry Dorsey and the grandson of C. Marcellus Dorsey, Pastorelli's old nemesis. Charles had applied to Curley at the behest of his grandfather, who wanted another priest in the family.[20]

Curley appeared more receptive to the idea of black priests, at least black Josephites, than he had previously. Writing in December, 1942, to H. M. Smith, president of the New Federated Colored Catholics of America, the remnant of Thomas Turner's original organization, Curley expressed the hope that "the Josephite Fathers will be able to get vocations from our colored boys . . . and that the day may soon come when we shall have . . . Negro priests who will cater to their own people." Curley's change of heart may have stemmed from a hope that black priests would serve as an antidote to radicalism in the black community. In a letter to the Reverend Aloysius Coogan, editor of *Catholic Missions*, for example, the

18. Edward V. Casserly to Louis Jungman, February 27, 1943, copy in Casserly-McNamara Papers; CMB, April 8, 1943, in JFA.

19. In 1939, the Holy See had added the name of Washington, D.C., to that of Baltimore in the title of the see. The complete separation of the two sees occurred six months after the death of Archbishop Michael Curley. On January 14, 1948, Patrick A. O'Boyle was installed as the first resident archbishop of the archdiocese of Washington, D.C.

20. Interview of Charles H. Dorsey, Jr., by Stephen J. Ochs, October 12, 1983.

staunchly anticommunist Curley fretted over what he saw taking place within that community: "The colored people were never more race conscious than they are at this time. Communism is making inroads into the race." [21]

Curley held conferences with George A. Gleason, the Sulpician rector of St. Charles College, and also with Casserly, who advised the archbishop that he should accept Dorsey if the boy wanted to join the archdiocesan clergy. Curley argued, however, that so young a boy as Dorsey could not endure the discrimination he would encounter at St. Charles College. Casserly thereupon agreed to accept him into Epiphany Apostolic College, and Curley promised to pay his tuition. [22]

On August 21, 1943, demonstrating the tight rein he held on society affairs and also his penchant for treating subordinates as errand boys, Casserly asked Timothy J. Holland, the vice-rector of Epiphany College, to send Dorsey a formal application blank, adding, "I have already accepted him as a student for first year high school work." During the summer of 1943, he also admitted a second black student, Dudley Darbonne from Beaumont, Texas. [23]

Casserly's moves delighted the young Turks among the Josephites, an increasingly significant group since two-thirds of all Josephite priests had been ordained since 1930. Joseph Hennessy also applauded Casserly's admission of Dorsey and Darbonne and made an optimistic prediction: "It should be easy to develop the 'Go to Epiphany' habit in New Orleans. Congratulations on our two new Negro students." He then added fervently, "God speed the day when we really have interracial education at St. Joseph's Seminary . . . and interracial rectories on the missions." The veteran missionary indicated, however, that not all Josephites shared his enthusiasm and that "some of the boys are worried about it." [24]

21. Archbishop Michael Curley to H. M. Smith, December 5, 1942, in S-1722, Archbishop Michael Curley to Aloysius Coogan, November 25, 1942, in C-1503, copies of both in AAB.

22. Charles H. Dorsey, Jr., interview, October 12, 1983; Archbishop Michael Curley to Charles H. Dorsey, Sr., July 21, 1943, copy in D-1139, Joseph M. Nelligan memorandum, August 10, 1943, in D-1140, both in AAB; O'Dea interview, August 10, 1983.

23. Edward V. Casserly to Timothy Holland, August 21, 1943, copy, Francis Schmutz to Edward V. Casserly, July 26, 1943, both in Casserly-McNamara Papers.

24. Edward V. Casserly to Edward Brunner, April 15, 1945, copy, Joseph Hennessy to Edward V. Casserly, August 25, 1943, both in Casserly-McNamara Papers.

The following summer, Casserly expanded his efforts to recruit black students for Epiphany Apostolic College. In a letter dated June 12, 1944, he urged Josephites "to be solicitous about vocations" and listed a series of virtues he believed his priests should watch for in prospective candidates, including thrift, humility, modesty, and obedience. He also advocated "a studied avoidance of the company of the opposite sex," attendance at mass, frequent reception of the sacraments, love of prayer, devotion, "no attraction for things of the world," and "a good Catholic background." He cautioned against soliciting individuals as candidates and counseled his men instead to keep the subject of priesthood alive in the minds of young people through vocation talks in the upper grades of parish schools, yearly vocation sermons, and confirmation preparation classes. "Encourage and nurture vocations when you detect them," he exhorted them, especially "through conferences, surveillance, and special care in confession." He approved the use of charity or parish funds in order to provide needed items for poor boys and girls preparing to enter religious houses of training. Those who lacked proper qualifications or anyone about whom the priests had the slightest doubts he adamantly insisted they discourage or refuse to sponsor.[25] Mike McCormack praised the letter, calling it "complete in every detail and a real guide for us on the missions in recommending an individual to our college or seminary rectors."[26]

Casserly's vocation letter set into motion a chain of events that climaxed in a struggle between him and Edward Brunner, his appointee as rector of Epiphany College, over the question of accepting black students. Casserly had sent Brunner to Epiphany as rector in 1943 "to tighten up" the institution. A tall, white-haired, distinguished-looking gentleman of sixty-three, who still wore spats on his shoes and suffered from a plethora of ailments, real and imagined, Brunner had served the society in a number of posts prior to 1943. Those included pastorates in New Orleans and rectorships of Epiphany and St. Joseph's Industrial School. He had also functioned as something of an apologist for Pastorelli's policies regarding black candidates, defending them in general chapters and in the "battle of the letters" with Jesuits William Markoe and John

25. Edward V. Casserly to Reverend and Dear Father, November 29, 1947, copy in Casserly-McNamara Papers. This 1947 letter repeated the points made in the letter of June 12, 1944, which I could not find.
26. Mike McCormack to Edward V. Casserly, June 17, 1944, in Casserly-McNamara Papers.

LaFarge in 1930. He commanded the respect of many Josephites, who chose him as a delegate to the 1942 general chapter. Unlike Schmutz, his immediate predecessor at the college, Brunner did not consider himself a rubber stamp for Casserly. During his second tour as rector of the college, he intended to run it his own way.[27]

Casserly and Brunner first clashed over black candidates in the summer of 1944. Taking their cue from Casserly's vocation letter, Josephite pastors encouraged young men from their parishes to request applications for admission to Epiphany. On June 9, 1944, with the approval and support of his pastor Father McCormack, Edward Satterfield of St. Theresa Parish in Orange requested an application from Brunner. Brunner sent all of Satterfield's correspondence to Casserly, noting that the young man's draft board had rejected him for "emotional instability." Impressed by Satterfield's "very intelligent letter," Casserly told Brunner that he saw "no indication of the trouble found by the Selective Service." In order to protect the society and to do justice to Satterfield, however, Casserly asked McCormack, Satterfield's former pastor Michael Flaherty, since stationed at Our Mother of Mercy Parish in Houston, and Roderique Auclair, who did not know Satterfield, to interview the young man. Upon receipt of their advice, Casserly informed Brunner, he would render a decision in the case.[28]

After meeting with Satterfield, both Flaherty and McCormack (Auclair could not attend) found him quite acceptable, though he did not have an encouraging family background. McCormack explained that "the primary reason for non-acceptance in the service was an active mind just a click ahead of the examining board, plus an answer to prayer." Casserly passed on the reports to Brunner, leaving the decision on Satterfield to the rector and the college faculty in accordance with paragraph fifty-five of the Josephite constitutions, which stipulated that the faculty make the final decision on admissions.[29]

27. Edward Brunner to Edward V. Casserly, July 24, 1943, Edward V. Casserly to Joseph Lally, July 8, 1944, copy, both in Casserly-McNamara Papers; interview of Mario Shaw, O.S.B., by Stephen J. Ochs, July 9, 1982.

28. Edward Brunner to Edward V. Casserly, June 9, 1944, Edward V. Casserly to Edward Brunner, June 12, 1944, copy, both in Casserly-McNamara Papers.

29. Michael Flaherty to Edward V. Casserly, June 24, July 5, 1944, Mike McCormack to Edward V. Casserly, July 4, 1944, Edward V. Casserly to Edward Brunner, July 7, 1944, copy, all in Casserly-McNamara Papers.

Brunner, however, had serious reservations about Satterfield. He demanded that the young man obtain a written opinion, from either the draft board or a reputable psychiatrist, stating that he possessed the emotional stability necessary for the priesthood. Brunner did not explain why he believed that a Texas draft board had the competence to render an informed judgment on the emotional requirements for priesthood. He claimed that "we are dealing with potential dynamite in the case of this young man" and cited the draft board's description of Satterfield as "decidedly allergic to group living." More important, he took exception to Satterfield's stated objections to joining the army because of his bitterness over the unjust treatment that blacks were receiving in the United States. Brunner considered such an attitude "thoroughly dishonorable," totally inappropriate in one who aspired to the priesthood, and indicative of a lack of humility; he regarded Satterfield as a potential "trouble making priest."[30]

Casserly's response revealed a vastly different perception of black people. Disagreeing with Brunner's assessment of Satterfield, Casserly said, "Frankly, I am inclined to favor his case." Satterfield's writing ability particularly impressed Casserly, the more so since the young man received his high school education in the generally poor schools of the South. Casserly quickly noted, however, that he did not consider intellectual ability the most important factor in judging a potential candidate for the priesthood. He referred to his letter on vocations sent the previous year, which emphasized spiritual qualities, including the virtue of humility. Casserly's definition of that virtue, however, differed significantly from Brunner's. "I should be slow to say," he argued, "that recognition by a Negro of the adverse conditions that he has had to face in the South and even in the North necessarily indicates that he lacks a proper humility. . . . The thinking Negro cannot help but have mental attitudes developed in him." Casserly expressed little surprise that Satterfield, like many black Americans, resented the injustices blacks had borne and therefore lacked sympathy for the war effort. Casserly sarcastically pointed out that apparently millions of whites, with far less reason than blacks, lacked complete sympathy for the war effort and that "soldiering is on a draft basis for that reason." He

30. Edward Brunner to Edward V. Casserly, July 8, 21, 1944, both in Casserly-McNamara Papers.

also questioned the objectivity of southern draft boards and speculated that Satterfield's board probably recognized him as the "type of Negro who might be troublesome to them later on if he could come home a veteran with an even better right to demand justice."

Dismissing Brunner's fear that Satterfield might become a troublemaking priest, Casserly approvingly predicted: "Some of our colored priests of the not so far distant future will do some complaining about the disabilities that are forced upon them, both civilly and ecclesiastically. That seems bound to come unless they adopt what the Negro calls 'Uncle Tom's' ways." He contended that an Uncle Tom posture would harm blacks and whites alike. "Unless the latter are jabbed from their smug complacency about wrong," he declared emphatically, "they will go down to hell . . . and the Negro will go along subject to the next generation." Casserly insisted that Epiphany College, Mary Immaculate Novitiate, and St. Joseph's Seminary would correct any tendencies toward twisted thinking in any Josephite candidate, black or white. He agreed, however, that Satterfield should produce a certificate of mental health from a competent psychiatrist in order to remove the stigma of rejection by the draft board. Once Satterfield secured the required certificate as Casserly had directed, Brunner was to submit the application to the faculty. Casserly reminded the rector that in the case of admissions, the faculty had a deliberative, not simply an advisory, vote.[31]

Brunner's alarm about Satterfield's application involved far more than concern about the qualifications of a particular applicant, however. The Satterfield application, and others like it, in Brunner's view represented a grave threat to the society. On July 26, 1944, Brunner reported to Casserly that Epiphany College had twenty-two students listed for the approaching academic year, with half a dozen other prospects, including two black applicants: Satterfield and Prentice Polk, a young man from Tuskegee whom the Reverend Leo Farragher had recommended highly. Brunner noted that if the college accepted Satterfield and Polk, it would then have four black students for the 1944–1945 school year. He therefore enclosed a separate letter on the issue of black students and requested that Casserly place it in the file "as my long considered—and much

31. Edward V. Casserly to Edward Brunner, July 24, 1944, copy in Casserly-McNamara Papers.

argued at Chapters—opinion on this problem—which is not ours but the bishops."[32] Brunner's letter signaled the beginning of the old guard's last stand.

Admitting that he now represented minority opinion within the society, Brunner marshaled the arguments of an older generation of Josephites against accepting black students. He reminded Casserly that fifty years earlier the Josephites under Slattery had taken up the cause of a "native colored clergy," but the results had not been good. He recalled the frustration and heartache that Slattery experienced because of his "uncompromising do-it-now determination" in fighting the bishops over black priests. Slattery learned, according to Brunner, a lesson that "many of our over-zealous and do-it-now advocates do not seem to know or properly consider: we . . . are not in charge of Dioceses and do not have the final say in the placing of men." As a result of that reality, he claimed, both John Dorsey and John Plantevigne had suffered emotional breakdowns. Brunner reaffirmed his desire for black priests but argued that, despite the expressed wishes of Rome, conditions had changed imperceptibly in the South. The Josephites, therefore, had little reason to believe that they could place black priests on southern missions once they educated and ordained them. He pointed out that only the diocese of Lafayette had a significant number of black priests, and those priests worked only in a solidly Catholic area. Brunner told Casserly that if he really believed conditions had improved, he could easily test the situation by sending Chester Ball to a southern diocese that had relatively few Catholics. "The result might be enlightening," Brunner observed, "but I do not think it would be good for the soul of the priest involved."

For the future welfare of the society and of the black men involved, Brunner advocated what he called "the only safe policy." He urged Casserly to tell any qualified black applicant that the Josephites would gladly admit and educate him at Epiphany Apostolic College and St. Joseph's Seminary, free of cost, "but only on condition that he come to us from a Bishop . . . who will accept him as his candidate whom he will ordain and incardinate into his diocese." Such a policy, he insisted, would clearly show where the Josephites stood on the issue and would place the burden "where it

32. Edward Brunner to Edward V. Casserly, July 26, 1944, in Casserly-McNamara Papers.

belongs without getting the Society into hot water with the authorities." Brunner stressed that the Josephites could not "go on accepting these young men without limit without knowing where they will be accepted."

Since he could not assemble the faculty for a decision on Satterfield because they were on summer vacation, Brunner interpreted Casserly's approval of the young man as settling the issue. He promised Casserly that he would send an application to Satterfield, along with a request for a statement from a psychiatrist. He also sent Casserly the correspondence from the black candidate recommended by Leo Farragher and characterized Farragher as writing "with all of the enthusiasm and inexperience of the zealous young missioner" and failing to take into account what would happen to the young man should he become a priest. "Let me have your decision," Brunner resignedly wrote Casserly. "I have already given mine."[33]

Casserly and Brunner continued to skirmish throughout the summer of 1944 as young Josephites such as Farragher and Harry Maloney of Corpus Christi Parish in New Orleans forced Brunner's hand by referring black candidates to the college. On August 5, 1944, Brunner sent Casserly the correspondence from two more black candidates and argued that, even if he could assemble them, the faculty of the college should not decide an issue "of such truly great import for the men concerned and for the Society." He repeated his arguments about the difficulties of placing black priests and, though agreeing with Casserly that ultimately the work of evangelizing the black race belonged to black people, observed that "the work is their work" but "the Society is not theirs, nor will the difficulties into which this may plunge the Society be theirs." He worried that "this thing may well cancel out our usefulness, if . . . we try to force the issue," and he warned that the Josephites could not afford to forget "that we are mere agents," working at the bishops' pleasure. To Casserly's assurances that when he went south he would sound out the bishops about their willingness to accept black priests, Brunner skeptically predicted that the superior would find "a great deal of hedging and dodging." Even if bishops gave favorable replies, Brunner cautioned, "their successors are not bound by them."

33. Edward Brunner memorandum, to Edward V. Casserly, July 26, 1944, in Casserly-McNamara Papers.

While requesting Casserly's definite opinion about the black applicants on hand and guidelines for dealing with any additional candidates, Brunner also recommended a solution to what he saw as a looming problem. He indicated that Epiphany College would probably have six black students in the fall and predicted that "new applicants will most certainly come next year, and the following years—till we might well have a large number here." In order to avoid such an undesirable situation, he recommended that the college inform any new black applicants that "OUR QUOTA IS FILLED" [Brunner's emphasis]. He asserted, however, that Casserly should not leave such a crucially important decision involving the future of the society in the hands of the faculty and rector; he even asked Casserly to excuse him from voting if the superior left the matter up to the college.[34]

In his reply, Casserly insisted that black applicants be given the same opportunity for admission as white applicants. He conceded the difficulty of assembling the college faculty during the summer months, when most applications arrived at the college, but suggested that the faculty consider those students "as being received only under special probation for the first year so that the real acceptance would come at the close of the first year at the college." Meanwhile, he and the faculty at Epiphany would have to rely on the integrity and common sense of the priests who recommended the black candidates "to keep us from being burdened with any who would not measure up." However, Casserly declared the standard that would be applied to every case: "It shall be our duty to make decisions that will be just to . . . the subject . . . and the . . . Society. We must face the issue with a Christian and priestly courage."

Turning to the individual black applicants, he instructed that Satterfield produce papers from a psychiatrist and that the other three, as required by the Josephite constitutions, take written examinations. These would be prepared by Epiphany faculty members on the major subjects the candidates had studied in school and would be administered in the rectories of their respective parishes. If time and circumstances made examinations seem impracticable for three of the applicants, Casserly recommended that "their in-

34. Harry Maloney to Edward V. Casserly, August 7, 1944, Edward Brunner to Edward V. Casserly, August 5, 1944, both in Casserly-McNamara Papers.

tellectual qualifications be determined during their probationary year at the college." With the faculty's recent decision to allow Dudley Darbonne to repeat a year because of academic difficulties still fresh in his mind, Casserly reaffirmed his conviction that students "should be dismissed unless they can make their grades from year to year." Brunner followed Casserly's instructions and informed the four black applicants that he would admit them on one year's probation, with definite acceptance contingent on their first year's performance.[35] By the end of the summer of 1944, it appeared that the superior general had conclusively resolved the issue.

Brunner, however, had not yet surrendered and continued to press for implementation of a quota system. At an October faculty meeting, he told his teachers that "the standard for the Colored students should be particularly high because of the greater difficulties and trials that will be theirs in the priesthood." On December 31, 1944, he notified Casserly that the faculty would drop Darbonne because of poor grades and insufficient intellectual ability. "We should have dropped him before this," Brunner wrote, "but, knowing the criticism we used to get in the past, whenever we dropped a colored boy, we gave him a chance, and then some, to make good." He also enclosed a letter from Rosamond Shaw (who later changed his first name to Mario) of St. John's Parish in Montgomery, asking for an application. Refusing to treat black applicants as he did white ones, Brunner told Casserly that he would not respond to Shaw until Casserly advised him what he wanted done in the case. Casserly declined to play Brunner's game, returning Shaw's letter to Brunner and reminding him that he need not submit each application from a black boy for approval. "It is quite proper," he wrote, "to handle them in the same way that you would handle applications that come from white boys through the medium of the whole faculty." Casserly conceded, though, that Brunner might well write to the pastors of black applicants for more detailed testimonials than were ordinarily required for white applicants.[36]

35. Edward V. Casserly to Edward Brunner, August 23, 1944, copy, Edward Brunner to Edward V. Casserly, August 25, 1944, both in Casserly-McNamara Papers. For whatever reason, Satterfield never enrolled in Epiphany College.

36. EAC faculty meeting minutes, October, 1944, p. 63, in JFA; Edward Brunner to Edward V. Casserly, December 31, 1944, Edward V. Casserly to Edward Brunner, January 4, 1945, copy, both in Casserly-McNamara Papers.

Shaw's experience with Joseph Hennessy, his pastor at St. John's in Montgomery, illustrates how some Josephites recruited black students from their parishes for Epiphany Apostolic College. One day in January, 1944, Hennessy asked Shaw, the fourteen-year-old son of a relatively prosperous, professional, black Catholic family and a junior in high school, to leave the classroom at St. John's for a drive into the country. As they drove, Hennessy talked about the racist editorials then appearing in the Montgomery *Advertiser* and asked why Shaw had not written any refutations. Hennessy also spoke about other problems facing blacks and the Josephite missionaries who ministered to them. He drove up to a one-room schoolhouse on a cotton plantation owned by the McLemore family. As they approached the school, Hennessy and Shaw could see barefoot and poorly clad men, women, and children working in the fields.

Moella Matthews, the teacher at the school, told Hennessy and Shaw that the children attended the twelve-grade school only on rainy days; on fair days they worked in the fields. Hennessy turned to Shaw and observed that the people on the plantation remained in a state of virtual slavery, bound to the land by debt and illiteracy. He asked Shaw what the young man planned to do about the situation. Shaw responded that in ten or fifteen years, presumably after he had made his fortune, he would give part of it to the church so that Hennessy could help them. Hennessy told Shaw that God needed committed people, not money. They got back into the car and motored toward Montgomery. As they drove back toward the city, Hennessy spoke to Shaw about the real happiness found in serving God by helping others. That night, Shaw decided to become a priest.[37]

Approximately three weeks after Casserly had told Brunner to proceed on the Shaw application, on January 23, 1945, the Epiphany College faculty devoted most of its meeting to discussing the issue of admitting black students. Brunner told the faculty that he had recently received three applications from black youths and that he projected several more before the next school year. Repeating his familiar argument that bishops would not accept black priests after ordination and that those priests' lives would become "discouraging and unbearable," he suggested that "a quota ought to be set on colored applicants in justice to the applicants themselves and to protect the future welfare of St. Joseph's Society." He reiterated,

37. Mario Shaw interview, July 9, 1982.

nevertheless, his willingness to accept any candidate sent by a bishop who offered to ordain him for his diocese. After presenting his views, Brunner then asked the faculty for their opinions.

The discussion revealed a generational split in the faculty, with a slim majority supporting Brunner. Timothy Holland, Harry Kane, Michael O'Brien, Lawrence MacClellan, and William McLane, all older priests, voiced their agreement with the rector, whereas Cornelius Sexton led the younger opposition. Sexton acknowledged the difficulties involved in accepting and training black students but argued that "we should consider primarily the supernatural element." He then appealed to their trust in God: "If God gives a vocation . . . we cannot justly turn them down merely because we have a certain number. We should trust God's Providence to take care of difficulties." Joseph Murphy, Edward Bowes, and Frank Dalsey seconded Sexton's argument, though Dalsey suggested that because of the greater difficulties that they would face as priests, the black applicants should meet higher intellectual and spiritual standards than the white students. Higher standards, he explained, would set a "natural quota." Brunner objected that a different standard for black applicants would give rise to the accusation of discrimination. The meeting closed with a majority concluding that the superior general and the council of consultors, rather than the faculty, should decide the question.[38]

The issue of a quota for black students became entangled with the application of Rosamond Shaw. By the middle of February, 1945, neither Joseph Hennessy, the pastor who had suggested that Shaw request an application and who had also personally written Brunner on the boy's behalf, nor Shaw himself had received a reply from the rector. On February 14, 1945, Hennessy complained to Casserly about the situation. Several days later, Casserly directed Timothy Holland, the acting rector of Epiphany College while Brunner recovered from an illness, to acknowledge receipt of the two letters. He instructed Holland, moreover, to have Shaw take a written examination, prepared by the college faculty, in the subjects for which he earned credits in high school. Holland explained to Casserly that part of his anxiety about an early decision on Shaw stemmed from his understanding that in 1943 Casserly had approved a quota system for the college that allowed for the admission of only a given number of black students. He confessed that he did

38. EAC faculty meeting minutes, January 23, 1945, pp. 71–73.

not know definitely whether Casserly had indeed established such a quota or what Casserly thought about "a large number of colored boys here." Holland described himself as agreeing with Brunner "that we hasten slowly with what we have until we see how they will turn out."[39]

Casserly attempted to dispel Holland's misgivings, especially his fear that the admission of large numbers of black students would alter the nature of the society. He admitted that Holland's understanding about a quota "was not totally in error," hastening, however, to explain that he meant a natural quota based on ability and qualifications. Casserly assured the acting rector that he need not fear "a revolutionary change in the color of the student body" if parish priests and faculty observed the conditions that the superior had set down for the admission of candidates. Through examinations by the college faculty, Casserly asserted, "we can very well control things so as to avoid any unfavorable situation." He insisted, however, that "in everything we shall be honest: with God, with ourselves, with the people we serve." He declared that he would consider expediency only as his last criterion, though he would consider it.[40]

Brunner formulated a very different definition of a quota, despite his earlier protestations that neither he nor the faculty should decide such an important issue. Beginning in March, 1945, he moved to implement his idea. At a faculty meeting on March 6, 1945, he argued that "the fact that Colored priests have not been accepted for the work in dioceses seems an indication from God that we should not freely take applications." He promised the faculty that when bishops agreed to accept black priests into their dioceses, he would gladly open the doors of Epiphany to a "limited number of qualified applicants." Later in the meeting, he also advised the faculty that he had prepared a questionnaire for black applicants. Its purpose was to gather information about the family background, the intentions, and the intellectual and spiritual qualifications of the applicant so that the college would have "some guarantee of the boy's stability and ability before accepting him."[41]

39. Joseph Hennessy to Edward V. Casserly, February 14, 1945, Edward V. Casserly to Timothy Holland, February 17, 1945, copy, Edward V. Casserly to Joseph Hennessy, February 17, 1945, copy, Timothy Holland to Edward V. Casserly, March 4, 1945, all in Casserly-McNamara Papers.

40. Edward V. Casserly to Timothy Holland, March 8, 1945, copy in Casserly-McNamara Papers.

41. EAC faculty meeting minutes, March 6, 1945.

On March 16, 1945, eleven days after Boston's archbishop Richard J. Cushing announced that his archdiocesan seminary would give equal consideration to every candidate, regardless of race, Brunner finally responded to Hennessy, and to the Reverend Edward Murphy of St. Peter Claver Parish in New Orleans, who had also written about a black candidate. Brunner attributed his delay in answering their letters to two factors: illness and "the pause given us by the number of colored applicants, now that it is rapidly being noised abroad that we are taking them." He noted that Epiphany Apostolic College had six black students at the moment and that he had five applications from blacks on his desk; he forecast that he would receive at least another dozen applications before September. Claiming that "the character of our Society is going to change radically if any large number are accepted" and that the men themselves did not want "to see the Society turned over" to blacks, Brunner informed Hennessy and Murphy that he had instituted "a limited quota, which is presently filled." He advised them that he would make exceptions only in the case of "a quite exceptional applicant . . . always conditioned, in our institution, by the quota." He asked Hennessy and Murphy to circulate his letter among Josephites in the South so that they would become aware of the attitude of the college. In a postscript to Murphy, Brunner concluded: "We can only be certain that God's providence is taking a hand when the Church authorities give the 'go' sign. They are the ordinary channels of God's will; and theirs is also the responsibility."[42]

On March 19, 1945, the Feast of St. Joseph, Brunner apprised Casserly of the quota, calling it "the only practical solution." According to George O'Dea, Casserly "hit the roof." Three days later, he brought Brunner's letter to the attention of the general council, which was composed of Louis Pastorelli, William Murphy, and Charles B. Winkler. They unanimously concluded that Brunner had exceeded his authority in setting a quota and decided, moreover, that "colored students are to be subjected to the same tests as the white students."[43]

42. "First Colored Priest in Boston to be Ordained," *Catholic Herald*, March 9, 1945, clipping in Black Priests file, JFA; Edward Brunner to Joseph Hennessy, March 16, 1945, Edward Brunner to Edward Murphy, March 16, 1945, both in Casserly-McNamara Papers.

43. Edward Brunner to Edward V. Casserly, March 19, 1945, in Casserly-McNamara Papers; O'Dea interview, August 10, 1983; CMB, March 22, 1945, pp. 20a, 21a, in JFA.

On March 23, 1945, Casserly notified Brunner of the council's ruling. He explained that neither he nor the council objected to the moral or intellectual qualifications that the rector specified, as long as they applied equally to both white and black candidates. "I had said as much," Casserly reminded him, "in a circular letter . . . on the subject of vocations." He told Brunner the council was of one mind in finding that the rector had exceeded his authority when he set a quota at the college, because the society constitutions conferred no such power on rectors of houses of training. In addition, Casserly pointed out, the constitutions did not allow the rector to act alone on the admission of even a single student but required him to obtain the deliberative vote of the faculty, though Casserly noted that he and Brunner agreed they could, in some cases, postpone that vote until the end of the student's first year at the college and consider the months previous to the vote a probationary period.

Casserly scolded Brunner for telling Murphy and Hennessy that the Josephites had no prospects of placing black priests after ordination. He reminded the rector that black priests already served in two dioceses where Josephites worked and informed him that when he directly proposed the appointment of black Josephites to parishes in New Orleans, Archbishop Rummel assured the superior general that he did not object. Casserly expressed confidence that "other dioceses in which we work will also accept colored priests for service and before the first candidate we have now will be ready for ordination—at least eight years—there will be more conversions if such are necessary among the bishops." He asked Brunner to make the proper retractions to the priests he had written, since Casserly did not want "to be forced to issue a letter to our whole membership going into these points." Spelling out his attitude in the matter, Casserly declared, "I am much more afraid to have to face God on the basis of injustice in handling the problem than I am in having to face men on the charge of not giving sufficient consideration to matters of expediency as dictated by social conditions and personal views of individuals."[44]

Brunner defended his action, claiming that he had not exceeded his authority, because a majority of the faculty had voted in favor of the quota. Instead, he questioned the authority of the superior general and the council to adopt on their own a new policy that would

44. Edward V. Casserly to Edward Brunner, March 23, 1945, copy in Casserly-McNamara Papers.

affect every member of the society. "I do not take second place to anyone in my desire to see a colored clergy," Brunner declared, "but I do not think there is any obligation whatever on St. Joseph's Society to turn itself over to them, as will inevitably happen, in the long run unless a quota is established." Brunner also complained bitterly, and with some justification, about the superior's unwarranted interference in the college, which included his selecting books for some courses. Brunner accused him of having developed "into just another Big Boss" like Pastorelli, and he asked that the superior not reappoint him as rector when his term expired the following year. Casserly obligingly informed Brunner that he had already decided against reappointment "because of your physical condition."[45]

Although a lame duck, Brunner remained a tenacious opponent, refusing to concede defeat. He told the college faculty on April 10, 1945, that "the matter of accepting Colored students has not been settled definitely" and asked the general council to reconsider its decision. Ironically, given Brunner's dire predictions about the difficulties of placing black priests, only five days before the faculty meeting, Archbishop Curley, who had not had a black priest stationed in his archdiocese since Father Dorsey's death in 1926, voiced "no objection whatsoever" to Casserly's appointment of Chester Ball as pastor of the Josephite mission in Glen Arden, Maryland. Brunner's objections to the admission of large numbers of black students, however, focused by then on the danger he believed they posed to the future identity and character of St. Joseph's Society.[46]

On May 6, 1945, at Brunner's request, the general council reconsidered the issue of a quota at Epiphany College and reaffirmed its original decision, explaining that the authority given by the constitutions to the rector and faculty regarding the admission of students had to do with individual applicants and did not refer to considerations of any particular group. The power to set policy belonged only to the general chapter, which selected a superior general and a general council to carry out the business of the society during the six-year intervals between chapter meetings. Along with

45. Edward Brunner to Edward V. Casserly, March 26, 1945, Edward V. Casserly to Edward Brunner, April 15, 1945, copy, both in Casserly-McNamara Papers.

46. EAC faculty meeting minutes, April 10, 1945, in JFA; Joseph M. Nelligan to Edward V. Casserly, April 5, 1945, Edward Brunner to Edward V. Casserly, April 19, 1945, both in Casserly-McNamara Papers.

news of the council's decision, Casserly sent Brunner five applications from blacks that he had held, pending the council's ruling. He claimed to have given "no consideration to the color of the applicants" and asked Brunner to "please give . . . each one, a just consideration." The five black applications, added to the seven already on his desk, appalled Brunner. He judged that only two of the five possessed "the necessary groundwork." But even more than that, he believed "no society anywhere takes up an unlimited number of a racial type, without soon finding the necessity of division." He assured Casserly, nevertheless, that he would submit all of the applications to the faculty. "I shall not treat them unjustly," he promised, "as I appreciate very keenly my responsibility."[47]

Casserly could not let Brunner's characterization of his policy stand unchallenged. "Our policy," he countered, "is definitely not 'unlimited' with respect to our acceptance of colored candidates." He pointed to the limits imposed by canon law, by the Josephite constitutions, and also by the academic examinations. "I do not think," he concluded, "that many will be able to get by these restrictions." In an apparent attempt to guarantee that the college would have some idea of the qualifications of black applicants and also to conciliate Brunner, Casserly added an additional restriction: the Josephites would consider only those black applicants who came from Josephite parishes. Casserly ordered Brunner to refer black applicants from non-Josephite parishes to the religious communities or diocesan seminaries of the priests who served them. The rule applied only to black students; all of the white students at Epiphany of course came from non-Josephite parishes. Casserly further assured Brunner that his fear about the society changing color would never materialize. He expressed the hope, however, that in time the Josephites would become international, or non-national, since "the communities that have become truly non-national are the strongest." Taking note of Brunner's report about a dearth of applications from white boys, Casserly recalled that from the beginning of his administration he had recognized the need for vocations and had ordered special prayers for that intention. He suggested to Brunner that the applications from boys of Josephite parishes, especially because they were black, indicated God's will and his answer to their prayers.[48]

47. Edward V. Casserly to Edward Brunner, May 6, 1945, copy, Edward Brunner to Edward V. Casserly, May 15, 1945, both in Casserly-McNamara Papers.
48. Edward V. Casserly to Edward Brunner, May 19, 1945, copy in Casserly-McNamara Papers.

Josephites on the missions who had qualified lads wanting to enter Epiphany Apostolic College attempted to enlist Casserly's help
in order to circumvent Brunner's obstructionism. Joseph Hennessy,
for example, fearing that Brunner might mistreat Rosamond Shaw
if he kept pressing the issue and also aware that Casserly had not
renewed Brunner's term as rector, convinced Shaw to enroll at
Xavier University for a year before applying again to Epiphany.
In the meantime, he put Shaw into contact with the Reverend
Thomas Dodd at St. Thomas Church in Metairie, Louisiana, a
close friend of both Hennessy and Casserly. In December, 1945,
Dodd arranged for Shaw to meet Casserly during one of the superior
general's visits to New Orleans. Casserly quizzed Shaw informally
in Latin and mathematics and then told him that he would sponsor him. The next September, Shaw entered Epiphany College.
(Shortly before his death on December 26, 1951, Brunner apologized to Shaw for having opposed his admission.) [49]

In New Orleans, Stephen J. Hogan of Blessed Sacrament Parish
and Anthony Kiel of St. Joan of Arc Parish adopted similar tactics
for their parishioners. After receiving Casserly's assurances that the
society accepted "those who can satisfy the highest standards,"
Hogan encouraged Elmo Townsend to begin the application process
for Epiphany by sending a letter to Casserly, who then forwarded it
to Brunner. Anthony Kiel also recommended a student: Joseph C.
Verrett. The previous spring, Kiel had engineered a meeting between Casserly and the eleventh grader in the Verrett home following a wedding at which the superior general officiated. After talking
with young Verrett and inspecting his report card, Casserly advised
him to finish his senior year at Xavier Preparatory and then apply to
Epiphany. On receiving Verrett's letter of inquiry in May, 1945,
Casserly personally recommended him to Brunner, suggesting that
the rector probably remembered both the Townsend and Verrett
families from his years in New Orleans. [50]

Having lost the battle over formal quotas, Brunner resorted to

---

49. Joseph Hennessy to Edward V. Casserly, May 20, 1945, in Casserly-
McNamara Papers; Mario Shaw interview, July 9, 1982.

50. Stephen J. Hogan to Edward V. Casserly, May 24, 1945, Edward V.
Casserly to Edward Brunner, June 4, 1945, copy, both in Casserly-McNamara
Papers; interview of Joseph C. Verrett, S.S.J., by Stephen J. Ochs, May 29, 1985;
Edward V. Casserly to Joseph Verrett, June 4, 1945, Edward V. Casserly to An-
thony Kiel, June 4, 1945, Edward V. Casserly to Edward Brunner, June 4, 1945,
copies of all in Casserly-McNamara Papers.

questioning the "spiritual qualifications" of black applicants as a way of forestalling their acceptance. He acknowledged that he recalled the Townsend family and admitted that "this boy has something that approaches what we should demand." Still, he expressed doubts about whether both boys possessed "the supernatural motive" necessary for a true vocation. Referring to the black students already there, Brunner judged that all could "make the grade, in an average way, mentally, but they all lack the spiritual quality that I would wish to see." He argued that a black man who wanted to become a priest "must, undoubtedly be a saint and a scholar . . . to show the world and especially Bishops, that they can be the real article . . . men of zeal and piety whom their own people will look up to." Looking back over the years at those who were accepted into the college, Brunner concluded that "the recollection is none too encouraging." He informed Casserly that he had advised Townsend, a fifteen-year-old, to wait a year or two before applying to Epiphany in order to enable him to study the question of a vocation and all it entailed. Since Verrett had already finished high school, Brunner sent him an application.[51]

Casserly refused to budge in the contest of wills and continued to apply pressure. He challenged Brunner's disparaging characterization of the black students at Epiphany Apostolic College, telling the rector he could not accept the notion that "the white boy has a monopoly on spiritual qualities necessary in candidates for the priesthood or that they are found only rarely in the colored boy." Casserly faulted Brunner, moreover, for acting counter to prevailing thought on vocations in recommending to Townsend that he wait a few years before applying to Epiphany. "Ordinary thought in such matters," Casserly informed him, held that "there is danger of a vocation being lost in this way." When the superior general received a letter from Jerry Milinez, another black applicant from New Orleans who hailed from Corpus Christi Parish, he passed it on to Brunner, noting that he knew Milinez and "would receive him just as I would the Townsend boy."[52]

Inevitably, Casserly had his way: Elmo Townsend, Joseph Verrett, and Jerry Milinez entered Epiphany Apostolic College in September, 1945. Verrett was placed in the special Latin class for those

51. Edward Brunner to Edward V. Casserly, June 9, 1945, in Casserly-McNamara Papers.

52. Edward V. Casserly to Edward Brunner, June 19, July 31, 1945, copies of both in Casserly-McNamara Papers.

with weak classical backgrounds. Milinez and Townsend entered first and fourth years of high school, respectively. Brunner reacted to their arrival by telling the faculty that "because of the difficulties peculiar to the Negro priest," teachers should demand more of the black students "in intelligence and piety."[53] He had less than a year remaining as rector, however, and he knew that he had lost not only the battle but also the war. The admission of Verrett, Townsend, and Milinez to Epiphany signaled the end of formal opposition to Casserly's policy and the beginning of what became a steady stream of black students at the college.

Throughout the struggle with Brunner, Casserly remained far more confident than the rector about the prospects for black priests in the United States. He took comfort from what he regarded as tangible evidence that the climate for black priests in the American Catholic church had improved considerably in the space of a few years. Between 1934 and 1945, for example, twenty-six black men received holy orders, compared to only fourteen during the previous eighty years. All but seven of those ordained after 1934 had received at least part of their training at St. Augustine's Seminary. With the ordination in September, 1945, of the Reverend William H. Adams, the seventeenth black Divine Word missionary, the number of black priests serving in the United States reached twenty-one. Four black priests also worked in Africa, two in Trinidad, and one in British Honduras.[54] Additional developments in other religious communities and in dioceses in the South between 1944 and 1948 convinced Casserly that the Josephites could safely proceed with developing black priests of their own.

While Casserly dueled with Brunner throughout 1944 and 1945, John LaFarge attempted to persuade Jesuit authorities to take positive action to open the powerful Society of Jesus to blacks. Writing on August 24, 1944, to Zacheus J. Maher, the American assistant to the Jesuit superior general, LaFarge proposed that at least one of the Jesuit provinces in the United States admit a black man to study for the priesthood. (The New England province already admitted black Jamaicans to its theologate, but they returned to Jamaica fol-

53. Verrett interview, May 29, 1985; EAC faculty meeting minutes, September, 1945, p. 91, in JFA.

54. "High Church Dignitaries Will Participate in Seminary Rites," *Catholic Action of the South* (New Orleans), October 4, 1945, clipping in Casserly-McNamara Papers. In its count of black priests serving in Africa, the article failed to include the Reverend Adrian Esnard, C.I.C.M.

lowing their studies.) Not surprisingly, LaFarge already had a candidate in mind: a young black man who came from a solid family and had compiled an excellent record at St. Peter's College in Jersey City. LaFarge explained that when the candidate had applied to the Jesuits' New York province, the provincial told him he could not accept him because "there would be no place to use him in the New York Province." LaFarge asked for Maher's opinion "upon the general principle of refusing admission to an *otherwise qualified*, fully qualified candidate, solely upon racial grounds." He promised not to quote Maher but explained that he intended to report Maher's opinion when he met with the New York provincial about the matter. LaFarge volunteered his own opinion that if the society stationed a black Jesuit "right in our own home works" in the New York province, "people would take him for granted much more readily than one suspects, and he would have the cooperation of many more among Ours [Jesuits] than one may now anticipate."[55]

LaFarge's request, among others, evidently convinced Maher of the need to issue a policy statement on the admission of qualified blacks into the Society of Jesus. After consultations, Maher drew up a statement that he submitted, on May 3, 1945, to the provincials of the American assistancy of the Society of Jesus, which was composed of all the American provinces, for their discussion. Maher stated that "the basic principle in determining the admission of any candidate is not the good he may derive from admission, but the good the Society may hope to secure by admitting him." He declared that no province should exclude a candidate "merely because of his color." If, however, a provincial judged that color would impede a candidate's usefulness in a given province, the provincial should try to find a province in which he could function usefully; that province, whether in the American assistancy or any other, should accept him. Since the Jesuits usually left the admission of candidates to the local provincial, Maher concluded that he could do no more than establish a general norm.

Clearly indicating his desire that the provincials define *usefulness* broadly, Maher appended to his statement some observations by an anonymous Jesuit, "whose judgement . . . you respect." The anonymous priest cautioned provincials against determining usefulness on

55. Albert S. Foley, S.J., *God's Men of Color: The Colored Catholic Priests of the United States, 1854–1954* (1955; rpr. New York, 1969), 310; John LaFarge to Zacheus J. Maher, August 24, 1944, copy in Box 16-23, LaFarge Papers.

the basis of the current situation, since black candidates accepted in 1945 would not finish their studies until 1958. The sheer fact of admitting a black candidate, moreover, might prove advantageous by making the society's attitude unequivocally clear and by delivering a blow at prejudice. Finally, an intelligent and spiritual black Jesuit would create his own usefulness, especially in the interracial field. The author of the observations conceded, however, that regional conditions would affect utility.[56]

LaFarge applauded Maher's statement and the appended observations. He added another angle to the discussion of the term by suggesting that the presence "of an occasional Negro in our ranks is an answer to a very frequent and harmful type of Communist propaganda" and therefore very useful. The next year, the Missouri and Chicago provinces of the Society of Jesus accepted black novices to study for the priesthood.[57]

Edward C. Kramer, who had served as the director general of the Catholic Board for Mission Work Among the Colored People for twenty-two years and who had arranged seminary education and placement for several black priests, was, like LaFarge, trying to convince his superiors—in his case, the American bishops—to address systematically and comprehensively the issue of black diocesan clergy. An alumnus of the North American College in Rome and therefore a former classmate of many American bishops, Kramer lobbied his episcopal friends and acquaintances (and probably the apostolic delegate) through a steady stream of visits and correspondence. In October, 1944, he sent a memorandum on the question of black diocesan priests to each of the six members of the executive board of his organization: Archbishops Spellman of New York (the president), Stritch of Chicago, and Curley of Baltimore and Bishops Morris of Little Rock, Gerow of Natchez, and James A. Griffin of Springfield, Illinois. He hoped that his memorandum would spark discussion at the board meeting and convince at least one of the prelates to introduce the issue at the annual meeting of the American hierarchy.

Kramer based his argument on a quotation from the recently deceased bishop John A. Duffy of Buffalo, who wrote that "the prob-

56. Zacheus J. Maher to Provincials of the American Assistancy, May 3, 1945, copy in Box 16-23, LaFarge Papers.

57. John LaFarge to Zacheus J. Maher, June 3, 1945, copy in Box 16-23, LaFarge Papers; interview of William B. Faherty, S.J., by Stephen J. Ochs, May 2, 1985; "Admit First Negro," *New World* (Chicago), September 27, 1946, clipping in Black Priests file, JFA.

lem of the colored priest is larger than a diocesan one and will grow with the years." To combat this problem, Kramer argued, the episcopate needed to devise a general policy regarding black diocesan priests. He recommended that a department of the NCWC "canvass the colored situation and the future needs both for priests and sisters of color." Although he acknowledged the administrative board of the conference would, at first, maintain that those questions properly belonged to individual bishops within their dioceses, Kramer insisted that "no one diocese is in a position to canvass the situation entirely and to meet the increasing demands." He urged that the topic be placed on the administrative board's agenda, so that "the rest of us might be in a position to follow a policy that would open the way toward a solution of . . . the preparation of priests and sisters of color for work among their own people."

Describing himself as a prudent and temperate man, Kramer explained that "a series of circumstances . . . is forcing me to bring the cause of the colored priest to your Excellency, and through your Excellency, to all our Archbishops and bishops." His responsibility as director general of the mission board involved raising money for the construction and support of Catholic schools among blacks. He pointed out, however, that the title of director general led many black Catholics, priests, and even bishops to assume mistakenly that his powers extended beyond those of a simple priest. Some bishops advised black men to write to Kramer or sent them to him for help in becoming priests; some bishops went so far as to tell Kramer that he had the duty of finding a bishop to sponsor black men whom they could not use. Over the course of twenty-two years, he managed to assist only 4 black men to ordination: 2 in Rome and 2 in Prague. In addition, as a result of his appeals, Bishop William A. Griffin of Trenton accepted 2 black students in 1943 to study for the diocesan priesthood. In the meantime, Kramer observed, many had requested aid but had fallen by the wayside because he could not help them.

Kramer charged that the existence of St. Augustine's Seminary provided Catholic America with a way to ignore the cry for black priests. When people such as Kramer complained that blacks had no chance to be priests, others simply said, "Let them become Divine Word Missionaries." As a result, 340 black students from thirty-one states had enrolled at St. Augustine's since its opening. By January 6, 1944, the date of the last ordination, only 17 of the 340 had reached the priesthood as members of the Society of the Divine Word. Although Kramer rejoiced over the 17, he nevertheless observed that "the loss is tremendous." Noting the fine native clergies in Africa and South America, he denied that the fault for so few black priests in the United States lay with blacks. Even pagan Japan, he pointed out, with only 117,000 Catholics, boasted of a Japanese archbishop, 2 bishops, 117 native priests, 127 brothers, and 700 sisters. Meanwhile, the approximately 350,000 black Catholics in the United States had only 17 Divine Word missionaries, 1 Josephite, and 3 diocesan priests. "The fault lies," Kramer wrote, "in the policy that would have every colored boy be a member of a specific religious Order, to which then must be . . . added the sad fruits which flow from fears and prejudices." He requested that the members of the board bring the issue before the annual assembly of the episcopate.[58]

In his acknowledgment of Kramer's letter, Stritch opined that raising money for black schools would be "fruitless . . . if the way is not opened to the priesthood for Colored boys." He promised to respond sympathetically to "any action that would impress upon the bishops the urgency of the problem." At their meeting on November 17, 1944, however, though they discussed racial problems and debated the merits of endorsing a permanent federal Fair Employment Practices Commission, the bishops did not formally consider the question of black diocesan priests.[59]

Kramer, nevertheless, continued to hammer away in meetings and through correspondence with bishops on what he called "the burning question of the priesthood for the Negroes." All the while he kept Casserly posted on his progress. In late August, 1945, for example, he stopped by the Josephite headquarters in Baltimore and left for Casserly's inspection letters exchanged between him and bishops about black priests. Casserly thanked the mission board director for allowing him to read the correspondence, because it gave him additional insight into the thinking of the bishops. He assured Kramer of his support for Kramer's campaign on behalf of black diocesan clergy.[60]

Although a growing number of northern bishops appeared will-

58. Edward Kramer to Archbishop Michael Curley, October 9, 1944, in K-1113, AAB.

59. Cardinal Samuel Stritch to Edward Kramer, October 14, 1944, copy in Samuel Cardinal Stritch Papers, AAC; minutes of the annual meeting of the American hierarchy, November 17, 1944, in AUSCC.

60. Edward V. Casserly to Edward Kramer, August 20, 1945, in Casserly-McNamara Papers.

ing to accept at least a token black seminarian or two for their dioceses, most of those bishops maintained strict quotas and usually would consider only those black candidates who came from their own dioceses. Unlike black students at Epiphany College, blacks in diocesan seminaries often found themselves the only black persons in their institutions, besides the janitors and kitchen help.[61]

In the South, the efforts of Casserly, Kramer, and Joseph F. Eckert, the provincial of the Divine Word southern province (which had been erected in 1940), to convert southern bishops on the issue of black priests began to bear fruit. In conversations with Casserly and Eckert during 1944 and 1945, Archbishop Rummel, the South's most important prelate, assured both men of his willingness to allow the Josephites and the Divine Word Missionaries to station their black priests in his archdiocese.[62] At the jubilee banquet celebrating the twenty-fifth anniversary of St. Augustine's Seminary, in November, 1945, Rummel went even further. He spoke earnestly about the need for more black candidates for the diocesan clergy and gave the impression to those present that he was determined to have black diocesan priests and would take the necessary steps to achieve that end. Impressed by the archbishop's apparent sincerity, Joseph Busch, the rector of St. Augustine's Seminary, asked the house council of the seminary to consider the matter. As a result, the council proposed to Eckert that the Divine Word Missionaries offer to educate black diocesan candidates of southern bishops in the high school at St. Augustine's Seminary. The diocesan students would study at St. Augustine's only through high school; after graduation the Divine Word candidates would go to their novitiate in Wisconsin, and the diocesan students would need to pursue their studies elsewhere.

The members of the house council viewed their proposal as a way of protecting against falling enrollment at St. Augustine's as seminaries in the North opened their doors to black students. More important, they also reasoned that if St. Augustine's were not available, black students sponsored by southern bishops for the diocesan clergy would have to go North, since seminaries in the South still barred them. Most blacks, however, did not have enough money

61. John LaFarge to Vernon L. Thornley, June 27, 1946, copy, Vernon L. Thornley to John LaFarge, June 11, 1946, both in Box 10-11, LaFarge Papers.

62. Edward V. Casserly to Edward Brunner, March 23, 1945, copy in Casserly-McNamara Papers; Joseph F. Eckert to Archbishop Joseph Rummel, January 15, 1946, copy in Provincial's Correspondence, SPA.

to go North. The council concluded, therefore, that "if we open our doors to secular students, then bishops and priests can give students more encouragement, since they would have a place to send them."[63] One drawback, however, was that the plan would perpetuate the tradition of segregated seminary education in the South by providing southern bishops with a minor seminary to which they could send their black students for high school. The Divine Word Missionaries viewed their plan as nevertheless providing a beginning for black diocesan clergy in the South. When black students finished high school at St. Augustine's, bishops would have to find another minor seminary where black students could study philosophy. Perhaps that pressure would force them to consider opening their own minor seminaries to black students.

In early January, 1946, Eckert met with Rummel to discuss the proposal. Before making a decision, however, the archbishop decided to solicit the opinions of the bishops of the New Orleans ecclesiastical province. Eckert told Rummel that he would refrain from submitting the plan to the Divine Word superior general for approval until he learned what the reaction of the southern episcopate was. He assured Rummel that the superior general would undoubtedly accede to the wishes of the hierarchy in the matter, for the hierarchy "has been responsible for the success of the seminary."[64]

On February 4, 1946, Rummel solicited the views of his suffragan bishops and also of the ordinaries of the dioceses of Savannah, St. Augustine, Charleston, Nashville, and Louisville to Eckert's proposal. Describing the plan as "a forward step in the discharge of our responsibility to the Colored Race," he carefully noted that the plan covered only the preparatory education of the candidates; following high school, they would have to pursue philosophy and theology studies at seminaries in the North. Rummel made clear his own belief that "a way must eventually be found for giving to worthy Colored prospects the opportunity to become diocesan or secular priests."[65]

63. Minutes of the house council, November 29, 1945, Joseph Busch to Dear Fr. Provincial, December 3, 1945, copy, both in SASA.
64. Joseph F. Eckert to Archbishop Joseph Rummel, January 15, 1945, copy in Provincial's Correspondence, SPA.
65. Archbishop Joseph Rummel to Bishop Thomas Toolen, February 4, 1946, copy in Archbishop Thomas J. Toolen Papers, AAM.

Several old guard bishops opposed Eckert's recommendation. Bishop Toolen of Mobile, for example, expressed skepticism about the feasibility of black diocesan priests in the South and concluded that "it will be better if they were members of a community rather than seculars." He voiced his hope that the Society of St. Edmund, or Edmundites, which operated black missions in his diocese and which had a black candidate from Mobile, would, after the man's ordination, station him in the Mobile diocese, so long as he had "someone to keep a finger on him." Bishop Morris of Little Rock echoed Toolen's sentiments. Although he acknowledged that each race should have its own priests, Morris, like his counterpart in Mobile, suggested that the time had not yet arrived in his diocese "when Colored secular priests can be placed in charge of our Colored parishes," because of prejudice and the numerical weakness of the church. Repeating a recommendation he had been making for more than twenty years, Morris suggested that bishops watch black priests in religious communities to see how well they succeeded in parishes and missions before giving black secular priests charge of those parishes.[66]

Rummel's old friend, Bishop Gerow, who presided over a diocese that included the whole state of Mississippi, which numbered only 39,014 white and 4,844 black Catholics, agonized over the plan. On the one hand, he noted, Catholic instincts prompted him to say that every black person with a vocation should have the opportunity to enter the ranks of the local or diocesan clergy. The Episcopalians in Mississippi, for example, had had black ministers subject to the white Episcopalian bishop for many years with "no serious difficulty, even in general meetings of the clergy." Gerow reasoned, moreover, that any young man who entered the preparatory course at St. Augustine's Seminary would not attain ordination for at least ten years, during which time race relations would probably continue to improve.

On the other hand, Gerow worried, unless a diocese had a group of black diocesan priests who could freely associate among themselves, a lone black priest would have to possess extraordinary spiritual strength to endure the isolation and prejudice of his fellow

66. Bishop Thomas Toolen to Archbishop Joseph Rummel, February 7, 1946, copy in Toolen Papers; Bishop John B. Morris to Archbishop Joseph Rummel, February 19, 1946, copy in Bishop John B. Morris Papers, ADLR. The second page of the letter is missing.

white priests. If he broke under the pressure and failed, he could set back for a generation the work of developing black diocesan clergy. Then, too, white sisters conducted many of the Catholic schools on black missions; a black pastor exercising authority over white sisters could lead to trouble in the local community. A black pastor, therefore, would probably require black sisters. Finally, because black candidates would have to study philosophy and theology in northern seminaries, Gerow feared that their association with white students for six years might make it difficult for them to readjust to the South. He admitted that times had changed since the bishops of the New Orleans province last considered the issue in 1935, but, Gerow observed to Rummel, "the improvement has not gone as far as you and I would desire." Despite his reservations, however, and like a majority of the southern ordinaries, Gerow cautiously approved the plan. He noted that the proposed course of study at St. Augustine's Seminary would compel no bishop to accept any particular individual for his diocese, though it would exert upon him "some degree of moral pressure to adjust his plans so that eventually he may admit a Colored clergy."[67]

Discussion among the bishops about using St. Augustine's Seminary for their black candidates apparently prompted a similar suggestion from a Josephite. On August 16, 1946, Father Lally of St. Peter's Parish in Dallas suggested to Casserly a plan whereby the Josephites would erect a house of studies at Bay St. Louis for black Josephite students. The students would have community exercises and meals at the Josephite house but would take their high school, philosophy, and theology courses at St. Augustine's Seminary. Such a plan, Lally argued, would "relieve the Society of some embarrassing results from having both races at Newburgh and especially Washington." He added, "Maybe later on the Bay St. Louis place could be staffed by some of our Colored priests."[68]

Lally's plan failed to impress Casserly, who called it "clearly unacceptable" because it would have "the evident mark of subterfuge about it." Casserly knew that black Catholics were, in the words of

67. "An Appeal from the Heart of the Southern Missions," *Backyard Mission Field*, clipping in SASA; minutes of the meeting of southern bishops, November 14, 1946, copy in Bishop Jules B. Jeanmard Papers, ADL; Bishop Richard O. Gerow to Archbishop Joseph Rummel, February 12, 1946, copy in Bishop Richard O. Gerow Papers, ADJ.

68. Joseph Lally to Edward V. Casserly, August 16, 1946, in Casserly-McNamara Papers.

the Reverend James F. Faherty of Our Lady of Mercy Church in Beaumont, "clamoring for Colored priests . . . because they think that the Church is holding out on them." Insisting that Josephite policy manifest openness, frankness, and honesty, Casserly declared, in his characteristically blunt manner, "If that brings embarrassment to anyone, I can only say that anything else must certainly bring embarrassment before Christ." [69]

In the summer of 1946, newly appointed cardinal Samuel Stritch, acting in his capacity as chairman of the American Board of Catholic Missions and at the urging of Archbishop Cicognani, brought additional pressure to bear on the southern bishops. Stritch arranged through Rummel for a September meeting in New Orleans with the bishops of the South in order to discuss the black apostolate and obtain their recommendations for a special program aided by the mission board. [70]

Stritch met with the 14 southern ordinaries, including Archbishop Rummel, in the archbishop's residence at 11 A.M. on the morning of September 19, 1946, following the meeting of the Catholic Committee of the South. The cardinal told the assembled prelates that the Holy See wanted more action in the black dioceses, and he received their pledges to accept "worthy candidates of the Colored race for the diocesan clergy." The bishops also discussed the need for more Catholic schools for blacks. Stritch then invited each of the bishops to formulate plans for his own diocese and to apply to the American Board of Catholic Missions for funds. Meanwhile, he kept Cicognani informed of developments. At its October meeting, the mission board appropriated an additional $20,000 for new schools for blacks in each of the southern dioceses. [71] As of October, 1946, 511 priests worked on the black missions in the United States. They were joined by 1,800 sisters, 475 of whom were black. Approximately 5,000 black students studied

69. James F. Faherty to Edward V. Casserly, August 19, 1946, Edward V. Casserly to Joseph Lally, August 21, 1946, copy, both in Casserly-McNamara Papers.

70. Cardinal Samuel Stritch to Archbishop Amleto Cicognani, June 6, 1946, Cardinal Samuel Stritch to Archbishop Joseph Rummel, June 6, August 5, 1946, copies of all in Stritch Papers.

71. Bishop Jules Jeanmard to Edward Kramer, June 14, 1947, copy in Jeanmard Papers; minutes of the special meeting of the American Board of Catholic Missions, November 18, 1946, in American Board of Catholic Missions file, AUSCC; Cardinal Samuel Stritch to Archbishop Amleto Cicognani, September 24, 1946, copy in Stritch Papers.

in Catholic high schools, colleges, universities, and seminaries, and 60,000 black children attended black parochial schools. Many others attended integrated parochial schools.[72]

At a meeting held in November in conjunction with the annual gathering of the American hierarchy at Catholic University, the southern bishops reaffirmed their pledge to Stritch and unanimously approved a resolution declaring themselves in favor of "negro priests among the diocesan clergy" and pledging "mutual cooperation in the training of, and in the adjustment of, such priests in the various Southern dioceses." Bishop Richard Gerow reported that St. Augustine's Seminary would accept black students for preparatory seminary training and that the major seminary of the archdiocese of Cincinnati, Mount St. Mary of the West, would provide their philosophy and theology.[73]

At least 2 southern bishops moved quickly to open their seminaries to blacks. By the time of the September conference with Stritch in New Orleans, Rummel had already accepted Aubrey Osborne, a young man from the Josephite parish of All Saints, just outside the New Orleans city limits, to study for the archdiocesan priesthood. Osborne completed his college studies at St. John's Abbey Seminary in Collegeville, Minnesota. In 1948, Osborne, along with Bernard Dunn, entered Notre Dame Seminary, the major seminary of the Diocese of New Orleans, after an informal poll conducted by seminary authorities indicated no serious opposition to the presence of blacks. In September of 1951, Rummel arranged for the desegregation of St. Joseph's College, the archdiocesan preparatory seminary, which was conducted by Benedictines. In June, 1953, Osborne was ordained by Rummel in St. Louis Cathedral. The other receptive prelate was Bishop Jeanmard, in whose diocese most of the black Divine Word missionaries labored. In the summer of 1947, he accepted his first black candidate, Vernon Dauphin, for the diocesan clergy and sent him also to St. John's Abbey Seminary. Although Dauphin left the seminary the following year, another of Jeanmard's candidates, Louis LeDoux, persevered and received holy orders on December 27, 1952. Jean-

72. See [LaFarge?] sermon delivered to the Catholic Interracial Council of Detroit, 1946 (Typescript in Box 16-21, LaFarge Papers).

73. Minutes of the meeting of southern bishops, November 14, 1946, copy in Jeanmard Papers.

mard thus became the first bishop of the Deep South to ordain a black man for the diocesan clergy.[74]

Bishop Gerow moved more slowly than his 2 episcopal friends in New Orleans and Lafayette. Shortly after attending the conference of southern bishops in November, 1946, Gerow, who was an ardent admirer of Stritch, told Father Eckert that "one of the Colored priests could do an excellent job at Mound Bayou," a heavily Protestant black town located in the Delta country. Up to that time, Gerow, who had ordained most of the black Divine Word missionaries, had not considered it prudent to station any black priests in his diocese outside Bay St. Louis. A lack of funds delayed the Mound Bayou project until October, 1949, when John W. Bowman, a black Divine Word missionary and a former military chaplain, opened a mission there. In that same year, near Bowling Green, Kentucky, Benedictine monks originally from St. John's Abbey established a small interracial priory that they named St. Maur's.[75]

Other dioceses followed in ordaining and incardinating black priests, if much more slowly. The diocese of Alexandria ordained its first black priest, August L. Thompson, on June 8, 1957. The Rev-

74. J. E. McKee to Edward V. Casserly, October 11, 1946, in Casserly-McNamara Papers; interview of Msgr. Charles J. Plauché, by Stephen J. Ochs, July 15, 1983; Foley, God's Men, 302; interview of David Melançon, O.S.B., by Stephen J. Ochs, December 27, 1984; Bishop Jules Jeanmard to Edward Kramer, June 14, 1947, Bishop Jules Jeanmard to Vernon Dauphin, July 27, 1948, Cardinal Giuseppe Pizzardo (prefect of the Congregation of Seminaries and Universities) to Bishop Jules Jeanmard, August 18, 1950, Louis LeDoux to Bishop Jules Jeanmard, November 22, 1952, Bishop Jules Jeanmard to Roland Fournier, June 14, 1951, copy, all in Jeanmard Papers; Consultors Minutes, September 5, 1950, p. 82, in ADL; Foley, God's Men, 213, 301.

75. Bishop Richard O. Gerow to Joseph F. Eckert, November 21, 1946, copy in Gerow Papers; Foley, God's Men, 190–91; Colman J. Barry, O.S.B., Worship and Work: St. John's Abbey and University, 1856–1956 (Collegeville, Minn., 1956), 315; Alexander Korte memorandum to Abbot Alcuin Deutsch, [1946?], Alexander Korte to Abbot Alcuin Deutsch, September 28, 1946, February 2, 11, 15, 1947, Bishop Francis R. Cotton to Alexander Korte, April 10, 1948, Bishop Francis R. Cotton to Abbot Alcuin Deutsch, October 29, 1949, all in Abbot Alcuin Deutsch Papers, SJAA; "Plan Monastery for Negroes and Whites," Sun (New York), April 1, 1949, "St. John's Opens Dixie Priory," Minneapolis Tribune, April 4, 1949, Joe Creason, "One Faith—Two Races," Courier-Journal Magazine (New Orleans), December 14, 1952, pp. 6–7, all clippings in Black Priests file, JFA; Foley, God's Men, 258.

erend Joseph Dyer, ordained for the diocese of Jackson, did not join the ranks of its clergy until August 16, 1974. Cordell Lang and Hayden Michael Hill were ordained for the archdiocese of Mobile on May 19, 1979, and May 28, 1988, respectively. May 28, 1988, was also the date of the ordination of Lois Warren Harvey, the diocese of Little Rock's first black priest. As of May, 1988, the diocese of Lafayette had ordained only one black priest in addition to Louis LeDoux, though it had incardinated several others. From Aubrey Osborne's ordination in 1953 to 1988, 5 black priests were ordained for the archdiocese of New Orleans, and 7 black priests were incardinated there.[76]

The willingness of Rummel and Jeanmard to accept and ordain black candidates, together with the pledges of other southern bishops to accept blacks for their diocesan clergy, had important ramifications for the Josephites. The New Orleans archdiocese, for example, contained the largest number of Josephite parishes and missionaries. Rummel's actions reassured Casserly that, Brunner's fears notwithstanding, the Josephites would have places to assign their future black priests. Casserly, however, would not be the one to make those assignments.

At the July, 1948, general chapter of St. Joseph's Society, in what Casserly later described as "a rejection" rather than an election, the Josephites decided that they had had enough of the New York boss and in his place elected fifty-two-year-old Thomas P. McNamara, a veteran of the Louisiana missions, as the sixth superior general of the society. The election represented a reaction against Casserly's autocratic style and his apparent insensitivity to Josephites on the missions, rather than a repudiation of his policies. Indeed, the new superior general and his righthand man, George O'Dea, Casserly's protégé, continued and expanded the recruitment of black vocations for the Josephites. Casserly became a so-

76. See Frances B. Boeckman, archivist of the diocese of Jackson, to Stephen J. Ochs, January 14, 1988, Beverly Walker, archival assistant of the diocese of Alexandria, to Stephen J. Ochs, January 15, 1988, both in the possession of Stephen J. Ochs, Silver Spring, Md.; interview with archbishop's office, archdiocese of Mobile, April 4, 1988; Sr. Catherine Markey, archivist of the diocese of Little Rock, to Stephen J. Ochs, January 14, 1988, in the possession of Stephen J. Ochs, Silver Spring, Md.; *Arkansas Catholic* (Little Rock), May 20, 1988, in Black Priests file, JFA; Rev. James F. Geraghty, vice chancellor and archivist, to Stephen J. Ochs, January 13, 1988, Rev. James C. Moragne, vice chancellor for spiritual affairs, archdiocese of New Orleans, to Stephen J. Ochs, May 13, 1988, both in the possession of Stephen J. Ochs, Silver Spring, Md.

ciety consultor and also pastor of St. Peter Claver Parish in Baltimore. In 1954 he became rector of St. Joseph's Seminary; in 1960 he was appointed pastor of St. Benedict the Moor Parish in Washington, D.C. He left pastoral work at the age of seventy in 1966 but accepted the post of Josephite treasurer. After serving in that capacity for five years, he retired in 1971. He died on October 17, 1982.[77]

Although it spanned only six years, Casserly's administration marked a turning point for St. Joseph's Society. He established twenty parishes and missions and an equal number of schools. He sent priests to graduate school, thereby strengthening the educational institutions conducted by the society. Largely as a result of his efforts and vision, in 1948 the Josephites won the right to staff St. Augustine's High School in New Orleans, which he hoped would eventually prove to be a source of black Josephite vocations.[78]

Less defensive than Pastorelli, Casserly promoted Josephite participation in organizations such as the Catholic Committee of the South, where, he said, Josephites "might both learn and teach." Dan Cassidy's interracial club in Baltimore, John Doyle's farm cooperative and credit union in Ames, Texas, and the street preaching of some younger Josephites all reflected Casserly's emphasis on studying and employing modern methods of evangelization. Casserly also effectively used Chester Ball, the society's lone black priest, "to show the Josephite flag" in the black Catholic community by preaching retreats and giving numerous speeches before Catholic and non-Catholic groups. Casserly, moreover, encouraged his men to foster religious vocations among black girls in Josephite parishes and urged numerous congregations of sisters to accept black candidates into their communities. He managed the financial affairs of the society so skillfully that when he left office, St. Joseph's Society owed not a single penny.[79]

77. Hogan interview, December 29, 1982; O'Dea interview, August 10, 1983; see obituary, assignment sheet, and biographical sheet in Edward V. Casserly File, JFA.

78. Edward V. Casserly to Archbishop Joseph Rummel, March 5, 1948, copy in Casserly-McNamara Papers.

79. Edward V. Casserly to Walter Mulroney, April 13, 1944, copy, Edward V. Casserly to John Doyle, March 26, 1947, copy, John Doyle to Edward V. Casserly, May 27, February 19, 1945, Edward V. Casserly to Chester Ball, April 3, 1947, copy, Edward V. Casserly to Mother David, April 27, 1946, copy, all in Casserly-McNamara Papers; O'Dea interview, August 10, 1983.

Casserly's most important contribution, however, lay in the realm of black vocations for the priesthood. Benefiting from the support of young Josephites and reassured by the new-found willingness of some southern bishops to accept black priests into their dioceses, Casserly overcame the final opposition of the old guard led by Edward Brunner, and reclaimed a crucial part of Slattery's legacy. In a real sense, St. Joseph's Society recovered its identity. Freed from energy-sapping struggles with black Catholics and with themselves over the issue of black priests, the Josephites reassumed their role as champions of a black clergy, thereby identifying more closely with the aspirations of the black Catholic community that they served. Casserly left a reinvigorated society to his successors, just as the civil rights revolution began in earnest.

Chapter X

A NEW BEGINNING, 1948–1960

This incident was clearly a violation of the obligation of reverence and devotion which Catholics owe every priest of God, regardless of race, color, or nationality. Every Catholic priest who enjoys the approval of his . . . superiors must be acceptable to our Catholic people.
—ARCHBISHOP JOSEPH F. RUMMEL, OCTOBER 14, 1955

Thomas P. McNamara, a pleasant, low-key, kindly man, served as superior general of the Josephites from 1948 until 1960. He left the day-to-day administration of St. Joseph's Society in the hands of his able and dynamic vicar general, George F. O'Dea, a close associate of Edward V. Casserly. Practically speaking, O'Dea ran the society for McNamara from 1948 until 1960, years that witnessed the intensification of the civil rights struggle. From its inception as a religious institute in 1893, and except for the eight-year hiatus between the death of Charles Uncles in 1933 and the ordination of Chester Ball in 1941, St. Joseph's Society had included black priests among its members. Under Casserly, however, and fully ten years before the Supreme Court's landmark *Brown* v. *Board of Education* decision in 1954, which declared segregation in public schools unconstitutional, the Josephites had begun to integrate their society more thoroughly. Two months after the *Brown* decision, Josephite delegates to the general chapter unequivocally committed St. Joseph's Society to promote integration throughout the Catholic church and the United States and called upon their fellow Josephites to lead in efforts to secure "a full Catholic and American life" for blacks.[1]

1. Minutes of the general chapters, July 7, 1954, in JFA.

As part of their commitment to integration, McNamara and O'Dea continued and expanded Casserly's policy of encouraging and recruiting black vocations. The Josephites ordained four black priests between 1955 and 1960, and with over two score of black students and seminarians at Epiphany Apostolic College and St. Joseph's Seminary, they anticipated increasing numbers of black Josephite priests by the midsixties. Unlike earlier Josephite superiors, McNamara and O'Dea were able to assign black Josephites to the Deep South for the first time in almost forty years. Just as the Supreme Court ruled in favor of blacks in the *Brown* decision, so, too, within the Catholic church two southern prelates, Bishop Richard Gerow of Natchez-Jackson and Archbishop Joseph Rummel of New Orleans, took stands in defense of black priests in 1954 and 1955 that clearly signaled a new era.

Between 1946 and 1960, black enrollment at Epiphany Apostolic College, Mary Immaculate Novitiate, and St. Joseph's Seminary grew steadily, soon surpassing the numbers found there during John R. Slattery's administration. By October, 1953, Josephite recruitment of black students had produced such drastic changes at the college (see Table) that Thomas F. O'Connor, the rector, felt compelled to write McNamara about the "vocation situation," describing it as "the most important problem the Society is currently facing."[2]

During the five years between the 1949–1950 and 1953–1954 school years, total enrollment declined from a high of sixty-three in 1950–1951 to a low of thirty-eight in 1953–1954. What is more dramatic, the proportion of black students to white students completely changed. In the 1949–1950 academic year, there had been eleven black students and forty-two white students (a ratio of 21 percent to 79 percent). By the 1953–1954 school year, however, there were twenty-two black students and sixteen white students (58 percent to 42 percent). Many Josephites believed that the drop in white enrollment resulted from the increased number of black students. Of the ten new students at Epiphany in 1953, seven were black and only three were white; the first- and second-year high school classes were completely black. The entire high school department of sixteen students had only four whites, whereas the college department had thirteen white and nine black students.

2. Thomas O'Connor to Thomas P. McNamara, October 16, 1953, in Edward V. Casserly-Thomas P. McNamara Papers, JFA.

Table

EPIPHANY APOSTOLIC COLLEGE ENROLLMENT FIGURES,
ACADEMIC YEARS 1946–1947 TO 1953–1954

Year	Black Students	White Students	Total Enrollment
1946–1947	4	43	47
1947–1948	8	42	50
1948–1949	8	41	59
1949–1950	11	42	53
1950–1951	14	48 (49)*	62 (63)*
1951–1952	17 (18)*	40 (41)*	57 (59)*
1952–1953	24	27	51
1953–1954	22	16	38

* Sources disagree on figures (EAC faculty meeting minutes, September [?], 1946, September 26, 1947, September 24, 1948, in JFA; Thomas O'Connor to Thomas P. McNamara, October 16, 1953, in Casserly-McNamara Papers).

Despite the enrollment statistics and conventional wisdom, O'Connor contended that "thus far, the number of colored students has in no way affected the number of white boys we have." He maintained that Epiphany would have begun the 1953–1954 academic year with only sixteen students "if we did not have the colored boys." Nevertheless, he predicted that continued predominance of black students would prevent the Josephites from securing many white vocations in the future. "Unless the entire complexion of the Society is to change (no pun intended)," he wrote, "I think we should do everything in our power to secure more white vocations." O'Connor insisted that the solution lay not in limiting black vocations but in a concerted effort to secure white ones. "It would be flying in the face of Divine Providence to reject possible vocations because of color," he argued, "and I would feel in conscience bound to resign before becoming party to such action." He urged that the Josephites instead do everything possible to see that future enrollments reached at least 50 percent white.[3] Fears about a permanent change in the composition of the college proved premature, however. The surge in the number of vocations for religious

3. Thomas O'Connor to Thomas P. McNamara, October 16, 1953, in Casserly-McNamara Papers.

communities and the diocesan priesthood that characterized the middle and late fifties brought greater numbers of white students to the college and restored racial balance.[4]

Epiphany Apostolic College offered four years of high school and the first two years of college. The small classes and intimate atmosphere (there were only fourteen students in the high school in 1952) helped compensate for a faculty not always distinguished in its academic degrees, enthusiasm, or teaching ability. During the late forties and early fifties, many Josephites viewed the college as a desolate and isolated assignment, lacking the importance or prestige of parish work. That attitude began to change somewhat during the early fifties, when some of the men whom Casserly had sent to graduate school took up posts at the college and eventually moved into administration.[5]

The curriculum, like that of most other Catholic minor seminaries and many Catholic high schools, emphasized a classical education. A typical junior in the high school took Latin, Greek, English, religion, mathematics, and chemistry. A standard first-year college schedule included religion (Christian doctrine), sociology, Greek (New Testament), English, Latin (Ovid), and French. A college sophomore might study Latin (Plautus, Cato, and Cicero), English, U.S. history, biology, religion (apologetics), and Greek. Before the push for more professional standards and accreditation began in 1954, Timothy Holland, the dean of students and the director of the bookstore, often determined a student's academic schedule on book day by asking him for his grades from the previous year and then simply handing him the books in the subjects that Holland believed he should study.[6]

In addition, special Latin courses of study in both the high school and the college enabled students entering Epiphany with weak Latin backgrounds to catch up with the other students. The special Latin students took English, religion, and two classes of Latin each

4. Interview of Peter E. Hogan, S.S.J., August 30, 1983, interview of Robert E. McCall, S.S.J., June 24, 1982, both by Stephen J. Ochs; James Hennesey, S.J., *American Catholics: A History of the Roman Catholic Community in the United States* (New York, 1981), 287.

5. Interview of Peter E. Hogan, S.S.J., by Stephen J. Ochs, December 29, 1982; Thomas O'Connor to Thomas P. McNamara, May 15, 1952, in Casserly-McNamara Papers.

6. Interview of Eugene P. McManus, S.S.J., by Stephen J. Ochs, June 10, 1985; Joseph C. Verrett transcript from EAC, in Joseph C. Verrett file, JFA; interview of Joseph C. Verrett, S.S.J., by Stephen J. Ochs, May 29, 1985.

day. After successfully completing a year in special Latin, students entered the appropriate level of the high school or college, depending on their previous educational background. After his year of special Latin, for example, Joseph Verrett, who had already graduated from high school, went into the first year of college.[7]

Beginning in 1949 with the arrival of Peter E. Hogan, one of the men whom Casserly had sent to graduate school, students at Epiphany also studied black history and the race problem in their U.S. history class. Since standard history texts presented a negative picture of blacks when they mentioned them at all, Hogan used such novels as Kenneth Roberts' *Lydia Bailey* to provoke discussions about the objectivity of the depictions of blacks. He also incorporated material from books by John Gillard and by black historians such as John Hope Franklin and Carter Woodson and used articles from the *Journal of Negro History*. Convinced that they could not adequately prepare students to deal with contemporary problems, especially those involving race, if the students lacked information, Hogan and his allies on the faculty eliminated the rule that prohibited the minor seminarians from reading newspapers. The New York *Times* thus became standard reading fare at the college. Hogan also used the Catholic Students' Mission Crusade unit at the college as a forum for structured study and discussion groups on race and American government. One former Epiphany College student echoed the views of many when he recalled, years later, that Hogan put him in touch with black history and with his own blackness long before it became fashionable or publicly acceptable.[8]

Black and white students lived, studied, and played together harmoniously at the college with little apparent race consciousness. Even in the heat of athletic contests or occasional teenage fist fights, racial epithets almost never appeared. Initially, black students often faced a difficult period of adjustment at Epiphany, many having traveled great distances from home into a predominantly white, northern, Irish Catholic environment. The period of homesickness and culture shock, however, lasted a relatively short time for most, and the black students quickly came to feel at home. Stuffed into

7. Interview of Bishop-elect Eugene A. Marino, S.S.J., by Peter E. Hogan, S.S.J., August 13, 1974 (Typescript in JFA), 25–26; Verrett interview, May 29, 1985.

8. Hogan interview, December 29, 1982; taped memoir of Thomas Honoré, October 21, 1983, in JFA.

open dormitories on the top two floors of the four-story college building, the students developed close friendships that crossed racial boundaries. One black student described the college as "a happy, close knit boarding school, with plenty of outdoor activities like sledding and baseball."[9]

In the late forties and early fifties, approximately half of the students at Epiphany came from Boston or its environs. The grand St. Patrick's Day celebration every year reflected the Boston-Irish dominance of the college. For a time, a kind of Boston-versus-the-rest-of-the-world attitude prevailed among the students. As the number of black and white southern students increased, however, the annual Thanksgiving football game among the students, which had previously pitted the Boston students against everyone else, changed to a North versus South contest.[10]

Black students ran the gamut in terms of abilities. Some, such as Joseph Verrett, Rosamond Shaw, Elmo Townsend, Charles Hall, Elbert F. Harris, and Vernon P. Moore, led their classes. Charlie Dorsey's winning personality, athletic ability, and intelligence made him popular with teachers and classmates alike, and in 1952, Elbert Harris, an eighteen-year-old sophomore from Harriston, Mississippi, became the dean of the student body, an office akin to the student government president at other schools. The outstanding quality of a number of the black students inspired and reassured others who arrived at Epiphany, nervous and insecure, from small schools in the South. Of course, some black students, Dudley Darbonne and Prentice Polk, for instance, struggled academically and never made the grade. Other black students from the South, coming from substandard schools, had to enroll in the special Latin class for a year. Both Verrett and Harris, later academic giants among their peers, spent their first year at Epiphany in special Latin. The special Latin class was not, however, the exclusive preserve of black students. In 1952, for example, only three of ten in special Latin were black.[11]

Black students encountered little overt racial discrimination from the faculty, though at times some administrators and teachers

9. Verrett interview, May 29, 1985; interview of Charles H. Dorsey, Jr., by Stephen J. Ochs, October 12, 1983; Honoré memoir, October 21, 1983; Marino interview by Hogan, 25–26.

10. Marino interview by Hogan, 26; Hogan interview, December 29, 1982.

11. Marino interview by Hogan, 25, 28–29; interview of Mario Shaw, O.S.B., by Stephen J. Ochs, July 9, 1982.

appeared insensitive to southern boys. After hearing Rawlin B. Enette of Port Arthur read aloud for the first time in the refectory, for instance, Arthur J. O'Leary, the rector, publicly voiced his disgust for the way Enette spoke. He later summoned Enette to his room, told him that he did not know how to speak properly, and made him practice speaking into a tape recorder. When an Irish boy arrived sporting an Irish accent, however, O'Leary and some of the other priests appeared to relish it. On another occasion, Edward D. Eichman, the prefect of discipline, admonished a northern boy from a good high school for lack of effort because Elbert Harris and Joseph Messina, two southern boys, one black and the other white, had higher grades in mathematics. Sometimes southern boys misinterpreted academic rigor for insensitivity. Much to the annoyance of some students, for example, Robert E. McCall insisted that, irrespective of their regional dialect, they use standard English correctly. Educated men used standard English, McCall and other Josephites reasoned, and they wanted to train priests whose educations would compare favorably with those of any other priest or educated man in the country.[12]

The faculty policy of dismissing first-year students at midyear for academic difficulties was a source of anxiety for black students from substandard southern schools. That policy changed, however, as a result of the efforts of Peter Hogan, who became vice-rector and dean of studies in 1954. Hogan believed that well-intentioned, highly motivated, and normally intelligent students could master the college's six-year program if they were given adequate individual attention by teachers and a reasonable amount of time to adjust to a new environment and to academic expectations. He therefore encouraged his faculty to tutor students outside regular class periods and convinced the council to rule that no student could be dismissed at Christmas.[13]

Although the students at Epiphany Apostolic College enjoyed a close community life in a protected environment largely devoid of racism, the outside world occasionally intervened. The students lived a regimented life and remained on campus except for twice weekly hikes and a weekend visit to the nearby city of Newburgh for three hours of shopping. While isolation from the world repre-

12. Interview of Rawlin B. Enette, S.S.J., by Peter E. Hogan, S.S.J., March 9, 1971 (Typescript in JFA), 152, 155–56; Marino interview by Hogan, 25; McCall interview, June 24, 1982; Hogan interview, August 30, 1983.

13. Hogan interviews, December 29, 1982, August 30, 1983.

sented the common ideal of most preparatory and major seminaries, the tense racial situation in Newburgh also prompted the Josephites to try to limit the visits of their students to the city. A center for black migrant workers who picked fruit in the orchards of Orange County, Newburgh also contained a black community that pre-dated the Civil War. White citizens of Newburgh employed black labor but attempted to disfranchise blacks in the city. White bar-bers in the town refused to cut the hair of the black Epiphany Col-lege students for fear that they would lose their white customers. The black students, therefore, went to the barbershop in the black section of town, which reportedly exposed them to lewd talk and carnal temptations in the surrounding neighborhood. Early in 1952, after a black student allegedly contracted syphilis, O'Leary placed the barbershop off limits to the black students without telling them the reason. The black students felt discriminated against, especially since the white barbers would not cut their hair. Hogan insisted that if the black students could not go to the barber, then neither should the white students. Hogan and Eichman convinced a white barber from Newburgh to come out to the college (about three miles from the city) to cut the students' hair. The college even-tually even purchased a barber's chair to make the haircutting ses-sions more comfortable. On another occasion, when Mary Le Page, a secretary at the college, became ill, Eichman asked white students to donate blood for her but skipped the black students until one of them asked sarcastically, "What's wrong? Don't you want Al Trav-is's [a black student's] blood?" [14]

After graduation from Epiphany Apostolic College, students en-tered Mary Immaculate Novitiate for a year of intensive spiritual reflection and formation that included two 8-day retreats, one at the beginning and one at the end of the year. In the novitiate, the novices studied the Josephite constitutions and gained a clearer understanding of the Josephite apostolate. At the end of the noviti-ate, if they were recommended by the novice master, novices made their first temporary promise and became members of St. Joseph's Society. Between 1948 and 1955, two or three blacks made their novitiate each year. In 1956 and 1959, the number of black novices ballooned to eleven and ten, respectively. [15]

14. *Ibid.*; EAC faculty meeting minutes, February 4, 18, 1952, pp. 117, 119, in JFA; Enette interview, 361.

15. Enette interview, 152; list of black students in novitiate, in Mary Immacu-late Novitiate file, JFA.

Rawlin Enette found the novitiate year particularly difficult, in part because he was confronted with elements of racism within the society. According to Enette, in May, 1953, a priest on the noviti-ate staff summoned him to his room shortly after returning from a retreat. The priest had heard that Earl L. Chachere, a black priest working in the Lafayette diocese, had created a stir at Blessed Sac-rament Church in New Orleans when during a sermon he errone-ously accused the Josephites in the parish of having refused him a place to sleep during his visit to that city. The novitiate priest furiously demanded to know whether Enette knew either Chachere or Joseph Richardson, a black seminarian who had been dismissed earlier. Enette answered that he had seen Father Chachere once in his life and knew Richardson only by sight. The staff member there-upon told Enette that he would not recommend him for the major seminary. When Enette asked the reason, he exploded, "You damn Negro guys ought to keep your damn mouths closed, that's why." Enette demanded that the priest put his complaints in writing—a demand that evidently brought him back to his senses. He simply waved Enette off, saying, "O.K. Oh, go ahead, go ahead."

During his exit retreat from the novitiate, Enette again encoun-tered what he regarded as racial stereotyping. On the first night, the retreat master, who had never met him, called him to his room and told him that at dinner that evening he had noticed Enette and had said to himself, "Here is a guy with an ultra-superior attitude." He told Enette that the Josephites had no place for men filled with pride and that they had gotten rid of Casserly for that reason. He then advised the black novice to quit the Josephites. Enette pointed out that none of the faculty had corrected him for that particular fault, and he flatly refused to quit. Seven more times during the re-treat, the retreat master unsuccessfully advised him to leave.[16] Hap-pily for the Josephites and their black candidates, incidents such as these were apparently isolated and uncommon.

Following the successful completion of the novitiate, candidates went to St. Joseph's Seminary in Washington, D.C., for two years of philosophy and four years of theology. Josephite seminarians pre-pared for the priesthood in much the same, traditional way as most other seminarians. The philosophy courses were Thomistic and in-cluded logic, epistemology, cosmology, ethics, metaphysics, and theodicy. The theology courses ran in a cycle that included moral

16. Enette interview, 165–68.

and dogmatic theology, scripture, church history, canon law, and the sacraments. Teachers emphasized memorization and recitation from manuals and textbooks written in Latin. Nothing in the curriculum specifically addressed working among blacks, though the library contained works on black literature, history, sociology, and religion.[17]

Outside of the classroom, however, through Catholic Students' Mission Crusade activities, guest speakers, and the experience of living in an integrated religious community, the Josephite seminarians received their orientation in black work. After he arrived at St. Joseph's Seminary in 1955, Robert McCall, another of Casserly's graduate school men, made the New York *Times* and the Washington *Post* available to the seminarians, who were thus able to follow the growing civil rights movement and to discuss it among themselves and with their teachers. A steady stream of priests from the missions, moreover, visited the seminary and almost always spoke to the students about their work. The seminarians' apostolic activity involved teaching catechism in black parishes on Sundays. Black seminarians, most of whom had endured racism firsthand, shared their experiences with their white classmates. Visits home during the summer months also enabled seminarians to catch up on current events.[18]

As at Epiphany, black and white seminarians at St. Joseph's lived together harmoniously. An incident in 1950 involving Joseph Verrett and a group of his white seminary friends illustrates how oblivious seminarians could become about race. Verrett, Walter A. Cerbin, Gerard J. Gfroerer, Joseph T. Leonard, and Joseph J. Miller went out for a walk one afternoon and found themselves at the Hot Shoppe restaurant on Rhode Island Avenue. Without thinking, the members of the group entered the restaurant and began to take their seats. At that point, the waitress approached and informed them that she could not take Verrett's order because the establishment did not serve blacks. Gfroerer became indignant and objected loudly. The waitress, nevertheless, remained adamant, and since Verrett was becoming increasingly embarrassed by the scene, the group left the restaurant. When older seminarians learned about the incident, they raked Miller over the coals for having put Verrett

17. Verrett interview, May 29, 1985; McCall interview, June 24, 1982.
18. Hogan interviews, December 29, 1982, August 30, 1983; Verrett interview, May 29, 1985.

into such a mortifying position. Verrett, who came from the segregated city of New Orleans, later explained that he and his friends had become so used to one another that they simply forgot about segregation in Washington. After the incident, Verrett's friends called Howard University for the name of a restaurant that served racially mixed groups. On their next free day, Verrett and his comrades went to the Zanzibar, a Chinese-owned restaurant on Fourteenth Street that catered to a black clientele. Verrett's companions found themselves in the unfamiliar position of being the only white people in the establishment.[19]

In their day-to-day relations with students, faculty at St. Joseph's Seminary appeared to treat black seminarians no differently than white seminarians. When it came time to evaluate seminarians as to their suitability for the priesthood, however, they looked for specific qualities in black seminarians. They used the terms "docile" and "balanced on the race question" to describe the best black candidates. They later explained that docility indicated "an openness to instruction," not a groveling personality. In the fifties, with integration as the society's ideal, "balanced on the race question" meant that the seminarian wanted to work in an integrated society and showed evidence of the judgment and stability needed to deal with injustice without becoming embittered, emotionally unstable, or an embarrassment to the society. The Josephites did not want angry young men, nor did they want men who stressed blackness; in the context of the fifties, the Josephites and many others, both black and white, viewed such an inclination as extremism, smacking of separatism.[20]

Later critics of the Josephites accused them, with some justification, of training "white" black men. Indeed, integration in the 1950s usually meant adaptation by blacks to white contexts, almost never the reverse. Although Epiphany Apostolic College and St. Joseph's Seminary made some changes to accommodate the influx of blacks, Afro-American Josephite students and seminarians basically had to conform to a white world. At a time, however, when most northern residential neighborhoods were rigidly segregated and many Catholic schools in the North and most in the South remained entirely white and when white citizens' councils and Ku

19. Verrett interview, May 29, 1985.
20. Joseph L. Waters to Thomas P. McNamara, April 30, 1960, in St. Joseph's Seminary file, JFA; McCall interview, June 24, 1982.

Klux Klansmen used intimidation and violence to oppose school desegregation, the interracial communities at Epiphany and St. Joseph's Seminary appeared light years ahead of most American institutions.

As Verrett and his fellow seminarians pursued their studies amid integrated settings during the late forties and early fifties, Chester Ball, the single black Josephite priest, carried on a ministry notable for its lack of controversy. In 1943, with Archbishop Curley's permission, Casserly appointed Ball pastor of the Josephite mission church of St. Joseph's in Glen Arden. An all-black town of fifteen hundred, one-third of whom were Catholics, Glen Arden was located four miles northwest of the city limits of the District of Columbia. While pastor of St. Joseph's, Ball enrolled in graduate school at Catholic University and secured his master's degree in speech in 1949. He taught speech at St. Joseph's Seminary and conducted retreats, lectured, and preached extensively, often on race problems, before such groups as the Catholic Committee of the South and Catholic University seminarians. In August, 1952, Ball became the first black pastor in Washington, D.C., when he assumed the pastorate of Epiphany Parish in Georgetown. Ball continued to teach at Catholic University and St. Joseph's Seminary and made weekly trips to Baltimore to teach psychology and catechetics to the Oblate Sisters of Providence.[21]

The Catholic clergy in the nation's capital received Ball cordially. He maintained friendly relations with Washington's liberal archbishop Patrick O'Boyle and participated on an equal basis with other priests in archdiocesan celebrations and events. Ball's uneventful pastorate probably eased whatever apprehensions O'Boyle may have had about accepting black candidates for the ranks of the diocesan clergy. Ball paid a high price, however, for fitting in. Already possessing a light complexion, he used skin creams and hair straighteners to whiten his appearance even more. He craved acceptance and maintained a jovial demeanor to earn it. Although he spoke on the race question, he carefully avoided any appearance of militancy. Ball's identity problems resulted in a breakdown and a period of hospitalization in 1960. He died on July 15, 1970.[22]

21. Joseph M. Nelligan to Edward V. Casserly, April 5, 1945, Chester Ball to Thomas P. McNamara, August 19, 1952, both in Casserly-McNamara Papers; Albert S. Foley, S.J., *God's Men of Color: The Colored Catholic Priests of the United States, 1854–1954* (1955; rpr. New York, 1969), 232–33.

22. Foley, *God's Men*, 233–34; William B. Swanson, to George F. O'Dea, November 9, 1960, in Charles Chester Ball file, JFA.

The expanding numbers of black seminarians at Epiphany Apostolic College and St. Joseph's Seminary reflected the commitment of the Josephites to racial justice within their own society and also within the church and nation. The numbers also mirrored a more hospitable environment for black seminarians and priests in the Catholic church. Developments in the South made a significant contribution to this growing acceptance of black seminarians and priests.

In particular, more seminaries in the border states and upper South opened their doors to blacks. In the spring of 1950, for instance, in response to an inquiry from Washington's archbishop O'Boyle, George A. Gleason, the Sulpician rector of St. Charles College in Catonsville, informed Monsignor James E. Cowhig, chancellor of the archdiocese of Washington, D.C., that since the laws of the state of Maryland did not prohibit any elementary or secondary schools from admitting black students, he and the faculty would accept black candidates from the archbishop. As a result, James B. Joy entered St. Charles College in September, 1950. Joy had such light skin that it took weeks before students realized that an Afro-American student had enrolled in the college. In the Deep South, both Jeanmard and Rummel continued to sponsor black seminarians and ordained black priests (LeDoux and Osborne) for their dioceses in 1952 and 1953, respectively. Liberal bishop Vincent S. Waters of Raleigh followed suit in 1953 when he accepted Joseph L. Howze, a convert from the Josephites' Most Pure Heart of Mary Parish in Mobile and a future bishop, to study for his diocesan clergy. Howze became the first black man since James Augustine Healy to serve as the ordinary of a diocese, when he was named bishop of the diocese of Biloxi in 1977.[23]

At St. Augustine's Seminary in Bay St. Louis, the opposite phenomenon occurred. Beginning in 1943, black seminarians from there not only took their two-year novitiate in integrated settings at East Troy and Techny but also spent their first two years of college at either Techny or Epworth, Iowa, before returning for philosophy to Bay St. Louis. Then in September, 1950, four white seminari-

23. St. Charles College faculty minutes, May 16, 1950, in RG-4, Box-6, James E. Cowhig to Archbishop Patrick O'Boyle, May 23, 1950, copy, in RG-4, Box-19, George A. Gleason to James E. Cowhig, June 12, 1950, copy, all in SAB; interview of John W. Bowen, S.S., by Stephen J. Ochs, October 28, 1983; Bishop Joseph L. Howze, curriculum vitae, July 3, 1985, copy in JFA; interview of Benjamin M. Horton, S.S.J., by Stephen J. Ochs, July 17, 1984.

ans, the first appreciable number of whites ever to enroll at St. Augustine's Seminary, arrived at Bay St. Louis to study philosophy. Their Divine Word superiors had told them that if they went to St. Augustine's for philosophy, they would have to stay through theology. Two years later, in 1952, a white student, Marian ("Buddy") Brignac, entered the high school. By 1955, the Divine Word Missionaries had abandoned the policy of assigning all black students to St. Augustine's Seminary; they sent seminarians to either Bay St. Louis or Techny purely on a regional basis, without regard to color. A white southerner, therefore, was assigned to Bay St. Louis, a black northerner to Techny. At St. Augustine's Seminary in 1955, five of the fifty minor seminarians and thirteen of the twenty-seven major seminarians were white. The faculty numbered thirteen white and six black priests.[24]

On January 1, 1953, in an action fraught with symbolism and described by Albert S. Foley, a noted Jesuit historian and sociologist, as signifying "the coming of age of the colored priesthood . . . in the United States," Pope Pius XII, who had named eight of the world's ten black bishops, appointed Divine Word missionary Joseph O. Bowers, a forty-two-year-old West Indian native and a graduate of St. Augustine's Seminary, as bishop of Accra, in the Gold Coast. On April 22, 1953, Cardinal Francis Spellman consecrated Bowers a bishop before a large crowd in Bay St. Louis. Bowers became the first black man elevated to the office of bishop in the United States since James Augustine Healy of Portland in 1875. The Pittsburgh *Courier* trumpeted the event with huge headlines that proclaimed, "CATHOLICS HAIL NEGRO BISHOP." William C. Bauer, the Divine Word southern provincial, called the consecration a unique historical event for the South. "Never before did such an event take place," he wrote, "when the whites vied with the colored in honoring a member of the Negro race." Before assuming his duties in Accra, Bishop Bowers undertook an extensive personal appearance tour throughout the United States in order to raise money for his missionary diocese and to allow black Catholics to see a bishop of their own race. He celebrated a solemn pontifical mass in New Orleans' St. Louis Cathedral and ordained two black

24. Interviews of Francis A. Theriault, S.V.D., by Stephen J. Ochs, July 18, 1983, June 11, 1985; "Integrated Seminary Ordains 31st Negro," *Catholic Messenger* (Davenport, Ia.), July 7, 1955, in Black Priests file, JFA; John LaFarge to Albert S. Foley, February 2, 1955, copy, in Box 15-17, in John LaFarge Papers, GUA.

seminarians at St. Augustine's Seminary, the first time that a black bishop in the United States had ordained black priests.[25]

Foley claimed that Bowers' consecration also showed "the advancing maturity of the Catholic Church and its white hierarchy in the United States." In the early fifties, the cautious acceptance of black priests reflected a more liberal stance on race relations by several southern bishops. On October 1, 1949, for example, at the request of Josephites and Divine Word Missionaries, Rummel canceled a holy hour service planned for the observance of the golden jubilee of the archdiocesan Holy Name Society when city park commissioners insisted on racial segregation as soon as the procession of parish Holy Name societies entered the city stadium. Three years later, in 1952, Rummel ordered the integration of all Holy Name societies in New Orleans parishes. On June 25, 1951, again in response to entreaties from Josephite and Divine Word priests along the Gulf coast, Bishop Gerow repeated his earlier declaration that "the colored people are not to be discriminated against in any way as regards seating in our churches."[26]

Still, Josephite activists remained unsatisfied with the efforts of southern bishops. In March, 1952, Roderique A. Auclair, a twenty-five-year veteran of the black missions who was stationed at St. Anne de Beaupre Church in Houston, sent a scathing letter to the editor of the *Priest* after reading an anonymously written article, which appeared in the May, 1951, issue of the magazine. Entitled "Black Priest," it detailed the painful experiences endured by a black priest from the South. In his letter, Auclair castigated the leaders of the Catholic church in the South for having created an "enforced caste system . . . for the defenseless Negro." Auclair

25. Foley, *God's Men*, 219; William C. Bauer to Gustav J. Schultheiss, April 27, 1953, copy in Provincial's Correspondence, SPA; "History-Making Event Recorded in Mississippi," Pittsburgh *Courier*, May 2, 1953, "Cathedral Will Be the Scene of Bishop's Pontifical Mass," *Catholic Action of the South* (New Orleans), July 8, 1953, "Bishop Bowers Stays Here in Tour of U.S.," *Catholic Review* (Baltimore), July 31, 1953, clippings of all in Black Priests file, JFA.

26. Foley, *God's Men*, 219; Philip S. Olgivie, executive secretary of Catholic Committee of the South, to Mary Sabusowa, American Council on Race Relations, October 24, 1949, copy in Box 28-15, LaFarge Papers; "Archbishop Hits New Orleans Bias," *Times Picayune* (New Orleans), October 2, 1949, clipping in Black Priests file, JFA; McManus interview, June 10, 1985; Robert Grant to Charlie [?], November 23, 1952, in Robert Grant file, JFA; Bishop Richard O. Gerow to priests of the diocese, May 23, 1951, copy in Bishop Richard O. Gerow Papers, ADJ.

claimed that the bishops in the South had always considered blacks a problem and had "never hesitated to placate the white pharisees, the 'Talmadges' and the 'Bilboes.'" Arguing that segregation and discrimination "are still rampant in the Catholic Church," Auclair objected that priests and bishops taught blacks "the supremacy of the white race" instead of "the dignity of the human being." He declared, "We are more concerned with the color of faces and ancestry than we are with the salvation of immortal souls."[27]

Auclair's letter stung Gerow, who, in his own letter to McNamara, demanded a retraction and an apology. Gerow also indicated that he wanted to speak with McNamara about other Josephite actions "of the same nature." McNamara disavowed Auclair's letter, apologized for it, and suggested that the matter be dropped to avoid a further airing of the "ridiculous charges." He then rebuked Auclair, reminding him that the Josephites needed the good will and friendly support of the bishops, "since we have many parishes and missions in these dioceses." He specifically faulted Auclair for unfairly vilifying Gerow and Rummel and pointed out that if Auclair "had made the necessary distinctions in your all-embracing charges, perhaps we would not have the problem of trying to soothe over a very ticklish situation." He ordered Auclair to apologize immediately to Gerow. "No one admires your zeal . . . more than I," McNamara wrote. "However, your tactless statements . . . are needlessly and unfairly antagonizing our ecclesiastical superiors. We have enough headaches of our own without adding this one."[28]

A year later, in a move that no doubt found favor with Auclair, Rummel issued a five-page pastoral letter that was read on March 15, 1953, in all Catholic churches throughout the New Orleans archdiocese. In the letter, Rummel called for an end to segregation in church life. Anticipating a Supreme Court decision on segregation, he argued that Catholics could do much to hasten peaceful adjustment to the end of segregation in society by eliminating it first in Catholic life. Pointing to common membership in the Mystical Body of Christ and citing progress already achieved in integrating some aspects of church life, Rummel directed that "there be no further discrimination or segregation in the pews, at the Communion

27. R. A. Auclair to the editor, "Protests Southern Intolerance," *Priest*, VIII (March, 1952), 232–34.
28. Bishop Richard O. Gerow to Thomas P. McNamara, March 17, 1952, in Casserly-McNamara Papers; Thomas P. McNamara to Roderique Auclair, March 25, 1952, in Roderique A. Auclair file, JFA.

rail, at the confessional, and in parish meetings." Two months later, Bishop Waters went further, ordering an end to all segregation in the Catholic church in North Carolina and abolishing all separate churches for blacks. Following the historic *Brown* decision on May 17, 1954, Bishop William L. Adrian of Nashville integrated the parochial schools of that city, despite local ordinances to the contrary; and in Little Rock, Bishop Albert L. Fletcher declared that black Catholic children would "be admitted to any Catholic school available in places where there is no Catholic school especially for them." In San Antonio, Archbishop Robert Lucey had already effected the desegregation of Catholic institutions with relative ease.[29]

In the crucial archdiocese of New Orleans, the archdiocesan school board issued a statement, shortly after the *Brown* decision, that called the Supreme Court's ruling morally, if not legally, binding on the parochial school system. Rummel left the impression at a subsequent news conference that desegregation of the parochial schools would begin in 1955. In the meantime, however, the Louisiana legislature reaffirmed its commitment to segregation and its determination to oppose the decision. In order to thwart Rummel's planned integration of the parochial schools, members of the legislature formulated bills to remove the subsidies that the state gave to Catholic schools in the form of free textbooks, school lunches, and bus service for parochial students. Rummel feared that the loss of the subsidies would strike hardest at black Catholics, who, for the most part, needed them worse than did white Catholics. Although archdiocesan officials knew that federal courts would probably rule against the legislature's actions, they also realized that legal maneuvering could take years. In addition, some of Rummel's own consultors opposed the integration of the Catholic schools.[30]

Southern bishops recoiled in the face of the massive resistance that swept the South in the wake of the *Brown* decision. Bishop Gerow commented in his diary about the southern response: "The South has become frantic in its attack upon the Supreme Court and its attempts to thwart the decision. Citizens Councils have been organized . . . to bring economic, social, and other pressure upon any

29. William A. Osborne, *Segregated Covenant: Race Relations and American Catholics* (New York, 1967), 46, 75; "Urged Race Bias Halt," *Colored Harvest,* LXIII (May, 1953), 1; Osborne, *Segregated Covenant,* 46–47.

30. Osborne, *Segregated Covenant,* 79–81; McManus interview, September 9, 1983.

persons who . . . seem at variance with . . . 'Our Southern way of Life.'" Legislators in Louisiana and Mississippi became particularly enraged at the Catholic church in 1956 after Rummel publicly denounced segregation as sinful and morally wrong. In March, 1956, for example, the Mississippi state senate passed a bill denying tax exemptions "to any property . . . utilized on a non-segregated basis." The bill also provided that "if one property belonging to a certain corporation or society or body should forfeit this exemption then this forfeiture would apply to all other properties of that corporation or group or association within the state." Joining forces with the Episcopal and Methodist bishops of the state, Gerow and the Reverend Joseph B. Brunini of Vicksburg lobbied the governor and key members of the legislature against the bill. The governor announced his opposition to it on the grounds of separation of church and state, and the bill was not introduced into the House.[31]

Faced with the legislature's threats, the emergence of white citizens' councils, and the prospects of serious violence, Rummel backed away from desegregating Catholic schools; the impasse continued until 1962. In a classic understatement, Rummel told the American Board of Catholic Missions that "the problem creates many difficulties and anxieties." In 1959, a Catholic journal reported that, with the exception of North Carolina, only 2 out of 745 parochial schools in the states of the Deep South had desegregated their student bodies.[32]

In New Orleans and in other southern dioceses, the continued activism of Josephites who chafed at the slow pace of racial integration in the church added to the anxieties of Rummel and his fellow bishops. At their July, 1954, general chapter, two months after the *Brown* ruling, the Josephite delegates enthusiastically and unanimously approved a society commission on integration, with regional divisions "to work with the bishop in order to accomplish integration in the best possible way." They also adopted a policy statement on integration that applauded *Brown*, declared segrega-

31. Bishop Richard O. Gerow Diary, March 23–24, 1956 (Typescript in Richard O. Gerow Papers, ADJ).

32. Archbishop Joseph Rummel to American Board of Catholic Missions, October 1, 1954, copy in Peter J. Kenney Papers, JFA; Osborne, *Segregated Covenant*, 82–89; Philip A. Grant, Jr., "Archbishop Joseph F. Rummel and the 1962 New Orleans Desegregation Crisis," *Records of the American Catholic Historical Society of Philadelphia*, XCI, (March–December, 1980), 59–66; Glenn Jeansonne, *Leander Perez, Boss of the Delta* (Baton Rouge, 1977), 263–69; Osborne, *Segregated Covenant*, 47.

tion an "immoral and . . . vicious sin," and called on Josephites to exert leadership and use every opportunity to work "towards practical means of integrating the Negro into Catholic life." The statement also urged Josephites to identify themselves, "always discreetly and in a priestly manner," with Catholic civic movements working for results in society that paralleled those in the church, all the while sedulously avoiding "movements that are radical or even suspect." Specifically, the chapter recommended organizations such as the Catholic Committee of the South, the Catholic interracial councils, the local units of the urban league, and the Southern Regional Council.[33] The NAACP was noticeably absent from the list.

On October 20, 1955, Rummel complained to McNamara that the Josephites in New Orleans "are following a policy of urging rather immediately integration between the white and colored races." He cited Josephite agitation regarding Holy Name societies, sodalities of the Blessed Virgin, and Catholic Youth Organization (CYO) programs and demanded to know whether it represented official society policy or "was inspired by local agreement among the Josephites serving in the parishes of the New Orleans Archdiocese." Somewhat defensively, the embattled archbishop told McNamara that no one should question his desire to recognize the rights due to blacks, especially black Catholics. Then Rummel declared his considered position: "It is my conviction that integration cannot be forced down the line on all fronts, especially at the present time when the controversy over integration in the schools is the subject of serious tension. Efforts to press for integration in parish societies, the Catholic Youth Organization, playground programs, etc. would only multiply our difficulties."[34]

McNamara replied diplomatically, assuring Rummel that the Josephites, though opposed to segregation, realized that the archbishop could not eliminate the long-established pattern "in a day, or a month, or a year." He applauded Rummel's "Christ-like attitude" toward the evil of segregation and his efforts to wipe it out, as far as possible, in the archdiocese of New Orleans. McNamara sent the archbishop a copy of the society's statement on integration and assured him that he would remind Josephites stationed in the archdiocese of official Josephite policy.[35] In effect, McNamara stood by

33. Minutes of the general chapters, July 7, 1954, in JFA.

34. Archbishop Joseph Rummel to Thomas P. McNamara, October 20, 1955, in Casserly-McNamara Papers.

35. Thomas P. McNamara to Archbishop Joseph Rummel, November 4, 1955, copy in Casserly-McNamara Papers.

his men; Josephites in New Orleans continued to press Rummel on integration.

Although they were impatient with the pace of integration in many southern dioceses, the Josephites nonetheless appreciated the strong stands taken by Gerow in 1954 and Rummel in 1955 in defense of black priests. These prelates' decisive actions helped ensure that the desegregation of the Catholic priesthood would continue uninterrupted and that black Josephites assigned to the South would not suffer the fate of their forebears.

In 1952, the Reverend Herman A. (Martin) Porter, a black member of the Priests of the Sacred Heart of Jesus and a teacher of English and religion at Divine Heart Seminary in Donaldson, Indiana, wrote an article entitled "Color Line in Catholic Churches," which appeared widely in the Catholic press. Porter reported that he had encountered no racial discrimination while doing weekend pastoral work in white parishes and voiced the opinion that "there should be little hesitation to accept Negro boys qualified for the priesthood for general diocesan or religious order work among white people in the North."[36]

The idea of black priests ministering to whites touched a tender nerve in many white Catholics. Porter's article brought a letter from a Mrs. C. to the editor of the *Indiana Catholic and Record* of Indianapolis. She expressed a definite opinion: "No, we would not welcome a colored pastor. It is not necessary. Let them work among their own people. I believe in colored priests, but not in white people's churches. This our non-Catholic husbands and wives would not accept." In the same issue, the paper's editorialist observed that "Mrs. C. . . . was exposing the stand of a large group of Catholics, and we think this portion ought to be questioned." The editorial writer unintentionally revealed why black priests represented such a serious threat to white supremacy: "Every Catholic recognizes the office of the priesthood as that of an ambassador of Christ. The priest preaches in the name of Christ, he forgives sins in the name of Christ, he offers the Holy Sacrifice in the name of Christ. To reject or discriminate against Christ's instrument, Christ's ambassador on the basis of . . . color is an appalling insult to Christ himself." The editor of the *Indiana Catholic and Record* received numerous letters in response both to Mrs. C.'s letter and to the accompanying edi-

36. "Color Line in Catholic Churches," *Catholic Herald Citizen* (Milwaukee), February 2, 1952, clipping in Black Priests file, JFA.

torial; a majority of those published sided with the editorial stand of the newspaper but a significant minority agreed with Mrs. C.[37]

The question of black priests ministering to whites surfaced again in July, 1953, during the Third Annual Vocational Institute at Fordham University, attended by representatives of more than one hundred religious communities in the United States. These representatives approved a resolution written by John LaFarge that condemned racial discrimination against applicants for admission to any Catholic seminary or religious congregation. LaFarge also commented that "Negro priests and religious are doing a fine job among their own race." He quickly amended his statement, however: "It should not be necessary that they be consigned to race ministrations. Negroes are quick to sense this subterfuge and resent it as a trap and a surrender to racism." LaFarge maintained that "the work of black priests will never be on a sound and healthy footing as long as they are barred from ministering to other than their own race."[38] In Mississippi and Louisiana, Bishop Gerow and Archbishop Rummel found themselves confronting that very issue.

Robert E. Pung, the rector of St. Augustine's Seminary, frequently received requests from pastors in Mississippi and Louisiana for priests from the seminary to help out in parishes during weekends, periods of illness, and vacations. Pung had an arrangement with M. J. Costello, pastor of St. Clare's Parish in Waveland, Mississippi, approximately three miles west of the seminary, to supply a priest every Sunday. On February 2, 1954, Pung informed Gerow that some parishioners in Waveland "showed signs of resentment" when Carlos Lewis, a black Divine Word priest, arrived to say mass.

Gerow responded quickly, reassuring Pung that he had done the right thing in sending Lewis to Waveland. "If an emergency arises again or for other reasons you feel that it would be good to send him or one of the other priests, I want you to feel that is all right," Gerow wrote. "If any of the people don't like it, then that is their

37. "Opinions, Mrs. C. to the Editor" and "Lucky for Some Catholics that Christ Wasn't Colored," both in *Indiana Catholic and Record* (Indianapolis), February 15, 1952, clippings in Black Priests file, JFA. For letters to the editor, see "Opinions, T. G. M. to Editor," February 29, 1952, "E. D. to Editor," February 22, 1952, "Mrs. C. H. to Editor," March 28, 1952, "Naomi Blair to Editor," February 29, 1952, "Lucille Knopke to Editor," February 29, 1952, all in *Indiana Catholic and Record* (Indianapolis), clippings in Black Priests file, JFA.

38. "Religious Orders Score Racial Bias," religious news service press release, July 31, 1953, in Box 18-5, LaFarge Papers.

responsibility and not ours." He added, however, that in order to avoid embarrassment to the black priests, Pung should "exercise a certain amount of judgement" as to when and where he sent them. To emphasize his support for Pung and the black priests, Gerow sent Costello a copy of his letter to Pung, along with his personal congratulations to Costello for what he termed Costello's consideration in the matter.[39]

Gerow's letter relieved Pung. The following Sunday he again sent Lewis back to Waveland, since all the other priests at the seminary already had regularly scheduled visits to make. A few whites reportedly walked out of the church when they saw Lewis. Before the black priest returned to St. Augustine's Seminary from Waveland, Pung received a telephone call from a man who identified himself as Mr. Bourgeois. Bourgeois wasted no time on amenities with Pung: "We have had enough of this nonsense in our church. Don't you ever send another 'nigger' down here to this church. We don't stand for this." Pung interrupted the caller, telling him that Father Costello had requested a priest from the seminary and that both Costello and Bishop Gerow had given permission for either a black or white priest to say mass at St. Clare's. Bourgeois warned Pung that the next time he sent a "nigger" to Waveland, he would have to "come and get him." Then he hung up.

That afternoon Costello telephoned the seminary. Pung informed him about the incident, and Costello identified Fred Bourgeois as a troublemaker. When Pung advised Costello that he would stick to the established schedule and send a white priest the next Sunday, followed by black priests William Adams and Lewis on succeeding Sundays, Costello objected. "It is too hot to send any more colored Fathers down," he claimed. "It won't work." Pung expressed his disappointment over Costello's lack of courage and pointed out that so few people had walked out of the church that Lewis had failed to notice them leaving; besides, over three communion rails of people received the Eucharist from Lewis' hand, thus demonstrating that the vast majority of the white congregation had no difficulties in being ministered to by a black priest. Pung told Costello that in view of Gerow's stand on the issue and the principle involved, he could not promise to send always a white priest to the parish. Costello urged Pung to write a letter to Bourgeois about the

39. Bishop Richard O. Gerow to Robert Pung, February 4, 1954, in SASA.

matter, which he did. He also enclosed a copy of the letter, along with a full report on the new developments, to Gerow.[40]

Pung minced no words in his February 12, 1954, letter to Bourgeois. He termed Bourgeois' actions and attitudes "un-American" and "lawless." He told him, furthermore, that if Bourgeois wished to consider himself a good Catholic (a claim he had made on the phone), then he had to obey his lawful superior in the church, his bishop, and adhere to the teaching of the church that clearly proclaimed the essential unity and equality of all people as children of God, regardless of color. To emphasize his point, Pung quoted the Apostle John: "If anyone says, I love God, and hates his brother, he is a liar." Pung scoffed at Bourgeois' threats, pointing out that the history of the saints and martyrs of the church "should . . . convince you that no threat can scare a loyal priest into denying any doctrine of Christ by word or action." Declaring his intention of sending to Waveland "any priest who is available . . . and whom I think . . . qualified to take care of the task," Pung concluded by asking God's blessing and forgiveness for Bourgeois' "rash words" and by enclosing a copy of Bishop Gerow's letter of February 4, 1954.[41]

In his letter to Gerow on the same day, Pung expressed gratitude for the bishop's earlier expressions of support and also for his concern about possible embarrassment to the black Divine Word missionaries. Pung assured Gerow, however, that the black priests themselves had told him they would willingly accept the threat of "a little embarrassment" as part of their duty to stand up for the teachings of the Catholic church and of Jesus Christ. On the Thursday following the incident at Waveland, Archbishop Rummel, who had probably heard about the episode from Gerow, raised the matter during a meeting with Pung and assured him that his views coincided with Gerow's. Rummel also told Pung that since the New Orleans archdiocese suffered from a shortage of priests, he would like to use Divine Word missionaries for weekend work in selected parishes.[42]

After receiving Pung's report, Gerow stood firm. Although cautious about integration in other situations, he evidently believed

40. Robert Pung to Bishop Richard O. Gerow, February 12, 1954, copy in SASA.

41. Robert Pung to Fred Bourgeois, February 12, 1954, copy in SASA.

42. Robert Pung to Bishop Richard O. Gerow, February 12, 1954, copy in SASA.

the Lewis case involved such a clear-cut issue of respect for the priesthood and for the authority of the bishop that he felt constrained to support Pung and Lewis. He contacted Costello and insisted to him: "This matter has reached the point where we simply can't back down. We have to stand up for the principle and we cannot let Bourgeois or anyone else cause us to violate the principle." He invited Costello to meet with him at the Oblates of Mary Immaculate Seminary in Pine Hills, Mississippi, to discuss the situation. Obviously trying to bolster Costello's resolve, Gerow congratulated him for having adopted "the right attitude" following the initial complaints about Lewis. "Just at present I do not know what steps are necessary," Gerow concluded, "but . . . we just can't back down on this thing."[43]

Fred Bourgeois, meanwhile, visited Pung on Wednesday, February 18, and denied making the threatening telephone call. Evidently, news about the call had spread, upsetting a number of people in Waveland who thoroughly disapproved of such tactics. Then, too, the copy of Gerow's letter that Pung had sent to Bourgeois left little doubt that the bishop intended to support Pung and Lewis. Following his meeting with Bourgeois, Pung met with Costello, who had just conferred with Gerow. Pung and Costello agreed that the rector would furnish a priest for Waveland through May, but since he could not guarantee a priest during the summer months because of other commitments for many of his men, the two decided to allow the arrangement between St. Clare's and St. Augustine's Seminary to lapse. The new agreement clearly relieved Gerow, who viewed it as a way of supporting basic principles while also providing for the gradual elimination of a potential source of greater trouble. "For the good of the cause," he wrote Pung, "it would be wise not to let matters go to the point where there would be an open break . . . yet at the same time, we cannot back down on fundamental principles."[44]

Pung thanked Gerow for his backing and reported that, at the request of Archbishop Rummel, St. Augustine's Seminary would begin furnishing black and white priests on Sundays for two parishes in New Orleans. The pastors of the two parishes had decided to say nothing about the arrangement to their parishioners unless

43. Bishop Richard O. Gerow to M. J. Costello, February 18, 1954, copy in SASA.

44. Bishop Richard O. Gerow to Robert Pung, March 1, 1954, Robert Pung to Bishop Richard O. Gerow, March 3, 1954, copy, both in SASA.

asked directly by individuals. They also intended to ignore any remarks or opposition that might arise.[45] Rummel's invitation to the Divine Word Missionaries set the stage for a dramatic public confrontation in the archdiocese of New Orleans.

In August, 1955, Robert Pung became provincial of the southern province of the Society of the Divine Word. Effective as of September 1, 1955, Archbishop Rummel approved Pung's appointment of Clement Meyer as pastor of Our Lady of Perpetual Help in Belle Chasse, Louisiana, and for its missions at Jesuit Bend and Myrtle Grove, about fifteen miles south of New Orleans. Each of the three congregations included black and white parishioners, who sat on opposite sides of the aisle in church. All three lay in Plaquemines Parish, the stronghold of District Attorney Leander Perez, the political boss of the Delta, a die-hard segregationist, and a Catholic. Each weekend, a priest from St. Augustine's Seminary traveled to Belle Chase or its missions to say mass on Sunday, since Father Meyer could not cover the whole area.[46]

Gerald Lewis, the brother of Carlos Lewis and a mathematics and science teacher in the high school department of St. Augustine's Seminary, drew the assignment of saying mass at St. Cecilia's Chapel in Jesuit Bend on October 2, 1955. Lewis had celebrated mass that September for a racially mixed congregation in Edgard, Louisiana, without incident. Although he had received no prior warning that whites would object to a black priest at Jesuit Bend, Pung had some misgivings; he therefore made it a point to ask Rummel for permission to send one of the black priests to Jesuit Bend to assist on Sundays. The seventy-nine-year-old Rummel, who was suffering from glaucoma and who, at that time, also found himself deeply embroiled in the crisis over desegregating the Catholic schools in New Orleans, replied that since the Divine Word Missionaries administered the parish, Pung had every right to send a black priest to Jesuit Bend. In addition, the archbishop promised to step in if any problem arose. He asked only that Pung inform him prior to sending a black priest to Jesuit Bend for the first time.[47]

45. Robert Pung to Bishop Richard O. Gerow, March 3, 1954, copy in SASA.

46. Archbishop Joseph Rummel to Robert Pung, August 26, 1955, in SASA; Jeansonne, *Leander Perez*; Robert Pung to Stephen J. Ochs, April 30, May 27, 1985, in the possession of Stephen J. Ochs, Silver Spring, Md.

47. "Negro Priest Barred; Mission Is Rebuked," New York *Times*, October 15, 1955, "Parishes Placid in Racial Dispute," New York *Times*, October 16, 1955, "Masses Cut as Parish Scorns Negro Priest," *Advocate* (Newark), October 22, 1955, clippings of all in Black Priests file, JFA; Pung to Ochs, April 30, 1985.

Despite his clearly stated support for Pung, Rummel's handling of earlier cases may have unintentionally created the impression that whites could effectively veto black priests in their parishes. Some pastors in the New Orleans archdiocese had privately asked the Divine Word Missionaries to send only white priests as substitutes. On April 26, 1955, for example, Rummel had advised Pung that Monsignor Joseph A. Wester, pastor of St. Francis de Sales in Houma, Louisiana, needed a Divine Word priest on weekends; but the archbishop recommended that "under present conditions it would not be advisable to appoint as a regular helpmate . . . one of the Colored members" of the community. Instead of insisting that Wester accept any priest available, Rummel asked Pung to arrange for a white priest to help the monsignor. Other parishes in New Orleans also balked at accepting black priests. Rather than resort to fiat, Rummel attempted to persuade two of the pastors to accept black priests for help on Sundays.[48]

On Saturday night, October 1, 1955, Father Meyer warned Lewis that he might encounter trouble when he went to say mass at St. Cecilia's Chapel in Jesuit Bend the next day. About 12:30 A.M. on Sunday morning, Lewis was awakened in the rectory of Our Lady of Perpetual Help by a telephone call. An anonymous caller warned him not to offer mass at Jesuit Bend. As he had done with similar threats he received prior to saying mass in several white parishes in New Orleans, Lewis shrugged off the call. As he drove up to St. Cecilia's Chapel about 7:25 the next morning, however, he noticed a police cruiser parked in the chapel driveway and two armed, uniformed men standing with a small group of parishioners in front of the church. In the church yard, three parishioners, led by J. B. Perez, brother of Leander Perez, politely told Lewis that they, as delegates of the people of the parish, would neither allow him to enter the church nor permit any black to say mass in a white parish. With police standing around in the yard watching the scene, Lewis judged that the group had the backing of the law. He therefore did not argue but got back into his car and returned immediately to Belle Chasse to report the incident to Father Meyer. After speaking with Meyer, he proceeded to Myrtle Grove, where he was scheduled to celebrate the 9:30 A.M. mass. Meyer, meanwhile, drove to Jesuit Bend, where he found Perez and told him that he wanted no

48. Archbishop Joseph Rummel to Robert Pung, April 26, 1955, in Provincial's Correspondence, SPA; Pung to Ochs, May 27, 1985.

trouble in Myrtle Grove. Lewis celebrated mass in Myrtle Grove without incident. In his brief sermon, he mentioned the occurrence in Jesuit Bend, and after the service, six people came into the sacristy to express their regret.[49]

Angered and pained that white parishioners of St. Cecilia's had thus insulted the priesthood, Rummel immediately ordered the suspension of services at the chapel in Jesuit Bend and reduced from three to two the number of masses offered each Sunday at Our Lady of Perpetual Help in Belle Chasse. In a letter to the three communities involved, the archbishop explained his actions. He denounced the behavior of the whites at Jesuit Bend as "an act of injustice, uncharitableness, and irreverence . . . clearly a violation of the obligation of reverence and devotion which Catholics owe to every priest of God, regardless of race, color, or nationality." Rummel declared that his punitive measures would remain in effect until Catholics of the area expressed their willingness to accept whatever priest he sent to them. He thanked the group of Catholics at Myrtle Grove who had communicated to Lewis their sorrow over the outrage.[50]

Rummel took no further punitive measures against the three parishioners who had actually interfered with Lewis. As a result of the suspension of services at Jesuit Bend, some blacks, such as Mrs. Geneva Dobard, who had no means of traveling to Myrtle Grove or Belle Chasse, missed mass. She nevertheless observed that "the church is better off closed than the way it was."[51]

The overwhelming majority of Catholic newspapers around the country praised Rummel's actions. Most significant, on October 17, 1955, reportedly acting on direct instructions from the Vatican Secretariat of State, L'Osservatore Romano ran an unusual front-page editorial that deplored the behavior of the members of St. Cecilia's congregation and applauded Rummel's response, calling it "prompt, admirable, pastoral, and Catholic." The editorial claimed that Rummel's action "stirs every Catholic with Christian pride"

49. "Parishes Placid in Racial Dispute," New York Times, October 16, 1955, "Men Who Barred Black Priest Censured," New York Times October 31, 1955, clippings of both in Black Priests file, JFA.

50. "Organize Ban on Negro Priests," Catholic Exponent (Youngstown, Ohio), November 8, 1955, "Negro Priest Barred; Mission Is Rebuked," New York Times, October 15, 1955, clippings of both in Black Priests file, JFA.

51. "Parishes Placid in Racial Dispute," New York Times, October 16, 1955, "Faithful Divided on Closed Church," New York Times, October 17, 1955, clippings of both in Black Priests file, JFA.

and declared that anyone who impeded a priest from offering mass committed a sacrilege. It urged American Catholics to join the fight against racial prejudice, which it described as inhuman and as "a sin against the nature of the Catholic creed." Support from such an important source clearly buoyed the archbishop.[52]

Black American leaders hailed Rummel and also the Vatican. On October 18, 1955, A. Philip Randolph, president of the International Brotherhood of Sleeping Car Porters and veteran civil rights leader, conveyed his "heartfelt commendation and appreciation for the vigorous, courageous, and uncompromising stand" taken by the Vatican newspaper in support of Rummel. The next day, Channing Tobias, chairman of the board of the NAACP, wrote Pope Pius XII expressing his pleasure at reading "of the magnificent stand which the Vatican has taken with respect to racial discrimination" in the Jesuit Bend incident. On behalf of the NAACP, he thanked the pope for his leadership "in efforts to eradicate racial discrimination in the Christian Church." Tobias added, "The Roman Catholic Church in this country has played a vital role in the desegregation of schools and churches under the leadership of such representatives . . . as Bishop Vincent Waters, Archbishop Joseph Rummel, and Archbishop Joseph Ritter."[53]

On November 8, 1955, the "Louisiana sacrilege" became formally institutionalized. One hundred whites met at Belle Chasse and formed a citizens' council to keep black priests from offering mass in the area. The group claimed that it had obtained more than 250 names on a petition protesting the assignment of black priests to Plaquemines Parish. "The archbishop," said Arthur Bergeron, one of the council's leaders, "is trying to compel us to go against the way we were raised and the things we believe in." The petition characterized integration as contrary to church teaching and the assignment of black priests to white churches as a step toward breaking down segregation barriers. "If no white priest is available," declared Joseph Sendeker, who presided over the session, "let the church remain closed." He appointed a committee to draft a charter for the citizens' council.

52. "Vatican Commends New Orleans Prelate," New York Times, October 18, 1955, "Vatican City Daily Praises Archbishop's Action in Condemning Racial Prejudice," Catholic Action of the South (New Orleans), October 23, 1955, clippings of both in Black Priests file, JFA.

53. Carlos Lewis, S.V.D., "Jesuit Bend's Unknown Sequel," St. Augustine's Messenger, XXXIII (January, 1956), 6; "Letter Sent to Pope Pius XII," Colored Harvest, LXVII (December, 1955), 1.

The following evening, residents of the area boycotted a meeting at Our Lady of Perpetual Help Church in Belle Chasse, called by Father Meyer, to explain the Church's teaching on the issue. Five people at most appeared for the meeting, which normally would have drawn two hundred to three hundred. On November 10, 1955, in an attempt to clarify matters and to defuse charges from his opponents, Rummel issued a statement denying that Father Lewis had gone to Jesuit Bend as a regular assistant. Rummel asserted that he never intended to appoint a black priest as the regular assistant pastor.[54]

In a letter dated December 2, 1955, and read in the churches in Belle Chasse and Myrtle Grove, Rummel appealed to parishioners "to let justice and charity take the place of hatred and prejudice." He demanded that the leaders of those who had opposed Father Lewis give "an expression of sincere sorrow over the grievous offense which they committed." He asked them to consider prayerfully the teaching of the church "about the dignity of every true priest of God and the respect and confidence which we owe to his person and services." The day following the reading of the archbishop's letter, Meyer sent each member of his parish a card that read: "In conformity with the teaching of the Church on the dignity of the priesthood and the dignity of the human person, I regret the offenses committed in our community against this teaching. Henceforth, I will accept any priest appointed to give us Sunday Masses and other services." In a covering letter, Meyer asked his parishioners to sign and return the cards. "This letter is not meant to antagonize," he assured his people, but he also warned that they stood in serious danger both of losing the privilege of receiving the sacraments and of excommunication. "This is a matter of our Holy Faith," he pleaded. "It is a doctrine to which all must submit."[55]

54. "Negro Priests Opposed in Petition," *Evening Sun* (Baltimore), November 10, 1955, "Organize Ban on Negro Priests," *Catholic Exponent* (Youngstown, Ohio), November 18, 1955, "Action at Jesuit Bend Misinterpreted by Group," *Catholic Action of the South* (New Orleans), November 20, 1955, "Parishioners Shun Meeting on Issue of Negro Priests," *Catholic Transcript* (Hartford, Conn.), November 17, 1955, clippings of all in Black Priests file, JFA.

55. "'Let Justice, Charity Rule,' Plea in Jesuit Bend Situation," *Catholic Herald Citizen* (Milwaukee), December 17, 1955, "Parishioners Support Segregation Despite Prelate's Plea for Justice," *Pilot* (Boston), December 15, 1955, "Full Text of Archbishop's and Pastor's Messages Refutes False Statements," *Catholic Action of the South* (New Orleans), December 18, 1955, clippings of all in Black Priests file, JFA.

Most parishioners refused to submit. Following the reading of Rummel's letter and the distribution of the cards, the white opposition, led by Leander Perez, organized protests. Perez denounced the desegregation movement as communist-inspired and advised whites to combat it by organizing a greater New Orleans citizens' council of fifty thousand and by demanding that the Louisiana legislature outlaw the NAACP. A spokesman for the intransigent white parishioners of Jesuit Bend made a public broadcast over a New Orleans television station in which he claimed that the overwhelming majority of the Catholics of Jesuit Bend and Myrtle Grove believed strongly that the archbishop should not command under penalty of excommunication that they give lip service to "a dogma, doctrine, order, or request . . . that is contrary to their sincere beliefs and convictions."

In a second letter to Meyer, Rummel called the television statement "definitely subversive and contrary to the obligation which every Catholic has to accept the teachings of our Holy Church, especially in matters of 'dogma or doctrine.'" Rummel received public expressions of support from the New Orleans Archdiocesan Council of Catholic Women, which reaffirmed its devotion to "the priesthood of Jesus Christ and His duly ordained priests irrespective of their color." The New Orleans chapter of the Catholic Committee of the South sent letters to each of the approximately 250 families in the Belle Chasse parish and its missions, reminding them that the priest received his authority from God, not man. Father Lewis, who continued to serve other mission chapels, received nearly fourscore letters, from persons overseas and in the United States, expressing shame and indignation over the incident.[56]

The Jesuit Bend congregation, however, adamantly refused to sign the pledge demanded by Rummel; St. Cecilia's, therefore, remained closed for more than two years. In March, 1958, Pung left for Rome to attend the society's general chapter. Lacking confidence in Peter Oswald, the assistant pastor in Belle Chasse, Pung explicitly instructed his assistant provincial to do nothing regarding Jesuit Bend until he returned. While in Rome, Pung was elected a general consultor of the Society of the Divine Word and thereupon

56. "Catholics Rap Rummel," Pittsburgh *Courier*, December 24, 1955, "Jesuit Bend Incident at Standstill Following Letter to Parishioners," *Catholic Standard and Times* (Philadelphia), December 23, 1955, "Deplore Stand on Negro Priest," *Catholic Review* (Baltimore), November 25, 1955, clippings of all in Black Priests file, JFA; Lewis, "Jesuit Bend's Unknown Sequel," 4–11.

resigned as provincial. During Pung's absence, Oswald, in an attempt to end the two-year dispute, collected signatures from some white parishioners in Jesuit Bend on a document stating that they would accept any duly ordained priest sent to them. Oswald reportedly managed to secure the signatures by quietly promising the people that the Divine Word Missionaries would never send another black priest to assist at St. Cecilia's. Whether Oswald did indeed make such a promise remains unclear, as does the role of the pastor, Frank Ecimovich. At any rate, Oswald presented the signatures to Rummel, who, though disappointed at the small number, nevertheless decided to reopen the chapel.[57]

In a letter to Ecimovich, Rummel set Easter Sunday, April 6, 1958, as the date for reopening St. Cecilia's. Prior to that date, he ordered three days of prayer in reparation for the original offense and in thanksgiving for its resolution. The triduum of prayer would begin in Belle Chasse and Myrtle Grove on Palm Sunday. Rummel noted "with supreme regret . . . that it has been possible to obtain only some inadequate expressions of sincere sorrow." Alluding to the coercive tactics of Leander Perez, Rummel attributed the reluctance of many to sign the cards to "certain intimidating influences which are equally deplorable." The archbishop explained, nevertheless, that he could not permit the closed chapel "to stand forever as a symbol of resistance to the authority of the Church and . . . contempt for the Holy Priesthood"; nor did he believe that he could indefinitely deprive "the majority of good and well meaning Catholics of the use of the House of God because of the obstinacy of a few." Finally, Rummel said, he could not ignore the example of Christ, who pleaded, "Father, forgive them, for they know not what they do." On Easter Sunday, as spider webs on some of the chapel windows of St. Cecilia's waved gently in the soft breeze off the nearby Mississippi River, Ecimovich celebrated mass for fifty-five white and twenty-five black parishioners.[58]

On his return from Rome in June, Pung learned about Oswald's alleged maneuvering and promptly informed Rummel. Pung's report upset the archbishop, who found himself in a bind. He thought that, the new information notwithstanding, he ought not reverse himself and close the chapel again, only two months after reopen-

57. Robert Pung to Stephen J. Ochs, April 30, May 27, 1985.

58. "Jesuit Bend Services to Resume," *Catholic Action of the South* (New Orleans), April 6, 1958, "Mass Said Again at Jesuit Bend," *Times Picayune* (New Orleans), April 7, 1958, clippings of both in Black Priests file, JFA.

ing it. Nature, however, providentially intervened: a hurricane destroyed St. Cecilia's Chapel. When Ecimovich and Oswald asked Rummel to rebuild it, he emphatically told them, "No!" Subsequently, the priest from Belle Chasse drove a bus to Myrtle Grove, about eight miles down the river, to say mass. On the way, he picked up black parishioners from Jesuit Bend. The whites drove themselves.[59]

Like so many of his actions in dealing with the knotty problem of race relations, Rummel's handling of the Jesuit Bend incident left him open to second-guessing. Prior to the incident, by his tolerance of certain pastors who refused to accept black priests for weekend help, he may unintentionally have given whites the impression that they could veto the assignment of black priests to their parishes. The Jesuit Bend incident differed from these private disagreements between Rummel and some of his pastors: it involved a public insult by laymen to a priest whom Rummel had authorized to say mass. As such, it represented a lay challenge not only to the archbishop's racial policies but also to his authority. Critics, including some Josephites, argued that rather than closing the chapel Rummel should have publicly excommunicated the three white parishioners who prevented Father Lewis from saying mass. Those same critics argued, moreover, that once Rummel closed St. Cecilia's Chapel, he should not have reopened it after receiving only a handful of cards promising to accept any priest sent in the future.[60]

Despite his critics' claims, Rummel's public stand in defense of black priests indicated that the cause of a black clergy had made significant gains. His actions contrasted sharply with those of previous archbishop of New Orleans James H. Blenk, who forty-six years earlier had refused permission to Josephite John Plantevigne to conduct a mission because he feared white reaction. Rummel's willingness both to allow black priests into his archdiocese and to support them in the face of opposition made it possible for a black Josephite to return at last to the Crescent City.

The ordination of Joseph Verrett in June, 1955, marked a new phase in the history of black Josephites. Verrett was the first black Josephite ordained since Chester Ball in 1941 and the first of the black students admitted by Casserly in 1945 to receive holy orders.

59. Robert Pung to Stephen J. Ochs, April 30, May 27, 1985.
60. John McShane to George F. O'Dea, July 24, 1958, in George F. O'Dea Papers, JFA.

He had distinguished himself throughout his college and seminary career: in March, 1955, when Casserly, then the rector of St. Joseph's Seminary, had asked the faculty for an appraisal of the deacon class, Timothy Holland described Verrett as "one of the two best in the class." Holland predicted that Verrett could do well on any assignment and "if not sent on for higher studies . . . should be the answer to some of the problems in the high school." Holland pointed out that "he would be good publicity in New Orleans, should be a good teacher, and probably would settle some of the situations which might be embarrassing to other priests."[61]

Verrett's imminent ordination also delighted other Josephites. During 1954 and 1955, John A. McShane, pastor of St. Lucy's in Houma, peppered McNamara with so many requests for Verrett's services that the exasperated superior general finally ordered him to cease his importuning because it had become known at the seminary, giving rise to jokes and causing embarrassment to Verrett. Andrew J. Eck, pastor of Verrett's home parish of St. Joan of Arc, became so excited about plans for Verrett's first mass there that he proposed a massive renovation and decoration of the church that would have cost ten thousand dollars. Once again, McNamara found himself forced to cool the ardor of another of his overly enthusiastic men, and he refused permission for such large expenditures.[62]

Despite the excitement surrounding Verrett's ordination, the Josephite administration handled the matter in a low-key manner, giving it no special publicity. The July–August issue of *Colored Harvest*, for example, ran a picture of the fifteen-man ordination class, the largest in Josephite history, without mentioning that one of the newly ordained, the relatively light-skinned Verrett, was black.[63]

Following ordination, Verrett returned to St. Joan of Arc Parish for his first mass. The next Sunday, he accepted the invitation of the irrepressible McShane to celebrate mass in Houma. After brief stints during the summer at All Saints Parish in Algiers, Louisiana, and Most Pure Heart of Mary Parish in Mobile, he reported to St. Augustine's High School in September, 1955. The talented and

61. Timothy Holland to Edward V. Casserly, March 30, 1955, in St. Joseph's Seminary file, JFA.

62. John McShane to Thomas P. McNamara, March 2, April 25, August 12, 1954, Thomas P. McNamara to John McShane, January 19, 1954, copy, A. J. Eck to Thomas P. McNamara, September 27, 1954, Thomas P. McNamara to A. J. Eck, October 4, 1954, copy, all in Casserly-McNamara Papers.

63. *Colored Harvest*, LXVII (July–August, 1955), 4.

personable Verrett quickly earned the respect and affection of faculty and students. He taught English and coached dramatics. An avid sports fan, he became almost a stepfather to some of the basketball and football players. Verrett also became involved in efforts to desegregate the Catholic schools of New Orleans, participating, for instance, in a series of eight public forums sponsored by the Commission on Human Rights of the Catholic Committee of the South, which produced a handbook on Catholic school integration.[64]

Verrett yearned to be accepted as a priest and as a man and resented being put on display as a black priest. Nevertheless, during his first years in New Orleans, he became, in his own words, "a professional invocation giver." He received invitations from groups and organizations throughout the city to bless street lights and golf courses and address boy scout troops and communion breakfasts. Verrett even received a special invitation from the chancery office each year to assist at the Holy Thursday blessing of the chrism by the archbishop; the other Josephites in the St. Augustine's High School community received only a general invitation. Verrett began sarcastically to refer to the chancery as "Hertz rent a Negro."[65]

Whereas some whites tried to use Verrett as their token black, others occasionally objected to his mere presence. The Josephite priests at St. Augustine's High School, like the Divine Word Missionaries at St. Augustine's Seminary, took turns on weekends substituting at parishes in New Orleans for priests who went on vacation, became ill, or found themselves shorthanded. In one case, shortly after the Jesuit Bend incident, Monsignor Magnus Roth, the German pastor of Holy Trinity Parish, asked the Josephites at the high school to send a priest to help him on Sundays. He assured them that they could send any priest they wished. The Josephites went through two rotations, and after Verrett's second visit to the parish, Roth called Frank Cassidy, the rector of the high school, and asked him not to send Verrett again, because he had received complaints from some members of the congregation. Cassidy sent Eugene P. McManus, a member of the faculty, an outspoken civil rights leader in the New Orleans archdiocese, and Roth's friend, to speak to him. McManus, purposely adopting a kindly demeanor, gently asked Roth why he had requested that Verrett not return to

64. Thomas P. McNamara to Joseph Verrett, September 8, 1955, in Joseph C. Verrett file, JFA; McManus interview, September 9, 1983; Verrett interview, May 29, 1985.
65. Verrett interview, May 29, 1985.

Holy Trinity. Roth replied that several white parishioners had telephoned to tell him that they did not "want any nigger priests." Roth, a peaceful, gentle man, wanted to avoid conflict and thought that a quiet arrangement with the Josephites would eliminate the problem.

McManus asked Roth how many phone calls he had received. When Roth replied, "Seven," McManus reminded him that Verrett had celebrated mass before a packed congregation. He queried the monsignor as to how he could allow seven isolated racist telephone calls to outweigh the dignity of the priesthood. Roth responded that he had "never thought of it that way" and told McManus to send Verrett the next week. The following Sunday, when Verrett arrived to say mass, the embarrassed Roth avoided him. The Josephites heard no more reports of hostile reaction at the parish. After the incident, the Josephites refused to accept assignments to white parishes unless the pastors knew that they had a black priest on the faculty and agreed to accept priests in rotation. Verrett remained at St. Augustine's High School until 1961. During his tenure, he became Josephite vocation recruiter for New Orleans in 1959 and assistant principal of St. Augustine's in 1960. A number of students from New Orleans were inspired by his example to enter Epiphany Apostolic College.[66]

Verrett's appointment to New Orleans symbolized a new era for black Josephite priests. The exclusion of a black Josephite from New Orleans in 1909 had helped trigger a long period of retrenchment in the society. Verrett's appointment there and the willingness of the archbishop to accept him returned black Josephites to the Deep South and completed a circle of events that had begun with John Plantevigne's ordeal. In June, 1959, four years after Verrett's arrival in New Orleans, a second black Josephite was assigned to a parish in the South. McNamara named Chester Ball as assistant at Our Mother of Mercy Parish in Houston. In assigning black priests in the South, McNamara and O'Dea adopted an assertive approach to bishops. They simply notified the ordinary of the appointment, without designating the race of the man. They resolved that if they encountered any resistance from a bishop, they would fight him, including appealing the matter to Rome. They ex-

66. McManus interview, September 9, 1983; Verrett interview, May 29, 1985; Joseph Verrett to Thomas P. McNamara, November 18, 1959, in Joseph C. Verrett file, JFA; Verrett interview, May 29, 1985.

perienced no opposition to the appointment of black priests.[67] The publication, on November 17, 1958, of a pastoral letter from the American bishops entitled "Racial Discrimination and the Christian Conscience," which condemned segregation as contrary to Christian teaching and declared that the heart of the race question was "moral and religious," gave added impetus to the cause of black priests.[68] The letter made it even more difficult for any bishop to refuse a prospective black seminarian or priest.

By the end of the decade, St. Joseph's Seminary had begun to produce additional black Josephite priests. The ordinations of Rawlin Enette in June, 1959, and of Charles Hall and Elbert Harris in June, 1960, brought the total to 5—the most that St. Joseph's Society had ever had at one time, though far less than the Divine Word Missionaries, or the Benedictines for that matter.[69]

In addition to the Josephites' Harris and Hall, 10 other black priests were ordained in 1960, a record number for the Catholic church in the United States. According to a survey conducted by the Society of the Divine Word, in 1960 the number of black priests had risen to 106, a paltry figure compared to the roughly 50,000 white priests, but a dramatic increase nevertheless over the previous decade. There were 15 more black clerics anticipating ordination in 1961, and another 50 black seminarians studying philosophy and theology would become candidates for ordination in the years up to 1966. Of the 106 black priests, 31 were diocesan; the remaining 75 belonged to seventeen religious communities. Among the religious institutes, the Divine Word Missionaries led with 33. The Benedictines counted 14; the Josephites and Spiritans numbered 5 each. The Conventual Franciscans followed with 3, whereas the Edmundites, White Fathers, and Blessed Sacrament Fathers each claimed 2. Nine other communities had 1 apiece.[70]

67. Thomas P. McNamara to Bishop Wendelin J. Nold, June 19, 1959, copy in Casserly-McNamara Papers; interview of George F. O'Dea, S.S.J., by Stephen J. Ochs, August 10, 1983.

68. "Discrimination and Conscience," *Colored Harvest*, LXXI (January, 1959), 4–5; minutes of the annual meeting of the hierarchy, November 11, 1958, in AUSCC. John F. Cronin, S.S., provides an account of events leading to the issuance of the pastoral—including the role played by Pope Pius XII—in "Religion and Race," *America*, June 30, 1984, p. 472.

69. Joseph L. Waters to Thomas P. McNamara, April 30, 1960, in Casserly-McNamara Papers.

70. "12 Negroes Ordained in Year," *Register* (national edition), August 28, 1960, clipping in Black Priests file, JFA.

A new day had apparently dawned for the Josephites and for black priests in the Catholic church. With 5 black priests and with black students and seminarians composing at least one-third of the enrollments at Epiphany Apostolic College and St. Joseph's Seminary, the Josephites entered the turbulent sixties confident that they had recaptured the spirit of their founder and that a steady stream of black Josephite priests would enable them to evangelize the black community more effectively and to contribute significantly to the struggle for a truly integrated priesthood, church, and nation.

Epilogue

UNFINISHED MISSION, 1960–1988

For the Josephites, the decade of the 1960s witnessed the best and worst of times. Josephites supported and applauded the gains of the civil rights movement, which culminated in the march on Washington in 1963 and the subsequent passage of the Civil Rights Act of 1964 and the Voting Rights Act of 1965. Within the Catholic church, Catholic interracial councils united to form a nationwide organization, the National Catholic Conference for Interracial Justice, and joined in 1963 with Protestants and Jews to form the National Conference on Religion and Race, which lobbied effectively for passage of civil rights legislation. Formal segregation ended in Catholic churches, schools, hospitals, and seminaries during the decade, and the number of black Catholics increased by 220,000, a gain of 35 percent, over half of whom were converts. By 1966, the number of black priests stood at 165; that same year, the Holy See appointed the Reverend Harold R. Perry, a Divine Word priest, as auxiliary bishop of New Orleans, making him the first black man to join the ranks of the American episcopacy since Bishop James Augustine Healy. Between 1960 and 1969, the Josephites began to reap the harvest of their fifteen-year recruiting effort among blacks, as they added 11 black priests (approximately one-fourth of the total of all new Josephite priests) to their ranks.[1]

As the decade drew to a close, however, optimism and hope

1. William A. Osborne, *Segregated Covenant: Race Relations and American Catholics* (New York, 1967), 40–41; John F. Cronin, S.S., "Religion and Race," *America*, June 30, 1984, p. 472; Osborne, *Segregated Covenant*, 233–34; James Hennesey, S.J., *American Catholics: A History of the Roman Catholic Community in the United States* (New York, 1981), 313; "Need Negro Priests," *Clarion Herald* (New Orleans), March 17, 1966, "Negro Appointed as U.S. Bishop," *Sun* (Baltimore), October 31, 1965, clippings of both in Black Priests file, JFA; Earle A. Newman, S.S.J., "List of Ordinands: 1930–1980" (Typed list in St. Joseph's Seminary file, JFA).

evaporated in the face of the revolutionary currents unleashed by the growth of black consciousness (often described by the term *black power*), the Second Vatican Council, and the Vietnam War. Although the full story will have to await the availability of sources and the cooling of the passions of the participants, the outline is clear. On April 18, 1968, 58 black priests, including several Josephites, met in Detroit and organized the Black Catholic Clergy Caucus, declaring that "the Catholic Church in the United States is primarily a white racist institution." Assuming the leadership role envisioned for them by Thomas Turner, the black priests demanded a black vicariate and the appointment of an episcopal vicar for all black Catholics in the country, a black-directed office for black Catholics within the framework of the United States Catholic Conference (successor organization to the NCWC), establishment of a black diaconate, increased recruitment of black men for the priesthood, incorporation of Afro-American culture into Catholic liturgies designed for blacks, inclusion of black history and culture in seminary curricula, and diocesan programs for training black leadership. The Black Catholic Clergy Caucus inspired the formation of other groups of black Catholics, including the National Black Sisters' Conference, the National Black Catholic Seminarians' Caucus, and the National Black Catholic Lay Caucus.[2]

Disillusionment with their church, which many criticized as paternalistic and Eurocentric, spread among black Catholics, including priests and seminarians. Some questioned whether it was even possible to remain "both black and Catholic." The question of race also exacerbated the vocation crisis that suddenly emerged in the church at the same time. One study estimated that between 1970 and 1975, 250 black seminarians withdrew from seminaries, 125 of 900 black sisters left their communities, and 25 of 190 black priests left the ordained ministry. Some observers calculated that as many as 20 percent of black Catholics no longer practiced their religion.[3]

2. "Statement of the Black Catholic Clergy Caucus, April 18, 1968," copy, "Negro Priests Describe Church as 'A White Racist Institution,'" *St. Louis Review*, April 26, 1968, clipping, both in Black Priests file, JFA; Joseph M. Davis, S.M., and Cyprian Howe, F.M.S., "The Development of the National Office for Black Catholics," *U.S. Catholic Historian*, VII, Nos. 2 and 3 (1988), 269; Hennesey, *American Catholics*, 324–25; Lawrence Lucas, *Black Priest/White Church: Catholics and Racism* (New York, 1970), 186–97. Lucas' book provides a clear, if somewhat extreme, expression of the anger, ideas, and objectives that underlay the rise of black power in the church.

3. Joseph A. Francis, "Black and Catholic—1," *America*, March 29, 1980, pp. 256–57; Hennesey, *American Catholics*, 324.

St. Joseph's Society found itself at the center of the crisis that engulfed the black Catholic community. Once again, as in earlier times of unrest, the predominantly white Josephites, often the most visible symbol of the church in the black community, came under attack from black Catholic activists, who accused them of paternalism, insensitivity to Afro-American culture, and failure to develop black leadership. On the last charge, the Josephites were particularly vulnerable since activists could dredge up the past and accurately point out that despite its being the only institute of Catholic priests devoted exclusively to ministry in the black community, St. Joseph's Society had, for a considerable period of its history, all but barred blacks from its college and seminary. In an attempt to dramatize what they called the failure of the Josephites to relate to the black community, representatives of the National Black Catholic Lay Caucus staged a sit-in at Josephite headquarters in Baltimore on March 27, 1971, and presented a list of general demands to Matthew O'Rourke, the Josephite superior general. The demonstrators called on the Josephites to "make black priests and brothers more visible in black communities," to develop a diaconate program "relevant to Black people," to sponsor programs to foster "the development of real Black leadership," and to institute an ongoing program of black awareness for all Josephite priests and brothers under the direction of the National Office for Black Catholics (established in 1970).[4]

The demand that they help develop a diaconate program relevant to blacks was ironic given the pivotal role played by Josephite superior general George F. O'Dea in convincing the National Catholic Conference of Bishops in 1967 to recommend to the Holy See the restoration of the Order of Permanent Deacons in the United States. On June 27, 1967, Pope Paul VI had authorized the restoration of that diaconate in the Roman rite, making it possible for qualified married men at least thirty-five years old to become deacons permanently, without going on to the priesthood. Following the pope's approval of the restoration of the order, the American bishops held prolonged discussions during three general meetings and seven meetings of the forty-member administrative committee of the National Conference of Catholic Bishops. On October 12, 1967, O'Dea sent a letter to Archbishop John F. Dearden, president of the conference, to Bishop Ernest L. Unterkoeffler, chair-

4. "Special Information Report on National Black Catholic Lay Caucus," [sent to all Josephites in spring, 1971] (Typescript in Joseph C. Verrett file, JFA).

man of the bishops' committee for the permanent diaconate, and to the seventeen ordinaries under whom the Josephites worked. He strongly urged the bishops to approve restoration of the permanent diaconate, arguing that "in this period of 'Black Consciousness,' it is imperative to have worthy Negro men in responsible positions in the Church." During the decisive November, 1967, meeting, the bishops referred to O'Dea's letter and subsequently approved the petition for restoration of the permanent diaconate in the United States. The Holy See gave its formal approbation in October, 1968.[5]

St. Joseph's Seminary in Washington, D.C., also became a focal point of tension and turmoil between 1967 and 1972 as black and white seminarians and faculty wrestled with the implications of black power, the counter culture, the Vietnam War, and the Second Vatican Council. Seminarians at St. Joseph's demanded greater academic and personal freedom. In addition, black seminarians clamored for an end to the imposition of what they termed Anglo-Saxon cultural norms and for permission to wear symbols of black identity such as Afro hairstyles and mustaches.

The atmosphere at the seminary became increasingly charged as the positions of both the older Josephites and the younger seminarians hardened in opposition to each other. The black power movement confused and threatened many of the faculty, white and black, who for years had championed the ideal of integration and who viewed the new attitudes, demands, and behavior of black seminarians as separatist, racist, un-Catholic, and ultimately inimical to the colorblind society that they had tried to build. Conversely, many black seminarians regarded much of the faculty as insensitive, irrelevant, white paternalists or as black Uncle Toms who did not understand the true black community and its need for autonomy and self-determination. Similarly, some questioned the underlying motivation of their white classmates, many of whom began to wonder whether they had any positive contribution to make among blacks or whether perhaps they suffered from a misguided white-man's-burden mentality. The crisis at the seminary culminated in 1972 with the transfer of faculty members and the departure of most of the black and many of the white seminarians; four black priests also left the society.[6]

5. See "Statement on the Josephite Permanent Deacon Program," in "Chapter of Renewal Position Papers, 1968–1971" (Typescript in JFA).

6. CMB, April 7, 1967, in JFA; interview of Peter E. Hogan, S.S.J., December 29, 1982, interview of Robert E. McCall, S.S.J., June 24, 1982, inter-

Although hurt and dismayed by the loss of so many talented black seminarians and priests and shocked by the animosity some black Catholics displayed toward them, the Josephites in the late sixties and early seventies struggled to understand and adapt to the changes sweeping through black America. They responded to the challenges from black Catholics more reflectively and less defensively than Pastorelli and his generation had done. They attempted to listen to the different segments of the black Catholic community and tried, through their chapter of renewal from 1968 to 1971, mandated by the Holy See in the wake of Vatican II for all religious institutes, to reexamine their ministry, both in terms of the spirit of their founder and in light of the rise of black consciousness. As a result, the Josephites renewed their commitment to serve Afro-Americans and pledged themselves to foster black leadership within their society and the church through programs such as the permanent diaconate, parish councils, and continued recruitment of black vocations.[7]

In keeping with the Josephites' commitment to promote black leadership, Superior General O'Rourke in 1971 appointed Eugene Marino as vicar general of St. Joseph's Society, second in command only to himself. In 1974, Carl Fisher, a newly ordained black priest, became director of vocations. Although the number of seminarians both in the Josephites and throughout the church plunged during the seventies, 5 of the 25 Josephites ordained during the decade were black.[8]

Gradually, the conflict and pessimism of the early seventies gave way to renewed hope for black Catholics and for the Josephites.

---

views of Joseph C. Verrett, S.S.J., May 29, June 1, June 7, 1985, interview of Joseph L. Waters, S.S.J., June 30, 1983, all by Stephen J. Ochs; interview of Bishop-elect Eugene A. Marino, S.S.J., by Peter E. Hogan, S.S.J., August 13, 1974 (Typescript in JFA), 36–37, 39–44; interview of Carl A. Fisher, S.S.J., by Stephen J. Ochs, July 12, 1985.

7. See, for example, "Aims and Goals," "Changing Black Community," "Academic and Spiritual Formation," and "The Permanent Diaconate," in "Position Papers Prepared for the General Conference, July 7 to July 27, 1971" (Typescript in JFA).

8. "Bishop Eugene A. Marino: The Path from Biloxi, Miss., Has Been Full of Surprises," Washington Post, July 23, 1974, clipping in Black Priests file, JFA; Fisher interview, July 12, 1985; Newman, "List of Ordinands: 1930–1980"; Earle A. Newman, "Editorial," "From the Beginning," both in Josephite Harvest, LXXXVI (Summer, 1984), 2–6.

The National Office for Black Catholics, established in 1970 in response to black demands, led to the formation of black secretariats
in many dioceses throughout the country. Many black parishes incorporated explicitly Afro-American symbols, themes, music, and
styles into their worship, and the ordination of 265 lay black deacons by 1984 added more blacks to positions of visibility in the
church. Despite the hemorrhage of black seminarians in the early
1970s and the mass exodus of priests that plagued the church during
that period, the number of black priests increased after the mid-
seventies, climbing to 300 by 1985.[9]

What is perhaps even more significant, between 1966 and 1988,
as the pool of black priests expanded, the Holy See responded to
black demands for positions of authority in the church by naming
thirteen black bishops, including three Josephites: Eugene A. Marino, auxiliary bishop of Washington, D.C., in 1974; John H.
Ricard, auxiliary bishop of Baltimore, in 1984; and Carl A. Fisher,
auxiliary bishop of Los Angeles, in 1986. Until May, 1988, only
one of the black bishops, Joseph L. Howze of Biloxi, served as an
ordinary. On May 5, 1988, however, Marino became the second
black ordinary and the first black archbishop in the United States,
when he was installed as archbishop of Atlanta.[10]

During the 1980s, the black bishops provided important leadership for an energized black Catholic community. In 1984, they
issued a pastoral letter on evangelization in the black community
entitled "What We Have Seen and Heard." In it they described
themselves as a "sign among many other signs that the black Catholic community in the American Church has now come of age."
They noted with concern, however, that blacks remained meagerly
represented on the decision-making levels of the church. The letter
inspired a movement for a national gathering of black Catholics,
which took place in May, 1987, when the National Black Catholic
Congress, the first such meeting since 1894, met in Washington,
D.C., to map out an agenda for black Catholic action. In August of
that same year, Pope John Paul II, during the course of his visit to

9. John Harfmann, S.S.J., *1984 Statistical Profile of Black Catholics* (Washington, D.C., 1985), iii, 8–9.

10. "Bishop Eugene A. Marino: The Path from Biloxi, Miss., Has Been Full of
Surprises," Washington *Post*, July 23, 1974, clipping in Black Priests file, JFA;
Fisher interview, July 12, 1985; Newman, "List of Ordinands: 1930–1980"; Newman, "Editorial," "From the Beginning," 2–6; *Josephite Harvest*, LXXXIX (Spring,
1987), 2; *Catholic Standard* (Washington, D.C.), May 5, 1988, pp. 20–27.

the United States, signaled his support for the black Catholic community by meeting privately in New Orleans with the black bishops and by addressing a gathering of black Catholics in the New Orleans Superdome. The pope's highly visible identification with the cause of black Catholics came as a result of an earlier representation to the Holy See by the black Catholic prelates, some of whom, including Marino, had traveled to Rome to present their case.[11]

The predominantly white Catholic hierarchy also manifested a greater sensitivity and receptivity to black Catholics. In 1979, for example, the bishops of the United States issued a pastoral letter, "Brothers and Sisters to Us," which acknowledged the existence of racism within the church, committed that institution to eliminating all forms of racial injustice, particularly in its hiring and business practices, and pledged to find ways for black Catholics to contribute their unique gifts to the church. In November of 1986, the National Conference of Catholic Bishops approved a National Secretariat for Black Catholics.[12] Reflecting the positive developments between 1975 and 1985 (as well as an influx of Haitian refugees), the black Catholic population increased by 60 percent, from 916,854 to approximately 1,500,000, though it still lagged far behind the approximately 11,000,000 black Baptists and 4,000,000 black Methodists.[13]

The Josephites could take justifiable pride in the hopeful developments occurring in the black Catholic community during the 1980s. Through their pastoral center, parishes, priests, and black bishops, they had played a significant role in the revitalization of black Catholicism. Still, black vocations remained in short supply. The approximately 300 black priests for roughly 1,500,000 black Catholics translated into 1 priest for every 5,000 people, as com-

11. *Catholic Standard* (Washington, D.C.), May 5, 1988, p. 25, September 20, 1984, p. 5; *National Catholic Reporter*, March 8, 1985, p. 8; June 5, 1987, pp. 1, 8; Edward K. Braxton, "The National Black Catholic Congress," *America*, July 18–25, 1987, pp. 29–37; *Mentor*, August–September, 1987, pp. 1–3, 6, 8, 12, 15–18; Bishop Eugene A. Marino memorandum and enclosures to Bishop Moses B. Anderson, S.S.E., *et al.*, March 16, 1987, copy in JFA; *Mentor*, November–December, 1987, pp. 1, 3, 7, 8, 9–11.

12. Rev. Edward K. Braxton, "Black Catholics in the United States: An Historical Perspective" (Typescript in JFA).

13. Hennesey, *American Catholics*, 324–25; Harfmann, *1984 Statistical Profile of Black Catholics*, iii, 8–9; "Black Catholics," *America*, August 23, 1986, p. 63; *Encyclopedia of American Religions* (2nd ed.), 276–79, 399–401. For reflections on being black and Catholic, see *America*, March 29, 1980, pp. 256–77.

pared to 53,522 priests in 1989 for 53,496,862 U.S. Catholics, an overall ratio of 1 priest for every 800 people. By 1988, over forty years after Casserly had resumed active recruitment of black vocations, the Josephites counted only 12 black priests (and 2 bishops and 1 archbishop) among their declining membership of 151. In their formation program, 4 of 7 seminarians and 4 of 5 college students were black.[14]

Obviously, neither the Josephites nor the church in the United States had managed to overcome the shortages created by earlier discrimination. Still, significant progress had occurred. Between 1960 and 1988, the number of black Catholic priests had increased by 200 percent, and the twenty-two years between 1966 and 1988 had seen 13 black men raised to the episcopacy. Although the Reverend George Stallings, with his founding of Imani Temple and his calls for an African-American rite, complete with its own liturgy and bishops, struck a responsive chord in a number of black Catholics who felt alienated from the church, the majority appeared resolved to follow the trail blazed by Archbishop Marino, pushing from within the institution for full inclusion in its life. The differing paths of the two men nonetheless highlighted a question that lay at the heart of the black Catholic experience and, more particularly, at the center of the struggle for black Catholic priests in the United States: Could blacks participate fully in the life of the predominantly white Catholic church? Until the mid–twentieth century, the answer, despite the early efforts of the Josephites, had clearly been "No!" By 1988, after years of struggle marked by important advances but also marred by the persistence of racism in the church, the elevation of Archbishop Marino, the spiritual heir of John Slattery, Charles Uncles, John Dorsey, and John Plantevigne held out the hope that one day the answer would be a resounding "Yes!"

14. Felician A. Foy, ed., *1989 Catholic Almanac* (Huntington, Ind., 1988), 429; statistics on the Josephites furnished by Agnes Rembus, secretary to the superior general, May 20, 1988.

Appendix A

D	Diocesan
C.I.C.M.	Congregation of the Immaculate Heart of Mary (Missionhurst or Immaculate Heart Fathers)
C.M.F.	Missionary Sons of the Immaculate Heart of Mary (Claretians)
C.P.	Congregation of the Discalced Clerics of the Most Holy Cross and Passion of Our Lord Jesus Christ (Passionists)
C.Pp.S.	Society of the Precious Blood
C.S.Sp.	Congregation of the Holy Ghost (Holy Ghost Fathers or Spiritans)
C.SS.R.	Congregation of the Most Holy Redeemer (Redemptorists)
M.M.	Catholic Foreign Mission Society of America (Maryknoll)
M.S.SS.T.	Missionary Servants of the Most Holy Trinity
O.C.S.O.	Order of Cistercians of the Strict Observance (Trappists)
O.F.M.Conv.	Order of Friars Minor Conventual (Conventual Franciscan Fathers)
O.S.B.	Order of St. Benedict (Benedictines)
O.S.C.	Canons Regular of the Order of the Holy Cross (Crosier Fathers)
O.SS.T.	Order of the Most Holy Trinity (Trinitarians)
S.A.	Society of the Atonement (Atonement Fathers)
S.C.J.	Congregation of the Priests of the Sacred Heart of Jesus (Sacred Heart Fathers)
S.D.S.	Society of the Divine Savior (Salvatorians)
S.J.	Society of Jesus (Jesuits)
S.M.A.	Society of African Missions
S.S.E.	Society of St. Edmund (Edmundites)
S.S.J.	Society of St. Joseph of the Sacred Heart (Josephites)

S.S.S.   Blessed Sacrament Fathers
S.V.D.   Society of the Divine Word (Divine Word Missionaries)
W.F.   Society of Missionaries of Africa (White Fathers)

Black Priests, 1854–1960 by Year of Ordination

The list includes those ordained in the United States and those Americans ordained overseas.

YEAR	PRIEST'S NAME AND AFFILIATION	PLACE OF ORDINATION
1854	†Healy, James Augustine (D)	Paris, France
1858	Healy, Alexander Sherwood (D)	Rome, Italy
1864	Healy, Patrick Francis (S.J.)	Liège, Belgium
1886	Tolton, Augustine (D)	Rome, Italy
1891	Uncles, Charles Randolph (Mill Hill-S.S.J.)	Baltimore, Md.
1902	Dorsey, John Henry (S.S.J.)	Baltimore, Md.
1905	*Esnard, Adrian (C.I.C.M.)	Louvain, Belgium
1907	Burgess, Joseph C. (C.S.Sp.)	Chevilly, France
	Plantevigne, John Joseph (S.S.J.)	Baltimore, Md.
1910	Theobald, Stephen Louis (D)	St. Paul, Minn.
1923	*John, Joseph Alexander (S.M.A.)	Harlem, N.Y.
1926	DuKette, Andrew Norman (D)	Detroit, Mich.
1927	Derricks, Archibald Augustine (O.SS.T.)	Rome, Italy
1933	*Lane, William Leroy (D)	Latrobe, Pa.
	Logan, Charles A. (D)	Los Angeles, Calif.
1934	Bourges, Anthony (S.V.D.)	Bay St. Louis, Miss.
	*Grau, William C. (D)	Rome, Italy
	*Marin, Philip (D)	Bay St. Louis, Miss.
	*Murphy, Max E. (D)	Prague, Czechoslovakia
	Rousseve, Maurice (S.V.D.)	Bay St. Louis, Miss.
	Smith, Vincent (Mary Simon, O.C.S.O.) (S.V.D.)[1]	Bay St. Louis, Miss.

1. Vincent Smith left the Society of the Divine Word and took solemn vows as a Trappist in 1951. He assumed the name Mary Simon.

	Wade, Francis Guy (S.V.D.)	Bay St. Louis, Miss.
1935	*Jones, Theldon Francis (D)	Prague, Czechoslovakia
1937	*Glover, Francis Marcus (W.F.)	Carthage, Tunisia
	*Howard, Clarence J. (S.V.D.)	Bay St. Louis, Miss.
	Wells, Orion Francis (S.V.D.)	Bay St. Louis, Miss.
1939	*†Bowers, Joseph Oliver (S.V.D.)	Rome, Italy
	*Bowman, John Walter (S.V.D.)	Bay St. Louis, Miss.
	Chachere, Carmen George (S.V.D.)	Rome, Italy
	*Dauphine, John W. (S.V.D.)	Bay St. Louis, Miss.
	Woods, Leo (S.V.D.)	Bay St. Louis, Miss.
1941	Ball, Charles Chester L. E. (S.S.J.)	Washington, D.C.
	Leedie, Alexander J. (S.V.D.)	Bay St. Louis, Miss.
	Martin, Leander Joseph (S.V.D.)	Bay St. Louis, Miss.
	Williams, Maxim Andrew (S.V.D.)	Bay St. Louis, Miss.
	*Wilson, George C. (S.V.D.)	Bay St. Louis, Miss.
	*Winters, Richard (S.V.D.)	Bay St. Louis, Miss.
1944	†Perry, Harold R. (S.V.D.)	Bay St. Louis, Miss.
1945	Adams, William Henry (S.V.D.)	Bay St. Louis, Miss.
	Butler, Joseph Paul (D)	Trenton, N.J.
	Chachere, Earl Lawrence (Austin, M.S.SS.T.)[2]	Washington, D.C.
	Jones, Thomas Campbell (D)	Trenton, N.J.
	Winters, Arthur C. (S.V.D.)	Bay St. Louis, Miss.
1947	Faustina, John Marcellus (S.S.E.)	Burlington, Vt.
	*Meyer, Prosper Edward (O.S.B.)	Collegeville, Minn.
	Porter, Herman A. (S.C.J.)	Milwaukee, Wis.
1948	*Sayles, Bartholomew (O.S.B.)	Collegeville, Minn.
	Shepherd, Harvey (O.S.B.)	Collegeville, Minn.
	Simpson, Allen Matthew (D)	Youngstown, Ohio
1949	Figaro, Mark (S.V.D.)	Bay St. Louis, Miss.
	Lambert, Rollins (D)	Chicago, Ill.
	*†Lewis, Carlos (S.V.D.)	Bay St. Louis, Miss.
	*Washington, Curtis (S.V.D.)	Bay St. Louis, Miss.

2. Earl Chachere left the Trinitarians in 1950 and was incardinated by the diocese of Lafayette. Austin was the name he assumed when he took perpetual vows for the Trinitarians.

1950	Cunningham, Leonard Aloysius (C.S.Sp.)	Norwalk, Conn.
	†Francis, Joseph Abel (S.V.D.)	Bay St. Louis, Miss.
	Mosley, James Edward (D)	St. Paul, Minn.
1951	Anderson, Joseph Warren (D)	Omaha, Nebr.
	Carter, Peter J. (D)	Buffalo, N.Y.
	Figaro, Egbert (C.S.Sp.)	Dayton, Ohio
	La Bauve, John (S.V.D.)	Bay St. Louis, Miss.
	†Olivier, Leonard (S.V.D.)	Bay St. Louis, Miss.
	Rodgers, William J. (D)	Brooklyn, N.Y.
1952	Boucree, Thaddeus (S.V.D.)	Bay St. Louis, Miss.
	Gopaul, Paul (S.S.E.)	Burlington, Vt.
	Hicks, Eugene J. (D)	New York, N.Y.
	LeDoux, Louis Verlin (D)	Lake Charles, La.
	*Lewis, Gerald (S.V.D.)	Bay St. Louis, Miss.
	McKnight, Albert (C.S.Sp.)	Brooklyn, N.Y.
1953	Osborne, Aubrey (D)	New Orleans, La.
	Patterson, Bernadine Joseph (O.S.B.)	St. Louis, Mo.
	Singleton, Hubert (S.V.D.)	Lake Charles, La.
	Thorne, Vance (S.V.D.)	Bay St. Louis, Miss.
1954	McCall, Aidan Maurice (O.S.B.)	Collegeville, Minn.
	*Thornton, Lawrence P. (S.V.D.)	Techny, Ill.
1955	*Bertrand, Joseph E. (C.SS.R.)	Esopus, N.Y.
	Clinch, Columban (O.S.B.)	Kansas City, Kans.
	*Jackson, Charles L. (D)	Fort-de-France, Martinique
	King, William E. (C.M.F.)	Claretville, Calif.
	Nearon, Joseph Roy (S.S.S.)	Rome, Italy
	Powell, Elmer Sylvester (S.V.D.)	Bay St. Louis, Miss.
	Tarlton, Gilbert (O.S.B.)	Collegeville, Minn.
	Verrett, Joseph C. (S.S.J.)	Washington, D.C.
	Ward, Martin de Porres (O.F.M.Conv.)	Albany, N.Y.
1956	Brown, Theophile W. (O.S.B.)	Collegeville, Minn.
	Davis, Cyprian (O.S.B.)	St. Meinrad, Ind.
	Rivers, Clarence (D)	Cincinnati, Ohio
	Salmon, Harold (D)	New York, N.Y.
	Shaw, Mario Rosamond William (O.S.B.)	Collegeville, Minn.

1957	Clements, George H. (D)	Chicago, Ill.
	Coakley, Charles L. (O.S.B.)	Collegeville, Minn.
	Guidry, Joseph (S.V.D.)	Bay St. Louis, Miss.
	*Guidry, Raymond (S.V.D.)	Bay St. Louis, Miss.
	Joyner, John (C.S.Sp.)	Norwalk, Conn.
	LeDoux, Jerome (S.V.D.)	Bay St. Louis, Miss.
	Robinson, James P. (S.S.E.)	Selma, Ala.
	Thompson, August Louis (D)	New Orleans, La.
1958	Allen, Philip J. (D)	St. Louis, Mo.
	†Anderson, Moses B. (S.S.E.)	Burlington, Vt.
	Hadden, Thomas P. (D)	Rome, Italy
	Henry, Vincent de Paul (O.F.M.Conv.)	Washington, D.C.
	Muschette, Emilian (O.S.B.)	Washington, D.C.
	Nadine, Jerome Eugene (D)	Syracuse, N.Y.
	Oliver, William R. (S.V.D.)	Bay St. Louis, Miss.
	Pittman, Robert (S.S.S.)	Rome, Italy
	Robinson, John Fisher (S.V.D.)	Bay St. Louis, Miss.
	Toussaint, Jean (D)	Lafayette, La.
1959	Clarke, Aloysius Roland (O.S.B.)	Washington, D.C.
	Enette, Rawlin B. (S.S.J.)	Washington, D.C.
	Hardin, Boniface (O.S.B.)	Indianapolis, Ind.
	†Howze, Joseph Lawson (D)	Raleigh, N.C.
	Lucas, Lawrence E. (D)	New York, N.Y.
	*Rogers, Leslie (M.M.)	Maryknoll, N.Y.
1960	Alleyne, Lawrence (S.D.S.)	Washington, D.C.
	Brooks, Jerome (Bernard O.) (C.P.)[3]	Louisville, Ky.
	Carmon, Dominic (S.V.D.)	Chicago, Ill.
	*Davis, Boswell Ambrose (O.S.B.)	Nassau, Bahamas
	Hall, Charles A. (S.S.J.)	Washington, D.C.
	Harris, Elbert F. (S.S.J.)	Washington, D.C.
	Leake, Conrad (S.A.)	Garrison, N.Y.
	Potts, Donald Gerard (O.S.C.)	Fort Wayne, Ind.
	Rodney, John J. (S.V.D.)	Techny, Ill.
	Taylor, Benedict M. (O.F.M.Conv.)	Washington, D.C.

3. Jerome was the name Bernard O. Brooks took when he professed his vows as a Passionist.

Violenus, James A. (D)	New York, N.Y.
Wilson, Gene R. (C.Pp.S.)	Celina, Ohio

SOURCE: Josephite Fathers Archives

* Served outside the United States for at least some, if not all, of his priestly career.

† Elevated to bishop later in his priestly career.

Appendix B

GROWTH OF CATHOLICISM AMONG BLACKS, 1890–1960

TOTAL BLACK CATHOLIC POPULATION

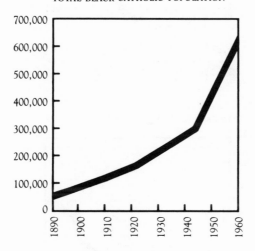

ANNUAL NUMBER OF BLACK CONVERTS

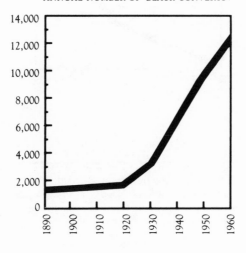

PRIESTS ASSIGNED TO THE BLACK APOSTOLATE

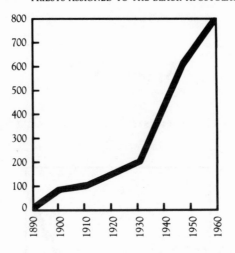

PREDOMINANTLY BLACK CHURCHES

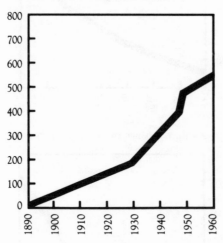

SOURCE: Reports of the Secretary to the Commission for Catholic Missions Among the Colored People and the Indians, in Richard A. Lamanna and Jay J. Coakley, "The Catholic Church and the Negro," in Philip Gleason (ed.), *Contemporary Catholicism in the United States* (Notre Dame, 1969), 171. Reprinted with the permission of the University of Notre Dame Press.

Bibliographical Essay

This essay discusses the sources that I found most helpful and does not include every source consulted or cited.

PRIMARY SOURCES

ARCHIVAL AND MANUSCRIPT COLLECTIONS

The single most important source for this study was the Josephite Fathers Archives, in Baltimore, Maryland. In addition to collecting primary sources over the course of nearly forty years, Josephite archivist Peter E. Hogan, S.S.J., has also assembled an extensive library of books, journals, and other printed materials on Catholic and Afro-American history, making the Josephite archives a center for the study of black Catholicism in the United States. The papers of the Josephite superiors general, from John R. Slattery through Thomas P. McNamara, covering the years 1893–1960 and occupying approximately 117 linear feet, formed the research backbone of this book. The Alfred B. Leeson–John R. Slattery Papers are thoroughly indexed by both correspondent and subject and are easy to use. In addition to letter boxes, the Leeson-Slattery Papers include four letterpress books and two copy books, along with a private data book into which Slattery and Louis B. Pastorelli vented their spleen. The Thomas B. Donovan, Justin McCarthy, and Louis B. Pastorelli papers, though not completely indexed when I used them, are well organized, with each letter box containing a list of correspondents by date. The Edward V. Casserly–Thomas P. McNamara Papers and the George F. O'Dea Papers are, for the most part, still in their original files and have not been processed.

Other materials in the Josephite archives also proved quite valuable. The John T. Gillard Papers produced letters and newspaper clippings that were especially helpful in tracing the conflicts between the Josephites and Thomas Wyatt Turner, John LaFarge, S.J., and William M. Markoe, S.J. The papers of Albert S. Foley,

S.J., pioneering historian of black priests in the United States, are an important, though as yet unprocessed collection, containing Foley's research notes, drafts of articles and papers, unpublished manuscripts, and statistical data on black priests. The minutes of the general chapters of St. Joseph's Society of the Sacred Heart, or Josephites, and of its council, the society consultors, provided me with an important window into these key Josephite decision-making bodies. Parish and personal files of individual Josephites, black students' files from 1884 to 1915, minutes books of faculty meetings at Epiphany Apostolic College and at St. Joseph's Seminary and the student journals from those two institutions, and a historical biography file on most black priests in the United States, all yielded a wealth of information. The T file contains copies of theses, dissertations, articles, scholarly papers, and unpublished manuscripts, including a copy of William Markoe's illuminating memoir, "An Interracial Role, Memoirs of William M. Markoe, S.J., 1900–1966." The miscellaneous file holds a wide assortment of pamphlets, booklets, and other printed matter.

The Josephite Fathers Archives also house copies from other archives of records and manuscript collections that are pertinent to the history of the Josephites and black priests. Among the most important are the twenty-seven rolls of microfilm of the Mill Hill Fathers Archives, many of them transcribed into notebooks. Cited as the Mill Hill Fathers Papers throughout this book, the collection consists of copies of three letterpress books, Mill Hill Provincial Records, American correspondence with Mill Hill, minutes of chapter meetings between 1875 and 1924, and Canon Peter Benoit's invaluable diary, in which he recorded his observations of the conditions of blacks in the Catholic church and the South during a trip in 1875. The Mill Hill Fathers Papers are especially important for ascertaining the receptivity of Herbert Vaughan, Benoit, and Mill Hill missionaries in the United States to the idea of black priests and for following the evolution in Slattery's views on the subject. The Mill Hill Fathers Papers are also indispensable for an understanding of the factors that led Slattery to push for the separation of the American Josephites from their English parent organization. Copies of documents from the Archives of the Archdiocese of New Orleans, particularly the correspondence between Archbishop James H. Blenk and John J. Plantevigne, proved especially helpful.

Professor William L. Portier generously made available to me the microfilm of an extraordinary unpublished manuscript, the "Biographie de J. R. Slattery," from the Papiers Houtin, *Oeuvres*, LIV, NAF 15741–42, Bibliothèque Nationale. Despite its title and the fact that most of it is written in the hand of French modernist Albert Houtin, this four-hundred-page manuscript is actually an autobiography composed by John R. Slattery. The work is divided into twenty-one chapters that cover Slattery's life from 1851 until 1911. It proved useful in filling in gaps left by other sources. Written after Slattery's apostasy, the "Biographie" is basically an apologia and is filled with biting, unflattering characterizations of most of the prominent Catholic clergy in whose circles Slattery moved. It must, therefore, be used critically and in conjunction with other sources. Its acerbic, sometimes nasty tone notwithstanding, the "Biographie" describes Slattery's close association with leading Americanists like Archbishop John Ireland, Walter Elliott, Bishop John Keane, and especially Denis O'Connell and establishes a connection between Slattery's Americanism and his later modernism.

Although Slattery devotes only one chapter, Chapter XI, "Mon experience chez les gens de couleur," exclusively to an account of his work among blacks between 1877 and 1903, other chapters contain illuminating material. Chapter XVI, "La Crise," provides important background information about Slattery's "sabbatical policy" for black seminarians and his controversial sermon at John Dorsey's first mass. Chapters XVII to XIX give a detailed account of Slattery's crisis of faith and his "long goodbye" to the church. The "Biographie" suggests an important link between Slattery's daily contact with the scandal of racism in the church (especially among its clergy) and his growing intellectual and spiritual disillusionment with Catholicism.

In addition to the Josephite Fathers Archives and the "Biographie de J. R. Slattery," the archives of St. Augustine's Seminary and of the southern province of the Society of the Divine Word, both located in Bay St. Louis, Mississippi, provided important sources for this book. Both archives contain a wealth of documents pertaining to the efforts of the Society of the Divine Word to develop a black clergy. The provincial's correspondence files in the province archives produced a copy of John Albert's 1913 letter to the apostolic delegate. Most of my research was centered in the St. Augustine's Seminary Archives, which consist of several filing cabinets crammed with letters, reports, unpublished manuscripts, and house council minutes spanning the period 1914–1960. The seminary archives hold a surprisingly large number of copies of letters that passed between provincials of the society in Techny, Illinois, and various members of the hierarchy, particularly Bishop Richard O. Gerow. That I was thus able to sketch the story of the founding of St. Augustine's Seminary and the eventual ordination and placement of its first four black priests from these letters was particularly fortunate, for the archives of the Chicago province of the Society of the Divine Word were closed to me.

The papers of Bishops Gerow and John E. Gunn, in the Archives of the Diocese of Jackson, and of Daniel F. Desmond and Jules B. Jeanmard, in the archives of the dioceses of Alexandria and Lafayette, respectively, contain items that flesh out the story of St. Augustine's Seminary, the stationing of black Divine Word missionaries in the South, and the acceptance of black candidates for the diocesan priesthood in the South. Both Gerow and Desmond kept extensive diaries. Desmond's journal provides rich detail concerning the 1934 meeting of southern bishops with Cardinal George Mundelein and Archbishop Amleto Cicognani, during which Desmond offered to provide a place in his diocese for the four new black priests of the Society of the Divine Word.

The Society of African Missions Archives, in Tenafly, New Jersey, and the Archives of the Diocese of Savannah provided valuable material from the papers of Ignatius Lissner, S.M.A., and Bishop Benjamin J. Keiley that revealed Lissner's efforts in 1920 to secure the backing of two congregations of the Roman Curia, the Congregation for the Propagation of the Faith and the Consistorial Congregation, for the erection of a seminary for blacks and for the appointment of an episcopal vicar for blacks in Georgia. Documents from the Society of African Missions Archives also shed light on the difficulties Lissner experienced in trying to find an assignment for the Reverend Joseph John.

Information gleaned from copies of the papers of Thomas Wyatt Turner, which were made available to me by Marilyn W. Nickels but which are now housed in the manuscript division of the Moorland-Spingarn Research Center at Howard University in Washington, D.C., figured significantly in this study. The papers reveal the perspective, goals, and methods of the most prominent lay, black, Catholic leader of the first half of the twentieth century and provide insight into why black Catholics viewed the struggle for black priests as so crucial to their attainment of full rights within the church. The national council minutes of the Knights of Peter Claver for the year 1920, found in the A. P. Tureaud Papers, in the Amistad

Research Center at Tulane University in New Orleans, detail the expulsion of C. Marcellus Dorsey from that organization for his attacks on the Josephites.

Several archives hold correspondence that sheds light on the trials suffered by John Dorsey and John Plantevigne. Items from the Bishop John B. Morris Papers, in the Archives of the Diocese of Little Rock, particularly Monsignor J. M. Lucey's long report in 1907 to Bishop Morris, proved invaluable in my piecing together the story of Dorsey's ordeal at St. Peter's Parish in Pine Bluff, Arkansas. Similarly, the papers of Bishops Edward P. Allen of Mobile and William J. Kenny of St. Augustine, Florida, and the archives of the Sisters of the Holy Family, in New Orleans, and of the Sisters of the Blessed Sacrament for Indians and Colored People, in Cornwells Heights, Pennsylvania, all yielded important letters from, to, or about Dorsey or Plantevigne. The archivist of the Holy Ghost Fathers at the Spiritan Archives in Pittsburgh also provided documents showing how Josephite difficulties with black priests during the first decade of the twentieth century convinced the Spiritans to accept no more black candidates.

The superbly indexed papers of Cardinal James Gibbons and Archbishop Michael J. Curley, in the Archives of the Archdiocese of Baltimore, furnished for this study important materials that spanned the years 1893–1948. The Sulpician Archives in Baltimore yielded several letters from John Dorsey and Joseph Griffin to Edward Dyer concerning Slattery's sabbatical policy for black students. The papers of John LaFarge, at the Georgetown University Archives in Washington, D.C., especially his letters to the American assistant of the Society of Jesus, reveal the importance that LaFarge attached to the development of a black clergy and his influence in moving the Society of Jesus in the United States to open the doors of its seminaries to blacks.

The plight of the handful of blacks in northern seminaries during the late 1920s and early 1930s is graphically revealed in documents supplied by the St. Vincent Archabbey Archives, in Latrobe, Pennsylvania, and the Archives of the Diocese of Cleveland. The papers of Bishop Thomas S. Byrne of Nashville and Archbishops John T. McNicholas of Cincinnati and Thomas J. Toolen of Mobile yielded copies of important reports or letters to the apostolic delegate that proved useful in discerning the attitudes of missionaries and bishops toward black seminarians and priests and in charting the efforts of the Holy See on behalf of a black clergy. The Archives of the

United States Catholic Conference (USCC), in Washington, D.C., were helpful for the minutes of the meetings of the administrative committee of the National Catholic Welfare Conference (NCWC), as well as for the minutes of the annual meetings of the hierarchy and of the meetings of the American Board of Catholic Missions (ABCM). The NCWC-USCC Papers, in the Archives of the Catholic University of America, Washington, D.C., produced an important report in 1919 on Josephite missionary activity sent from Pastorelli to the American bishops.

The Samuel Cardinal Stritch Papers, in the Archives of the Archdiocese of Chicago, though neither indexed nor processed, were particularly valuable in piecing together the story of how Stritch, working in tandem with Archbishops Joseph Rummel and Cicognani, secured the pledge of southern bishops to accept blacks into their diocesan seminaries. The file on St. Maur's Priory in the Alcuin Deutsch Papers at the St. John's Abbey Archives, Collegeville, Minnesota, details Benedictine efforts to establish an interracial priory in the South in the 1940s.

Copies of documents relating to the Catholic church within the present borders of the United States from the Archives of the Congregation for the Propagation of the Faith, deposited in the Archives of the University of Notre Dame, reveal the unsuccessful efforts of William A. Williams, an antebellum black man, to become a priest. The eight volumes, to date, of the series begun by Finbar Kenneally and continued by Mathias C. Kieman and Alexander Wyse, *United States Documents in the Propaganda Fide Archives: A Calendar*, compiled by Anton Debevec (8 vols.; Washington, D.C., 1966–), helped me to locate and request materials from Notre Dame.

Several collections of potentially great value were either lost, inaccessible to me, or closed. Unfortunately, it appears that, except for copies of Monsignor John E. Burke's diary (located in several archives, including the Josephite archives), the papers of the Catholic Board for Mission Work Among the Colored People have either been destroyed or lost. The microfilmed copies of the voluminous records of the Commission for Catholic Missions Among the Colored People and the Indians (Negro and Indian Commission), located in the Archives of the Bureau of Catholic Indian Missions, in Washington, D.C., contain little material on black priests. The archives of the Apostolic Delegation to the United States are deposited in the Vatican Secret Archives in Rome and are open only through 1923. The Reverend Cyprian Davis, O.S.B., has recently been able to do some research in this collection, the results of which will be noted later in this essay. The papers of Archbishop Rummel are located in the chancery of the Archdiocese of New Orleans and are not available for research; neither are most manuscript materials in the Josephite archives that are dated after 1960, because many of those involved in the turmoil that rocked St. Joseph's Society in the late 1960s and early 1970s are still living.

INTERVIEWS

Many individuals graciously consented to interviews that provided me with important information. Father Hogan also made available to me transcripts of interviews. Following is a list of the persons interviewed, along with brief descriptions, and the dates of the interviews: Anthony Bourges, S.V.D., one of the first four black Divine Word priests ordained at St. Augustine's Seminary, July 11, 1983; Earl Counters, nephew of the Reverend John Dorsey, November 2, 1983; Sister Audrey Marie Detiege, S.S.F., archivist of the Sisters of the Holy Family, December 22, 1983; James F. Didas, S.S.J., former editor of *Colored Harvest* and former rector of St. Joseph's Seminary, October 7, 1983; Charles H. Dorsey, Jr., former student at Epiphany Apostolic College, grandson of C. Marcellus Dorsey, and grandnephew of the Reverend John Dorsey, October 12, 1983; Olga Dorsey, daughter-in-law of C. Marcellus Dorsey and mother of Charles H. Dorsey, Jr., November 2, 1983; William B. Faherty, S.J., director of the St. Stanislaus Jesuit Historical Museum in Florissant, Missouri, May 2, 1985 (by telephone); Carl A. Fisher, S.S.J., black Josephite priest (now auxiliary bishop of Los Angeles) and student leader during the late 1960s and early 1970s at St. Joseph's Seminary, July 12, 1985; Albert S. Foley, S.J., historian and sociologist, May 3, 1985 (by telephone); Peter E. Hogan, S.S.J., Josephite archivist and former teacher at Epiphany Apostolic College and St. Joseph's Seminary, December 29, 1982, August 30, 1983, numerous conversations between 1978 and 1988; Benjamin M. Horton, S.S.J., Josephite missionary who baptized Bishop Joseph L. Howze, July 17, 1984; Eugene A. Marino, S.S.J., auxiliary bishop of Washington, D.C. (now archbishop of Atlanta), black Josephite, and former student and teacher at both Epiphany Apostolic College and St. Joseph's Seminary, December 6, 1983; Robert E. McCall, S.S.J., former teacher at Epiphany Apostolic College and former professor at St. Joseph's Seminary, June 24, 1982; Eugene P. McManus, S.S.J., former teacher at St. Augustine's High School and a leader of Catholic integration forces in New Orleans (now Josephite superior general), September 9, 1983, June 10, 1985; David Melancon, O.S.B., former rector of St. Joseph's College in St. Benedict, Louisiana, December 27, 1984; George F. O'Dea, S.S.J., former aide to Edward V. Casserly and former Josephite superior general, August 10, 1983; Monsignor Charles J. Plauché, former chancellor of the archdiocese of New Orleans, July 10, 1985 (by telephone); Agnes Rembus, former secretary to Edward V. Casserly and current secretary to the Josephite superior general, July 9, 1983, May 20, 1988; Mario Shaw, O.S.B., former student at Epiphany Apostolic College and St. Joseph's Seminary, July 9, 1982; Francis A. Theriault, S.V.D., former rector of St. Augustine's Seminary and one of the first white students to attend St. Augustine's Seminary, July 18, 1983, June 11, 1985 (by telephone); Joseph G. Vath (now deceased), bishop of Birmingham, former secretary to Archbishop Joseph Rummel, July 22, 1983; Joseph C. Verrett, S.S.J., black Josephite priest, former teacher and assistant principal of St. Augustine's High School, and former assistant rector and dean of studies at St. Joseph's Seminary, May 29, June 1, June 7, 1985; Joseph L. Waters, S.S.J., former professor at St. Joseph's Seminary, June 30, 1983. Taped copies of most of these interviews are available at the Josephite Fathers Archives.

Father Hogan also made available to me typescripts of interviews he conducted with the following people: John H. Clouser, a convert of John Dorsey and a former supreme knight of the Knights of Peter Claver, January 2, 1978; Rawlin B. Enette, S.S.J., black Josephite priest and former chairman of the southern region of the Black Catholic Clergy Caucus, March 9, 1971; Bishop-elect Eugene A. Marino, S.S.J., August 13, 1974; Vincent D. Warren, S.S.J., veteran missionary and staunch champion of a black clergy, October–November, 1965.

CORRESPONDENCE

The Reverend Robert Pung, S.V.D., former rector of St. Augustine's Seminary and former provincial of the southern province of the Society of the Divine Word, responded to my questions about the Jesuit Bend incident in two letters, dated April 30 and May 27, 1985.

Extensive clippings from both secular and diocesan newspapers in the black priests file in the Josephite archives facilitated my research. Clippings from the Baltimore *Afro-American* (most of them critical of the Josephites) for the period 1918–1940 appear frequently in the Pastorelli and the Gillard papers. Issues of *Colored Harvest* (changed to *Josephite Harvest* in 1960), first published by the Josephites in 1888, provide an abundance of reports on mission life from Josephites in the field. These include detailed accounts both of the parish missions conducted by Dorsey and Plantevigne and of the catechetical work done by "suspended" black seminarians. *Colored Harvest* also reported on developments at Epiphany Apostolic College and St. Joseph's Seminary.

During the 1880s, Slattery and John H. Greene used *St. Joseph's Advocate*, published from 1883 to 1890, the American supplement to Mill Hill's *St. Joseph's Foreign Missionary Advocate*, to campaign for black priests. They incorporated essays, one written by Bishop Francis A. Janssens of Natchez, explaining the need for a black clergy, as well as reports on the activities of black priests in Africa and at the Propaganda's college in Rome and on Augustine Tolton's reception in Quincy, Illinois. The black priest file also contains copies of articles by and about black priests and seminarians from *Colored Harvest*, *St. Augustine's Messenger*, a monthly produced by St. Augustine's Seminary, and *Our Colored Missions*, the magazine of the Catholic Board for Mission Work Among the Colored People. The John R. Slattery Papers contain numerous newspaper clippings, as well as copies of many of the more than twenty articles that Slattery penned for *Catholic World* between 1883 and 1899. Among the most important on the development of a black clergy are "The Seminary for the Colored Missions," *Catholic World*, XLVI (January, 1888), 547–49; "Native Clergy," *Catholic World*, LII (March, 1891), 882–93; and "A Catholic College for Negro Catechists," *Catholic World*, LXX (October, 1899), 1–12. A copy of Slattery's public announcement of his apostasy from the Church, "How My Priesthood Dropped from Me," *Independent*, LXI (September 6, 1906), 565–71, can also be found in his papers. The yearly reports of bishops to the Commission for Catholic Missions Among the Colored People and the Indians, compiled and published under the title *Mission Work Among the Negroes and Indians* (changed to *Our Negro and Indian Missions* in 1926), provide some useful details, though researchers should beware of putting too much confidence in the figures given for the black Catholic population in many dioceses, since they often represent inaccurate estimates.

For contemporary developments in the Black Catholic community, I relied on *Freeing the Spirit,* the journal of the National Office for Black Catholics, *Mentor,* a national black Catholic newspaper that began publishing in 1987, the National Catholic News Service's *Origins* (which includes the text of the 1984 pastoral letter "What We Have Seen and Heard," issued by the nation's black Catholic bishops), *Catholic Standard* (Washington, D.C.), *National Catholic Reporter,* and *America.* The proceedings of the National Black Catholic Congress of 1987 can be found in *U.S. Catholic Historian,* VII, Nos. 2 and 3 (1988), 299–356.

MEMOIRS AND AUTOBIOGRAPHIES

Thomas Honoré, a former black Josephite priest, provided me with a taped memoir, dated October 21, 1983, of his years at Epiphany Apostolic College and St. Joseph's Seminary. Three leaders in the Catholic interracial movement have produced memoirs or autobiographies. George K. Hunton's *All of Which I Saw, Part of Which I Was: The Autobiography of George K. Hunton, as Told to Gary MacEoin* (Garden City, N.Y., 1967) provides the most extensive discussion of the ways in which the Catholic Interracial Council of New York attempted to encourage the development of a black clergy. John LaFarge's autobiography, *The Manner Is Ordinary* (New York, 1954), mentions very little on the subject, though his earlier books, *Interracial Justice* (New York, 1937) and *The Race Question and the Negro: A Study of the Catholic Doctrine on Interracial Justice* (New York, 1944), state his arguments in support of a black clergy. Lawrence Lucas' angry *Black Priest/White Church: Catholics and Racism* (New York, 1970) reflects the influence of the black power movement on a black Catholic clergyman in the late 1960s and early 1970s. Joseph M. Davis, S.M., and Cyprian Lamar Rowe, F.M.S., recount their experiences as the first two directors of the National Office for Black Catholics in "The Development of the National Office for Black Catholics," *U.S. Catholic Historian,* VII, Nos. 2 and 3 (1988), 265–89.

BOOKS

That the priest held a revered position in the eyes of Catholics is, of course, central to the controversy over the ordination of black priests. The sacral nature of the priesthood is emphasized in the catechism authorized by the Third Plenary Council of Baltimore, *A Catechism of Christian Doctrine* (New York, 1886), and its later editions, such as *The Baltimore Catechism with Explanations* (Chicago, 1918). These catechisms came to be widely used in the Catholic community, and they express the concept of priesthood held by most Catholics.

SECONDARY SOURCES

Since black Catholics constitute only about 2 percent of the Catholic population in the United States, historians of the Catholic experience in this country have produced relatively few studies either of the black Catholic community or of those who served them. References to black Catholics or Catholic missionary work among blacks in general church histories, biographies, or other scholarly works are often brief and superficial. Some important work, however, has recently appeared.

Students of any aspect of American Catholicism should first consult two bibliographies: John Tracy Ellis and Robert Trisco (eds.), *A Guide to American Catholic History* (2nd ed.; Santa Barbara, 1982), and James Hennesey, S.J., *American Catholic Bibliography 1970–1982*, Working Paper Series 12, No. 1 (Cushwa Center for the Study of American Catholicism, Notre Dame, 1982), along with his *Supplement to American Catholic Bibliography 1970–1982*, Working Paper Series 14, No. 1 (Cushwa Center for the Study of American Catholicism, Notre Dame, 1983). Two indispensable reference works are the *Official Catholic Directory* (New York, 1912–) and the *New Catholic Encyclopedia* (15 vols; New York, 1967) and its supplements, Vol. XVI, *Supplement 1967–1974* (Washington, D.C., 1974), and Vol. XVII, *Supplement 1974–1979* (Washington, D.C., 1979).

The struggle for black Catholic priests should be understood within the larger contexts of Catholic, Afro-American, and American religious history. Stephen Neill traces the development of Catholic and Protestant indigenous clergy in mission areas throughout the world in *A History of Christian Missions* (Rev. ed.; Harmondsworth, Eng., 1986). J. Derek Holmes, *The Papacy in the Modern World, 1914–1978* (New York, 1981), highlights the efforts of Popes Benedict XV, Pius XI, and Pius XII in the twentieth century to encourage the formation of "native clergies." For an overview of

Afro-American history, John Hope Franklin and Alfred A. Moss, Jr., *From Slavery to Freedom: A History of Negro Americans* (6th ed.; New York, 1988), is superb. Sydney E. Ahlstrom, *A Religious History of the American People* (New Haven, 1972), is the best survey of American religious history and includes two chapters on black religion, one focusing on the rise of black churches following the Civil War and the other on black religion in the twentieth century. Albert J. Raboteau, *Slave Religion: "The Invisible Institution" in the Antebellum South* (New York, 1978), W. E. B. Du Bois, *The Negro Church* (Atlanta, 1903), E. Franklin Frazier, *The Negro Church in America* (New York, 1964), C. Eric Lincoln, *The Black Church Since Frazier* (New York, 1974), Joseph Washington, Jr., *Black Religion: The Negro and Christianity in the United States* (Boston, 1984), Gayraud S. Wilmore, *Black Religion and Black Radicalism: An Interpretation of the Religious History of Afro-American People* (2nd ed.; Maryknoll, N.Y., 1983), and Carter Woodson, *The History of the Negro Church* (Washington, D.C., 1929), remain the standard references for the history of Afro-American religion in the United States.

Two recent surveys attempt to incorporate blacks more fully into the story of American Catholicism: James Hennesey, S.J., *American Catholics: A History of the Roman Catholic Community in the United States* (New York, 1981), and Jay P. Dolan, *The American Catholic Experience: A History from Colonial Times to the Present* (Garden City, N.Y., 1985). Hennesey sketches the unsuccessful efforts of William A. Williams in the mid-nineteenth century to become a priest and provides helpful statistics regarding the loss of black seminarians and priests in the late 1960s and early 1970s. Dolan blames racial discrimination for the lack of black clergy but does not expand on the statement. I relied on both books in attempting to place the struggle for black priests within the context of the history of the Catholic church in the United States.

Several books and articles attempt to survey the relationship between the Catholic church and Afro-Americans. John T. Gillard, S.S.J., pioneered in the field with *The Catholic Church and the American Negro* (1929; rpr. New York, 1968), which he then followed with *Colored Catholics in the United States* (Baltimore, 1941). Gillard's books contain valuable historical information, as well as, up to the time of their publication, the most accurate statistics on black Catholics and the Church's missionary efforts among blacks. His works are also important as primary sources because they reflect the attitudes of the Josephite leadership on a number of issues, including the question of black priests.

William A. Osborne provides a historical account of Catholics and blacks, rich in anecdotes and personality profiles, in "A Freeman's Odyssey," *Jubilee*, III (September, 1955). In a later book, *Segregated Covenant: Race Relations and American Catholics* (New York, 1967), Osborne combines sociological and historical approaches in tracing the story up to 1966. Following a historical account, he describes the pace of integration in Catholic institutions in the various sections of the nation. He is critical of the church for its tendency to accommodate itself to prevailing local customs and social norms and for its failure to challenge racism more forthrightly. Richard A. Lamanna and Jay J. Coakley in "The Catholic Church and the Negro," in Philip Gleason (ed.), *Contemporary Catholicism in the United States* (Notre Dame, 1969), explore the role played by the institutional church and individual Catholics in the struggle for racial justice. The article contains helpful tables and graphs, which chart the progress of Catholicism among blacks. The authors attribute the historic dearth of black priests in the church to "overt discrimination and lack of encouragement" and confidently proclaim that "this discrimination has all but ended." They also express reservations about the emergence of "black consciousness" among Catholic clergy.

An indispensable book for the study of black Catholic priests is Albert S. Foley, S.J., *God's Men of Color: The Colored Catholic Priests of the United States, 1854–1954* (1955; rpr. New York, 1969), a collective biography of the approximately seventy-five black priests ordained between 1854 and 1954. Based largely on interviews and on some archival work in the southern province archives of the Society of the Divine Word, Foley's book consists of biographical vignettes, almost all undocumented. He had to omit many controversial aspects from his sketches because of pressure from religious superiors. Foley also authored *Bishop Healy: Beloved Outcaste* (New York, 1954), a biography of Bishop James Augustine Healy, the first black priest and bishop in the United States. In the biography and more explicitly in "Bishop Healy and the Colored Catholic Congress," *Interracial Review*, XXVIII (May, 1954), 79–80, Foley shows that Healy chose not to identify himself publicly with specifically Afro-American movements. For a biography of Augustine Tolton, another of the early black priests, see Sister Caroline Hemesath, *From Slave to Priest: A Biography of the Rev. Augustine Tolton (1854–*

1897), First Afro-American Priest of the United States (Chicago, 1973). Hemesath considers Tolton the "first Afro-American priest" because both of Tolton's parents were black, which was not true of Healy's parents. The greatest weakness of the book is her use of "imaginative recreations" to fill gaps created by a lack of sources. Each of the three books on black priests suffers from an overly pious tone, occasioned, at least in part, by a desire to refute old charges that black priests lacked the intelligence, morality, and sanctity of white priests.

J. D. Fage (ed.), *The Cambridge History of Africa: From c. 500 B.C. to A.D. 1050* (8 vols.; Cambridge, Eng., 1978), and Basil Davidson, *The African Slave Trade* (Boston, 1980), furnish information about black priests in fourth-century Ethiopia and sixteenth-century Congo, respectively. Peter Guilday, *The Life and Times of John England* (2 vols.; 1927; rpr. New York, 1969), Richard C. Madden, *Catholics in South Carolina: A Record* (Lanham, Md., 1985), and Leo R. Ryan, "Pierre Toussaint, 'God's Image Carved in Ebony,'" *Historical Records and Studies* (United States Catholic Historical Society), XXV (1935), establish that in 1836, John England of Charleston became the first American bishop to ordain a black man, albeit in Haiti. Guilday's biography also highlights the vulnerability of the Catholic church in the South and vividly describes England's efforts to disassociate the church from charges of abolitionism hurled by its enemies. Colman J. Barry, O.S.B., *Worship and Work: Saint John's Abbey and University, 1856–1956* (Collegeville, Minn., 1956), includes a section on the founding of St. Maur's interracial priory in 1949.

Randall M. Miller has described the Catholic church's missionary efforts among blacks up to Reconstruction as a "Failed Mission." Several historians explore different aspects of that failure. Although they deal with areas outside the United States, both Leslie R. Rout, Jr., *The African Experience in Spanish America, 1502 to the Present Day* (Cambridge, Eng., 1976), and Carl Degler, *Neither Black nor White: Slavery and Race Relations in Brazil and the United States* (New York, 1971), by noting resistance to the ordination of black priests in the Catholic empires of Spain and Brazil, helped me to view the problem of black clergy in the United States as part of the larger problem of developing indigenous clergy in mission areas. Randall M. Miller and Jon L. Wakelyn (eds.), *Catholics in the Old South: Essays on Church and Culture* (Macon, 1983), present a superb collection of essays by historians that explore the tension between southern regional and Catholic religious cultures. The essays address such topics as Jesuit slaveholding, congregations of religious women (black and white) in the South, the development of Colored Catholic Creole culture, the institutional establishment of the church in the South, and Catholic missionary efforts among blacks. All point to the conclusion that the institutional church conformed to local norms and conditions in a region where it was weak and vulnerable.

Volume I of Gilbert J. Garraghan, *The Jesuits of the Middle West* (3 vols.; New York, 1938), and Stafford Poole, C.M., and Douglas J. Slawson, C.M., *Church and Slave in Perry County Missouri, 1818–1865* (Lewiston/Queenston, N.Y., 1986), should be read in conjunction with R. Emmett Curran's essay, "'Splendid Poverty': Jesuit Slaveholding in Maryland, 1805–1838," in Miller and Wakelyn (eds.), *Catholics in the Old South*, for an understanding of clerical slaveholding in the United States.

Madeleine Hooke Rice, *American Catholic Opinion in the Slavery Controversy* (New York, 1944), Joseph Brokhage, *Francis Patrick Kenrick's Opinion on Slavery* (Washington, D.C., 1955), and Charles P. Connor, "The Northern Catholic Position on Slavery and the Civil War: Archbishop Hughes as a Test Case," *Records of the American Catholic Historical Society of Philadelphia*, XCVI (March–December, 1985), 35–48, explain the theological and social bases for Catholic toleration of the institution of slavery during the antebellum period. They also point out that the nativism espoused by many abolitionists served to reinforce Catholic identification of abolitionism with social and political radicalism. Dennis Clark explores the roots of the longstanding antagonism between blacks and Irish Catholics in "Urban Blacks and Irishmen: Brothers in Prejudice," in Miriam Ershkowitz and Joseph Zikmund II (eds.), *Black Politics in Philadelphia* (New York, 1973), 15–30.

Thomas W. Spalding's excellent biography, *Martin John Spalding: American Churchman* (Washington, D.C., 1973), further illustrates the general Catholic opposition to abolitionism and emancipation, but it also recounts in great detail Spalding's largely unsuccessful attempts during the Second Plenary Council of Baltimore in 1866 to persuade the American bishops to adopt more effective means for reaping a "golden harvest" among the freedmen. Edward J. Misch's exhaustively researched and encyclopedic "The American Bishops and the Negro from the Civil War to the Third Plenary Council of Baltimore, 1865–1884" (Ph.D. dissertation, Pontifical Gregorian

University, 1968) goes far beyond the scope of its title in thoroughly describing and analyzing the Catholic bishops' attitudes and policies (or lack thereof) toward Afro-Americans from the antebellum period through 1890. Misch's dissertation provides the best account available of the Third Plenary Council's deliberations and decisions concerning the black apostolate.

Protestant efforts to evangelize the freedmen far outstripped those of Catholics. Joe M. Richardson, *Christian Reconstruction: The American Missionary Association and Southern Blacks, 1861–1890* (Athens, Ga., 1986), recounts the efforts, achievements, and failures of the best known and most important of the freedmen aid societies. That opportunities for leadership, full participation, and self-determination played a key role in drawing blacks to predominantly black Baptist and Methodist churches is shown in Chapter 42 of Ahlstrom's *A Religious History of the American People*, in Raboteau's *Slave Religion*, in Wilmore's *Black Religion and Black Radicalism*, in Machel Sobel's *Trabelin' On: The Slave Journey to an Afro-Baptist Faith* (Westport, Conn., 1979), and in Clarence E. Walker's *A Rock in a Weary Land: The African Methodist Episcopal Church During the Civil War and Reconstruction* (Baton Rouge, 1982).

Blacks also had more opportunities for ordained leadership in many "white" Protestant denominations, such as the Protestant Episcopal and the Methodist Episcopal churches, than they did in the Catholic church. David C. Reimers, *White Protestantism and the Negro* (New York, 1965), J. Carleton Hayden, "The Black Ministry of the Episcopal Church: An Historical Overview," in Franklin D. Turner (ed.), *Black Clergy in the Episcopal Church: Recruitment, Training, and Development* (New York, 1978), 1–19, and "After the War: The Mission and Growth of the Episcopal Church Among Blacks in the South, 1865–1877," *Historical Magazine of the Protestant Episcopal Church*, XLII (December, 1973), 403–27, and Robert A. Bennett, "Black Episcopalians: A History from the Colonial Period to the Present," *Historical Magazine of the Protestant Episcopal Church*, XLIII (September, 1974), 231–45, all suggest that the creation of segregated general conferences in the Baptist and the Methodist Episcopal churches and the tradition of married, rather than celibate, clergy in the Protestant Episcopal church help explain the greater willingness of those Protestants to countenance black ministers and priests. Focusing on six ministers of independent black Presbyterian and Congregational churches, David E. Swift, in *Black Prophets of Justice: Activist Clergy Before the Civil War*

(Baton Rouge, 1989), emphasizes the crucial importance of black Protestant clergy in antebellum black protest and reform movements. During that same period, of course, black Catholics had no corresponding Afro-American clerical leaders.

Several works treat the arrival and first years of the Josephites in the United States. J. G. Snead-Cox's *The Life of Cardinal Vaughan* (2 vols.; London, 1910), a biography of the founder of St. Joseph's Society of the Sacred Heart for the Foreign Missions (Mill Hill Fathers) furnishes important information about Herbert Vaughan's original aims in sending the Mill Hill Fathers to the United States and includes his vivid impressions, gathered during visits to the United States, of the plight of blacks in the Catholic church during Reconstruction. Richard H. Steins, in "The Mission of the Josephites to the Negro in America, 1871–1893" (M.A. thesis, Columbia University, 1966), recounts the difficulties faced by the Mill Hill Josephites during their first twelve years in the United States and explains the factors that led to the independence of the American branch in 1893. John Rooney, M.H.M., in "A Divorce of Sorts," *Millhilliana*, No. 4 (1985), examines from the Mill Hill perspective Slattery's efforts to create an independent American society.

William L. Portier offers an insightful analysis of Slattery's proposals and arguments for evangelizing blacks in "John R. Slattery's Vision for the Evangelization of American Blacks," *U.S. Catholic Historian*, V, No. 1 (1986), 19–44. Robert Emmett Curran, S.J., gives useful information about the group of liberal, New York-Irish clergy who supported Slattery's efforts to develop black priests in "Prelude to 'Americanism': The New York Accademia and Clerical Radicalism in the Late Nineteenth Century," *Church History*, XLVII (March, 1978), 48–65. Two master's theses that deal with aspects of Slattery's plans for developing a black clergy are William J. Jauquet, "Epiphany Apostolic College, 1889–1925" (M.A. thesis, University of Maryland, 1976), and Laurence A. Schmitt, S.S.J., "John R. Slattery and the College for Black Catechists, Montgomery, Alabama, 1900–1920" (M.A. thesis, Washington Theological Coalition, 1977).

The Americanist and modernist crises in the Catholic church, which figured so prominently in Slattery's life, have been studied exhaustively. I found Robert D. Cross, *The Emergence of Liberal Catholicism in America* (Cambridge, Mass., 1958), and Christopher J. Kauffman, *Tradition and Transformation in Catholic Culture: The*

Priests of Saint Sulpice in the United States from 1791 to the Present (New York, 1988), especially helpful on Americanism. Recent scholarship emphasizes a connection between Americanism and modernism. I drew heavily on William L. Portier, "Modernism in the United States: The Case of John R. Slattery," in Ronald Burke, Gary Lease, and George Gilmore (eds.), *Varieties of Modernism* (Mobile, Ala., 1986), 77–97, and William L. Portier, "Catholic Theology in the United States, 1840–1907: Recovering a Forgotten Tradition," *Horizons*, X (February, 1983), 317–33. Margaret M. Reher, "Americanism and Modernism—Continuity or Discontinuity," *U.S. Catholic Historian*, I (Summer, 1981), 87–103, also proved helpful. For more traditional interpretations that emphasize discontinuity between Americanism and modernism, see Michael DeVito, *The New York Review: 1905–1908* (New York, 1977); Michael Gannon, "Before and After Modernism: The Intellectual Isolation of the American Priest," in John T. Ellis (ed.), *The Catholic Priest in the United States: Historical Investigations* (Collegeville, Minn., 1971), 293–384; and Thomas T. McAvoy, "Liberalism, Americanism, Modernism," *Records of the American Catholic Historical Society of Philadelphia*, LXIII (December, 1952), 225–31.

Both H. Shelton Smith's *In His Image, but . . . : Racism in Southern Religion, 1780–1910* (Durham, N.C., 1972) and George M. Fredrickson's *The Black Image in the White Mind: The Debate on Afro-American Character and Destiny, 1817–1914* (New York, 1971) explain the prevailing racial ideology in the United States during the years in which Slattery and his immediate successors wrestled with the issue of black priests. The evolution of Catholic racial parishes in New Orleans at the turn of the century is described by Dolores Egger Labbe, *Jim Crow Comes to Church: The Establishment of Segregated Catholic Parishes in South Louisiana* (2nd ed.; Lafayette, La., 1971). Margaret Law Calcott, *The Negro in Maryland Politics, 1870–1912* (Baltimore, 1969), analyzes the declining political fortunes of blacks in the state where the Josephites were headquartered. Helpful analyses of anti-Catholicism in the United States can be found in Ray Allen Billington, *The Protestant Crusade, 1800–1860* (New York, 1938), William E. Gienapp, "Nativism and the Creation of a Republican Majority in the North before the Civil War," *Journal of American History*, LXXII (December, 1985), 529–59, John Higham, *Strangers in the Land: Patterns of American Nativism, 1860–1925* (New Brunswick, N.J., 1955), and Chapter

XXII in C. Van Woodward, *Tom Watson: Agrarian Rebel* (New York, 1938).

Henry J. Koren, in *The Serpent and the Dove: A History of the Congregation of the Holy Ghost in the United States, 1745–1984* (Pittsburgh, 1985), illustrates how the difficulties the early black Josephites experienced with bishops of the South and the subsequent decision by Josephite administrators to restrict the admission of blacks into Josephite seminaries led the Holy Ghost Fathers to stop admitting blacks into their seminary. Koren also describes the lobbying efforts of Joseph Anciaux and Archbishop Alexandre Le Roy with the Holy See, and Mother Katharine Drexel with the American bishops, that led to creation of the Catholic Board for Mission Work Among the Colored People.

Until relatively recently, the black Catholic community has received little attention from scholars. Indeed, most of the works discussed in this essay so far, with the exception of the few biographies of black priests, focus on the largely white institutional Church in its dealings with blacks. There are, however, an increasing number of articles and books that give the black perspective. Cyprian Davis, O.S.B., in "Black Catholics in Nineteenth Century America," *U.S. Catholic Historian*, V, No. 1 (1986), 1–17, sketches the contours of early black Catholicism, highlighting significant individuals, both lay and clerical. In a later article, "Black Spirituality," *U.S. Catholic Historian*, VII, nos. 2 and 3 (1988), 39–46, his description of the Society of the Holy Family, an antebellum prayer group, offers a glimpse into the heretofore largely unexplored world of black Catholic spirituality. Black women religious played a key role in fostering vocations to the priesthood. In "A Minority of a Minority: The Witness of Black Women Religious in the Antebellum South," *Review for Religious*, XL (March, 1981), 260–69, Michael J. McNally briefly narrates the difficult early days of the two largest communities of black sisters, the Oblate Sisters of Providence and the Sisters of the Holy Family. In this context, see, also, Grace Sherwood, *The Oblates' One Hundred and One Years* (New York, 1931), Sister M. Reginald Gerdes, O.S.P., "To Educate and Evangelize: Black Catholic Schools of the Oblate Sisters of Providence (1828–1880)," *U.S. Catholic Historian*, VII, Nos. 2 and 3 (1988), 183–99, and Sister Audrey Marie Detiege, *Henriette Delille, Free Woman of Color: Foundress of the Sisters of the Holy Family* (New Orleans, 1976). David [Thomas W.] Spalding, C.F.X., "The

Negro Catholic Congresses, 1889–1894," *Catholic Historical Review*, LV (October, 1969), 337–57, traces the rise and fall of a vital lay black Catholic movement at the close of the nineteenth century. In "The Federated Colored Catholics: A Study of Three Variant Perspectives on Racial Justice as Represented by John LaFarge, William Markoe, and Thomas Turner" (Ph.D. dissertation, Catholic University of America, 1975), which was published recently as *Black Catholic Protest and the Federated Colored Catholics, 1917– 1933: Three Perspectives on Racial Justice* (New York, 1988), Marilyn W. Nickels picks up the story of lay black Catholic activism in the second decade of the twentieth century in the person of Thomas Wyatt Turner, and she delineates lay black Catholic efforts to end discrimination in the church and to secure black priests. Nickels' biographical sketch of Turner, entitled "Thomas Wyatt Turner and the Federated Colored Catholics," in *U.S. Catholic Historian*, VII, Nos. 2 and 3 (1988), 215–32, deftly captures the personality and spirit of black Catholicism's leading spokesman during the first half of the century.

Thomas Turner and the federation generated a steady stream of petitions and letters to the Holy See. Their actions were not in vain, for Rome played a crucial role in opening American seminaries to blacks. Gerald P. Fogarty's *The Vatican and the American Hierarchy from 1870 to 1965* (Stuttgart, 1982) provided me with valuable background for evaluating the actions of the Roman Curia and the pope on behalf of black Catholics. Cyprian Davis, O.S.B., "The Holy See and American Black Catholics: A Forgotten Chapter in the History of the American Church," *U.S. Catholic Historian*, VII, Nos. 2 and 3 (1988), 157–79, describes correspondence from 1904 to 1921 in the files of the Apostolic Delegation in the Vatican archives that shows the concern of the Holy See over both the condition of black Catholics in the United States and the dearth of black priests. The revealing letters that passed between Archbishop Giovanni Bonzano and Cardinals Gaetano De Lai and Willem van Rossum were most helpful in establishing Bonzano's personal opposition to black clergy and the cardinals' growing impatience with what they regarded as foot dragging by the delegate and the American episcopate over the issue of providing for more black priests in the United States.

Fogarty's *The Vatican and the American Hierarchy*, Anthony J. Kuzniewski's *Faith and Fatherland: The Polish Church War in Wisconsin, 1896–1918* (Notre Dame, 1980), and Richard M. Linkh's

American Catholicism and European Immigrants (1900–1924) (New York, 1975), with their accounts of the efforts of Germans, Poles, and Oriental rite Catholics (most of them Ruthenians) within the United States to secure bishops of their own nationalities or rites, help place black Catholic agitation for priests within the tradition of ethnic conflict within the church. At the same time, however, these studies throw into stark relief the unique character of discrimination against blacks in that, unlike other ethnic groups in the United States (except perhaps for Oriental rite Catholics, because of the issue of a married clergy), blacks were denied not only bishops but also priests of their own race.

Charles W. Malin, S.V.D., "Integration of the Catholic Clergy in the United States, The Divine Word Missionaries' Chapter" (M.A. thesis, Marquette University, 1964), is a solid piece of scholarship that narrates the story of the founding of St. Augustine's Seminary and the ordination and placement of its first four black priests. Malin's thesis helped me fill lacunae in my own research, especially concerning the debate over whether to accept black seminarians into full membership into the Society of the Divine Word.

Harvard Sitkoff describes the 1930s as the "seedtime" of the civil rights movement in *A New Deal for Blacks: The Emergence of Civil Rights as a National Issue: The Depression Decade* (Oxford, 1978). Within the Catholic church, the decade of the 1930s was a watershed in the struggle for black priests and for interracial justice. Edward S. Stanton, S.J., analyzes LaFarge's thought in "John LaFarge's Understanding of the Unifying Mission of the Church, Especially in the Area of Race Relations" (Ph.D. dissertation, St. Paul University, 1972). Paul E. Czuchlewski offers a perceptive analysis of Catholic liberals and the race problem in "Liberal Catholicism and American Racism, 1924–1960," *Records of the American Catholic Historical Society of Philadelphia*, LXXXV (March–June, 1974), 144–62.

The readmission of black students to Catholic University in 1936, after almost twenty years of exclusion, was an event fraught with both symbolic and practical meaning for the church, black Catholics, and the Josephites. The most valuable accounts of the policies of Catholic University regarding the admission of black students are Blase Dixon, T.O.R., "The Catholic University and the Racial Question, 1914–1948," *Records of the American Catholic Historical Society of Philadelphia*, LXXXIV (December, 1973), 221–24;

Albert S. Foley, S.J., "The Catholic Church and the Washington Negro" (Ph.D. dissertation, University of North Carolina, 1950); and C. Joseph Neusse, "Loss and Recovery of Interracial Virtue: Desegregation at the Catholic University of America" (Paper presented at the annual meeting of the American Catholic Historical Association, Washington, D.C., December 28–30, 1987).

Richard M. Dalfiume, "The Forgotten Years of the Negro Revolution," *Journal of American History*, LV (June, 1968), 90–106, highlights World War II as a catalyst for racial change in American society, a thesis supported by Casserly's opening of Epiphany Apostolic College to black applicants and by the pledges of southern bishops to Cardinal Stritch to accept black candidates for their diocesan clergy. Katherine Martensen, in "Region, Religion, and Social Action: The Catholic Committee of the South, 1939–1956," *Catholic Historical Review*, LXVIII (April, 1982), 249–67, describes the rather ineffectual efforts of Catholic liberals in the South to address their region's economic and racial problems.

Some studies have been done on integration and the church on the local or the diocesan level. The Jesuit Bend incident in 1955 was part of the larger struggle for desegregation going on in the Archdiocese of New Orleans. See, for example, Philip A. Grant, Jr., "Archbishop Joseph F. Rummel and the 1962 New Orleans Desegregation Crisis," *Records of the American Catholic Historical Society of Philadelphia*, XCI (March–December, 1980), 59–66, and Glenn Jeansonne, *Leander Perez, Boss of the Delta* (Baton Rouge, 1977). Donald J. Kemper, "Catholic Integration in St. Louis, 1935–1947," *Missouri Historical Review*, LXXIII (October, 1978), 1–22, and William Barnaby Faherty, S.J., "Breaking the Color Barrier," *Universitas*, XIII (Autumn, 1987), 18–21, deal with the integration of Catholic institutions in a border state. Peter E. Hogan, S.S.J., gives a somewhat sympathetic picture of Archbishop Michael Curley of Baltimore in "Archbishop Curley and the Blacks" (Paper presented at the spring meeting of the American Catholic Historical Society, Louisville, April 16, 1983).

For a thoughtful exposition of the status of black Catholics in the church in 1980, see the section entitled "Black and Catholic," in *America*, March 29, 1980, pp. 256–77. Up-to-date statistical data on black Catholics can be found in George Shuster, S.S.J., and Robert M. Kearns, S.S.J., *Statistical Profile of Black Catholics* (Washington, D.C., 1976), and in John Harfmann, S.S.J., *1984 Statistical Profile of Black Catholics* (Washington, D.C., 1985).

Index